LORD PELHAM.

[See pages 74 and 499.]

HISTORY
— of —
PELHAM
MASSACHUSETTS
FROM 1738 TO 1898

Including the Early
History of Prescott

EARLY SETTLEMENT OF THE TOWN.—ESTABLISHMENT OF SCHOOLS.—THE FRENCH AND INDIAN WARS.—THE REVOLUTIONARY WAR.—SHAYS REBELLION.—SKETCH OF CAPT. DANIEL SHAYS.—CHURCH HISTORY.—THE REBELLION OF 1861-5.—SKETCHES OF NOTABLE MEN, NATIVES OF THE TOWN, ETC., ETC.

By

C. O. Parmenter

HERITAGE BOOKS
2011

HERITAGE BOOKS
AN IMPRINT OF HERITAGE BOOKS, INC.

Books, CDs, and more—Worldwide

For our listing of thousands of titles see our website
at
www.HeritageBooks.com

A Facsimile Reprint
Published 2011 by
HERITAGE BOOKS, INC.
Publishing Division
100 Railroad Ave. #104
Westminster, Maryland 21157

Originally published:
Amherst, Massachusetts
Press of Carpenter & Morehouse
1898

— Publisher's Notice —
In reprints such as this, it is often not possible to remove blemishes from the original. We feel the contents of this book warrant its reissue despite these blemishes and hope you will agree and read it with pleasure.

International Standard Book Numbers
Paperbound: 978-0-7884-1845-7
Clothbound: 978-0-7884-8634-0

Table of Contents.

SETTLEMENT OF PELHAM.

North of Ireland Scotchmen learn of America—Memorial to Governor Shute of Massachusetts sent by Rev. Mr. Boyd in 1718—One Hundred families sail for Massachusetts and land in Boston August 4, 1718—From Boston to Worcester—Then to Pelham in 1738—Description of Equivalent Lands purchased—North of Ireland Scotchmen in 1738, ... 7 to 13

PROPRIETORS' RECORDS.
1738 to 1743.

First meeting of Proprietors held at Worcester February 26, 1738-9—Articles of Agreement for purchase of Land made and indented October 20, 1738—Survey of the tract purchased with plan of the same and names of those who drew Home Lots—First meeting of Proprietors held on the newly purchased tract first called Lisburn, August 6, 1740—Various meetings of Proprietors previous to the Incorporation of the Town 1743—Meetings of Proprietors' organization until 1767, ... 13 to 67

THE COMMUNION TOKEN.

Distributed to Members on Lecture Days—Gathered Again After Communion Service, ... 68 to 74

INCORPORATION OF THE TOWN OF PELHAM—TOWN MEETING RECORDS.
From 1743 to 1763.

First Town Meeting held April 19, 1743, at the call of Robert Peibols—Full list of Officers Chosen—Voted to Establish Schools in 1744—Annual Town Meeting Records—Petition to General Court to Legalize Acts of Town Officers in 1753—Invoices Given in for Taxation in 1760—The Town Presented at Court in 1762 for "Voluntarily Omitting and Neglecting to Provide Themselves with a Learned and Able Orthodox Minister"—Illegal Killing of Deer in 1763, and Penalty therefor, ... 74 to 116

From 1763 to 1776.

Call of Rev. Richard Crouch Graham to Settle in 1763—Objectors Thereto—Warning of Objectionable Families to Leave Town—Pewing the Meeting-house in 1766—Allotment of Pews—Disagreement with the Shutesbury Selectmen About Town Lines in 1769—Town Vendue in 1769—Death of Rev. Mr. Graham in 1771—Rev.

Andrew Bay Supplies the Pulpit in 1772—Patriotic Response to the Boston Committee of Correspondence, 1773—Call to Rev. Nathaniel Merrill in November, 1774—Letter of a Pelham Man in the Army at Charlestown, 1775—Committee of Safety Chosen 1776 —Handbill from the Court of Independency 1776 . . 116 to 132

From 1777 to 1786.

Valuation of Property for Taxation Established 1777—Rev. Mr. Merrill's Appeal 1779—Large Increase of Salary 1780—Measures Taken to Secure Men for the Army 1781—Bounties Offered—Action Taken to Procure Beef for the Army—Daniel Shays on Committee of Safety 1781—Selectmen Refuse to Call a Town Meeting 1782— Trying to Settle with the Three and Six Months Men 1783 – Allowance to Soldiers in the Late War 1785—The Town Votes to Have a Bank of Paper Money Made 1786, . . . 132 to 157

From 1786 to 1797.

Petition of certain inhabitants of Belchertown in 1786—Convention at Bruce's Tavern, July 31, 1786—Mutterings about "Grievances" in Town Meeting—Delegates to Convention at Hatfield in August, 1786—Second Parish Organized 1786—Choice of Delegates to Attend Constitutional Convention, 1787—First Justice of the Peace Appointed, 1788—Families Warned to Leave Town in 1790-91— First General Appropriation for the Poor, 1790—Support of the Poor First Sold to Lowest Bidder 1794—Laying Out Road to the Valley, 1795—Stipulation Concerning the Poor, 1797. 157 to 168

From 1797 to 1809.

Tranfer of Pews in the Old Meeting-house, 1798—Permission Voted to build "Horse Shades," 1799—Sale of Town Lands at Vendue, 1801 —Opposition to the Building of Turnpike, 1802—A Town Pound Established, 1804—Robert Lotheridge Sells His Pew in the Old Meeting-house—Voted to hold one-third of the Town Meetings in the Second Parish, 1805—Attempts to have the Toll-gate Abolished, 1806—Samuel and Andrew Hyde Petition to have their Lands Set Off to Amherst, 1807, ... 168 to 176

From 1809 to 1815.

Two Candidates for Representative to the General Court, 1809—Taxes Upon the People, 1809—The Abercrombie Brothers, Isaac and James, Candidates for Representative, 1810—The 6th Mass. Turnpike Corporation Tries to Discontinue Their Road Through Town, 1810—County Road to Enfield Laid Out, 1811—Governor Petitioned to Restore the Two Military Companies to their Former Regiments, 1812—Fear of a Draft for the War of 1812—Wages of Detached Soldiers Raised, 1814—The East Parish asks to be Set Off as a Town by Itself, 1815, ... 176 to 183

CONTENTS.

From 1815 to 1824.

New Pelham—Order of Notice from the General Court to Show Why the Prayer of the Second Parish Should Not be Granted, 1819— The Town Votes Against Revising the Constitution, 1820—The Last Act of Opposition to Setting Off the Second Parish—The Town Rejects All of the Eleven Amendments to the Constitution, 1821—The East Parish Succeeds in Getting Set Off from the Old Town, 1822—Large Number Supported by the Town in 1822,—Sale of Common Lands and Proceeds go for Repairs on the Meeting House, 1823, ... 183 to 190

From 1824 to 1861.

Council Called to Dismiss Rev. Winthrop Bailey in 1825—Great Flood of 1828 Does Damage—Ziba Cook Elected Representative by One Majority in 1829—Stove Used in Meeting House for the First Time in 1831—New Town Hall Wanted in 1835—Money Secured from the United States Treasury in 1837—Wanted to Change the Name of the Town in 1840—Libraries Established in 1842—Scheme for Two Town Halls in 1842—Old Meeting House Changed for Town Hall in 1844—Old Meeting House Rented in 1846—Many Candidates for Representative in 1850-51—Voted to Surrender the Charter in 1854-56—Enrolled Men in 1861, . , . 190 to 205

From 1862 to 1897.

Action for the Relief of Soldiers' Families, 1862—Draft for Men in 1863 —Heavy Taxes After the War—Number of Schools Reduced from Eight to Four in 1874—Few Town Meetings Annually After That— Blizzard of 1888—Death of Sylvester Jewett, 1892—History of the Old Meeting House, ... 205 to 223

Schools—From 1744 to 1897.

Establishment of Schools in 1744—School Committees—Appropriations of Schools for Each Year from 1744 to 1897, . . 223 to 234

Mills, Manufacturies, Etc.

Lands for Mills, 1739—Corn Mill, 1755—Stinson's Sawmill, 1760—Hamilton's Sawmill, 1785—Barlow's Sawmill, 1787—Town Takes Action, 1791—Mills Built on Home Lot 56, 1803-4—Many Owners of Mills in the Hollow—Stephen Fairbank's Carding Machine, 1815— Shoe Peg Business on Pergy Brook—Land for Mill at West Pelham, 1739—Scythe Shop and Foundry—Carding Machine, 1808— Jillson's Mills, 1820—Various Owners of Mills—Fishing Rod Business, 1858—Montague City Rod Co—Brown's Turning Shop—Charcoal—Stone Quarries—Miscellaneous Manufacturing—Innkeepers and Retailers—Merchants—Justices of the Peace—Physicians— Blacksmiths, ... 234 to 261

Religious Societies.

The First Presbyterian Church History gathered from the town and parish records, the old church records having been lost or destroyed —From the Records of the Second Presbyterian Church and Parish of Pelham from 1786 to 1822—Confession of Faith—Records of Church at Pelham Center from 1822 to 1897—Quakers or Friends —Baptists at Packardville—The Methodists, Beginning with the Labors of Rev. Isaac Stoddard in 1831—Union Society at Packardville Organized 1869, ... 261 to 294

Rev. Robert Abercrombie and the Church at Pelham.

His Call to be their Pastor in 1742—Protest Against His Settlement in 1743—Ordained August 30, 1744—Sermon by Rev. Jonathan Edwards of Northampton—Home Lot No. 1 turned over to Mr. Abercrombie as the First Settled Minister—Troubled to Collect His Salary in 1746-7—Charged by the Presbytery with Conduct Contrary to Presbyterian Principles and Rules Governing the Church, and Forbidden to Preach at the Church in Pelham—Suppliers Appointed by the Presbytery—Final Suspension in 1754—Suit against the Town for Arrears of Salary in 1756—Statement of Differences with the Presbytery made by Mr. Abercrombie in Letters to a Friend, ... 294 to 319

Stephen Burroughs, The Supplier.

Obtained a Situation as Supplier in Spring of 1784—Preached Acceptably Four Sundays—Reengaged for Four Months—Read an Old Sermon at a Funeral—Given a Text from which to Preach with Little Time for Preparation—Proved his Ability to Preach Extempore—With One Sunday More to Preach was Found to be an Imposter—Fled in the Night—Pursued by the Indignant People—Fracas at Rutland—Came Back to Pelham in the Night to His Friend Lysander—Passed Counterfeit Dollars in Springfield and was Imprisoned—The Hay Mow Sermon, . . 320 to 340

Pelham in the Wars.

French War—Revolutionary War—War of 1812—Mexican War—The Great Rebellion—A Full Company of Men in the French and Indian War, 1757—Opening of War of Revolution—Ironclad Oath of Pelham Men.—Capt. David Cowden's Company of Minute Men April 19, 1775—Old Muster Rolls—Names of Men—The March to Cambridge in the War of 1812—Pelham Men in the Great Rebellion—Sketches of the Men and the Regiments in which they Served, ... 341 to 365

The Shays Rebellion of 1786–87.

Capt. Daniel Shays, a Pelham Man—Gathering of Debt Burdened Men in Conventions—Lists of Grievances Formulated—Opposition

to Lawyers in General Court—Opposition to Sittings of the Courts
—Terms of Court Prevented by Armed Men—Court Houses in Possession of Armed Insurgents—Gov. Bowdoin Calls Out the Militia
—Warrants Issued for Arrest of Insurgent Leaders—Gen. B. Lincoln Given Command of Militia—Gen. Shepherd's Detachment
Guarding the Arsenal at Springfield—Shays Marches to the Attack
—Repulsed—Several Men Killed—Flight of Capt. Shays and Men to
Pelham—Gen. Lincoln Pursues—Shays' Men Dispersed at Petersham, ... 366 to 390

CAPTAIN DANIEL SHAYS.

Born at Hopkinton—In the War of the Revolution—In Pelham After
War—A Friend of Landlord Conkey—Met Debt Burdened Men at
Conkey's Tavern—Drilled them in Use of Arms—Became Rebel
Leader—Fled from the State—Was Pardoned in 1788—Removed to
State of New York—Did not Prosper in Business—Drifted to
Livingston County—Died in 1824 After Living in Extreme Poverty
at Sparta, ... 391 to 402

SETTLEMENT OF SALEM, N. Y., BY PELHAM PEOPLE IN 1764.

James Turner and Joshua Conkey First Settlers of Salem—Journeyed
Through the Forests on Foot in 1761—Took Up Lands—Went Back
to Pelham for the Winter—Made Permanent Settlement in 1764—
Hamilton McCollister Joined the Pioneers—The Settlement Known
as New England Colony—Were Men of Character—Had Highest
Esteem for Religion—First Sermon Preached was in the Cabin of
James Turner, ... 403 to 411

PROFESSIONAL AND BUSINESS MEN, NATIVES OF PELHAM.

The Record a Good One—Have made their Mark as Professional and
Business Men in Many States—Wells and Edward Southworth,
Business Men—Daniel, James and Austin W. Thompson, Leading
Physicians of Northampton—Ira P. Rankin, Business Man and
Government Officer, San Francisco—Dr. James Dunlap of
Northampton—Dr. Harvey Willson Harkness, Scientist, San Francisco—Judge Ithamar Conkey of Amherst—Col. James N. Smith,
Railroad Builder, Brooklyn—Nathaniel Gray, San Francisco—
Rev. Aldin Grout, Missionary—William Smith Otis, Inventor, Etc.
—Dr. Israel H. Taylor of Amherst, ... 412 to 446

JOHN SAVAGE AND JOHN STINSON.

Prominent Citizens of Pelham in the Middle of the 18th Century, but
not Natives of the Town, ... 446 to 449

CONCERNING THE WOMEN OF PELHAM.

Reputation for Industry—They Introduced the "Little Wheel" for
Spinning Flax—They Taught Its Use—They Spun and Wove Linen

—Also Wool, and made the Cloth into Garments—Made Domestic Braid from Rye Straw—Braided or Platted Palm Leaf into Hats—Wove Palm Leaf into Webs for Shaker Hoods—Marriages—Published Intentions of Marriage—Births—Form of Death Record, Etc., ... 450 to 469

MOUNT LINCOLN.

Description of the Mountain—Many Towns Seen from its Summit—Beacon Fires During the Revolution—Station for Geodetic Survey—Heighth Above Tide Water—Uncle Reuben Allen, 470 to 472

OLD BURIAL PLACES.

A Sketch of each of the Eleven Burial Places of Pelham—The Old Burial Ground at the Center—The West Burying Ground—The Quaker Burying Ground—The Arnold Burying Ground—The Johnson Family Burial Place—The Smith Private Burial Ground—Burial Ground near George Knight's—Packardville Burying Ground—The Valley Cemetery—The West Pelham Burying Ground—The Cemetery on the Prescott side of the East Hollow, . . 473 to 481

TAVERNS AND LANDLORDS.

The Tavern of Thomas Dick—The Old Conkey Tavern—Dr. Hind's Tavern on Pelham East Hill—Kingman's Tavern on the West Hill—Cook's Tavern—The Orient House—Hotel Pelham, 482 to 487

OLD ADVERTISEMENTS, ETC.

Stray Cattle and Horses—Taken in Damage and Otherwise—Clear Description of Animals—"Marks for Creaturs", Posting of Warrants for Town Meetings, ... 488 to 490

STORIES—PLEASANT AND OTHERWISE.

De Rex vs. Hyde—Rev. Robert Abercrombie and the Church Committee—Rev. Dr. Parsons of Amherst and the People of Pelham—Farmer Harkness and the Traveler—Crimes—Prince Dwelly Loses His Life—Charles Stetson Shot April 11, 1881—Marion Montgomery Kills His Son December 26, 1882, . . . 491 to 498

SKETCH OF HENRY PELHAM—1696-1754.

From Memoirs of Henry Pelham, by William Coxe, Vol. 2, 301-304, ... 499 to 501

REPRESENTATIVES TO THE GENERAL COURT—502-503.

TOWN OFFICERS.

Moderators of Annual Town Meetings—Town Clerks—Town Treasurers—Town Selectmen—1763 to 1898 Inclusive, . . 503 to 508

List of Illustrations.

	Page.
Lord Pelham, Facing Title Page.	
Pelham Center from the North,	7
Plan of Town of Pelham, with Home Lots,	25
Second Plan of the Town, Three Divisions of Land,	30
Capt. Thos. Dick's Gravestone,	51
Upper Reservoir, Apple Trees in bloom, May, 1898,	51
The Token,	68
Town Meeting, March, 1897,	77
Capt. Benjamin Page's House, Rankin Farm,	98
Abijah Fales' Farm House,	98
L. W. Allen's Sawmill,	116
S. F. Arnold's Residence,	116
The Rocking Stone,	132
House on Joel Grout Farm, Owned by Henry Cook,	132
Stephen Rhodes' Residence,	157
C. P. Hanson's Residence,	157
The Jewett, or Harkness House, in Winter,	176
J. R. Anderson's House, in Winter,	176
To the Cider Mill,	205
On the Sandy Road to Amherst Market,	205
Sylvester Jewett,	217
The Communion Service of the Scotch Presbyter'n Church,	217
The Old Pulpit of the Old Meeting House,	217
The Old Meeting House,	217
William Gilmore's Invoice for Taxation, 1760,	221
First Town Meeting Warrant,	222
Residence of Mrs. A. Morgan,	223
The "City" School House,	223
The Valley School House,	229
The Valley Bridge,	229
Dam and Bridge, West Branch,	236
Up the Valley of the West Branch, from the Cemetery,	236
Dam at Fishing Rod Factory, West Pelham,	242
Montague City Fishing Rod Company's Factory,	242
Residence of David Shores,	245

	Page.
Charcoal Kilns, near Pulpit Hill, Pelham Hollow,	245
M. E. Boynton's Residence,	254
Tombstone of Edward and Elizebeth Selfridge,	254
Pelham Center from the South,	282
Daisies Among the Graves, Old Burying Ground,	282
Union Church, Packardville,	288
M. E. Church, West Pelham,	288
Autograph Manuscript by James Conkey, 1746-7,	301
The Protest,	302
The Grave of Adam Johnson,	302
Receipt or Discharge Given by Rev. R. Abercrombie,	312
Stephen Burroughs,	322
View in West Pelham, near the Fishing Rod Factory,	341
Falls on Pergy Brook, Pelham Hollow,	365
Amherst as seen from Pelham Before 1850,	365
Home of Capt. Shays in Pelham	391
Abial Robinson Farm House,	391
Facsimile of Capt. Shays' Handwriting,	393
Up the East Hill, (Prescott)	399
Wells Southworth,	412
Edward Southworth,	414
Ira P. Rankin,	417
Dr. James Dunlap,	418
Dr. Harvey Willson Harkness,	421
Judge Ithamar Conkey,	425
Birth Place of Judge Ithamar Conkey,	425
Col. James N. Smith,	428
Nathaniel Gray,	430
Rev. Aldin Grout.	432
The Buffum Brook,	432
Otis Patent Steam Excavator,	436
Thomas Buffum,	440
Dr. E. Ward Cooke,	444
Uncle Eseck Cook Farm House,	444
Mrs. Betsey Otis Smith,	461
Tower on Mount Lincoln,	470
Boiling Cider,	470
View from the Enfield Road Toward Pelham Center,	471

	Page.		Page.
The Reuben Allen Place,	472	Ziba Cook's Tavern,	484
The East School House,	472	Waterfall on Dunlap Brook,	484
Samuel Davis' Residence,	472	Orient House, West Pelham,	486
The Old Graveyard, Center,	474	Hotel Pelham,	486
J. W. Keith's Residence,	474	View from West Bury'g Ground,	498
Tomb in Smith Private Cemetery,	477	View of Prescott from the North,	498
The Arba Randall Farm House	477	High Water in the West Branch, 1897,—Vanstone's Mill and Bridge,	507
The Old Conkey Tavern Sign,	482		
The Old Conkey Tavern,	482	Stone Bridge, Dunlap Brook,	507

Errata.

Page 17—Fifth line from the bottom Abraham Should be Adam.

" 76—Sixth line from bottom read 1742 in place of 1752.

" 265—Fifth line from top read Andrew for William.

PREFACE.

After earnest and repeated solicitation on the part of friends, who set forth the desirability and the urgent need of the work being done, the task of preparing a history of the Town of Pelham has been commenced and it is expected that the work will be carried forward and up to January 1, 1896—158 years from the first settlement of the town.

It will be evident to all who give the subject a little thought, that the history of this town must be largely a transcript of the existing records. All that can be made known to the public must be drawn from that source. The earnest, zealous, strong-minded Scotch Presbyterian settlers finished their labors long years ago. We cannot appeal to them for facts,—their record of events is all we have.

These records consist of town and parish record books mostly. The old Presbyterian church records have disappeared within the past twenty years, and thus one very interesting source of information concerning the social, religious and family life of these people is beyond our reach.

In the records accessible, we have little or nothing respecting the social or family life of the people. The records of Marriage Intentions, Marriages, Births and Deaths contain all that there is concerning the wives and daughters. No record of their work appears. We know they spun wool and flax, they wove the stout cloth for their husband's and son's wear, as well as for themselves. They knitted the yarn, they sewed the cloth into garments—but there is no hint or intimation in the records of their having any part in the social or business life of the settlement.

Exciting events required action by the town; but the record of such action fails to convey to us anything of the active stirring interest which the events themselves developed among the people. We cannot hear the animated discussion and debate, which we know occurred often, and was long-continued and sharp, as we read the dull record of their decisions.

The plan thus far pursued has been to give every town meeting record a careful reading, and to copy whatever might be of interest to anyone interested in the history of the town. In many instances.

the complete record of town meetings, including the warrants under which they were held, have been copied entire and will be so printed.

Names of town officers are given—not every year; and every officer, but for many years the full roster of officers, down to tythingmen and "Hog Constables", are given. The purpose being to get as many names of inhabitants in print as possible.

The action of town meetings upon all matters of peculiar or extraordinary interest will be given in full, especially action of the town during the stirring times of the Revolutionary war. The names of all who served in that struggle, and all those that were drawn into rebellion against the state government, under Capt. Daniel Shays, will be given, so far as they are obtainable.

Shays Rebellion will be given ample space, and the entire correspondence between Gen. Lincoln, in command of the state militia at Hadley, and Capt. Daniel Shays and other insurgent leaders while they with their 1100 followers were occupying East and West hills in Pelham in the bleak winter of 1787, will be included.

The Stephen Burroughs episode will not be omitted, nor will any other event of interest or importance of which there are accessible records.

The entire contents of the book containing the Records of the Lisburn "Propriety", excepting the descriptions of the 183 lots of land into which the tract was divided in the three divisions, have been copied, and a reproduction of the plans of the surveys of William Young in 1739, which he submitted, and were made a part of the record, have been prepared for the work. · A line drawing of the old Meeting House, where for 153 consecutive years the people of the town have gathered for town meetings, has been prepared in a plate for printing in the book; also a half-tone plate of the old Conkey Tavern in the Hollow, which was burned in 1883.

The above is a brief outline of the work proposed, and the preparation will continue, but no further printing will be done until some expression of the demand for the completed work is obtained, in order to decide how many volumes may be disposed of. The responses received from people who may desire such a history as may be gathered from the materials available will determine how many volumes shall be printed or whether any completed ones shall issue. C. O. P.

February 3, 1896.

PELHAM CENTER FROM THE NORTH.

"THERE IS NO TOWN SO POOR

THAT ITS PAST HASN'T FURNISHED SOMETHING

WORTH EMBALMING FOR POSTERITY."

—*Boston Transcript, February* 23, 1898.

The First Settlers of the Town of Pelham.

The people who settled in Pelham in 1738-9 were of Scotch origin, as many of the sturdy names would indicate if it was not definitely known that they were such. They came to this country from Ireland and were commonly called Scotch–Irish, though nothing was more offensive than the term Irish as applied to them, and the only reason why it was ever attached to them came from the fact that these people and their ancestors had lived in the North of Ireland for many years. They were Scotchmen living in Ireland, and as they hailed from that island on their arrival here, it was natural that while their real nationality was quite apparent, their coming from the Green Isle caused the use of the double name to express their nationality.

The history of these Scotch people in Ireland, and the reason of their being there, may properly be given here briefly.

During the reign of James I. his Catholic subjects in the north of Ireland rebelled, and upon the suppression of the rebellion two million acres of land, comprising nearly all of six northern counties, came into possession of King James as sole owner.

His Scotch and English subjects were offered liberal inducements in the way of grants of land, and in other formal ways, to leave their own country and homes and settle upon these vacated lands in the north of Ireland, from which the Catholic Irish had been expelled.

Believing that good homes could in this way be secured, large numbers of Scotchmen of strong Presbyterian faith settled upon these lands as early as 1612. In the reign of Charles II. there were further accessions to their numbers, but it was in the latter part of the century, during the reign of William and Mary, that by far the larger number migrated.

In their new homes they were allowed to worship according to their own faith and forms of worship, but were obliged to contribute one-tenth of their income in support of the clergy of the established church. They also became aware of the fact that they were only tenants of the crown, and could never own the lands they cultivated in fee.

The natural emnity between their Catholic–Irish neighbors in adjoining counties, and these sturdy Scotch Presbyterians was of such a nature that it did not render their condition one to be desired, or to be long endured, and they began to cast about for relief.

They had heard of America, and had learned something about it from one who had been there and returned to them, and they desired to know more. In the year 1718, they sent Rev. Mr. Boyd to Massachusetts to present an address to Governor Shute, in which their desire to settle in New England was expressed. The address borne by Rev. Mr. Boyd was signed by more than two hundred men, nine of them being ministers of the gospel, besides three other graduates of the University of Scotland, and among the signatures are found the names of John Gray, William Johnson, James Gilmore and James Alexander, who were among the first settlers of this town, in 1739. Also the names of Alexander Dunlop, M. A., Thomas Dunlop, and Andrew Dunlop, doubtless ancestors or relatives of James Dunlap, who was in Pelham as early as 1743, and probably earlier.

The following is a copy of the Memorial, as printed in Parker's History of Londonderry, N. H.

MEMORIAL TO GOV SHUTE

To His Excellency the Right Honorable Collonel Samuel Suitte Governor of New England.

We whose names are Underwritten, inhabitants of ye North of Ireland, Doe in our own names, and in the names of many others of our Neighbors, Gentlemen, Ministers, Farmers and Tradesmen, Commissionate and appoint our trusty and well beloved friend, the Reverend Mr. William Boyd of Macasky, to His Excellency the Right Hororable Collonel Samuel Suitte Governor of New England, and to assure His Excellency of our sincere and hearty inclinations to transport ourselves to that very excellent and renowned Plantation upon our obtaining from his Excellency suitable encouragement. And further to act and Doe in our Names as his Prudence shall direct.

Given under our hands this 26th day of March, Annog. Dom 1718.

The favorable report brought back to Ireland by Mr. Boyd caused the larger part of those who had signed the above Address to Gov. Shute to convert their property into money, and as many as one hundred families embarked for Boston in five ships, where they arrived in safety, August 4, 1718. They were the descendants of Scotchmen who went from Argyleshire in Scotland, in 1612, and settled upon the lands in Ulster county, Ireland, from which the rebellious Catholic subjects of King James had been removed because of their rebellious action.

It is said that a goodly portion of these people remained in Boston and with other Scotch people already there, organized the first Presbyterian church, and Rev. John Moorhead was pastor. Some went to Andover. Sixteen families left in a body, and finally settled at Nutfield—now Londonderry, N. H. Others of them, and probably some of the first settlers of Pelham, went from Boston to Worcester, and settled, but the colony dispersed later, some, as we have said, being in the colony that purchased the tract of 16,662 1-2 acres included in the towns of Pelham and Prescott, of Col. John Stoddard of Northampton.

Others of those who landed in Boston went west and settled in the state of New York. Some families settled in Spencer, some in Stowe, some in Hopkinton, a few passed over into Connecticut. There were fresh arrivals in the years following 1718, and with the pioneer families were among the settlers of Palmer and Colraine, in this state, as well as Pelham, and probably other towns.

Just when the negotiations began for the purchase of the tract of land on which these Scotch Presbyterians settled does not appear, but the closing of the bargain is shown in the Articles of Agreement.

DESCRIPTION OF THE TRACT OF EQUIVALENT LAND PURCHASED BY THE NORTH OF IRELAND SCOTCHMEN IN 1738.

The lands purchased of Col. John Stoddard of Northampton were a portion of a large tract known as the Equivalent lands, which is now included for the most part in the towns of Belchertown, Ware, Pelham, a portion of Prescott and a portion of Enfield. Prescott was a part of Pelham up to 1822, and the part set off from Pelham was equivalent land, but territory not of the equivalent lands has been added on the north.

The designation "Equivalent lands" was adopted and applied at the time the state of Massachusetts made a grant of the tract abovementioned to the state of Connecticut as an equivalent for the towns of Woodstock, Somers, Enfield and Suffield in the last named state, which, through some blunder or error in surveying, were supposed to be within the boundaries of the state of Massachusetts for many years. After it became certain that the south line of Massachusetts was not far enough south to include these four towns within its limits and that the towns were in the state of Connecticut, the state of Massachusetts instead of acknowledging the error and giving up control over these towns, still claimed and exercised jurisdiction over them. As an offset to this absurd claim, and instead of giving up the claim, the state of Massachusetts offered to give the state of Connecticut a tract of wild land equal in extent to that of the four towns named, as an equivalent. After sixty-five years of controversy 107,793 acres were granted and accepted by the state of Connecticut in full satisfaction of the absurd claim. The state of Connecticut held the legal title to the tract of equivalent lands, but it was always under the jurisdiction of Massachusetts.

As early as 1716 Connecticut began selling the Equivalent Lands, and the whole tract brought but £683, or about one farthing per acre. A company formed in Boston, of which Hon. Jonathan Belcher, a former governor of the state, was a member, purchased a large portion of the tract. Men in Northampton also purchased, Rev. Jonathan Edwards being an owner of equivalent lands at one time. All the money from the sales went into the funds of Yale College.

Probably there were no land syndicates in those early days of the modern pattern, booming settlements on these wild lands, but the price per acre (one farthing) which Connecticut realized for her Equivalent Lands, and the price paid Col. Stoddard, per acre, by the North of Ireland Scotchmen (2 1-3 pound new tenor) indicates that there were thrifty land speculators in those days, looking for customers upon whom they could unload at an advance. After a time the people living in the four Connecticut towns threw off the control Massachusetts had exercised, preferring the jurisdiction of the state they resided in to that of Massachusetts.

The negotiations of Robert Peibols, blacksmith, and James Thornton, yoeman, and both of Worcester, was for a tract of land about three and one-half miles wide and seven and three-quarters miles in length,—the several range lines running due east and west, and contained 16,662 1-2 acres. Its west line was the east line of Hadley (now Amherst). The tract consists mainly of two high ridges of land running north and south across the tract and the Great Hollow lying between. In this hollow, with its abrupt sides, the west branch of Swift river runs south, and combining with the east branch below Enfield, forms a sizable stream for manufacturing purposes.

From the east line of Amherst to the top of Pelham West Hill it is a little more than six miles, and in that distance there is a rise of about nine hundred feet. The old meeting house is not quite 1200 feet above tide water, but Mount Lincoln and another elevation a little south of the center is quite 1200 feet above tide, while Amherst center is but 300 feet above tide level. From the West Hill east to the Hollow, the descent is abrupt and continues for about two miles. When the West Branch is crossed; then for about two miles, the up grade is sharper if anything than the descent from the west. When the summit of East Hill is reached, straight west over the Hollow and at about the same level, is the West Hill in full view. The descent to the east from the East Hill begins at once and ends on the plains of Greenwich, through which flows the waters that make the east branch of Swift river. These two ridges are by no means smooth and rounded, but are broken into ravines along either slope, down which flow the sparkling rivulets on their way to the lower ground. On the westward side of the West Hill is a deep depression, known as the Valley, which leads out towards Amherst.

Judge Ithamar Conkey, in his centennial address at Pelham, January 15, 1843, spoke of this tract as follows:

"This town and the adjacent territory, previous to their being settled, were distinguished as being excellent hunting grounds—they abounded with deer and other valuable game, and much damage was undoubtedly done to the lands by those persons who resorted here for that purpose. It was a practice among the hunters, in those days, to set a line of fires, encircling a large plot of ground, which, burning in every direction, would gradually encompass the game in a narrow circle and so it would become an easy prey to its pursuers. Thus in process of time the native forests, which were extensive and valuable, and which covered the lands with a dense foliage were nearly destroyed, and much of the vegetable substance which usually collects in a forest were consumed, thereby rendering the lands less productive and much less valuable.

This practice was continued many years, and the fires were known to burn in some parts of the territory, especially in the low marshy places, for several months together. But the lands which had been thus burned over were soon covered with a species of wild grass—growing rapidly and luxuriantly—thus giving it the appearance of an extensive rolling prairie, and affording very excellent pasturage for cattle. For many years great numbers of cattle and horses were sent out from the towns on the Connecticut river to graze on these hills during the summer season, and to make the pasturage sweeter and facilitate its growth, the practice of burning over the lands was continued a considerable time after the first settlement of the place, and in fact until the inhabitants of the town chose a committee to prosecute the offenders and thus save their lands from further destruction."

Of the wisdom of the settlers in selecting this tract, Judge Conkey says: "Could we be transported back to those days and view this land as it was thus situated, see the natural make and construction of the soil,—the beautiful streams of water which flow through it, the granite formations and the easy and natural facilities for improvement, when compared with some of the adjoining territories, we should be convinced of the wisdom and good judgment manifested in the selection. No spot of ground east of Hadley and west of the then existing settlements in Worcester county could be found more favorable to successful agricultural improvement."

The condition of the soil, at the time of the purchase, despite the frequent burnings was doubtless more fertile than at present, a fact that applies to most hill-town tracts, and the east hill was better than the west for agricultural purposes, not being as stony and rough as the west hill. Rye, oats, corn and other grains were raised, as well as flax. The forest growth is remarkable in regard to quickness with which newly cleared land will clothe itself again, and this fact has been the reason why the people for the last fifty years have been able to furnish lumber, railroad ties, and wood to neighboring towns, in large quantities; in fact, relying upon this method, and the furnishing of stone for building purposes, for income rather than upon the raising of agricultural crops for the market. Potatoes of the finest quality are produced, and have always been considered better than those raised along the Connecticut Valley.*

From the common on the west hill near the old meeting house there is a fine view of the Connecticut valley, and to the north-west Greylock, the highest land in the state can be seen, and also the

---

* The potato is said to have been raised in Pelham as early as 1740, or ten years before the people of Amherst and Northampton raised them. The potato was regarded as a curiosity rather than for use as food at that time, and was coarse grained and rank in taste. It is said Josiah Pierce of Hadley raised eight bushels in 1763, to the great wonder and astonishment of his neighbors who wondered what he could do with them. The potato was regarded by some as a sort of forbidden fruit, and a hill or two was planted in gardens as a curiosity. It is said that Rev. Jonathan Hubbard of Sheffield came near being handled by the church for raising twenty bushels in one year, it being thought a matter of sufficient importance for the church to take action upon as a moral question.

Green Mountains of southern Vermont. Almost due east, Wachuset, the next highest mountain in the state, is visible, and looking northeastward, across the hill-top village of New Salem, Monadnock looms up across the state line in New Hampshire. The air upon these two hilltops is pure and healthful, and the Great Hollow between is not swampy or malarious, the soil being light and sandy and more easily cultivated than in portions more rough and stony along the slopes.

BOOK NO 1

This Book belongs To the
Proprietors of ye Northerly Half of
a Tract of Equivalent land Lying on ye
East of Hadley &ct
& is Libo A   JOHN CHANDLER JUN
                     Proprietors Clerk
Lisburn So Called.

WORCESTER SS—WORCESTER FEB 26 1738-9.

John Chandler Jun Esq being chosen clerk of the Proprietors of a tract of land lying in the county of Hampshire East of and adjoining to Hadley which James Thornton Robert Peibols and others purchased of John Stoddard Esq was sworn to a faithful discharge of his office the day and year above said by me
                          WILLIAM JENISON
                               Justice of the Peace

Entered from Original by
     JOHN CHANDLER JUN
         Proprietors Clerk.

Articles of Agreement Indented and made ye twentyeth day of October seventeen hundred and thirty eight Between Robert Peibols of Worcester in the county of Worcester and Province of Massachusetts Bay in New England, Blacksmith, on the one part and James Thornton of Worcester aforesaid yeoman on the other part witnesseth, That Whereas on the 26 day of September last past the said Robert Peibols and James Thornton have Jointly covenanted and contracted with Honorable John Stoddard of North Hampton in ye County of Hampshire Esq for one fourth part of that tract of Equivolent Lands Lying Easterly of Hadley (Except eight hundred acres) which he bought of the Executors of Dame Mary Saltonstall Late of Boston D'sd which land was Laid out by Matthew Allen Roger Wolcott and Ebenezer Pomroy Esqr for Twenty nine Thousand Eight hundred & seventy four Acres, And also for one Eighth part of said Tract of Land which said John Stoddard purchased of Capt Roswell Sallonstall of Brandford in the county of New Haven and also for an Eighth part more of said tract of land which fell to or belonged to said Stoddard by Division, making the whole ye one Half of said Tract of Land Excepting Eight hundred part of ye fourth part which ye said Stoddard Purchased of the Executors of Dame Mary Saltonstall as aforesaid.

And Whereas they have covenanted to pay for the Same as follows Viz : Fifteen hundred pounds within Twelve months from the 26th day of September as Aforesaid & Three Thousand pounds more in Eighteen Months from said Date, and both sums to sd Stoddard, and Also the Sum of Nine hundred pounds to Josiah Willard of Boston Esq and the other Executors of Said Dame Mary Saltonstall aforesaid Deceased on or before the 30th day of June 1739, and the further sum of Nine hundred Pounds more to said Executors on or before the Thirtieth Day of June 1740 Together with Lawful Interest from the 30th day of June last Past and also the sum of Five hundred to ye Aforesaid Roswell Saltonstall at or before the Seventh Day of September next Ensuing, and the Further sum of Five Hundred pounds on or before ye Seventh day of September which will be in the Year of our Lord 1740, Together with Lawful Interest Therefor from the Seventh of September last Past, All said sums of Money amounting unto the Sum of Seven Thousand and three hundred pounds and are to be paid in Bills of Credit of ye Old Tenor & for which the said Robert Peibols and James Thornton are within six months from the Said Twenty sixth day of September last past to procure and Deliver him said Stoddard Good and Sufficient Bonds Executed by Persons of Sufficient Estate & such persons whose Bonds shall be to said Stoddards Acceptance of a certain Instrument of that well Executed and called an Indenture under the Hands and Seals of said John Stoddard Robert Peibols and James Thornton will fully and at large appear Reference thereto being had.

And Whereas the Said Robert Peibols & James Thornton being fully determined to Bring forward the Settlement of Said Lands by Settling fourty Families thereon in the Space of three years from Date hereof Viz Each of them Twenty familys. And in order to proceed therein with the more despatch as well as the better to enable them Raise the money for which they are Joyntly to pay for the Purchase as aforesaid and for the building and Erecting a Meeting House for the Publick Worship of God and Settling a Minister and laying out of suitable and convenient Highways and for Making all needful Bridges causways and Roads in said Settlement they do by these Presents Each one for Himself and for his Heirs executors and Administrators Absolutely covenant and engage to ye other in ye Way and Manner following. That is to say. Imprimis, the said Robert Peibols for Himself and for his Heirs executors and adms engages to present proper security in the time and Manner Aforesaid to said Stoddards Acceptance for the one half of all ye aforesaid sums of Money. And the said James Thornton for himself and for his heirs Executors and Administrators engaged to procure proper Security in ye time and Manner aforesaid to Said Stoddards Acceptance for one half of all the aforesaid sums of Money.

Secondly—That they will forthwith or with as Much speed as conveniently they can, have said land Measured and Bounded and then proceed to lay out Sixty one Lots of One Hundred Acres Each so as best to Accommodate them for Settlements, in the doing of which they will lay out Needful and convenient Roads and ways all which Lotts shall draw an equal proportion in all after Divisions till the whole of said Land shall be laid out.

Thirdly, that one of said Lots shall Immediately be Sequestered and Sett Apart for ye settled Ordained Minister in said Plantations with all future drafts and the Same is hereby Ratified to him his heirs and assigns forever, and to be laid as convendable as the same may be and they Oblige themselves to Ratify and Confirm ye same to ye Person who shall be first settled and Ordained as Aforesaid for the Incouragement of those persons they shall admit as Partners or Settlers with them.

Fourthly, that as soon as ye said Ministers Lot shall be sett off that then the said Robert Peibols shall have the Liberty of Choosing Two lots In that he sees cause without Draft and when he has so done then the said James Thornton shall have Liberty to choose two lots as he sees cause without Draft. That the remaining lots shall be numbered and drawn for by said Partys or those they shall admit as partners or Settlers with them—so that each party shall have with those who held under them Thirty Lots.

Fifthly, That the charges arising in said Plantation by the surveying and bounding of ye whole of said tract and Laying out the lots as aforesaid and the After Divisions, all needful ways and Roads and Making Bridges and Causways and the settling of a Minister and building and finishing a Meeting House and all unforeseen Charges for ye proposing and compleating what is aforementioned shall be borne by the Persons owning the said Lotts Viz—One Lott to pay one sixtieth part and so proportionately for what each party shall own.

Sixthly, The said Robert Peibols engages for himself and for his heirs executors and Administratsrs To have with himself Twenty familys of Good Conversation Settled on the Premises who shall be such as were Inhabitants of the Kingdom of Ireland or their Decendants being Protestants and none be admitted but such as bring good and undeniable Credentials or certificates of their being Persons of good conversation and of the Presbyterian Persuasion as used in the Church of Scotland and Conform to the Discipline thereof unless they shall otherwise agree hereafter, said families to be actually settled on the premises in three years from the date hereof Each to have a House of at least Eighteen feet Square and Seven feet studd well Inclosed and made Habitable and upon one of said hundred Acre lots, and have three acres part thereof improved by Plowing and Mowing and the said James Thornton engages for himself for his heirs executors and adms to have with himself Twenty families settled on the Premises in the time and way and Manner and in all regards as discribed as aforesaid nothing excepted or Rejected and who shall each one perform as to laboring and

Improving as aforesaid   Viz as is to be done on the part of said Robert Peibols.

Seventhly, That each party have liberty in his own name and right to dispose of his share and Interest in the premises as he sees cause to Inable him fully to comply with what they respectively have engaged to do as herein already stated.

Eightly—That in the first and all future Divisions all Persons who shall be admitted as Partners or Settlers shall have a vote in proportion to his Right in all Meetings Hereafter to be called unless Debarred by some Previous contract.

Ninthly—They Each one engage for themselves and all those who shall hold under them that none of them shall take any cattle to Feed in ye woods in ye bounds and Limits of the aforesaid Settlement in the Sumor season but what are their own property unless ye settlers hereafter shall agree to ye same and, Finally, that they will with convenient speed procure a Legall Meeting of ye Proprietors of said Lands as soon as they have heard of all or part of their settlers, and in the proprietors book entered the foregoing articles of Agreement as ye foundation of their Settlement and future Intending. Hereby Covenanting for themselves and for their several and Representative Heirs executors administrators and assigns that they will proceed agreeable to what is above written on the Forfeiture of Five Hundred pounds by him who shall Fail to be paid to the other besides Treble Damages.

In Witness whereof the Party to thees Presents have hereunto affixed their Hands and Seals the day and year aforesaid.

It is agreed Notwithstanding aforemention that Peibols shall choose one of his two Lots then Thornton one, Then Peibols his Second Then Thornton his Second.

ROBERT PEIBOLS   (Seal)
JAMES THORNTON   (Seal)

Signed Sealed and Delivered
in presence of us
    MATHEW GRAY JUN
    JOHN CHANLDER JUN

WORCESTER SS--WORCESTER OCTOBER 26, 1738

Robert Peibols and James Thornton The Subscribers personally appearing and respectively Acknowledged the foregoing Instrument containing Seven Pages to be their act and deed before Me

JOHN CHANDLER JUN Im-Pa

Entered from the Original by
    JOHN CHANDLER JUN Clerk.

DEED FROM COL. STODDARD.

To all people to whom these presents shall come. Greeting

Know ye that John Stoddard of North-Hampton in ye County of Hampshire in the Province of the Massachusetts Bay in New England, for and in

THE FIRST SETTLERS.

Consideration of the Sum of Seven Thousand three Hundred Pounds in bills of Public Credit of ye Old Tenor in hand already Received of the Persons hereafter named the Receipt whereof he doth hereby Acknowledge and himself thereby fully satisfied and contented, hath given granted, bargained and sold, And by these presents doth fully freely Clearly and Absolutely Give grant, Bargain sell Release convey and confirm unto them their heirs and Assigns forever one half (excepting Eight Hundred acres) of that tract of equivolent land Lying and being in ye County of Hampshire bounded Westerly on Hadley, Southwardly on another Tract of Equivolent land Commonly called Cold Spring Township, Eastwardly on land called Quabbin North on land now called Wells Town, Which Tract of land was laid out by Mathew Allen, Roger Woolcott, and Ebenezer Pomroy Esq^{rs} for Twenty nine Thousand Eight Hundred and Seventy four acres, A More particular Discription of which land does appear by Abar (Cohun) entered in ye Secretaries office in Boston, which half part (Excepting Eight Hundred acres as aforesaid) by a Division lately Made by the owners or proprietors of said Equivolent Land is laid seperatly and contained in ye first lott and does contain ye whole of said lott (excepting thirty eight acres two Roods and thirty three perches which belongs to Mr. Elisha Williams (Doct) of Yale College, which lott Lyeth on the north part of said Equivolent Land and from said line Extends South one Thousand and Eleven Rods and Eleven feet to Monuments Raised at Each End and does Extend from Hadley bounds on the west to the East Bounds of said Equivolent land, A more particular description of which lot may be seen in ye Deed of Partition bearing date ye seventh day of September 1738, which said half (excepting as aforesaid) the said John Stoddard doth hereby sell and confirm as aforesaid, to the following persons and in ye following proportion (viz) To Robert Peibols five sixtieth parts; To Patrick Peibols one sixtieth part; To Robert Lotheridge two sixtieth parts, to William Gray Jun one sixtieth part, To John McConkey, one sixtieth part, To Alexander McConkey one sixtieth part, To Alexander Turner one sixtieth part, to John Stinson one sixtieth part, to James Hood one sixtieth part, To Adam Johnson two sixtieth parts, To Ephraim Cowan one sixtieth part, To George Cowan one sixtieth part, To Samuel Gray two sixtieth parts, To John Gray Jun three sixtieth parts, To Thomas Dick one sixtieth part, To John Dick one sixtieth part, To John Alexander one sixtieth part, To James Allexander one sixtieth part, To James McAllach one sixtieth part, To Samuel Thomas one sixtieth part, To James Taylor two sixtieth parts, (All the above named persons are of Worcester In the County of Worcester, except George Cowan who is of Concord in the Couuty of Middlesex) To John Fergerson of Grafton one sixtieth part, To James Gilmore of Boston two sixtieth parts, To Abraham Patterson of Liecester in ye County of Worcester one sixtieth part, To Thomas Lowden of Leicester one sixtieth part, To John Chandler of Worcester one sixtieth part, To John Johnson of Shrewsbury one sixtieth part, To Adam Clark of Worcester one sixtieth part, To James Thornton of Worcester fourteen sixtieth parts.

To have and to hold the aforesaid half part of equivolent land (except the Eight Hundred acres as before excepted) and in that part thereof above described with ye Appurtenances and Priviliges thereto belonging, To them the above named persons, their heirs and assigns forever according to their several and Respective proportions as before expressed, to their several and Respective proper use benefit and behoof forevermore, and the said John Stoddard for himself his heirs etc, Doth covenant and engage to and with the before named persons their Respective heirs and assigns, that before and until the ensealing thereof as ye true sole and lawful owner of the premises and stood seized thereof in his own right in Fee simple and had in himself good Right and full power and Lawful authority to Grant bargain sell aliene Release convey and confirm the same as aforesaid and that free and Clear and Clearly executed acquitted and discharged of and from all leans and other Gifts grants Bargains Sale Lease, Mortgage, Wills, entails, Joyntures, Thirds, Executions and Incumbrances whatsoever, and the said John Stoddard doth hereby further Conenant and engage the before granted premises with ye Appurtenances to them the before named persons and other Respective heirs and Assigns forever; to warrant secure and defend against the Lawful Claims and demands of any and every person and persons whatsoever. In Witness whereof he hath hereunto set his hand and seal this twenty first day of January in the twelfth year of the Reign of our Sovereign Lord George of Great Britain as King Annogy Dom 1738-9 John Stoddard and a seal signed sealed and Delivered in presence of ye witness Elisha Marsh, Cor-nel Waldo

WORCESTER SS WORCESTER FEB 1738

John Stoddard Esqr Subscriber to the foregoing Instrument personally Appearing freely Acknowledged the same to be his act and Deed

Before me WILLIAM JENISON Justice of Peace.

HAMPSHIRE SS SPRINGFIELD FEB 3d 1738-9

Received and Recorded in ye Records of Deeds for the County of Hampshire Lib⁰ L. Folio 220 &ct

Pr WM PYNCHON JUN Redr

Entered from the Original Deed
Pr JOHN CHANDLER Proprietors Clerk

APPLICATION FOR THE FIRST MEETING, FEB. 2, 1738-9.

To the Honorable John Stoddard Esq one of His Majestys Justices of the Peace for the County of Hampshire. Ss. We the Subscribers Proprietors of the Northerly half of that Tract of Equivalent Land (Excepting Eight Hundred Acres) Lying and being in the County of Hampshire bounded Westerly on Hadley, Southerly on another Tract of Equivalent Land commonly called Cold Spring Township, Easterly on Land called Quabbin, North on Land now called Wells Town, Humbly apply to you Honr & Pray you will please to Grant a Warrant directed to some one of us, Requiring ye person to whom the same is directed pursuant to law to warn and notifi all the Proprietors of said Tract of land to Assemble and meet together on Monday the 26th day of Feb'ry Currant by Ten of the Clock in the forenoon at the present Dwelling House of Capt Daniell Heywood in Worcester. Then and there to transact the following Particulars

I.   To Choose a Moderator for said Meeting.
II. To Choose a Clerk for said Proprietee.
III. To Agree upon a Suitable Method for bringing on a Speedy Settlement of said Lands, and in order thereto—1st to Choose a committee and surveyor to take an exact survey of the whole tract of Land, and to see it well bounded out, & 2dly to lay out Sixty one home lotts so as best to Accommodate a Settlement.
 3dly To lay out suitable Roods & ways
 4th To Grant a lot or Right to the first settled Minister.
 5th To Draw Lotts according to Each ones Interest.
 6th To Agree upon Proper Methods for laying out all aforesaid Divisions.
 7th To Raise Money for defraying all Charges proper to be born by ye Proprietors heitherto and also for Defraying the Charges that may arise for the future Viz for building a Meeting House Settling a Minister, Making Bridges Causways and Roads and for defraying any Unforeseen Charges that may arise in perfecting and Compleating the settlement of the place.
IV To Agree how Meetings shall be called for the future and to Pass orders for the Managing Improving Dividing or Disposing of said lands, and finally to do any other thing Conducive to the good of the community Herein you will greatly Oblige Sr Your Honors Humble Servants
  Worcester February 2 : 1838-9

> ROBERT BARBER
> ROBERT LOTHERIDGE
> JOHN DICK
> PATRICK PEIBLES
> JOHN CHANDLER JUN
> JAMES THORNTON
> ROBERT PEIBLES
> WILLIAM JOHNSON
> JOHN STINSON
> SAMUEL GRAY.

WARRANT FOR FIRST MEETING OF PROPRIETORS.

HAMPSHIRE SS
  [L. S.]   To Patrick Peibles of Worcester In the County of Worcester & one of the foregoing Subscribers Greeting.
  Pursuant to the foregoing Application you are hereby Required In His Majestys name to Warn aud Notifi (Agreeable to the Direction of the law in that Case Made and Provided) the Proprietors of the Tract of Land within mentioned to Assemble & Meet at the Time & place within mentioned. Then and there To Transact on all or Such of ye Particulars in Said Application Named as they shall see cause, Hereof you are not To Fail And make due and timely Return hereof and of your doings herein,

Given under my hand and seal at North Hampton this Second day of February in ye 12th year of the Majestys Reighn Anno Dom⁰ 1738-9
JOHN STODDARD.

WORCESTER FEB 2d 1738-9.
By Virtue of the within warrant I have notified ye Within Proprietors to meet at the time and place within Mentioned to Transact on the within Affairs, by Posting up a Notification in the Town of Hadley on which the land adjoins And one in the town of Worcester where the Proprietors Mostly Dwell.   Attest   PARTRICK PEIBLES
Entered from the Original Application & Warrant.
Pr JOHN CHANDLER JUN Proprietors Clerk

NOTIFICATION TO THE PROPRIETORS.

Pursuant to a Warrant to me Directed by the Honorable John Stoddard Esq, One of His Majestys Justices of the Peace for the County of Hampshire

The Proprietors of the Northerly half of that Tract of Equivalent Land (Excepting Eight Hundred Acres) Lying and being in the County of Hampshire, bounded Westerly on Hadley, Southerly on Another Tract of Equivalent Land Commonly Called Cold Spring Township, Easterly, on land called Quabbin, North on land now called Wells Town, are hereby notified to Assemble and meet together on Monday the 26th day of February Currant by Ten of the Clock in the forenoon, at the Present Dwelling House of Capt Daniel Haywood in Worcester, Then and there to Transact on the following particulars, Viz

    I   To Choose a Moderator for said Meeting.
   II   To Choose a Clerk for said Proprietee.
  III   To Agree upon suitable Methods for bringing on a speedy settlement of said lands, And in order thereto

First, to Choose a Committee and Surveyors to take an exact survey of the whole Tract and see it well bounded out &

Secondly to lay out Sixty one Home Lotts so as best to accommodate a Settlement

Thirdly, To lay out suitable Roads and Ways.

Fourthly, To Grant a Lot or Right for the first Settled minister.

Fifthly, To draw Lotts according to Each ones Interest.

Sixthly, To Agree upon proper Methods for laying out all after Divisions

Seventhly, To Raise Money for defraying all the Charges proper to be born by the Proprietors hitherto; and also for building a Meeting House, Settling a Minister, Making Bridges Causeways & Roads and for defraying any Unforeseen Charges that may arise in perfecting and Compleating the Settlement of the Place.

  IV   To Agree how Meetings shall be called for the future, and to Pass orders for the Managing, Improving, Dividing or Disposing of said Lands, and finally to do any other thing Condusive to the good of the Community.

Given under my hand and this second Day of February Anno Dom 1738-9
PATRICK PEIBLES.
Entered from the Original
Pr JOHN CHANDLER JUN Proprietors Clerk

THE FIRST SETTLERS.

First Meeting of the Proprietors, Feb. 26, 1738-9.

Att a meeting of the Proprietors of the Northerly half of that Tract of Equivalent Land (excepting Eight hundred Acres) Lying and being in the County of Hampshire, bounded westerly on Hadley, Southerly on another tract of Equivalent Land commonly called Cold Spring Township, Easterly on land called Quabbin, North on land now called Wells Town, Regularly assembled and Mett Together at the Dwelling House of Capt Daniel Heywood in Worcester on Monday the twenty sixth day of February at 10 a clock in ye forenoon, At which meeting the following Votes Passed Vizt

John Chandler Jun Esq was chosen Moderator by a Unanimous Vote.

John Chandler Jun Esq was chosen Clerk by a unanimous vote and sworn to the faithful discharge of his office by William Jenison Esq in the meeting before ye proprietors.

Voted That the Clerk be desired to purchase a book at the charge of the proprietors and that he first enter in the Same the Grand Agreement made and Executed Between James Thornton & Robert Peibles Oct 20th 1738 which is now voted as the foundation of the Settlement and Direction in future proceedings they having just purchased the premises of the Honorable John Stoddard Esq and Took the Rest of the Proprietors in as partners on the thirty first day of January last and many of them in Consequence of obligations or Agreements made in writing on aforesaid thirty first day of January, and that the Grand Deed or Instrument be so Recorded and then the Application to said Stoddard for this present Proprietors Meeting &ct with the warrant & Warning and then the proceedings of this and all other future meetings. Said Records to be done at the charge of the Propriety,—Ordered that Messrs Andrew McFarland Robert Lotheridge & Samuel Gray be a Committee with the Assistance of a Surveyer all on oath to take an exact Survey of the whole Tract of land and bound the same out well, and then to lay the same out into six Equal Ranges, The Range lines to Run East and West and between Each Range to leave two perch wide for a highway except between the Center Range where they are to leave four perch wide for a highway That then they do in the Center of the whole Tract or as near as they in their Judgments Shall think proper lay out Ten Acres for a Meeting House Place burying place and Training field from which a highway four perch wide shall be left North and South from the North and South of the whole Tract, and that then the Committee proceed to lay out Sixty one Home Lots, the Standard to be One Hundred acres and that they proportion the lotts for Quality so as to make them as Equal as may be. That they Lay out one of said Lotts for the first Minister as nigh the Meeting House as ye land will Admit off.—And that then they proceed to lay out ye Sixty Lotts, in ye doing of which they are to lay out the best of ye lands, and that such land as is not suitable for the Homelotts as aforesaid to Lye for after Divisions. And in Case a number of lotts Exceeding three are laid out adjoining in one Range that they leave land for a highway between so that between every three lotts at least There be a highway of two perch wide.

Voted that the Committee take Such Pilotts with them as they Shall Judge Necessary at the Charge of the Proprietors.

Voted that there be an exact Plan of the whole Tract Made and the Sundry Range lines laid down thereon to be Numbered as follows. The Range on the South Side to be called the First Range, and so to proceed Northward to the sixth Range on the North side, And that the land laid out for ye Meeting House &ct be Duly laid down on the Plan as also Each & every of ye Sixty one Lotts. That the Range lines & lotts be very well bounded and Marks therein made so thick as to be at anytime Easily found.

Voted that the Comette have nine Shillings per Diem Allowed them for their Service and Subsistance. And they were sworn in the Meeting to the faithful Discharge of their Trust by John Chandler Jun Esq.

Voted that William Young be the Surveyor, who was Sworn in the Meeting to the faithful Discharge of his office and that he have fourteen Shillings pr Diem for his service and Subsistance, and he is hereby Directed to keep an exact Journal of the whole affair and to return a fair Plott of his whole proceedings in all regards as Aforesaid, And in case of his being Indisposed or otherwise not attending the Service that then the Comittee and Clerk choose some other suitable person to perform the same.

Voted, that James Allexander be an assistant to said Comittee and have the same wages (vizt) Nine Shillings Pr Diem he finding himself.

Voted, that before the lotts are drawn Vizt, the fifty six Lotts, (after Robert Peibles and James Thornton have chosen their two lotts Each which they may do at anytime when laid out and ye Ministers Lott) be all of them numbered on the Plott, Vizt, from six to Sixty one and the Ministers Lott to be number One, And their four Lotts Number Two, Three, four, five,—And that after they are drawn a Return be wrote of every mans Lott with ye Point of Compass and length of line and the Corner bounds to be entered at large in ye Proprietors Book And the Original to be delivered to the owner of the Lott, Said ye Return to be signed by ye Comittee & Surveyor or Otherwise as the Proprietors shall order.

Voted that the fifth sixth & seventh particulars under the third General head or Article be Referred to the adjournment of this Meeting—then to further Consider on.

And then the Meeting was by a vote of the Proprietors adjourned to this place on the first day of May next at Ten of the Clock in the forenoon.

      Attest JOHN CHANDLER JUN Moderator

The Aforesaid Votes were passed

      Attest JOHN CHANDLER JUN Proprietors Clerk

SECOND MEETING OF THE PROPRIETORS, MAY 1, 1739.

At a meeting of the proprietors aforesaid held by Adjournment from February 26, 1738-9 to May 1 1739 at Ten a Clock in the forenoon and then met at the Dwelling House of Capt Daniel Heywood in Worcester. The Comittee appointed for Surveying the lands belonging to the Proprietors and for laying out Sixty one homelotts made Report, and by the Surveyor William Young laid before the proprietors a Plan of the whole Tract and Also of said home lotts— Said Lotts being numbered from one to Sixty one, which was approved off & ordered to be recorded, and whereas they are but twenty five of said lotts fully compleated it was Voted that the Remainder be done at the charge of the Society. It was also Voted that whoever draws the Thirty Second, fifty fourth, & Sixty first Lott or any of them, may have Liberty to Drop fifty acres off either lott at one end or side in a regular figure & have the same laid out in any of ye Undivided lands at the charge of the Society. And it was also Voted that Said lands be for ye future called ye Lisburn Propriety.

Voted the Lotts No 7 & No 8 which now contain One Hundred and Eleven acres have added to each of them at the West end of said lotts Ten Acres, ye whole width of Said Lotts. Voted that Lot No 1 with the After Divisions befor the first Settled Minister, That No 2 & No 3 be two of Robert Peibles Lotts and No 4 and No 5 be two of James Thorntons Lotts, And then the Proprietors proceeded to draw their Lotts and Here follows a List of the names of the Proprietors and the lotts they drew &ct.

NAMES OF THE PRESENT PROPRIETORS AND THE LOTTS THEY DREW.

Names of Proprietors	No. of Lotts	Names of Proprietors	No. of Lotts	Names of Proprietors	No, of Lotts
Ministers Lott		James Thornton	1	Samuel Gray	21
Robert Peibols		Adam Patterson	2	Robert Barber	22
Robert Peibols		James Gilmore	3	Robert Barber & }	23
James Thornton		Adam Clark	4	William Jonhson }	24
James Thornton		John Chandler Jr Esq	5	Alexander Turner	25
(The foregoing Lotts were without Draft)		John Alexander		John Gray	26
		John Johnson		John Stinson	27
John Dick		James McAllah	6	James Alexander	28
Patrick Peibols		Robert Lotheridge	7	John Fergerson	29
John Gray		John Chandler Jn Esq	8	James Thornton	30
John Gray		James McConkey	9	Adam Johnson	31
John McConkey		William Johnson	10	James Thornton	32
William Gray Jr		James Taylor	11	James Thornton	33
James Thornton		Adam Johnson	12	Alexander McConkey	34
James Thornton		James Hood	13	James Taylor	35
James Thornton		William Thornton	14	Robert Lotheridge	36
Thomas Dick		Samuel Thomas	15	Thomas Lowden	37
Robert Peibols		James Thornton	16	Samuel Gray	38
James Gilmore		Andrew McFarland	17	Andrew McFarland }	39
Mathew Gray		James Breakenridge	18	& Mathew Gray }	40
James Thornton		Mathew Thornton	19	Robert Peibols	41
George Cowen		Ephraim Cowen	20		42

Lotts values right column: Samuel Gray 43, Robert Barber 44, William Jonhson 45, Alexander Turner 46, John Gray 47, John Stinson 48, James Alexander 49, John Fergerson 50, James Thornton 51, Adam Johnson 52, James Thornton 53, James Thornton 54, Alexander McConkey 55, James Taylor 56, Robert Lotheridge 57, Thomas Lowden 58, Samuel Gray 59, Andrew McFarland & Mathew Gray 60, Robert Peibols 61

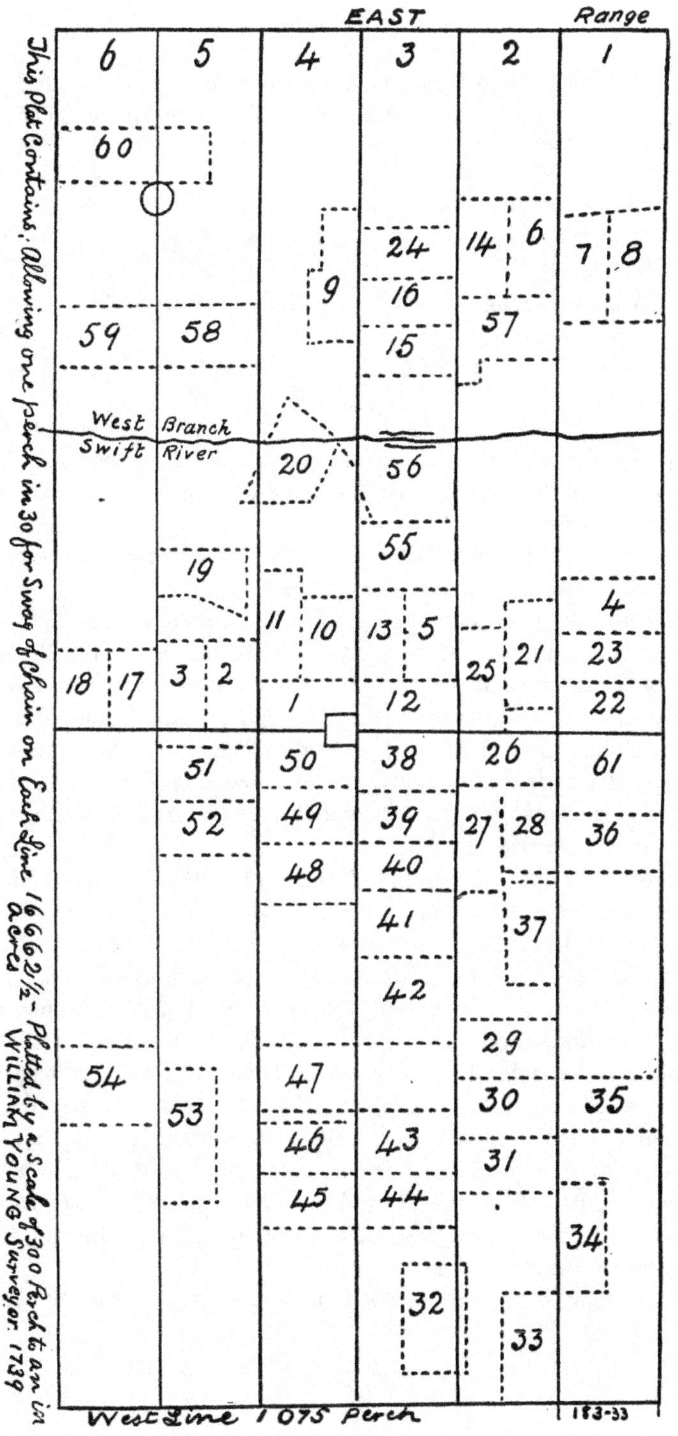

This plat contains, allowing one perch in 30 for Sway of Chain on Each Line 1666 2/3 acres — Platted by a Scale of 300 Perch to an in WILLIAM YOUNG Surveyor 1739

EAST — Range

| 6 | 5 | 4 | 3 | 2 | 1 |

60

59 | 58

24 | 14 | 6 | 7 | 8
9 | 16
| 15 | 57

West Swift Branch River

20 | 56
55
19
11 | 10 | 13 | 5 | | 4
18 | 17 | 3 | 2 | | 25 | 21 | 23
| 1 | 12 | | 22

51 | 50 | 38 | 26 | 61
52 | 49 | 39 | 27 | 28 | 36
48 | 40
41 | 37
42
29
54 | 53 | 47 | 30 | 35
46 | 43 | 31
45 | 44 | 34
32 | 33

West Line 1075 Perch — 183-33

The Comittee laid before ye proprietors an Account of the charge of Surveying the whole Tract and of Sixty one Home Lotts, and is as follows Vizt

			£ s p
Andrew McFarland	22 Days	a 9s	8—18—0
Robert Lotheridge	22 Days	a 9s	9—18—0
Samuel Gray	22 Days	a 9s	9—18—0
William Young	22 Days	a 14s	15— 8—0
James Allexander	23 Days	a 9s	10— 7—0
To Andrew McFarland for Pilotts &ct			2—11—6
			58— 0—6

Voted that the above sums as in enntry—Unto the sum of Fifty Eight Pound & six pence be allowed and paid to the above persons by the Treasurer.

Voted that the sum of three pound be paid Patrick Peibles for a Journey to North Hampton &c by the Treasurer.

Voted that thirty Shillings be allowed & paid to Captain Daniel Heywood for the expenses at his house this meeting by the Treasurer.

Voted that the sum of fifteen pound be allowed and paid towards the Making a Road to the Meeting House and from thence into East Hadley so called Vizt a Bridle Road, and John Gray and James Allexander are appointed a Comittee To see ye same located in the most Suitable place for Publick Advantage and According to their best Discretion.

Voted that the Remainder of the Lands be all Laid out in two Divisions, one to be called a Second Division and ye other the Final Division. and that the Standard for the Second Division be Fourty Acres, and that the Lotts be laid out Quantity for Quality, taking the best of the land, and that the lotts be numbered from one to Sixty one and drawn for as the home lotts were. And that the Remainder be laid out into Sixty one Equal parts and numbered and drawn as the Second Division, and that the lotts in both Divisions be well bounded out and a fair plan returned both of the home lotts Second Division & Final Division, and a Return Made and Signed by ye Comittee & Surveyor of both Divisions in one Return to be Recorded in the Proprietors Book & the Original Delivered to the Respective owners of Said Lotts,—

Voted that Robert Peibles Ephraim Cowan and John Stinson be

the Comittee with ye Assistance of William Young the Surveyor to Accomplish said work by ye Last day of October next, and that the Comittee have nine Shillings each pr Day & the Surveyor fifteen Shillings pr day they finding themselves and to be on oath,—and they were all sworn to the faithful Discharge of their Trust in the Meeting by John Chandler Jun Esq.

Voted That William Thornton be an Assistant to said Committee, and he have nine shillings pr Day he finding himself.

Voted, That William Young ye Surveyor doe with ye Assistance of William Thornton and John Dick perfect ye Surveying of the Home Lotts and that it be done as soon as May be, that said Young have fourteen shillings pr day and said Thornton & Dick each nine shillings pr Day for said Service, finding themselves, and they were sworn by John Chandler Jun Esq

Voted that the Clerk Draw all needful Copys for the Comittees and Surveyors Instruction.

Voted, That a Tax Assessment of Three Pounds a Right, amounting to the Sum of One Hundred and Eighty pounds be assessed For Defraying the charge that have and may arise in performing the said service and for such other things as the Society shall order & appoint & that the money may be collected by the first day of November next and paid into ye hands of the Treasurer.

Voted That William Gray Jun Andrew McFarland and John Chandler Jun Esq be a Comittee & Assessors for ye Propriety—The said William Gray Jun & Andrew McFarland were sworn to the faithful Discharge of their Trust in ye meeting by John Chandler Jun Esq.

Voted that Robert Barber be the Collector of the Propriety—and he was sworn to ye faithful discharge of his Trust in ye Meeting by John Chandler Jun Esq.

Voted that John Chandler Jun Esq be Treasurer to the Propriety, —and he was sworn faithfully to Discharge the Respective Dutys of an Assessor and Treasurer by William Jenison Esq.

Voted That the Assessors do forthwith make said Assessment of three pounds on each Right and that the same be collected by ye time Aforementioned.

And then the Meeting was by vote of the Proprietors adjourned as also ye Affairs in ye Warrant not yet acted on To this place on the

First Day of November next at Ten of the clock in the forenoon.
     Attest JOHN CHANDLER JUN Moderator.

 All the foregoing votes were passed.
     Attest JOHN CHANDLER JUN Proprietors Clerk.

THIRD MEETING OF PROPRIETORS, NOVEMBER 1, 1739.

Att a meeting of the Proprietors Held by Adjournment from May 1, 1739 to November 1, 1739 At Ten of the Clock in ye forenoon and then Mett at the House of Capt Daniel Heywood in Worcester.

The meeting not being full the Matters to be Transacted not being fully prepared, It was Voted that the Expenses being fourty Shillings be paid by the Treasurer, and then The Meeting was by a vote of the Proprietors adjourned as also the Affairs in ye Warrant not yet acted on To this place on Monday the fifth Instant at Ten a Clock in the forenoon.
     Attest JOHN CHANDLER JUN Clerk Proprietors.

FOURTH MEETING OF THE PROPRIETORS, NOVEMBER 5, 1739.

Att a Meeting of the Proprietors Aforesaid Held by adjournment from the First Instant to this 5th day of November 1739 at Ten a Clock in ye forenoon and then Mett at the House of Capt Daniel Heywood in Worcester.

An account of the Charge for Completing the Division being laid before ye proprietors for allowance and approving the following sums due to the following Persons Vizt

  To William Young Surveyor 13 Days at 14s £9 2s 5d
  To William Thornton   13 days at 9s 5 17 0
  To John Dick   13 days at 9s 5 17 0
                 £20 16 0

Voted that the above sums amounting Unto the Sum of Twenty pounds sixteen shillings be Allowed and paid to the above persons by the Treasurer. Pursuant to a vote of the Proprietors of ye first of May last William Johnson who drew the Thirty Second Home lot on first Division Dropt fifty acres thereof at ye Southeasterly corner and to take the same at the Northwesterly corner of the Home lott Number Twenty in the Forth Range & is called No 32.

James Thornton by his assignee, Hugh Gray Dropt fifty Acres on the Easterly end of the Home Lott Number fifty four and Took it in the fifth Range between No 53 & 46 & 47 and is called No 54.

Also Robert Peibles Dropt fifty Acres on the southerly side of the Home lott num sixty one and took it in the fourth Range between No 15 & 58 & is Called No 61.

A Plan of the Second and Third Divisions including the first Division was presented and allowed by the Proprietors and ordered to be Recorded or added to the Book of Records.

RANGE 6   5   4 EAST 3   2   1 RAN

7-3	29-2	61-3	19-3	28-2	46-3
15-3	5-3	7-3	20-3	18-3	17-3
60	6-3	25-2		14	6	7	8
	59-2	26-2	24		
8-3	58-2	27-2	9	16	57	60-2
17-3	57-2	30-2	15		13-3
59	58				
31-2	1-3	4-3	21-3	32-2	14-3	12-3
9-3	3-3	2-3	22-3	33-2	15-3	11-3

West Branch Swift River

10-3	36 37 38	39 10-3			25-3
34-2	35	2-2 2-2	2-2	20	5 6	28-3
23-3	41-2 40-2	32	22-3 24-3	46-3	26-3
	75-2 74-2				27-3	20-2
24-3	19	21-2 1-3	55	19-2	
12-2				18-2	5
11-2	1-3	11 10	13 4	17-2	
10-2				25	21	23
18	17	3	2	1	12		22
		29-2			17-2	56-2
30-3	51	50	38	26	61	
31-3	52	49	39	27	28	36
32-3	43-2	48	40		49-3
	44-2				
33-3	45-2	5-2	41	60-2	37	50-3
48-3 47-2	35-3	6-2		55-2	51-3
46-2	47-3	34-3	42		
		53-2			52-3
54	8-2	46-2 4-2	47	2-2 29-2	29	35
	53			3-2	30	
36-3	7-2	46	43	31-	54-3
47-3 54-2	48 2	45	44	22-2	55-3
60-2	49-2			23-2	
39-2 31-2	50-2		59-3	60-2	
38-3	37-3	45-3		34	34
40-3	39-3	44-3	32	33	56-3
42-3	41-3	43-3		57-3	
1-2	48-3	58-3			

1075 Perch   WEST   183½ Rods

Scale 300 Perch to the inch — 166 63/64 Acres in Plat

2480 Perch

THE FIRST SETTLERS. 31

Voted that the Surveyor with ye late Comittee Vizt Ephraim Cowan forthwith or as soon as may be Compleat the Third Division at ye charge of ye Proprietors.

Voted that whoever Draws the Second Division No 40 May have Third Division No 4, second Division No 41 3d Division 56, 2d Division No 56, 3d Division 6,—2d Division 17,—3d Division 44.

Here follows the List of the first Division as formerly Drawed with the numbers of the Second and Third Division as drawn by the proprietors.

Persons names.	1st Div	2d Div	3d Div	Persons named.	1st Div	2d Div	3d Div
Ministers Lott	1	56	6	William Johnson	32	50	10
Robert Peibles	2	52	13	James Taylor	33	51	29
Robert Peibles	3	11	28	Adam Johnson	34	31	19
James Thornton	4	16	1	James Hood	35	13	27
James Thornton	5	40	4	William Thornton	36	55	20
John Dick	6	17	44	Samuel Thomas	37	25	16
Patrick Peibles	7	45	7	James Thornton	38	3	14
John Gray	8	27	34	Andrew McFarland	39	39	5
John Gray	9	8	50	James Brakenridge	40	54	24
John McConkey	10	61	35	Mathew Thornton	41	58	45
William Gray	11	60	48	Ephraim Cowan	42	24	52
James Thornton	12	42	38	Samuel Gray	43	9	26
James Thornton	13	22	55	Robert Barber	44	19	33
James Thornton	14	12	58	Robert Barber and Wm Johnson }	45	29	22
Thomas Dick	15	18	8
Robert Peibles	16	6	42	Alexander Turner	46	36	12
James Gilmore	17	41	56	John Gray	47	37	11
Mathew Gray	18	26	25	John Stinson	48	21	18
James Thornton	19	14	9	James Alexander	49	46	61
George Cowan	20	10	41	John Fergerson	50	47	21
James Thornton	21	34	57	James Thornton	51	1	30
Adam Patterson	22	23	51	Adam Johnson	52	15	32
James Gilmore	23	33	36	James Thornton	53	5	43
Adam Clark	24	30	53	James Thornton	54	57	2
John Chandler	25	59	39	Allex McConkey	55	53	3
John Alexander	26	49	17	James Taylor	56	20	46
John Johnson	27	43	54	Robert Lotheridge	57	38	46
James McAllah	28	32	15	Thomas Lowden	58	2	59
Robert Lotheridge	29	7	40	Samuel Gray	59	28	23
John Chandler	30	4	31	Allex'r McFarland and Mathew Gray } 60		44	47
James McConkey	31	35	37
				Robert Peibles	61	48	60

Memorandum—here follows an Acct of ye Owners of some of the Above Lotts Vizt, Such as have purchased since ye Home lotts or first Division was Drawn, And the Second & third Divisions Are laid out to said persons and the Return so made Vizt

		1st Div	2d Div	3d Div
William Crossett	Home Lott	57	38	46
Andrew Mclain	do "	14	12	58
James Gilmore	do "	38	3	14
John Peibles	do "	16	6	42
John Clark	do "	19	14	9
William Gray Jun	do "	53	5	43
Mathew Gray	do "	45	29	22
Robert McClain	do "	41	58	45
Hugh Gray	do "	54	57	2

The Second & Third Divisions to said Persons Accordingly.—

The Committee for surveying the Second and Third Divisions laid before the Proprietors An Acct of ye Charges Thereof and it is as follows Vizt

```
To William Young for Thirty eight   a 15s is  £28—10—0
To Robert Peibles        35 days    a 9s is   15—15—0
To Ephriam Cowan         25 days    a 9s is   11— 5—0
To John Stinson          38 days    a 9  is   17— 2—0
To William Thornton      38 days    a 9  is   17— 2—0
To William Young for Drawing the Returns
                          3 days    a 9s is    2— 5—0
                                             ─────────
                                              £91.10.—0
```

Voted that the above sums amounting unto the sum of Ninety one Pound Nineteen shillings be allowed and paid to the Above persons by the Treasurer.

Whereas at the Meeting held on the first day of May Last (1739) there was a sum of fifteen pounds allowed for and towards making a Road in Said property as pr ye votes appear and it now appearing that instead of said sum there has been expended on said affair More Labour than was at first Judged Needful. Wherefore Voted that the following Sums be granted to the following persons for said work and what the same shall Amount to more than said sum of fifteen pounds shall be paid out of ye Taxes Assessed or that may be hereafter assessed on the Propriety Vizt

To James Allexander	7 Days	£3— 3—0
To John Johnson	6 Days	2—14—0
To William Thornton	6 Days	2—14—0
To James Gilmore	6 Days	2—14—0
To Allexander McAllah	6 Days	2—14—0
To William McConkey	6 Days	2—14—0
To Robert McKee	3 Days	1— 7—0
To John Gray	3 1-2 Days	1—11—0
To Ephraim Cowan	1 Day	9—0
To James Brakenridge	2 Days	18—0
To Robert Peibles	1 Day	9—0
To James Hood	1 1-2 Days	13—6
To James McConkey	4 1-2 Days	2— 0—6
		£24—1—6

The further sum now granted being Nine Pounds one shilling & six pence Ordered the whole to be paid by the Treasurer.

(The above sum of £24—1—6 was for building the bridle path to the Meeting house and into East Hadley, or Amherst which they voted to do May 1, 1739.)

Voted that a tax or assessment of twenty-five Shillings A Right, Amounting unto the sum of Seventy pounds be granted for further defraying ye charges that have or may arise on ye proprietors to be Surveyed by ye comittee or assessors already chosen, or they or part of them and to be collected and paid unto ye proprietors Treasurer at before ye fifteenth day of April next, To be by him paid to defray ye Charges already (or which may hereafter be) Allowed of by the Proprietie, And the Meeting with the Articles not acted upon was adjourned by a vote of the propriety to meet at this place on Tuesday the fifteenth day of April next at Ten of the Clock in the forenoon.

     Attest JOHN CHANDLER Clerk Proprietors
The aforesaid votes passed.
    Attest JOHN CHANDLER Clerk Proprietors

FIFTH MEETING OF THE PROPRIETORS, HELD BY ADJOURNMENT FROM NOVEMBER 5 1739 TO APRIL 15 1740.

Att a Meeting of the Proprietors aforesaid, held by Adjournment from November 5th 1739 To April 15 1740 at Ten a Clock in the forenoon and then Mett at the House of Capt Daniel Heywood in Worcester.

An Acc't of the Charges for compleating ye Second and Third Divisions yet being laid before the Proprietors for Allowance.

Voted—That the sum of Eighteen pounds be allowed to William Young Surveyor, for 24 days service as aforesaid and drawing the Return & Seven shillings for paper ye whole being Eighteen pounds 7 shillings, And Also ye sum of five pound Seventeen Shillings to Ephraim Cowen assisting therein &ct being 13 days.

```
            18— 7—0
             5—17—0
           £23— 4—0
```

The above sums amounting to twenty three Pounds four Shillings, Allowed and Ordered to be paid by the Treasurer.

Voted, that James Thornton Robert Peibles James McAllah—Mathew Gray & John Gray a Comittee Impowered by the Proprietors to Request of the Clerk of said Proprietie a Warrant for Calling of a new Meeting as they shall see cause.—The Meeting to be held in the Lisborne propriety. The warrant to Express time and place of Meeting and what is to be Transacted therein—Notifications to be put up in some Publick place in said Proprietie & also in ye Town of Worcester the time by law Required before said Meeting.

Voted, that as often as five or more of ye proprietors shall Judge there is a newsesity from time to time of said Proprietors. The Clerk for the time being upon Application to him Made by said persons in writing under their hands setting forth what they Apprehend newssary to be Transacted shall give a warrent for the same, which warrant shall (till ye proprietors Otherwise Order) be Posted up in some Publick place in said Proprietie and also in the Town of Worcester àt Least fourteen days before the time of the Meeting.

Voted That James Thornton and William Gray and Andrew McFarland be a Comittee fully Impowered To Settle Accounts with the present Treasurer John Chandler Esq for ye Taxes already Granted, allowing his own acct out of the same which amounts To the sum of Twenty Eight Pounds Eighteen shillings with a Reasonable allowance for his service as Treasurer, and that they give him proper discharge and Report as soon as may be to the proprietors & what they do to be obligatory on ye Proprietors.

Voted, that this Meeting be Disolved And it was accordingly so declared by ye Moderator.

      Attest JOHN CHANDLER Proprietors Clerk.

The Aforegoing Votes were passed by the Proprietors & Entered by my own hand.

      Attest JOHN CHANDLER Proprietors Clerk.

Here follows the Returns of ye Home lotts & Second & final or Third Division. These consist of a description and bounds of each of the sixty-one home lotts and also of the sixty-one lots in the Second Division and the sixty-one in the third division. The full description of all these lots would be monotonous reading, that few would care to wade through, and so we give only a few full copies of these descriptions, but enough to show how the record was made. With three divisions of land, each drawn by lot and each series numbered from one to sixty-one must have led to much confusion. It was only by the sheerest luck that a man drew his three parcels of land and had them adjoining each other. Oftener the three parcels were several miles apart, and consequently comparatively valueless for cultivation for the party who drew them. Doubtless there were exchanges made, whereby a parcel drawn by one farmer, but far from his home lot on which he lived, could exchange for a parcel near by, but drawn by a farmer several miles away, to their mutual advantage.

Home Lot No. 1, or the lot set apart for the first settled minister, and the one that Rev. Robert Acercrombie had, with Second Division No. 56 and Third Division No. 6, will serve to illustrate the inconvenience of getting land by lot, or drawing for it as in a lottery.

"No. 1—Ministers Lott—Is a home Lott Laid out to the first Settled Minister in the Lisburn Propriety, Viz, Lays in the fourth Range & Lays Quantity for Quality Containing one Hundred Acres, it Lys In two parts, ye first Lays adjoining the Meeting House Lott, it Bounds Northerly & Southerly on ye Range Lines. Westerly on home Lott No 50 partly and partly on the Meeting House Lott & Easterly on home Lott No 10 partly and partly on home Lott No 11. The Southwest Corner is a stake and stones hence N : 40 perch to a state and stones thence west 20 perch to a stake & stones, Runs from thence N. 143 perch to a stake and from thence East 87 perch

& four tenths of a Perch to a stake and stones, thence S. 183 perch to a stake & stones, from thence to ye Corner first mentioned, Contains Ninety five acres; ye Second is bounded Southerly by home Lott No 56, W. by home Lott No 55 N & E by—third Division No 24 the Southwest Corner is a Stake and Stones Runs from thence E five Degrees South 40 Perch to An Elm tree from thence N 20 Perch to a stake and stones from thence W, five Degrees S: 40 perch to a heap of Stones, thence to the first Corner Containing five Acres, out of the first there is a highway of four Peach Wide to be allowed out on the South side.

Surveyed in April 1739 Pr

WILLIAM YOUNG Surveyor.

ROBERT LOTHERIDGE
SAMUEL GRAY } Comittee
ANDREW MCFARLAND

Entered by JOHN CHANDLER Proprietors Clerk

No 56 is a Second Division Laid out to the Minister in the Lisburn propriety & it Lays in the first Range & Lays Quantity for Quality Containing 50 Acres the S. W. Corner is a stake & stones from thence it Runs North 52 perch & three quarters to a Chisnut tree from thence it Runs E. 152 Perch to a pople stadle from thence it Runs 52 Perch & 3 Quarters to a stake & stones & from thence to ye Corner first mentioned it Bounds South on the South line of the Town N. on home Lott No 61 E. on ye 4 Perch high way Running Cross the Town & W. on home Lott No 36.

No 6 Is a Third Division Laid out to ye Minister In ye Lisburn Propriety & it Lays in ye 5th Range & contains 107 acres the S. W. Corner is a chisnut tree & from thence it Runs C 14 Perch to a heap of stones North from thence 183 perch to a heap of stones from thence 183 perch to a heap of stones from thence E 45 perch to a heap of stones from thence N 26 perch to a heap of stones thence E 10 3-4 perch to a heap of stones from thence N 39 1-4 perch to a stake & stones thence W 55 perch to a heap of Stones from thence S 248 Perch to a heap of stones from thence W 4 Perch to a white oak tree & from thence it Runs to the Corner first mentioned it Bounds S. on ye Range Line partly & partly on 3d Division No 5 E on 2d Division No 29 partly and partly on 3d Division No 7 N on 3d

No 15 & W. on home Lott No 60 partly & partly on 2d Division No 59.—Surveyed in Oct 1739"
Pr WM YOUNG Surveyor.
Entered by JOHN CHANDLER Proprietors Clerk.

The Ministers Home lot was at the center of the town, that is ninety five acres of it, and five acres nearly two miles east in the "Hollow."

Second Division No 56, 50 acres, was on the south line of the town about two miles from lot No 1.

Third Division No 6, 107 acres, was in the 5th Range and nearly to the east line of the town, five miles or more from the home lot.

WARRANT FOR FIRST MEETING OF THE PROPRIETORS HELD ON THE NEWLY PURCHASED TRACT CALLED LISBORNE PROPRIETY AUGUST 6, 1740.

To James Thornton one of the Proprietors of the Lisborne propriety so Called in the County of Hampshire. Greeting—

Upon application made to Me the subscriber Clerk to said propriety by the said James Thornton Robert Peibles James McCallough Mathew Gray and John Gray that a new Meeting of Said Proprietors may be Called and to be held at Lisborne you are therefor hereby Directed agreeable to the votes of said Proprietors and the application to me made to notifie the Proprietors of the Lisborne propriety aforesaid that they assemble and meet on Wednesday the Sixth Day of August nixt at Eight of the Clock in the forenoon at the Dwelling House of John Fergerson In said Lisborne : by Posting up a Copy of this warrant there and also in the town of Worcester then and there to Transact on the following articles : first to Choose a Moderator of said Meeting.—Secondly to Choose a new Clerk to impowr him to Receive the Book and Papers of the present Clerk and to Give his Rec't for them.— Thirdly to Grant what money may be nessary for building and finishing a Meeting House or part thereof, also for settling a minister, or having preaching for the present or for so long a time as the Proprietors shall think proper, also to Grant for making Bridges Causeways Highways and Roads as may be needful and agree upon proper Methods for altring those that are alredy laid out or sequestered for that purpose if there shall be occasion thereof and to do anything needfull and necessary for the bringing forward the setelment of the place and also to Chouse a Treasurer and Colector for Colecting and Receiving future Taxes—and also to Grant Money for such other Services as have been already done or ordered to be done or that may at said meeting be agreed upon or for any other unforeseen Contingent Charges and Maik Return hereof with your doings herein to said Proprietors. at the time and place of Meeting.

Dated in Worcester this 22d day of May Anno Dom 1740
JOHN CHANDLER Proprietors Clerk.

First Meeting of Proprietors at Lisborne Propriety August 6th 1740.

At a meeting of the Proprietors of Lisborne Propriety so Called meet and Assembled on August the 6th 1740 first James Thornton was chosen Moderator—Secondly William Gray was Chosen Proprietors Clerk.—Thirdly Voted that the Meeting House be 46 feet in leanth and 36 in weadth.

Forthly Voted that there be one hundred and twenty Pounds in Pairt for a meeting house to be Colected aginst the first day of May nixt ensuing.

Fiftly Voted that there be One Hundred and twenty pounds in part for a meeting house to be collected against the first day of May nixt ensuing.

Sixthly—Voted that James McCoulough James Thornton and Samuel Gray be a Comeety to agree with a workman to rease a Meeting house and in Close it and lay the under floor and hinge the Doors and mack the windo frames.

Seventhly Voted that the settling of a minister be a jorned for the Present.

Eighthly, Voted that there be thirty Pounds Colected for Present Preaching until the third Tusday of May nixt.

Nintly, Voted that there be a cart Bridge Ericted on the Revor Commonly Called the West Branch.

Teenthly Voted that Robert Lotridge Samuel Gray and James Gilmor Jir be a Comeety to regulat and repar the Roads and to buld the Bridge menchond on the ninth vote.

Eleventhly Voted that there be three days work Doan for each Lot upon the highways the Bridge Excepted.

Twilthly Voted that there be Fighty days works Doon upon the Middel road and North upon the Cros Road and Eighty Days doon upon the Second Road and the Cross road South and twenty days on the East hill from the Rever where it is most needful.

Thirteenthly Voted that this work is to be doon and perficted betwixt the 9th and 20th of September nixt.

Forteenthly Voted that there be alowed for Each Man six shillings per Day and three shillings for one yock of oxen and one shilling for a Cart per day.

Fifteenthly Voted that Each lot work one day at the Bridge and a man to be allowed Eight shillings per day at said work and said work is to be perficted on the 27th and 28th Days of August nixt.

Sixteenthly Mathew Gray was chosen Proprietors Treasurer.

Seventeenthly, John Gray was chosen Colector.

Eighteenthly Voted that William Gray James Thornton and James McColouagh be assessors for the Propriety.

Nineteenthly Voted that the Meeting is ajorned to the third Tusday of May nixt to the Dwelling House of John Fergerson at teen of the Clock in the forenoon.

JAMES THORNTON Moderator.

Recorded by WILLIAM GRAY Proprietors Clerk.

MEETING, MAY 19TH, 1741.

At a Meeting of the Proprietors of Lisborne so Called upon ajournment from August the 6th to May the 19th 1741 then meet and Assembled.

First Voted that there be one hundred and twinty pounds Collected for the second payment of the meeting house.

Secondly Voted that there be Colected forty Pounds for to pay Debts and to pay for Preaching till the nixt Meeting.

Thirdly Voted that Robert Peibles Mathew Gray James Thornton James McCoulough and John Alexander be a Comeety to proceed for the reasing of the Meeting house.

Forthly Voted that there be forty days work doon upon the midel Road and twinty days work to be doon upon the second Road, the work is to be doon on the tuesday and wensday of June nixt and there is to be alowed for each days work teen shillings and for one yock of oxen five shillings per day.

Fiftly Voted that Samuel Gray has exchanged the four Rod Road in his Land with the Propriety.

Sixtly That John Alexander has exchanged with the Propriety the two Rod Road running through his land.

Seventhly Voted that the Moderator Clerk Treasurer and Colector be chosen nixt meeting.

Eightly Voted that the meeting is ajorned to the first tusday of september nixt at Eight of the Clock in the fornoon at the dwelling house of John Fergerson.

JAMES THORNTON Moderator.

Recorded by WILLIAM GRAY Proprietors Clerk.

Meeting of Proprietors Lisborne Propriety, Sept. 1, 1741.

At a meeting of the Lisborne Propriety so Called from ajornment from the 19th of May to the first of September 1741 then meet and Assembled.

And First was chosen James Thornton Moderatour.

Secondly, Was chosen William Gray Proprietors Clerk.

Thirdly Voted that there be two Colectors Chosen.

Forthly Voted that there be one humdred Pounds Assessed for the last payment of the Agreement for the Meeting house.

Fiftly Voted that Mathew Gray was Chosen Proprietors Treasurer

Sixtly Voted that James Alexander was Chosen the first Colector.

Seventhly, Voted that James Thornton was Chosen the second Colector.

Eightly, Voted that Mathew Gray go to Londonderry to the Presbeters Comeety with a Call for the Rev. Mr. Johnson.

Nintly, Voted that the meeting house be seet upon the land that is Cleared upon the west sied of the Cros Road where it may be thought properest by James Thornton James McCoulough and Samuel Gray.

Teenthly, Voted that the meeting is ajorned to the twenty forth day of this instant September to the house of John Fergerson at nin of the clock in the for noon.

JAMES THORNTON Moderator.

Recorded by WILLIAM GRAY Proprietors Clerk.

Meeting of Proprietors Lisborne Propriety, Sept. 24, 1741.

At a meeting of the Proprietors of Lisborne Propriety so Called upon ajournment from Sept. the first to September 24th 1741 then meet and Assembled &

First Voted that the seventh vote of the meeting held on September the first 1741 is Reconsidered.—

Secondly Voted that ther be a Equalety of what money was paid for Preaching in our first begining.—

Thirdly Voted that George Cowan Andrew Macllom and John Dick be a Comeety to Reckon with Robert Pebles for what money has been paid towards Preaching.

Forthly, Voted that James Taylor is Chosen Colector.

Fiftly Voted that the meeting is a journed to the first tusday of

November nixt to the Dwelling House of John Fergerson at nin of the Clock in the for noon.

Recorded by WILLIAM GRAY Proprietors Clerk.

JAMES THORNTON Moderator.

MEETING OF PROPRIETORS LISBORNE PROPRIETY NOV. 3, 1741.

At a meeting of the Proprietors of Lisborne Propriety so Called upon a journment from September the twinty fourth 1741 to November the Third then meet and Assembled and

first Voted Robert Pebles Keep a minister when he comes to be our suplayer at twelve shillings per week.

Secondly, Voted that the peper of Charges for tranchant Preaching of twenty one Pounds Eleven shillings and six pence be assessed upon the propriety.

Thirdly, Voted that Mathew Gray be alowed three Pounds for his going to London Derry.

Forthly Voted that the Meeting is a jorned to the second tusday of May nixt at nin of the Clock in the for noon at the dwelling house of John Fergerson.

Recorded by WILLIAM GRAY Proprietors Clerk.

JAMES THORNTON Moderator.

MEETING OF PROPRIETORS LISBORNE PROPRIETY MAY 11, 1742.

At a Meeting of the Proprietors of Lisborne propriety so called upon a journment from November the third 1741 to May the Eleventh 1742 then meet and Assembled and

First Voted that the meeting be a jorned for half an hour to the house of John Fergerson for to Chous a Moderator at the Meeting on said day after the afor said a jornment.

First Voted and was chosen Samuel Gray Moderator.

Secondly Voted that we interceed with Mr. Robert Abercrombie to be our Suplayer as far as he can for this Summer.

Thirdly, Voted that the meeting is a jorned to the 18th day of this instant May at Eight of the Clock in the for noon to the dwelling house of John Fergerson.

Recorded by WILLIAM GRAY Proprietors Clerk.

SAMUEL GRAY Moderator.

A Warrant for the first Meeting of the Proprietors held in the Meeting House, and the first meeting where the Propriety is designated as Pelham, May 16, 1743.

HAMPSHIRE SS

To William Gray of Pelham in the County of Hampshire. Greeting.

Whereas nine of the Proprietors of Pelham formly Lisborne have made application to me the subscriber for a warent for Calling a Meeting of the Proprietors of said Pelham to be held at the meeting house in said Pelham on the Sixteenth day of may nixt at teen of the Clock in the forenoon in order to Choose assessors to assess a Tax of One penny per acre Granted by the General Court on the Lands in said Propriety in the year 1742 and also for the Proprietors to Consider and determine whither the Proprietors will raise any money to purchas Elisha Williams Esqr right of Land in said Townshipe and appoint some Person to Receive a deed of the same and order if so the Assessors to Assess said money.

These are therefore in his Majestys name to require a meeting of the said Proprietors at said time and place for the ends and purposes aforesaid and you are hereby required to post up notification in som Publict Place in said Pelham fourteen days before the time for holding said meeting setting forth the Time place and occasion there of unter your hand Hereof feal not. Deated at Hatfield this 29th day of April 1743.

ISREAL WILLIAMS Justes Pace—

Recorded by WILLIAM GRAY Proprietors Clerk.

By Vertue of the within warent I have notified the Proprietors of Pelham by posting up a notification by the sied of the meeting house door May 16th 1743.

By WILLIAM GRAY Proprietors Clerk.

At a meeting of the Proprietors of Pelham Lawfully warned to meet at the meeting house May the 16th 1743 and then was chosen John Gray Moderator.

Secondly, Voted William Gray William Croset and John Hamilton was chosen assessors to assess a Tax of one penny per acre Granted by the General Court in the year 1742—

Thirdly Voted that Robert Lotridge Ephraim Cowan and James Thornton be a Comeety to Receive a deed and gave boand for the money of Elisha Williams Esq land lying in the Townshipe of Pelham

Forthly, Voted the meeting ajorned to tne 24th day of May current at the meeting house of Pelham then and there to Receive the return of the afore said Comeety at two of the Clock in the afternoon.

JOHN GRAY Moderator.

Recorded by WILLIAM GRAY Proprietors Clerk.

MEETING OF PROPRIETORS MAY 24, 1743.

At a meeting of the Proprietors of Pelham upon ajornment from May the 16th 1743 to May 24th then meet and Voted that the meeting be ajorned to the 26th of May Corrent at twelve of the Clock at the meeting house of said Pelham and on the 26th of May then meet and ajorned said meeting to the first tusday of July nixt at two of the Clock in after noon at the meeting house of said Pelham.

JOHN GRAY Moderator.

There is no record of any action at the meeting adjourned to the first Tuesday of July, 1743, and from the fact that a warrant for a new meeting was issued by Israel Williams of Hatfield on petition of nine proprietors, for a meeting on the 18th of August, it is probable that there was some illegallity in the manner of issuing the warrant under which the meeting had been acting, and the adjourned meeting was disregarded, and the proprietors entered a petition for a new warrant from Israel Williams, a justice of the peace, living at Hatfield.

WARRANT ISSUED BY ISRAEL WILLIAMS, JUSTICE PEACE.

HAMPSHIRE SS.

To William Gray one of the proprietors of the Townshipe called Pelham in the County of Hampshire Greeting.

Whereas nine of the Proprietors of the Afore said Township have made application to me the subscriber one of his Majestys Justice of the Peace for said County for the Calling of a Meeting of said Proprietors to be held and keept at the meeting house in said Pelham on the 18th day of Augst nixt at three of the clock in the afternoon in order to Receive the request of a Comeety appointed to Purchase Elisha Williams Esqr Right of Land in said Townshipe as by the same under the hand of the said Proprietors bearing date the 26th day of July Instant will appear.

These are therfore in his Majetstys name To require a meeting of the said Proprietors at the time and place and for the end afore said and you are required to Post up notifications here of in some Publict place in said Pelham forteen days at least before the time for holding of said meeting, here of they nor you may feal. Dated at Hatfield the 30th day of July in the seventeenth year of his Ma'st Reign anno Domine 1743.

ISREAL WILLIAMS Justice Peace.

Recorded by WILLIAM GRAY Proprietors Clerk.

MEETING PROPRIETORS OF PELHAM AUG. 18, 1743.

At a Meeting of the Proprietors of Pelham Lawfully warned there meet and Assembled on Aug the 18th 1743 And then first was Chosen John Gray Moderator.

Secondly, We Received the report of the Commeety sent to Purchase Elisha Williams Esqr Right of Land in our Townshipe and the Report is that they have purchased said land for the sume of thirty Eight Pounds according to the old tenor and

Thirdly it is Voted that said money be paid out of the land taxes.

Forthly Voted that the meeting is ajorned to the last tusday of October nixt at three of the Clock in the Afternoon at the Meeting house of said Pelham.

JOHN GRAY Moderator.

Recorded by WILLIAM GRAY Proprietors Clerk.

By vertue of the above warant I have notified the Proprietors of Pelham by Posting up notification by the Sied of the Meeting house Door of time and place within menconed by me.

WILLIAM GRAY Proprietors Clerk.

(Return of the above Warant Put under the meeting by mistake.)
WILLIAM GRAY Proprietors Clerk.

WARRANT FOR MEETING PROPRIETORS SEPT. 28, 1743.

HAMPSHIRE SS

To William Gray of Pelham In the County of Hampshire.

Whereas you and Eight more Proprietors of Lands within the Townshipe of Pelham afore said have by writing under your hands Dated September the 10th 1743 applayed to me the subscriber for a warent to Call a meeting of said Proprietors for the Purposes hear after mentioned you are therefor Required to Post up a notification under your hand in som publick place Requiring said Proprietors to meet and assemble togeather at the meeting house In said Pelham on Wendsday the 28th Day of this Instant September at teen of the Clock in the for noon then and there to agree on a method for Calling in the debts Dne to the Proprietors and getting accounts of Debets and Credets and to Receive the meeting house from those that Built it and to agree on a meathod for Calling Proprietors meetings for the futer.

Given under my hand and seal this 12th day of September 1743 in the 17th year of his Majests Reighn.

ELEEZER PORTER Justice Peace.

Recorded by WILLIAM GRAY Proprietors Clerk.

By Vertue of the within warent I have notified the Proprietors of the Town of Pelham by Posting up a notification by the sied of the meeting house door to meet at time and Place within menshoned.

Dated at Pelham Sept the 28th 1743.

WILLIAM GRAY Proprietors Clerk.

THE FIRST SETTLERS. 45

MEETING OF PROPRIETORS OF PELHAM, SEPT. 28, 1743.

At a meeting of the Proprietors of the Town of Pelham warned according to Law to meet at the meeting house of said Pelham on Sept 28th 1743 then meet and assembled on said day and was chosen Samuel Gray Moderator—

First Voted William Gray James and Robert Peabels to be a comeety to Receve the accounts of the Proprietors.

Secondly Voted that the meeting is ajorned to the 8th day of November at the meeting house of said Pelham at teen of the Clock in the for noon.

SAMUEL GRAY MODERATOR.

Recorded by WILLIAM GRAY Proprietors Clerk.

MEETING OF PROPRIETORS OF PELHAM, NOV. 8, 1743.

At a meeting of the Proprietors of the Town of Pelham meet and Assembled upon ajornment from Sept 28th 1743 to November 8th.

First Voted that there be a Commeety Chosen to Agree with Mr. Robert Abercrombie for what time he has been with us and the Commeety is George Cowan John Clark and John Gray and then was voted on said day part of the debts perfixed to Each Persons name—and then said meeting was ajorned to the ninth of November at nin of the Clock in the for noon at the meeting house of said Pelham then meet and was chosen John Gray Alexander Konkey and James Thornton a commeety to agree with a suitable Person to Keep our Minister and also to provid for his horse Keeping and then was Chosen Robert Pebels James Thornton and William Gray to be a commeety to see what of the Proprietors Vots is nidfull to be Recorded and also what Recepts will be given out to those that the the Proprietors is indebted to also.

Voted that John Konky tack Care to shut the meeting house Doors—also

Voted that John Stimson James Thornton John Johnston John Gray and George Cowan be a Commeety to Repare to the Clerk for warent to Call Proprietors meetings for the future—

Now folowes the sums granted and perfixed to there names.

Recorded by WILLIAM GRAY Proprietors Clerk.

SAMUEL GRAY Moderator.

THE SUMS VOTED AND RECORDED TO EACH MANN, NOV. 8, 1743.

All these debts are according to the Old Tenor, and are Debets due to the Proprietors.

	£ s d		£ s d
to John Gray for Glass	64 01 09	to James Johnston	00 10 06
to Mr Robert Abercrombie	100 00 00	to John Dick	01 10 00
to Robert Pebles	05 00 00	to Robert Pebels	00 11 00
to Solomon Boltwood	03 05 00	to Ephraim Cowan	01 10 00
to Alexander Turner	00 13 00	to John Johnston	00 12 00
to Samuel Gray	01 00 04	to John Stoddard Esqr	02 16 00
to James Alexander	01 10 00	to Mr. Hopkins	09 00 00
to Adam Peteson	01 14 00	to Timothy Dwight	02 00 00
to James Thornton for Mr Caldwell	08 04 00	to Matthew Gray	06 10 00
		to Samuel Gray	07 00 00
to James Thornton Andrew McFarland and William Gray to be paid to Cornal Chandler	08 09 10	to Alexander Konkey Jun	01 07 00
		to John Dick	03 00 00
		to George Cowan	01 10 00
		to Alexander Turner	00 13 00
to James Thornton and Ephraim Cowan to be paid to Elisha Williams Esq	38 00 00	to John Gray	01 01 06
		to John Konky	00 16 06
		to Alexander Konky	03 10 00
to John Crawford for Rum to the Meeting house raising	11 05 00	to James Taylor	01 07 00
		to William Konky	02 15 00
to Robert Pebles for 53 Wics boarding of the minister.	37 00 00	to William Croset	01 08 00
		to William Gray for service down for the time past in Recording for Proprietors.	01 08 00
to William Konky	03 05 00
to James Alexander	01 10 00	*Here begins the grants of those that Paid for tranchant Preaching to wit*	
to James Thornton,	05 02 00
to William Gray to Mr Abercrombie for hors keeping the first winter	02 13 02	to Robert Pebles	04 05 00
		to William Gray	01 01 00
		to John Fergerson	01 00 00
to Alexander Turner	00 07 00	to Ephriam Cowan	01 00 00
to Robert Pebels	03 10 00	to John Gray	04 11 00
to John Gray	05 00 00	to Robert Lotridge	02 01 00
to Patrick Pebels	01 03 00	to James Konky	00 10 00
to Robert Lotridge for hors keeping	03 08 00	to James Hood	00 02 00
		to James Gilmore jun	00 05 00
to John Stinson	00 06 00	to James Alexander	00 05 00
to John Gray	01 18 00	to Mathew Gray	01 12 06
to Robert Lotridge	00 10 00	to Samuel Gray	01 06 00
to Robert Pebels	01 05 00	to James Gilmore jun	00 13 00
to James Thornton	00 10 01	to James Johnston	00 10 00
to James McColough	01 10 00	to William Crosett	00 10 00
to John Gray	01 04 00	to John Alexander	60 03 00

THE FIRST SETTLERS. 47

	£	s	d
to Andrew Macklam	00	03	00
to Robert Macklam	00	03	00
to James Thornton	00	03	00
to James McColouogh	00	03	00

Now follows Debets Paid to the Proprietors.

	£	s	d
to Robert Pebels	26	19	00
to James Thornton	14	11	00
to John Gray	12	14	06
to William Gray	04	11	00
to Alexander Konky	04	17	00
to Matthew Gray	08	02	06
John Konky	00	16	06
to Robert Pebels	01	13	04
to William Konky	05	10	00
to Robert Pebels	02	02	05
to Robert Pebels	01	13	04
to John Dick	02	09	04
to Patrick Pebels	00	03	00
to Robert Pebels	04	01	00
to Mr Robert Abercrombie	100	00	00
to Mr Hopkens	09	00	00
to George Cowan	01	01	00
to Robert Peebles	02	13	04
to John Craford	11	05	00
to Samuel Gray	05	01	00
to Adam Pateson	01	14	00
to Alexander Turner	01	13	00
to Solomon Boltwood by his order to Matthew	03	05	00
to John Alexander the affuls of a bulock to James McColough in Tallow and Molassas			
to Robert Lotridge	05	19	00
to Robert Pebles	04	17	00
to Samuel Gray	04	05	4
to William Crosett	01	18	00
to John Johnson	00	15	00
to John Alexander	00	14	00

	£	s	d
to James Alexander	03	05	00
to Mr Robert Abercrombie	02	13	02
to John Gray for Gleaze to the Meeting house	64	01	09
to James Dayton	04	07	00
to James Taylor for paying of Mr Hopkens	04	00	00
to John Johnston for paying of Mr Hopkens	03	00	00
to John Fergerson	01	00	00
to James Gilmor sen	00	15	00
to Robert Pebels	01	02	06
to James Johnson for Mr Hopkins to James Johnston	01	00	06
to Robert Pebels	04	06	00
to Robert Maklam	06	03	00
to John Stinson	00	06	00

This nine pounds to Mr Hopkens was paid to those that paid out the said money.

	£	s	d
to James Hood	00	04	00
to James Gilmor Jun	00	12	00
to James Thornton Andrew McFarland and William Gray to pay John Chandler jun	08	04	10
to James Thornton and Ephraim Cowan to pay Elisha Williams Esq	38	00	00
to Andrew Macklam	60	03	00
to William Gray	04	11	04
to John Stoddard Esqr	02	16	
to Timothy Dwight Esq to John Dick	02	00	08
to William Gray	10	18	00
to Ephraim Cowan	02	10	00
to Isreal William Esq	01	17	00
to William Gray	04	13	00

WARRANT FOR MEETING OF PROPRIETORS APRIL 26, 1744.

HAMPSHIRE ss. To William Gray Proprietors Clerk of the Town of Pelham and County of Hampshire Greeting.

These are therefore in his Majestis name to will and require you forth with to warn the Proprietors of said Town by Posting up notifications in som publick Place within the said Town of Pelham to Meet and Assemble themselves at the Meeting house of said Town on Thursday the 26th day of this instant April at nine of the clock in the fore noon then and there.

I   To chouse a committy to tack care of what common land belongs to the said Proprietors so as it may be put to the use of the Proprietors—

II   To Chouse a Committy to luck after William Young's money due to him from the Propriety.

III   To Chouse a Commeety and apoint them with full Powr to do what may be nessery to reas and Cause be brought unto the treasury the Taxes Assessed upon the Proprietors to end these debets may be with all Conveneant speed Paid according to there order.

IIII   to See if the Propriety will consult to renew the lines of all there divisions of lands.

V   to all that have any Debets or Credits to bring them in to said meeting.

VI   to see if the propriety will allow Thomas Dick any allowance of adition towards building of the meeting house.

Hearof feal not and mack return of your doings som time before said Meeting to one of us Subscribers as witness our hands and seal this 3th day of April anno domni 1744 and in the seventeenth year of his majesties Reigne &c James Thornton George Cowan John Stinson John Johnston John Gray Commeety.

By vertue of the within Warrent I have warned the Proprietors to meet at time and Place above mencioned by Posting up a notification by the meeting house Door April 26th 1744

Pr WILLIAM GRAY Proprietors Clerk

MEETING OF PROPRIETORS OF PELHAM APRIL 26TH 1744.

At a meeting of the Proprietors of the Town of Pelham Legally assembled on thursday the 26th of April 1744 then meet on Said day and was chosen Samuel Gray Moderator.

I   Voted that John Stinson Samuel Gray and Robert Pebels be a Comeety to luck after what Common Lands belongs to the Propriety.

II   Voted that James Konky Patrick Pebels and John Jonston be a Comeety with full Powr to do what may be nesshry to reas and Cause to be brought unto the Tresery the Taxes assessed upon the Proprietors to the end these Debets may be with all Conveneant Speed Paid according to there order.

III   Voted that Every neighboure meet and renew there lins of all there Lands by the first day November nixt.

IIII   Voted the sums of money set to each Persons name being due to them by said Proprietors to wit all old tenor

THE DEBETS PAID
Paid to the undernamed

	£	s	s
to Alexander Thomson	01	10	00
to Samuel McLachay	15	00	00
to Robert Pebels	01	00	00
to Mr Robert Abercrombie	63	00	00
to Robert Pebels	02	03	00
to Ephraim Cowan	05	06	00
to John Gray	14	17	00
to Mr Robert Abercrombie the sum of	42	00	00
to Robert Pebels	32	18	07
to James Thornton	00	16	06
to William Gray	02	19	08
to John Hamilton	01	04	00
to Alexander Thomson	04	10	00

DEBTS DUE

	£	s	s
to Mr Robert Abercromcie	63	00	00
to Ephram Cowan	05	00	00
to William Young	03	00	00
to John Gray for hors keeping	14	17	00
to Samuel McLakey	15	00	00
to Robert Pebels for Bording	14	00	00
to William Gray	01	10	00
to Robert Pebels	00	12	06
to James Thornton	00	07	06
to John Hamilton	01	04	00
Granted to Alexander Thomson	03	00	00

September the 18th 1743

V Voted that Robert Pebels James Thornton and William Gray be a Comeety to geve out orders for the above Debets and to mack up accounts with James Alexander and James Taylor Colectors.

SAMUEL GRAY Moderator

By WILLIAM GRAY Proprietors Clerk.

WARRANT FOR MEETING OF PROPRIETORS JULY 24 1744

To William Gray Proprietors Clerk of the town of Pelham and County of Hampshire Greeting

These are therefor in his Majestes name to will and Require you forthwith to warn the Proprietors of said Town by Posting up notification in som publick place within the town of Pelham to meet and assemble themselves at the meetinghouse of said town on tuesday the twinty forth day of this instant July at Eight of the Clock in the for noon then and there—

I To Consider what is nessary to be done with Regard to the Lands Claimed by Road Town and Sealam formly supposed to belong to the Proprietors and to apoint what ever they judge Requisite in that affaire—

II To hear what may be Laid before the Proprietors by there Committee appointed to agree with one to bulde the meeting house and to order whatever they may find necessary for the finishing of that business.

III To enquire what there Committee appointed to erase the Taxes alredy assessed have don in that matter—and to enlarge there Power if found necessary and appoint others in place of such or all of them who cannot or refuse to serve.

Hereof feal not and mack due return of your doings to one of us the subscribers before said meeting as witness our hands and seal this ninth day of July One thousand seven hundred and forty foure and in the Eighteenth year of his majestes Reighn.

By vertue of the above warent I have warned the Proprietors by posting up a notification by the side of the meeting house door to meet at time and place above mencioned July ye 24th 1744

By WILLIAM GRAY Proprietors Clerk.

MEETING OF PROPRIETORS JULY 24 1744

At a Meeting of the Propretors of the town of Pelham on tusday the 24th day of July 1744 then meet on Said day and then was chosen Robert Pebels Moderator

I Voted that there be a commeetty Chosen to tack all proper methods to see what Land is lost by Preambling the lins by Road Town and Sealom. The said Commeety is John Stinson John Konky and James Gilmor sen the said Commeetty is appointed to bring what each Lot has lost that Lys upon the said lins.

II Voted that Thomas and John Dicks be alowed the sume of thirty pounds according to the old tenor in case they Deliver up there bounds which they Received of the Commetty that agreed with them to bueld the meeting House

III Voted that Thomas Dick be a Commeety man in the room of John Johnson to tack Care of the Taxes alredy essessed according as it is menshoned in the vote in Aprill the 26th 1744 also that the said Commeety is alowed by vote to Call Timothy Dwight Esq for there assistance when need Requires.

IIII Voted that this meeting is ajourned to the first tusday of October next at Eight of the Clock in the for noon at the Meeting house of said Pelham to Receive the returns of the above Commeettys

ROBERT PEBELS Moderator

Paid to Thomas Dick by order of the Treserer the sum £15, 00 s, 00 p.

ADJOURNED MEETING OF PROPRIETORS OCT 2 1744.

At a meeting of the Proprietors of the Town of Pelham Upon ajornment from the 24th day of July 1744 to the 2th of October following to Receive the Report of the Commeete chosen to see what Land is lost in runing our lin betwixt us and the town of Road town Sealom and then was chosen Thomas Dick Moderator in Place of Robert Pebels being absent and was

Voted that this meeting is ajorn'd to the 30th of this instant October at Eight of the Clock in the for noon at the meeting house of

GRAVE STONE OF CAPTAIN THOMAS DICK, WEST BURYING GROUND.

AMHERST WATER COMPANY'S UPPER RESERVOIR, APPLE TREES IN BLOOM.

said Pelham for ter see what meathod will be taiken as to the said land lost upon our north lin

THOMAS DICK Moderator

Paid to John Dick by order of the Treasurer the sum of £15-00-00

ADJOURNED MEETING OF PROPRIETORS OCT 30 1744

At a meeting upon ajorment from October the 2th 1744 to the 30th of said October there Meet on said day and there was Voted that those that lost there Land by Perambulating the lin betwixt us and Road Town and Sealom shall have Reasonoble Recestucion fore the same as shall be ajudged by a Commeety yet to chosen.

This meeting is by vot ajorned to the second tusday of March nixt furder to consult what meathods may be taeken about said Land at teen of the Clock in the for noon at the Meeting house of Said Pelham

THOMAS DICK Moderator

ADJOURNED MEETING OF THE PROPRIETORS MARCH 12 1745

At a Meeting of the Proprietors of Town of Pelham upon ajornment from the 30th day of October 1744 and from said October it was ajorned to the 12th day of March nixt then meet on said day and was chosen John Gray Moderator by Reason of Thomas Dick being absent First Voted that James Konky go to Kings Town to see if he can prevent the Selling of the Property for money Borowed by them from Samuel Fergerson and said James Konky is to do it in what meathod he can when he gos their.

This Meeting is ajorned by vot to the Second tusday of August nixt at teen of the clock in the fore noon at the Meeting House of said Pelham forder to Consider the afearn of Said Land

JOHN GRAY Moderator

ADJOURNED MEETING OF THE PROPRIETORS AUGUST 13 1745

At a meeting of the Proprietors of the Town of Pelham upon ajornment from the 12th day of March 1744 to the 13th of August 1745 then meet on said day and was chosen Thomas Dick Moderator by reason of John Gray being absent and by Vot this Meeting is ajourned to the last tusday of September nixt at twelve of the Clock at the Meeting house of said Pelham forder to Conseder the ofear of the land thats a wanting on our north line

THOMAS DICK Moderator.

Adjourned Meeting of Proprietors Sept 24 1745

At a Meeting of the Proprietors of the Town of Pelham upon ajornment from the 13th of August 1745 to the 24th day of September folowing there meet on said day and was Chosen James Konky Moderator, by Reason of Thomas Dick being absent.

First Voted that there be a Commeette Chosen to see what each Lot Coms Short in the North Reange Betwixt the Cros Road and the west end of Said Reange—the Commeette Chosen is to wit James Alexander James Konky and John Clark

By vot this Meeting is ajourned to the last tusday of November nixt at teen of the Clock in the for noon at the Meeting house of Said Pelham forder to Consider the offear of the land Lost on our north Lin

James Konky Moderator

By William Gray Proprietors Clerk.

As the next meeting was called by a warrent it shows that this much adjourned meeting failed to meet on the last Tuesday of November 1745. A marginal note explains the result.

"A meeting upon ajornment, and now this meeting sinks by not meeting." The sinking of the meeting allowed rest and further consideration before the next meeting of the Proprietors which was not called until the following April when the question of "Land lost by Preambling" was taken up again.

Warrant for Meeting of Proprietors April 8, 1746

To William Gray Proprietors Clerk for the Town of Pelham and County of Hampshire--Greeting—These are thefore in his Majestes name to will and Require you forth with to warn the Proprietors of the Town of Pelham by notification to meet and assemble them selves at the meeting house of said Pelham on tusday the Eight day of April at nin of the Clock in the for noon then and there to Consider of a Meathod to meak Satisfaction to those of the Propriety that Lost Land by Preambling our town lin by Road town and Sealom at the desire of Samuel Gray

2ly to see if the Propriety will Chuse a Commeette to go and talk with our first Commeette to Wit Andrew McFarland Robert Lotridge and Samuel Gray to see if they will Make Satisfaction for there not Running the line according to these Directions and also upon there Refusal to Mack Satisfaction said commeette to be impowered to Procecut said Commeette at the Law for there non Performanse which Caused our Second Commeette to go astray in the laying out our Second and third divisions which is Lickly to Cost the Preprietry a Great deal of truble and Charge

THE FIRST SETTLERS. 53

5ly To see if the Propriety will chuse a Commeette to luck after what Common land belongs to the Propriety.

Heare of feal not and Mack due return to one of us the Subscribers sum time befor said meeting as witness our hands and seal this third day of March A. D. 1745–6 and in the nineteeth year of the Reigne of our Souvraine Lord George the Second of Great Brietaen King &c

Commeette JAMES THORNTON
GEORGE COWAN
JOHN STINSON
JOHN JOHNSON

By Vertue of the within Warrant I have notified the Propriety by Posting up a notification by the side of the meeting house door to meet at time and Place within mencioned by me
WILLIAM GRAY Proprietors Clerk

MEETING OF PROPRIETORS APRIL 8, 1746

At a meeting of the Proprietors of the Town of Pelham on tusday the Eight day of Aprill 1746 then meet on Said Day and was Chosen Thomas Dick moderator.

First Voted that there be no Commeette Chosen to Viue the Land that was Lost on our north lin by Road Town and Sealom.

Secondly Voted that there be a Commeette Chosen to talk with the Commeette that Laid out the hom Lots of said Town

Thirdly Voted that said Commeette is George Cowan James Alexander and John Johnston. Said Commetee is George Cowan James Alexander and John Johnston. The Return of Said Commettee is that Samuel Gray will maake no Satisfaction till the Law Macks him and Robert Latridge Pleads not Gilty for the Reason that he was over Pour'd by the Rest of Said Commeette

Fourthly Voted that the above said Commeette is not to truble the other Commeette at ye Law which Laid out the first Lots

Fiftly Voted that there be no Commeette to luck after the Common land for the Present

THOMAS DICK Moderator.

Recorded by WILLIAM GRAY Proprietors Clerk

The above is the last regularly called meeting of the Proprietors that was called and held at the meeting house where the action of the meetings was spread upon the Proprietors Book and the temper of the meeting, judging from the record, was to quit fretting and fuming about "Land lost by Preambulating by Road Town and Sealom" on the north line of the town. That it was a substantial dropping of the question there can be little doubt, for at least a dozen years and more, and when it was next agitated it was more in the form of individuals seeking to have the Proprietors recompense them for alleged loss of land. Whether the loss complained of was caused by a land grab on the part of the people of Road Town and Sealom (Shutesbury and New Salem) or that the shortage was due to mistakes in surveying we are unable to determine. It may have been from defective surveying and from difficulty in finding the exact line between the towns and not chargeable to any intent on the part of Roadtown people to grab land belonging to the inhabitants of Pelham.

From April 8, 1746 until April 27 A. D. 1760 the Original Proprietors Book had no line written upon its pages.

At that time there was a revival of the charge of loss of land and under the last named date we find the record of Thomas Dick taking the oath as Proprietors Clerk, preparatory to calling a meeting of the Proprietors to Consider the matter of the lost land. It will be noticed that none of the meetings of the proprietors were called or held at the meeting house but at private houses of proprietors and mostly if not wholly at the house of Thomas Dick who seems to have been the prime mover or organizer of the new campaign to recover lost lands.

THOMAS DICK SWORN AS PROPRIETORS CLERK.

HAMPSHIPE SS APRIL 27 1761

Then Thomas Dick of Pelham in the same County upon Declaring himself to be Chosen Clerk of the Lisburn Propreity, So Called in said Pelham was Sworn to the true and faithfull Discharge of his trust in that office according to the best of his Knowledge & Discretion

Coram C. PHELPS Justice Peace

Entered from the Original

Pr THOMAS DICK Proprietors Clerk

WARRANT FOR PROPRIETORS MEETING MAY 28 1761

HAMPSHIRE SS: To Robert Lothridge hereafter named Gent, One of the Proprietors of a Tract of Land in Pelham in sd County Called the Lisburn Propriety—Greeting—

Whereas application In writing bearing Date the twenty sixth day of March last hais been made to Me the Subscriber one of his Majestys Justicies of the Peace for the County of Hampshire by Robert Lotridge Thomas Johnston Alexander Turner Thomas Dick Mathew Gray, five of the Proprietors of a large Tract of land lying in Pelham in the County of Hampshire Called the Lisburn Propriety—Bounded Northrly Partly by Roadtown and partly by New Salem, Easterly by Greenwich, Southerly by a range of the Equivalent land formerly owned by Whittlesey and Hall and Westerly by the District of Amherst, which tract was Originally owned and held in Common by a body of Proprietors, and whereof the Partion is not to this day Compleated—Requesting a Warrant for Calling of a meeting of sd Proprietors to be Holden at the House of Thomas Dick Inholder in Pelham aforesaid on Wednesday the twenty eight day of May next at ten of the Clock in the forenoon for the purposes folowing to wit—In the first place to Choose a Moderator for Sd Meeting.

Nextly to Chuse a Clerk to enter and Record the Votes and doings of the Proprietors—Also to Consider and determine whether there hais not been a very great error made in laying out of all the Lots in Said Propriety that were Supposed to have been laid adjoining on the north line of Sd tract much to the wrong and loss of the Proprietors to whom Sd Lots were laid out, the then Sd five Proprietors supposing that by reason of a mistake of said line Considerable land has been assigned to Sd Proprietors in part of satisfaction of their share in Sd tract of land which never was any part of the same and therefor Cannot be held by them to whom Sd lots was laid out. Allso if the Proprietors when met shall be satisfied that such an error as the above said has been Committed to desire some method whereby to make Satisfaction to Such Proprietors as have been Injured thereby.—Also to Consider and Determine whither they will proceed to divide the Lands in Sd tract that have hitherto lain in Common and Undivided, and in what manner. You are therefore hereby required to notify and warn the Proprietors of Sd tract of land that they Assemble themselves at the time and place above specified then and there to Consider and Act upon the articles above mentioned which Warning you are to give them by Posting up a notification in writing in some public place or places in Sd Town of Pelham fourteen days at lest before the day above mentioned for holding Sd meeting to wit ye twenty eight day of May next therein setting forth particularly the time place and business of Sd meeting herein before mentioned.

Hear of you may not fail and you are to make return of this precept with your doings in obedience thereto fairly Indorsed thereon Into said Meeting at the opening of the same,

Given under my hand and seal at Northampton in Sd County of Hampshire this ninth day of April Anno Dom 1761 in the Thirty third year of His Majestys Reighn

JOSEPH HAWLEY

Entered from the Original by THOMAS DICK Proprietors Clerk
Pelham May 28 1760

Pelham May 28 1760—By Vertue of the above warrant I have notified the Proprietors to meet at times and place thereon mentioned by setting up a notification at Worcester and Pelham

ROBERT LATRIDGE

Entered from the Original THOMAS DICK Proprietors Clerk

MEETING OF PROPRIETORS MAY 28 1760

At a Meeting of the Proprietors of the Lisburn Propriety Called on the 28 day of May 1760 at the House of Thomas Dick Inholder.

First Thomas Dick was chosen Moderator

Secondly Thomas Dick was Chosen Clerk.

Thirdly Patrick Pebels chosen to get Colonal Timothy Dwight William Young and Mr Rust in order to find the true line on the north side of the above named propriety

Forthly Voted that William Crosett Alexander Turner and Robert Lothridge be a Commeete to search out what common land is in Sd tract above and make report to the Proprietors when next met

Fiftly Voted that this meeting is ajorned to tusday the twenty third of September next at ten of the Clock in the forenoon to said Dicks

Recorded by THOMAS DICK Proprietors Clerk.

ADJOURNED MEETING SEPTEMBER 23 1760

At a meeting of the Proprietors aforesaid held by adjournment from May 28 1760 to Sept 23 1760 at ten oclock fornoon and then met at the Dwelling house of Thomas Dick above said in Sd Pelham

First Voted that those Proprietors that hais lost Land on the north line of the Propriety have Satisfaction at the Judgment of a Commete to be chosen for that business

Secondly Voted that David Huston John Craford and William Harkness be a Commeette to vew the Land lost on said line and to value the same

Thirdly Voted that the Said Committee make return of their doings to the Propretors when next meet.

Forthly Voted that Capt Robert Lotheridge Alexender Turnor and William Crosett be a Commeette to sell what Common lands belongs to the Proprietors that there is no claim to or Return of.

Fiftly Voted that there be two shillings and Eight Pence laid on each sixteeth part of said Property to defray charges

Sixtly Voted that Thomas Dick be Treasurer for said Proprietors

Seventhly Voted to adjourn said meeting to the twenty fifth day of December next to Meet at one o clock afternoon at the Dwelling house of Thomas Dick Inholder at Pelham aforesaid.

Recorded by THOMAS DICK Proprietors Clerk

ADJOURNED MEETING DEC. 25 1760

At a meeting of the Proprietors aforesaid held by ajornment from September 23 1760 to Dec. 25, 1760 at one of the Clock afternoon and then met the dwelling house of Thomas Dick in Pelham Inholder.

First Voted that Alexander McCulogh and Patrick McMullen is added as Commetee men to Prise the Land lost on the north side of said Property

Secondly Voted that Thomas Dick Alexander McColough and John Dick be a Commete to expose the Proprietors Lands for Sale for payment of Rates as there shall be ocation

Thirdly Voted Patrick Peobels for servis done the Property.

Sixtly Voted that this meeting is adjourned to May 27, 1761 at one oclock afternoon to Meet at the Dwelling house of Thomas Dick in Pelham aforesaid

Recorded by THOMAS DICK Proprietors Clerk

ADJOURNED MEETING MAY 27 1761

At a meeting of the Proprietors of the Lisburn Propriety so called held by ajournment from December 25 1760 to May 27 1761 at one o'clock afternoon at the Dwelling house of Thomas Dick in Pelham Inholder

First Voted that the meeting is adjurned for one hour to meet at this place

Secondly Voted that the aprisement rendered by the Commeetee to prize the land lost on the north lins of said Pelham is excepted.

Thirdly Voted to send a petition to the Genaral Court to help us concerning said land

Fourthly Voted Thomas Dick to carry on said petition

Fiftly Voted that this meeting is adjourned to the last Monday of June next to meet at one oclock afternoon at the Dwelling house of Thomas Dick Inholder in said Pelham

Recorded by THOMAS DICK Proprietors Clerk

Warrant for Proprietors Meeting June 9, 1761

HAMPSHIRE S. S.—To Thomas Johnston hereafter named one of the Proprietors of a large tract of land in Pelham in Sd County—Greeting.

Whereas Application in writing dated the first day of March has been made to me the subscriber one of his majestys Justices of the Peace for the Sd County of Hampshire by Thomas Johnston Patrick Peebles John Conky John Clark and Robert Lotheridge, five of the Proprietors of a large tract of Land in Pelham aforesaid called the Lisburn Propriety lyeing in Comen, the proportion of each Proprietor therein being stated, Bounded northerly by Shutesbury and Partly by New Salem, Easterly by Greenwich, South by a Reange of the Equivalent land formerly owned by Whitelsy and Hall and Westerly by the District of Amherst requesting a warrant for the warning of a Meeting of the Proprietors of Sd tract to be holden at the Dwelling house of Thomas Dick Inholder in said Pelham aforesaid on Wendsday the ninth day of June next at one of the Clock afternoon for the purposes folowing to wit

In the first place to chose a Clerk to enter and Record all those votes and orders that shall be made and passed in the meeting of Sd Proprietors.

Also to Consider and determine whether there hais not been a great Error made in laying out all the Lots in Sd tract that were supposed to have laid adjoining the North line of Sd tract to the great wrong and loss of those particular Proprietors to whom Sd lots were laid out they the five Proprietors apprehending that by reason of a mistake of said line Considerable land has been assigned to said particular Proprietors in part satisfaction of thare shares in said tract which never was any part of the same nor did belong thereto and lying Northward of Sd line and therefore cannot be held by the Particular Proprietors to whom Sd land was laid out and thereby a deficulty hais hapened to them of the quantity of land in Sd tract which was supposed to have been aloted to them—also if the Proprietors when met shall be satisfied that such an Error as the above Sd has been Comited to devise and order some Method whereby to make satisfaction to such Proprietors as have been Injured thereby—Also to Consider and determine whither they will proceed to set out and alot the lands within Sd tract that have not hitherto been laid out and in what Manner

You are therefore in his. Majestes name hereby required to notify and warn the Proprietors of said tract of Land that they assemble themselves at the time and place above Mentioned which warning you are to give them by posting up notification in writing under your hand in some publick Place or places in said Town of Pelham fourteen days at least before the day above mention for holding said meeting therein particularly setting forth the time place and business of Sd meeting herein before mentioned

Hereof you may not feal and you are to make Return of the presents with your doing in obedience to the same fairly certified thereon under your hand into said meeting at the time aforementioned for holding the same.

Given under my hand and seal at Northampton in Sd County this eighth day of May A. D. 1762 in the Second year of his Majestys Reighn.

JOSEPH HAWLEY

Entered from the Original by THOMAS DICK Proprietors Clerk

RETURN OF WARRANT

By Virtue of a Warrant to me directed under the hand and seal of Joseph Hawley one of his Majestys Justices of the peace I have warned the Proprietors of the Lisburn Proprietie so called to meet at the Dwelling House of Thomas Dick at one oclock afternoon Wednsday ninth day of June 1762 acording to the Direction in Sd Warrant

THOMAS JOHNSON

Entered from the Original Pr THOMAS DICK Proprietors Clerk

MEETING OF PROPRIETORS JUNE 9 1762

At a meeting of the Proprietors of the Lisburn Proprietie so called, at the Dwelling house of Thomas Dick in Pelham Inholder on Wensday the ninth day of June 1762 at One oclock afternoon the folowing Proprietors personally appeared Viz. Capt Robert Lothridge two Rights, Lieut John Stevinson one—John Dick one Robert McColough one, Robert Meklem one John Conky one, James Taft one, Daniel Gray one, Alexander Turner one George Cowan one Thomas Johnston one George Patterson one John Clark two Patrick Peebles three Thomas Dick two Moses Gray one John Peebles one—

First Chosen Thomas Dick Moderator

Secondly Chosen Thomas Dick Clerk

Thirdly Chosen Thomas Dick to prefer a petition to the General Court to have the Proprietors land taxed to pay for land lost by Perambulating the lines between them Salem and Roadtown or any other Method they shall think proper.

Forthly—Voted that this Meeting is ajourned to the first Monday in October next at One Oclock afternoon at the house of Thomas Dick in Sd Pelham

The above Vots were passed—

Attest THOMAS DICK Proprietors Clerk

REPORT OF COMMITTEE CHOSEN TO APPRAISE THE LAND LOST

An appraisment on Record of a tract of land that is cut off the several lots on the North Range together with number of acres each lot has lost in Said Rainge

ALEXANDER MCCOLOCH
DAVID HUSTON
PATRICK MCMILLEN, Committee

The Sum of the Appraisement of the Same.

Division	No	Acres	Value Per Acre		
3d	7	24;32	£0-5-4		
3d	15	17;20	0-1-4		
Home Lot	60	24.144	0-2-8		
3d	8	23.119	0-5-4		
3d	17	5-32	0-1-0		
Home Lot	59	29.63	0-5-4		
2d	31	9.40	0-4-0		
3d	9	122-00		15 acres too much-	More than the
3d	10			17 " " "	records gives
2d	34	16.35	0-2-8		
3d	23	18.50	0-1-4		
3d	24	0.146	0-1-0		
2d	12	17.00	0-1-0		
2d	11	22.00	0-1-0		
2d	10	7.40	0-9-0		
2d	9	12.40	0-5-4		
H. Lot	18	63-132	0-5-4		

To this appraisement the Committee made solemn oath to its truthfulness as follows—

HAMPSHIRE MAY 27 A D 1761

Then the within named Alexander McColoch David Huston Patrick McMillen all of Pelham within said County Apprising made sollem oath to the truth of the above and within apprisement according to the list therein exhibited

Coram C. PHELPS Justice Peace

Entered from the Original Pr THOMAS DICK Proprietors Clerk

According to the sworn statement of this committee there was a loss of about 431 acres of land in the Sixth Range in a length of nearly eight miles and the sworn value per acre on the average would be about three shillings, sixty pounds perhaps, all told. Hardly enough to pay for the trouble and expense incurred in endeavoring to get a settlement during all the years the matter was agitated.

The subscription to the oath by the Committee appointed to appraise the lost land is the last entry on the book until 1767 when the clamor for the lost land opened afresh, as will appear.

Warrant for Proprietors Meeting March 16 1767

HAMPSHIRE S.S. To Hugh Johnson one of the Proprietors of a tract of land in Pelham in the County of Hampshire Called the Lisburn Propriety Greeting—

Whereas Application hath been made to me the Subscriber one of his Majestys Justices of the Peace for the County above Sd by Seven of the Proprietors of the land above mentioned for a Warrant to Call a Meeting of Sd Proprietors as soon as may be for the purposes hereafter to be mentioned —These are therefore in his Majestys name to require you forthwith to notifie the above named Proprietors to meet at the dwelling house of Thomas Dick Inholder in Sd Pelham on Monday the sixteenth day of March next at ten oclock in the forenoon then and there after a Moderator chosen to act on the following articles viz to Make Choice of such officers as they shall find needful.

Secondly To agree on Method for calling meetings of the Proprietors for the future

Thirdly To Enquire what became of the petition that was sent to the General Court to get money laid on to pay those that lost land on the north side of the Town of Pelham

Forthly To Agree on some method to recompense those that lost land as aforesaid

Fifthly To make provision for the payment of those that have done service for the Property

Sixthly To see if the Proprietors will agree to sell what Common land they have and what method they will proceed in to do it if so.

Hearof fail not but have you this warrant at the place when and time when this meeting is set as within with return of your doing thereon.

Given under my hand and seal at Hadley the nineteenth day of February Anno Dom 1767 and seventh year of the Kings Reighn

         EBENZEER PORTER Jus Peace.
Entered from the Original by THOMAS DICK Proprietors Clerk.

Pelham March 16th 1767 By Virtue of the within Warrant I have notified the Proprietors of the within Mentioned Property by a notification set up to meet at time and place within mentioned

         HUGH JOHNSON
Entered from the Original THOMAS DICK Proprietors Clerk

PROPRIETORS MEETING MARCH 16 1767

At a meeting of the Proprietors of the Lisburn Propriety so called at the Dwelling House of Thomas Dick in Pelham on Monday the sixteenth day of March 1767

Chosen Hugh Johnston Moderator—

Secondly Chosen George Patteson Thomas Dick and Hugh Johnson to be a Committee to Call Meetings for the future

Thirdly Voted that the said meetings shall be warned by setting notifications in some publick Place in Said Town of Pelham

Forthly Voted that Joseph Hawley Esq shall be consulted to see how we shall conduct ourselves in Selling the Roads and other Common Lands

Fiftly, Voted, to Thomas Dick for money laid out for Proprietors and for service done them twelve pounds Lawful money—

Sixthly Voted to Alexander McCulough for Service done twelve shillings

Seventhly Voted to John Gray for service done four shillings—

Eighthly Voted to the heirs of David Huston, Deceased, twelve shillings—

Ninthly Voted to Patrick Peebles one pound twelve shillings and four pence

Tenthly Voted to Hugh Johnston one shilling and four pence

Eleventhly Voted to adjourn said Meeting to the first Monday in April next to one of the Clock afternoon to meet at the Dwelling House of Thomas Dick Inholder in Pelham above said '

HUGH JOHNSTON Moderator

The above votes were passed

THOMAS DICK Proprietors Clerk

PROPRIETORS MEETING APRIL 6 1767

At a meeting on adjournment from Monday the Sixteenth day of March 1767 to Monday the sixth day of April 1767

First Chose John Gray Moderator

Second Voted to bring Joseph Hawley Esq out to our next meeting to counsel with him about our affairs in our present Dificulty—

Thirdly Voted to Adjourn this Meeting to Thursday the fourteenth day of April currant to meet at 10 oclock foornoon at the Dwelling house of Thomas Dick in said Pelham

JOHN GRAY Moderator

The above votes were passed attest

THOMAS DICK Proprietors Clerk

PROPRIETORS MEETING APRIL 14 1767

At a Meeting on adjournment from Monday the Sixth day of April to tusday the fourteenth day of said month.

First Voted to rais money on each one owning land in the Propriety acording to what he poses for Charges arisen on the Property

Second Voted to assess one half peny per acer on each Mr Abercrombees and Mr Grahams lots they live on Roads and Common Land excepted

Thirdly Chosen Thomas Dick Hugh Johnston and Ebenezer Gray Assessors—

Forthly Chose Patrick Peebles Colector to gather Said Rates—

Fifthly Voted to sell the Common Lands and what Roads can be sold according to Law belonging to the Propriety—

Sixthly Chose John Dick George Patterson and Alexander McColough to be Committes to sell the Common Land and Roads and to give titles.

Seventhly Voted to Adjorn Said meeting to the general election day it being the 27 day of May next at ten oclock in the foornoon at the Dwilling House of Thomas Dick in said Pelham

JOHN GRAY Moderator

The above votes were passed

Attest THOMAS DICK Proprietors Clerk

PROPRIETORS MEETING MAY 27 1767

At a Meeting of the Proprietors of the Lisburn Propriety so called on adjornment from tusday the fourteenth day of April 1767 to May twenty seventh next folowing then on said day.

Chose Hugh Johnston Moderator for said meeting

Voted to adjourn said meeting to tusday the eight day of September next folowing at ten oclock forenoon at the Dwelling house of Thomas Dick in Sd Pelham

HUGH JOHNSTON Moderator

The above votes were pased

Attest THOMAS DICK Proprietors Clerk

PROPRIETORS MEETING SEPTEMBER 8 1767

At a meeting of the Proprietors of the Lisburn Propriety so called on adjornment from May 27 1767 to tusday the eight day of September folowing then meet

First Voted to recall a vote Voted April the 14th 1767 wherein they voted to assess one half penny per acre on each acre of land to pay charges on said Propriety—

Second Voted to assess on each acer of land belonging to the Propriety three farthings pr acer to pay charges arisen on the Property except what has been laid out by the Proprietors for Publick uses—

Thirdly Voted to adjorn said meeting to Tusday the twenty ninth day of September current to four oclock afternoon to meet at the Dwelling house of Thomas Dick in Pelham Inholder

         HUGH JOHNSTON Moderator

 The above votes were pased

      Attest THOMAS DICK Proprietors Clerk

WARRANT FOR PROPRIETORS MEETING AUGUST 21 1767

HAMPSHIRE SS. To Thomas Dick clerk of the Proprietors of Town of Pelham & County of Hampshire Greeting.

These are therefore in his Majestys name to will and require you forthwith to warn the Proprietors of Said Town known by the name of Lisburn Propriety to meet at the hous of Said Dick on fryday 25th of Agust next at one of the clock afternoon on consideration of the folowing purposes & hereafter Mentioned & after a Moderator Chosen to act on the folowing

1 first to Consider what to do in withstanding Sd Dick in the Common court of Common Pleas in Said County on the last tusday of Agust next

2ly If they do they are to nominat a man for Said business

3ly If they do not chuse to stand the law they are to consider what method to decide the Grevances of said Dick and others complaining in the same cause of Said Dick

Hereof fail not and make return sometime before said meeting to one of us the subscribers as witness our hand and seal 31st of July Anno Domini 1767 and in the seventh year of his Majestys Reign

       HUGH JOHNSTON } Proprietors Committee
       GEORGE PATTERSON

Entered from the Original Pr THOMAS DICK Proprietors Clerk

NOTIFICATION.

Pursuant to Warrant under the hands and seal of Hugh Johnston and George Patterson Committee of the Proprietors in Pelham called and known by the name of Lisburn Propriety to me directed I hereby warn and notify said Proprietors to meet on Friday the 25th day of Agust currant at one of the Clock afternoon at my Dwelling house in said Pelham and after a Moderator chosen

First to Consider what to do in withstanding me in the Common Court of Common Pleas to be holden at Springfield the last day of Agust current

Secondly If they do they are to nominate a man for said business

Thirdly If they do not chuse to stand the law they are to consider what method to decide the grievance of I and others complaining in the same cause that I do

Dated at Pelham this first day of Agust Anno Domini 1767

        THOMAS DICK Proprietors Clerk

Meeting of Proprietors August 21, 1767

At a meeting of the proprietors of the Lisburn Propriety so called at the House of Thomas Dick in Pelham Inholder on Friday the 21 day of Agust 1767 at one of the Clock Afternoon

1st Chosen Hugh Johnston Moderator

2ly Voted to adjorn said Meeting to four of the Clock afternoon of said day

3ly Voted that they will not stand me in the Law in a case wherein I sue for money laid out and service done for them to be heard and tried at the court of Common pleas to be holden on tusday the 25th day of Agust current at Springfield in this County of Hampshire

4ly Voted that they will not stand me in the Law in another case wherein I have sued the Proprietors a division of the third division of lots in Sd Pelham

5ly Voted that the meeting is adjorned to tusday the eighth day of September Current at one of the Clock afternoon at this place

HUGH JOHNSTON Moderator

The above votes were passed

THOMAS DICK Proprietors Clerk

Meeting of the Proprietors Sept 8 1767

At a Meeting of the Proprietors of the Lisburn Propriety on adjornment from Fryday the 21st day of Agust 1767 to tusday the Eight day of Sept next then met on Said day and adjourned the meeting to tusday the 29th of Said month to five oclock afternoon.

HUGH JOHNSTON Moderator

The above vote was passed

THOMAS DICK Proprietors Clerk.

The above is the last entry in the Proprietors Record Book, leaving one half of the book blank waiting for the record of the adjourned meeting which was to be held on the 29th of September, but no record is found here or elsewhere and the doings of the Lisburn Propriety at the Dwelling House of Thomas Dick were ended and forever. How they settled the lost land trouble, or how they concluded a settlement with Thomas Dick after voting "not to stand him in the law" cannot be stated for lack of data.

Why the meetings of the Proprietors were excluded from the

meeting house and were held at the tavern of the renowned Thomas Dick does not appear. Why the business of the Propriety should remain dormant from 1746 until 1760, then for two years be pressing, —then no record of action for five years, and to close abruptly after a short campaign of a few months in 1767, with Thomas Dick filling nearly all the offices and the active campaigner for the Proprietors,—with several suits at law against his fellow Proprietors, and the record to end with the suits unsettled and the "Lost Land" claim unsatisfied we would be pleased to give information upon, but must leave them in the unsatisfactory manner the record leaves all these matters.

We have copied everything in this first Record Book except the monotonous and hardly intelligible descriptions of the 183 parcels of land distributed to the proprietors in three separate divisions by lot. It is easy to see how there might be uncertainty and trouble concerning the lands, not only in the north or sixth range but all over the town.

There were five range roads that were reserved in the distribution of the lands and when they were not built the land was allowed to those whose lands the roads crossed, or from whose lands the two rods in width was reserved, either by sale or by exchange, which must have been liable to tangle matters. To this may added the great liability to inaccuracies in the survey of such a large and uneven tract in the short space of time allowed for the work. The Surveyor, William Young, submitted a plan of the first division of 61 lots in April 1739 which was accepted, a copy of which is appended. Then he submitted another plan later in the same year which included the first second and third divisions. A copy of this plan is also included here. In this last plan, the surveyor places first division numbers 7 and 8, 150 to 200 rods farther east than in the first plan. No. 6 and 14 of first division are moved East the same distance in the second plan. First division No. 20 is placed in Ranges 3 and 4, instead of in 4 and 5 in the first plan. First Division No 56 is in Ranges 2 & 3 in the Second Plan and wholly in Range 3 by the first plan. No 58 and 59 of First division are also moved east the whole width of the lots in the second plan. Surveyor Young makes the entire width of the town 1075 rods and reports the width of each of the six ranges 183.33 rods. This gives a width for the town of 1100 rods instead of 1075 as recorded, and a width for each range of $179\frac{1}{6}$ rods. The restored copy of the second plot or plan containing 1st 2d and 3d divisions or lots we do not claim as perfect in all respects as the plot in the old record book has been thumbed so much by so many people in the 156 years since it was made a part of the record as to be nearly obliterated. In regard to location of many of the small lots of the 2d and 3d divisions the lines are completely effaced. We submit it for what it is, without vouching for absolute reliability in the reproduction, but hope it may be of interest in tracing the location of the three divisions of land to each proprietor.

It is well to remember that while the " Standard was forty acres " in the second and third or final division many of the lots in these two divisions contain over 100 acres. The best lands were selected in the first division for home lots and they averaged about 100 acres each while in the second and third divisions the poorer land was measured into lots at a standard of 40 acres to each man, and the surveyor and committee put in quantity to make up what was lacking in quality. This will explain the phrase "Quantity for Quality" which occurs in the discription of each lot in the several divisions.

It was deemed advisable to continue with the records of the Proprietors book until the record closed, and then take up the records of the town under the Act of Incorporation in 1743. As there was a town record and a proprietors record kept for some years, and they cannot be as intelligently interpreted together as if given separately.

Before entering upon the history of the town as found in the records following the Act of Incorporation, we offer an interesting matter of history as a sandwich between the Proprietors Records and the Town Records.

THE TOKEN,

Used by the Scotch Presbyterians of Pelham.

The Scotch Presbyterians who settled the town of Pelham brought with them all the stern orthodoxy of the Presbyterian church of Scotland. They insisted for years upon a rigid inquiry and investigation into the antecedants of all who applied for admission as partners or settlers within their borders and for many years required that those who came "should be such as were Inhabitants of the Kingdom of Ireland, or their Decendants, being Protestants, and none to be admitted but such as bring good and undeniable credentials or certificates of their being persons of good conversation and of the Presbyterian persuasion as used in the Church of Scotland and conform to ye Decepline thereof." They adhered to the creed, the doctrines and the government, and discipline of the Scotch Presbyterian church to the letter, and brought with them all the church customs and practices that were prevalent in Scotland, and among the Scotch who had made their homes in the North of Ireland for many years previous to coming to Massachusetts. There had been no falling away from the true faith or the observances of the church,—but on the contrary there was the same rigid observance and requirement, the same faithful performance of all and every rule of church government as was required in the old country.

All this being true it is no matter of surprise that they continued to guard admission to the town itself by rigid safe guards, and to the communion table by the use of the Token,—the visable symbol of the faithful and devout communicant, which was a time honored custom in Scotland and one they adhered to in Ireland, and one they did not forget in their new home.

The use of the Token is of ancient origin and they have been employed for many different purposes. The Token as used by the church dates back to the Reformation and beyond and was employed by the church in Scotland before 1600 as is shown by ancient church records. Many different metals and substances have been employed; lead or pewter being perhaps the more common, and the shape and style of Tokens much varied; some were oval, some round, others square or oblong, and they had various marks, words, mottoes or figures stamped upon them, and sometimes a date.

The term Tokens and tickets were substantially the same, and the latter term was often used in referring to the use of the Token. Communion Tokens is more expressive of the purpose for which they were used, or better still, Tokens of admission to the Lord's Table. In Scotland on the Saturday before the communion, or on the day of examination, the minister in person, the clerk, or some of the elders specially appointed for the work, distributed the Tokens to all present who were entitled to them, and none were admitted to the communion table on the Sunday following except such as had a Token.

In some instances the church doors were guarded and none were admitted save those who had a Token of lead as a guarantee of their right of entrance.

It was considered disreputable for members to absent themselves from the Lord's Table, and members who were unable to be present on the Saturday previous, when the Tokens were distributed, would sometimes try to obtain one through some friend who was present at the distribution, or try to pass with another's ticket or Token. If the deception became known the offender was punished. Sometimes counterfeit tokens, or pieces of money were dropped in the hand of the minister or elder when collecting the Tokens at the close of the service. Persons detected in such sacreligious deception were punished by the church in a manner that prevented a repetition of the offence.

It was this time honored custom that the settlers of Pelham brought with them and which was observed for a long time probably as long as the strict Presbyterian creed and discipline were adhered to, or until the change to Congregational form of church government. The Tokens used by the Scotch Presbyterians of Pelham were made of lead, of the size in the engraving, which was made from a photograph of real genuine Tokens used at Pelham. They were distributed at the preparatory lecture, before the day of communion, and they were collected at the close of the communion service and kept in a bag made for their reception. That they were much used is indicated by the rounded corners and other marks of use and age.

The letters P. P. in relief upon the bits of lead were understood to stand for Pelham Presbyterian. They are said to have been used wherever the Presbyterian church was established in the United States. They were in use at Londonderry, N. H. and the device adopted there was L. P. signifying Londonderry Presbyterian; also at Chelsea and Sutton. It is also stated that a church in Boston used the Token until recent years.

The Tokens from which the accompanying engraving was made are a small remnant of those used at Pelham, and are probably the only two in existence within the town.

Alice Morse Earle in her valuable book on "The Sabbath in Puritan New England" attributes the introduction of the Token in Pelham to Stephen Burroughs. She says: "The notorious thief and forger Rev. Stephen Burroughs, that remarkable rogue, organized and introduced to his parishoners the custom of giving during the month a metal check to real worthy and truly virtuous church members, on presentation of which check the bearer was entitled to partake of the communion."

She describes the Token, or "check" as she terms it as follows: "Many of the thin chips called Presbyterian checks are still in existence. They are oblong discs of pewter about one inch and a half long bearing the initials P. P." Doubtless Stephen Burroughs, —the smart active boy of nineteen summers did many wicked things, was a sacriligious wretch perhaps, but to attribute the introduction of the Token to the staid Presbyterians of Pelham, during his services as "supplyer" for barely twenty Sabbaths in the spring and summer of 1784 is highly presumptuous and improbable. That Burroughs could "organize and introduce" to these Scotch people any new church custom while Rev. Robert Abercombie, a graduate of Edinburgh University and a former pastor was still living in the town could not be accepted as possible if there was no authenticated records of the use of the Token in the churches for centuries previous to the appearance of the wily Burroughs in Pelham, and showing that it was in use in Scotland before the ancestors of the people living in Pelham had migrated to the north of Ireland. It is much more reasonable to suppose these people continued a custom in use in the Presbyterian church to which they belonged long before they settled Pelham.

We quote once again from the "Sabbath in Puritan New England" to show why the Tokens of the Pelham Presbyterians are not common in the old town to-day: "A clergyman of the Pelham church gave to many of his friends these Presbyterians checks, which he had found among the disused and valueless church properties and the little relics have been carefully preserved." This quotation is generally accepted as substantially true, but does not convey any good reason why any clergyman going out from his labors at Pelham should assume that any church property that had come down from the time of the first settlers in 1738 were valueless, because not in use. Many Presbyterians in New England to-day may never have seen or even heard of the communion Token, because the use of it has been abandoned save in exceptional instances.

Robert Shiells in his "Story of the Token" describes the manner of distributing the Tokens in the churches in Scotland, at the close of Thursday's services, and the "lifting" or gathering them in while the communicants were seated at the sacramental table. "Sometimes they were distributed on Fast days, when the people were dismissed and the minister and elders stood in front of the pulpit. As the members filed past, those who were in good standing and worthy to communicate were handed a small piece of metal known as a Token."

In some churches an annual list was made up of those who were to be refused Tokens, but they were not those who were really liable to excommunication. Of the solemnity and importance attached to the distribution of the Tokens, Shiells quotes the words of Rev. George Gillespie, minister of Strathmiglo, Scotland, who said, "He never gave a Token of admission to the Lord's supper without a trembling hand and a throbbing heart."

The manufacture of the lead Tokens was easy and simple. They were either cast in a mould or struck up with a die in just the same manner coins were formerly made. The keeping up of the needful supply of Tokens devolved upon the minister; and sometimes when a new minister was ordained or installed over a church the mould in which the Tokens were cast was turned over to the new pastor.

In the Story of the Token, already referred to the author refers to the general use of the Token in Scotland and gives many interesting incidents in connection with their use. "In 1590 the sessions of St. Andrews Edenburgh paid for the Token-moulds and 2000 Tokens." "At Galston in 1634 a man had to make public repentance and pay a fine of ten shillings for giving away his Token." "At Mauchline in 1771 a young lad going forward to his first communion, excited and oblivious of minor matters handed the elder a sixpence. This was a heinous offence. The boy was called before the session, when he expressed great sorrow, but this did not save him from being formally rebuked for his sacriligious heedlessness and admonished to be more careful in future."

· In 1727 the following entry occurs in the church book of Ettrick, Selkirkshire, Scotland. " The session met to distribute Tokens but finding that a horserace was to come off before communion Sabbath, forbade any member to attend and decided to hold over the Tokens until after the race." The collection of Tokens has become a popular fad in Scotland, and in the United States there are collectors who are engaged in gathering them. Mr. John Reid, 13 Wellmeadow Blairgowrie, Scotland, is said to have upwards of 5000 Tokens in his collection.

We will close this extended notice of the Token and its use in Scotland and in Pelham by what seems to us a more probable theory of its introduction and use among the Presbyterians of Pelham than that of Alice Morse Earle. Rev. Robert Abercrombie has already been mentioned in this connection and it is proper to state further that he was the first settled minister of the town of Pelham. A Scotchman by birth and education, he commenced his labors among the people of Pelham in 1742 and was ordained August 30, 1744. The meeting house was not completed at that time and the church probably not fully organized in all respects until then, so that it seems fair to suppose that Rev. Mr. Abercrombie himself might have been the one to decide what device should be upon the Token for use in Pelham and see to procuring the moulds for casting them, as that duty was laid upon pastors by custom in Scotland as Mr. Abercrombie very well knew, and were the records of the Presbyterian church in Pelham accessible they would quite probably disclose the circumstances of the adoption of the Token. To show the standing and acknowledged ability of Mr. Abercombie and his influence among the Presbyterians of New England we quote from Sprague's Annals of the American Pulpit Vol. III, page 16 of the Historical Introduction : " Notwithstanding Presbyterianism has never prevailed extensively in New England, it has had a distinct and independent existence there from a very early period. The French church of Boston, which was formed of Huguenots in or about the year 1687 was the first church organized on a Presbyterian basis ; but it was continued no longer than while their public worship was conducted in the French language.

The first Presbyterian organization in New England of any permanence dated to about the year 1718 when a large number of Presbyterians with four ministers imigrated to this country from the North of Ireland. For sometime in cases of difficulty the ministers and elders were wont to assemble informally, and hold what might be called pro re nata meetings ; and occasionally when they were unable to reach a satisfactory result, they asked advice of the Synod of Ireland.

This state of things continued till the year 1745 when the ministers resolved as preparatory to the step they were about to take, to observe in connection with their congregations, the third Wednesday of March as a day of fasting, humiliation and prayer.

On the 16th of April following the Rev. Messrs. John Moorhead of Boston, David McGregorie of Londonderry, N. H., Robert Abercrombie of Pelham, with Messrs. James McKeon, Alexander Conkey and James Hughes, met at Londonderry and being satisfied as to the Divine Warrant, with dependence upon God for counsel and assistance, they, by prayer, constituted themselves into a Presbytery, to act, so far as their present circumstances will permit them, according to Word of God and the constitution of the Presbyterian church of Scotland, agreeing to that perfect rule. This body was called "The Boston Presbytery" and met according to adjournment in that town on the 13th of August, 1745."

INCORPORATION OF THE TOWN OF PELHAM.

It was while the Proprietors of Lisburn were absorbed with the great business of settling a first minister that the legislative action took place under which the people organized the plantation or settlement as a town and began their career as the eleventh town organization west of Worcester County.

The several acts of the General Court,—the call for the first town meeting, and the doings of the meeting follow.

The selection of the name Pelham for the town doubtless came from the fact that Lord Pelham was travelling in this country at the time. It has been said that Lord Pelham, pleased to learn that a town had selected his name to be placed in the act of incorporation, signified his pleasure by sending from England a bell for the meeting house. If one was sent it never arrived in Pelham. The reason why the bell did not reach its distination, it has been said, was caused by the fact that no money was forthcoming to pay the freight charges on its arrival in Boston, and that after waiting in vain for payment on the freight bill the bell was sold to the Old South Church. If Lord Pelham was so kind and thoughtful as to order a bell sent over from England it was very unfortunate that he did not open his purse and pay for its free delivery in Boston, if not in Pelham.

It is doubtful about a bell being sent at all, but as the pleasant story has been told many times in connection with the naming of the town it can do little harm to give it a place here. Unless there was some good and sufficient reason, such as the hope of getting a bell or some other valuable consideration, we fail to understand why the very pleasant sounding name of Lisburn or New Lisburn, first selected for the name of the settlement was discarded to honor Lord Pelham. No one, so far as we are advised has ever been able to give a reason why these people first gave the name Lisburn or New Lisburn to their new settlement on the hills of Eastern Hampshire so we offer what seems to be a fairly good supposition, to say the least. Down on the extreme southern border of County Antrim Ireland, on the banks of the river Lagan is located the town of Lisburn, celebrated for its manufacture of damasks and fine linen goods, said to have been established there by a settlement of Hugeuenots after the Revocation of the Edict of Nantes. Perhaps some of the settlers of Pelham came from Lisburn and suggested the name for the new plantation. Certainly those people who came to Massachusetts in 1718, brought with them the "little wheel" for spinning flax and this alone would indicate that they were well acquainted with this center of linen manufacture, if they were not actual residents of Lisburn. The wives and daughters of the early settlers of Pelham were noted as skillful spinners of flax and weavers of linen.

Anno Regne Regis Georgie Seccondo Decimo Sexto
An act for erecting a tract of Land Commonly Called New Lisborn Lying in ye County of Hampshire into a Township by ye Name of Pelham.

Whereas there are a Considerable Number of Families Settled on a tract of Land Commonly called New Lisburn Lying in the County of Hampshire Who have Represented to this Court that they labour under great Difficulties By reason of their not being incorporated into a Township Be it therefore Enacted by the Govnr Council & House of Representatives that the Lands aforesaid be and hereby are Erected into a Seperate and Distinct township by the Name of Pelham—the Bounds Whereof to be as Follows Viz—Bounding Easterly on a tract of Land Commonly Called Quabin granted to a Number of Canada & Narragansett Soldiers Southerly on a Lot of Equivalent Land so Called belonging to Rev Mr Edwards & Mrs Rebecca Hauley—Westerly on ye East Bounds of the Town of Hadley & Northerly partly on a New Township Commonly called Roadtown and Partly on a New Township Commonly Called New Salem & that ye Inhabitants on ye Land aforesaid be and hereby are vested with all ye Power Priviliges & Immunities Which ye Inhabitons of other towns within this Province are or by Law ought to be vested with—Decr: 28,—1742—This Bill having Been Read three sev l times in Ye House of Representatives—Pased to be Enacted   J CUSHING Speaker.

Decr.: 28: 1742 This Bill having been read three several times in Council —Pased to be Enacted   J WILLARD Sec'ry

Jan,y 15, 1742   By the Governor.—I consent to ye Enacting of this Bill—
WILLIAM SHIRLEY
Copy: Examined Pr J WILLARD Sec'ry

In Ye House of Representativs April 1 1743 ordered that Mr Robert Peibles one of Ye Principal Inhabetans of the New Township Lately erected Named Pelham in the County of Hampshire be & hereby is fully authorized & impowered upon due Publication or Notice Given to Assemble the Inhabitons of said Town to Choose

all town officers who shall stand till ye anniversary Meeting in March Nixt—
<blockquote>Sent up for Concurrence. F CUSHING Speaker
In Council April 1st 1743—Read & Concurid, J WILLARD Sec'try
Consented to W SHIRLY
Copy Examined pr J WILLARD Sec'ty</blockquote>

Province of Massachusetts Bay.—Whereas the Generall Court or assembly of s'd Province by their order of the first of April Current have authorized and empowered the subscriber hereoff (upon due notice or publication given) to assemble the Inhabitants of the town of Pelham in the County of Hampshire to choose all town officers who shall stand till the anniversary meeting in March next.

Pursuant thereto these are therfore to Warn and Notifie the free-holders and other inhabitants of s'd town qualified by law to vote in Town affairs that they assemble themselves at the Meeting House in s'd Pelham on Tuesday the Nineteenth day of April current at nine of the Clock in the forenoon for the choosing Town officers for s'd town as aforesaid.

Dated at Pelham this ninth day of April in the sixteenth year of His Majestys Reighn
Annoy Dom'ni 1743 ROBERT PEIBOLS

Pelham April 9 1743
Then I Posted up a Notification for colling a Town Meeting in Pelham by fixing it on the side of the Meeting House (by the door) in s'd Pelham of the which Notification the within is a true copy.
As Attest ROBERT PEIBOLS.

The meeting to organize under the act of incorporation was held according to the above notification. The act incorporating the town was passed by the General Court on the 28 of Dec 1752, and became a law by the addition of the Governor's Signature on the 15th of January 1743. At that time there were only the towns of Springfield, Northampton, Hadley, Hatfield, Northfield, Sunderland, Brimfield, Westfield, Sheffield and Stockbridge in the state west of Worcester County that were incorporated, Pelham making the eleventh.

TOWN MEETING, MARCH, 1897.

TOWN MEETING RECORDS

From 1743 to 1763.

Petition to General Court to Legalize Acts of Town Officers in 1753.—Invoices Given In for Taxation in 1760.—The Town Presented at Court in 1762 for " Voluntarily Omitting and Neglecting to Provide Themselves with a Learned and Able Orthodox Minister.—Illegal Killing of Deer in 1763, and Penalty Therefor.

RECORD OF FIRST TOWN MEETING UNDER THE ACT OF INCORPORATION, HELD APRIL 19, 1743.

Officers chosen to stand to ye anniversary meeting in March, 1744:

Selectmen—Alexander Conky, Robert Pebils, John Alexander, John Gray, Robert Lotheridge.

Town Clerk—William Gray.

Town Treasurer—John Stinson.

Surveyors—James Taylor, John Conkey, John Johnson, Ephriam Cowan.

Tythingmen—Andrew Maklem, James McConel.

Constables—George Cowan, James Hood.

Fence Viewers—Thomas Hamilton, Alexander Tower.

Hogreeves—William Conky, John Blair.

Assessors—William Gray, Samuel Gray, & William Croset.

Officers to Prosecute ye Law Respecting Killing Deer—Robert Maklem, John Lucore.

Officers to Prosecute ye Law about Burning of Woods—John Hamilton, Hugh Gray.

At a Leguall town meeting in Pelham April ye 19th, 1743 John Stoddard Esq'r Being first Chosen Moderator the town Made choice of ye Several Persons above Named to ye Several offices to Which Their Names are Respectively Affixed.

test JOHN STODDARD, Moderator.

Pelham April ye 19 1743.

Then all ye Persons Named in ye above List took ye oaths to their Respective offices Belonging Except the Selectmen and John Lucore

Cor^m JOHN STODDARD Pac^e Justice.

The town was now fully organized under the act of incorporation and a full board of town officers elected. The meeting house was far enough advanced towards completion so that it might be, and in fact was in use for preaching the gospel, and now the business which the settlers placed before the almost everything else was in order, viz.—

THE SETTLING OF THE FIRST MINISTER.

Matthew Gray had been dispatched to Londonderry, N. H. with a call to Rev. Mr. Johnson to settle in Pelham, but for some unexplained reason the call was not accepted and the people were obliged to look farther.

It was the first of September, 1741 that Matthew Gray bore the call to Rev. Mr. Johnson, and not until May 11, 1742 that the vote was taken "to interceed with Rev. Robert Abercrombie be our supplayer as far as he can for this summer." The peculiar form of the vote passed would indicate that Mr. Abercrombie had some engagements which would prevent his preaching at Pelham continuously, but they hoped by judicious intercession he might be induced to preach for them a portion of the time. Owing to the importance of the business of settling the first minister in the town and the singularly interesting history of the pastorate of Rev. Robert Abercrombie over the church at Pelham, it has been thought advisable to place all matters pertaining to his settlement, pastorate and dismissal, as well as incidents of his life in the town after his retirement from the ministry, in a separate chapter, where all such matters of fact and record could be perused more in detail, and separate from other ordinary town business and history. Space has been set apart for that purpose and the reader is referred to it.

ANNUAL TOWN MEETING, MARCH 5, 1743–4.

First Was Chosen John Stinson Moderator.

Selectmen—Ephriam Cowan, John Stinson, George Cowan, Matthew Gray and John Clark.

Town Clerk—William Gray.
Assessors—James Conky, John Hamilton, Alexander Tower.
Constables—John Johnson, Thomas Hamilton.
Town Treasurer—John Stinson.
Surveyors of High Ways—Patrick Pebels, Alexander Tower, William Conky, Robert Lotheridge.
Tything men—Thomas Hamilton, James Alexander.
Fence Viewers—John Conky & Samuel Gray.
Hog Reveevs—Hugh Gray & Robert Maklem.
Committee to Run Lines with Neighboring Towns—Robert Lotheridge, Sam^{ll} Gray, James Alexander.

Ye meeting is adjourned for two hours to swear ye Officers and to Dismiss one Constable and Chuse another.

JOHN STINSON, Moderator.

MEETING MAY 26, 1743.

Voted Col Timothy Dwight is chosen Moderator.

Voted there be a Committee Chosen to Provide Sermon till such Times as We can orderly Proceed to ye Calling of a Minister.

Voted y't John Stinson, John Johnson and James Conky be a Committee to Provide Sermon.

Voted that said com'ttee is to Invite such Person or Persons as they think Proper to be Improved in Said Service.

Voted that there be a Committee Chosen to Invite three ordained Neighboring Ministers to Keep a Day of fasting and Prayer With us and to consult With ye same whome we Shall Call to be our Minister.

Voted that Ephriam Cowan, Samuel Gray & Robert Pebels be a Committee to invite three Ministers to Keep a Day of fasting and prayer with us.

Voted y't there Be a Committee Chosen to Provide Glass to Gleas the Meeting House and to Build a Pulpit and to finish ye under Pinning of ye Meeting house at ye Charge of ye town and said Work to be Done Before Winter.

Voted y't ye select Men to Wite Robert Pebels, Alexander Conky, John Alexander, John Gray & Robert Lotheridge Be a Committee to Provide ye Glass and Glasing of ye Meeting house and to Build a Pulpit & under Pine y'e s^{d} House at y'e charge of the Town.

Voted that y'e aforesaid Committee for Bulding a Pulpit is to Buld a Pulpit for Dignitee Like unto haddley third Precinct.

Voted that there be y'e Sume of Eighty four Pounds old tenor Expended on High Ways this year to Be Rased on y'e town Each man an Inhabitant in this is to have Liberty to Do three Days Work at High Ways this year y't May be Levied by a Reat Made By y'e Pols & Estates.

Voted that there be allowed to each Man Eight Shillings per Day & a team of four Cattle Eight Shillings per Day for a full Day Work.

Voted that Each Surveyor of High Ways is to take Notice how Much any Person Comes Short Eather by Himself or his tame of Doing a Reasonable Days work & to Note down in his Count how much any Person so falls Short & that such Person Be abated so much of the aforesaid Prices.

Voted y't y'e select Men are Directed to Provide Sutable Cloath & have it Made up to Covire Coffins With in Buring of our Dead at the charge of y'e town.

Voted y't y'e Committee appointed to Invite three of Neighboring Ordained Ministers to assist us at a Day of fasting and Prayer to Seek to God for Direction in y'e Choice of a Minister & to Desire ye Ministers to Attend on ye Last tusday of June Nixt at ye Meeting house abovesaid—all y'e above s[1] Articles Were Voted Affirmatively —test

TIMOTHY DWIGHT Moderator.

There seems to have been some hitch in the committee chosen to "invite the three neighboring ordained ministers" to assist in the proposed day of fasting and prayer and a warrant was issued for a town meeting, containing the following articles only.

WARRANT.

First to See if or Not they will adjourn ye fast Day that Was appointed— till longer time.

2[ly] to See if or Not they will ye Committee appointed for that Purpose to appoint ye Day.

Hereof fail not etc—

MEETING JUNE 21, 1743.

At a Leguall town In Pelham June ye 21st 1743.—at said meeting John Stinson was Chosen Moderator.

Voted y't ye Day appointed in Our Meeting May ye 26th for fasting & Prayer is adjourned to Longer time.

Voted that ye Committee appointed for Inviting Ministers to Keep ye fast that they are to appoint ye time when they Can have it Done With the Best Conveney

JOHN STINSON Moderator.

ANNUAL MEETING MARCH 4, 1744-5

Then meet on said Day and was Chosen as Follows
Matthew Gray Moderator
Selectmen.—Alexander Conky, Robert Pebels, John Gray, James McCulloch, Thos Dick.
Town Clerk.—William Gray
Constables.—Alexander McCulloch & James Gilmore.
Assessors.—William Gray, William Crossett, Thos Dick.
Town Treasurer.—James Conky
Surveyors of High Ways.—John Clark, James Allexander, Robert Meklem, Nathaniel Gray, John Hamilton, John Stinson.
Tything men.—William Conky & John Blaire
Hog Rives.—James Taylor & Samuel Gray.

Meeting adjourned to April 9th 1745 when a number of roads were consented to by owners of lands through which they passed and among them it was " Voted that ye Road laid out From ye North East Corner of Mr Abercrombies lot to ye Meeting house as it is marked –   –   –   Consent to ye above vote

R. ABERCROMBIE—"

"Voted that ye Road Laid out From Hadley line to ye south end of Robert Lotheridge^s Barn as it is Marked & from thence By ye south end of s^d Lotheridges Rey field as ye Road Now Goes & so to ye Range Road Betwixt s^d Lotheridges & Ephriam Cowan, said Road is to be two Rods in width.—

Consented to by Andrew Meklem, James Conky, John Crawford, Robert Lotheridge."

The above record must have been that of the laying out of the present road from Amherst line east to Home lot No. 29, drawn by Robert Lotheridge, or about two miles from Amherst line. It then ran north until it joined the Second Range road between Lot No. 29 and Lot No. 42, the latter owned by Ephriam Cowan. The second range road is the one that ran due east, up over the hill, past the Collins Brailey farm and came out at the Cross road about half a mile south of Pelham center, and thence to the east line of the town. The Collins Brailey farm is now owned by Stephen Rhoads.

It is supposed that the first bridle path to East Hadley followed the middle range as far as possible down through the Valley and over the side of the mountain to Amherst, keeping on the north side of what is now known as Amethyst Brook.

Some articles from Warrant for a town meeting dated April 26, 1744:

"First to see How Many Days Works Each Pole will Work at y'e Highways this Present year.

2ly To see what the Town will do concerning a scole for this Present year

3ly To See if ye town Will alowe anything for Killing Rattle Snaks for Two Months thats April & May.

4ly To see if y'e town Will alow ye Constables to post up notifications to Warn town Meetings For y'e futter—

5ly To See if y'e town Will Clean ye Buring ground & fence y'e Same & Clean about the Meeting house.

MEETING APRIL 26, 1744.

Then Meet on ye said Day & Was Chosen Sam'l Gray Moderator.

1st Voted that Each Pole work four Days on ye High ways

2ly Voted that their be a Scole Keept in town For y'e Space of two Months one Month at ye Dwelling house of Ephriam Cowan and one Month at ye Dwelling house of William Gray's—

3ly Voted that ye Constables Post up ye Warnings for town Meetings for ye futur.

4ly Voted that ye Collectors & ye Constables from ye Beginning have four pound yearly a Cording to ye old tenor.

5ly Voted that there be one Acer of land Fenced with a good Stone wall and also that Robert Pebels, Samuel Gray & Robert Lotheridge over See ye Bulding of ye s^d Wall at their own Charge.—

6ly Voted Their be two men Chosen to build ye said Wall.

This meeting is adjourned to ye 8th Day of May Nixt at 4 of ye Clock in ye After Noon to Consider ye voted of fencing ye buring Place.

At meeting on adjournment from April ye 26 1744 to May ye 8th. Then Meet to Consider of ye Method of fencing ye Buring place & was voted y'^{t} ye fifth vote is Recald & it is voted y^t ye Sixth vote is Recald—Also

Voted y' y'e Buring Place be fenced With Good five Real fence ye Reals ten feet Long & twelve Lengths to each Quarter, also

Voted to agree with a Sutable Person to fence ye s^d Buring Place—

Also it is agreed y^t John Conky do ye above s^d fence & he is to have five pounds Ten Shillings Reward for said work aCording to ye old tenor.—Also voted that James Gilmore sen John Stinson & Sam^{ll} Gray be a Committee to see that the above s^d fence be Sufficiently Done by ye first Day of Octr Nixt.

SAM'L GRAY Moderator.

In a warrant for a town meeting dated May 14, 1745, are these articles,—the meeting being called at seven o'clock in the forenoon.

To see whats Proper to be Done about ye Gleass of ye Meeting house That Was Sued for.

To see what Method will be taken in Building a Pound. (No action taken concerning the Pound at this meeting.)

Voted that James McColloch & Robert Lotheridge be a Committee to go to Major Williams to see to stop ye action y^t he Sued for of ye Meeting house Gleass

JAMES McCOLLOCH Moderator.

The obvious reason for calling a town meeting at seven o'clock in the morning was to take action in season to stop an impending lawsuit which Major Williams instituted to recover pay for glass used in building the meeting house.

ANNUAL MEETING MARCH 3, 1745–6.

Then Meet on s^d Day & Was Chosen

George Cowan Moderator

Selectmen—Alexander Conky, James McCulloch, Adam Petteson, John Clark, Robert Meklem.

Town Clerk—John Dick

Assessors—William Gray ye 3^d, William Crossett, John Dick.

Constables—Thomas Dick, Andrew Meklem

Treasurer—James Conky

Surveyors—Edward Selfridge, Matthew Gray, John Stinson, John Wason, Thomas Hamilton & William Crossett

Tythingmen—John Conky, James Hood

Hog Rives—Allexander Conky Jun, David Thomas.

Fence Viewers—William Conkey, James Gilmore Jun.

MEETING APRIL 15, 1746.

The principal business of this meeting was presentation of Debt and Credit, and voting the amounts due to each man to whom the town was indebted for services.

"Meet on Said Day and was Chosen
William Gray, Moderator.

First Voted that Samuel Gray be allowed one Pound sixteen shilling old tenor for Carring a Notification to Roadtown & Salem

2^{ly} Voted Robert Pebels one Pound twelve shilling

3^{ly} Voted Samuel Thornton one Pound twelve shilling

4^{ly} Voted William Gray three Pound four shilling

5^{ly} Voted John Gray four Pound thirteen shilling

6^{ly} Voted Alexander Conky, James McCulloch, & John Gray each one Pound ten shilling

7^{ly} Voted William Conky fifteen shilling

8^{ly} Voted James McColloch ten shilling

9^{ly} Voted James Gilmore one pound

10^{ly} Voted John Stinson one pound

11^{ly} Voted John Conky one pound

12^{ly} Voted That William Young be alowed one Pound old tenor for Running the North line if Demanded

13^{ly} Voted John Stinson & John Gray one Pound

14^{ly} Voted James Allexander eight shilling

15^{ly} Voted John Stinson one Pound Eleven shilling overpaid by him

16^{ly} Voted John Conky two Pound for taking Care of ye Meeting house

17^{ly} Voted William Crosset Sixteen shilling

18^{ly} Voted Negatively y^t Thos Dick^s order be Returned

19^{ly} Voted Thomas Dick eight shilling

Ye vots from ye first to the Nineteenth is Debt & Credit allowed to the Persons Named."

Voted that ye Delinquents Work out ye Remainder of their Work at ye Pound & that there Be Men Brought from Several Quarters to Work & be alowed as much as att ye Roads Work—

Voted y^t Thomas Dick be oversier to have ye remainder of ye Work Don at ye Pound—

Voted that there be five Pound Raised to Buy a town Book for ye use of ye town.

Annual Meeting March 2, 1746-7.

Then meet on said Day and was Chosen Thomas Dick Moderator
Town Clerk—John Dick
Treasurer—James Conky
Selectmen—George Cowan, William Gray 3^d, James Thornton, James McConel, Ephriam Cowan.
Assessors—William Crosset, John Dick, & James Thornton.
Constable—For the East End, Robert Meklem
Constable—For the West End, Edward Selfridge
Surveyors—For the West End, James McColloch, John Blair & John Gray.
Surveyors—For the East End, John Hamilton, John Pebels & John Clark.
Tything Men—For the East End, Robert McKee
Tything Men—For the West End, John Savige
Fence Viewer—For the West End, John Stinson
Fence Viewer—For the East End, John Conky
Hogs Reve—For the East End, James Taylor
Hogs Reve—For the West End, Thomas Johnson

Meeting March 19, 1746-7.

"Voted that James Thornton, Matthew Gray, Patrick Pebels & Thomas Johnson is to Oversee the Finishing ye Pound.

Voted also that Each Man that Refuses to Work shall Pay ten Shilling for every Day Deficit.

Voted that there be a Reat Made on ye Pole of ten Shilling for each Pole that Will Not Work."

James Thornton, Moderator.

In April of the previous year Thomas Dick was chosen to oversee the work of finishing the pound, but it had not been done, and now four men were chosen to oversee work on the pound, and measures were adopted to compel men to work.

Annual Meeting March 7, 1747-8.

Then Meet on said Day and then was Chosen James Thornton Moderator

Selectmen—James Thornton, George Cowan, Ephriam Cowan, James McConel & John Clark

Town Clerk—John Dick
Treasurer—James Conky
Constable for West End—William Gray ye 3^d
Constable for East End—William Gilmore
Assessors—John Dick, William Gray Jun, James Thornton & Thomas Dick.
Surveyors—Robert King, Thos Hamilton, aDam Petteson, John Stinson, John Pebels
Tythingman for the West End—Allexander Tower, James Dunlap
Tythingman for the East End—Patrick Pebels, John Hamilton, Thomas Cochran
Fence Viewer for the West End—John Blair.
Fence Viewer for the East End John Conky.
Field Driver for West End—John Johnson.
Voted y^t John Johnson be no field Driver.
Hogs Rive for West End—James Gilmore.
Hogs Rive for East End—William Linsey.

PROTEST—We the Subscribers Enter our Protest against ye unlawful Proceedings of this Meeting. ROBERT PEBELS,
PATRICK PEBELS.

We the subscribers enter our Protest against ye Proceedings of this Meeting. THOMAS COCHRAN,
JOHN HAMILTON,
JAMES TAYLOR.

There was a town meeting April 12, 1748, and the warrant called upon the town to "Bring in their Debt and Credit" also To see How Many Days ye town will Work at ye Roads this Year
To see Wither the Hogs Will Run In ye Commons or be Sutt up.
Voted y^t Each Pole Work two Day ye Roads this year
Voted y^t ye hogs is to Run at learge this year
JAMES THORNTON Moderator.

MEETING AUGUST 11, 1748.

Two Articles in Warrant

1st To see if the town will be Willing to lett Every Man Have Powder out of the town Stock as fare as Every Man Paid.

2^{ly} to see if the town Will be Willing to Have a Rate made to Bay a Buring Cloth for ye Use of ye town.

Voted that every Man Have Powder & Lead as fare as they Have Paid & have itt out of ye Present town Stock.

Voted that there be a Buring Cloth bought, also voted there be twenty pound Made in a Rate to buy the same.

WILLIAM GRAY 1st Moderator.

ANNUAL MEETING MARCH 6, 1748–9.

Then meet on said day and was chosen Thomas Dick Moderator

Town Clerk,—John Dick

Treasurer,—James Conky

Selectmen,—Thomas Dick, John Fergerson, John Johnson, John Hunter, John Dick.

Assessors,—John Fergerson, Thomas Dick and John Hunter.

Constable for ye East end—John Clark.

Constable for ye West end—Ephraim Cowan.

Tythingman for ye West end—John Edeger.

Tythingman for ye East end—John Hamilton.

Surveyors for ye East end—William Conky George Cowan William Crosett James Gilmore

Surveyors for ye West end—William Fergerson Allexander Tonrer James McConel.

Fence Viewer for ye West end—John Stinson.

Fence Viewer for ye East end—John Conky.

Hog Rives—Edward Selfidge and John Conky.

Meeting adjourned to First day of April next at nine of the Clock in the forenoon.

ANNUAL MEETING MARCH 5, 1749–50.

Then meet on said day and was Chosen James Conky Moderator.

Town Clerk—John Dick.

Treasurer,—George Cowan

Selectmen,—Ephraim Cowan, James McCollock, James Conky William Crosett and John Conkey

Assessors—Thomas Dick William Crosett and James Conky.

Constable for ye West end—John Lucore

Constable for ye East end—John Hamilton.

Tythingman for ye East end—Thomas Cochran

Tythingman for ye West end—Joseph Rinken

Surveyors for ye West end—John Crawford Jun John Savige David Cowden and Ephraim Cowan.

Surveyors for ye East end—Adam Johnson, James Gilmore Andrew Meklem and William Gilmore.

Hoge Rive for ye East end—Daniel Gray

Hoge Rive for ye West end—Robert McCollock

Fence Viewer for ye West end—Robert Blair.

Fence Viewer for ye East end—James Taylor.

This year seems to have been a quiet one among the people, there having been but one town meeting from March 5 1750 to March 4 1751, and that was to bring in the "Debt and Credit" and settle with all that had done work for the town.

Annual Meeting March 4, 1751.

Then meet on said Day and then was Chosen William Crosett, Moderator—

Town Clerk—John Dick.

Treasurer—George Cowan

Selectmen—Ephraim Cowan James McColloch John Conky James Conkey and William Crosett.

Assessors—William Crosett, Thomas Dick and James Conky.

Constable for ye East end George Petteson

Constable for ye West end Robert King.

Road Surveyors for ye West end John Savige David Thomas John Crawford Jun and David Cowden.

Road Surveyors for ye East end Robert Meklem William Conky and John Clark

Tuthingman for ye East end James Taylor.

Tuthingman for ye West end Edward Selfridge

Fence Viewer for ye West end John Blair

Fence Viewer for ye East end John Pebels

Hog Rives for ye East end James Hamilton

Hog Rives for ye West end John Johnson

Voted Negatively that the town refuses to open ye Range Road for the Convenency of George Cowan also voted that the town His aproven of ye Roads that ye Selectmen Viewed for the Convenancy of the Inhabitons of Pelham.

We ye Subscribers Do Acknowledge our Selves contented to establish the Roads when ye Selectmen viewed through our Lands as

Witness our hands George Cowan Thomas Hamilton Thomas McMullan Joseph Rinken.—

We ye Subscribers Inhabitons of Pelham Do Protest against the unregular Proceedings at their Annual Meeting March 4th 1751—In not purging the Meeting and alowing Voters as ye Law Directs, Robert Pebels James Taylor John Hunter, Thomas McMullen Adam Petteson Thomas Hamilton John Gray Thomas Dick Edward Selfidge John Hamilton

WILLIAM CROSETT Moderator.

MEETING APRIL 30, 1751.

Thomas Dick alowed £1—8s for making Rats

James Conkey alowed 17s—4d for making Rats

Ephraim Cowan ⎫
James McCollock ⎬ each alowed 2s 8d for running Line between Hadley and this town
John Conky ⎭

John Conky alowed 6s—8d for taking care of Meeting house.

William Crosett alowed 17—4d for running line between Quabin and this town.

Voted that each pole work three Days att the Roads

Voted that each Delinquent Pole pay 3 shilling lawful money per Day

Voted that ye Hogs Run at Large this Present year.

Voted that there be one acre and a half fenced with stone wall for buring yard

Voted that Each Pole work one Day at ye Buring yeard also voted that Each Delinquent Pole pay three shilling lawful money,

Voted that Cart or Slide & one Pare of Oxen be Equal to one Pole for this Present year at the Buring yeard,

THOMAS DICK Moderator.

ANNUAL MEETING MARCH 2, 1752.

Then meet on said Day and was Chosen William Crosett—Moderator

Town Clerk.—John Dick

Treasurer.—John Hamilton

Selectmen.—John Savige Patrick Peebils John Johnson John Blair Thomas Johnson.

Assessors.—David Cowden David Thomas Daniel Gray.

Constables.—Patrick McMullen & James Conky.

Tythingmen.—John Pebels & Robert Blair.

Surveyors.—Thomas Cochran Andrew Meklem William Conky Hugh Johnson John Savige Allexander McCollock Robert Lotheredge Hoge Reevies Jonathan Gray John Lucore.

Meeting April 8, 1752.

Meet on said Day and was chosen John Savige Moderator

First Voted that John Conkey is allowed five shilling and four pence for lawful money for taking care of the Meeting house.

2^{ly} James Conky is allowed seventeen shilling four pence for making Reats Eight Days and a half

3^{ly} Thomas Dick is allowed seventeen shilling and four pence for making Reats eight days and a half

4^{ly} William Crosett is allowed thirteen shillings for making Reats six days and a half.

5^{ly} Daniel Gray is alowed Eight Shilling for a jorney of his Horse to Boston

6^{ly} Voted that the assessors is alowed to assess forty four pound Nine Shilling for ye Support of Gospel for this present year

7^{ly} Voted that there is eight Pound alowed for the support of a school the Present year

8^{ly} Voted that there be a Committee chosen to provide a schole Master

—Said Committee is John Stinson Robert Lotheridge & Andrew Meklem

9^{ly} Voted y^t Each Pole Work two Days at ye Roads and one Day at ye Buring Yeard

10^{ly} Voted that ye hogs Run at large this Present year

12^{ly} Voted that John Starling and Thomas Lowdan is freed from there Reats for this Present year

John Savige Moderator.

Annual Meeting March 5, 1753.

Then Meet on said Day and was Chosen James Conky Moderator.

Town Clerk,—John Dick

Treasurer,—Thomas Dick

Selectmen,—Patrick Peebels Thomas Johnson John Savige John Blair George Cowan

Assessors,—John Fergerson David Thomas Daniel Gray.

Constables,—William Crosett for the East End John Blair for the West End

Voted that the old Surveyors stand for the Present year.

Petition sent to the General Court.

By reason of the failure to administer the oath to the town officers elected in the spring of 1753 it became necessary to apply to the General Court to legalize the acts of these men and the following petition was sent to Boston by the selectmen of 1753:

To his Excellency William Shirley Esq Captain General & Governor In Chief & to the Honorable His Majestys Council and House of Representatives in General Court assembled Dec 1753.

The Petition of the Selectmen of the town of Pelham Humbly Showeth—That the Said town at their Meeting in March Last for the Choice of Town Officers through inadvertancy neglected to Administer the oath respecting the Bills of Credit of the other Governments unto the Several officers that were then Chosen which causes great Difficultys among us—We humbly request your Excellency & Honor to enable us to Call a Meeting of Said Town for the choice of Officers & that they may be Qualified according to law or otherwise relieve us as in your Wisdom you shall see fit and as in duty bound shall ever Pray

George Cowan
Patrick Peebles
John Savige
John Blair
Thomas Johnson

In the House of Representtives Dec. 12, 1753.

Whereas the town of Pelham in the County of Hampshire when they chose their officers to the respective offices in Said Town in March Last omitted administering to them the oath appointed by Law of this Province of the 22^d of His Present Majests Reign Respecting Bills of Credit of the Neighboring Governments appointed to be taken by such officers by Means Whereof the several officers in said town are vacant & thereby Great Inconveniences & Difficulties Have arisen to said town which Cannot be Remedied but by ye aid & Interposition of this Court—Therefore ordered that Eleazer Porter Esqr be directed & Hereby Impowered to Issue His Warrant Directed to some Inhabitant of said Town—Requiring him to warn and give Notice to the Inhabitons of said town as by said warrant shall be appointed to make choice of such officers for said town as shall be Necessary & acording to Law ought to be chosen yearly for transacting the affairs of said Town & the Inhabitons Being so Met are Hereby Impowered to Make Choice of Such officers and such Officers so Chosen—Having first Taken the oath aforesaid & the oaths of their Respective offices Shall have the Like Power in their Respective offices as by Law they would have had on their being Chosen acording to ye Directions of the Law in the Month of March & Qualified as aforesaid

       Sent up for Concurrence
            F HUBBARD Speaker
In Councel Dec 12 1753
    Read & Concurred THOMAS CLARKE Dep^t Secry
      Consented to WILLIAM SHIRLY.

Hampshire ss March ye Eight one thousand Seven Hundred & fifty four

To John Savige of Pelham in the County of Hampshire (Porsuant of the Within order of the Great and General Court) In His Majestys Name you are Required to Notifie & Warn all the Freeholders and other Inhabitons of said Pelham Qualified to vote in town Meetings to assemble themselves together at the Meeting house in said Pelham on the twenty Eight of this Month at Nine of the Clock in ye forenoon then & there to Make Choice of all Necessary town officers which by Law towns are obliged to Make Choice of & Make Return of your Doings thereon to your Inhabitons so assembled.

Given under My Hand & Seal ye Day and Deate Above said
           ELEAZER PORTER Justs *Coram*.

By Vartue of the Within Warrant I have Warned the Inhabitons of Pelham above said to Meet at time & Place above mentioned

Pelham March ye twenty Eight one thousand seven hundred & fifty four
              JOHN SAVIGE.

ANNUAL MEETING MARCH 28, 1754.

Then meet on said Day & was chosen

William Crosett, Moderator

Town Clerk,—John Dick.

Treasurer—Thomas Dick.

Selectmen—Thomas Hamilton Alexander Torner John Fergerson David Thomas William Conkey

Assessors,—John Fergerson David Thomas Daniel Gray.

Constables,—John Conkey Robert McCollock

Surveyors,—Archibald Crosett Patrick McMullen Thomas Hamilton Alexander Conkey John Blair Thomas Johnson Wm Fergerson

Hog Rieves,—Allexander McNut Joseph Rinken

Fence Viewers,—Daniel Gray Robert Blair

Meeting, April 16, 1754.

Allowed six shillings to John Conkey for taking care of the Meeting house.

Allowed John Savige and John Blair 8s—8d for Getting a Preacipe from the court to Hold Meetings.

Voted to Petition the General court for a Help from ye None Inhabitons for finishing ye Meeting house

Voted that each Delinquent Pole pay two shilling

"Voted that William Crosett Thomas Dick & John Dick be a Committee to Look over the town Vots & lay the same Before ye town they think Not Proper to be Recorded

Voted that there be a Bridge Bult over the West Branch where the Road is Newly Confirmed by the Town."

Adjourned to the third Tuesday in May and again to the 27th of May.

"Voted that there be one Half penny per aker Laid on the None Inhabitons Lands"

JAMES CONKEY Moderator.

The vote to build a bridge over the West Branch makes it clear that the road across the river had been changed and a new bridge was required.

The laying a tax of one penny per acre upon the lands of all known Inhabitants to raise money to repair the Meeting house could not have been a burdensome demand, and the evident intention was to oblige all landowners to contribute.

Annual Meeting, March 3, 1755.

Then meet on Said Day and Was chosen Thomas Dick, Moderator.

Town Clerk,—John Dick.

Treasurer,—George Cowan.

Selectmen,—Thomas Hamilton Allexender Turner John Fergerson William Conky & David Thomas.

Assessors,—David Thomas John Fergerson & Daniel Gray.

Surveyors,—William Harkness, Allexender Turner John Johnson, James Fergerson Arcebald Crosett, William Crosett William Conkey, James Cowan, David Cowdin.

Constables,—Patrick McMullen & Thomas Johnson.
Fence Viewers.—James Hamilton & James Harkness.
Hogreeves,—Robert Hamilton Hugh Johnson.

At the above meeting several roads were established and we copy the agreements made and signed consenting to roads established by the selectmen.

"Pelham March Ye 3^d 1755

These are to Signifie that We alowe a Rode of one Road In Width on the West side of the Second Division Lot No. Six Now in our Posission Beginning at the four Rode Road & to Run as fare North as ye land Now in ye Posession of John Edegar   And to be Improved by said Town So Longe as We may Peacably Posses & Injoy the Range Road Laid out on the North of said lot viz. the timber
As Witness our Hands
John Gray
Thomas Dick

These are to Signifie that We the subscribers is Willing that the Road shall be Improved by said town as Laid out By the Selectmen, Viz: one Rode In Width through John Grays Land & two Parch through John Edegers John Blairs & James Fergersons Lands
As Witness our Hands
James Fergerson
John Blair
John Edeger

These May Certifie that I am Willing to Let ye Road go where it now Dos Between Matthew Grays & ye Corn Mill Having ye Range Rode Equivelent
John McFarland

These may signify that I allowe a Road of two Parch Wide from My North East Corner of My Lote No 37 to the Range Road as Witness my Hand
Pelham March 25 1755   David Thomas

Neither Mr. Thomas nor the selectmen give any hint of the direction of this road, but it must be assumed that Mr. Thomas could have no authority to allow road building on land not his own so the road he consented to above must have been built from the Northeast corner of lot No. 37 on the plan South to the first range road:

"These may certifie that We alowe ye town to confirm the Road as is laid out through our Lands as Witness our Hands Patrick Peebles Robert Peebles
Pelham March 25 1775"

By a reference to the plan of the town it will be seen that the home lots of Patrick and Robert Peebles were No. 7 and No. 16 respectively, and the road referred to was somewhere south of Prescott center.

"We Ye Subscribers Desire ye town to Confirm a Road of two Parch Wide by the House of Daniel Grays North from the Range Road to his North Line Likewise from John Peebles North West Corner to ye County Road of one Rode in Width for ye Benefite of Daniel Gray as Witness our Hands

JOHN PEEBLES
March 25 1755   DANIEL GRAY.

John Peebles is on record as owner of lot No. 16, perhaps by purchase of Robert Peebles, consequently it may be assumed that Daniel Gray lived in that part of the town and would be benefited by the highway.

"March the twenty first 1755
Then Laid out a Road from Allexander Turners South East Corner Into John Grays Land along his South Line till it Comes up the Hill Into the Great Road Which Road is on ye South Side of the Mark't trees two Parch Wide by us.

JOHN FERGERSON }
WILLIAM CONKEY } Selectmen
DAVID THOMAS   }

"These May Certifie that the town May Have a Road in my Land two Parch Wide as itt is now Laid out if I may Have ye Range road as far as said Road Goes in my Land as Witness My Hand.

JOHN GRAY.
Pelham March ye 25 1755"

Alexander Turner drew Houselot No. 46 and John Gray No. 47. The location of the latter is substantially the same as the farm of Levi Moulton and the farm known as the Joseph G. Ward place.

MEETING, APRIL 24, 1755.

The April business meeting was known as the "Debt & Credit" meeting for the reason that at this April meeting men brought in their bills for labor and the bills were considered in open meeting and allowed or disallowed according to the temper of the meeting. There was much adjusting and settlement of accounts at this particular meeting and it is interesting in its way.

"Then Meet on said Day and was Chosen William Crosett, Moderator.

first Voted that the town His aCepted ye aCount that Thomas Dick Give In for His Being treasurer.

2^ly Thomas Dick is alowed £2—3s—0—2 fathings for being treasurer four years.

3^ly Voted that Robert Hamilton is Cleared from His Reats ye year 1751.

4^ly Voted that John Allexander Jun is Cleared from His Reats in ye Lists

5^ly Voted that William Conkey & John Dick each of them is allowed 1s—4d for Mending ye Meeting House Windows.

6^ly John Conkey is allowed Six shilling for taking care of the Meetinghouse.

7^ly John Fergerson David Thomas & Daniel Gray each allowed Six shilling for taking care of ye Invoyice.

8^ly That Robert Peebles is alowed £2—13s—4d for ten Weeks Boarding Preachers.

9^ly That Mr Dickinson is alowed £2—12s for Preaching and Mr McClintock is alowed £4—8s for Preaching also that Mr. John Houston is alowed £5—8s for Preaching

10^ly John Blair & John Clark each alowed one Pound for Going to Boston to the Presbytrie.

11^ly James Johnson is alowed £1—10s—8d for going to the Presbytrie at Newberry.

12^ly Robert Peebles is alowed £1—6s—8d for entertaining the Ministers Presbytrie time.

13^ly Robert Hamilton is cleared of His Pole Reats for this year.

14^ly John Johnson John Clark & John Blair each alow'd £1, for going to East town Presbytrie.

15^ly David Thomas is alowed ten Shilling for going to Londonderry for Advice.

16^ly that there be Six Pound for the support of a Scole for ye Present year.

17^ly Voted that the Hogs Run at Large this Present year.

18^ly Voted that ye Line be Run Between New Salem Roadtown & this town by Cornel Timothy Dwight.

19^ly that there be Forty Pounds for Repairing ye Roads ye Persent year—also voted that said Money be Laid on Pols & Reatable Estate.

20ⁱʸ Voted that Each Pole be alowed two Shilling pr Day at the Roads this Present year.

21ⁱʸ Voted that there be forty five Pound Assessed for the support of ye Gospel for the Present Year.

22ⁱʸ Voted that the Scole Be Keep at the Meeting-house & the East Hill & the West End each place to Have there Proporsheable Share Also voted that ther be a Scole House Buielt at the Meeting-house—Likewise voted that there be a Scole House Built at the West End—also voted that there Be a Scole House Buielt at the East Hill.

WILLIAM CROSETT Moderator.

ANNUAL MEETING, MARCH 1, 1756.

Then meet on said day and there was Chosen
William Crosett—Moderator.
Town Clerk—John Dick.
Treasurer—John Fergerson.
Selectmen—John Fergerson, David Thomas, Thomas Johnson, John Blair & James Harkness.
Assessors—John Fergerson, David Thomas, Daniel Gray.
Constables—Jonathan Gray & William Harkness.
Surveyors — John Conky, Robert Meklem, Archibald Crosett, George Cowan, George Petteson, John Gray, James Harkness, Edward Selfridge, James Fergerson, William Fergerson.
Fence Viewers—William Conkey, David Cowden.
Hoge Reeves—John Conky, Robert Blair.

The only important matter of record at this annual meeting besides the choice of officers is the following—

" This may Certifie that I Am Willing the Cross Road Go round the East side of ye Pond Hole In My Land two Parch Wide for the Use of the Town So long as I Injoy the Road In the Pond Hole

Witness My Hand
Pelham March 1 1756.   GEORGE PETTESON."

MEETING, MARCH 24, 1756.

John Conky allowed four shillings for taking Care of the Meeting house.

Robert Peebles allowed £3—16s for keeping the Minister and His Horse fifteen Weeks.

The Committee to Wite John Savige, George Cowan & James Johnson is allowed One Pound for Going to the Presbytrie at Boston.

Voted £40 for support of the Gospel the Present Year.

Voted that the town be Divided Into five Parts as Relating to Schools.

WILLIAM CROSETT, Moderator.

ANNUAL MEETING, MARCH 7, 1757.

Meet on said Day and there was Chosen
William Crosett—Moderator.
Town Clerk—John Dick.
Treasurer—John Fergerson.
Selectmen—Archibald Crosett, William Crosett, Patrick McMullen, Thomas Hamilton, James McConel.
Assessors—John Fergerson, David Thomas, James Harkness.
Constables—Thomas Cochran, James Dunlap.
Surveyors—John Peebles, James Berry, William Linsey, George Pettison, William Conkey, Robert King, John Crawford, Matthew Gray, Thomas Dick & William Selfridge.
Fence Viewers—James Harkness, Jonathan Gray.
Hogreeves—Oliver Selfridge, James Cowan.

MEETING, APRIL 12, 1757.

Various sums allowed—
David Thomas 5s—4d for taking the Province Invoice.
William Fergerson 14s—8d for His Meere to Boston & Newbery.
William Conky 12s for one Jorney of His Horse to Boston.
John Gray £1—3s for Keeping ye Ministers six Weeks.
Robert Peebles £2—12s for Keeping ye Ministers fourteen Weeks.
Voted £40 for the support of the Gospel this Present Year.
Voted that the Hogs run at Large.

ANNUAL MEETING, MARCH 6, 1758.

Meet on said day & there was Chosen
William Crosett—Moderator.
Town Clerk—John Dick.
Treasurer—John Fergerson.

CAPT. BENJAMIN PAGE'S HOUSE.

ABIJAH FALES' FARM HOUSE.

Selectmen—William Harkness, Allexander McCallock, John Hunter, John Crawford & William Conky.

Assessors—John Fergerson, William Crosett & Hugh Johnson.

Surveyors—John Gray Jun, Andrew Maklem, Allexander Conky, James Thompson, John Hamilton, John Gray, William Harkness, James McConel, James Fergerson, Thomas Dick.

Fence Viewers—Daniel Gray & Capt Robert Lotheridge.

Hogreeves—Isaac Gray & James Cowan.

It was at this meeting that the first action was taken for assistance to the poor, £10 being allowed for the support of Thomas Lowden's family, and it was "Voted that Capt Robert Lotheridge, John Crawford & William Harkness Be a Committee to Receive the Money or Corn or Meal for said Lowdens family." It was also "Voted that Thomas Lowden is to Continue in the Dwelling House Where He is." The intention doubtless was to assist the unfortunate Lowden at his home rather than to remove him to other quarters.

MEETING, MAY 26, 1758.

Debt and Credit was brought in, and various sums allowed or voted.

John Conky allowed six shilling for taking care of Meeting house.

Alexander Turner fourteen shilling for tending Court at Springfield.

John Crawford six shilling for Moving Thomas Lowden's Hay.

James Harkness six shilling for taking Invoice and Making Reats.

John Fergerson and David Thomas six shilling each making Reats.

John Gray £3—15s for Boarding Minister.

Thomas Hamilton, 6 shilling for tending the Corps of Mr. Baker.

Robert Peebles 8 shilling for bording Minister Sacrament Time.

Voted £40 for the Support of the Gospel this Present Year.

Voted £13—6s—8d for Support of School the Present Year.

Voted £8 for Repairing ye Roads.

Each Pole is allowed three Shilling per Day on Roads.

Eighteen pence for one Pare of Oxen and Eighteen pence for a Cart per Day.

Lastly Voted that the Hogs Run at Large this Present Year.

WILLIAM CROSETT, Moderator.

Meeting, Sept. 23, 1758.

This meeting seems to have been called mainly to choose a town treasurer in place of John Fergerson who had been elected at the previous Annual Meeting, and the cause for this action as recorded, was "By Reason of Said Fergerson's Removal."

John Fergerson had been a prominent citizen from the very first, and drew home lot No. 50, located west of the Meeting house and close to the ten acres set apart for "Common, training field, and burial ground." It was at the log house of John Fergerson that the first meeting of the Proprietors was held after they took possession of the land and had time to build houses, and the date of the meeting was Aug. 6, 1740.

Mr. Fergerson had been with the people of Pelham for nearly twenty years, a valuable aud trusted citizen whose removal to some other portion of the country must have been a serious loss. Where he removed to the records give no hint. There were others of the name in town at that time but there have been none of the name for many years. Besides John Fergerson there were James, Robert, Samuel, and William, possibly sons of town treasurer John, or his brothers.

Annual Meeting, March 5, 1759.

Then Meet on Said Day and was Chosen
John Crawford—Moderator.
Town Clerk—John Dick.
Treasurer—Alexander McColloch.
Selectmen—William Crosett, James Berry, William Clark, David Cowden, Robert McColloch.
Assessors—Hugh Johnson, William Crosett, John Hunter.
Constables—Alexander Conky, James Fergerson.
Surveyors—John Dick, Alexander McNutt, John Clark, James Harkness, Alexander Turner.
Field Drivers—David Cowden, Thomas Cochran.
Hog Reeves—William Conky, William Fergerson.
Fence Viewers—John Blair, William Selfridge.
Deer Reeves—Hugh Johnson, James Tompson.

There had been officers to enforce the law against "Killing Deer" since 1743 but the office of Deer Reeve appears for the first time, and such officers chosen. And at a meeting May 24, 1759, the warrant called for action in relation to choosing a man to represent the town at the Great and General Court, but no action was taken on the article, at least there is no record of such action. This was the first time anything is said about sending a man to the General Court from the town.

Annual Meeting, March 3, 1760.

Meet on said day and was Chosen
William Crosett—Moderator.
Town Clerk—John Dick.
Treasurer—Allexander McColloch.
Selectmen—James Harkness, Thomas Johnson, William Fergerson, Thomas Dick, Robert Lotheridge.
Assessors—Thomas Dick, William Crosett, John Dick.
Surveyors—William Harkness, John Blair, William Conkey, Isaac Gray.
Field Driver—John Gray.
Hog Reeves—John Gray, David Cowden.
Deer Reeve—George Pettison.

Meeting, Oct. 2, 1760.

There was a committee chosen to Place School houses and it was " Voted that there be a Man or Men chosen to go to the Jersey to Gett a Minister to Supply the Pulpit—also Voted that John Crawford is Chosen to go to the Jersey to Gett a Minister to Supply the Pulpit."

The journey to Jersey on horseback was no small undertaking at that time but the need of a settled minister was urgent.

That the settlers of the town were industrious, hard-working men cannot be questioned but the material evidences of their success clearing up and subdueing the wild tract they had settled upon are very limited, and consist of certain invoices handed in by them for taxation. A small package tied with a homespun linen yarn which was found among waste papers and documents in boxes at the town clerk's office and containing about two score of these schedules dated in April and May, 1760, twenty-two years after the tract was purchased, give some idea of their success. Eight of these invoices are those of first settlers who drew " home lots," and the others must have settled in town soon after the first settlers drew their lots. These invoices of property for taxation are written upon small scraps of paper, and give the personal property for taxation, such as stocks of cattle and horses, grain on hand, also the number of acres of tillage land, mowing and orcharding, also dwelling-houses, barrels of cider, tons of hay, etc.

John Conkey's list was as follows:

Polls	1	Tillage acres	8
Dwelling house	1	Bushels of Rye	4
Horses	1	Indian Corn	30
Oxen	2	Oats	14
Cows	4	Orcharding—acres	1½
Sheep	13	Sydor—barls	5
Swine	1	Mowing—acres	14
Pasturing a Cow—acres,	4	Tons of hay	12
Keeps Cows	2		

PATRICK PEEBLES LIST.

Polls	3	Wheat—Bushels	3
Dwelling Houses	2	Rye—Bushels	31
Oxen	4	Indian Corn—Bushels	40
Cows	7	Oats—Bushels	60
Sheep	30	Orchard—Acres	3¾
Swine	1	Cyder—Barrells	26
Pasturage—Acres	38	Mowing—Acres	35
Keeps Cows	12	Tons of hay	25
Tillage Acres	15	Barley—Bushels	1¾
Peas—Bushels	5		

THOMAS LOWDEN.

Polls	1 not rateable	Tillage	2
House	1	1 Corn—Bushels	16
Horse	1	Mowing Acres	3
Cows	2	Tons hay	2

WILLIAM GRAY.

Polls	3	Tillage	14
D-House	1	Rye	60
Horses	1	Indian Corn	25
Oxen	4	Oats	60
Cows	7	Orchid	1 acre
Sheep	10	Barrels Sider	6
Pasture	11	Mowing land	17 acres
Keeps Cows	4	Tons Hay	12

Thomas Cochran—Envoyce.

Mowing Land Ackrs	15	Cape one Hors	
Pols	one	Sedr Barls	12
Dweling House	one	Indn Corn Bushels	17
Hors	one	Reay Bushels	21
One York of Oxen		Ots Bushels	8
Cows	4	hey tons	10
Swine	5	Pastr one per ackr	
Sheep	8	Swamp Hay tons	3
Orchard one Acker and thre quarters		Peas bushels	5
Telag Land ackrs	9		

John Peebles.

Poles	1	Tilig	7
Horses	2	Corn Indon	12 B
Houses	1	Wheat	25 B
Oxen	2	Oats	13 B
Cows	8	Syder Barls	10
Sheep	18	Mowing	18
Swin	0	Tons of Hay	12
Pastor	13 acrs	Mowing Land	8—10
Keeps	8 cows		

Jonathan Gray.

Pasture acres	14	Tons of Hay	6
Keeps Cows	5	Fresh Meadow hay	2
Polls	1	Tilige acres	7½
D House	1	Rye bushels	4
Horses	2	Indian Corn bushels	20
Oxen	2	Oats	16
Cows	3	Orchard acres	2
Sheep	9	Sydor	20
Swine	1	Mowing land	11

Robert Maklam.

Howses	1	Wheat	15
Horses	2	Rie	15
Oxen	6	Orchard land acres	1¾
Cows	0	Syder	9
Sheep	10	Mowing	17
Swine	0	tons o hay	15
Pasturing acres	9	Oats bushels	31
Keeps Cows	2	Money at interest	£1—7s10
tilige acres	7	Polls	1
Corn bushels	53		

WILLIAM GILLINOR'S INVOICE.

Poul	1	Scider—Barls	13
hours	1	Mowing land—ackers	15
Oxen	2	Tillage—ackers	9
Cows	6	Corn—Bushels	30
Swine	1	hay touns	12
Sheep	17	peaster—ackers	2
one house 2 roms	1	Keeps cows	2
Orched—Ackers	2		

May ye 19 1760 & c.

THOMAS JOHNSON.

Poles	2	Tons of hay, about	13
House	1	Oats about (bushels)	25
Oxen	3	Wheat	2½
Cows	5	Indian corn	30
Sheep	26	Horses	2
Swine,	4	Pastring for 4 cows	4
Rie, (bushels) about	19	Orchard acres	1½
Cyder-Barrels	32½	Mowing land acres	20
Tillage about 7½ acres	7½		

JOHN CLARK.

Poll	1	Pastrage (acres)	5
Dwelling house	1	Keeps cows	3
horse	1	Plow land acres	5
Oxen	2	Mowing land acres	18
Cows	5	Tons of hay	12
Sheep	9	Rye—bush	3
Orchard acres	1	Indian Corn	30
Cyder barls	11	Swine	4
Oats—bushels	10		

JAMES FERGERSON.

Pole	1	Rye bush	6
Dwelling house	1	Wheat "	7
Horse	1	Indian Corn	2
Cows	3	Oats	6
Tillig land (acres)	5	Mowing land—acres—	8
Tons of hay	6		

JOHN ANDERSON.

Polls	1	Orchard—acres	3½
D House	1	Mowing "	5
horse	1	Rye Bushels	15
Cows	1	Indian Corn	18
Tons hay	4		

JAMES THOMSON.

Pools	2	Swine	5
House	1	Tileg land—acres	10
Horses	3	Rye Bushels	20
Oxen	4	Corn "	70
Cows	6	Mowing land—acres	16
Tons of hay	16		

ROBERT McKEE.

Pool	1	Plow land acres	2
Horses	1	Mowing land "	3
Cows	2	Indian corn bush	2
Sheep	2	Rye	3
Tons of hay	2		

ALEXANDER TURNER.

Pelham ye 30th April 1760

Three acres of orcharding produces 14 Barrels yearly.
12 acres of Mowing produces 8 tuns of hay yearly
8 acres and a half of tillage produces 20 Bushels of Rey
30 bushel of Indian Corn and 15 bushels pettates yearly
2 acres of pasteridge Keeps 2 cows yearly—
Stoke—one youk of oxen, 3 cows, 1 hors, 6 sheep.
2 Polls, 1 Dwelling house

THOMAS HAMILTON, JUN.

Polls	1	Hors	1

JAMES STON.

Polls	1	Mowing land acres	7
Hors	1	twilig land	6
oxen	2	tuns of hay	9
cows	2	corn bushels	25
sheep	6	Rie "	20
swine	0	oats	8

The name attached to this list cannot be determined.

Pols	1	Sheap	0
hors	0	moing land acres	9
oxen	0	tilig land "	2
cows	2	tons hay	4
swine	0	fresh meadow	

WILLIAM CONKY.

1 Pool, 1 Hors, 2 oxen, 4 Cows, 5 acres plough Land, 6 acers Mowing Land, 4 tune hay, 30 bushels Ingen Corn—20 bushels English Grane—Wheat 17½ bushels, Rye 2½ bushels—a true acounte to the best of My Judgment.

James Conky.

- 1 Pool
- 1 Hous
- 2 Cows
- 2 Horses
- 6 Sheep

- 3 acres plow land
- 4 acers Mowing Land
- 10 Bushels wheet
- 4 tuns hay

John Gray's Invoice.

Poals	1	Inden Corn	25
Dwelling hous 18x24	1	Rie	12
Horses	1	Oats	18
Cows	3	Ackers of Tillag	3
Sheep	8	Ackers of Moaging	6
Swine	2		

John Edgar.

Polls	1	Rye	9
Hous	1	Indian Corn	20
Oxen	2	Orchard	1
Cows	2	Tuns of Hay	3
Swine	3	Mowing Land acres	6
Tillage	4½		

John Croser.

Polls	2	Wheat	4
Dwelling Hous	1	Rye	16
Horse	1	Oats	8
Oxen	2	Mowing Acres	6
Cows	4	Paster Acres	3
Swine	4	Tons of Hay	6
Tillage	7		

Rosanna Peteson.

Dwelling House	1	Mowing	5
Horse	1	tons hay	2
Cows	1	Paster keep Cows	1
Tilege	½		

John McFarland.

polls	1	Tillage 5 acers	5
Dwelling House	1	Mowing	9 acres
Cows	2	Tuns of hay	4
Orched 1 acer ½	S 6		

James Hood.

Pols	1	Corn	20 Bushels
hous	1	Wheat	3 Bushels
horses	1	Rie	10 Bushels

Oxen	2	Oats	3 Bushels
Cows	9	Orchard	1 acer
Sheep	5	Syder	3 Barls
Swine	1	Moing	9 aCres
Pastor	1	Money	£24—6—8
P feed	1 Cow	Tons hay	10
Tilig	5 aCers		

JAMES HARKNESS.

Dwelling House	1	Horses	2
Pols	2	Oxen	2
Mowing Land	14½	Cows	6
Tons Hay	11	Swine	1
Tillege	3	Sheep	17
Pastridge	6	Wheat	10
Keeps Cows	3	Rye	12
Orchard	1½	Indian Corn	60
Sydor	1	Oats	20

Not attested
Recorded

ISAAC GRAY.

Polls	1	Wheat	17
Horses	1	Rye	5
Dwelling house 16 x 19		Indian	30
Oxen	2	Orchard—Acer	1
Cows	4	Sydor Barels	12
Sheep	9	Mowing	12
tillage	3	Hay tuns English	10

JAMES HALBERT.

Polls	1	Sheep	6
Horse	1	Swine	1
Cow	1	Money at Interest £22-10-11½	

THOMAS HAMILTON.

Dwelling House	1	Fresh Meadow	6 acres
Poles	2	Orchard	2 acres
Oxen	4	Inden Corn	60 Bushels
Cows	5	Wheat	10 Bushels
Sheep	11	Rie	4 bushels
Swine	2	Oats	35 Bushels
Horse	1	English Hay	8 Tuns
tillage	6 acres	Fresh Hay	4 Tuns
English Moing	12 acres	Sydor	20 Barals

Paster 6 acres capable to paster 13 Cows

DAVID COWDEN.

Dwelling hous	1	tilidg Land acres	7
Pole	1	of Mowing Land acres	7
Hors	1	of rye bushels	14
Cows	2	of Corn bushels	19
Oxen	2	of barley bushels	3
Sheep	2	of oats bushels	25
Swine	3	Orchard Acres	2

Of hay bracks and bushes—tuns 6

MARGARET THUSTEN.

Dwelling house	1	tillige	5
Pols	2	Corn	30
Horse	1	Rey	4
Oxen	2	Mowing land	8
Swine	4	Hay	6

ESTER ALEXANDER.

Polls not Rateable	1	Tillage	1
Dwelling House	1	Oats	10
Horse	1	Orchard aCres	1
Cows	4	Sydor	8
Pasture	4	Mowing	7
Keeps Cows	2	Tuns of Hay	5

ALEXANDER McNITTS' INVOICE.

Pools	1	Moyaing Land	6
Dwelling house 19 by 26		tillage land	3
Oxen	2	Indin Corn	25
Cows	3	Rie	10
Sheep	10	tons of hay	3

PER JNO YOUNG.

A Just and true acount of what I have that is rateable to the best of my knowledge.

1 Poll	2 Horses
three acres of paster	1 Cow
One of Mowing	Drags to the Value of £50—00—0

JAEMS SLOAN.

Polls	2	tilige	4
houses	1	Corn	22
Horses	1	orchard sider	3
oxen	2	Mowing	13
Cows	6	tons of hay	13
Sheep	33	Ray	8
Swine	1	Wheat	0
Pastridge	0	Oats	11

John Linsey.

Pols	1	tillage 6 acus	
House	1	Inen Conn	30 B
Horse	1	Wheat	7 B
Oxen	2	Ray	16 B
Cows	2	Oats	20 B
Swine	2	Orchad ¾ S	1 B
Pastridge	1	Hay	10 tone
Keeps 1 Cow		Money	£12

Archibald Croset's Invoice.

Poals	1	Ackers of tillige land	5
Dwelling house	19 by 37	Ackers of orchard	3
Horses	2	Buchels of Corn	45
Cows	3	Buchels of Rie	20
Sheep	13	Buchels of oats	23
Ackers of Mowing Land	12	Barrels of Sider	3
tuns of hay	9		

Edward Selfridge.

Poles	1	Orchard acres	1½
Dwelling hous	1	Cyder Barrels	4
Horse	1	Mowing acres	14
Oxen	2	Hay tons	7
Cows	4	Barley bushells	2½
Swine	3	Oats Bushels	8
tillage acres	11½	pasturage acres	1
Indun Corn Bushels	28	Keeps a cow half	
Rye Bushels	26½	Peas & oats bushels	12

Oliver Selfridge.

Pelham May ye 19th 1760

Of Mowing an acre and quarter—1 tun of hay
Of Corne land one acre—ten Bushels corne
Of new land three quarters of an acre—three Bushels of wheat
One horse one Cow one hog

Margerett Kidd.

Cows	2	tuns hay	5
Swine	1	Syder—barls	1

Nearly all of the grains enumerated in the invoices were used as food by the settlers, and they certainly had plenty for home consumption. Only four men returned money at interest, and only one includes potatoes among his crops for taxation.

James Hood, James Halbert, John Linsey and Robert Maklem returned money for taxation, the aggregation of surplus capital of these four men for which they were honest enough to return for taxation was £60–4s.–7d.–3far.

These men were probably looked up to with the same feeling of awe and fear as working men of to-day regard the modern millionaire.

The independent and original spelling of each of the tax payers has been retained in copying the invoices and is interesting. On the back of each scrap is endorsed the word "Recorded" and some have also the word "attested," indicating that some of the tax-payers made oath to their invoices while others did not. Only a few of the farmers remembered to date their schedules after making them out.

From these invoices of thirty-eight men and four women we learn that these forty-two farmers had given in for taxation, after only twenty-two years had passed away since they bargained for this tract of wild land, the following list of personal property:

42 Horses,	375 Bushels of rye,
137 Cows,	256 " oats,
61 Oxen,	833 " corn,
132 Sheep,	140 " wheat,
56 Swine,	53 Barrels of cider,
284 Tons of hay.	

The list of invoices may not be complete for the whole town, but it is all that it has been possible to find of such an early date. They are written upon small scraps of paper, some of them only two or three inches square, the printed copy of William Gilmore's invoice being a fair sample of all, and one of the few in the package bearing a date. James Conkey, James Hood, Thomas Lowden, John Gray, John Conkey, Patrick Peebols, William Gray and Alexander Turner were among those who drew home lots in 1739, and their farms can be located by referring to the plan of the town. The others whose invoices are given it is impossible to locate, as they came to town after the drawing of home lots and purchased lands or farms already under cultivation, or had taken up new lands by purchase of original settlers.

The first census of Pelham was taken in 1765 and the number of inhabitants at that time, twenty-six years after the drawing of home lots in 1739, was only 371. Consequently it is fair to assume that there were not more than 300 men, women and children in the town when the foregoing invoices were given in for taxation. As small families were the exception and large ones the rule in those days it is evident that the list of invoices comes much nearer being a full list of farms at that time than otherwise. Allowing seven persons for the forty-two farms or families represented and it comes close to a complete list of the taxable property in 1760.

ANNUAL MEETING, MARCH 2, 1761.

Then Meet and was Chosen
Thomas Dick, Moderator.
Town Clerk—John Dick
Treasurer—Allexander McColloch
Selectmen—Thomas Dick, David Houston, David Cowden, Robert McColloch, John Dick
Assessors—Thomas Dick, William Crosett, John Dick
Surveyors—Isaac Gray, Thomas Hamilton, Allexander Conkey, George Petteson, William Harkness, John Blair, Allexander McColloch, Allexander Turner.
Constables—William Fergerson, John Peebles
Wardens—John Crawford, Robert Meklem
Fence Viewers—John Croser, William Conky
Hog Reeves—Aaron Gray, William Gray
Deer Reeves—Isaac Gray, James Turner.

MEETING SEPT. 8, 1761.

"£17–6s–8d was voted to Repair the Bridge on the West Branch to Make it Passable—said work to be done this fall.
£6–10s was voted to send a man to Pennsylvania after a Minister. Voted that the scole be continued the whole year."

ANNUAL MEETING, MARCH 1, 1762.

Then meet & First Was Chosen
Hugh Johnson Moderator
Town Clerk—John Dick
Treasurer—Thomas Dick

Selectmen—Hugh Johnson, James Cowan, Robert Meklem, George Petteson & Isaac Gray

Assessors—John Hamilton juner, David Cowden & Hugh Johnson

Constables—Mathew Gray and John Gray Jn^r

Surveyors—James Thompson, Daniel Gray, Thomas Cochran, Patrick McMullen, William Harkness, Joseph Rinken & Robert McColloch.

Fence Viewers—Allexander McNutt & James Turner.

Hog Rives—James Thompson & William Edger.

Wardens—Hugh Holland & William Conkey.

Voted, by the town that the selectmen take Care of Sarah Davison Three Months at the Towns charge.

"Protest—We the Subscribers Enter our Protest against ye vote of The Town taking care of Sarah Davison Three months.
GEORGE COWAN,   JAMES COWAN."

Rev. Mr. McDowell was preaching in Pelham at this time but no minister had been settled since Rev. Mr. Abercrombie's dismissal in 1754, and the town had been presented at court for this neglect, as will be learned by action at the meeting August 18th, which follows:

WARRANT FOR A MEETING AUGUST 18, 1762.

"First To See if ye Town Will Chuse a agent or Agents to appear for said Town and Answer the Presentment of the Grand Jury to be Considered at the Nixt Court of General Sessions of the Peace to be Held at Springfield in & for the said county on the Last Day of August Current for Wickedly & Willingly Neglecting to provide themselves of an orthodox Minister for the three years Last Past Contrary to Law."

Thomas Dick was chosen Moderator of this important meeting and action on the first article resulted as per record.

"First Voted that Capt John Savige is Chosen agent to Represent the Town to answer to the Presentment at the General Sessions of the Peac at Springfield ye Last Tuesday of August Currant."

The fifth article in a warrant for a town meeting Sept. 21, 1762, is copied herewith:

"Fifthly, To have the Town Consider Whether they will chuse a Agent to Sue out & Present a Write Csheray in order to Revers the Last Judgment of Ye Court of Sessions that the town of Pelham settle a Minister as the law Directs by Nixt November Court and in Case they Don't the Court Shall Do it for them &c.

James Harkness was chosen Moderator of this meeting and when the fifth article was reached—the record says—

"Fifthly Voted that there is Nothing Acted on the fifth article of the Warrant."

"DE REX VS. PELHAM. LAST TUESDAY OF AUGUST COURT OF SESSIONS. 1762.

The Grand Jurors for Our Soverign Lord the King for the body of the County of Hampshire do on their oaths present that the Inhabitants of the Town of Pelham in s^d County for the space of three years last past have voluntarily omitted & Neglicted to provide themselves of an able and learned and orthodox Minister of good conversation to dispense the Word of God to them and that the said Inhabitants during all the term aforesaid have voluntarily and wickedly neglected to take due care for the procuring and settling and Encouragment of such Minister among them which neglect of said Inhabitants is Contrary to the Law of this Province in such Case provided the Peace of Said Lord the King his Crown and Dignity which presentment was made at the last term of Court and signed Nathaniel Kellogg foreman. And now comes before the Court the said Inhabitants of Pelham aforesaid by John Savage Gent'^{n} their Agent, and being put to plead and answer for the Presentment they say they are in Nothing guilty thereof and of this they put themselves on the Country. A jury being sworn according to Law to try the issue between our Soverign Lord the King and the Defendants—after a full hearing on their oaths say the Defendants are Guilty.

It is therefore Considered by the Court that the said Inhabitants of Pelham aforesaid do provide themselves of an able learned orthodox minister of good conversation to dispense the Word of God to them by ye next term of this Court at the farthest & they pay the Costs of Prosecution &c."

TUESDAY NOV. 9th 1762.

Whereas the Inhabitants of the Town of Pelham upon presentment made against Them for being destitute of a Minister &c and of which they were found guilty at a Trial before the Court at the last term thereof, were ordered to provide Themselves of an able learned orthodox minister of good Conversation to dispense the word of God to them by this Term of ye Court at the furtherest and it hath not yet been certified to this Court whether they have performed s^d Order. It is therfore ordered by this Court that the s^d Inhabitants of Pelham be summoned to appear before his Majesty's Justices at the next Court of General Sessions of the Peace to be held at Northampton &c that they may show to ye Court what they have done in Obedience to the fore recited order etc. Summons was made accordingly.

DE REX VS. PELHAM FEB 8 1763.

The Inhabitants of the Town of Pelham who were Summoned to appear at this Court pursuant to the summons which was made for this purpose agreeable to the order of this Court at the last Term thereof to testify to the Court what they have done in obedience to the order of the Court at their last term in August last now Come before the Court by John Savage their Agent and offer to show to the court that they have endeavored to Comply with the said order last abovesaid and this Court having heard the said Inhabitants as to their attempts to perform the s^d order and the Court being satisfied that they have been endeavoring a compliance with the same and it also appearing to the Court that the s^d order be not fully performed the said Inhabitants are still pursuing such Methods as may effect a performance thereof. It is therefore ordered that the Matter be continued to the next term of Court that the Court May further advise and determine therein. And it is also ordered that said Inhabitants pay ye cost of the prosecution heretofore and now carried on against them in the premises, taxed at five Pounds 19–7 & that the Execution be awarded accordingly.

DE REX VS. PELHAM 1763.

The Inhabitants of the town of Pelham who were summoned to appear at this Court the last term thereof to testify to the Court what they have done in Obedience to the Order of the Court at their Term in August last now come before the Court by John Savage their Agent and offer to Show to the Court that they have Endeavored to Comply with the s^d Order last above said and this Court having heard the s^d Inhabitants as to their Attempts to perform the s^d Order and the Court being satisfied that they have been endeavoring a Compliance with the same, and it also apearing to the Court that tho the s^d Order be not fully performed the s^d Inhabitants are still pursueing such Methods as may effect a performance thereof. It is therefore ordered that the matter be Continued to the Next Term of this Court that the Court may further advise and determine therein —And it is also ordered that the s^d Inhabitants pay ye Cost of the Prosecution heretofore and now carried on against them in the premises taxed at 19 7 and that the Execution be awarded accordingly.

May 8th 1763.

DE REX VS. PELHAM AUG. 30 1763.

It being now fully certified to this Court that the Town of Pelham have settled a Minister agreeable to an order of this Count at a former Session thereof. It is ordered that they be not further held to Answer respecting that Matter. It is also ordered that the Execution be Issued for the Costs therefor taxed against the Said Town.

ILLEGAL KILLING DEER IN PELHAM IN 1763.

Killing deer in defiance of law and in disregard of the deer reeves chosen by the town was the cause of quite a number of Pelham men paying the penalty at the bar of the court as is shown by the court records which we copy.

"DE REX VS. COWAN, COURT OF SESSIONS, FEB. 8, 1763.

John Worthington Esq attorney to our Soverign Lord the King in this behalf here instantly informs and gives this Court to understand that James Cowan the Second of Pelham in the County of Hampshire, yeoman, at s^d Pelham on the sixth day of January last past did wittingly and willingly Kill one Grown wild Deer and then and there had in his possession the raw flesh and raw skin of the same Deer Contrary to one Law of this Province in that case made and provided against the Peace of the said Lord the King his Crown & Dignity. And now comes before the Court the said James (being held by recognisance for this purpose) and being put to plead to the foregoing Information he pleads that he is guilty.—The Court having Considered of the offence do order that the said James pay a fine of ten pounds lawful money to be the one moiety thereof to his Majesty for the support of the Government &c & the other moiety of the same to William Boltwood of Amherst Gent'^{n} the original Informer in this case, and costs of Prosecution taxed at one pound 3-8. The said James Declaring here in this Court his inability to pay said fine, It is further ordered that he be disposed of in Service to any of his Majesty^s subjects for ye space of two Months from ye time of ye Sale of said James—standing Committed &c

Sold for 25 " (Shillings)

There were several cases of the same kind tried in the same court, and among them was James Halbert of Pelham. Halbert was convicted and being in no better condition to pay his fine, he was disposed of in service for two months for 30 shillings.

We learn from the cases of Cowan and Halbert that the deer reeves made a business of watching for deer slayers and when they obtained positive evidence against a man they made it known to some sheriff who complained, arrested the offenders and when convictions resulted the sheriff and the informer received half of the fine. If the poor fellows who were convicted of killing deer could not pay the fine their services were sold for several months to the highest bidder. So it was with Cowan and Halbert.

From 1763 to 1776.

Call of Rev. Richard Crouch Graham to Settle in 1763.—Objectors Thereto.—Warning of Objectionable Families to Leave Town.—Pewing the Meeting-house in 1766.—Allotment of Pews.—Disagreement With the Shutesbury Selectmen About Town Lines in 1769.—Town Vendue in 1769.—Death of Rev. Mr. Graham in 1771.—Rev. Andrew Bay Supplies the Pulpit 1772.—Patriotic Response to the Boston Committee of Correspondence, 1773.—Call to Rev. Nathaniel Merrill in November, 1774.—Letter of a Pelham Man in the Army at Charlestown, 1775.—Committee of Safety Chosen 1776.—Handbill From the Court for Independency 1776.

Meeting, Jan. 24, 1763.

In the warrant for this Meeting were these important articles:

First, To take into consideration whither they will Settle a Gospel Minister under and in Subjection to the Authority of the Presbyterie—Whose Authority we are at present Professed Subjects to Commonly Called Boston Presbyterie.

Secondly whether they will choose Mr. Richard Crouch Graham who at Present Supplys the Pulpit in this town, to be the Gospel Minister above Described.

"Thirdly, What Incouragement the Town of Pelham will be Pleased to Give Him to Settle Amongst them as to a Present Settlement.

Forthly What His Annuall Mentainance or Yearly Sellary Shall be While he Remains our Minister acording to the above Presbitarel Establishment.

William Crosset was chosen Moderator of this Meeting and the record informs us that the town "First Voted that the first Article is Concord With as it is Mentioned in the Warrant.

Secondly Voted that Richard Crouch Graham is to be thare Gospel Minister as is above Discribed.

L. W. ALLEN'S MILL.

S. F. ARNOLD'S RESIDENCE.

It was voted to call Richard Crouch Graham to settle with them and £100 lawful money voted to him if he should accept the call. They also voted that his salary should be £60 à year.

Not all were satisfied with this action however, for Thomas Cochran, James Taft, Joshua Gray, Mathew Gray, Joseph Rinkin, James McConel, David Cowden, John Stevenson, William Clark, John Dick, John Blair, Oliver Selfridge, William Fergerson, Aaron Gray, James Harkness, William Harkness, William Selfridge, James Fergerson, Ephraim Cowan, William Gray and Moses Gray protested against the action of the majority in calling Mr. Graham. It will be remembered that William Fergerson, John Dick and James Fergerson protested against the action of the town in voting to settle Rev. Robert Abercrombie as their minister, and twenty years later we find them protesting against the settlement of Mr. Graham, which can but prove that the chronic objector was not unknown at that early day.

MEETING, FEB. 15, 1763.

At a town Meeting on the 15th of February, 1763, the selectmen were chosen a committee to "Employ Workmen to finish repairs on the Meeting House as fare as the Stoof will finish," and Mathew Gray was allowed five shillings and four pence for "Warning Curtis Clemens & his wife out of the Town." Patrick Pebels was allowed "One Shilling & Three pence for Making a foot Lock for John Davison." John Gray was allowed five Shilling & four pence for "Warning the Widow Elisebeth Queen out of Town."

James Pebels was allowed "one Shilling for taking care of John Davison an insane man." William Conkey was "Allowed Four Shilling & Eight Pence for going to Oxford for Mr. Cambel," who probably was a "Supplyer" for the pulpit. David Cowden, Hugh Johnson and John Hamilton were allowed 12 shilling and 6 shilling respectively for work taking the Invoice, and John Gray was allowed £6—15s—11d for the same kind of service. Voted Robert Maklem £1—18s and John Alexander 12 shilling, all for the very honorable business of "Boarding Ministers."

At a Meeting on the 3d of May, 1763, £20 addition was voted to Mr. Graham's salary, but the addition was not to become a tangible fact until the year 1766 and to make it more tantalizing the additional vote reads "And to Pay four Pound at the End of every three Year Till Said Addition be Paid."

In a warrant for a Meeting Dec. 2, 1763, the following article appeared : First, to see if the town will agree upon a time when Mr. Graham's Salery should commence,—and it was voted that the selary should commence at the time of his ordination.

At a Meeting Jan. 20, 1764, £8 was voted for the support of Thomas Lowden, and the General Court was petitioned for liberty to sell lands of Elinor Gray, who had already been assisted by the town and £5—7s was allowed for her support that year. The poor woman died not long after and had no further need of lands or assistance from the town.

The ordination of Mr. Graham had taken place and the bills had been reported to the town, and the allowances made as follows : "John Gray is allowed £6—17s—6d for Charges at Ordination time, and £1—7s—6d for His trouble at Ordination time." Elisibeth Clark is allowed 4s for "Tendance at ordination time." John Gray was allowed £5—17s "for Boarding ye Ministers." James Turner had an allowance of 8s for boarding two ministers ordination time, and John Savige 12s for "Pastring Horses Ordination time."

MEETING, FEB. 2, 1765.

It is quite probable that the meeting house had been without pews up to this time, though doubtless there were enough benches to accommodate the people on Sundays and at the frequent town-meetings, but better accommodations were at hand, as witness the following vote, dated February 2, 1765 : "Seventhly—Voted that the Whole body of the Meeting House is to be made in Plain Pews."

In some way inhabitants that were not acceptable persisted in coming into the town, for at an adjournment of this same meeting to the 4th of March following, James Halbert was allowed 3s. for "Warning Benjamin Whitney & his Wife out of this Town."

Daniel Gray was elected "Surveyor of wheat for the ensuing year in 1765."

We learn also that a new house had been erected for Rev. Richard Crouch Graham, and "that there is a two Rode Road Established from ye two Rode Road South of Mr. Graham's new House by s^d House to the County Road.—Consented to by R Crouch Graham March 4 1765."

The above is given to show how indefinitely many of the roads were laid out and consented to, rendering it almost impossible at this late day to locate them or even to make a fairly good guess where they were or where they led to.

Sept. 23, 1765. Two pounds were voted to buy weights and measures and William Fergerson was chosen sealer of these very necessary articles for the year 1765.

MEETING, FEB. 28, 1766.

John Dick was allowed 10 shilling for sending for the temporary acts for twenty years past, and as Andrew Shaw and family were objectionable people, Robert Hamilton was allowed 3s for " Warning them out of the town and recording the warrant."

This seems to prove that some legal process was resorted to in ridding the town of new settlers that did not come up to the standard that had been set up. Action upon the ninth article of the warrant for this meeting is recorded as follows: " Voted that the Town Has agreed on a Method to Pew or Repair the Meeting House and that a Committee be chosen to lay out the Grounds in the Meeting House Round the Sids of Said House,—Said Committee is Thomas Dick, John Hunter and John Dick. The two Dicks were carpenters, and were the builders of the Meeting House and competent men to have on a committee to " Pew " the house. £100 was voted for the work.

MEETING, MARCH 27, 1766.

It was voted that twenty-seven Pews be built, twenty-four below and three in the front Gallery. It was also voted " that two familys is to sit in one Pue,"—Voted that Said Peus is to be divided by two years of the old Invoice & the Last Inventory,—Voted that the two highest in the Rats Draw the Highest Pew,—So on agreeable to this Method till the Whole is Comprehended.—Voted that the Men that Draws Said Pews Give Nots of Hand to the treasurer for said Money & Said Money to be paid a year hence.

Thomas McMullen Entered his protest against the action above recorded.

The Meeting of March 5, 1767 had little of note beyond allowing money for services rendered to the town. David Cowden was allowed 5s for "Making Stocks, Lock and Kie," for which they had doubtless found use.

Allotment of Pews.

The Appraisal of the Meeting House Pews was made by Thomas Dick and Archibald Crossett, March 28, 1766. They also made the allottment.

Pew No. 1—£6—18s, Patrick McMullen, Thomas Johnson.
" " 2—£6—00s, Patrick Peebles, John Peebles.
" " 3—£5—10s, Daniel Gray, Mathew Gray.
" " 4—£5—2s, James Berry, James Thompson.
" " 5—£5—1s, Robert Maklem, William Gilmore.
" " 6—£5—00s, Thomas Dick, James Sloan.
" " 7—£4—18s, George Pettison, William Gray.
" " 8—£4—12s, John Dick, James Hood.
" " 9—£4—10s, John Savige, James Harkness.
" " 10—£4—8s, Hannah Lothridge, John Gray.
" " 11—£4—6s, Robert King, William Crossett.
" " 12—£4—00s, Ichabod Crossett, Thomas Hamilton.
" " 13—£3—14s, John Blair, Thomas Cochran.
" " 14—£3—12s, John Hunter, Isaac Gray.
" " 15—£3—10s, Robert McCulloch, Hugh Johnson.
" " 16—£3—6s, Alexander Turner, David Cowden.
" " 17—£3—2s, William Harkness, James Dunlap.
" " 18—£3—1s, John Conkey, Elizabeth Selfridge.
" " 19—£3—00s, Jonathan Gray, John Clark.
" " 20—£2—15s, William Fergerson, John Stevenson.
" " 21—£2—10s, Andrew Maklem, Alexander Conkey.
" " 22—£2—8s, Ephriam Cowan, John Lucore.
" " 23—£2—2s, John Gray Jun, James Taylor.
" " 24—£2—00s, David Huston, Alexander McCulloch.
" " 25—£1—18s, James McConel, John McCartney.
" " 26—£1—17s, Sarah Cowan, James Cowan.
" " 27—£1—00s, John Lindsay.

The above allotment did not satisfy the people however and it was sometime before it was finally settled. At a Meeting on August 6, 1769 "It was voted that the elderly Men and their Wives be seated in the front part Seats Below, Provided they clear them on Sacrament Days.—Voted that the front seats all round the Gallery be seated by the Present Valuation, and only the Heads of familys sit in said Seats.

August 31, 1767 Alexander Conkey, Clerk of the Market acknowledged the reception from the selectmen of the various Weights and Measures and gave a receipt for them.

MEETING, MARCH 31, 1768.

March 31, 1768 " Robert Hamilton was allowed 3s for One Gallon of Rum for Raising the Bridge, "and John Peebles jun 1s for " Making a branding iron for the town." Nov. 16 of the same year, Samuel Hyde, James Gilmore and George Thompson were voted " Liberty to build a Pew over the Women's Stears," and James Campbell, Andrew Hamilton, James Cowden, William Cowden, David Conkey Jun, John Harkness, John Maklem and Jonathan Hood were voted liberty to build a pew over the "Men's Stears." From other matters of record it appears that the persons to whom these liberties were voted were young men who wished seats in the Meeting House for their own special use.

April 11, 1799. It was voted that the Town Pew be moved to where it first stood and the Nixt Pew be as Large as the town Pew and the Corner Pew to have the rest of the ground. John Dick, Hugh Johnston and Archibald Croset were chosen to provide shingles to finish Roof of the Meeting house and to Imploy Workmen to Do Said Work.

In the town records for the year 1769 is the following entry which shows that the trouble about the north line was still unsettled.

Pelham, March the twenty third one thousand seven hundred and sixty nine. Pursuant to a Notification issued by us the subscribers Selectmen of Pelham Requiring the selectmen of Shutesbury meet us at the Northwest Corner of the township of Pelham and from thence pramble the line Between Said towns have attended Said Service the Day above written and there meet John Child and Silas Wild Selectmen of Shutesbury and Preambled said Line until we came against the Land of John Chamberline and there said Child and Wild refused further to Preamble said Line also giving the line from thence Eastward not to be the true Line Between said towns.

ROBERT MAKLEM, WILLIAM CONKEY, DAVID COWDEN,
                                                Selectmen of Pelham.

Meeting, March 24, 1769.

Pelham March the 24 One Thousand seven hundred and Sixty Nine. Pursuant to a Notification Issued by us the Subscribers—Selectmen of Pelham Requesting the Selectmen of the District of New Salem to Meet us on the North Line of the township of Pelham aforesaid where the townships of Shutesbury and New Salem meet with said North line of Pelham have attended said service and there meet with Lieut. Foster, Isreal Richardson and Jeremiah Ballard selectmen of Said District the Day above—Said Selectmen of Said District Refused to Preamble the North line of Pelham with us Alledging the line we Claimed as the North line of the township of Pelham was Not the true line of said township but verbally agreed with us that upon a true copy of the Grant of the Equivalent Land being Procured so as thereby to obtain a certainty of the North East Corner of said Equivalent Land that they would extend a line from thence Due West Point of Compass the line between said towns.

ROBERT MAKLEM, WILLIAM CONKEY, DAVID COWDEN,
Selectmen of Pelham

The following is a copy of a document which bears the heading :

"TOWN VENDUE.

Sold at Publick Vendue at ye Meeting House of Pelham ye 26 of Oct^{hr} 1769 to ye Persons Under Named Said Sums Set Down in old tenor viz.

	£00--19s—00d
Patrick Peebles 2 heaps of Shingles	
And^w Ebercrombie Three heaps of Shingles	01—07 —06
Ebenezer Gray one heap of Shingles	00—15 —00
Eisha Divenport two heaps of Shingles	01—19 —06
Thos Johnston one heap of Shingles	01—12 —00
William Conkey one thousand of Nails	01—00 —00
Joseph Rinken one thousand of Nails	00—19 —00
Patrick Peebles one thousand of Nails	01—00 —00
Thos Johnston one thousand of Nails	01—00 —00
William Conkey one thousand of Nails	01—03 —00
And^w Meklem one thousand of Nails	01—00 —00
And^w Ebercrombie one thousand of Nails	01—02 —00
Patrick Peebles seven hundred of Nails	00—17 —00
John Conkey Jun one Binch	00—10 —00
Patrick Peebles two Plank	00—07 —00
Hugh Johnston " "	00—07 —00
Patrick Peebles Nine Joyce	00—10 —00
John Dick Joyce	00—09 —00
Joseph Rinken Plank	00—09 —00
	£17—06 —00

GEORGE PATTISON Vendue Master."

PAID BY DICK, OLD TENOR.

Paid in Cash by John Dick to Thomas Dick for Rum	£co—17s—o6d
Paid by John Dick in Change	oo—10 —oo
Paid Hamilton for Rum	co—15 —oo
Troble Vendue Days	02—oo —oo
For Collection	02—co —oo
Old tenor town Money	£6—02 —o6

The town vendue 128 years ago seems to have been quite a social occasion judging from the quantity of liquor purchased by town Clerk John Dick with the town funds for use at that gathering. Just how the town came to have so many heaps of shingles and so many thousands of nails that they felt it necessary to sell to the highest bidder is not so easily determined, but probably the Meetinghouse had been given a new roof after thirty years of service by the first roof that had been placed upon it, and these heaps of shingles and thousands of nails were left over and were distributed to those in need of them at vendue.

MEETING, JULY 12, 1770.

The matter of additions to Rev. Mr. Graham's "Sallery" came up for further consideration at a Meeting held July 12, 1770, and it was reaffirmed by vote that the bargain was as follows: "That there was to be a Standing Addition to Mr. Grahams Sallery of four Pounds at the End of Every three Years till it Amounts to from Sixty Pound to Eighty and there to Stand while he remains our Minister." In January, 1771, a committee was chosen to "Call the Men to an Account that had the care of the Town Stock of Ammunition." Osborn Brown and family were warned out of town in that same year, and James Hunter was allowed the legal fee of three shilling for executing the order.

MEETING, APRIL 16, 1772.

The record of a town meeting on the 16th of April, 1772, has the following singular entry: "Voted that Widow Graham Supply the Pulpit Four Sabbath Days." Rev. Mr. Graham died on the 25th of February, 1771, in the 32[d] year of his age and in April, 1772, this vote requiring Widow Graham to supply the pulpit four Sabbaths was passed. As there were no women preachers in those days, we cannot believe that Mrs. Graham was to supply the pulpit by preaching herself, and are forced to the conclusion that from her own scanty means she was expected to pay the expense of a "Supplyer" for four Sabbaths.

The following September a Meeting was held and it was "Voted That the Selectmen is impowered to give Thomas Johnson a order on the Treasurer for the Charge of the Funerul when Mr. Graham was buried, Which is £1—18s—5d," also "voted that Thomas Dick, James Harkness, Thomas Cochran, William Crossett, John Dick and Robert Hamilton be a Committee with the Elders to treat with the Reverend Mr. Bay for a further trial in order for a settlement;" but as no Mr. Bay was ever settled he either did not grant the further trial, or a further trial was unsatisfactory. Yet on the 14th of October, 1772, it was "Voted that there is Eighty Pound granted for the Reverend Mr. Andrew Bay by way of Settlement, provided he settle Among us."

MEETING, MARCH, 1773.

In March, 1773, it was "Voted that there is Sixty Pound Granted for the support of the Gospel provided Rev. Mr. Bay don't settle among us."

Three families were warned out this year (1773) and John Alexander was allowed the fees for doing the business and recording the warrants. And at the same Meeting the vote calling Mr. Bay to settle was recalled. The history of the Rev. Mr. Bay episode forces one to believe that these people hardly knew their own minds.

MEETING, NOV. 16, 1773.

At an adjourned Meeting held on the 16th of November, 1773, a committee chosen on the 9th of the same month reported as follows in answer to a communication from the committee of correspondence in Boston.

To the Committee of Correspondence in Boston, Gentlemen:

We have considered your Circular letters and are Not a little Shoked at the attempts upon the liberties of America, from Such Beginnings of Oppression upon the properties of the french Did that ill fatted & worse pated Lewis the thirteenth by the Cruel Craft of a richlieu with Bribes Lucrative posts Underhanded Treacheries fines imprisonments Banishments & Most treacherus and Bloody Masucries utterly sap the very foundations both of civil and Religious Liberty and establish arbitrary power in that new Kingdom of Slaves.

We replid back also upon the unhappy Reign of the Stuart family & bloody Struggles to subdue a free people to Nonresistance and Passive obedience. We have still a More feeling sense of the worth of our Liberties by the total loss of them in the conquered Kingdom of Ireland When altho made of the same one Blood they have a yoke of Iron Put upon there Necks & they must Serve their Conquerers with as much of their Money and Blood as they are pleased to demand and Sustain More Intolerable oppressions from these Legislative Masters & Unfeeling Landlords than some of the Barbarious Nations compared by the Ancient Romans before the Wars of there Empire.

This so greivous a yoke upon the Western Isle which neither they nor their fathers were able to Bear has driven them by hundreds & by thousands to bide a final adue to their otherwise Dear Native Land & Seek a peaceful Retreat from the bane of Oppressions in this American Wilderness.

Depending upon the faith of the Nation for all the priviliges Charterd to the American Colonies, we Cannot therfore but be greatly Alarmed at the News of the Incroachments upon the Natural and Chartered Rights of this Province where we have our abode. We drained our purses and Spiled not a little of our Dearest blood in the late War in defense of our Gracious King against frainch perfidy and Indian Barbarity in hops he would be a father to this Country and Protect our lives and all our Rights & Liberties. Nor can we tamely Surrender these Liberties Recieved with the Expense of so Much Blood and treasure from Cruel Saviges to the More unnatural invaders we cordially acquiess in Revolution Principls, we utterly Detest a Popish pretender to the throne.—We wish the Illustrous house of Hanover may long sway the Brittish Septer in truth & Justice,—we pray that in Righteousness the throns of His Present Majesty May be Established and be far from oppression & that he May Sit and Rule on a Quiet and unmolested throne in truth & Rightiousness till he Retorn at Last to a More Glorious throne above. But if When we look for Judgment behold there is a cry of oppression, if the Glorious things Prescribed for the Western Kingdom Shall Extend there baneful Influences thrae thus American Territory^s—if our money be taken from us Without our Consent, why not our Lands & Even our lives. We fear Whereunto these things May Grow. But after all the Detail of Greivances you Were pleased to Send us. We are obliged in Justice & Gratitude to acknowledge that We have many Invaluable Priviliges Not as yet Wrested from us & we take it as no Small Token of the Divine Displeasure that we are so far threatened & Deprived as we are as Members of the Community Both for our own and the General Good we humbly offer as our opinions that we Study to be Quiet & do Nothing Rashly and avoid as much as Possible the Reproach of Muttny as moving Sedition, or in any Degree hurtful to King or Province. And let us have Patience alonger in our humble Suits for Justice to the British throne—in a Pious & Manly Sense of the worth of our Liberties.—Still Struggling by Lawful & Constitutional Measures to vindicate our Natural & Pactioned Rights let us do no Wrong, But Rather be wronged as we Learn by Doctor Sibs: that the wronged Side is the Safer Side. But if at length all our Humble Petitions for our own Natural or Promised Rights Shall be baffled & Refuge on Earth and Hops of Redress Shall fail us we trust We Shall be Wanting in nothing in our power by Laudable & Wholesome Counsel to Unite With our Dear Countrymen for our Mutual Good and Shall Venture our Properties & Lives in Executing any Plan Pointed out by the Supreme Ruler and as the innate and Principles of Self Preservation & love to our Posterity may oblige us. —Tho we would not be Munnors & Complainers Especially for Wrongs we do not Suffer, Nor Rashly Speak Evil of Dignities, Nor Represent those Called Benefactors as traitors to our Country Byond the truth of facts. Nevertheless we would unite our Testimony against all the Real Greivances Prescribed for us at this or any future Period, and if things Should Eare Long Proceed to an unhappy Rupture Betwixt the Mother Country and these Plantations, which Heaven forbid, We are Not at Present Much Intimidated with that Pompous Boasting on the other Side of the Water, Viz. that Great Brittain Could Blow America unto Attoms as we Cosider the Sighs of the oppressed & Good Wishes of Milions in the Mother Country to the Liberty and Weal Both of themselves and their own flesh, their Beloved Americans. We trimble not so much for our Selves in that Case in Particular as for the Rehealim in General and lest the Pillars of State should fall and we be left to Shift for our Selves without any Earthly King to Save us.

But we pray a Merciful Ruler to Avert Such a Judgement and not Suffer the things that Belong to the Nations peace to be hide from our Eyes so We Remain united with our breathren in the Common Cause of American Liberty.

ROBERT HAMILTON, JOHN HAMILTON, THOMAS COCHRAN, DAVID COWDEN, GEORGE PETTESON, Committee.

REPORT OF COMMITTEE ACCEPTED NOV. 16, 1773.

The above extraordinary document was submitted to the patriotic citizens of the town assembled in town meeting at the Meeting House on that chill November day, and the record of their action follows:—

"Approved by vote of the town without Contradiction. It was also Resolved that the thanks of the town be returned With the above to the Said Committee in Boston for their honest faithful kind & Patriotit Zeal and Care in Stating our Rights & Showing us our Grievances and Giving such timely Notice.

Also Resolved at the Said Meeting that the Committee be & Remain as a Committee to Receive & Lay Before the town any further Intelligence that May be at any time Received from Boston Respecting our Liberties.

JOHN CRAWFORD, Moderator.
Attest JOHN DICK, Town Clerk."

MEETING, APRIL 7, 1774.

At a Meeting of the town held on the 7th of April 1774 we find the following votes recorded.

Hugh Johnson was chosen Moderator.

£70 voted for support of the Gospel.

£30 voted for the support of Schools.

£60 voted for Making and Repairing highways.

Robert Hamilton was allowed five shilling that he lost in John Clark's Rats.

James Gilmore was allowed four shilling for "Warning Amos Whitting and family out of this town."

George Petteson was allowed 12 shillings "that Doct' Jels Creach Kelog Charged for one visit to James Hyde in the year 1770."

Jeremiah Jackson was allowed 2 shillings for a "Warding Staff."

Daniel Gray was allowed £5—12s "for going to the Jersey College after a Minister."

William Fergerson was allowed 12s for taking care of the Meeting House the Past year.

Voted that "Timothy Ingram is Cleared of his Rats that is in John Alexander's List." (on account of sickness in his family)

Meeting, Oct. 3, 1774.

The town was beginning to feel the pressure of British power and resented all attempts at oppression. In a warrant for a meeting held on the 3d of October, 1774 was an article reading as follows:

"To see if the town will make an addition to the Committee of Correspondants" and James Harkness, James Halbert, Ebenezer Gray and Daniel Gray were added to that Committee.

The town had been without a settled Minister since the death of Rev. Richard Crouch Graham in 1771 and dependent upon "Suplyers," but on the 23d of Nov., 1774 a call was extended to Rev. Mr. Nathaniel Merrill to settle as Minister of the town and £70 voted in the way of a settlement and £80 yearly salary so long as he continued as their Gospel Minister.

Meeting, Dec. 27, 1774.

A Committee consisting of William Harkness, William Crossett, Alexander McCulloch, Hugh Johnson and John Dick was chosen and named "A Committee of Inspection" whose duty was to follow the instructions of the Continental and Province Congresses.

Meeting, August 28, 1775.

It was "Voted that there is Preperation to be made for the Instalment of the Rev. Mr. Merrill—and that said Preperation be for Ministers and other Gentlemen of Liberal Education, and that there is a Committee to be chosen to Provide for Said Gentlemen—said Committee is Thomas Cochran, Robert Hamilton and James Halbert."

James Halbert was also chosen assessor at this meeting "In the Room of Ebenezer Gray now in the War."

JOHN CRAWFORD, Moderator.

Ebenezer Gray is the first town officer of whom we find mention of being in the war early in 1775, but that there were men from the town at the front early in that year is proven by the following letter which we copy from the original.

Charlestown, Agust the 4th, 1775.
Frand Dick these Linds I write to you and your famaly hoping that they will find you all Wall as they Lave my Boy and I hart hole heer all this time thank God for it and we are all pretty Wall that Belongs to Pelham and as for News you must Reed the prants because I cannot send you any that is Sarten to Depand upon for truth only you Need Not Bee afraid of the Daviel in Pelham this Summer for he has his handful to Dow heer and I know that hee is ashamed of his under taken Salfridge is wall and Sands his Love to all Inquiring frands Capt Cowden Sands his Love to you all! Excuse my writing Sir when you Look on the paper and Reed the above writing So Know more at prasant But I Remain your Loving frand and humbul Sarvant.

JOHN WHITE.

Waltham Brown is Wall—so no more
Sir go and Reed the whole to my wife and you will abladge me much

Loving Wife and Children—I hope that these will find you all wall as they Lave us—I must Bee Short! gat 2 or 3 Bushel of Solt as quick as you Can for it will Bee Deer and what the Barn will Not Winter the Saller Sall and give them as good a Chance as you Can and as for my Coming home I Can Not if you Sant ten men in my Room—Do as wall as you Can So No more at prasant But I am your Loving Husban till Dath

JOHN WHITE

From this above interesting letter we learn that at the time it was written all the men belonging in Pelham were well, which leaves us to infer that there was quite a company of Pelham men at Charlestown. Probably Capt. Cowden and his company of Pelham men were there.

COMMITTEE OF SAFETY CHOSEN.

March 29, 1776, a Committee of Safety was chosen. Thomas Cochran, John Hamilton, George Petteson, Ebenezer Gray, Peter Bennett, Daniel Gray and James Dunlap constituted this committee.

Jonathan Gray was allowed £1 14s expense money for bringing up Mr. Merrill and family,—and Widow Hamilton was allowed £2 2s for the journey of her late husband to the Presbyterie.

William Conkey was allowed £1 for conveying provisions to Watertown, which without doubt were for the support of soldiers from the town, or others in the army.

Up to about this time the selectmen in directing the constables to warn the voters of a Town Meeting had used the following form:

HAMPSHIRE SS.

To John Rinkin & Eliot Gray Constables of the town of Pelham within the County of Hampshire Greeting. You are hereby required to warn & give Notice to all the freeholders and other inhabitants of the town of Pelham Duly Qualified to vote in town affairs to meet togither on the 31 Day of Dec Current to act upon the following Particulars &c.

WILLIAM HARKNESS, HUGH JOHNSON, JONATHAN GRAY & JAMES DUNLAP, Selectmen of Pelham.
Dec. 23, 1776.

The first appearance of the new form was at the next recorded meeting and was as follows:

HAMPSHIRE SS.

To Mr Eliot Gray & John Rinkin Constables of the town of Pelham within the County of Hampshire Greeting—You are in the name of the People & Stats of the Bay Colony to warn and give Notice to all the freeholders and other inhabitants of the town of Pelham Qualified to vote in town affairs to assemble and meet togither on Monday the 17 Day of March Current.

Dated at Pelham, March 3, 1777.

WILLIAM HARKNESS, HUGH JOHNSON, JONATHAN GRAY, JAMES DUNLAP, Selectmen of Pelham.

The form was soon changed to read—"In the name of the people of the state of Massachusetts Bay" or "In the name of the people of the Colony of Massachusetts Bay" etc.

Under date of Jan. 7, 1776 and with the underwritten marginal note we find the following:

HAND BILL FROM THE COURT FOR INDEPENDENCY.

In the House of Representatives.—A resolve of the late House of Representatives Passed on the tenth of May, 1776 that the Inhabitants of each town in this Colony ought in full meeting warned for that Purpose, to Advise the Person or Persons who should be Chosen to Represent them in the Nixt Genrul Court, Whether, Should the Honorable Congress for the Safety of the Colonies Declare them Independents of the Kingdom of

Great Brittain, they, the Said Inhabitants will Solemnly Engage With themselves and fortunes to support them in the Measure, and, Whereas said Resolve though Published in the Public News Papers yet it has since Been Manifest to the Present House that Some Actions in said Colony were not so Seasonably favored with the said Points as to have it in their Power to Instruct their Representative Agreable to Advice in said Resolve had they so Minded. So that the General Assembly are unable to Collect the Sentiments of Many towns in said Colony on so Interesting & Important a Subject & as towns who had Seasonable Notice Have given their Representatives Instructions to Comply fully with the late House aforesaid Whose number to the honor of their Constituents are Very Numerous, and as some of the United Colonies have of late Bravely Refused to subject themselves to the tyranical yoke of Great Brittain any longer by Declaring for Independence—therefore Resolved, as the opinion of this House that such towns as have not Complied with the Resolve Aforesaid Whither they are Represented or not, duly warn a town Meeting for such purpose as soon as may be. that their sentimets may be fully known to this House agreeable to fermore Resolve of the late House of Representatives & that one hundred & fifty hand bills be forthwith Printed and Sent to such towns for the Purpose aforesaid. By Order of the House: T. WARREN, Speaker.

By order of this hand Bill We Have Warned & Given Notice to the Inhabitants of Pelham East & West of the Cross Road Qualified to vote in town affairs to meet according to orders.

Pelham, June the Eighteenth, 1776.

ELLIOT GRAY & JOHN RINKEN, Constables.

MEETING, JUNE 20, 1776.

Record of the above warned meeting:

"Att a meeting of the freeholders & other Inhabitants of the town of Pelham meet and Assembled togither on Thursday the twentieth day of June 1776 then meet and first was Chosen Daniel Gray, Moderator. Secondly, Voted by Unanimous Vote that we are willing to Come Under Independuncy from under the yoke of the King of Great Brittain, Provided the Contnental Congress see fite in their Wisdom to Establish Independence in the Colonies for their Safety.

DANIEL GRAY, Moderator.

That the town had already quite a number of men in the army is shown by action in town meeting on Dec. 31, 1776, when Abizer Edson and Andrew Abercrombie were chosen assessors "in room of John Hamilton and James Caldwell McMullen Gone to the War."

James Caldwell McMullen and Rev. Richard Crouch Graham are the first names that appear on the records with what is commonly known as a middle name up to this time. Hitherto no ink was wasted in writing out long names upon the books and there was no ambitious desire to bestow such names upon the children born to the early settlers. There was not a man among them that was hampered with a middle name. James or John was a common name and considered enough to place before any surname, consequently the appearance of the middle name must be noticed as an innovation. If attention is given to this matter it will be noticed that the middle name did not increase very fast and there were very few up to 1800 and beyond that date.

From 1777 to 1786.

Valuation of Property for Taxation Established 1777.—Rev. Mr. Merrill's Appeal 1779.—Large Increase of Salary 1780.—Measures Taken to Secure Men for the Army 1780.—Bounties Offered.—Action Taken to Procure Beef for the Army 1781.—Daniel Shays on Committee of Safety 1781.—Selectmen Refuse to Call a Town Meeting 1782.—Trying to Settle With the Three and Six Months Men 1783.—Allowance to Soldiers in the Late War 1785.—The Town Votes to Have a Bank of Paper Money Made 1786.

April 14, 1777. "It was voted that the East Hill School Quarter be divided Into two Squadrens Provided they build their Schoolhouses on their own Cost Without any troble or Cost to the town."

William Crossett "Was allowed £1 for Carring Down Provisions to the army at Cambridge" and Hugh Johnson, Abraham Livermore and Alexander Conkey were each allowed the same amount for the same errand and journey.

THE ROCKING STONE.

HOUSE ON JOEL GROUT FARM.—NOW OWNED BY HENRY COOK.

Meeting, May 12, 1777.

"May 12, 1777, it was Voted that there is £18 allowed to each man that Will Inlist in the Continental service for three years," but at an adjourned meeting this vote was "Recaled" and it was "voted that all those men which have served Personally or Engaged a man in the Service of the United Stats shall have Credit for so many months as they have served or engaged in said service."

Hugh Johnson was moderator at a meeting Dec. 23, 1777, when the valuation of property for taxation was fixed.

20s. was laid on each acre of home lot not improved, 10s. laid on each acre of third division, 15s. on each acre in second division, and the valuation of personal property for taxation was as follows:

"One pair of oxen four years old is	£18
Cows at three years old,	£ 6
Steers at three years old,	£ 6
Steers and Heifers at three years old,	£ 4
Yearlings at	£ 2
Calves,	£ 1
Horses at three years old,	£12
Colts at two years,	£ 6
Yearling Colts,	£ 4
Spring Colts,	£ 2
One Sheep,	9s.

Mr. Merrill's Salary Increased.

April 14, 1777, £60 was added to Mr. Merrill's salary in 1778, and the next vote recorded was that rams be shut up from the first of August till the fifteenth of November yearly.

Meeting, May 15, 1778.

May 15, 1778, "£92-13s.-2d. was granted for Clothing sent to the Contental Soldiers, to be assessed in the first Assessment assesed by the Assessors."

Meeting Jan. 24, 1779, is thus recorded:

"John Crawford, Moderator. Voted that this meeting be adjourned to the House of Joseph Packard, Inholder. Voted that the Arms Coming from Boston be sold at Public Vendue to the Highes Bidder, None to bide But the training band & Larm list.

Voted that the Ammonition be Divided Equally. Voted that the steel be cut in Pound Peices & Sold at Public Vendue to the Highes Bidder."

MEETING, MARCH 29, 1779.

The money of the country had evidently become very much depreciated, for at a meeting March 29, 1779, £100 was voted for schools in place of £30 for the years previous and it was voted that each pole be allowed $5 per day on the roads. £250 was voted for repairing the roads where £60 had been the usual sum in previous years.

At the adjourned meeting on the same warrant it was also "Voted April 16, 1779, that the town has agreed to have a new Constitution formed, also Voted that they empower there Representative to vote for the calling of a state Constitutioual Convention for forming a new Constitution. WILLIAM CROSSETT, Moderator."

MEETING, MAY 12, 1779.

In a warrant for a town meeting called for May 12, 1779, the following articles appear after the one for choosing moderator.

"Secondly: To see if the town will Recall there Vote of April 16 in adding Sixty Pound to Rev. Mr. Merrills yearly Sallery as we think it is not sufficient to Mentain a Gentleman and his family.

Thirdly: If the town Recall Said vote to see what Honorable addition the town will Pleas to add to his yearly sallerry.

Fourthly: To see if the town will Allow Money for those families Which there Men Are Gone into the Service."

The record of the action of the town upon this warrant is not long but was decisive. On the second article it was "voted to recall the vote of April 16 of the same year in adding £60 to Rev. Mr. Merrills sallery for the present year."

"Thirdly, Voted that there is four Hundred and twenty Pound added to the Rev. Mr. Merrils Sallery.

Lastly Voted, that there is Nothing Acted on the Last Article of the Warrant. DANIEL GRAY, Moderator."

The warrant for a meeting on the 4th day of June of the same year is interesting and is addressed to Mr. James Peibols and Reuben

Lotheridge, Constables. The first article is to choose a moderator,. and other articles in the following order:

Secondly to See if the town Will make an Addition of Two Hundred & fifty Pound to the Highway Rate as we suppose there is Some Misunderstanding in the former vote, or if note the Above Sum, any other Sum the town shall think Proper.

Thirdly, to See if the town Recall there Vote of the twelth of this Instant Granting the Rev. Mr. Merrill four Hundred & twenty Pound Addition to His Sallery for this present year as it is very burdensome to many who are Groning under Heavy taxes Already.

Forthly to See if they Will Agree to Mak the Addition by a Volentry Superscription for no one Can Dout but how (who) have been so free for laying it on in a tax will be as free in thare Superscription—so that there Dear Brethren May Riceive the two Above Articles is at the Requist of a Number of the Freeholders of Pelham.

Fifthly—if the town will Recall the third article of this Warrant & Don't. act on the forth Article, to see what Honorable Addition the town will be Pleased to Make to the Rev Mr Merrills Stated Sallery for this Present year.

Hereof fail Not and Make Return to one of us the subscribers sometime before Said Meeting. Given under our Hands and Seal Dated at Pelham May the 26 one thousand Seven hundred & Seventy Nine & in the fourth year of Independence.

   HUGH JOHNSON, JOSEPH PACKARD, JONATHAN HOOD,
                Selectmen of Pelham.

Daniel Gray was chosen moderator and further action under this above warrant follows: Under second article, " Voted that there is Five hundred and fifty Pound Granted by Way of addition to the Two Hundred & thirty Granted for Repairing the Highways for the Present year.

Thirdly, Voted that there is nothing acted on the third article of the Warrant.   DANIEL GRAY, Moderator."

It will be seen that the third and fourth articles were practically ignored and the former vote of £60 addition to Mr. Merrill's salary having been recalled, because it was believed to be much too small an addition, the newly settled minister was left with only the original salary voted at the time of his being called, the additional appropriation of £420 with the currency much depreciated, and the addition was not paid for a long time.

MEETING, JUNE 25, 1779.

This town meeting had nothing to do with ministers' salaries or highway matters but upon more important and pressing business.

The meeting was warned to meet at the meeting house, June 25, 1779, and there were only two business articles in the warrant after the one for choosing a presiding officer.

Article Second. To see if the town will come into any Method to inable Commition officers to Raise Men for the Contenantal Service & for the Militia.

Thirdly to see if the town will Come Into any Method to Make an Equality throughout said town by assessment or any other Method they shall think Proper.

Action on the second article of the foregoing warrant:—"Voted that the town is Come Into a Method to Assess a sum of Money to Raise the Present Quota of men to be paid by those that are Delinquent in order to bring Every Individual upon a Proper Everidge,— the tax and other Charges to be Raised in the Common Method of Town Charges.

Thirdly. Voted that there is a committee to be Chosen to Assist the Militia Officers in Hiring Men to go into the Contenintel & Militia Service.

Forthly. Voted that there is five men to be Chosen as a Committee to find those men. Said Committee is Daniel Gray, Samuel Hyde, John Rinken, Andrew Abercrombie & William Dunlap.

HUGH JOHNSON, Moderator."

MEETING, AUG. 16, 1779.

The warrant for a town meeting on the 16th of August, 1779, had the following articles:

"Secondly, to see if the town will agree to Send a Delgate to Cambridge for the Sole Porpuse of forming a New Constitution, said Convintion is to Sit on the first Day of Sept. Nixt.

Thirdly, to see if they will chuse a Man or Men to take Into Consideration the Prices of Marchandise and Contry Produce and to Make such Regulations as they shall think Proper to Act on.

HUGH JOHNSON, JOSEPH PACKARD & GEORGE PETTESON, Selectmen."

Action on the second article resulted as per record: "Voted that Joseph Packard is Chosen a Delegate to Go to Cambridge to Sit in Convintion for the Sole Purpose of forming a New Constitution.

Forthly. Voted there is nothing acted on the third article.

JOSIAH DUNBAR, Moderator."

MEETING, AUG. 27, 1779.

A meeting called on Aug. 27, 1779, was for action on less important matters than matters of state and was to see if the town would stand up behind its constables who had sold land for taxes.

The second article explains: "To see if the town will support Adam Clark Gray and Mathew Gray, Constables, in an action Commenced against them by Obediah Dickinson of Hatfield for Selling some of his Land for taxes."

"Thirdly, to see if the town will chuse a man as Delegate or Delegates to Go to Northampton to meet a County Convintion in order to state the Prices of Such County Produce & Marchandise as shall come before them —and any other article that the town shall think Proper when Assembled."

The town ignored the second article which involved the constables by a record as follows: " Voted that there is nothing acted on the second article."

"Thirdly—Voted that Thomas Johnson is Chosen a Delegate in Behalf of said town to meet the Convintion at Northampton the Second Wednesday of September Nixt.

Forthly—Voted that there is a Committee to be chosen to state the Pricese of Articles,—Said Committee is Thomas Johnson, Peter Bennet, John Rinkin, Timothy Packard & Mathew Clark.

HUGH JOHNSON, Moderator."

MEETING, SEPT. 27, 1779.

The town was called together on the 27th of September, 1779, to act on the following business:

"Article Second to see if the town will accept the Resolves of the Convintion in Regard of Stating the Prices of Contry Produce or Not if they Do to order the Committee Chosen to state the same in this town.

Thirdly:—To see if the town will Chuse a delegate to Go to Concord to a State Convintion for to sit there on the Second Wensday of October Nixt in order to State the Prices of Marchandise and Other Contry Produce.

Forthly to see if the town Will come into Any Method to Inable the Selectmen to Provide Money to Get the Contenental Cloathing & any other Article they shall think Proper when assembled."

The town acted as follows: " Secondly, Voted that the town has Excepted the Prices of Sundry articles that the Convintion that meet at Northampton agreed on.

Thirdly. Voted that Capt David Cowden is Chosen a delegate to

Represent the town at the Convintion to Meet at Concord the Second Wensday of October Nixt.

Forthly Voted that the Selectmen are allowed to Draw Money out of the treasury to pay for Soldiers Clothing.

Isaac Gray, Moderator."

Meeting, Dec. 10, 1779.

On the 10th of December, 1779, the town was called to act upon " the following Particulars at the Request of Rev Mr Merrill, the following articles with the Reasons are Set Down &c."

"Secondly, As I have Disposed of My farm to have the Advice of the town as to Laying out my Money or not for Another to there Satisfaction.

Thirdly, to know the Will and Pleasure of the town Respecting my staying among them or not, I think its Noised by some as if it was not Desired, Maks me uneasy Not being Willing to Crowd upon any People and as my State is now at Such Looss Ends to Determine my mind about laying out my money.

Forthly—if it the Pleasure of the town I should Stay to Know what the town is Willing Chearfully to vote for my Support towards making up my Sallery for the Insuing year as I am unwilling to take it but from Chearful Givers & if they are Willing to Make up my sallery as they have Mr Williams and Mr Baldwins and others I will be as free that they shall take out my Proportionable Part of Extrorny Charges so that I be no more Burdensom than when I first Came amongst them, and as I think its said by some as if they were Deceived on aCount of my familys Circumstances and tho I did What I could that they might not be Decieved even then so I am Willing if they are Dissatisfied that they should act thare Pleasure. Now Undecieved about it & and as my Last years Sallery is out Sometime Past & the money about spent togither with Sum Hundreds of Pounds put in of my Personal Estate.

Fifthly, to see what the town will alow Adam Clark Gray and Mathew Gray, Constables, to Compleat the Loss they have sustained by the Seal (sale) of Leu^t Dickinsons land."

Action on this warrant follows: " Voted, that there is nothing acted on the second article of this warrant.

Thirdly—Voted that there is four hundred and twenty Pound voted as an Addition to the Rev Mr Merrills Sallery for the Present Year.

Forthly Voted that there is nothing allowed Adam Clark Gray & Mathew Gray Relating to the Case Between Leu^t Dickinson and them.
Capt John Thompson, Moderator."

While the town seems to have been negligent in paying Rev. Mr. Merrill's salary promptly, and it had forced him to draw upon personal funds for the support of himself and family, it must be remembered that the struggle for liberty was going on in the land, and every town in the state, including Pelham, were straining every nerve to furnish their respective quota of men and supplies; taxation was frequent and heavy to raise money to meet the many and various heavy expenses of a public nature, and it is not strange that some of the demands for money were not met as promptly as they should have been. That the minister's salary was behind some of the time is not surprising although the support of the Gospel was considered one of the most important duties resting upon them as a community.

The appeal of Rev. Mr. Merrill to the town as recorded in the foregoing warrant for a town meeting was evidently carefully considered and the prompt action of the people in town meeting assembled was undoubtedly most satisfactory to Rev. Mr. Merrill and is certainly a most agreeable record for us whose eyes are permitted to scan the faded record more than one hundred years after the recording officer spread it upon the book.

Another Middle Name.

Adam Clark Gray is the third name that appears on the books up to this time with the middle name or initial. This particular Gray and Matthew Gray were constables of the town and in some unexplained way had involved themselves in loss of money by selling lands of Lieut. Obadiah Dickinson of Hatfield for unpaid taxes. An article in the foregoing warrant was to see if the town would allow money to these public servants to remunerate them for their loss in the service of the town but the constables were doubtless chagrined and perhaps angered when the voters refused to act upon the article in their interest. They did not give up the fight for their rights however, for in the very next warrant for a Town Meeting appeared an article calling upon the town to act upon this claim of the two Grays, constables. Another article in the same warrant was " To see if the town will Come Into some Safe Method in order to Stop the Collection of the last tax Come to Pelham from the State Treasurer for the Present as we Suppose a part of it to Rise from the Distribution Fleet at Pennobscut, or any other article the town shall think Proper to Act on Relation to the same." The meeting was held Jan. 28, 1780. The selectmen were chosen a committee to settle with the two Grays, constables, thus proving that persistence in the right is the safe course. "Lastly voted that there is nothing acted on the last Article of the Warrant.

JOHN THOMPSON, Moderator."

MEETING FEB. 18, 1780.

The next Meeting was called for Feb. 18, 1780, and the second article was " To see what Method the town will Come into to pay the tax and Charges that has Arisen on thirteen lots that was Assessed and put into Reubin Lotheridges Constables hands to Collect and no Person Appearing to pay the taxes the Said Reuben Lotheridge posted said Lots for Seal as the law Directs, but Could not sell them."

"Hugh Johnson was Chosen Moderator and it was voted that there is a man or men to be Chosen to Purches those Lots that Can't be Sold by the Constable at Vendue, Said Committee is Isaac Gray & William Dunlap. This Meeting is Continued by Agreement to the House of Mr. Abercrombie at four of the Clock in the Afternoon,—Meet according to the above adjourment and first voted to pay the tax & Charge that May Arise on the Lots Aftermentioned to wite Third Division No 37, 17, 16, 14, 7, 5, 2. Second Division 31 Third Division No. 47 and Intervening Charges that shall or may arise on Said Lots for the space of three years and to take the Constables Discharges if now owner appears within said term of time."

ADJOURNED MEETING.

At a meeting on March 23, 1780 "Three thousand pounds was allowed for Repairing of the High Ways the present year."

This shows how much depreciation there had been in the value of the Currency up to this time. It was also "voted that there is £2000 added to Rev Mr Merrills £500 for the Present year."

THE NEW CONSTITUTION SUBMITTED TO THE PEOPLE OF PELHAM, MAY 9, 1780.

In the warrant for a town meeting, May 9, 1780, was one article after the one for choice of a Moderator which was as follows:

Secondly to see What sanction the Town Will Put on the New form of Government or Constitution, or any other article the town Shall think Proper to Act on.

HUGH JOHNSON, JACOB EDSON
THOMAS JOHNSON, SAMUEL HYDE
JOHN RINKEN, Selectmen.

The meeting was called at 9 o'clock in the forenoon and William Crossett was chosen Moderator.

About the Second article we find this record:—" Secondly—that there is a Committee to be Chosen to Inquire into the New Constitution said Committee is Doct Robert Cutler, John Thomson, Thomas Johnston, John Crawford, and John Hamilton. This Meeting is continued till five aclock in the afternoon of said Day May 9th then Meet a Cording to Said adjournment & Continued by a Second adjournment till Monday the twenty Second day of Said May Corrant at ten of the Clock in the forenoon to Recieve the Report of Said Committee With Regard to the New Constitution. Meet according To appointment & first Voted that this Meeting is adjourned for one Hour to the Meeting house.

Meet & first Voted that Each Pole at the age of Sixteen years & Upwards His a Right to Vote for there officers. Secondly—Voted that the New Constitution is Concord With Agreeble to the Committees Remarks on the same.

WILLIAM CROSET, Moderator."

The above record shows that the people of the town promptly accepted the new constitution and placed themselves in line with all other patriotic communities in the state.

The meeting of May 22, 1780, was for the choice of a man to represent the town at the great and general court which was to assemble at Boston on the last Wednesday of May, and Capt. John Thompson was chosen to represent the town for the session of 1780.

MEETING, JUNE 15, 1780.

June 15, 1780, the town was called together to consider the question of taking a new Valuation of the " Rale and Personal Estate," and the Assessors were instructed to go from " House to House Round the whole town and make a new valuation."

Another important question for consideration was the choice of a " Committee of Safety " and John Thompson, Isaac Gray, Andrew

Abercrombie, Timothy Packard and John Maklem were chosen to act in this capacity.

Isaac Gray was Moderator.

The town had been called upon to furnish more men for the army, but just how many is not stated in the record, but a town meeting was called on the 20th of June, 1780.

"To see what Method the town Will Come into to Raise the Men now Caled for into the Service. Thirdly, to see what encouragement the town Will Give Said men."

The action of the town upon this warrant was peculiar.

After choosing John Thompson Moderator there was an adjournment for "one Houre" and on reassembling "voted that the Delinquents Raise the Present Cotow of Men Called for." "Also voted that James Pebles is allowed the Rats of that Land that Reuben Lotheridge sold at Public Vendue. Lastly, Voted that there is No Credit to be Sold by any man in the town."

The delinquents were to raise the men called for, and nothing seems to have been done to encourage them to enlist.

Meeting July 3, 1780.

The warrant for the Meeting held July 3, 1780, at one o'clock in the afternoon gives information as to the number of men the town had been called upon to furnish.

The language of the warrant follows: "Secondly—as the General Court has Called in the Most Pressing Manner for the town of Pelham to Raise Seventeen men more than was first Required and as those that Were Indeted are brought Principly to the Present Averige, to see What Method the town will take to Raise said Men and any other article the town Shall think proper to act upon."

The action of the town upon this warrant in answer to the pressing demands of the General Court for more men we copy from the record: "Voted that men be Raised for the War by Pole & Real & Personal Estate for the Futter as other taxes is Raised. Fifthly voted that the Selectmen is Impowered to Heire the Contenental Soldiers as Chape as they Can—Either in Speci or Silver or Contenentel Money.

JOSEPH PACKARD, Moderator."

It was not an easy matter for the selectmen to raise the number of men the General Court had demanded as the town was called together again August 24, 1780, to act upon the matter of filling the quota of men,—and the question was placed before them in the following form :

"Secondly—To see what Directions the town Will Give the Selectmen Concerning two Six months men they Cannot Raise by Hire nor by Drafting. Thirdly to See what Method the town will come into to Raise Money to Procure Clothing for the Army."

The meeting was at once adjourned after choosing Joseph Packard Moderator, to the 6th of September at nine o'clock A. M. and on assembling on that day it was "Voted that there is twenty-five pound Granted to Buy Shirts, Stokens and Blankets for the Support of the Army.

Secondly, Voted that the town Stock of Powder that is come to the town is to be sold out Both to the training Band and Larmlist.

Thirdly Voted that John Bruce is allowed three hundred & four Pound Sixteen Shilling for Lodging the Ministers Presbyterie Time.

Fourthly—Voted that Joseph Packard is Allowed two Hundred & Sixty four Pound six shilling for tending the Convention at Boston.

JOSEPH PACKARD, Moderator."

FIRST GOVERNOR ELECTION, SEPT. 4, 1780.

The Meeting for the choice of the first Governor under the new constitution was held on the fourth day of September, 1780 and is of interest as it shows the number of votes cast in the town. The result of the balloting is copied from the report of the meeting.

"Made choice of the Honorable John Handcock Esq Governor for the Ensuing year by a full vote containing Sixty one votes.

Made choice of the Honorable James Bowdoin to be Leu^t Governor & his son rly seven vots Mr. Samuel Adams two vots. Made choice of Con^l Bliss of Wilbreham Noah Goodman of South Hadley Caleb Strong of Northampton Doctor Mathers of Westfield each forty Vots for Counclors."

The stirring times did not allow the people much rest; there were calls for men, for clothing and other supplies all the time.

Oct. 20, 1780 the town voted as follows: "Voted that the town has Agreed to Procure the beef that is sent for.

Thirdly—Voted that there is a committee to be Chosen to Procure Said Beef. Said Committee is Caleb Keeth, Mathew Clark & John Maklem.

Voted that the Remainder of the old Stock that is at William Blairs house be sold at Publick Vendue this Ivining. Also Voted Andrew Abercrombie is to have the Care of what is left of the New Stock,—this meeting is continued till tusday nixt at three of the Clock in the afternoon at the Meeting house of said town to Receive the Report of Said Committee.

Voted that the Above Committee is to take care of the Cattle they have Purchased & Deliver them to the Commisery.

JOSEPH PACKARD, Moderator."

The raising of the quota of men called for had not been accomplished as we judge by action taken at a meeting held Dec. 21, 1780 when it was

" Voted that there be a Committee chosen to Procure these Men Called for—said Committee is Daniel Gray, David Cowdin & Nathaniel Samson."

The Meeting adjourned to Jan. 4, 1781 to hear and act upon the report of this committee when it was

" Voted, that there is fifty Shilling pr Month Granted by the town as a Bounty agreeable to the Court Act. Ray at three & four pence pr Bushel or Money Equivalent thereto to Each Soldier that will Inlist for three years or During the War.

Secondly—Capt Daniel Gray was chosen to Represent the town at the Convintion at Northampton Provided said Convintion Do Meet.

DANIEL GRAY Moderator."

MEETING JAN. 18, 1781.

A meeting held January 18, 1781 had one important article in the warrant as follows:

" To see what Method the town will take to Procure the beef Required of this town Agreeable to the Act of the General Court Deated Decr the fourth one thousand seven hundred and eighty, or any other article the town Shall think Proper when Assembled.

Daniel Gray was Chosen Moderator, and Secondly, " Voted that there be a man Chosen to Go to Northampton to Enquire of the

Commisary what they Give pr Hundred In Money or Grain for Beef.

"Thirdly Voted that Capt Daniel Gray is Chosen a Committee man to Go to Northampton to Enquire at the Commisary the Price of Grain & how he will Change for Beef. This Meeting is continued till the twenty-fifth of this Instant. Meet and then it was voted that there is three hundred & Nine Pound Granted to Procure the Beef for the Continental Army."

MEETING, FEB. 26, 1781.

At a Meeting held on Monday the 26th day of February, 1781 it was

"Voted that there is £1200 continental Money Granted for the Support of the Gospel.

Thirdly that Hugh Johnston is allowed for Assessing Rats twenty nine days £230 and John Rinken £208 for twenty six days assessing Rats.

Fourthly—John Conkey is allowed fourty five Pound for taking Care of the Meetinghouse the past year. Ebenezer Gray allowed £90 for being treasurer the past year. John Maklem & Kaleb Keeth are each allowed £3 7s for purchasing the beef for the Army.

Adjourned to the 5th day of March 1781 and then Chose John Thompson, Samuel Hyde, Jonathan Hood, John Rinkin and Andrew Abercrombie a Committee to "Settle the Everidge"—also voted that ye former Committee viz Daniel Gray, David Cowden, Nathaniel Samson is freed from Being a Committee to Raise Men for the War.

JOSEPH PACKARD, Moderator."

The meeting of March 5, 1781, was the Annual Meeting for the choice of officers and little other business was done.

Anjourned to the 9th day of March when Jonathan Hood, John Thompson, Daniel Sheas and Aaron Gray were Chosen as the "Committee of Safety."

The record of this Annual Meeting is notable from the fact that the name of Daniel Sheas, or Shays, appears for the first time on the town books in the capacity of a town officer, and shows that the man who a few years later was to become the leader of a remarkable rebellion against the state government, was a citizen of the town for quite a number of years before the discontent took the form of open rebellion.

Meeting, Mar. 22, 1781.

£6000 was voted for the repairing of highways. It was also "Voted that there vote of Dec. 21, 1780 granting the Soldiers to be Raised fifty Shilling per Month the old way is Recald by said town. —Voted that the Assessors is to Class the town into ten Classes to Raise the Soldiers as Called for. Also Voted y" one of the Committee of Safety meet the Convention at Hatfield the twenty seventh of March Corrant. John Crawford, Moderator."

On the 18th of May, 1781, there was a town meeting when it was "Voted twenty three Hundred and twelve pound ten shillings old Contenental Money to be Assessed to Enable the treasurer to Settle with Rev. Mr. Merrill."

Meeting, July 17, 1781.

The warrant for a meeting, July 17, 1781, had the following important articles:

" To see what Measure the Town will Take in the order to Rase four thousand two hundred and thirty nine pounds of Beef for the Army as quick as it is Called for in the Court Orders. Also to warn a Meeting to be held on said Day at three o'clock afternoon at the same place of all the Mail Poals of twenty one years old and upwards to Make choice of Militie officers that is wanting in said town Acording to the New Constitution."

The above is written in a different hand-writing from records of former meetings, all having been in substantially the same hand almost from the incorporation of the town, John Dick having served as town clerk thirty-five years.

Action upon the above article concerning beef was as follows: "Voted to Rase the Beef sent for by the Court—thirdly voted that there shall be a Committee to purchis said beef. Committee is Caleb Keaith, Alexander Berry and John McLeane.

Forthly Voted Seventy five Pound in hard Money or Grain Equivolent thereto to Enabel the above mentioned Committee to Purchis the above mentioned Beef.

Fifthly, Voted that the Bounty Granted for the six and three months men by the Court which served in the year 1780 shall be assessed. John Thompson, Moderator."

Meeting, July 25, 1781.

"Voted to Raise Hard money to Purchis the Sixth part of Beef now called for.

Thirdly voted to Raise Hard Money to Purchis the Second Sixth part of s^d Beef.   CALEB KEITH, Moderator."

At a meeting July 30, 1781, there were important articles in the warrant, among them this one:

"To see if the town will reconsider a vote passed April Last to Raise £2312 10s Contenantal Money to Redeem a Note Given to Mr Merrill by the Treasurer."

The town assembled and Joseph Packard was chosen moderator. The meeting was then continued to Friday, the 3d of August. Assembled as per adjournment, and another continuance or adjournment was voted for "teen Minits" to Landlord Samson's in said town. What this special adjournment to the tavern of Landlord Samson's was for does not appear on the record. We only know that there was such an adjournment and on reassembling they passed the following vote, and this is all that resulted. "Voted thirty Pounds to be assessed in Hard Money for the supply of the Pulpit." This indicates that Mr. Merrill had been dismissed.

There was a town meeting on the 27th of August, 1781, with the following articles in the warrant:

"Secondly, To see what the town will do Concerning Raising the Remainder Part of the Beef called for by the General Court.

Thirdly, to see if the town will Reconsider a vote Passed to Divide the town into two Compenys or Divide in any other Method that the town shall see fit—Also to warn Both the Train Band and Larm List that they appear at time and Place to Chuse officers."

"Voted that the Committee formerly Chosen to Purchis the Beef last Caled for from the Court is to give thare Obligations for Hard Money for s^d Beef.

Thirdly, Voted forty Shillings per hundred for the above Mentioned Beef if it cant be Purchased under.

Forthly—Voted to Recal a vote Pased on the 17th of July Last of Seventy five Pound Hard Money or Grain Equivolent to Purchis Beef."

MEETING, OCT. 25, 1781.

The voters were called together again on the 25th of October, 1781, to consider the question of beef and the six and three months' men. The warrant asked for action on the following particulars:

"Secondly to see what Method the Town will take in order to Purchis the Beef that is Delinquent for the year 1781."

"Voted to Chuse a man to Go to the Superintendant to see about an Execution supposed to be Against the Town for Beef.

Secondly Voted Nathaniel Samson to be the Man.

Voted to Rase the Beef Called for by the Superintendant that he has a Execution against the town for.

Secondly Voted that Doc^t Nehemiah Hinds be a Committee Man to Purchis s^d Beef.

Voted that this meeting is continued by adjournment twenty Minits to Landlord Bruce'^{s}.—Meet According to Adjournment and Voted & Chose John Bruce to Hire a three years Man to serve in the Continental Army for the town of Pelham.

CALEB KEITH, Moderator."

Nov. 28, 1781, the town was called together and after voting that "the Selectmen shall not Give out Orders to the six and three month^s men—and that their shall be a Average—the meeting was Continued to the 12th of Dec at nine o'clock in the morning, when it was voted that the Average shall be from the Beginning of the War.

Secondly Voted that the Average shall be Settled by a Committee out of town Said Committee to be Daniel Shaw of New Salem, Capt Isaac Powers of Grenidge, and Capt Metoon of Amherst.

Voted that the orders for Raising the six and three months men Shall be Precured and Red in the town, and that Doct Nehemiah Hinds Procure the above mentioned orders.

Voted that the Average Money shall be settled according to Debt and Credit. NEHEMIAH HINDS, Moderator."

MEETING, JAN. 9, 1782.

"Fifthly, Voted Not to Allow Credit Dun in other towns to be Brought into the Averege.

Sixthly, Voted that those New comers that have Cominto the town of Pelham During this Present Ware Shall be Looked upon an Equateble Level at the time of there Coming in with the Inhabitants of s^d town Respecting Services Dun in this Present War.

Seventhly Voted to Chuse a Committee to take the Credit and Settle the Average in Case it Give Satisfaction to the town, if not to be Left to the former Committee out of town s^d Committee to Consist of Seven—James Taylor, Daniel Gray, John Renkin, Daniel Shess (Shays), John Peibols, Doct Nehemiah Hinds, Joseph Peckerd. Also Voted that Capt John Thompson is to attend the above Committee to give what Light into the Credit he Can."

The action of the town at the above meeting concerning the issuing of orders to the six and three months men was not satisfactory to quite a number of voters and their protest not being heeded and their petition for a town meeting ignored by the selectmen, a petition to a justice of the peace to issue a call for such a meeting was made, which we copy in full.

WARRANT FOR MEETING, JAN. 22, 1782.

HAMPSHIRE SS

To Abiah Southworth, Mathew Brown, Isaac Backer, Constables of the town of Pelham in the County of Hampshire and Commonwealth of Massachusetts, Greeting,—Whereas Application has Been made to Me the Subscriber by John Conkey Jun, James Thompson, Hugh Johnston, Robert Selfridge, William Croset, William Balden, Thomas Thompson, Thomas Montgomery, Andrew Abercrombie, James Abercrombie, Isaac Conkey, Jacob Proute, John McLem, and Caleb Keith, Inhabitants of the town of Pelham Qualified to vote in town meetings this fourteenth day of January in the Year of Our Lord 1782 that at said Pelham on the 12th day of Jenury Instant there was Grate necessity and occasion of a Town Meeting for Sertain Business of Publick Concern to the Said Town and the Inhabitants their to be Don, that is to say to see whether the town will Recall the Vote Past the Ninth Day of Jenury Instunt Allowing the Selectmen to give Orders to the Six and three months men for the Stats Average or to see if the town will stop the Giving of Orders till such time as the Average is Settled and that by Reason and Necessity as aforesaid they the said Persons Aforesaid Did then and there make Due Application in writing unto the said Selectmen of the said town of Pelham Requiring them to Issue there Warrant according to Law for the Calling a Meeting of the Inhabitants of said town to be Assembled to act upon the Business Matters and Articles as aforesaid and that the Selectmen aforesaid having Before them the Application Aforesaid Did then and thare Unreasonably Deny to Call such meeting as aforesaid on the Public reason aforesaid and Making Application to Me the Subscriber as one of the next Justices of the Peas for and within the same County for a Warrant to issue in Due form of Law Calling a Meeting of the Inhabitants of said town to act on the Matters and Articles aforesaid. These are therfore in the name of the Commonwealth of Massachusetts to Require you forthwith to warn all the Freeholders and Other Inhabitants of the town of Pelham lawfully qualified to Vote in town meetings that they assemble at the Meetinghouse in Pelham on Tuesday the twenty second Day of Jenury Instant at two of the Clock in the afternoon then and their after a Moderator Chosen to see whether the town will recall the Vote Pased the Ninth Day of Jenury instant allowing the Selectmen to give orders to the Six and three Months Men for the Stats Average or to see if the Town will stop the giving of Orders till such time as the Average is settled.

Given under my hand and seal Jan 14, 1782

JOHN CHES WILLIAMS, Jus of Peas.

The meeting called under the above warrant was a short one and resulted in a reconsideration of the vote of the 9th of January: "Voted that the vote passed Jenury the Ninth day of this instant Respecting the Selectmen to Give orders to the six and three months men is Recalled   THOMAS JOHNSON, Moderator."

"Settling the Average" was something desirable but not so easily accomplished. It had been left to a committee from surrounding towns. Committees of this town of Pelham had endeavored to settle it but it would not down.

A warrant was posted for a meeting Feb. 4, 1782, the meeting to be held Feb. 8, giving only four days notice.

"Thirdly to see if the town will Chose one or more Agents to Meet the Agents from the other towns in this County at Hadley on Monday the eleventh day of February Instant.

Forthly, to see if the town will Com in to Som effectual method to Settle the Average according to Law."

Acting on the third article "It was Voted that three Delegates should attend the County Convention Viz: Capt Daniel Shass (Shays) Aaron Gray and Jonathan Hood, Committee of Safety. Voted to chuse a Committee in town to Settle the Average—said Committee to Consist of thirteen, Viz: Daniel Gray, Jonathan Hood, Samuel Hyde, Hugh Johnston, Nehemiah Hinds, James Taylor, John Harkness, Caleb Keith, John Renkin, Samuel Samson, William Croset, John Peebles, James Dunlap. Secondly Voted that the above Committee is to Velow the Town's Don in the Service."

This last paragraph we interpret to mean that this committee of thirteen was instructed to make a valuation of what the town had done during the war up to this time to assist in settling the vexed average.

"Voted to sink the state and town Average from the beginning of the War and to Rais the Men for the future for the Present War in Equal Proportions as other taxes are Raised. Secondly Voted to Withdraw the bill of State Everage out of the Constables Hands.
                    NEHEMIAH HINDS, Moderator."

The regular Annual meeting for the choice of officers was held on the 18th of March, 1782 and the voters shelved David Cowden, Nehemiah Hinds, Daniel Gray, Caleb Keith and Joseph Packard, the board of selectmen that had refused to call a town meeting on petition, and by a vote of hand chose a new board consisting of Aaron Gray, Joseph Hamilton, Jonathan Hood, William Dunlap and Thomas

McMellin; and Mathew Clark, Caleb Keith, Capt. Daniel Shays,. Capt. Isaac Gray, Lieut. John McLem, Committee of Safety.

MEETING, MAY 13, 1782.

At a town meeting held on 13th of May, 1782, Henry McCulloch and Thomas Johnson were chosen delegates to attend a convention to be held at Hatfield on the following day. It was further voted to choose a committee to instruct the delegates to the convention, and Caleb Keith, Ebenezer Gray, William Dunlap, Mathew Clark, and Dr. Nehemiah Hinds were chosen for that duty and after the discharge of the duties laid upon them the town accepted the instructions as good.

It did not require very long notice to the freeholders and other inhabitants of the town to assemble them in town meeting, for the record shows a warrant bearing the date August 5, 1782, warning the voters to assemble at four o'clock on the afternoon of the 6th of August, the main business being to choose delegates to sit in county convention at Colonel Murray's in Hatfield on the following day. Daniel Gray and Thomas Johnston were chosen delegates and then Hugh Johnson, John Hamilton, Samuel Hyde, Henry McCulloch and John Renkin were chosen a committee to instruct the delegates in their duties. This done, the meeting adjourned for one hour and a half to the house of Landlord Bruce to give the committee time to instruct the delegates; at the expiration of the hour and a half the voters reassembled at the meeting house and hearing the report of the instructions given the delegates, the instructions were accepted by the town. Samuel Hyde was moderator.

There was a town meeting called on the 19th day of September, 1782 to " see what method the town would come into to pay the men for their Beef Bought in 1781," and it was "voted that the Selectmen examine into the Debt of the town and find out what the town is in Debt for Beef. JOSEPH PACKARD, Moderator."

The town was not called together again in town meeting until Jan. 22, 1783, and the only business was to choose wardens for the town under a new law of the General Court. James Taylor and Reuben Lotheridge were chosen. Nehemiah Hinds was moderator.

No more town meetings until March 3, 1783, which was the regular annual meeting for the choice of officers.

March 26, 1783, there was a meeting for general purposes. Henry

McCulloch was allowed 12s. for attending county convention, Capt. Shays, 12s. for attending a county convention, and officers of the town were voted various sums for their services. Three shillings per day was voted for workmen on the highways, etc.

The people of the east parish of Pelham began the agitation for having that part of the town set off by itself, and articles had appeared in several warrants for action upon the question and at an adjourned meeting, June 30, 1783, the matter was brought up and decided in the negative.

Meeting, March 25, 1784.

At this meeting the old question of paying the six and three months men their bounty money came up and the following is the record: "Voted to pay the six and three months men that was raised in the year 1780 thare several Bountys according to the States Everage, but they also voted to take advice of an attorney to see what method the town will take to settle an Everidge. The meeting was continued by adjournment to the house of Landlord Bruce for a quarter of an hour—then met and Vandued to Mathew Clark the Collection of the Bills taken out of Abraham Livermore[s] hands if Clark provide sufficint bondsmen. Samuel Hyde, Moderator."

April 14, 1784 there was a town meeting when a committee consisting of Dr. Nehemiah Hinds, Aaron Gray, Andrew Abercrombie, Capt. John Thompson, Nathaniel Sampson and Thomas Johnston were chosen to act as follows: "To treat with the six and three months men and Likewise every other Inhabitant of the town in order to Settle the Lose of the Late War in some shorter method than making a Everidge." This meeting was adjourned three times, and then was dissolved without further action.

On the 26th of May, 1784, the town voted £450 to settle with the six and three months men, and this probably cleared the vexed question from the town docket.

The question of an "Everidge" was on again and while we may not grasp the matter completely, it was a desire to learn just what the town was indebted to the state after the services of the town to the state during the war, which had recently ended, was duly credited.

On Friday, Feb. 4, 1785, the voters were called together again to act on these articles:

" 2ly to see if the Town will Petition the General Court to Chuse a committee to make an Everidge for the Town of Pelham—awaiting that the Verdict shall be Decicive.

3ly If the Town is not a mind to Petition the General Court then for the Town to Value the Tours Done in the Late war in order to settle the Everidge."

The assembled voters did not take kindly to the proposition to petition the General Court but " Voted to Choose a Committee out of town to Make an Everidge. Daniel Shaw of New Salem, Col McClallen of Coldrain and John Powers of Shutesbury is s^d Committee." Esquire Powers of Greenwich was afterwards selected in place of Daniel Shaw.

It was also " Voted to Chuse a Committee of three in order to Notify and appoint the Setting of the Above Committee and Likewise to lay before the s^d Committee all Papers Respecting Raising Men and all town votes that Respects the same—Said Committee is not to Communicate anything to the Above Committee or Suffer any other Person excepting under oath.—John Rinken, Lt Sampson and Mathew Clark is said Committee." it was also " Voted that the Result of Said Committee Shall be Decisive.

SAMUEL HYDE, Moderator."

The inhabitants of Pelham living on the East Hill and beyond had been dissatisfied for some time because of the long distance to travel to church and town meetings—they were obliged to go down the hill on which they lived into the valley of the West Branch and then climb to the top of the West Hill where the meeting house was located; there were frequent town meetings on week days, and on Sundays they were obliged to go over the same hard road again until they felt it a burden more than they could bear. They were desirous of having a meeting-house on the East Hill for worship on Sundays and petitions had been offered to the town on several occasions; articles had been in the warrants for town meeting asking that the east part of the town might be set off as a town by themselves, but " Nothing was acted " on such articles,—but the people in that part of the town were not discouraged thereby, nor did it turn them from the purpose they had set their hearts upon, but were more determined than ever to effect some sort of separation.

In the warrant for a town meeting, May 9, 1785, there appeared the following article:

"2dly To see if it is the minds of the Town to sett off the East End of Pelham Relative to a Petition that May be Presented for that Purpose."

The town promptly considered the petition and action followed as per vote:

"2dly Voted to Sett off the East Part of the Town as far as the West Branch of Swift River unto a distinct Town by them Selves.
SAMUEL HYDE, Moderator."

The result of this vote was not so sweeping as the language would indicate, and did not make a new town at once, but it made it possible to establish the East Parish and was the entering wedge which caused a division of the town of Pelham and the incorporation of that part of Pelham east of the West Branch of Swift river as Prescott in 1822.

The meeting, July 18, 1785, was an important one. There was but one article in the warrant which we copy.

"2dly to see if it is the Minds of the Town to Abide by the Prisel of Towrs as the Committee out of town Prised the Towrs or Make Such alteration as the Town shall think Proper or any other article the Town shall think Proper to act upon."

Action on above article:

"Firstly Voted to Allow Those men that Did Service in the Late war in the year 1783 (viz) the Eight Months Men Per Month Nine Pence.

2dly Men that Served six weeks in the year 1775 Per Month Nine Pence.

3dly Voted to Allow Those men that Did Service in the year 1776 at ticonderoga Dorgester White Plains and Morriston Per Month one Shilling.

4^{thly} Voted to alow for Towers Done in the year 1777 (viz) at Moser Creek Stilwater Benington alarm Taking Burgoin and Ticonteroge Per Month one Shilling.

5^{thly} Voted to alow for Service in the year one thousand Seven hundred and Seventy eaight (viz) Towers at Springfield Clerecreek Roadiland and New London Per Month Nine Pence also for Towers in 1779 (viz) Eaight Months men to fill up the Towns quota for three years—nine months men to fill up the Vacancy of the Army and Eaight months men of the militia Per month one Shiling.

7^{thly} Voted that David Sloan and John Harkness Should be alowed one year Each—for Robert Conkey^s Service in the three years Service, and the s^d Credit withdrawn from Alexander Conkey.

8thly Voted to alow those men that Bought Credit of Thomas Montgomery the Credit they Bought of him.

9thly Voted to alow John Barber Nine Months and a half in the Nine Months.

10thly Voted to Chuse a Committee to Make up a Bill of the Service Done in the Late War s^d Committee Lt Sampson, Mathew Clark and John Rinken. EBENEZER GRAY, Moderator."

July 19, 1785, a warrant was issued calling a meeting on Thursday, August 4, 1785, containing one article:

"To see if the Town will Grant a sum of money in order to Settle the Everidge according as the Town Prised the Towers and any other article the Town Shall think Proper to act upon."

MEETING, AUG. 4, 1785.

"Voted to Raise the Sum of fifty Pounds twelve Shilings and Two Pence two farthings in order to Settle the Service Done in the Late War (viz) Service Done from Seventy five to Eaight.

SAMUEL HYDE, Moderator."

The people of Pelham were feeling the after results of a long and expensive war; there was a scarcity of money and what there was in circulation was much depreciated; debtors were pressing for payment, and in common with many other towns and communities the clamor for a further issue for paper money took possession of the people of this town, and found expression in town meeting held Jan. 26, 1786. A full transcript of the warrant and the action thereon follows:

WARRANT FOR MEETING, JAN. 26, 1786.

HAMPSHIRE Ss

To Mr John Conkey, Constable for the Town of Pelham Greeting we Command you that you Warn and Give Notice to all the freeholders and other Inhabitants of Pelham Qualified to Vote as the Law Directs to Assemble on Monday the 30th Day of Jan'y Instant at one of the Clock in the Afternoon at the meeting house in s^d Pelham to act on the following Articles (Viz) first to Chuse a Moderator—Secondly to See if it is the minds of the Town to have a bank of Paper money made and any other article the Town Shall find Necessary when Conviened.

Hereof fail not and make Due Return of the Warrant to one of us the Subscribers Sometime before s^d meeting—Given under our hands and Seal this twenty Sixth Day of Jan^{ry} one Thousand seven hundred and Eighty Six JOHN BRUCE, JAMES TAYLOR, MATHEW CLARK, TIMOTHY PACKARD,
Selectmen of Pelham.

Town Votes for Paper Money.

"Att a Meeting of the freeholders and other Inhabitants of the Town of Pelham Legally Assembled on Monday ye 30th Day of Jan^ry 1786 Then Meet and first was Chosen Hugh Johnston Moderator.

2dly Voted to have a Bank of Paper money made.

3dly Voted to Chuse a Committee to Petition the General Court to make s^d mony.

4^thly Voted that the Selectmen be s^d Committee.

5^thly Voted that Thomas Johnston be added to s^d Committee.

The people of Pelham had been through the hard struggle of the Revolution and had responded to all calls as promptly as it was possible for them to do; they were patriotic, but they were not possessed of abundant wealth and the long years of war had borne heavily upon them. The war had but recently ended when in 1784, they were humiliated as well as angered by a four or five months' experience with Stephen Burroughs, a wolf in sheep's clothing, who came among them as a supplyer when without a settled minister. The year 1786 had now opened—a year of much turmoil and excitement throughout the state and especially in this portion of the state. Capt. Daniel Shays was one of the town wardens and he began to gather the discontented grumblers together and drill them in the use of arms. They also began to organize themselves by conventions here and there, and formulating long lists of grievances for which they demanded redress, and to secure which, later in the year, bodies of armed men attempted to force the state to grant. It is quite probable that nearly all of the men in the town were in active sympathy with the insurgent movement although not a word concerning the rebellion of that year is found upon the records, except a word or two about "Public Grievances."

Meeting, May 19, 1786.

The only business of importance was the choice of "Thomas Johnston to represent the town in the General Court for the present year."

STEPHEN RHODES' RESIDENCE.

C. H. HANSON'S RESIDENCE.

From 1786 to 1797.

Petition of certain inhabitants of Belchertown in 1786.—Convention at Bruce's Tavern, July 31, 1786.—Mutterings about " Grievances" in Town Meeting.—Delegates to Convention at Hatfield in August, 1786.—Second Parish Organized, 1786.—Choice of Delegates to Attend Constitutional Convention, 1787.—First Justice of the Peace Appointed, 1788.—Families Warned to Leave Town in 1790-91.—First General Appropriation for the Poor, 1790.—Support of the Poor First Sold to Lowest Bidder 1794. —Laying Out Road to the Valley, 1795.—Stipulation Concerning the Poor, 1797.

Certain citizens of the north part of Belchertown became desirous of becoming inhabitants of Pelham and a petition embodying their desires was presented to the voters of Pelham in town meeting assembled June 21, 1786, for action thereon.

"The Petition of a Number of Inhabitants of the Town of Belshertown Humbly Showeth that we Request you would put an Article in your Next Warrant for Town Meeting to See if your Town will vote to Recieve s^d Petitioners together with all the Lands Described in said Petition, Viz :—So far south and east as Mr. Jacob Edsons South and East Line, and so far south and west as the south and west Range of Wm Jedediah Ayeres Land and we your Petitioners as in Duty bound shall Ever Pray. To the Selectmen of Pelham, Francis Stratton, Jedediah Ayers, John Barrus, Thomas Thurston, John Whight, David Conet, John Stratton, John Woods, We the Subscribers Jointly and severally agrees and Covenants with the Town of Pelham, Provided they vote to Receive said Petitioners or Subscribers, that We Our Heirs Executors or Administrators will Never vote to Remove said Pelham Meeting House from the place where it now stands, as witness our hands,

FRANCIS STRATON, JOHN BARRUS, THOMAS THURSTON, JOHN WOODS, JEDEDIAH AYERS JUN, JOHN WHITE."

The above petition was considered, and it was "Voted to Recieve to the town of Pelham a Number of Inhabitants of Belsherton with their Lands as is Sett forth in their Petition."

On the south border of the town which was originally a straight line running due east and west there is now a break and a portion of the town is south of the original layout. This is believed to be the tract of land described in the above petition.

The proviso appended to the petition which bound the petitioners, their heirs and assigns, never to take any steps looking to the removal of the "Meeting-House" from its position at the center of the town was unquestionably made a part of their petition to prevent opposition by some who believed the addition of a few families on the south border of the town might lead to a demand that the meeting-house be moved to a more central position.

Agitation for the Redress of Grievances, 1786.

It was believed that the Legislature for the year 1786 would be called upon to redress certain grievances under which the people were suffering and the interest of the people in the action of the General Court about to be chosen is shown in the following articles of the same warrant:

" First, To see if the Town will approve of the Instructions the Committee gave the Representative and Pass all votes Relative thereto.

3dly To see if the Town are Desirous of having a Redress of Publick Grievances and vote anything Relative thereto or any other article the town shall think proper to Act upon when Assembled."

Action on the first article is given as per record: "Voted not to accept of the Instructions of the Committee to the Representative—also Voted to Dismiss said Committee.—Voted to chuse a Committee to Instruct the Representative this Present Year—the Committee to consist of five—that Mathew Clark, Joseph Hamilton, John Rinken, Hugh Johnston and Nathaniel Sampson is said Committee.
                    Nathaniel Sampson, Moderator."

Article three of the above warrant, for "Redress of Publick Grievances" seems to have received no consideration by the meeting, not even a vote to "pass the article" or "nothing acted on 3d article," which was a common record when articles in a warrant were not considered. If there was action on it, as there might have been in the excited state of the people, the record was not spread upon the book.

Convention at Landlord Bruce's Tavern.

The next meeting was on Friday, July 28, 1786, and the warrant contained but one article.

" 1stly For the Town to Chuse a Delegate or Delegates to Meet in Convention on Monday the thirty-first Day of this Instant at ten o'clock in the forenoon at the house of Landlord Bruce's in Pelham and Pass any vote Relative thereto or any other article the Town shall think Proper to act upon when Assembled."

Action on above article: " Nehemiah Hinds was chosen Moderator. Caleb Keith and John Rinken were chosen as Delegates to represent the town in Convention at Landlord Bruce'^{s} on the 31st Instant.

2dly Voted that there shall be a Committee of ten to Instruct s^d Delegates.— Said Committee is Joseph Hamilton, Thomas Johnston, Joseph Packard, Mathew Clark, Doct Hynds, John Peebles, Hugh Johnston, Ebenezer Gray, James Taylor and Captain John Thompson."

The meeting was continued by adjournment to Monday the 14th of August next at 5 o'clock P. M. Dr. Hynds being absent, Ebenezer Gray was chosen Moderator—and it was " Voted to chuse a Delegate or Delegates to Attend Convention at Hatfield on Tuesday the 22^d of this Instant—Voted that Caleb Keith and Mathew Clark are said Delegates."

For what purpose the convention was called at Landlord Bruce's we find no record, but can assume that it was for the consideration of the " publick grievances " in some form or other; that the duties of the delegates to the Pelham convention were considered of a weighty nature, and to have an important bearing for the good or ill of the town, is made evident by the fact that ten of the first citizens of the town were chosen to confer with them and give them final instructions to guide their action in the convention assembled at the house of Landlord Bruce. There is no record of action in the convention.

The convention at Hatfield on the 22^d of August 1786, which Caleb Keith and Mathew Clark were to attend was in session for three days with delegates from fifty towns to consider the causes of the general uneasiness and dissatisfaction among the people; and the convention formulated a list of twenty-five grievances under which the people were suffering. Similar conventions gathered in many parts of the state during the summer and autumn of this year until the excited people were in open rebellion against the state government.

Meeting, Oct. 17, 1786.

"Voted that Lieutenant Packard and Captain Shays shall be delegates to meet in convention in Hadley on the first Tuesday of November. Then voted to continue the meeting by adjournment to Monday, the 23d day of this instant at 12 o'clock, at the meeting-house in said town. Then met according to appointment—the same moderator continued—then voted to excuse Captain Shays and Lieutenant Packard from serving in convention. Voted that Caleb Keith and Samuel Hyde should serve in their room.

SAMUEL HYDE, Moderator."

This was the last time Capt. Daniel Shays was elected to serve the town by the people of Pelham.

Meeting, Oct. 3, 1786.

That portion of the town east of the west branch of Swift river having formed a separate parish to be known as the East parish, it became necessary to decide what grants should be assessed upon the town and what expenses should be borne by the two parishes. It was voted that the selectmen consult with the East parish committee and agree upon what grants should be assessed upon the town.

John Hamilton, Lamond Gray, Andrew Abercrombie, Joseph Packard and Nathaniel Sampson was chosen a committee to consult the neighboring towns in order to petition the General Court.

The exciting times caused by being in open rebellion against the state government, and its leader a citizen of the town, occupied the attention of the people so completely that they may not have had time for town meetings had the voters been at home, as they probably were not during the last few months of this year (1786) and for a month or two of the year 1787, or until the collapse of the rebellion.

After the adjourned meeting of October 23 the town was not called together again until the warrant was posted for the regular annual town meeting March 29, 1787, and there was a continuance until the 24th of April without any business being transacted beyond the choice of Alexander Berry, moderator, followed by the choice of the usual officers for the year.

Meeting, April 2, 1787.

The Shays Rebellion was substantially ended and the voters of Pelham were probably all at home except Capt. Daniel Shays and

Henry McCulloch. The General Court had passed a law requiring all men elected to office to subscribe to an oath of allegiance before taking the oath of office, and the following transcript from the record of this meeting makes it clear that the best men of the town were actively engaged in the rebellion or in sympathy with it.

"The following persons have taken and Subscribed to the Oath of Allegiance as Directed by Law previous to the oath of office. John Rinkin, John Harkness, Andrew Abercrombie, Alexander Berry, Nathaniel Sampson, Ebenezer Gray, William Conkey jun, John Bruce."

Subscribing to the oath of allegiance was required of all officers for a few years, and then the law was not enforced, perhaps repealed.

After the east part of the town had become a parish by itself the call for town meetings warned the inhabitants to meet and assemble at the old or West parish meeting-house and the west branch of Swift river was the line between the two parishes. The highway surveyors were directed to recognize the river as the limit of their respective districts while repairing roads. Surveyors in the East parish came down to the river and those belonging in the old parish went no farther than the river. There were separate collectors chosen for the two parishes, to collect town taxes, John Barker having the collection of taxes for the West or old parish vendued to him in 1787 at 12d on the pound and Lieut. John Hamilton had the collectorship of the East parish the same year at 12d. on the pound.

The work of framing a constitution for the country which had been through a long and costly war for liberty had been accomplished and conventions were called in the various states to submit it for adoption or rejection.

A meeting was called Nov. 26, 1787,

"To chuse a Delegate to Set in Convention at Boston to approve of the States Constitution."

Nathaniel Sampson was chosen Moderator, and then it was "voted to Continue this meeting by adjournment to the house of Landlord Bruce for a quarter of an hour."

Just where Bruce's tavern was located cannot now be determined, but it could not have been far from the old parish meeting-house; had it not been near, the assembled voters could not have adjourned to Bruce's tavern from the meeting-house for a consultation and returned to the meeting-house again within fifteen minutes. The record says that they "Met according to appointment," and "Made choice of Mr. Adam Clark to Represent the Town in the Convention to Ratify or Reject the Constitution."

The next business on the record: " Voted to Chuse a Committee of five to Instruct s^d Delegate.—Said Committee is Caleb Keith, John Conkey, Abiah Southworth, Doct Hynds and Joseph Packard.
NATHANIEL SAMPSON, Moderator."

MEETING, FEB. 25, 1788.

This warrant had but one article in it, but one of no less importance than "To see if the Town will Reccommend some Proper Person for a Justice of the Peace to the Governor and Counsel."

Action of the meeting: " Voted to Reccommend Deacon Ebenezer Gray to the Governor and Counsel for a Justice of the Peace. Voted that the Selectmen make out a Petition to the Governor and Counsel that they would Grant a Commition to Deacon Ebenezer Gray for a Justice of the Peace.   CALEB KEITH, Moderator."

Dea. Ebenezer Gray was a man of integrity, honest, faithful and much respected by the people, as is shown by his being chosen town treasurer for many years, and elected upon many important committees where intelligence, honesty and good sound judgment were required.

MEETING, APRIL 7, 1788.

At this meeting the following record was made: " Voted to Remit Capt Shays Rats in Capt. John Conkey's Rate Bills," thus showing that the rebel captain neglected to pay his taxes before leaving town, and that he was not expected to return to town again.

MEETING, FEB. 6, 1789.

This meeting was called Feb. 6, 1789, to act upon an article as follows:

" First to see if the Town as they have not had an Equeal Chance with thair Breatheran by Reason of thair not having a Precept Seasonably to see if the Town will Petition the General Court for an Equel Chance with thair Breatheran for a New Choice for a Representative and to act on any other Article the Town shall think Proper when Convened."

The meeting was organized at one o'clock in the afternoon by the choice of Capt. John Conkey, moderator, and then it was " Voted to adjourn said meeting to Landlord Shurtlief's until five oclock of s^d

day. Then met and it was voted that the Selectmen send a Letter to the General Court and Inform them of the Neglect of the Precept Respecting the Representative."

The location of Landlord Shurtlieff's tavern was doubtless near the meeting-house; and the fact of the town not being represented in the General Court because the precept did not arrive in season to call a meeting as directed in the delayed document was a matter that demanded consideration before action was taken by vote. There was no heating apparatus in the meeting-house and consequently not a comfortable place for consultation on the afternoon of a February day in an old-fashioned winter, and for this good and sufficient reason we have a right to suppose the adjournment was made to Shurtlieff's tavern, where the voters could deliberate and decide upon their action in comfort before the blazing fire-place at the tavern. When the plan of action had been decided upon the voters reassembled at the meeting-house according to the terms of adjournment and directed the selectmen to write a letter of explanation to the General Court, and at the same time praying to be given authority to elect a representative so that the town might not be deprived of the right of representation accorded to other towns.

The Town Exercised on Account of the Poor.

Since the settlement of the town the policy had been to exercise a close and rigid scrutiny upon those who desired to make a home in the town; not only to see that they were desirable morally speaking but also for the purpose of making sure that they would make citizens not likely to become an expense to the town by reason of poverty. The thrifty Scotchmen had succeeded in keeping the poor and shiftless out of the town, warning out such as came in without first securing permission to enter, and by forcible removal if there was a disposition on the part of any new comer to disregard the notice to leave the town. In spite of all the care exercised by the leading citizens, sickness and distress would fall upon some, and assistance from the town was the only alternative.

Meeting, April 12, 1790.

The first general appropriation for the poor was made at the 12th of April meeting, 1790, recorded as follows: "Voted to allow 6 Pounds for the Support of the Poor the present year."

The first board of overseers of the poor, or a committee whose duties were substantially those of overseers of the poor of modern times, was chosen at the same meeting by this recorded vote: " Voted to choose a committee of three to Inspect the poor for the Present year."

Meeting, May 4, 1790.

It was voted to give a bounty for killing crows:—" Voted one shilling in Town Security for each Crow that is killed in the town by the 15th of June Next by the Inhabitance of s^d Town. Voted that any Person that shall kill a crow or crows shall carry the same to one of the Constables of s^d town and he to give a certificate for the Number of Crows that is killed. Mathew Clark, Moderator."

In the warrant for meeting, June 4, 1790, was this article :

" To see if it is the mind of the Town to Petition the General Court setting forth the Badness of the Roads and our Inability to keep them in Repair Praying that they would grant the Town liberty to work out thair state Taxt on the County Road."

It was voted to petition the General Court as per article and Andrew Abercrombie and Abiah Southworth were chosen a committee to assist the selectmen in the " Draught of a proper petition."

The meeting was called at 4 p. m. and the meeting was " adjourned to the house of Landlord Shurtlieff to meet again at half an hour after Eight oclock this Instant."

This adjournment to the Shurtlieff tavern was not because the meeting-house was cold but to give the selectmen, and assisting committee, better opportunity to formulate a petition to the General Court. The voters met at 8-30 that evening at the meeting-house and it was " Voted that the Town Except the Draft of the Petition that the Committee Drew. Abiah Southworth, Moderator."

Copy of a warrant issued to Constable Benoni Shurtlieff, dated Jan. 31, 1791, by the selectmen :

" To Lieut Benoni Shurtlieff, Constable You are Directed to Warn and give notice unto Isaac Doge of Charlton in the County of Worcester, Laborer, Georg Eliot Middleborough in the County of Plymouth, Thomas Thompson Taylor, forrenor, James Tally, a Transent Person, Moses Buttler of Hardwick in the County of Worcester, Laborer and James Watkins of Hardwick in the County of Worcester, Laborer who has lattly come in this town for the Purpose of abiding etc. Thairfore that they Depart the

Limits thairof with their Children and others under thair care within fifteen days—Also the Widow Robeson of Connicticut State, a transent parson who has lately come into this town not having obtained Consent etc."

All of the persons named were ordered to depart the limits within 15 days and the warrant was signed by the selectmen.

The return of the constable is unique :

" HAMPSHIRE SS

February 19, 1791—By Vartue of this warrant I have warned all of the within Named Persons as this Warrant Directs Except Watkins family and thair not to be found in my presint and Eliot I left a Summons according to Law   BENONI SHURTLIEFF, Constable of Pelham."

As we contemplate this wholesale midwinter warning out to a considerable number of men, women and children, we can but be more impressed with the abounding contempt for shiftlessness and improvidence displayed by these Scotch citizens of the town. Had they issued their mandate to " Depart the Limits " earlier in the season, or postponed it until spring, we should not have felt so much like charging them with exhibiting a heartlessness that is not pleasant to to entertain against such thoroughly good people as we believe these sturdy Presbyterians to have been.

The meeting Oct. 20, 1791, was for very important purposes, best expressed by quoting the warrant. The first article was to see about a mill being built on the west branch. The next article marks the proposed introduction of a practice not commendable, but it was one in common use in many towns for years,—now happily departed from and abandoned.

" To see if the town will set up at Vandue the Cost of William McFall and his wife for one year."

The unmistakable intention of the above article was to set up the cost of maintaining the unfortunate McFall and wife at vendue to the lowest bidder, but it does not say that. Possibly they thought it might be construed to mean the highest bidder, and caused a halt, for there is no record of action on this article. Action upon the mill privilege will be found in the chapter about mills, etc.

" May 10, 1791, the Preambleation of the Line Between Pelham and Amherst. Began at a Heap of stones at the Southwest corner of Pelham and ran North 2d 15m west and found seven old Marks and Boundarys, several of which we Marked with the Letter PA (viz) a Large Pine tree against Harkness improved Land also another Pine tree at the North end of a Pon hol against Col Mattoons Land, another Pine tree about eight Roads North of Pelham Road, another Pine tree against Capt Parkers Lot, also an oak tree about ten Rods South of the River, also a large white oak tree against Hodgdons Land all of which trees we marked P. A. and ⊕ and Renewed the Northwest Corner of Pelham, which is a large Heap of Stones, by putting a Stake, said line is Run by Justice Dwight, Surveyor.

Annual Meeting, April 2, 1792.

The meeting was adjourned to April 17 and it was then "Voted to Chuse a Committee and to Provide for the Support of the Poor the present year. Chose James Dunlap, Lt Benoni Shurtlieff and Robert Makliam, for s^d Committee." A committee had been chosen in 1790 "To Inspect the Poor," and then excused from serving; the election of the above committee to provide for the support of the poor comes the nearest to overseers of the poor that the town had come, up to this time. It was found that the poor could not all be ejected from the town by a constable, and provision must be made for them. This year Justice Ebenezer Gray, David Huston and Jeremiah McMillen were serving the town —not as hog reeves, but under the more dignified title of " Hog Constables."

There was a regularly warned meeting held this same 17th of April for other business.

Dr. Nehemiah Hinds petitioned for a favor professionally, as the warrant indicates:

" To see if the town will grant Dr Hinds Liberty to set up a Pest House in s^d town Providing it shall be set in such a place as shall be thought safe for the Inhabitance of s^d town."

The vote was favorable to the project of the doctor, and is thus recorded :

" Voted Dr Nehemiah Hinds Liberty to set up anocalation House in said Town Provided it is set in such a place that the Inhabitance will not be Exposed to catch the Infaction."

Annual Meeting March 3, 1794.

"Voted to set up the Cost of Keeping of Mr. McFall and wife to the Lowest Bidder. Struck off to William Baldwin for £8 10s for one year, the Doctors Bill Excepted."

Mr. William Baldwin stands first on the long list of those who followed his lead and supported this plan of dealing with the unfortunate by bidding off the poor to support at the inverted vendue, or lowest bidder.

" Minits of a road altered by the Selectmen on the road leading from the County road to what is Called the Valley, the alteration is as follows (viz.) Beginning about twenty rod East of whare said road leaves the County road at a White pine staddle north of the road where now traveled, then bearing North of East to a white pine Staddle and then to a pich pine tree and then to a white pine tree by the mill brook a little north of the Bridge that is over the Mill brook. S^d trees is on Mr. John Harkness' land and are marked on the south side. Then keeping the road where it is now traveled to the bottom of the hill, then leaving the said road on the north of a chestnut tree marked on the south side, from thence East bearing south still in John Harkness land to the new Dug Way to land lately owned by Major Egleston, then through said Eglestons land to John Rinkins land, from thence to an old seller where Torrance lately lived and from thence to the road now travelled. S^d road is laid out two rod wide southerly of the Marks."—Pelham, April 6, 1795.

MEETING, April 6, 1795.

Under a separate warrant the town was called to act on business contained in the following article :

" For the purpose of Collecting their Sentiments on the Needsessity or Expedeency of revising the Constitution in order to Amendments agreeable to the Provition made in S^d Constitution."

Vote on above article: " Five voats for revising and fifty-six against revising."

MEETING, AUGUST 25, 1795.

" Voted for the town to set up posts and Bords at the corner of the roads through S^d town to Direct Travellers to the Next town where S^d road leads. DAVID CONKEY, Moderator."

The assessors of Pelham one hundred years ago had very different methods in making up the valuation for taxation from those of to-day, when the valuation is fixed somewhat close upon the real value of farm property. In 1795 the valuation of all the property in Pelham, including 209 polls and the non-resident lands, amounted to only $6028.05. Squire Abbott's valuation was placed at $190 and then a line was drawn across it as though it was a mistake. Dr. Nehemiah Hinds valuation for taxation was only $157, and yet the doctor paid the highest tax of any man in town, though it was only about $24 annually. They made the valuation very low and the rate sufficient to raise all the money needed for public purposes.

Annual Meeting, March 6, 1797.

"Voted to adjourn this meeting to Ensign John Coles for fifteen minnits, then meet and first voted to adjourn this meeting for ten minnits to the meetinghouse then meet and first was voted to set up the keeping of Mr. McFall and wife to the lowest bidder, the Purchaser is to return him with as much Property as he Receives with him S^d Town is to pay all Extraordinary Doctrine, Struck of the keeping of Mr McFall and wife to Matt Clark for £14 10s."

The meeting adjourned to the first Monday in April following. In the mean time Matt Clark repented him of his purchase and asked to be relieved of his bargain. The record concludes as follows:

" Then met according to the above adjournment and first voted to Except Mr. James Latham in the room of Mr. Matt Clark, the keeping of Mr. McFall and wife was struck of to Mr Matt Clark at £14 10s which sum S^d Latham is to have."

The unfortunate Mr. McFall and wife had similar experience for many years.

From 1797 to 1809.

Transfer of Pews in the Old Meeting-house, 1798.—Permission voted to build " Horse Shades " 1799.—Sale of town lands at Vendue, 1801.—Opposition to the Building of Turnpike, 1802.—A town Pound established, 1804.—Robert Lotheridge sells his pew in the Old Meeting-house.— Voted to hold one-third of the town meetings in the Second Parish, 1805.—Attempts to have the Toll-gate Abolished, 1806.—Samuel and Andrew Hyde petition to have their lands set off to Amherst, 1807.

Meeting, March 20, 1797,

was called especially and only for action on this one article:

" To see if the Town will grant Liberty for the anoculation of the Small

Pox in said Town and Establish a House or Houses for the Caring on the same for any length of time that they shall judge best when convened."

Action on above article was prompt and decisive. "Voted not to have the anoculation of the Small Pox in town.

WILLIAM CONKEY, Moderator."

CONTRACT FOR THE CARE OF THE POOR.

Mr. McFall and wife were struck off again for £16 to Joel Conkey and Lieut. Jeremiah McMillen, under the following written agreement:

"Pelham April 4th 1798. This may certify that Lt Jeremiah McMillen and Joel Conkey has agreed Before us that Conkey is to take McFall and his wife this year for Sixteen Pounds without the cow, and Conkey to have the cow towards the Sixteen Pounds, if the Town Consent to sell her for what sum Conkey and the Town shall agree for at the Aprisal of Men such as Conkey and the town shall agree upon these to the other selectmen of Pelham.

NEHEMIAH HINDS, ALEXANDER BERRY, DAVID CONKEY, JOHN PEEBLES, Selectmen."

The transfer of pews in the first parish meeting-house from one to another was made by deed in due form. Here follows the deed of Jonathan Killogg to Levi Gray. The deed conveys one-quarter of Killogg's pew, and is the same pew that Andrew Abercrombie sold to Killogg on the 25th of June, 1796, for $13. The sum Gray pays for one-quarter indicates over 100 per cent. advance in the value of pew property in two years.

"Know all men by these Presents that I Jonathan Killog of Pelham in the County of Hampshire, cordwainer, Do in Consideration of Seven Dollars to me in hand paid by Levi Gray of town and County above Named, do Bargain with and sell unto the said Levi one 4th of a Certain Pew in the West Parish Meeting House, s^d Pew is situated under the Gallery Stairs at the South East Corner of the Meeting House ¾th of s^d Pew is improved by Ezekiel Baker and Samuel Rodes and is Bounded west by Dr Southworths pew, North by the Alley to the stairs, East by the stairway, south by the walk of s^d meeting house, to have and to hold the above one 4th of s^d pew free from all Incumberance of Every Name or Nature and that the s^d Jonathan do Warrant secure and Defend the same to the s^{id} Levi his heirs and Assigns against all Claims and Demands Whatever, in Witness hereof I have set my Hand in Presents of JONATHAN KILLOGG

Attest, CHRISTOPHER PATTEN
Pelham Dec 12th 1798"

Meeting, Sept. 10, 1799.

The main business of this meeting is set forth in article two of the warrant:

"To see if the Town will grant a privilege to a Number of their Inhabitance to Build Horse Shades near the first Parish meeting house where the Town shall see fit."

It was "Voted that their is a privilege to any Person that has a mind to Build Horse Shades,—Voted to chuse a committee to see where it is Most Convenient to Build Horse Shades on the Town Land, s^d Committee is Dea Gray, Nahum Wage and Jonathan Hood.—said committee reported that their opinion is that it is most convenient to Build Horse Shades on the south side of the grave yard wall. DAVID CONKEY, Moderator."

Meeting, May 5, 1800.

The vendue master's services were called in at this meeting as per record:

"Voted to set up Francis Straton to the Lowest Bidder by the week to the next Annual Meeting, they that bids him oft is to Bord wash and Nurse him in Common health and the Extraordinary Doctring Nursing and Clothing is to be paid by the Town in time of Sickness,—Struck of to Ebenezer Wright at six shillings a week."

Meeting, Nov. 2, 1801.

Originally there were ten acres of land set apart at the center of the town for a common, training field and burying ground, and by the plan of the tract containing the first division into homelots it will be seen that a portion of this ten acres was taken from lot No. 1 or the minister's lot. Some of this land was east of the burial ground and the town had been called upon to lease or sell it in a number of town meetings. In the warrant for this meeting was the following article:

"To see if the town will sell the land belonging to said Town lying East of the Graveyard and North of the turnpike road at the Request of a number of Petitioners, and pass all votes Nesessary to carry such sail into effect."

Action on article as recorded: "Voted to sell the land Belonging to the Town East of the Graveyard and North of the turnpike road as far south as the south side of the school house, with a reserve of the Land the school house stands on and the Cross Road.—Voted to sell said land at Publick Vendue, and to chuse a Committee to accomplish said Sale.—Nehemiah Hinds, David Conkey and John Rinken Committee. Voted that the above Committee shall guarantee to the purchaser that the Town shall not Use their land Southerly of the school house and North of the turnpike road, for any use except a Common. NEHEMIAH HINDS, Moderator."

About this time the people became somewhat excited by a proposition to build a turnpike from Belchertown to Greenwich and Hardwick which would leave the town sidetracked, and they began to work in opposition to the project upon information received from Capt. Isaac Abercrombie, then representative at the General Court.

MEETING, FEB. 1, 1802,

Was called to act on a matter of public interest as per article:

"To see if the town will send a Memorial to the General Court against the proposed turnpike Road from Belchertown to intersect with the Sixth Massachusetts turnpike somewhere between Major Powers of Greenwich and General Warners in Hardwick according to the Request of a Letter sent to the Selectmen of Pelham by their Representative."

The people assembled and "Voted that the Selectmen shall send a remonstrance to the General Court against the proposed turnpike in behalf of the town. JOHN RINKEN, Moderator."

MEETING, SEPT. 17, 1802.

It was "Voted to chuse two agents to attend on the Committee appointed by the General Court of the Commonwealth to Examine and report to the said General Court Respecting the Expediency and Utility of the Road Petitioned for by Benjemin Hooker and others to be Established as a turnpike Road at Esqr Fields in Greenwich on the 21 day of this instant. Chose Esqr Isaac Abercrombie and Dea Nathaniel Sampson agents for the above purpose."

MEETING, NOV. 1, 1802.

Was called to consider a very important proposition as set forth in warrant:

"To see if the Town will consider the Request of a Committee from New Salem in Joining the Neighboring towns Respecting or otherwise providing a work House for the Reception and employment of the Poor at the joint expense and for the Common Benefit of such towns and Chuse an Agent or a Committee to meet at the House of John Smith, Inholder, in New Salem on the first Monday of January Next at Eleven oclock A. M. with such Instructions as the town shall think Proper."

Meeting dissolved without action on the article.

The people of Pelham had known but little about the poor; the word pauper is not found on the records up to the receiving of the above proposition to build a Work House for the common benefit of the neighboring towns, including Pelham. Probably for fifty years from the incorporation of the town they had kept the poor from settling in the town, or warned them out if such persons came into the town without first obtaining permission to settle, and consequently were not in sympathy with the proposition from New Salem. They did nothing to encourage poverty or shiftlessness, and perhaps thought building a work house would encourage people to apply for aid, and who would prefer a snug home in a work house rather than being vendued to the lowest bidder.

MEETING, SEPT. 7, 1804.

"Voted to raise $70 to purchis town stock of military stores for the town. Dr. Hinds, David Conkey chosen committee to purchis the town stock.

Voted $70.99 to defray the expense of building a bridge over Swift river, so called.

Voted to set up Samuel Nash's boarding and washing by the week to the lowest bidder until next annual meeting unless it proves he is not an inhabitant of the town, then struck of as proposed above to Nahum Wage the Keeping of Samuel Nash at Ninety-Nine cents per week."

MEETING, NOV. 5, 1804.

The sole business of this meeting was to consider the question of building a pound. The last one built was at the southwest corner of the graveyard near the meeting-house; it was built of wood and had probably become useless by this time.

"Voted to build a Pound in said Town. Voted that the Pound shall stand on Mr Hach's land below the Blacksmith shop on the Rite hand side of the turnpike Road. Voted that the Pound is to be made with a stone wall of five feet thick at the bottom and six feet and one half high with a Squair timber on the top of Eight inches squair."

Voted to chuse a committee of three men (Viz) Esqr Abercrombie, Doct Hinds and Landlord Hach to build said Pown

SAMUEL JOSLINE, Moderator."

DEED OF A PEW IN THE FIRST PARISH MEETING-HOUSE.

Robert Lotheridge' Deed to Freedom Chamberlain. Know all men by these Presents that I Robert Lotheridge of Pelham in the County of Hampshire and Commonwealth of Massachusetts Cordwinder, in Consideration of ten Dollars paid by Freedom Chamberlain jun of Pelham in the County and state aforesaid Cordwinder the receipt whereof I do hereby acknowledge—do Hereby grant sell and convey unto the said Freedom Chamberlain a certain half of a Pew in the first Parish Meeting house in Pelham upon the Lower floor—Said Pew stands in the southwest corner of the Body Pews in said meeting house formerly belonging to My Honored Father Reuben Lotheridge Decest, with reserve of one seat for my Honored Mother so long as she remains a widow or Removes from said Pelham. To have and to Hold the above granted premises to the said Freedom his Heirs and assigns to his and thair use and behoof forever and do Covenant with the said Freedom his Heirs and assigns that I am lawfully Seized in fee of the above granted premises, that they are free of all incumbrances, that I have good right to sell and convey the same to the said Freedom and that I will warrant and Defend the same premises to the s^d Freedom his Heirs and Assigns forever Against the Lawful Claims and Demands of all Persons.

Dec. 24, 1804.   ROBERT LOTHERIDGE,
                                                  MARY LOTHERIDGE.

MEETING, APRIL 1, 1805.

"It was voted that one third of the town meetings should hereafter be held at the second parish meeting house."

MEETING, MAY 29, 1805.

The town was called together to consider the proposition contained n this article:

"Article 2 For the town to vote that all those Persons living on the turnpike Road to work out their proportion of thare Highway taxes the year ensuing on s^d turnpike Road Providing the Directors of s^d turnpike road will Discontinue the gate in s^d town of Pelham the year ensuing."

Israel Conkey was chosen moderator and Article 2 was passed over in short order and the meeting was at an end. We learn by this that the directors of the turnpike company had a toll gate in the town.

Meeting, Oct. 23, 1805.

There had been a vote passed to have one-third of the town meetings at the Second Parish. This was the first town meeting called at the Second Parish meeting house. For sixty-three years or more all town meetings were held at the First or West parish meetinghouse and the assembling of the voters on Pelham East hill must have been a day to be remembered. The business of the meeting was stated in the second article:

"For the Town to Grant a sum of money to Defray the unexpected expenses of Supporting the poor of said town."

As the fixed belief of the town from its settlement was that there should be no poor persons in the town this call for more money for the Poor was not pleasant, and when the second article came up the people promptly passed it over, but on second thought recalled it and "Voted to raise $100 to Defray town Charges." rather than "for supporting the Poor," as expressed in the warrant. Joseph Akers was moderator.

Meeting, Nov. 22, 1805.

The location of the school-house in the middle district of the first Parish was not satisfactory to some and this meeting was called to act upon the question of changing the location, and we copy the recorded vote: "Voted Liberty to have the school house in the Middle District of the West Parish of Pelham Removed to near the Eand of the stone wall North of Robert Ormstons store and on the East sid of the Cross Rode Leeding thairby provided Mr Ormston moves it on his own Cost and puts it in as good Repair as it now stands. Voted to Chuse a Committee of three,—said Committee is Lt Rinken, Doct Hinds and David Conkey. Voted that said committee is impowered to Transfair by Deed or otherways the Land the said school House now stands on for a school House spot Discribed in the second vote of said meeting. Voted to adjourn this meeting to Landlord Haches for one Hour. JOHN RINKEN, Moderator."

It seems that Mr. Ormston was in the mercantile business; he had a store, and was to pay the cost of moving the school-house. The place selected was on the east side of the cross road that crossed the middle range road; the middle range road running east and west, and the cross road north and south.

Annual Meeting, March 3, 1806

Was called at the West parish meeting-house, and after the officers were chosen the meeting adjourned to the Second parish meeting-house at 2 P. M. the same day to complete the list, and transact other unimportant business; quite an undertaking when we consider the condition of the roads in the month of March, and that the Second parish meeting-house was three and a half miles away.

After the first, second and third divisions of land were drawn by lot there were still portions of land left and termed common lands, and the third article of the warrant for this meeting had reference to such lands.

" 3^d to see if the town will Look up the Common Lands in said town and accertain what Number of acres thair are, and whether they will sell it, and pass all votes the Subject requires."

" Voted to chuse a committee to look up the Common lands so called—s^d committee is Isaac Abercrombie Esq Lt John Rinken and Joseph Akers. They also voted that the Proprietors book containing a record of all the lands in town should be lodged in the town clerk's office. Isaac Abercrombie, Moderator."

Meeting, Nov. 20, 1806.

Those living along the turnpike were not at all satisfied with the action of the voters who lived at a distance from the turnpike in voting at a former meeting to "pass the article" asking to be allowed to work out a portion of their taxes on the turnpike, and the town was called together again on the same business. This time the true inwardness of their desire is expressed in the wording of their article in the warrant. They asked as before to work out a portion of their taxes on the turnpike " Provided the turnpike gate in said town shall be kept open and free from tole." It was of no use—the voters away from the turnpike sat down on the proposition by "voting to Pass the Article. Joseph W. Hamilton, Moderator."

Meeting, March 2, 1807.

In the records of the west or first parish found elsewhere is the action of the parish upon the petition of Andrew Hyde and others living near the west border of the town who wished to be set off to Amherst as far as pertained to parochial purposes in 1812 ; but Article 7 of this warrant shows that an attempt to be set off from the town, with their farms, had been made by Samuel and Andrew Hyde, who lived in the southwest corner of the town on the farm now (1897) occupied by Hiram Ballou.

The article on which Samuel and Andrew Hyde asked action was:

"To see if the town of Pelham will vote to set off Samuel Hyde and Andrew Hyde from Said town and annex them to the Town of Amherst with their lands in Said town of Pelham."

The town voted to pass the article. The meeting was then adjourned to the east parish meeting house on the first Monday in May.   JOHN CONKEY, Moderator.

MEETING, MARCH 7, 1808.

It was voted to hold the May meeting at the East parish. Voted that the selectmen be a committee to examine the road from the turnpike to Samuel Arnold's house and report as they think best at the May meeting.

It will be noticed that Marson Eaton, the collector of the West parish for the year 1808, was on record to do the work for nothing and Joseph Akin, the collector for the East parish, was to do the work and pay two cents on each pound for the privilege.

From 1809 to 1815.

Two Candidates for Representative to the General Court, 1809.—Taxes Upon the People, 1809.—The Abercrombie Brothers, Isaac and James, Candidates for Representative, 1810.—The 6th Mass. Turnpike Corporation Tries to Discontinue Their Road Through Town, 1810.—County Road to Enfield Laid Out, 1811.—Governor Petitioned to Restore the Two Military Companies to their Former Regiments, 1812.—Fear of a Draft for the War of 1812.—Wages of Detached Soldiers Raised, 1814.—The East Parish asks to be Set Off As a Town By Itself, 1815.

The following is a copy of the Pelham tax bills, A. D. 1809:

"Committed to Jonathan Wood and Marson Eaton Collectors of said Town Containing the following Sums. Viz—State Tax set at 30 cents on poll, 2 cts on the Dollar contains the sum of $225.19

School Tax set at 61 cents on the pole and 4 cents on the
   Dollar Contain, $454.46
Town Grants and County Tax set at 61 cents on the Poll,
   and 4 cents on the Dollar Contains $454.39
Which they are to Pay to the said Treasurers Directed
   in these Warrants.

Pelham Sept 1809.   ·   JOHN RANKIN JUN) Assessors
                                                 ROBERT CROSSETT } of
                                                 DAVID CONKEY JUN.) Pelham."

EAST PARISH.

Atkins, Joseph	8 81	Hoar, John	8 84
Airs, Beunos	3 72	Hoar, Calvin	1 52
Ballard, Joshua	1 82	Jennings, Roswell	7 82
Baker, John	2 05	Knight, William	6 44
Berry, Alexander	10 67	Millen, Levi	2 32
Butler, Daniel	2 12	Millen, Jonathan	11 17
Brigham, Barnabas	8 44	Millen, William	14 27
Brigham, Liscomb	6 62	Miller, John & Rufus	9 44
Clifford, P. Daniel	1 52	Meklam, John	13 94
Crossett, James	4 62	Mills, Brigham	6 25
Conkey, Alexander	3 30	Mills, James	3 92
Conkey, James	1 70	Miller, David & William	5 53
Conkey, William	12 04	Powers, Isaac Doct	2 32
Conkey, Thomas	8 67	Richardson, Jonathan	9 14
Cooley, Obadiah	5 82	Sears, Roland	5 84
Crossett, Robert	8 72	Sloan, Samuel	7 94
Conkey, Alexander Jun.	3 30	Sloan, David & Gardener	5 42
Felton & Conkey	10 86	Staples, Elias	5 08
Felton, Nathan	4 75	Sloan, Samuel Jun.	1 52
Gray, Patrick Jun.	1 52	Sloan, Andrew	1 52
Gray, Patrick	3 75	Titus, Sylvester	5 27
Gray, Moses 2d	2 41	Taylor, Lyman	1 52
Gray, Jeremiah	1 52	Stockwell, Peter	4 12
Gray, Daniels heirs	2 00	Vaughn, Thomas	4 27
Green, John	1 52	Williams, Silas	4 12
Hunter, Wilkins	12 08	Wright, Gad	2 60
Hinds, Nehemiah	24 02	Wheeler, Edward	4 67
Hunt, Alden	1 52	Wright, Ebenezer	1 21
Hathaway, Jonathan	9 23	Wright, Gaius	2 19
Hyde, James	3 74		

WEST PARISH.

Abercrombie, Isaac	10 72	Harkness, Joel	4 62
Abercrombie, James	7 14	Houstin, Robert	6 72
Abercrombie, William	2 99	Heyden, Thomas	3 13
Andross, Stephen	4 56	Housten, David	3 29
Abby, Sabin	6 62	Hamilton, Joseph	8 14
Arnold, Samuel	10 86	Hamilton, Oliver	4 45
Do Cook Farm	1 00	Harlow, Thomas	1 36
Arnold, Ephraim	1 52	Hamilton, Isaac	1 52
Andross, Asa	2 32	Inman, William	3 29
Braley, Solomon	4 32	Johnston, Adam	7 50
Baldwin, William	1 62	Joslin, Joseph	6 67
Bryant, Ichabod	5 28	Janes, Stephen	4 37

Name	$	c
Boyington, Silas	5	44
Brown, Ezra	4	20
Brown, William	4	70
Butterworth, John	2	42
Bayington, Ebenezer	1	62
Bayington, Asa	1	25
Ballew, Stephen	1	22
Crozier, Artimus	3	91
Cook, Silas	1	90
Cook, Eseck	11	17
Do Preserved Farm	2	30
Cook, James	2	53
Cook, Adams	3	04
Clark, Samuel	4	07
Conkey, Isaac	5	22
Conkey, David 2^d	3	40
Conkey, Elisha	7	24
Cowen, James	7	09
Cowen, George Heirs	5	46
Conkey, David	4	86
Conkey, David Jun.	3	34
Conkey, John	4	85
Conkey, Isreal	4	48
Conkey, John Jun.	3	19
Conkey, Warren	1	52
Capron, Otis	1	52
Crawford, John & Levi	9	50
Curtis, Oliver	6	54
Conkey, Alexander	1	60
Carpenter, Daniel	2	12
Cowen, Willard	1	52
Conkey, Rheuben	1	52
Cowen, Josiah	1	52
Dwelley, Aaron	2	62
Dunlap, William	5	70
Dunlap, James	5	70
Dunlap, John	4	57
Danforth, Elijah	7	52
Davidson, Phineas	6	24
Dodge, Nathaniel	5	84
Draper, Lewis *	8	89
Dunbar, Josiah	1	52
Dodge, Daniel	2	52
Eaton, Marson	7	33
Do Southerbies Farm	1	10
Eaton, Walter	7	52
Edson, Seth	6	87
Failes, Sewel	3	55
Gilson, Riley	2	90
Gilson, Nathan	11	21
Gilson, Nathan Jun.	2	42
Gaskin, William	6	47
Griffin, David	1	52
Griffin, Jonathan	2	37
Grout, Joel	8	41
Gray, Ebenezer & John	15	58
Gray, John	5	82
Goold, Haffield	5	17
Greenwood, Daniel	5	00
Johnston, Silas	5	57
Kelley, Wing	8	89
do Allen Farm	1	80
King, Robert	3	82
King, Peter	8	37
Kingman, Henry	11	49
Do Washbun farm	2	00
do Ormston farm		80
Leach, Marvelous	6	17
Leach, Jonathan	5	20
Lincoln, Isaac	7	44
Miller, Samuel	1	52
McColluck, Henry	1	52
Miller, Moses	3	90
Macomber, George	5	02
May, Isaac	1	92
Newel, David Jr.	4	37
Newel, Levi	3	17
Otis, Isaac Jun.	2	32
Oliver, William	3	47
Packard, Daniel	5	07
Packard, Elijah	4	72
Packard, Thomas	2	75
Packard, Jonathan	6	64
Packard, Job	6	12
Packard, Eliab	6	17
Peso, Samuel	4	34
Packard, Jacob Jun	4	32
Peck, F Jesse	4	85
Potter, Olney Doct	9	12
Randall, Gideon	1	52
Randall, Ephriam	3	42
Rankin, John	8	97
Rankin, John Jun	5	97
Rankin, James	6	32
Reniff, Abisha	7	84
Rider, Isaac	3	91
Reniff, Morey	1	52
Smith, Oliver	6	66
Swan, Duty & Robert	3	60
Sterns, Jasper	2	92
Shaw, Asa	2	77
Smith, William	10	22
Tower, Isaac Jun	3	77
Do Shaw Farm		80
Turner, Elis	1	52
Taft, Jared	4	92
Tower, Isaac	1	52
Thurston, Paul	4	07
Thurston, Elisebeth	1	51
Thomson, James	3	00
Thomson, James Jun	4	27
Thomson, John Heirs	2	60
Thomson, Daniel	4	02
Thomson, Thomas	3	37
Terel, Noah	3	27
Taylor, John	5	24
Wheeler, Joseph	2	40
Do Baldwin farm		60

THE JEWETT FARM HOUSE.

J. R. ANDERSON'S HOUSE.

Gray, Elliot	5 72	Wood, Jonathan	7 32
Hannum, Plinne	4 34	Wood, Daniel	2 52
Harkness, John	8 12	Waiscoat, Rheuben	2 57
Harkness, David	5 02	Do Southwards farm	1 40
Hyde, Samuel	2 80	Ward John	3 52
Hyde, Andrew	3 52	Wilson William	3 02
Hannum, David	2 87	Wilson, William Jun	3 11
Hood, Jonathan	11 09	Wedge, Nahum	5 75
Hall, Lemuel	4 92	Wells, Augustin	2 27
Howard, Joseph	7 23	Williams, Henry	2 82
Harkness, Daniel	5 57		

The footings of these taxes will not equal the amounts called for in the warrant because of the non-resident taxes which are not given in the above list, but it shows the amount of every man's tax that was assessed that year.

The rate as stated in the tax bills as delivered to the collectors, was two cents on the dollar for the state tax, and four cents for the school tax and the same for town and county tax. Putting it another way, it was $20 on the $1000 for state tax, and $40 per $1000 for school and town and county. A very high rate but the valuation was low.

Fortunately we have the money value or cost of one farm that was taxed in 1809,—that of Samuel Arnold. Mr. Arnold paid $3000 for the farm in the year 1800 and probably that was a fair price for it in 1809 if worth $3000 in 1800. Eseck Cook purchased his farm in 1806 paying $3000 for it.

The price for taxation by the valuation in 1809 was exceedingly low, as appears when we separate the items that make up Arnold's total tax of $11.86. State tax, one poll, 30 cts., real estate $1.64, personal 22 cts., total tax $2.16. This sum less the poll tax is $1.86. As the tax rate is two cents on the dollar, the total of real and personal estate for purposes of taxation was only $93. But there were two rates, one of two cents on the dollar, and one of four cents on the dollar, and three separate taxes were assessed.

The school tax, four cents on the above total valuation of $93, and a poll tax of 61 cents, amounts to $4.35
The town and county tax is the same as the school tax   4.35
State tax as above   2.16
Cook farm, three separate taxes, 20, 40, 40=   1.00 $11.86

An examination of the list of taxes given for the West parish shows that the seven heaviest town tax-payers were Ebenezer and John Gray, $15.58; William Smith, $14.79; Henry Kingman, $14.29;

Samuel Arnold, $11.86; Nathan Gilson, $11.21; Eseck Cook, $11.17; Jonathan Hood, $11.09. In the East parish, comprising that part of Pelham which is now Prescott, the seven largest tax-payers were Dr. Nehemiah Hinds, $24.02; William Miller, $14.27; John Maklam, $13.94; Wilkins Hunter, $12.08; Jonathan Miller, $11.17; Felton & Conkey, $10.86; Alexander Berry, $10.67. Besides the three taxes above named, there was the parish tax for the support of the Gospel.

Meeting, May 7, 1810.

Was for choice of a representative to the General Court for the session opening on the last Wednesday of May instant. James Abercrombie received 69 votes; Isaac Abercrombie received 67 votes. The defeated candidate had served for several terms but failed of a re-election. His brother, James Abercrombie, being elected by a majority of two.

Both were sons of Rev. Robert Abercrombie, the first settled minister in the town. It was a contest that quite likely brought out a full voting strength of the town.

Meeting, Dec. 3, 1810.

The Sixth Massachusetts turnpike corporation was chartered and incorporated in 1799. The company had built a turnpike through the town and had collected tolls from the people, but had maintained the road at their own cost; for some reason, probably because the travel on the turnpike was not sufficient to make any money for the Company, they proposed to discontinue the part that ran through Pelham. This action was not pleasing to the people of the town and the warrant for the Dec. 3d meeting had the following article:

"To see what method the town will Take in Answer to Order of Notice from the Sixth Massachusetts Turnpike Corporation for Discontinueing said road through said town and pass any vote respecting the same they shall think proper."

Action of town on above article, first Major John Conkey was chosen moderator and then it was "Voted Unanimously to Remonstrate against the Discontinuance of that part of the Sixth Massachusetts Turnpike road through the town of Pelham. Voted to Choose a Committee of five to Draught a Remonstrance to send to the General Court, the selectmen to be the above Committee viz Major John

Conkey, Isaac Abercrombie, Andrew Hyde, Roland Sears and Jonathan Richardson.—Voted that Mr. James Abercrombie use his influence to oppose the Discontinuance of said road through Pelham."

Meeting, May 6, 1811.

This meeting was called to act upon to the proposition to lay out a County road from Amherst through the south part Pelham to Greenwich south line. It was a revival of the project started in 1809, the town opposing it at that time.

The article reads as follows :

" To see whether the Town will Chuse Agents to oppose a County Road being laid from Amherst to Greenwich through the south part of Pelham as the order of notice of John Williams and others shall show."

The opposition was of no avail, and the county road from Amherst to South Greenwich, now Enfield, was built in 1812.

Meeting, May 27, 1812.

"Voted, that the town of Pelham as a Town Petition the Executive that both the Militia Companys be reinstated to their former Regiments. Chose Isaac Abercrombie Esq, Capt Henry Kingman and Asa Shaw a committee to draft a petition and forward the same.

John Conkey, Moderator."

By the action of the town at the special meeting it appears that the town had two militia companies, and that for some unstated reason they had been deposed from a connection with certain regiments of militia and the action was to secure their reinstatement.

Meeting, Oct. 6, 1812.

This meeting was called to act upon the petition of Andrew Hyde and five or six other citizens of the town who lived near the west line of the town, near Amherst, who had grown tired of climbing up the hills to the first parish meeting house to attend the preaching of the Gospel on Sunday. They had petitioned before and been turned away, and more determined than ever petitioned the General Court.

The article covering the business in hand is here given :

" Article 2 For the Town to take into consideration the Petition of Andrew Hyde and others to the General Court to be set off with their Estates to the East Parish in Amherst and the Order of Notice thereon and vote and act as you shall think fit when met."

"Voted that the Selectmen of the town of Pelham be a Committee to Answer the General Court on the order of Notice sent to said Town.

Voted Not to set off Andrew Hyde and others to the town of Amherst as expressed in their petition.

JOHN RANKIN, Moderator."

MEETING, JULY 13, 1812.

The people of the town had began to fear that there would be a draft of men for the war with Great Britain which was now imminent, and the warrant expresses the desire of the people for action in advance of a draft.

"Article 3 To see what Money or Any the town will grant to the Men that are Drafted to go into the service in Case they should be called out, in addition to what is Established by law."

Acting on the above article it was " Voted to Allow Each soldier two Dollars bounty each, provided they are called into actual service; and make them up ten Dollars per month while they are in the service.

Isaac Abercrombie Esqr was chosen an Agent from the town to meet at Northampton at a County Convention the 14th of July Current. ISAAC ABERCROMBIE, Moderator."

MEETING, NOV. 7, 1814.

The main business for which this meeting was called being to raise the wages of detached soldiers. The article in the warrant was:

"To see if the town will raise the wages of the detached soldiers to twenty dollars per month."

The vote on the above article was "To raise the detached soldiers wages. Voted to give the detached soldiers five dollars per Month while in service including the want of Provisions in going to the place of destination."

MEETING, MAY 1, 1815.

Was called to act upon several important matters of interest, among them, the disposal of the common lands north of the graveyard at the West parish:

"Article 4 To see if the town will vote for the Second Parish in Pelham to be Incorporated into a town with the South part of New Salem."

They voted not to sell the common lands, but ignored the 4th article entirely or failed to record the action on that article.

The East parish people having been desirous of being incorporated into a town probably had this article placed in the warrant in order to test the sentiment of the people in the West parish, but were not gratified. They did not give it up however, for in the warrant for a

MEETING, MAY 17, 1815

the matter was brought before the town again under substantially the same article.

The meeting was called to order and Jesse F. Peck chosen moderator. The meeting was then adjourned for half an hour probably for informal consultation. Then met and voted to pass the article which had reference to the East parish being incorporated as a separate town, and chose a committee to remonstrate against it before the General Court where the East parish people proposed to go with their case. William Miller, Henry Kingman and Isaac Abercrombie were chosen a committee to oppose the East parish in the General Court.

From 1816 to 1824.

New Pelham.—Order of Notice From the General Court to Show Why the Prayer of the Second Parish Should Not be Granted, 1819,—The Town Votes Against Revising the Constitution, 1820.—The Last Act of Opposition to Setting Off the Second Parish.—The Town Rejects All of the Eleven Amendments to the Constitution, 1821.—The East Parish Succeeds in Getting Set Off From the Old Town, 1822.—Large Number Supported By the Town in 1822.—Sale of Common Lands and Proceeds Go For Repairs on the Meeting House, 1823.

MEETING, SEPT. 15, 1817.

Following the above meeting is the record of the perambulation of the town lines; beginning at a hemlock tree at the southwest corner of New Salem, going east to the east line of the town of Pelham, thence south between Pelham and Greenwich formerly Quabbin, until the southeast corner of Pelham was reached. We quote from the language of the record now: " Thence west to A stake at the N. E. corner of New Pelham, a white oak by the brook, S. W. of Abram Packards, from thence to a stone set up formerly for the S. E. corner of New Pelham which is now the corner of Enfield, Belchertown and Pelham—from thence to an oak the corner of Randalls land and Marked it P. B. a chestnut tree in the woods, another in corner of the wall, next a stake on the road S of Elijah Randalls, next a pitch pine Stake Southwest corner of New Pelham; a white oak stake the N W corner of New Pelham; thence west to a white oak tree on the road N of R Browns.—a stake on the road North of Pettengalls, a chestnut tree in the road, a chestnut tree on the top of the hill, a white oak on the line of the Hyde farm,—closed the line between Belchertown and Pelham at a stake standing W of the road and northerly from John Thayers and marked it P. B. & P. A."

They are now at the Southwest corner of the town of Pelham and we will not follow them further. Have copied that part of their record which speaks of New Pelham. This is the tract of land, being a part of Belchertown that was allowed to become a part of Pelham on petition of the inhabitants living thereon in the year 1786, and which juts out south from the south line of the town, which was a straight east and west line up to that time.

Henry Kingman was the surveyor in charge of the peramble and Levi Crawford was his assistant. The date of this record is Nov. 14, 1817.

The people living in the East parish had not outgrown their ambition to set up for themselves as a separate town. In another warrant from the one calling upon the people to elect a representative to the General Court was the following article calling for action this same 3^d of May 1819.

"2^d To see what the Town will do on the the order of notice from the General Court to show Cause, if any they have why the prayer of the petition of the inhabitants of the East parish to be set off with the south part of New Salem as a separate Town shall not be granted and act and do anything touching the same, as the Town may think proper."

"Voted Not to set off the East Parish as a Seperate town.

Voted Capt Henry Kingman, Jesse F. Peck and John Rankin jr a Committee to instruct the Representative respecting the East Parish getting off as a Seperate town.—said Committee to draw up a remonstrance against the East Parish getting off as a seperate town.

> ISAAC ABERCROMBIE, Moderator.
> ABIA SOUTHWORTH, Town Clerk."

MEETING, JUNE 7, 1819.

The irritation rendering this town meeting necessary arose from the action of the Sixth Massachusetts Turnpike Corporation as expressed in the one business article of the warrant:

"To see if the town will take Measures to Oppose the petition of the Sixth Massachusetts Turnpike which is gone forward to the legislature for throwing back upon the Town of Pelham said Turnpike road through said Town, and to act or do anything respecting the same that said Town shall think proper."

"Voted that the Selectmen of Pelham write to our Representative at the General Court to oppose an order of notice which we expect from the General Court through the instigation of the proprietors of the Sixth Turnpike Corporation."

The Turnpike Company had aroused the displeasure of the people long before by continuing to exact toll, and now proposed to throw the road back upon the town, which was accomplished.

Some concessions had probably been made to the people in the way of exemption from toll when on certain necessary business trips, and one of these is said to have been exemption from toll when going and returning from the grist mill. One toll gate was some distance west of the old meeting house, and one day the keeper refused to allow a boy to pass with a load of grain without toll, and having no money the boy was turned back. The night following this outrage, the gate disappeared, and in the morning the toll gatherer found the following poetical notice posted near where the gate had been:

> "The man who stopped the boy while going to mill,
> Will find his gate at the bottom of the hill."

The notice proved to be truthful,—as the toll man found his gate a mile or more down the hill toward Amherst.

MEETING, AUG. 21, 1820.

The warrant for this meeting was short:

"Is it expedient that Delegates should be chosen to meet in Convention for the purpose of revising or altering the Constitution of Government of this Commonwealth."

The action of the town was decidedly against revision or change, the vote standing as follows: For revision 23, against it 52.

There was a sudden change of sentiment among the people on the subject of revision or change in the Constitution, for in the face of the pronounced opposition expressed in the vote given above, the voters were called together on the third Monday of October following to choose a delegate to a constitutional convention.

Meeting, Oct. 16, 1820.

The warrant called the voters together to elect one delegate to meet delegates from other towns in convention in Boston on the third day of November next, for the purpose of revising the constitution of government of this Commonwealth.

Action of meeting: " Did then and there elect Rev. Winthrop Bailey to be their delegate for the purpose aforesaid."

Annual Meeting, April 2, 1821.

The last gasp of opposition to the East parish getting set off and incorporated as a town is shown in the two closing votes of this annual meeting :

" Voted to Instruct the Representative to oppose the East Parish getting off as a town.

Voted that the Selectmen remonstrate against their getting off as a town."

The population of Pelham by the census of 1820 was probably larger than at any other time in its history. And that portion of the town east of the west branch of Swift river being set off in 1822 the old town never increased in population sufficiently after that to come up to the numbers before the division.

According to the census of 1820 there was a population of 1278 in Pelham. Amherst has 1917, Ware but 1154, Northampton 2854, Hadley 1461.

Rejection of the Fourteen Amendments to the Constitution, Monday, April 9, 1821.

Tinkering the constitution was not in favor with the voters of Pelham as shown by the reception the fourteen amendments received at their hands when called upon to vote upon them, every one of them being rejected.

There were no more town meetings in the town until March 1822. The East parish had succeed in getting set off, and with a slice off from the south end of New Salem had been incorporated as the town of Prescott, Jan. 28, 1822. Consequently the familiar forms and faces of the voters residing east of the west branch, who had been coming to the West parish meeting house all their lives to attend town meetings, were seen no more. The records up to this time since 1738 cover the whole town, but from this date forward are separate and distinct. The number of voters will be less, the appropriations less, the number of officers less, and possibly the number of the poor fewer.

Meeting, April 1, 1822.

"Voted Lemuel Hall, Henry Kingman Esq and John Harkness a Committee to settle the demands against Pelham and Prescott.

Voted To Give the Town of Prescott the offer of supporting what that has gained a settlement within their Limmits, if not the town of Pelham will Support all the Poor and the town of Prescott pay their proportion for their support."

Meeting Adjourned to May 1, 1822.

At this adjourned meeting the business transacted was the disposition of the poor of the town for the ensuing year. The system was an objectionable one, but at the time this record was opened upon the town books it was the system adopted and practiced by many towns. Within thirty years all of the burden of the poor had come upon the town,—the pressure was great and the system adopted was for the purpose of making the burden as light as possible and not from any inhumanity or animosity felt toward the unfortunate poor. That there was so many relying upon the town for support in 1822 is something remarkable, and it is not easy to understand how there should be such an increase when in 1790 there was practically no paupers in town. We give the full record of the disposition of the poor for the year 1822. It will serve to fully illustrate the system, so that not so much space will need be devoted to this phase of town management hereafter.

May 1, 1822, Then met according to adjournment. "Voted to set up the Poor of Said town by families.

Voted That the Persons that bids off the poor shall Victual, doctor, nurse and clothe them, and return them with as good Clothing as when Received.

Voted that the sale of paupers of the town shall be confined to the town (i. e. no man from out of town would be allowed to bid.)"

There were close upon twenty-five persons supported by the town in 1822.

At the time the East parish was organized in 1786 it became necessary to organize the West part as a parish and to conduct its affairs as a separate organization, but now that the West parish comprised substantially the whole town the subject of returning to the town system of management of church affairs came up for consideration, and a parish meeting was called.

Parish Meeting, April 8, 1822.

"Voted to transfer all the parish papers into the hands of the town officers and do no more business as a Parish.

Voted to Constitute the Parish Committee to settle all demands against said Parish and then transfer all papers to the town officers.

Isaac Abercrombie, Esq., Moderator."

Town Meeting, May 1, 1822.

"Voted to raise $300 for Rev. Winthrop Baileys Salary for the year Ensuing and Voted to raise $25 for Contingencies."

Under this action the parish was abolished and the affairs of raising money for support of the Gospel and contingent expenses restored to the control of the town as of old.

Meeting, June 17, 1822.

The article under which this meeting was called was as follows :

"To see if the town will Condescend to let the Rev Mr Bailey preach in any other town or Towns such part of the time for the year ensuing as shall be agreed upon when Convened."

Recorded action upon above article : "Voted that Rev W Bailey Preach in the town of Prescott or some other town one fourth part of the time for one year from this date.

Isaac Abercrombie, Moderator."

Meeting, March 3, 1823.

"Voted to Choose a Committee to settle with the town of Prescott concerning the Paupers and divide said Paupers with said Prescott, and our Selectmen be the Committee.

Voted To adjourn this meeting till the first Monday of April at two oclock P M. Then met and voted to take off two hours of the adjournment and went on to do the business at 12 oclock at noon.

Voted to Give Martin Kingman leave to occupy eight rods of the town lands for a house.

Voted to choose three of a Committee to consult with the Town of Prescott concerning our Ecclesiastical affairs—and Isaac Abercrombie Esq, Dr Abia Southworth and Henry Kingman Esq be said Committee. Adjourned to May 5.—Met according to adjournment and Voted that the town keep a stock of Powder and Ball on hand, and the Soldiers may not Furnish themselves with powder and ball at our trainings in said town."

MEETING, MAY 28, 1823.

The town was called together to act upon the following article:

" To see if the town will assume the debt of arearages due from the Committee of the proprieters of the Meeting house for repairing the same on Conditions the town will vote to sell the Town and Common lands in said Town for that purpose, and also on conditions and in Consideration of the proprietors of the Meeting house yealding up and giving said town the right and privilege of holding Town Meetings in the same so long as said Proprietors shall Continue the same for a Meeting house."

The above warrant is in pursuance of and agreeable to the petition of John Taylor and others.

" Voted to sell the town lands and the proceeds applied to pay for repairs on the Meeting house on condition the town be allowed to hold town meetings in the Meeting house."

From 1824 to 1861.

Council Called io Dismiss Rev. Winthrop Bailey in 1825.—Great Flood of 1828 Does Damage.—Ziba Cook Elected Representative by One Majority in 1829.—Stove Used in Meeting House for the First Time in 1831.—New Town Hall Wanted in 1835. —Money Secured from the United States Treasury in 1837.— Wanted to Change the Name of the Town in 1840.—Libraries Established in 1842.—Scheme for Two Town Halls in 1842.— Old Meeting House Changed for Town Hall in 1844.—Old Meeting House Rented in 1846.—Many Candidates for Representative in 1850-51.—Voted to Surrender the Charter in 1854-56.—Enrolled Men in 1861.

In 1824 school houses were needed in the southeast and in the northwest school districts, and the assessors made out lists of non-resident property within these districts and assigned the lists to these districts. The northwest district had 1000 acres of non-resident land valued at $8000 to $10,000 for taxation to build school houses.

Meeting, Sept. 5, 1825.

This meeting was of more importance than the one just recorded. Rev. Winthrop Bailey was settled over the people of Pelham in 1815 and had been a faithful pastor for ten years but for some cause that does not appear in the record, his work among them was about to close, and the warrant for this meeting was to bring the matter before the people.

" Voted to choose three of a Committee to unite with Rev W Bailey in Calling the aforesaid Council. Made Choice of Henry Kingman Esq, Isaac Abercrombie Esq and Martin Kingman the above Committee.

Voted To raise one hundred and fifteen Dollars to reward the Rev Winthrop Bailey for services rendered to said town—up to his dismission.

Voted that the above Committee receive the Money Voted to said society by the Evangellical Missionary Society in Boston and pay the same to Mr Bailey.   Henry Kingman, Moderator."

Doubtless the council was called and the Rev. Winthrop Bailey was formally dismissed. The action of the Council was probably duly recorded upon the church books. The above is all the record of action by the town.

MEETING, AUG. 16, 1826.

"Article To see if the town will agree to find Pompons and feathers for the soldiers in lieu of the Money which has been paid in by the Conditional exempts."

"Voted that the town will furnish the Money to purchase Pompons and feathers and take money in the treasury paid in by the conditional exempts in lieu thereof.

Voted Capt Cyrus Kingman, Lt Alanson Chapin, Ensign Lemuel C Wedge a Committee to look up the Money paid in by said Conditional exempts.

Voted That Said Pompons and feathers when not in use shall be lodged with the clerk of the Company."

Adam Johnson, a liberal donor to Amherst College of funds to erect the Johnson chapel, had recently deceased and there was an unsettled claim of his estate against the town, and the town had a claim for taxes against the estate of Johnson. Oliver Smith, Jr., Ezra Brown and Reuben Westcott were chosen a committee to examine Johnson's claim against the town and the claim for taxes against the estate. They were to report at the annual meeting in March or April and at a meeting Nov. 27, 1826, it was "Voted to raise Four Hundred Dollars to pay a Claim of the Administrator on Adam Johnsons Estate against said town."

The desire to prosecute Martin Kingman as expressed by vote in the meeting of June 25, 1827, was subject for another town meeting on the 19th of November following, when the matter of choosing an agent to prosecute to final judgment came up. Isaac Abercrombie, a cool headed and able citizen was chosen Moderator, and the suit against Martin Kingman was disposed of effectually by vote as recorded.

"Voted Not to Choose an Agent to prosecute and Voted to instruct the Committee to discharge the Action now pending between the town and Martin Kingman, and they (the committee) be discharged."

The year 1828 was made memorable because of the great flood of that year which swept away bridges and caused great damage to the roads and necessitated the calling of a special meeting, Sept. 23, 1828, to raise money for the repair of the highways and bridges.

Henry Kingman was moderator. It was "Voted to raise $500 for the repair of the Highways injured by the late freshet.

Voted to raise $200 in addition to the above."

The damage to the town highways and bridges proved to be greater than estimated for at a meeting held Dec. 1, 1828, it was voted to raise $300 in addition to the $700 voted in September.

Meeting, May 4, 1829.

Was for the choice of a man to represent the town in the General Court to be convened in Boston on the last Wednesday of the current month of May.

There were three candidates in the field, and for the first time in years the vote for representative was recorded by the town clerk. The vote for Ziba Cook, 48, for Samuel Clark, Jr., 39, and for Cyrus Kingman, Esq., 8.

Lawsuits, 1829.

The town for some reason was involved in lawsuits this year. The records fail to explain just what the suits were for and we are shut up to the bare facts as stated.

At a meeting held in May, 1829, Cyrus Kingman, Esq., was chosen agent of the town to manage a suit commenced by Sally Smith against David Abercrombie.

At the same meeting Cyrus Kingman was chosen an assistant agent to help Martin Kingman to manage the suit brought against the town of Pelham by Abner Goodell.

At a meeting on the 16th of September Cyrus Kingman was chosen an agent to defend the suit brought by Ira Abercrombie against the town.

Meeting, Sept. 2, 1830.

This meeting was unimportant save in one or two particulars. It was at this meeting that the list of the poor people was increased by the addition of Mary and Rachel Johnson. It was voted that these two worthy but poor people remain in the hands of the selectmen until the first of November.

Building the wall in front of the center graveyard was struck off to Nathaniel Wheeler. The turf was to be taken off and the wall laid three and a half feet thick at the bottom and four and one-half feet high, capped with flat stones on the top, the front to be equal to Col. Cyrus Kingman's wall west of said wall. Mr. Wheeler had the job of building a gate with stone posts at the burying ground. Undoubtedly the same stone posts that stand there now. Wheeler was paid one dollar per rod for the wall and $5 for the stone posts and gate.

MEETING, APRIL 4, 1831.

"Voted to accept of a proposal made by David Goddard Jr of Petersham concerning taking and keeping the Canada Girls. The proposals is as follows viz—He is to take them at Sixty-five dollars per year from and after the Sixth day of May next and keep them free of Expense to the town so long as they all three live. Whenever one shall be taken away by Death he is to keep the others until the expiration of the year and return them free from expense to the town or Make a new bargain. He pays all funeral as well as other charges. Receives his Money for keeping them at Pelham."

The Canada or Kennedy girls were persons supported by the town.

MEETING, NOV. 14, 1831.

" Voted (Under General article) that the Subscribers for procuring a stove have a privilege of setting it up in the Meeting house providing they obtain it and support it throughout at their own expense.
                                    DANIEL THOMPSON, Town Clerk."

The history of this town meeting doubtless marks the time when the introduction of a stove into the meeting house, that since 1740 the good people of Pelham had sat in on Sundays and on many town meeting days without any fire save a few coals in the foot stoves monopolized by the women on Sundays. On town meeting days in cold weather the men were nimble in carrying adjournments for consultation to the tavern beside the great open fireplaces. The proposition to set up a stove in the meeting house was considered in the town meeting in a way to throw all the responsibility upon the "subscribers." They were granted the privilege of setting it up, but the voters did not propose to have the town made responsible for its support.

The election of representative had become an interesting feature of the annual election and in 1832 there were six candidates and the votes cast for each candidate we take from the record:

Reuben Westcott	1 Votes.
John Rankin Esq	2 "
Martin Kingman	2 "
Cyrus Kingman	5 "
David Conkey	29 "
Lewis Draper	60 "

Lewis Draper was elected by a majority of 21 votes.

Attest DAVID THOMPSON Town Clerk.

MEETING, MARCH 4, 1833.

" Voted—that whoever takes charge of the Meeting House the ensuing year shall take charge and care of the fire at all necessary and proper times, and sweep the Meeting House Every Month in the year Meeting or no Meeting.

Voted to set it up to the lowest bidder. Martin Kingman bid 2.75 and being the lowest bidder the same was struck off to him."

There were twelve town meetings in 1833 and five of them were called for no other purpose than to vote for Register of Deeds. The dates of these meetings were June 3, 1833, Aug. 29, Nov. 11, Nov. 23, Dec. 25. Giles C. Kellogg, Chauncy Clark and William Swan were the principle candidates and the meeting of Dec. 25, resulted as follows: Giles C. Kellogg, 38 votes; Chauncy Clark, 26 votes. We can conceive of no reason for so many trials for a Register of Deeds save a failure of any candidate to get a majority.

ANNUAL MEETING, MARCH 2, 1835.

"Voted to set up the Care of the Meeting House to the lowest bidder—To sweep said house when necessary—Also to make fires when occupied, and lock and unlock when used—Struck off to Jared T. Westcott at $2.00 for the year.

Voted that the Selectmen be a Committee to confer with Prescott authorities about building a bridge between the said Towns and report at April meeting.—Report was to build a bridge wide enough for two teams to pass and $250, was voted to build it.

CYRUS KINGMAN, Town Clerk."

Warrant for Business Meeting, Nov. 9, 1835.

2d " To see if the town will vote to build a town house for the accommotion of transacting town business.

3d To see if the town will vote to Accept of a Piece of land lying in the fork of roads above Learned O. Draper's for the Center of said Town and for the location of said House.

4th To Choose a Committee to Superintend the building of said house and secure a title of said land in behalf of said Corporation.

5th To see if the town will accept of the town house in Shutesbury as a pattern for said house.

6th To see if the town will Job out the building of said house to the lowest bidder therefor. With sufficient bonds, and make note of them accordingly, to be completed by first of Nov. 1836, and to the acceptance of superintending committee."

The meeting " Voted not to build a Town House." They tried again in 1836 and failed, that ended the matter.

Annual Meeting, March 6, 1837.

The choice of the school committee was effected after a singular spasm of backing and filling.

" Voted not to choose a school Committee for Examining School Teachers. Voted To reconsider the above vote.

Voted To Choose an Examining Committee of one person from each school district that may serve for nothing.

Voted To adjourn choosing an Examining Committee till the first Monday in April at one o'clock P. M.

Voted to choose a School Committee consisting of three persons to examine School teachers, make the necessary returns and go no father."

It was after all these votes in the order given, that the committee was chosen.

Meeting, May 1, 1837.

This meeting was for the purpose of considering and determining whether the town would agree to receive its proportion of the monies received and to be received by the Treasurer and Receiver General of this Commonwealth from the Secretary of the Treasury of the United States for deposit with this Commonwealth, in pursuance of an Act of Congress to regulate the deposit of the public money, approved June 23, 1836.

"Voted. That this town agrees to receive from the Treasurer and Receiver General of the Commonwealth its proportion of the Surplus Revenue of the United States, on deposit and will comply with the terms and provisions of the several acts passed by the legislature of said Commonwealth concerning the surplus Revenue.

Voted. That Martin Kingman is hereby authorized to sign a certificate of deposit for the sums of money he may receive from time to time from the Treasurer and Receiver General, thereby binding the town in its corporate capacity for the repayment to said Treasurer of the money so deposited, and any and every part thereof whenever it shall be required by said Treasurer, to be by him refunded to the Secretary of the Treasury of the United States.

Voted to pay the town debts out of the Surplus Revenue, and that the Selectmen put the remainder at interest in sums not to exceed one hundred dollars each, to be loaned to inhabitants in town, if sufficient applications are made, if not, in larger sums at the discretion of the Selectmen, they taking sufficient security for the same.

Attest RUFUS GROUT, Town Clerk.

The number of persons supported by the town had fallen from perhaps twenty-five in 1822 to five in 1838, and they partially self-supporting. This decrease was only temporary, and the number increased again within a few years.

ANNUAL MEETING, MARCH 2, 1840.

There were some people in town who believed that Lord Pelham had been honored sufficiently in the nearly one hundred years that the town had borne his name and were anxious to change the name Pelham to something else more fitting to the elevated location, and we find the following vote on the records as passed at this annual meeting: "Voted to petition to the General Court to change the present name of Pelham to Mt. Hermon."

The petition was not followed by the legislation they prayed for and Lord Pelham continued to be honored by the use of his name the same as for the almost completed century since the incorporation of the town.

MEETING, APRIL 4, 1842.

"Voted $105 for the common school libraries, it being the sum required of said town for the purpose of establishing District School

Libraries to enables the town to receive the same sum from the state, agreeable to a law passed by the legislature of 1841.

Voted George B. Pitman, Calvin D. Eaton, Ziba Cook, a committee to examine the records to see whether the Old Meeting House belongs to the town, or whether it has any interest in the same. Committee to make report at the next town meeting."

MEETING, JAN. 1, 1844.

The main business of this New Years' day meeting was to act upon the following article of the warrant:

Article 4. To see if the town will vote to sell the Old Meeting House, and if they so vote to see on what terms and conditions the Vestries of the Congregational and Methodist Churches in said town can be had and appropriated for the purpose of holding town meetings in them alternately and to take such measures for carrying the same into effect as shall be thought proper when convened. Agreeable to the petition of John Parmenter and others.

The meeting was organized with George B. Pitman as moderator, and when the fourth article was reached the only record of action is in the following words: "Voted to pass the 4th Article of the Warrant." Thus ended another attempt to change the place of holding town meetings from the Old Meeting House where they had been held for one hundred years.

MEETING, APRIL 7, 1845.

"Voted to lay a floor across the gallery of the Old Meeting House and move the stove now in the old Meeting house above and repair it suitable for a town house, meaning the upper part of the old Meeting house.

Voted to let out the repairing of the upper part of the old Meeting house to the lowest bidder; to be repaired as follows: Viz, To lay a floor, between the galleries, timbers shored up well on the underside, Glass put in the windows in the galleries and Chimney to be made from the top of the upper floor to the top of the roof. Struck off to C. D. Eaton to repair for the sum of $50, to be done first of Nov. 1845.

Voted that any person or persons who may choose may have the privilige to move the Old Meeting house back the bigness of the house, and thirty feet more, if any person or persons will move it at their own expense.

Voted to finish off the N. E. Corner of the Old Meeting house, for a hearse house by a partition up to the under side of the gallerys jointed and matched 16 feet by 12 feet—make suitable doors and hang them and wharf up so that it will be convenient to draw a hearse in and out of the door, and put a lock and key on the door.

MEETING, APRIL 6, 1846.

"Voted to accept of Asa Tomsons proposals for the rent of the lower part of the town house which is as follows. I Asa Tomson of Pelham agree to pay the town of Pelham six dollars a year for the rent of the lower part of the Old Meeting House in Pelham for a term of fifty years to myself and heirs and assigns provided I can have a privilige of making any repairs I shall think proper for converting the same into work shops or for any other purpose I shall think fit to appropriate the same. I am to have the privilige of Erecting a Chimney through the town hall area the same to intersect with a Chimney in the upper part of said house, the above rent to be paid annually so long as the town keeps the upper part in repair; and I am to have all the boards and lumber in the lower part of said house, and to have the privilige of taking off all tenantable repairs at the end of said term.

Pelham, April 6, 1846."

One cause of trouble among the people was the dissatisfaction with either the school districts or the highway districts, and sometimes there was dissatisfaction with both at the same time. Proposals for a change in highway districts or school districts appeared in the warrants for town meetings quite often and the year 1846 was notable in school district commotion.

MEETING, APRIL 23, 1849.

"Voted That the selectmen cause a room to be finished off in Southeast part of the town hall to keep the Weights Measures and Balances in, and the town books and papers."

MEETING, MAY 1, 1850.

Moderator, Chester Gaskill. "Voted, Thomas Buffum, Monroe Eaton, Olney Cook a committee to redistrict the town."

This committee attended to the duty assigned them and the record of their doings is spread upon the pages of the record book, and goes to show that there was at all times a prevailing dissatisfaction with the school districts, and a constant desire for change, but it would make monotonous reading if printed here.

MEETING, NOV. 25, 1850.

There had been one trial to elect a representative which failed, and this meeting was to give another chance. There were six good men who wanted to go. The voters were called together at "Ten of the Clock in the forenoon." The result of the voting was as follows for six candidates :

    Nehemiah W. Aldrich   80 votes.
    Israel H. Taylor   47 "
    Rufus Grout   10 "
    Chester Gaskell   10 "
    Lyman Jenks   3 "
    Alanson Chapin   1 "

The total sum assessed for the year 1850 as per assessor's report was as follows : Town grant $1550.00, overlayings $44.01, highway delinquences $55.20, total $1649.21.

MEETING, NOV. 27, 1850.

This was the third town meeting during the month and the business that called the voters together this time was set forth in article 2 of the warrant.

"Article 2. To see if the town will set off to Amherst the West Part of Pelham agreeable to the petition of John Russell and others."

The meeting was called at 2-30 o'clock of the short November afternoon and Daniel Purrington was elected Moderator. On article 2 the recorded action was decisive.

"Voted Not to set off the west part of this town to Amherst—the number of voters for setting off was eight. The number against setting off was eighty-six."

John Russell lived in the southwest corner of the town, on the farm now occupied by Hiram Ballou, and the same farm that Samuel Hyde tilled a century or so ago. He was six miles from Pelham center and attended church at Amherst. He was not satisfied with the vote and took his petition to the General Court the next year but did not succeed in getting set off.

Meeting, Nov. 10, 1851.

There was a contest for the office of representative to the General Court from Pelham this year. There were six candidates in the field, and the ballot on the first day resulted in no choice, the vote standing as follows:

David Abercrombie	72	votes.
Rufus Grout	59	"
Thomas Buffum	21	"
William Newell	5	"
Israel H. Taylor	1	"
Barney Wetherell	1	" = 159

Adjourned meeting, 10 A. M., Nov. 11, 1851. Result of the voting for representative to the General Court at Boston for the ensuing year, being the election of David Abercrombie.

A similar contest occurred in 1853 when it took two days. The first day Thomas Buffum received 55 votes; all others 55. At the next trial Mr. Buffum received 48; all others 42.

Meeting, Jan. 31, 1854.

This was a very important meeting and the warrant follows:

"2ᵈ To see if said Town is willing to give up and surrender her town Charter and become disfranchised as to all town priviliges and rights.

3ᵈ To act on the subject of having said Town divided in any legal way and manner and having the parts annexed to adjoining town, and to use any legal means to accomplish the same.

4ᵗʰ To Choose all Committee or Committees, officer or officers necessary or desirable to carry any or all of the above into effect and operation and to give them such instructions as said town may judge expedient when convened."

Action of the meeting:—"1ˢᵗ Made choice of David Abercrombie, Moderator. Voted to surrender this town's Charter according to the Warrant calling this meeting. Seventy three in favor (73). Thirty six (36) against.

Voted to Choose a Committee of three to Carry the same into effect—Minor Gold, Isaac B. Barrows, Grove W. Hannum chosen committee."

Special committees were also chosen to visit the adjoining town to forward the project in hand, and the above committee were instructed to take charge of that petition in the Legislature at Boston.

The cause of the action of the town in voting to surrender the charter cannot be explained to the satisfaction of all ; but the action of the people of the western portion of the town in seeking to have the legislature set off a good generous portion of the town to Amherst, and their persistence in this purpose led to a growing feeling that if the best portion of the town was ultimately set off, it would be better to go in at once to surrender the charter, give up the organization, and have the territory all divided up and annexed to the surrounding towns. It was while the people were thinking that there was a probability of a tract, a mile and a half or more wide, extending across the western end of the town, being annexed to Amherst by the persistent efforts of the people residing therein, that they suddenly gave in and endorsed the annihilation project by a two-thirds vote of those present and voting thereon.

The action of the people of Pelham became known to the people of Amherst and was not pleasing to them. A town meeting was called at Amherst on the 27th of February, 1854, and an expression of the majority of the voters was obtained by a yea and nay vote on the following resolution offered by Hon. Edward Dickinson :

" Resolved—as the sense of this town of Amherst, that as at present advised and in the present state of proceedings before the Legislature, on petition of the town of Pelham for leave to surrender its charter, and to be annexed to the adjoining towns, we are opposed to the surrender of its charter and to the annexation of any portion of its territory to the town of Amherst." On motion of Horace Kellogg the yeas and nays were ordered on the above resolution. Each voter's name was then called and 252 voters answered to their names as follows : In support of the resolution, 168 ; against it, 84.

It had been generally understood that Amherst would be pleased to accept of a strip of territory a mile or more wide across the west end of the town of Pelham, but the probability that Amherst would be asked to receive more than that if the charter was surrendered, caused the decision not to accept of any portion of it.

The action of Amherst as recorded caused a change of feeling among the people of Pelham as will be seen in the action of the March meeting.

At the annual meeting, March 6, 1854, there was a motion made to rescind the vote passed Jan. 31, to " Surrender the Charter " and it failed to pass, 84 voting for reconsideration and 87 against.

Instead of a two-thirds vote in favor of surrendering the charter, in a total of 109 votes at the first meeting, there was only the small majority of three against rescinding in a total of 171 votes, which was as full a vote as was possible to call out, for the excitement on the question was great and both sides were out in full force. The sentiment against the surrender of the charter and annihilation had set in, and the success of the project was doomed although not entirely abandoned. Nothing seems to have been done about it during the year 1855 but the agitation was renewed in 1856.

MEETING, MARCH 6, 1855.

John Russell and others were still pushing to be set off to Amherst and a petition from these parties was read asking the legislature to set them off to Amherst. It was then "Voted to instruct the selectmen to call a town meeting to choose an agent or agents to appear at Boston to object to the petition of John Russell, Sylvester Jewett and others being granted." This meeting was held on the 16th of March, 1855, and Calvin D. Eaton was chosen agent to go to Boston to oppose the aforesaid petition. Eaton was empowered to take one or more witnesses with him.

MEETING, JAN. 28, 1856.

This meeting was called for substantially, the same purpose as that of Jan. 31, 1854, viz., to consider the question of surrendering the charter of incorporation of the town.

"Voted to have the petition presented to the meeting and read for the information of the voters.—Miner Gold Esq read the Petition."

A motion was made to pass over the petition or article under which it had come before the meeting.

A division of the house was demanded on this motion and the petitioners and all in favor of the surrender of the charter swayed to one side of the town hall while those who opposed were arrayed on the other. The change in sentiment since the meeting of Jan. 31, 1854, was manifested when only sixteen could be counted for surrender, to seventy-three against.

"Voted not to surrender the charter."

A motion was made to set off John Russell and Sylvester Jewett to Amherst. "Voted not to set off John Russell and Sylvester Jewett."

This is believed to be the last movement to surrender the charter,

or to set off any portion of the town to Amherst or to other towns
adjoining, until 1867 when it was tried again and failed. This cause
of disagreement and contention removed, the people were more contented with their surroundings, although they had seen the gradual
decline in prosperity experienced by all hill towus. Very few of those
who were active in the proposition to surrender the charter are alive
now, and the episode is almost forgotten now that forty years have
passed since the unusual and almost unheard of action of voting to
surrender the charter occurred.

ANNUAL MEETING, APRIL 4, 1859.

The average amount of the annual appropriations for the years
just previous to the breaking out of the rebellion, and the distribution thereof can be studied by reference to the appropriations for
1859 which follow :

Voted $550 for schools, $800 for roads and bridges, to pay 12 cts.
per hour for labor on roads, $500 for support of the poor, $300 town
debts, $400 for contingent expenses, total $2550.

The appropriation for schools was divided proportionately among
the eight districts, and the prudential committee of the several districts employed teachers, purchased fuel, etc.

MEETING, MAY 24, 1860.

This meeting was called for a very singular purpose—one for
which the voters had never before been called together. Mr.
Fay of Brookfield had driven some cattle into town to graze during the summer, and the cattle were suspected of being tainted with
pleuro-pneumonia and the people were excited, fearing a spread of
the disease among the herds in town. James M. Cowan, Calvin D.
Eaton, Philander Bartlett, Dexter Thompson and Thomas Buffum
were chosen a committee to confer with committees from adjoining
towns in reference to the cattle disease and $100 was voted for use
in exterminating the pleuro-pneumonia. The infected district was
east of the highway leading from the center to Shutesbury and north
of the main highway leading from the center to Prescott. All persons were forbidden to remove any cattle from that district, and also
charged not to let them run at large, or to drive infected or exposed
cattle on the public highways.

The first recorded evidence of the existence of the civil war was in a warrant for a special meeting, Aug. 31, 1861, as follows:

Article 6. To see if the town will vote to raise money for the support of the families of Volunteers who have gone to the war or who may go, and how much.

"Voted to pass the 6th article."

Return of men liable to military duty as made out by the Assessors, Aug. 14, 1861 :—

Sylvester Jewett	Asahel Gates	Samuel B. Dodge
John Shaw	Marcus C. Grout	William B. Downing
William Myrick	Theodore Gold	Myron Buffum
Hiram Tuttle	Levi W Gold	Gilbert H. Firman
Charles O. Parmenter	William Hannum	Elon G. Firman
C. D. Gray	Lucian Hill	Albert A. Grout
George Tufts	Gilbert G. Hunt	Otis Griffin
Henry Barrows	Elbridge F. Horr	Ziza Hanks
Elisha Thornton	Russell Hildreth	Warner Hanks
A. S. Barton	Rufus P. King	Joseph Hunt
S. F. Arnold	George Knight	Joshua Nickerson
Henry Wheeler	Charles Kimball	John N. Pitman
D. N. Squares	Sanford Lovett	Stephen Rhodes
Stillman Abercrombie	Francis Latham	John Root
John B. Ward	O. S. Latham	Marcenus B. Richardson
Nelson Witt	Levi H. Moulton	Cyrenus T. Richardson
William Avery	John F. Moulton	Warren Randall
Franklin Bramble	John F. Nichols	Alonzo C. Randall
Tyler D. Aldrich	Joseph Park	John Rider
Olney Aldrich	D. F. Packard	George Shaw
Martin Aldrich	William F. Reed	E. S. Southwick
Sanford Boyden	John Shay	Timothy Twohig
Henry Conklin	C. H. Taylor	Richard Twohig
William Comstock	Philo Thompson	John Willis
Henry Cook	Lucian Winslow	Moses L. Ward
Aaron Cook	Joseph G. Ward	George Wilson
Nathan C. Canterbury	David H. Allen	Heman D. Eaton
James M. Cowan	Estus Barnes	Myrett E. Boynton
Francis Dodge	Emerson Bartlett	Harrison Horr
Seth Davis	Arctus J. Cadwell	Theodore F. Cook
Frederick R. Dane	Lemuel R. Chapin	George D. Davis
James Fales	Charles R. Cleveland	Israel Taylor
Russell W. Whipple	Lewis Dodge	
Milo W. Field	Hollis Dodge	

MEETING, NOVEMBER 1, 1861.

The question of help to families of volunteers came up under "Article 2. To see if the town will vote to raise money for the support of families of Volunteers as provided in an Act passed by the last Legislature or instruct the Selectmen or take any other action in relation thereto when convened."

TO THE CIDER MILL.

ON THE SANDY ROAD TO AMHERST MARKET.

" Voted to instruct the Selectmen to borrow as much money as is necessary to pay the families of Volunteers who have gone to War.
CALVIN D. EATON, Town Clerk."

From 1862 to 1892.

Action for Relief of Soldiers' Families, 1862.—Draft for Men in 1863. —Heavy Taxes After the War.—Number of Schools Reduced from Eight to Four in 1874.—Few Town Meetings Annually After That.—Blizzard of 1888.—Death of Sylvester Jewett, 1892.—History of the Old Meeting House.

MEETING, JULY 21, 1862.

This meeting, called while the people of the town were at work in the hayfields, shows the importance of the business they were called to act upon. The war of the rebellion was raging and volunteers had been going forth to fight for the country leaving their families behind them in needy circumstances, and the town was called together to take action as articles in the warrant prove.

" Article Second, To see if the town will vote to empower the selectmen to borrow money to pay the families of Volunteers now gone to war all sums they may be entitled, also the families of those volunteers which may go hereafter.

Article Fifth, To see what sums of money if any the town will vote to raise to pay as bounty to Volunteers.

Article Sixth, To see what means the town will take to raise this Bounty Money,—by borrowing it, or by taxation at the present time."

Acting on the second article the town " Voted to empower the Selectmen to Borrow Money to pay the families of Volunteers that have gone to the war or who may go hereafter,—a sum not exceeding Seven hundred dollars."

Acting on the fifth article the town " Voted to Authorize the Selectmen to borrow One Hundred dollars for Each Volunteer, Not exceeding ten in number, who may enlist under the Call of the Governor of Massachusetts from this town, and that the same be assessed in the next annual assessment of taxes in the town of Pelham.

Voted to take this question by Yeas and Nays and the vote was so taken, and the following voters answered Yes to their names and No as it is written against their Names."

The importance and the scope of this vote, and what it might lead to as a precedent, probably led to the decision to make the record by a yea and nay roll call. There was a little opposition to such large appropriations for the people of the town to pay, but the large majority were in earnest to put down secession and willing to contribute liberally for bounties and for the help of families of volunteers. There were few if any suspected of "secesh" opinions, and the fact that some men answered No, is not to be considered as exhibiting a lack of patriotic desire to crush the rebellion. It being the first record of a yea and nay vote the record is copied in full.

"Arnold, Samuel F	Yes	Hildreth, Russell	Yes		
Abercrombie, George	Yes	Jewett, Sylvester	Yes		
Buffum, Thomas	No	Jenks, Lyman	Yes		
Boyington, Silas	Yes	Knight, Philander	Yes		
Barrows, Henry	No	Kimball, Samuel	Yes		
Barnes, Ansel	No	Lesure, Jesse	No		
Barnes, Estus	Yes	Latham, F. A.	Yes		
Boyden, Sanford	No	Latham, O. S.	No		
Bartlett, Philander	Yes	Myrick, William L	Yes		
Bent, G. R.	Yes	Nichols, John	Yes		
Chapin, Lemuel R	Yes	Newell, Lemuel H	Yes		
Chapin, Luther	No	Rankin, Ansel A	Yes		
Clough, Warren	No	Randall, Arba	Yes		
Cook, Ziba	Yes	Presho, Zadock	Yes		
Cook, Lewis	Yes	Packard, David F	Yes		
Cook, Olney	No	Pitman, John N	Yes		
Cowan, J M	Yes	Randall, Alonzo	Yes		
Dodge, Lewis	Yes	Richardson, Marcene	No		
Dodge, Hollis	Yes	Randall, Warren	Yes		
Downing, Wm B	Yes	Shaw, George	Yes		
Davis, Samuel	Yes	Stone, Eliab	Yes		
Dowden, Wm H	Yes	Tuttle, Hiram	Yes		
Eaton, Calvin D	Yes	Thurber, William	Yes		
Fales, Abijah	Yes	Thompson, Dexter	Yes		
Firman, Albert	Yes	Thompson, Edmund	Yes		
Field, Milo	No	Thompson, George	Yes		
Gray, Horace	Yes	Tufts, George	Yes		
Gray, C. D.	Yes	Whipple, Russell jr	Yes		
Gates, Asahel	Yes	Ward, Moses L	No		
Grout, Marcus C	Yes	Ward, Hosea	No		
Gold, Miner	Yes	Ward, John	Yes		
Gold, Levi	Yes	Wilson, George H	Yes		
Hills, Lucian	No	Ward, Joseph G	Yes		
Hunt, Joseph	Yes	Ward, John B	Yes		
Hamilton, Joseph	Yes	Witt, Nelson	Yes		

Fifty seven voted in the Affirmative and Thirteen in the Negative.

CALVIN D. EATON, Town Clerk."

Meeting, Aug. 29, 1862.

This was another meeting called in the busy season of the Pelham farmers, but there had been a call for 300,000 men by President Lincoln and the business for which the meeting was called was laid before the voters in this article.

"Article 2ᵈ, To see what Measures or Means the town will take to raise her quota or proportion of the 300,000 men last Called for by the President of the United States.

Article 3ᵈ, To pass all votes necessary or judged Expedient in order to Carry out the aforesaid Means or Measures which the town when convened may see fit."

Sylvester Jewett was chosen moderator and the action of the town is shown in the following recorded vote :

"Voted that the Selectmen be hereby authorized and empowered to procure all money necessary by borrowing it for the town or drawing it from the treasury as most convenient, and pay the sum of One Hundred dollars to Each person Entitled thereto when Mustered into Service."

The vote on the above article was taken by the yeas and nays, 69 voting in the affirmative and three in the negative.

Meeting, Oct. 20, 1862.

The article that was the main feature of the warrant was :

"To See if the town will vote to pay the One Hundred dollars bounty to the five Men over our quota of nine months men that are now in Camp at Greenfield."

The response was prompt and to the point. "Voted to pay the five men now in Camp at Greenfield, over and above our quota, One Hundred dollars Each."

Meeting, April 4, 1863.

"Voted to allow the selectmen to borrow as much money as necessary to pay state aid to families."

Meeting, April, 23, 1863.

Moderator, John Jones. "Voted to Authorize the Selectmen to borrow a sum not Exceeding Eight Hundred dollars to pay the families of Volunteers and give town obligations for the same.

Voted To Instruct the Selectmen to withhold two months pay

from the families of Volunteers after the 1st of August next instead of one Month as they now do."

Meeting, June 20, 1863.

"Voted that John Jones be an Agent for the town of Pelham to go before the Commissioner and use all lawful means to get from our Soldier rolls all Soldiers that ought to be exempt, And to pay all reasonable expense he may be at."

The frequent calls for men to fill the quota of many towns in the state was greater than the number of those who would volunteer, and the authorities were obliged to issue a call for a draft in July 1863. The following is the list of men drafted at Greenfield, July 20, 1863, from Pelham.

George B. Davis
Philo Thompson
Nathaniel H. Cook
Frederic R. Dane
John N. Pitman
Albert Pratt
Hollis Dodge
Heman D. Eaton
John T. Fales
George A. Gardner
Calvin D. Gray

Solomon Slater
Gilbert H. Firman
Theodore F. Cook
Joel Cutting
James D. Mower
John S. Willis
William Squares
George H. Willson
Charles H. Jenks
Levi W. Gold

Meeting, June 1, 1864.

This meeting was called at 3 o'clock P. M. because it was in the busy season for farmers, and the important business for which the town was called together is set forth in Article 2 of the warrant:

"Article 2 To see what action the town will take in relation to procuring Substitutes for the Men that may be accepted on the present draft, and all future drafts, or to fill all future quotas without a draft, and also in relation to Compensating the men that were drafted and accepted in 1863 in this town."

"Voted to raise the sum of one hundred and twenty five dollars apiece for all persons who may volunteer and are accepted into the United States Service.

Voted to Authorize the Selectmen to borrow and pay one hundred and twenty five dollars each, for Seventeen Volunteers to fill the quota of the town of Pelham under the present, and future Calls for Men.

Voted that John Jones, David F. Packard, Cyrus A. Wade and Moses Redding be agents to procure Substitutes for all future Calls for men from this town.

Voted to Authorize the Selectmen to furnish the above agents with money sufficient to bear their expenses in recruiting."

SYLVESTER JEWETT, Moderator.
C. D. EATON, Town Clerk.

"MEETING, AUG. 16, 1865."

(This meeting was probably held in 1864.)

The record of this meeting is incomplete there being no warrant spread upon the book. The moderator is not given, nor is the fragmentary record signed by the town clerk. All of the record is copied.

"At a legal meeting warned by the Selectmen and assembled in the town hall August 16, 1864 They passed the following votes, viz.

Voted to pay $125.00 to Every man who shall be one to fill the present quota of Seven.

Voted that John Jones be an agent to obtain Men from any quarter he may think best to go, and to pay his necessary Expenses.

Voted to accept of Moses Redding's account as settled by John Jones.

Voted to dissolve this meeting."

MEETING, APRIL 3, 1865.

"Voted that the selectmen be authorized to borrow and appropriate the amount of money they can lawfully, for recruiting purposes."

MEETING, MAY 27, 1865.

The war was substantially over and no more men would be called for, and this meeting was called to take measures to equalize the burdens that had fallen upon individuals as outlined in the main article of the warrant:

"Article 2 To see if the town will appropriate Money to reimburse money contributed to furnish recruits according to an act approved April 25 1865 and if so to give instructions in regard to raising such money."

Moderator, Sylvester Jewett. "Voted to raise four thousand dollars to be divided pro rata among those who have paid money to fill the quotas of the town during the war.

Voted to adjourn this Meeting two weeks from to-day at 2 o'clock P. M."

Met according to adjournment, and passed the following vote June 10, 1865.

"Voted to reconsider the vote passed May 27, 1865 to raise four thousand dollars to be divided among those who have paid Money to fill the quotas of the town during the war."

The haste with which this liberal proposition was reconsidered is evidence that it was not given due consideration before it was first passed. The war was over now, and the large sums the town had been obliged to raise by borrowing and otherwise had made the rate of taxation high, and to pay interest and small amounts upon the debt, caused by the war expenses, kept the rate high for many years. The rate of taxation rose to $25 or more, on $1000 and hovered near $20 per 1000 for a long time.

The amount of money raised by taxation increased for a number of years after the war closed. The total amount raised by taxation for the year 1865 was $4270.79; for 1866, $4961.22; for 1867, $5321.21; for 1868, $5557.81; for 1869, $4436.92; for 1870, $5429.38; for 1871, $4874.98; for 1872, $5429.38.

To raise these sums by taxation when the valuation of the town was shrinking every year, and the population growing less each year, in common with other hill towns, caused the burden of taxation to rest heavily upon the people until the war debt was lessened by small appropriations yearly to apply upon the principal, thereby lessening the yearly interest charge until the town debt is now nearly wiped out.

Schools and School Districts.

There was much agitation and numerous town meetings during the year 1867 upon the question of schools and school districts. The first of these was held Jan. 30. There was a proposition to abolish the school districts, and it was voted to abolish them. Then they voted to set up four schools. Then committees were chosen to locate the school-houses. There was no unanimity of feeling, consequently no satisfactory conclusions were reached, and the meeting was adjourned to Feb. 13 when it was voted to have three schools. This proposition was not satisfactory to some and the meeting was adjourned to the first Monday in April, and the vote to have three schools was reconsidered. Then it was voted to support seven schools and to have them in the school-houses as at present located. This vote was not carried out because the town did not need so many schools, but the people did not seem ready to do what the more intelligent knew must be done ultimately, viz.: A reduction in the number of schools, and a relocation of the school-houses ; and meeting after meeting was held until the work was finally accomplished and the eight school districts abolished, and four schools established.

Special Meeting, Nov. 16, 1867.

For ten years there had been no agitation for setting off any portion of the town to an adjoining town, or for surrendering the charter, but the leading article in the warrant for this special meeting was to bring up the question of surrendering the charter and setting off the territory covered by the charter to the adjoining towns.

Alfred Taylor was chosen moderator of the special meeting, and there were nearly one hundred voters present on Saturday the 16th of Nov. The meeting being called at thirty minutes past twelve o'clock of the short November afternoon.

A motion was made to pass Article two and the motion was carried by a majority of two votes, 45 voting to dismiss the article and 43 against it.

A motion to reconsider the vote was made by John Jones, but the voters refused to reconsider, 46 voting to reconsider and 48 against it.

Meeting, April 6, 1868.

" Voted that the selectmen be instructed to hire a certain number of men to repair the highways and bridges in this town the ensuing year. Not to work themselves personally but to superintend the whole. And that the Superintendence shall not exceed in cost the expense of work on said highways."

The name of the man who made the motion which preceded the above vote is not on the record, but he was doubtless of a sarcastic turn of mind.

" Voted that sextons be paid for digging graves for all citizens of the town out of the treasury.

Voted to pay Freeman C. Carver four dollars for services as moderator."

Appraisal of the school houses as reported by the board of assessors, 1869: District No. 1 appraised at $325, No. 2 at $300, No. 3 at $200, No. 4 at $300, No. 5 at $300, No. 6 at $400, No. 7 at $100.

Meeting, May 22, 1869.

The people still resisted the inevitable and fought for seven schools as indicated by the following votes :

"Voted to occupy the seven school houses on their present locations.

Voted that the school committee be instructed to set up a school in district No. 1 and district No. 6 this fall and to set up seven schools next winter in the present school houses."

There was great damage by floods in Oct., 1869, and there was a special meeting to see about repairs.

Meeting, March 15, 1870.

Article 2^d To see if the town will consent to surrender its charter and divide its territory between the towns of Amherst, Prescott, Enfield and Belchertown as already petitioned for to the Legislature by the citizens of Pelham, and also to designate lines of division.

"Voted that we surrender our charter—86 in favor, 36 against.

Voted, that we draw a line straight across from the Northeast corner of Belchertown to the Northwest corner of Enfield, and merge all territory now belonging to Pelham in Belchertown or Enfield. And then starting at the center of the North line of Pelham, run parallel with the west line of said Pelham to the south line, merging all West of said line in the town of Amherst and all east of said line in the town of Prescott.

Made choice of John Jones, Ansel A. Rankin, Philander Bartlett and William B. Downing a committee to appear before the legislative committee."

Amherst refused to consider the proposition of annexation. The Legislature refused to grant the petition of the town for surrender of its charter. There has been no further effort to surrender the charter, although the town has lost much in inhabitants and in valuation since 1870.

There were eight town meetings during the year 1870 and almost the entire business was concerning schools or school-houses, and the vexed questions involved were not yet settled. The records of those meetings are interesting reading in some respects but on the whole becomes monotonous and tiresome. That the people, or some of them, should insist on having eight schools in town when there were not pupils for more than four seems strange, but it is to be accounted for by the fact that it was hard to consent to breaking up of the old system of school districts and allow the town to manage the schools with little regard to the old lines and associations. There were many meetings during three or four years, or until 1874 before the consolidation of the districts was affected.

MEETING, FEB. 8, 1871.

In the face of the failure of the petition to the Legislature for permission to surrender the charter of the town in 1870 Sylvester Jewett and Hiram Ballou petitioned the Legislature of 1871 to be set off to Amherst, and the meeting of the above date was called. Action of the meeting : Made choice of C. D. Eaton as agent for the town to oppose the petition of Messrs. Jewett and Ballou for a change of town line.

The petitioners failed in their attempt to get set off and the lines of the old town remained intact. The town would vote to surrender the charter, but would not allow one or two men to go.

The amount assessed upon the tax payers of Pelham for the year 1871 by the assessors was as follows : State tax, $625.00 ; County tax, $410.21 ; Town grant, $3700.00 ; Overlayings, $136.19 ; Delinquent, $538.00 ; Total, $5429.38.

ANNUAL MEETING, APRIL 5, 1875.

"Voted to change the time of holding the Annual meeting from the first Monday in April to the second Monday in March.

Voted to pay the Moderator two dollars for his services.

Voted that W. K. Vaille, S. Jewett and A. A. Rankin formulate by-laws for the town and report at next meeting.

A. C. KEITH, Town Clerk."

MEETING, NOV. 7, 1876.

The year 1876 is a remarkable one in the history of the town in there being only two town meetings during the year. The annual meeting in March, and the annual November election.

The consolidation of the school districts had removed a bone of contention that had caused much excitement for two or three years and the town had been called together often to wrangle over the subject. The year 1877 was like 1876 only two town meetings, the people being left to pursue the even tenor of their way, having no exciting public questions to consider in special town meetings, and so it was in 1878. There were only three meetings in 1879.

Annual Meeting, March 14, 1881.

After the election of officers, the following votes were passed:

"Voted that the Selectmen be instructed to let the town hall for dances only to select parties, who shall pay ten dollars per night for the use of the same, who shall be responsible for good order in the hall, and who shall employ a constable to preserve order, and that only temperate and orderly company shall at any time be admitted to the hall.

Voted to rent the town hall for three dollars per evening for religious dances.

Voted Sylvester Jewett $1.50 for services as Moderator.

ADAM COLE, Town Clerk."

Meeting, December 17, 1881.

This meeting was called to accept the bequest of Samuel Wright of Northampton, deceased, as explained in the warrant.

"Article 2. To see if the town will vote to accept of the bequest of the late Samuel Wright of Northampton of One Thousand Dollars the income of which is to be given annually to widows, aged and infirm persons and orphan children. All being residents of said town and not town paupers, and appoint a board of trustees to invest the same."

"Voted to accept the bequest with the conditions annexed.

Voted that the present board of Selectmen be appointed trustees.

S. JEWETT, Moderator."

The year 1886 was the fifth year in succession in which the people came together at the annual March meeting, chose their town officers, raised and appropriated the money for paying for all the town expenses, and then returned to their homes and contentedly attended to their own individual affairs until the November election of state officers, and a representative to the General Court for the district to which the town belonged. At no time except March and November were the voters called together in town meeting. Only ten town meetings in five years, hardly more than were held in a single year sometimes. This five years of restfulness from town meeting excitements was never equalled in the history of the town, and only once was there a term of years approaching this in its freedom from numerous town meetings. 1876, '77 and '78 were notable for having the number of town meetings reduced to its lowest terms, viz., two each year.

Annual Meeting, March 12, 1888.

This meeting was a notable one in the history of the town in some respects, although the work of electing officers and appropriating money proceeded without any peculiar incidents of note.

The snows of a century and a half had whirled around the old Meeting house in which the town meeting was held the twelfth of March, 1888, but the snow that day filled the air as it had never been known to do before, and the keen blasts from the north had been piling it up in drifts in every direction while the people were voting money and discussing the important questions covered by the articles in the warrant. When the meeting dissolved and the voters started out from the town hall they became aware that a blizzard was upon them such as none had ever seen before, and one that all records of great storms the town had suffered from before, came far short in comparison. The cold was intense and the fierce wind froze ears and cheek as the voters started out for their teams. Night was fast coming on and many who were detained longer than the rest found it impossible to make headway among the drifts, and the intense cold made the attempt positively dangerous. Something like twenty voters were obliged to stay over night, and the house of Town Clerk J. W. Keith was filled with the storm bound. Luckily an Amherst meat peddler was among those that the deep snow and the cold had obliged to seek the shelter afforded by Mr. Keith.

All night the storm howled and the fast falling snow piled the drifts higher, and when Tuesday morning dawned the impossibility of moving along the snow drifted roads, either on foot or by team was greatly increased, and the fury of the blizzard was still undiminished. All day Tuesday the beleagured ones were forced to remain the guests of Mr. Keith, and when the night closed down, though the storm had substantially subsided, the great drifts were impassable. On Wednesday a portion of the imprisoned voters succeeded in reaching their homes while those living farther away dared not attempt it, and not all succeeded in surmounting the drifts and getting home until Thursday.

But the meat peddler's sleigh had a pretty good stock of beef and pork, and all were well fed and made as comfortable as possible.

None of those who were obliged to quarter themselves upon Town Clerk Keith at that time will ever forget the blizzard of March 12 and 13, 1888, or the generous and hospitable manner in which Mr.

Keith entertained them during their enforced visit at his house. All reached their homes in safety however, but those who battled with the storm and the drifts that Monday night, did so after hours of hard struggle. Altogether it was probably the worst storm that was ever known in the town, certainly the only one that was given a record on the town books.

Sketch of Sylvester Jewett.

Special meeting Jan. 23, 1892 was called to elect a successor to Sylvester Jewett, Chairman of the board of Selectmen, who had died on the 10th of the month, and to fill another vacancy on the board caused by the removal from town of H. R. Davidson.

Mr. Jewett was not a native of Pelham but came to town with his family from Northampton March 1st, 1857, settled upon the Harkness farm which has the line between Amherst and Pelham for its western boundary. Mr. Jewett was an active man of 34, intelligent and competent, and at once took a deep interest in the affairs of the town. He was first elected upon the board of assessors in 1858, and from that time until his death there were but a few years that he was not an officer of the town, either as selectman, assessor, or as a member of the school committee. On the school board he was elected for three terms of three years each, and in all served eleven years. He served as assessor for thirty years, and for twenty years of the time was also on the board of selectmen, most of the time serving as chairman on both boards. For much of this time the selectmen were also the overseers of the poor, which increased the burden of responsibility upon the chairman not a little. Mr. Jewett was quite often chosen as Moderator of the annual as well as the special meetings, and in every position of responsibility he was called upon to fill, discharged the duties laid upon him with intelligence and faithfulness. Very few men have served the town with more desire for its best interests than did Mr. Jewett, and but one man has ever served for more years than he did. The office of town clerk was held from 1746 to 1781 by John Dick; but Mr. Dick did not serve the town in many other positions during that time. Mr. Dick served continuously for thirty-five years while Mr. Jewett served thirty years out of thirty-four as assessor, twenty as selectman and and eleven on the school board, making much the greatest service

SYLVESTER JEWETT.

THE OLD COMMUNION SERVICE.

THE OLD PULPIT.

the town has ever received from any one man. In politics Mr. Jewett was an anti-slavery man, and upon the formation of the republican party he gave his support to it, and labored zealously for its success and the overthrow of slavery. He was also active in religious work; being an active member and officer of the Second Congregational church at Amherst, but mingled freely with the Methodist people in religious work. In 1869 Mr. Jewett was nominated by the republicans of the Fifth Hampshire district, which included Belchertown, Granby and Pelham, for representative to the General Court. He was elected and made an honorable record for himself, the town and district, at the following session of the legislature. Sylvester Jewett was born at Northampton August 18, 1824, and was the son of Ansel Jewett, for many years a resident of Northampton, and was 67 years of age at his death.

THE OLD MEETING HOUSE IN PELHAM.
Where town meetings have been held for 154 consecutive years.

A SKETCH OF THE OLD MEETING HOUSE.
1739 TO 1897.

For the last ten years, or more, the people have moved quietly along from year to year, with little of startling interest for record upon the town books, or to any one who may have been interested in the town meeting records of earlier date, when matters of importance were pressing for consideration; consequently we have only made a record of town officers elected during these later years, which is to be found elsewhere. At the annual meeting in March, 1897 an appropration was made for repairs upon the town hall and the sum has been expended in sheathing the ceiling of the ancient building and in other needful repairs, so that now the old meeting house or town hall seems to be in condition for service to several generations yet to come; unless destroyed by fire or cyclone, as the huge yellow pine beams that were originally for the support of the galleries on one side and the two ends of the building, seem sound and strong enough to support the floor of the upper room now used as a town hall. In April 1845 it was "Voted to lay a floor across the gallery and move the stove now in the old meeting house above and repair it suitable for a town house, meaning the upper part of the old meeting house." Since that time the upper portion of the building has been used for town purposes and the lower part for storage, except a small room on the lower floor in the southwest corner used for the library, selectmen's room, and a vault for the town records, built in 1890. The repairs referred to above have added much to the appearance of the room, and to the comfort of the people who assemble for town meetings, and social gatherings.

The first record in relation to a meeting house was the vote at Capt. Daniel Heywoods house in Worcester, where the proprietors held a meeting Feb. 26, 1738–9, instructing the committee, which reads as follows:—"That then they do in the Center of the whole Tract as near as they in their Judgments Shall think proper lay out Ten Acres for a Meeting House Place, burying place and Training field &c." At the first meeting of the proprietors on the newly purchased tract Aug. 6, 1740, at the house of John Fergerson, it was "Voted that the Meeting House be 46 feet in leangth and 36 in weadth." At the same meeting £120 in part for a meeting house was voted. Immediately following this vote is another appropriation of £120, which some think was a second sum of £120 voted for the meeting house, but it is more probable that William Gray, proprietors' clerk, made two records of the same vote, although one is numbered "Fourthly" and the other "Fifthly".

May 19, 1741 it was "Voted that there be £120 collected for the second payment on the Meeting house." Sept 1, 1741 " Voted that there be £100 assessed for the last payment of the agreement for the Meeting House." The first meeting of the inhabitants of Pelham warned to be held in the Meeting House, was held April 19, 1743 for the choice of town officers under the act of incorporation.

That meetings for worship were held in the unfinished meeting house for sometime before April 19, 1743 is quite probable, for it was " Voted Aug 5th 1740 that James McCoulough, James Thornton and Samuel Gray be a Comeety to agree with a workman to rease a Meeting House and inClose it and lay the under floor and hinge the doors and mack the windo frames. " It would seem improbable that the meeting house was not sufficiently advanced so that meetings for worship or for gatherings of the proprietors on business could be held before April 1743. Those Scotch Presbyterians were not the men to allow the work on the meeting house to drag along two or three years before it was far enough advanced for holding meetings, but it might have been sometime before it was finished with gallery, pulpit and pews.

The acceptance of the act of incorporation and the choice of town officers did not end the business of the original proprietors, for they continued to hold meetings for sometime after that. The first proprietors meeting called at the meeting house was that of May 16, 1743, nearly a month after the first town meeting, and proprietors meetings were held there until April 8, 1746. About that time there was some unpleasantness between a portion of the proprietors and the town authorities and in consequence no more proprietors' meetings were called at the meeting house.

Religious meetings probably began to be held in the meeting house as soon as the " under floor " was laid and the " doors hinged " in the summer of 1740, although the final settlement with Thomas and John Dick, the builders, was not recorded until July 24, 1744, when it was " Voted that Thomas and John Dick be allowed the sum of £30 according to the old tenor in case they Delivered up their bounds which they Received from the Commetty that agreed with them to build the Meeting House."

There are no pews, or remains of the old square box pews on the ground floor of the ancient building but at the west end of the upper or town hall room, the stout yellow pine frame-work of the gallery seats are still intact. The pulpit was on the north side of the building and high enough to command a view of the gallery seats as well as of the pews beneath. A picture of that portion of the pulpit in which the minister stood and which was reached by a winding flight of stairs, accompanies this sketch. Above the preacher's head hung the " sounding board," which was deemed an absolutely necessary equipment in the days so long past.

In summer, on Sundays, and on lecture days, when no fires were needed, and during the long cold winters when none could be had, these Scotch Presbyterian men and women gathered at the meeting-house and listened to two long sermons, or a long lecture preparatory to the Communion table, and received from the hands of the pastor or elder the lead token that would admit the possessor to that ordinance ;—this they continued to do for many years, for not until 1831 was there any arrangement for warming the meeting house. Nov. 14th of that year it was " Voted that the subscribers for procuring a stove have a privilege of setting it up in the meeting house providing they obtain it and support it throughout at their own expense."

In 1839 the corner stone of a new church building was laid by Rev. Nathan Perkins of Amherst, and after nearly a full century of occupancy for religious worship the old meeting house was moved back into the old burying-ground. The town meetings had always been held in the meeting house up to that time, and are still held therein, making 154 years that all the important and unimportant matters of town business have been discussed and decided within its historic walls at town meetings, averaging eight to ten per year, since 1743. Here they met and consulted with each other and took action during the French and Indian war, the war of the Revolution, the war of 1812, the Shays Rebellion, and the war of the Rebellion. Altogether the old meeting house has been a very useful building, and about it gathers more of historic interest than attaches to any other similar structure in this part of the state.

May ye 19th, 1760 &c

Poul: — 1
hous: — 1
oxen — 2
cows — 6
swine — 1
sheep — 17
one house & — 2 rums
orched — 2 ackers
Scider — 13 barrals
Mowing land — 15 ackers
Tillege — 9 ackers
Corn — 30 bushall
Rye — 20 bushall
oats — 30 bushalls
hay: 12 town — —
peaster — 2 acker
William Gillmors
invouice

FACSIMILE OF WILLIAM GILMORE'S INVOICE.
See Page 104.

Prov'ce of Massachusett Bay

Whereas the Gen'll Court or Assembly of P. Prov'ce by their Order of the first of Aprill Curr't have Authorised and Impowered me the Subscriber hereof (upon due Notice or Publication given) to Assemble the Inhabitants of the Town of Pelham in the County of Hampshire to Choose all Town Officers who shall serve till the Anniversary Meeting in March next

Pursuant thereto these are therefore to Warn and Notifie the Freeholders and other Inhabitants of P. Town qualified by Law to Vote in Town affairs that they Assemble themselves at the Meeting House in P. Pelham on Tuesday the Nineteenth Day of Aprill Curr't, at nine of the Clock in the forenoon for the Choosing Town Officers for P. Town as afores'd,

Dated at Pelham the ninth day of Aprill in the sixteenth year of His Maj'ty Reign Annoq' Dom'i 1743.

Robert Peebels

A Copy

FACSIMILE OF FIRST TOWN MEETING WARRANT.
See Page 76.

RESIDENCE OF MRS. ANNETTE MORGAN.

THE "CITY" SCHOOL HOUSE.

SCHOOLS.
From 1744 to 1897.

Establishment of Schools in 1744.—School Committees.—Appropriations.

ESTABLISHMENT OF SCHOOLS IN PELHAM.

Notwithstanding all the great labour and expense attendant upon the purchase and settlement of this tract of land,—the clearing away and building of roads and bridges,—the clearing away of the forest, and the building of their log houses,—the breaking up of portions of their home lots for cultivation to raise crops for the sustenance of themselves and families,—the work of building the meeting house, besides the many other necessary matters demanding attention to make their homes and families comfortable;—yet it was but little more than a year after the act of incorporation, and organization under it, before they began to feel the importance of a school, and the necessary action on the part of the town, took place on the 26th of April, 1744. Samuel Gray was Moderator of the meeting, and the recorded vote is as follows.

" Voted that there be a scole Keept in town for ye Space of two Months, at ye Dwelling House of Ephriam Cowan, one Month, one Month at ye Dwelling house William Grays. "

Ephraim Cowan lived on home lot No. 42 and was probably the same farm known as the Collins Brailey place fifty years ago, and now owned by Stephen Rhodes.

William Gray lived on home lot No. 11 about a mile Northeast of the old meeting house, at the center of the town.

No appropriation or allowance was made for the cost of the school; nor was there any school committee chosen to employ school masters, —for it must be assumed that school masters were employed, as very few if any women were capable of filling the position of teacher at that early day. Nor is it probable that girls attended school when schools were first established. Sewing, knitting, spinning and weaving and the ordinary duties of housekeeping, was considered enough for women to know, and the girls acquired all that at home.

Meeting May 14, 1745.

It was " Voted that there be a scole Keept in town this Present year.—ye time for Keeping s^d scole is in ye Months of August and September and ye Place is at ye Meeting house in s^d Pelham. " No allowance of money was made to meet the expense,—and no bills were brought in to the debit and credit meeting for settlement for this year;—after that, fixed appropriations were voted for schools, and school committees came into use to hire school masters, etc., but school committees were not elected regularly at each annual meeting until about 1786.

1746. " It was Voted that there be Thirty Six Pounds Raised to Pay a Scole Master for Keeping Scole. "

" Voted y^t there be a Scole in ye town ye Six Months Insuing or as soon as Convency Will allow.

Voted that ye scole be Keept two Months at ye Meetinghouse & two Months at Ephriam Cowans & two Months at Alexander Conkeys. Voted that John Conkey, Thomas Dick & John Gray be a Committee to Provide a Scole Master for ye town for ye Six Months. "

Meeting March 11 1747.

It was " Voted that there be Scole in town Six Months, to begin at the first Day of June Nixt & to continue Six Months following,—Voted also that ye Scole is to go no further than ye Nole Betwixt James Taylors & Alexander Conkey's and two Months at ye Meeting House and to go no further than the Bridge at Ephriam Cowans —Voted that ye Scole Money be Assessed with the Debt & Credit Money. "

In 1748 it was " Voted that there be a Scole Six Months to begin the first of June Nixt and that the Scole be Keept as it was last year."

In 1749 it was " Voted that there be £140 old tenor for a Scole this present year to be Keept one third of ye Time at John Savige's and one third of ye Time at Samuel Taylor's and one third of ye time at ye Meeting House,—Said Scole is to be Keept, Month about at each Plase & said Scole is to Begin att ye Meetinghouse.

April 10, 1750. " Six Pounds thirteen Shillings and four Pence Lawful Money is Voted for Support of Scole for this Present year. "

In 1751. " £6-13-4^d was allowed for Scole this Present year and Patrick Peebles and John Savige and John Hunter be a Committee to provide Scole. "

In 1752. £8— was allowed for support of Scole and it was " Voted that there be a Committee chosen to provide a Scole Master, said Committee is John Stinson, Robert Lotheridge & Andrew Maklam. "

1753. " £5—6—8 allowed for Scole this year. "

1754. " £8—0—0 allowed for Schole the Present Year. "

" Voted that the town be divided in regard to the Scole—Voted Negatively that there be no Committee. "

April 24, 1755. " Voted that the Scole Be Keept at the Meeting House & the East Hill & the West End Each place to have thare Propor Sheable Share—Also Voted that there be a Schole House Built at the Meeting House.—Likewise Voted that thare Be a Scole House Built at the West End—Also Voted that there Be a Scole House Built at the East Hill. "

March 24, 1756. "Voted that there is £40 allowed for the support of a Scole for the Present Year—Voted that the town is to be Divided Into five parts—Also voted that thare be a Committee Chosen to Divide said town as relating to ye Scole—Said Committee is James Berry, Thomas Hamilton, George Petteson, Thomas Johnson & Alexander Turner. "

1757. " £13—6^s—8^d Voted for Schools the Present year and that James Berry, John Clark, David Cowden, John Blair & Thomas Johnson be a Committee to provide a School Master. "

1758. " The Allowance for Schools was £13—6^s 8^d. There was no action in relation to school houses or other school matter. "

1759.—" £40 was Voted in lawful money to be Raised to Defray charges already arisen, " but nothing said about how much of it was for schools.

1760. David Houston, Patrick McMullen, Thomas Hamilton. William Harkness and James Furgerson were chosen a committee to " Place the Scole Houses said Scole Houses to be Laid as other Reats. "

The School houses were placed in such Quarter of the town, and " Each Pole is allowed 3 Shillings pr Day at Building the Scole Houses "

1761. £18 was allowed for the support of School this Present year and " Voted that the Scole is to be continued the whole year. Voted that Each Quarter Build their own Scole Houses, and later, men were chosen to have charge of money appropriated for Schole houses in the several quarters of the town.

1762, £13—6ˢ—8ᵈ. 1763, £13—6ˢ—8. 1764, £13—6ˢ—8. 1765, £20. 1766, £20. £30 allowed for the support of Schools from 1767 to 1770.

In 1770 it was "voted that there is Alterations to be Made in the School Quarters and that the Under named Persons are set off by themselves as a School Quarter, To Wite—William Conkey, Alexander Conkey, James Taylor, James Pebels, Eliza Davenport, James Gilmore, John Anderson, John McCraken, John McCartney, James Hunter, James McCartney, John Hunter & William Hunter."

"Voted that the School Houses is to be Built & Repaired in Each Quarter of the town—Voted that there is £100 allowed for Building School Houses in Each Quarter of the town—Likewise that Said Money be Divided to Each Quarter as the School Rate is Devided."

The allowance for Schools ranged from £25 to £30 per year from 1771 to 1778.

1779. £100.

March 22, 1780. Because of the almost worthless character of the Continental Currency, it was voted to allow £1000 for Schools.

1781. The sum allowed for Schools this year was £1500. The people were under the crushing burdens of the struggle for liberty, but they did not neglect to vote a liberal allowance for the support of the schools.

1782. April 11, £30 was appropriated for schools.

1783, £40. 1784, £40. 1785, £40. For many of the years after schools were established, all that the records show about them is the amount allowed or voted for their support. Up to this time School Committees had been chosen but a few years.

1786. There was a return to the plan of electing a school committee for the better management of the schools this year, and Dr. Robert Cutler, Ebenezer Liskam, John Crawford, Timothy Packard, Deacon Mathew Gray and Jonathan Hood were chosen to that important service. £50 was allowed.

1787. School Committee—Ebenezer Liskam, James McMullen, James Taylor, John Crawford, Caleb Keith and Jonathan Hood.

At a meeting April 7th of this year it was "Voted Not to Devid the School Quarter where Dea. John Crawford is School Committee Man." £50 allowed.

1788. No record of School Committee this year. £50 allowed for schools.

1789. £50. No School Committee elected—In the Warrant for a town meeting May 4th of this year was this article :

" To see if the Town will come into some Method that Each School Rick Shall Build and Maintain their own School Houses—also to see if the Town will set off a School Rick in the South Part of the Town. Seth Edson, Caleb Keith and Stephen Pettingill were voted into the new Edition taken from Belchertown."

1790. School Commitee —James C. McMillen, Samuel Finton, David Conkey, Joseph Thompson, Lt. Henry McColloch, Lt John Rinkin, Jonathan Hood and John Straton.

At a Meeting Jan. 14, 1790 it was " Voted that the whole of the School Money belonging to the South Quarter should be divided into three parts—The one half to be for the Benefit of the Middle Quarter and the other half to be equally divided in the other two extreme parts—one by Mr. Seth Edsons and the other by the County road by Mr. Thomas Dick's." £60 allowed.

1791. Alexander Berry, James C. McMillin, Joseph Thompson David Conkey, Lt. Henry McColloch, John Straton, Jonathan Hood, John Barber. £60 for schools.

1792. Jonathan Hood, John Barber, Robert Houston, Joseph Thompson, David Conkey, James C. McMillin, Alexander Berry, John White. £60 allowed for schools.

1793. " Voted to Establish a school quarter out of the quarter south of the Meeting House and the quarter Dea. Crawford belongs to, with the center at the Meeting House. " Committee : James C. McMillan, Alexander Berry, David Conkey, Robert Houston, Joseph Thompson, John White, John Barber, Jonathan Hood. £60 for schools.

1794. Alexander Berry, James C. McMillin, William Conkey, John Peebles, Robert Houston, John Wright, Jonathan Hood, John Barber. £60 for schools.

1795. Alexander Berry, James C. McMillin, William Conkey, Thomas Thurston, David Harkness, Jonathan Thayer, Lt. John Rinken, John Peebles. £80 for schools.

" At a legal meeting of the Inhabitance of the South School Quarter on the Second of June 1795 it was Voted to Divide the School Quarter.

Voted to Make the Divition by the farms of Messrs Elisha Searl, Thomas Montgomery, Samuel Cheever, William Dunlap,—the aforementioned Farms to belong to the Middle or New School Quarter.

Voted for the School Committee to request the Town to establish the above Division."

By the above record the power of the School quarters, School Ricks, or school districts to change their boundries is plainly indicated ; in this instance at least there was a meeting of the people of the school quarter—a new line was established, and the School Committee requested to go forward and have the new lines established by the town."

1796. School Committee—Alexander Berry, Archibald McMillan William Conkey, John Peebles, Samuel White, Nathaniel Sampson, Daniel Harkness. £100 allowed.

1797. School Committee—Alexander Berry, David Wait, William Conkey, Eliot Gray, Capt. Isaac Abercrombie, Robert Houston, Eliab Packard, Dea. Nathaniel Sampson, Daniel Harkness. £100 allowed.

The following important votes in reference to building and repairing school houses were passed May 1, 1797. "Voted to raise a sum of Money to Build and Repair School Houses—Voted to Raise four Hundred Pounds to Build and repair school Houses."

"Voted to Choose a trustee in Each School Quarter in s^d Town s^d trustees is Robert Houston, David Conkey, Lt. John Rinkin, Capt. Isaac Abercrombie, Dea. Nathaniel Sampson, Alexander Berry, Joseph Hamilton, David Wait and Isaac Tower.

Voted that the Assessors Shall Commit District Lists of the Assesment of every School Rick to their Trustee Chosen for that Purpose whose Duty it shall be to Receive all or any Part of the tax and pay out for Labor and Material to Build s^d School Houses the Receipt of s^d Trustees is to Answer in Payment of the aforesaid tax.

Voted that in case any or a number of School Ricks shall not need the whole or any Part of the aforesaid tax to Build and Repair School Houses then it shall be the Duty of the Trustee by the Direction of a Majority of the School Ricks Notified for that purpose to apply to the assessors for a remit to pay the whole or such part of their taxes as is not needful for the purpose aforesaid.

Voted that the Assessors shall Commit the Assesment of the sum of money voted to Build or Repair School Houses to the selectmen soon as may be after the assesment.

THE VALLEY SCHOOL HOUSE.

THE VALLEY BRIDGE.

Voted that the Trustees shall make a return of each mans name belonging to their Rick.

Voted that the Trustees shall make a Return to the Selectmen of their doings sometime before the next Annual Meeting. "

1798. School Committee—Alexander Berry, Bobert Crosett, George Cowan, William Conkey, Benjamin Jewett, Jonathan Packard, James Rinkin, John Harkness, Ezra Shaw. £100 for schools.

At a meeting " May 1 1798 Dea. Nathaniel Sampson, Andrew Bannister and David Conkey were appointed a Committee to fix on a place where the School House shall stand in Dea. Ebenezer Grays School quarter. " But when the Committee brought in a report at an Adjourned meeting it was voted not to accept the report of the Committee and the Meeting was dissolved.

1799. School Committee.—Henry McColloch, Eliab Packard Jr, James Rinkin, Lt. John Harkness, James Cowan, Capt. Isaac Abercrombie. $350 appropriated.

1800. School Committee.—Moses Gray s^d, Robert Crosett, Thomas Conkey, William Conkey, James S. Park, Lt. Henry McCollock, Samuel Peso, Capt. John Harkness, John Barber. $450.

Having given what may be of interest concerning the schools from 1744 to 1800, only the school committees, and appropriations will follow to 1897.

The schools of the town from 1800 to 1850 were well attended, 60 to 70 pupils being often in attendance in a single school, and the boys and girls were kept in school during the winter term until 18 to 20 years of age and under competent male teachers. From 1825 to 1850 it was not uncommon to have a term of school during the autumn for the more advanced pupils, which was termed a " select school, " and these terms of school were often held at the center school house or old meeting house, under various teachers, Miner Gold was often at the head of these extra schools. After Prescott was set off in 1822 there were six flourishing schools and from 1850 there was an increase to eight schools, but with the number of pupils growing less until the schools were reduced to four, about 1874. The number of pupils of school age now (1897) is only 80.

1801. Joseph Little, William Miller, John Taylor, Levi Crawford, Joel Grout, James King, Ezra Shaw, John Barber, Dea. Nathl Sampson. $300.

1802. Capt. Jeremiah Miller, John Miller, John Taylor, Abisha

Reeniff, Harris Hach, Jonathan Packard, Paul Thurston, Dea. Sampson, John Barber. $400.

1803. Moses Gray 2^d, John Miller, James Abercrombie, Nahum Wedge, Joel Grout, James Washburn, Nathaniel Doge, John Barber, Nathaniel Sampson. $500.

1804. Bunis Ayres, John Baker, Alexander Conkey 2^d, Nahum Wage, Esquire Abercrombie, Isaac Tower, John Barber, Seth Edson, Jun, Nathaniel Sampson. $400.

1805. Capt. Gray, William Mellin, Elisha Conkey, Esq. Abercrombie, Jacob Packard, Jun., Paul Thurston, Dea. Sampson, John Barber. $450.

1806. Olney Potter, John Barber, Abiah Southworth, Jonathan Packard, Abial Lumbard, William Oliver, James Thompson, Jun., Lyscom Brigham, Nathan Felton. $450.

1807. Paul Thurston, Thomas Hayden, Marson Eaton, John Barber, William Smith, Wing Kelley, Capt. Moses Gray, Obadiah Cooley, Maj. John Conkey. $450.

1808. Thomas Vaughn, John Baker, Eliot Gray, Silas Williams, Asa Shaw, Oliver Curtis, Lt. David Hannum, John Barber, Jonathan Packard. $450.

1809. John Baker, Sylvester Titus, Alexander Conkey, Jun., Henry Kingman, Marson Eaton, Paul Thurston, John Rankin, Jun., Lemuel Hall, Eliot Gray. $450.

1810. Capt. Moses Gray, William Miller, Israel Conkey, Thomas Conkey, Levi Taft, Seth Edson, Jun., Samuel Peso, Lemuel Hall, John Rankin, Jun. $450.

1811. Isaac Powers, Peter Stockwell, Levi Crawford, Abiah Southworth, Henry Kingman, Samuel Peso, Lemuel Hall, John Gray, John Taylor. $500.

1812. Peter Stockwell, Constant Ruggles, Esq., Capt. John Taylor, Silas Boynton, Reuben Westcott, Seth Edson, Jun., Haffield Gould, Jesse F. Peck, Ephriam Randall. $500.

1813. Roswell Jennings, Jonathan Miller, David Conkey, Jun., Nahum Wedge, Daniel Packard, Jonathan Packard, Asa Shaw, Haffield Gould, Pliny Hannum, Paul Thurston. $500.

1814. Jonathan Richardson, James Hyde, Alexander Conkey, Oliver Hamilton, Daniel Packard, Jonathan Packard, Samuel Peso, Pliny Hannum, Silas Johnson. $500.

1815. Peter Stockwell, Barna Brigham, John Taylor, Isaac

Abercrombie, Henry Kingman, Paul Thurston, John Gray 2^d, Oliver Smith, Oliver Hamilton. $500.

1816. Alexander Conkey, Luther Chapin, Obadiah Cooley, Reuben Westcott, Moses Gray 2^d, Jonathan Packard, Elijah Randall, Olney Potter, Lewis Draper. $500.

1817. Ithamar Conkey, Joseph Pierce, Jr., Wm. Harkness. $500.
1818. Ithamar Conkey, Chester Gray and the Minister. $600.
1819. Rev. W. Bailey, Albigence King, Stacy Lindsay. $600.
1820. Rev. Winthrop Bailey, Stacy Lindsay, Isaac Briggs. $500.
1821. Rev. Winthrop Bailey, Jesse F. Peck, Stacy Lindsay, Dr. Albigence King, Josiah Pierce. $500.
1822. Dr. A. King, Isaac Briggs, Rev. Winthrop Bailey. $350.
1823. Rev. W. Bailey, Henry Kingman, John Rankin. $300.
1824. Rev. W. Bailey, Cyrus Kingman, Wells Southworth, Martin Kingman, Rufus Grout. $350.
1825. Rev. W. Bailey, Dr. A. King, Cyrus Kingman, Daniel Thompson, Rufus Grout. $350.
1826. Dr. Daniel Thompson, Rufus Grout, Wells Southworth, Alanson Chapin, Martin Kingman. $350.
1827. Rufus Grout, Isaac Briggs, Oliver Bryant, Miner Gold, Grove Hannum. $350.
1828. Miner Gold, John Parmenter, Rufus Grout. $350.
1829. Isaac Briggs, Dr. Daniel Thompson, Alanson Chapin. $350.
1830. Cummings Fish, Martin Kingman, John Parmenter. $350.
1831. Rev. Isaac Stoddard, Dr. Daniel Thompson, C. Fish. $350.
1832. Dr. D. Thompson, Cummings Fish, Ansel A. Rankin. $350.
1833. Miner Gold, Thomas Hayden Jr., Cheney Abbott. $350.
1834. Dr. Daniel Thompson, Cheney Abbott, C. Fish. $350.
1835. Rev. Luther Pierce, Dr. D. Thompson, C. Fish. $350.
1836. Rev. Luther Pierce, Dr. D. Thompson, Miner Gold. $350.
1837. George B. Pitman, Ammon Cook, Simon Cook. $350.
1838. Miner Gold, Cummings Fish, Alfred Taylor. $400.
1839. Dr. Nath'l Ingraham, C. D. Eaton, Isaac L. Brown. $400.
1840. Calvin D. Eaton, John Carter, Wm. C. Rankin. $400.
1841. Calvin D. Eaton, Chester Gaskell, Wm. C. Rankin. $400.
1842. Calvin D. Eaton, Chester Gaskell, John B. Hall. $400.
1843. Same as 1842. $400.
1844. Chester Gaskell, John B. Hall, Monroe Eaton. $400.
1845. John B. Hall, Monroe Eaton, Wm. Barrows. $400.

1846. William Barrows, Cheney Abbott, I. H. Taylor. $400.

1847. George B. Pitman, C. D. Eaton, David Abercrombie, James M. Cook, Lewis B. Fish. $400.

1848. Rev. A. C. Page, Rev. I. B. Bigelow, Abel Fletcher. $400.

1849. Rev. A. C. Page, Miner Gold, Chester Gaskell. $400.

1850. Chester Gaskell, Monroe Eaton. $400.

1851. Chester Gaskell, C. D. Eaton, Warren C. Wedge. $400.

1852. C. D. Eaton, Monroe Eaton, A. A. Rankin. $400.

1853. A. G. Craig, Philo D. Winter, Monroe Eaton. $500.

1854. A. A. Rankin, P. D. Winter, W. C. Wedge, C. D. Eaton, Miner Gold, Rufus Grout, Horace Gray. $400.

1855. Milo W. Field, Charles P. Aldrich, James M. Cook. $500.

1856. John Jones, P. D. Winter, A. A. Rankin. $500.

1857. John Jones, C. D. Eaton, A. A. Rankin. $700.

1858. John Jones, three years; A. A. Rankin, two years; C. D. Eaton, one year. $500.

1859. Rufus Grout for three years. $550.

1860. Miner Gold for three years. $550.

1861. Ansel A. Rankin. $500.

1862. William H. Dowden. $550.

1863. John Jones. $500.

1864. Ansel A. Rankin. $700.

1865. Sylvester Jewett. $600.

1866. John F. Dyer, S. Jewett, Robert Miller. $800.

1867. Ansel A. Rankin. $1000.

1868. Sylvester Jewett. $1050.

1869. C. H. Hobby. $1000.

1870. Mrs. Moses L. Ward, Mrs. H. B. Brewer for three years; C. D. Eaton, John Jones for two years; James Hanks, David Shores for one year. $1000.

1871. Miner Gold, Mrs. H. Brewer. $1000.

1872. S. Jewett, James Hanks, J. T. Hughes for three years; Jason Washburn, J. L. Brainard for two years. $1000.

1873. $1000.

1874. $1000.

1875. Jason Washburn for three years, W. K. Vaille for two years, Austin Rankin for one year. $900.

1876. John Jones. $700.

1877. Dr. Herman Heed for three years, Asahel Gates for one year. $700.

1878. Asahel Gates for three years. $700.
1879. John Jones for three years. $650.
1880. John F. Dyer for three years. $650.
1881. Timothy Sabin for three years. $600.
1882. Alfred Tuttle for three years. $600.
1883. S. Jewett, J. Jones for three years, J. L. Brainard for two years, Moses L. Ward, Wm. P. Montgomery for one year. $600.
1884. James Hanks, Asahel Gates for three years. $600.
1885. Charles B. Shores, Charles L. Ward for three years. $700.
1886. S. Jewett, Alfred Tuttle for three years. $700.
1887. M. E. Boynton, Dwight Presho for three years. $700.
1888. J. R. Anderson, H. R. Davidson for three years. $700.
1889. J. W. Knight, C. E. Humphrey for three years. $500.
1890. Myrett E. Boynton, Dwight Presho for three years. $500 and dog fund.
1891. John L. Brewer, Louise M. Brewer for three years.
1892. Mrs. J. L. Haskins, E. M. Harris for three years. $600.
1893. C. E. Humphrey, J. W. Knight for three years. $700.
1894. J. R. Anderson, H. S. Allen for three years. $400 and dog fund.
1895. Miss Louise M. Brewer, John L. Brewer, for three years. $400 and dog fund.
1896. C. E. Humphrey, Charles L. Ward, for three years. $600 and dog fund.
1897. J. R. Anderson, Henry S. Allen. $500 and dog fund.

MILLS, MANUFACTURIES, Etc.

Lands for Mills, 1739.—Corn Mill, 1755.—Stinson's Sawmill, 1760.— Hamilton's Sawmill, 1785.—Barlow's Sawmill, 1787.—Town Takes Action, 1791.—Mills Built on Home Lot 56, 1803-4.— Many Owners of Mills in the Hollow.—Stephen Fairbank's Carding Machine, 1815.—Shoe Peg Business on Pergy Brook.— Land for Mill at West Pelham, 1739.—Scythe Shop and Foundry.—Carding Machine, 1808.—Jillson's Mills, 1820.—Various Owners of Mills.—Fishing Rod Business, 1858.—Montague City Rod Co.—Brown's Turning Shop.—Charcoal.—Stone Quarries.—Miscellaneous Manufacturing. — Innkeepers and Retailers.—Merchants.—Justices of the Peace.—Physicians.— Blacksmiths.

The proprietors of the new town early made provisions for building mills for grinding their grain and for sawing lumber, but just the earliest date that a mill was put in operation no record has yet been found. In the description of Home Lot No. 56, provision was made for building a mill.

"No. 56—Is a Home Lott Laid out to James Taylor Iny^e s^d Lisburn Propriety & it Lays Iny^e Second and third Range & Lays Quantity for Quality Containing One Hundred & fifty acres. It Bounds N: on Third Division No 24 W: on third Division No 46 partly and partly on home lott No 55 & partly on Second Division No. 19 S: on third division No 28 partly and partly on third Division No 46 & East ony^e River ye N. E. Corner is a Maple tree from thence it Runs W 5 Degrees South 180 perch to a stake and stones from thence it Runs W 5 Degrees South 180 Perch to a Stake and Stones from thence South 136 perch to a stake and Stones from thence E to ye River and from thence to ye Corner first Mentioned, —a highway of two perch Wide to be allowed out ony^e N: Side of ye Range Line Running through Said Lott and Said Lott is allowed six perch wide ony^e West side of Ye River & twenty perch In Length—

Said Line beginning att ye South Line of ye above Named Lott & to proceed from thence Down ye River Likewise on ye East side of ye River adjoining ye former there is 20 perch Wide of Land Said twenty perch wide of Land is to Run In Length Beginning att ye Water of ye Pond and Run down ye River as far as forementioned on ye West side On ye River Doth, and no further, Said Land being allowed for ye Privilige of Building a Mill on ye River & Allowed all ye Land Upwards to Home Lott No 20 for Pond Room. Surveyed In April 1739."

The first allusion to a corn mill that is found upon the records, is in the record of the annual town meeting, March 3, 1755, when besides the election of officers several roads were consented to, and among them is the following entry:

"These May Certifie that I am Willing to Let ye Road go Where it now Dos Between Matthew Gray^s & ye Corn Mill, Having ye Range Rode Equivolent.   JOHN MCFARLAND."

John McFarland was not one who drew land, but he may have been a son of Andrew McFarland who drew Home lot, No. 39 ; also lot No. 39 second division, and a No. 60 third division. Home lot, No. 39, was half a mile west of the meeting house, no corn mill could be built there. Lot No. 39 second division was on both sides of the West branch in range 4, and the corn mill was probably on the river at that point.

The next mention of a grist mill in the town is found in a vote changing the location of a road in 1762, but it was not upon the lot No. 56, but might have been on the West branch at some point above or below lot 56. The vote referred to is as follows:

"Voted that the Road be Altered from Matthew Grays Toward ye Corn Mill about Four Rode or as far as the Surveyor will think proper."

Up to this time nothing had been done by the owner of lot 56 towards erecting a mill, as the proposition of Mr. Phelps to the town that same year indicates.

John Savige was scheduled as the owner of a sawmill on the valuation list as early as 1760, and on the same list John Lucore is listed as the owner of one half of a grist mill, also John Crawford for half of a grist mill ; perhaps they together owned one and the same mill.

Town Meeting, Sept. 14, 1762.

In the warrant for this meeting there was an article as follows:

"Article 4   To see if the town will grant Mr. Phelps the Stream and place to build a Grist Mill & Dam in and Upon the Branch of Swift River by the Bridge across it in the Highway leading from the Meeting House in s^d Pelham to William Conkeys Dwelling house in s^d Pelham if he Clear the Town of Damage."

On this article it was "Voted that There is nothing acted on the forth article."

When the survey of the Lisburn property was made the fine stream running through the Hollow could but suggest to the minds of the sturdy settlers the opportunity to locate a grist mill for the convenience of the people, and with home lot No. 56, was coupled the obligation requiring the one who drew that lot to build a mill; failing to do it, the land set apart for mill and pond was reserved for some one that would.

James Taylor was the fortunate man to draw lot No. 56, but up to 1762 he had failed to build a mill. Possibly it was the hope that Mr. Taylor would do so soon that led the people to disregard the proposition of Mr. Phelps.

At a meeting Oct. 20, 1791, the following article appeared in the warrant:

"To see if the Town will grant their right of Privilege thair is in the West Branch for the purpose of Erecting a Mill or Mills for the purpose of Grinding Grain to any Person or Persons who will appear to Engage to Erect s^d mills to the Exceptance of s^d Inhabitance of Pelham."

Action on the Above Article.

"Voted to take advice of some Lyor Respecting the Privilige of a Mill Place that is laid out on the West Branch that Runs through s^d Pelham.

Voted to Choose a Committee to inspect s^d matter,—Said Committee is Hugh Johnston, Lt John Rinken, Lt Nathaniel Sampson.

Voted to adjourn s^d Meeting to Thursday the third day of November next at one oclock in the afternoon.

Then Met and first voted to Raise a Committee to Enquire of Mr James Taylor the Reasons why he has not Built a Grist Mill on ye spot ye Proprietors laid out to his Lot for the Privilige of a Mill and if not Sufficient Reasons given, to Demand of him to Build a Mill.—

DAM AND BRIDGE ACROSS THE WEST BRANCH.

UP THE VALLEY OF THE WEST BRANCH FROM THE CEMETERY.

Chose Mr Hugh Johnston, Mathew Clark and Andrew Abercrombie a Committee for the purpose above."

No record has been found of the result of this action of the town. Whether James Taylor built the long delayed grist mill or whether some other man did, no one living can probably determine, and unless some record turns up to decide it the question must remain unsettled. It would seem probable that the earnestness with which the town took hold of the matter, as indicated by the record, that James Taylor or some other man was to be forced to improve the fine water privilege for the accommodation of the people without further delay. The people were doomed to still further waiting for the much needed mill, as the following records plainly prove. In a warrant for a town meeting, March 17, 1800, is the following article:

" To see if the Town will Improve the Privilige of Building Mills on the West Branch having Respect for the former vote of the Town."

Action upon the above article is recorded as follows:

" Voted to Chuse a Committee to see if the Mill Place that is laid out on the West Branch whether it Belongs to the Town or any other Person or Persons. Said Committee is Joseph Akers, Capt Isaac Abercrombie and David Conkey."

The meeting was adjourned for one hour, and on reassembling the following vote was passed:

" Voted that the Committee that was Chosen to inspect the Mill Place on the West Branch they are to Examine the Town Book and if they find that it is Voted to Doctor Hinds they are to Desist till they have further orders from the Town."

Dr. Nehemiah Hinds was a prominent man in town, and a man of property who was at one time the largest tax payer in the town, and it is evident that the people were not anxious to crowd the Doctor provided the records showed him to be the lawful owner of the undeveloped mill privilege on the West branch;—hence the vote ordering the committee to desist if they should find Dr. Hinds in legal possession.

In an old account book that belonged to William Conkey (Uncle Billy) there are entries showing the payment of money for millwright work in the years 1803 and 1804. Mr. Milo Abbott of Prescott is of the opinion that Uncle Billy Conkey was one of three men that built the first mill on the West branch at the place near the bridge where there have been mills for many years.

Felton & Conkey were taxed as a firm in 1809, but whether they were in company in the mill business the tax entry does not state. Ansel and Robert Conkey, sons of Uncle Billy, are believed to have been owners of the mills for ten years or so, perhaps longer, and then came Nathan Felton, who was proprietor for some time and sold to Mala Cowles of Belchertown, and his son Edwin Cowles operated them,—the sawmill on the east side and a grist mill on the west side of the stream. Cowles owned the mills from about 1840 until '48 or '49, and rented them to Leland, Gillett & Gilbert for the manufacture of axe handles.

William Holt of Dana purchased the mills of Cowles in 1852 or '53, and was the owner until he sold them to J. M. Cowan, who purchased them in 1854. Mr. Cowan and Marcus Grout were in partnership for awhile, as was L. M. Hills in the manufacture of bobbins. In 1867 Cowan sold out the mills and the business to Hills and Westcott of Amherst, who carried on the bobbin business until the shop burned in 1874. Hills and Westcott then divided the property, W. S. Westcott taking the property on the east side of the stream and H. F. Hills the property on the west side.

Westcott sold the mill on the Prescott side to Theodore F. Cook in 1873 and Cook built a new saw mill.

Hills sold his mill property on the west side of the stream to John Vanstone in 1881. T. F. Cook sold the sawmill to E. Downing of Enfield in 1889, and John Vanstone purchased it of Downing in 1891. Vanstone owns the property on both sides of the stream at present but the mills on the west side have gone to ruin.

Hamilton's sawmill is mentioned as standing in 1785,—location not definite. Also John Hoar's sawmill about that date. In 1790 there is mention of a sawmill, whose owner is not named, in a recorded vote as follows: " Voted that the road Laid from the Sawmill to William Conkeys be Shut up by two Gats one at Each end of s[d] Road with two Hors Blocks at each Gate." The mills referred to above were situated in the easterly part of the town, probably in the Hollow.

In the record of a road established for Dea. Ebenezer Gray and others in 1787 occurs the following mention of a mill:

" Beginning southerly of Dea Ebenezer Gray[s] house at the third range road and running as described by various turns to a laid out road from Shutesbury to Barlow's sawmill."

In 1805 there was an article in a town meeting warrant :

" To see if the town will grant that the Surveyors shall allow work Don at the Bridge by Barlow's sawmill in the present Highway tax."

Wood's sawmill is also mentioned in the same vote as near a bridge. Turner's sawmill is referred to as being on the county road, leading from Pelham to Leverett, in 1801.

April 3, 1815, it was " Voted to discontinue a part of the road running from William Conkeys to John Hoars Sawmill." This record does not locate John Hoar's mill but it was undoubtedly upon the West Branch near the farm of Thomas Conkey, about a mile north of the sawmill of John Vanstone, at the bridge across the West Branch. Calvin Chapin of Prescott says that John Hoar owned the privilege at that point on the stream and after he (Chapin) came to town in 1824, that John Baker built a mill on Hoar's privilege and was to have the use of the mill for twenty years, and then it was to become the property of Mr. Hoar. It is quite probable that John Hoar had a mill on that privilege previous to 1815, when the vote to discontinue the portion of road leading from William Conkey's tavern to John Hoar's sawmill was passed.

Early in the century, perhaps as early a 1815, one Stephen Fairbanks built or owned a mill on what is known as the Pergy brook, and not far from where the sawmill of David Shores now stands. Fairbanks had a carding machine in his shop or mill and received the wool from the farmers to be carded into rolls for greater convenience in spinning. He ran his carding machine for some years and then sold it to Cheney Abbott. Abbott continued the business for a number of years or until it run out, because the practice of spinning wool on the large wheel began to die out, and then Abbott sold his mill to Austin Conkey and Miner Gold, who added a story to the shop and started the manufacture of shoe pegs. The shoe peg business not having proved a success Mr. Gold turned his attention to the manufacture of shingles in place of pegs, and continued the business, after leaving the shop on Pergy brook, in the south part of the town, using steam power. Stephen Fairbanks and a man by the name of Briggs were also associated together in building or running a sawmill a little farther down the Pergy brook in a deep ravine and south of David Shores's sawmill, where there is much fall to the brook over the ledges of rocks; this was probably sixty or more years ago. Mr. Fairbanks finally became discontented with his surroundings and conditions, and built himself a covered wagon in which he and his family journeyed to the West, camping where night overtook them, sleeping in the covered wagon.

Farther up Pergy brook the foundations of a mill were to be seen sixty or seventy years ago and it is said that there was a gristmill there once, but who the owner was we have been unable to learn, as no one seems to remember seeing a mill there, but it is said that some of the foundation timbers are still to be seen in the bed of the brook.

Other Land Set Apart for a Mill.

"No 32 Is a Home Lott Laid out to William Johnson Jun Iny^e Lisburn Propriety & it Lays in the Second Range & Lays Quantity for Quality Containing one Hundred acres it bounds S : on third Division No. 57 partly & partly on third Division No. 58 partly & partly on Undivided Land E. on third Division 59 & W : on third Division 58 the S. W. corner to a stake & stones—from thence it Runs N. 120 Perch to a stake and Stones from thence it runs E. 200 Perch to a Whiteoak Staddle and Stones, from thence it runs S : 102 perch to a White Oak Tree, from thence W. 88 Perch to a Stake & Stones from thence it runs S. 91 Perch to a White Oak Tree & from thence to ye corner first mentioned,—A highway of 2 Perch Wide to be allowed out of the N. side of ye range line Running through said Lott & is allowed five acres more adjoining ye E. End of said Lott for a Mill place viz for land to build a Mill on for a mill yard & for Pond room Said Mill place Begins at a White Oak Tree being the N. E. of Said Lott Runns from thence E 15 Deg N 31 Perch to a White Pine tree from thence In such form as ye Water Raised by a Dam shall flow the N : Bounds of said Mill place to Run 4 Perch north from the Brook and as far E. As shall include s^d five Acres."
Another lot of 50 acres under No. 32 and situated in East Hollow went with the above described No. 32.

The five acres of land allowed to William Johnson, who drew Home lot No. 32 in the west part of the town for " to build a mill, Mill yard and for pond room " was upon the stream now known as Amethyst brook and from which water is now taken by the Amherst Water Company to supply Amherst with pure water.

This five acres of land, set apart for a mill is 250 rods east from the west line of the town and must have been the point in the ravine a little way up the stream from the mineral springs on the Orient grounds, so called, now owned by Mr. Fred Pitman of Washington, D. C. At this point early in this century there was a mill or shop owned by Isaac Otis for the manufacture of scythes and there was a small foundry connected, where small cast iron articles for household use were turned out. The approach to this mill site was by a road from the County highway, starting opposite the West Pelham burying ground near the residence of Edwin Shaw, traces of which are still to be seen, and another approach was from the Valley road some distance east of the Valley bridge over the Amethyst brook. This shop or mill was washed away in the great freshet of 1828, and the grindstone used there was found 25 years afterwards far down the stream by Edmund Myrick and Horace Gray.

Just the date of the development of the power of Amethyst brook at the site of the Fishing Rod factory and at the mill of Lewis W. Allen, a few rods below, is not certainly determined by any data that is accessible. On the site now occupied by L. W. Allen's saw mill and shop there has been a saw mill since 1805 and perhaps before that time.

September 30, 1805, Nathan Jillson purchased of Dea. Nathaniel Sampson the farm known for many recent years as the Rev. John Jones farm. His two sons Riley and Amasa were mechanics, as was also the father. The Jillsons owned the two mills, a sawmill where L. W. Allen now owns, and a small gristmill at the privilege now occupied by the Montague City Rod company. The first gristmill was near the north end of the dam of the Fishing Rod company, and the water was brought in a canal from a small dam farther up the stream.

Riley Jillson built a gristmill on the site of the Fishing Rod factory in 1820, and the two brothers carried on the gristmill and the sawmill farther down in company. Horace Gray came into possession of Amasa Jillson's half of the property 60 years or more ago, owning one-half of each mill, exchanged his half of the gristmill for Riley Jillson's half of the sawmill. About the year 1858, Mr. Gray, with his son C. D. Gray, started manufacturing of fishing rods in a small way. The sawmill and shop at the lower privilege were burned in 1851, and Gray rebuilt. About 1860 he sold his sawmill to Andrew

Mitchell and purchased the upper privilege. Mitchell died and Darius Eaton was the next owner. Eaton sold to L. W. Allen the present owner. Riley Jillson, the original owner of the gristmill, sold to Robert Cutler in 1845; Cutler added a sawmill, ran them both several years and sold to Buffum & Ward; this firm sold to Mr. Anthony and he sold to William Johnson, and the latter to a man in Palmer. Gray & Son then purchased this mill. They increased the fishing rod business greatly; C. D. Gray died in 1873 and the business was sold to Ward & Latham. Latham dropped out of the firm, and Joseph G. Ward was sole owner for some time. Leander L. and Eugene P. Bartlett were the next owners of the business. Leander L. sold to Eugene P., and in 1889 the Montague City Rod Company became the proprietors of the flourishing business, and from their three factories at Montague City and Pelham, Mass., and Post Mills, Vt., turn out three-fourths of all the goods that go into the market. The Pelham branch of the Montague City Rod Company is in charge of Eugene P. Bartlett as manager, and in good times perhaps forty hands are employed in manufacturing split bamboo fishing rods that go to all parts of this country and to Europe. Besides the split bamboo rods, which are made from bamboo poles imported from Calcutta and Japan, fine lancewood fishing rods are made. Three hundred different patterns and styles are included in their catalogue, from the fancy fly rod of a few ounces in weight to the heavy and strong rods for salt water fishermen.

About the year 1808, John Parmenter set up a carding machine in a building back of the sawmill, now owned by L. W. Allen, where the farmers from this and neighboring town brought their wool to be carded into rolls for spinning on the large spinning wheels by the great open fire-places in the farmers' kitchens by the skillful fingers of the wives and daughters, and after spinning into yarn it was woven into cloth, bed-blankets and the like. Connected with the business was a fulling and dyeing department where yarn was colored and cloth dyed and fulled for use.

Some insight into the business and the manner of conducting it is gathered from an old ledger in use at that time indicates that the carding and dyeing was paid for mostly in farm produce or labor.

DAM AT FISHING ROD FACTORY.

MONTAGUE CITY FISHING ROD FACTORY.

The Old Carding Machine.

Scraps from the Old Ledger.

Dr. Robert Cutler was credited with 95 cents worth of salt pork and $1.42 in cash July 29, 1808 ; showing that the Doctor had both pork and cash to spare. Captain Calvin Merrill was allowed $1.00 for 1 Gallon Cider Brandy, and $2.00 cash for "2 Knapt Hats," in July, 1809. Simeon Pomroy has the following credit: Sept. 24, 1810, " By 5 days labor on the dam $3.33 ;" Not very heavy wages for laborious work, repairing a mill dam. Andrew Hyde was credited $2.01 for three days work on dam, showing that 67 cents was considered fair pay for a day's work. The account with Rev. David Parsons was opened in August, 1808 and was closed in 1814 by a cash payment of $2.44. David Pomroy has the following credit, Nov. 23, 1812, " By fifty lb. of Beef at four Dollars per Hundred,— $2.00." Gen. Ebenezer Mattoon brought the wool from his flock of sheep to the carding machine firm from 1808 to 1817, paying nothing but cash.

The following credits and prices carried out, taken here and there without regarding names give an idea of workingman's wages and value of farm products :

1810	By 13 1-2 pounds veal	.53c	1822	By 16 Pounds Sugar at 12 1-2 cts.	2.00
1811	" 2 1-2 Bushels oats at 34	.86	1822	" One Sheep, 38 pounds,	2.00
1808	" 3 Cords 40 ft. of wood at $1.17	$3.87	1822	" 1 Days Work	.54
1808	" Setting two horses shoes	.17	1823	" 1 Bushel of Turnips	.25
1808	" Killing calf	.17	1822	" 7 pounds Veal at 4 cts.	.28
1811	" 12 pounds butter at 12 1-2 cts lb	1.50	1817	" Horse to Hatfield, 9 miles,	.36
1812	" Horse to Whately (10 miles)	.40	1820	" 6 1-2 Bushels potatoes at 33	1.98
1813	" 1 hoe	.83	1822	" 14 1-2 Skim cheese at 7	.87
1813	" 4 Brooms (Corn)	.50	1824	" 7 lbs Salt Pork at 10	.70
1815	" 2 Bushels corn	2.00	1822	" 3 yds Cotton Cloth at 25	.75
1818	" 2 yards cotton cloth 2-9	.92	1826	" 4 lbs Butter at 12 1-2	.50
1820	" 2 1-4 lbs Butter	.22			

Seventy-five years and more ago there was a sawmill in the ravine where the lower reservoir of the Amherst Water Company is located, owned by Savannah Arnold. The site of the stone dam of the Company is nearly identical with the dam that supplied the water for Arnold's sawmill located a few rods farther down the stream, the remains of the canal or raceway being still visible. The first mill was burned and John and Collins Brailey built another on nearly the same site.

Access to Arnold's and Brailey's mill was by a cart-road to the county highway near the residence of James Haskins, and another cart-road that crossed the brook by a bridge and came out on the valley side of the brook.

At the head of the pond that held water for the Brailey sawmill Amethyst brook divides, or rather the two brooks that unite to form Amethyst brook, come together. One comes from the northeast and the other brings water from the watershed southeasterly from the point of union; on the brook that comes from the northeast, high up on the hillside there was an old sawmill on the farm purchased by Eseck Cook in 1807, and in later years it was rebuilt in modern style, but the scarcity of timber and the introduction of the portable mill rendered the investment worthless, and the mill was allowed to go to decay,—time and the elements have nearly completed their work and it will not be long before not a vestige will be left. Owners following Eseck Cook were his sons, Nathaniel and Lewis Cook; then it came into the hands of Smith M. Cook and Asa Ober, but no business has been done there for years. It is probable that this was the site of Turner's sawmill described as "on the road from Pelham to Leverett."

On the branch of Amethyst brook that comes from the southeast there was at one time a turning shop, situated a short distance above where the two branches join to make Amethyst brook. It was owned by Ezra Brown, who lived on the north side of the turnpike near the Amherst Water Company's new reservoir, on the farm now occupied by John Hawley. At the turning shop Mr. Brown used to split out his timber and turn faucets. These he would take to Rhode Island and sell or exchange for cotton yarn.

Bringing home the yarn he would then sell it to the farmers, and the farmers' wives wove it into cloth for their families on hand looms. Mr. Brown built a new shop nearer his home, on the road accepted by the town in 1828 and leading across the ravine to George Buffum's and is described as "leaving the turnpike near Ezra Brown's new shop." In this shop Mr. Brown probably made the coffins, which he sold to the people when needed. These coffins he stained a bright red color which was the custom or fashion at that time.

Near the location of Ezra Brown's new shop W. J. Harris built a mill or shop for mechanical purposes in 1875, where he carried on a small business for several years and then sold out to the Amherst Water Company, as the site for their upper reservoir, in 1892.

RESIDENCE OF DAVID SHORES.

Charcoal Kilns near Pulpit Hill–Pelham Hollow

Sixty years or more ago Thomas Buffum and Levi Hall built a stone dam and sawmill on a small rivulet that finds its way down from the high lands northeast of the valley and crosses the highway near the old Buffum homestead, now owned and occupied by John A. Page. The mill was quite a distance north of the Buffum place, and was run but a few years. The remains of the old dam are visible by the roadside now.

About 1800 Oliver Smith built a dam on the head waters of the small brook that comes down from the base of Mt. Lincoln and flowing south finds its way into Hop brook in the neighborhood of Dwight, or Pansy Park, and erected a small turning shop on the county road leading from the Methodist church at West Pelham to Enfield. A small business was done at this shop for years after Oliver Smith passed away and the farm on which it stood came into the possession of Arba Randall. John Lyman, who lived near the shop used it for building wagon wheels, turning the hubs in the lathe.

Later the building was taken down and removed. The old dam remains on the north side of the highway, and the shop stood on the same side of the roadway. Persons passing along the roadway now can scarcely hear any sound of running water, so little of it coming down now from the hillside above, that one wonders how enough could be obtained to drive even a turning lathe.

Manufacture of Charcoal.

The burning of wood into charcoal or "coaling" as the business was termed has been carried on in a small way by individuals here and there about the town for many years. The usual practice was to pile up ten, fifteen or more cords of four foot wood into a cone shaped mass, cover it with earth and turf except an opening at the apex. Fire was then applied at the base and the work of the fire carefully watched night and day for a week or ten days until the fire had charred the wood completely. Then the charcoal burner loaded up a wagon, fitted with high side and end boards, with perhaps an hundred bushels of coal and with horse or ox team drew his load to Amherst or Northampton and peddled the coal from house to house.

In 1862 David Shores began the manufacture of charcoal at the "Hollow" on a larger scale, than the ancient method described above. He built large ovens or kilns of brick large enough to hold many cords of wood. When an oven is filled iron doors shut the wood in, only sufficient openings are left for draft, when the kiln is fired. These ovens require constant watching day and night just the same as the earth covered coal pit. Mr. Shores has three of these ovens and manufactures from 50,000 to 150,000 bushels annually according to the demand.

The charcoal is marketed at Springfield and Chicopee mostly. It is drawn to Enfield by horses and loaded upon cars,—and on its arrival at Springfield the coal is distributed to the various large manufacturers, such as Smith & Wesson, the U. S. Armory and the large hotels.

Mr. Shores has purchased woodland from time to time to supply wood for his ovens, until he is the owner of 1000 to 1200 acres. Land that he cut the wood from when he first began business has grown another covering of wood large enough for railroad ties or for wood to turn into charcoal.

In 1870 Mr. Shores built a sawmill on Pergy brook to saw the large trees into lumber. This sawmill is the last one erected in town and is a circular sawmill with the latest improvements, and is located not far from his residence and charcoal ovens.

Stone Quarries.

The business of quarrying stone for building purposes has been carried on for more than 75 years; just the time when the work began is not fixed. A Mr. Kimball from Amherst was one of the first in this line of business. Thomas Buffum began quarrying on a ledge on the east side of the highway leading from Buffum's to Abijah Fales', when he was 17 years old in 1827. Stones from this quarry were easily cut and hammered.

Abijah Fales opened a quarry near his house. John and William Harkness owned a quarry half a mile or more east of the Methodist church, now owned by George P. Shaw.

The largest quarry and the one from which the most stone has been taken is on the farm best known as the Joseph G. Ward farm. Ward followed Levi Hall as proprietor of the farm, and "Cooper" John Gray was the owner before Hall.

The first work upon this quarry of any magnitude was in 1820 when the college buildings at Amherst were begun. John Gray

THE VALLEY STONE QUARRY.

POURWAY OF THE AMHERST WATER CO.'S RESERVOIR.

owned the ledge or quarry at that time and he got out cut stones for steps and other uses about the buildings.

From the quarry on this farm a great many stone have been drawn by team to Springfield, Northampton, Easthampton, Ware and Amherst for use as window sills and caps,—hammered stones for steps and other purposes, and building stone for use in factories and public buildings. Flavel Gaylord of Amherst now owns the farm and quarry.

There have been great quantities of rough stone gathered in the pastures and drawn to Amherst for cellar walls, and the demand continues. The farmers thereby clear their fields of stone and get pay for their labor. They also get out railroad ties for which they find ready sale to the railroads. Quantities of cord wood are cut and drawn to Amherst market. Wood prepared for the stove is also drawn to Amherst. W. Orcutt Clough has been in the business 19 years, and has drawn 8000 one horse loads, all with the same horse. John L. Brewer and others are in the business.

Miscellaneous Manufacturing.

Horace Gray in connection with his business of sawing logs into lumber used to do quite a business in turning bedsteads and making hand screws of wood, previous to the burning of his mill in 1851.

About 1840, Daniel Purrington built a machine for sawing shoe lasts on the principal of the Blanchard Lathe and ran it in an annex to the gristmill of his father-in-law, Riley Jillson, for some years.

"Tanner" John Gray had a tannery on his farm in the valley, many years ago and the location of the vats can be seen still on the farm of Levi Moulton.

Obadiah Cooley was a distiller, and his distillery was situated near the highway half a mile east of the center of the town on the way to the hollow.

At the beginning of this century Solomon Fletcher had a tan yard, curry shop, bark house and beaming house, standing on land of Robert Crossett in the east part of the town. He sold to Benjamin Dix in 1802.

John Parmenter made ploughs for use in Pelham and the neighboring towns in a small shop at the west end of the town, and about the year 1840 contracted to build some that were shipped to Illinois.

John Harkness and his sons used to purchase French burr stone in the blocks as shipped to this country and made sets of mill stones for grinding grain, selling them on orders about the country and placing them in the mills ready for use. They quit the business previous to 1850.

Barney T. Wetherell and Job S. Miller did quite a business at one time cutting out staves for hogsheads. Their place of business was at Pelham center.

INN KEEPERS AND RETAILERS.

Intoxicating liquors were in common use as a beverage among the people generally all through the county and state at the time this town was settled. Sylvester Judd the historian of Hadley says, " the drinks of the early days were wines of several kinds, sack, beer, ale and strong water or aquavitae,—consisting of brandy distilled from wine and a liquor distilled from malt ;"—but wine and beer were the principal drinks until rum was brought from the West Indies. It was sometimes called " Kill Devil or Barbadoes liquor." The settlers of Hadley planted apple trees early after the settlement of the town in 1659 and cider was made as early as 1677. They pounded the apples in troughs as was the custom in England. There is no record of cider mills in New England previous to 1700. Cider became in great demand for distillation into cider brandy, and apple orchards became numerous in Hampshire county at the time of the Revolution and the people of Pelham were in the front rank in the apple orchard industry.

The returns of the assessors of the towns of Hadley, South Hadley, Amherst and Granby for the year 1771 are said to show that there was an average of four and one-half barrels of cider for each family produced that year, and Pelham is said to have made more cider that year than either of the four towns named. Cider mills were common and there was probably distilleries for turning cider into brandy in the town. One such institution of that sort is said to have been located in West Pelham near the house of E. P. Bartlett. The lot on which it stood was known for years as the " Still Pasture," and a depression in the ground in that pasture has been pointed out as the cellar or basement of the distillery. Who owned the distillery cannot now be determined. Obadiah Cooley had a distillery half a mile east of the center of the town.

The use of liquors as a beverage by all, and the need of some place in town to entertain travelers on horseback journeying through the place caused the application to the country courts for license as taverners and common victualers, and the first licensed inn-holder in Pelham was Thomas Dick, and his license was granted in 1749, and reads substantially as follows on the court record:

"License is Granted to Thomas Dick of Pelham to be an innholder and Taverner and Common Victualler in s^d town for the year ensuing for Selling Strong Liquors by Retail."

Thomas Dick continued to be licensed as innholder every year following 1749 until 1768, according to the records at Northampton; but an auction bill, dated Feb. 20, 1770, advertised a sale at the house of Thomas Dick, innholder.

In 1763 Thomas Dick was licensed to sell "Tea, Coffee and China ware out of his house in Pelham. The said Thomas to render the accounts and pay the duties required by the law of this Province."

The above license seems to indicate that Dick added to the business of merchant to that of innholder and furnished the common necessities of life for his fellow townsmen.

The location of Landlord Dicks' tavern cannot be determined with certainty. It is claimed that it was a mile west of the center of the town at the fork of the roads, and that the house now owned by William O. Kimball was the site and perhaps a part of the old tavern. But a reference to the plan of the town shows that Thomas Dick's land was all on the east side of the West Branch, as drawn by lot. Thomas Dick purchased a tract of land of Martha Gilmore in 1758—a part of lot No. 6, second division, in range 4,—this was near where some say his tavern was located. Thomas Dick died in 1774. In 1795 a Thomas Dick, probably a son of the original Thomas, transferred lands to Margaret Dick, which he described as "the farm on which I now live—bounded westerly on lands of Thomas Hincks and Benoni Shirtlieff—Northerly on range line—Easterly on the Cross Road—and Southerly on county road and by the Meeting house lot and burying ground." This is a complete description of home lot No. 50, originally drawn by John Fergerson. Possibly Thomas Dick, the original settler, purchased Fergerson's land and kept a tavern there,—and the son Thomas was an innholder on the same farm in 1784.

1772, William Conkey, senior, was licensed as innholder. The license being more particular in its terms than that first issue to Thomas Dick, and reads as follows:

"William Conkey of Pelham is licensed to be an Innholder Retailer and Common Victualer in his dwelling house there for one year next ensuing and the same William now here in court recognizes to ye Lord the King as principal in the sum of ten pounds and Messrs. Curtis Loomis of Southampton and Eli Parker of Amherst also came here and as sureties for the said William annexed to ye Reconysaizance prescribed for Innholders by act or law of this Province in such cases made and provided entitled an act for the Inspecting and suppressing of Disorders in licensed Houses etc."

1773, William Conkey was a licensed innholder.

During the years from 1774 to 1778, there was an intermission or suspension of the Inferior Court of Common Pleas in the county of Hampshire and consequently no records of licenses granted for those years, if they were granted ; possibly those already licensed was sufficient to continue as innholders during those years. Licensed innholders for the year 1778 were John Cole, Christopher Patten and Nehemiah Hinds; and Robert Ormston, John Cole and James Lindsley received retailers license. 1779, David Sloan, William Conkey, John Cole and Nehemiah Hinds were innholders and Asa Conkey, Andrew Abercrombie, Robert Ormston and Nathan Felton were retailers.

Robert Ormston was a merchant and it is possible that Felton was in the same business, as it was the custom for all country merchants or grocers to keep liquors to sell to their customers and to treat good customers to a drink now and then.

1780. Innholders, David Sloan, William Conkey and Samuel Sampson. Retailers, Andrew Abercrombie and Henry McColloch.

1781. Innholder, John Bruce. Retailers, Alexander Barry and Nathaniel Sampson.

1782. Innholder, Samuel Sampson. Retailer, Nathaniel Sampson. The Sampsons seemed to have a monopoly that year.

1783. Innholders, Samuel Sampson, William Conkey, John Bruce, Nehemiah Hinds. Retailers, John Conkey, jun., Alexander Barry, Nathan Rankin.

The license of Landlord Bruce reads as follow ; "John Bruce of Pelham is licensed to be an innholder in his house there for the year next ensuing & Samuel Sampson as principal in behalf of said John recognises to the Commonwealth in the sum of fifty pounds with sureties, viz., William Conkey and John Conkey jun., in the sum of

£25 each to keep good rule and order in his House and duly observe the laws made for the regulation of such houses and also to keep and render the accounts and pay the Duties the law requires."

It will be noticed that Bruce's bondsmen and sureties were in the same business and probably Bruce reciprocated the favor and doubtless his name could be found as bondsman or surety for some of those holding licenses that year.

1784. Innholders, William Conkey, John Bruce, Nehemiah Hinds, Thomas Dick. Retailers, Alexander Barry, John Conkey, jun., William Ashley.

1785. Innholders, John Bruce, Nehemiah Hinds. Retailers, John Clark, jun., Wm. Ashley, Elihu Billings, Ebenezer Gray.

1786. No record of innholder or retailers this year.

1787. Innholder, Nehemiah Hinds. Retailer, Wm. Ashley.

1788. Innholder, Benoni Shurtleiff. Retailers, Wm. Ashley, John Conkey, Isaac Abercrombie.

1789. Innholder, Nehemiah Hinds. Retailers, Wm. Ashley, John Conkey.

1790. Innholder, Benoni Shurtlieff. Retailers, Wm. Ashley, John Conkey.

1791. Innholders, N. Hinds, John Stickney, Benoni Shurtlieff. Retailers, John Conkey, Nathaniel Sampson.

1792. Innholders, and retailers same as in 1791.

1793. Innholders, Nehemiah Hinds, Benoni Shurtlieff. Retailers, Luke Montague, Jacob Packard, John Thompson, jun., John Stickney.

1794. Innholders, John Stewart Parks, Nehemiah Hinds, John Conkey, Lebbeus Howard. Retailer, Luke Montague.

1795. Innholders, John Conkey, N. Hinds. No retailers recorded.

1796. Innholders, John Conkey, Nehemiah Hinds, John Cole. Retailer, Asaph Lyon.

1797. Innholders, John Cole, Christopher Patten, Nehemiah Hinds. Retailers, Robert Ormston, David Hannum, Asaph Lyon.

1798. Innholders, John Cole, C. Patten, N. Hinds. Retailers, Robert Ormston, John Cole, James Lindsley.

1799. Innholders, John Cole, Nehemiah Hinds. Retailers, Robert Ormston, Nathan Felton.

1800. Innholders, Christopher Patten, Nehemiah Hinds, Harris Hatch. Retailers, Robert Ormston, Nathan Felton.

1801. Innholders, Harris Hatch, Nehemiah Hinds. Retailers, Robert Ormston, Harris Hatch, Nathan Felton.

1802. Innholders, Nehemiah Hinds, Harris Hatch, John Richardson. Retailers, Nathan Felton, Harris Hatch, John Richardson, John Conkey.

1803. Innholders, Harris Hatch, Joseph W. Hamilton, N. Hinds, Retailers, Robert Ormston, John Conkey, Nathan Felton.

1804. Innholders, Harris Hatch, Joseph W. Hamilton. Retailers, Nathan Felton, John Conkey, Robert Ormston.

1805. Innholders, Harris Hatch, Joseph W. Hamilton. Retailers, John Conkey, Nathan Felton.

1806. Innholders, Joseph W. Hamilton, Walter Eaton. Retailer, Marston Eaton.

1807. Innholders, Walter Eaton, Chelles Keep. Retailers, Marston Eaton, Nathan Titus, Isaac Conkey.

1808. Innholder, Walter Eaton. Retailers, Marston Eaton, Nathan Felton.

1809. Innholder, Walter Eaton. Retailer, Marston Eaton.

1810. Inholders, Nathan Felton. Retailer, Marston Eaton.

1811. Innholder, Eliphaz Packard. Retailer, Marston Eaton.

1812. No Innkeepers License. Retailers, Marston Eaton Luther Chapin.

1813. No Innkeeper Licensed. Retailers, Marston Eaton, Isaac Conkey.

1814. Innkeepers, William Smith, Amariah Robbins. Retailer, Marston Eaton.

1815. Innkeepers, Nathan Felton, Rebecca Smith. Retailers, Barna Brigham, Marston Eaton.

1816. Innholder, Nathan Felton. Retailers, Stacy Linzee, Barna Brigham, Isaac Abercrombie, Jr., Marston Eaton.

1817. Innholder, Marston Eaton. Retailers, Marston Eaton, Stacy Linzee, Isaac Abercrombie Jr.

1818. Innholder, Nathan Felton. Retailers, Packard & Kingman, Isaac Abercrombie, Jr., Stacy Linzee.

1819. Innholder, Stacy Linzee. No Retailers.

1820. Innholders, Martin Kingman, Nathan Felton. Retailers, Martin Kingman, Stacy Linzee.

1821. No Innholders. Retailers, Martin Kingman, Stacy Linzee.

1822. Innholder, Martin Kingman. Retailer, Martin Kingman.

1823. Innholder. Martin Kingman. Retailers, Martin Kingman, Wells Southworth.

1824, Innkeeper, Martin Kingman. Retailers, Abial B. Smith, Rufus Southworth, Martin Kingman.

1825. Innkeeper, Oliver Bryant. Retailers, Rufus Southworth, Martin Kingman.

1826. Innkeeper. Oliver Bryant. Retailers, Martin Kingman, Rufus Southworth.

1827. Innkeeper, Ralph Kellogg. Retailers, Martin Kingman, Bryant & Kingman.

1828. Innkeeper, Ralph Kellogg. Retailers, Martin Kingman, Lewis L. Draper, Bryant & Kingman.

1829. Innholders, Martin Kingman, Ziba Cook. Retailers, Martin Kingman, Lewis L. Draper.

1830. Innholder, Martin Kingman, Ziba Cook. Retailer, Martin Kingman.

1831. No Innholder licensed. Retailers, Lewis L. Draper, Martin Kingman.

1832. Innholder, Martin Kingman, center of the town, Ziba Cook Southwest part of the town. Retailers, Martin Kingman, Lewis L. Draper, at store in Southwest part of the town.

1833. Innkeeper, Martin Kingman. Retailer, Martin Kingman, at his shop center of the town.

1834. Innkeeper, Martin Kingman, Ziba Cook. No Retailers.

1835. Innholders, Martin Kingman, not Licensed to sell spirits. Ziba Cook, licensed to sell spirits. No retailers.

1836. Innholders, Martin Kingman, not licensed to sell spirits. No retailers.

1837. Innholders, Benjamin Randall, at his house on the county road from Amherst to Enfield, licensed to sell spirits. No retailers.

1838. Innholders, Martin Kingman, licensed to sell wine at his old stand ; Ziba Cook, licensed on application of the selectmen to sell wines, beer, ale, but not distilled spirits.

1839. Nathan Weeks, licensed as a retailer of wines and fermented liquors, at the store formerly occupied by Joel Packard.

1840-41. Innholder, Benjamin Randall.

1842-'43-'44. Innholder, Calvin D. Eaton.

1845. No licensed innholder.

1846-'47-'48. Innholder, Calvin D. Eaton.

1849. No license granted.

1850. William Newell, licensed an innholder and common victualler at his dwelling house and at the public house near the mineral springs which he had discovered on his farm. Calvin D. Eaton was also a licensed innholder that year.

No licenses granted from 1851 to 1861. Nor any of record from the last date until 1890, although the Orient house built in 1861, was kept open for summer guests and invalids until 1881 when it was burned. In 1890, Theodore F. Cook was licensed as a common victualler and opened Hotel Pelham at the center of the town, and has run the house as a hotel since that time to date.

MERCHANTS.

It is probable that Thomas Dick was the first merchant as well as the first tavern keeper, as in addition to his license as tavern keeper in 1763, he was " licensed to sell Tea, Coffee and China Ware out of his house in Pelham. The said Thomas to render the accounts and pay the duties required by the law of this Province."

Robert Ormston was a merchant in the town but at what date he opened business is not easy to determine. He was a licensed retailer of spirits, first in 1778, and as most of the grocers were retailers of spirits it may not be unfair to assume that John Cole and James Lindsley or Linsey and Nathan Felton, who were also licensed retailers for several years, may have been small dealers in groceries and other necessities, having stores in different parts of the town.

Robert Ormston who is known to have been a merchant, continued to appear as a licensed retailer of spirits down to 1804 as did Nathan Felton and John Conkey. Ormston's store was on the West Hill.

Marston Eaton's name appears the year after Ormston's ceases to appear. Eaton was a merchant and Nathan Felton continued to appear as a retailer down to 1810. Felton resided in that part of Pelham now Prescott.

Kingman & Packard were in company for a year or more from 1818 and then Martin Kingman was merchant and retailer at the center of the town. Not a little of his trade is said to have come from Amherst people who came out to Kingman's store for bargains. Kingman continued in the business of merchant and tavern keeper

M. E. BOYNTON'S RESIDENCE.

TOMBSTONE TO MEMORY OF EDWARD AND ELIZABETH SELFRIDGE.

for some years. He closed his career as innholder in 1838, and probably continued as a merchant well down to that time. He was a capable business man and used to take quantities of wood in exchange for goods, which he marketed at Amherst.

In 1823 the name of Wells Southworth appears as a licensed retailer. His store was a building on the south side of the Common, opposite the old meeting house and stands near, and a little west of Hotel Pelham, and is still owned by the Southworth family. Rufus Southworth was connected with the business for several years, keeping the goods usually sold at country stores in those days. The last license to Rufus Southworth as retailer was issued in 1826.

Wells Southworth sold out his store, also the homestead of the family, and removed to South Hadley Falls in 1828 and engaged in the mercantile business.

A syndicate, consisting of Jared T. Westcott, Cyrus Kingman, Lyman Jenks, Dr. I. H. Taylor, Asa Thompson, Lemuel C. Wedge, Chancellor Wheeler, and perhaps others, built a store east of Martin Kingman's tavern and store, with a shop in the upper story for making shoes about the year 1845, and Chancellor Wheeler conducted the business that was done there, the business having been first started in the house of Lyman Jenks, which has since been remodeled into Hotel Pelham. Wheeler died in 1850 and William Conkey, son of Warren Conkey, succeeded Wheeler. Job Miller was the next proprietor of the store, and was followed by Enos S. Richardson. Richardson was the village merchant for a number of years or until 1866 when Myrett E. Boynton purchased Richardson's interest and continued as grocer and postmaster in the same building until 1895 when it was burned, and another and better store was built. Mr. Boynton continues to be the only merchant and postmaster in town.

About the year 1828 Lewis L. Draper opened a small store opposite where the Methodist church now stands at West Pelham, in a building now used as a barn on the north side of the road just west of the church. Draper was licensed as a retailer of spirits, and the last year his name appears was 1832 when he was licensed "to sell in his store in the southwest part of the town."

Hardin Hemmenway of Shutesbury succeeded Mr. Draper, and after Hemmenway, Elijah Hills, a brother of Leonard M. Hills of

Amherst, occupied the store and dealt in palm-leaf hats, taking them in exchange for goods.

George L. Shaw, a son-in-law of Ziba Cook, was in business at this stand for a short time and then the store was closed.

William Barrows and Chester Gaskell reopened the store formerly occupied by Lewis L. Draper and others under the firm name of Barrows & Gaskell in 1847 or thereabouts, and put out split palm-leaf among the people of this town and Shutesbury to be braided into palm-leaf hats. They kept groceries and some dry-goods to supply their customers. The firm was not very successful and closed the business after running about a year.

In 1853 or '54 Chester Gaskell went in company with Warren C. Wedge in a building forty or fifty rods west of the Methodist church and now occupied as a dwelling by James Miller. Wedge had opened a shop for manufacturing shoes and kept a small stock of groceries and dry goods. The men both worked at shoes and tried to build up a paying business, but did not succeed as well as they had hoped, and the firm was dissolved after being in business for a short period, Wedge going to Chicopee to meet with better success in business.

In 1873, James A. Murray and John F. Murray of Boston obtained control of the asbestos lands on Butter Hill, and opened the mine for getting out the asbestos. J. F. Murray opened a grocery store in the building east of the Methodist church, afterwards used by Alfred Tuttle as a carpenter shop, but continued the business only a short time. The Murrays left the asbestos mine and the grocery business in 1874. John sold his goods to Martin D. Gold, who continued in the business about a year and then closed the store. Edwin J. Powell started in the grocery business in 1882. In 1884 he built a house and store opposite the Methodist church and opened for business as a grocer and butcher. The daily mail having been established between the center of the town and Amherst, a post-office was opened at the store. Mr. Powell was postmaster from March 30, 1887 to Aug. 1, 1893. The business venture not proving sufficiently profitable, Mr. Powell sold his goods to W. J. Harris, July 5, 1893. Harris ran the store about a year and gave up the business, and the post-office was discontinued in 1893.

Business at Packardville.

About the year 1840, Joel Packard and John Thurston, both Pelham men, built a shop at the south part of the town, on the county road from Amherst to Enfield, and started the manufacture of wagons under the firm name of Packard & Thurston, and since that time that hamlet has been known as Packardville. The wagons they built were good, strong, durable vehicles, being equipped with what was known as "thorough braces" instead of steel eliptic springs, which were then unknown. Packard & Thurston were practical workmen at the business themselves and employed a few men besides. The firm finally decided to remove their business to Belchertown, and did so, taking down the old shop and removing that as well as the business. The first store in this part of the town was opened by Anson Ramsdell and James Hanks at Packardville near where the roads cross. Ramsdell put in five or six barrels of liquor to sell with other goods. Hanks found that the liquor business was ruining the trade and sold it all out at once to an Enfield tavern keeper. They gave up business and removed to Hardwick.

In the year 1860, James and Warner Hanks of Greenwich came to Packardville and built a store on the site of the wagon shop and filled it with a suitable stock of dry goods and groceries and opened for business. They continued in business nine years and sold their stock of goods to Jared Gould, renting him the store. Gould ran the business for two years, when Elmer Whitney succeeded him. Mr. Whitney was in business for nearly two years when his health failed and he died.

Abraham Stevens was the next merchant at Packardville; he began business in January, 1873 and continued for nearly two years, when he died. Since then there has been no store at Packardville and the building has been taken down.

Silas S. Shores built a small store at the Hollow and used it for a flour and meal business for a short time previous to 1872, when he rented the store to J. Monroe Packard who put in a stock of groceries and a small line of dry goods. Packard continued the business for a year and a half and then relinquished the venture because of the limited trade. Mr. Shores still owns the building, which has since been converted into a dwelling.

Justices of the Peace.

Dea. Ebenezer Gray was commissioned as Justice of Peace on petition of the people in 1786, and was probably the first one in town up to that time. James Abercrombie, Isaac Abercrombie, John Conkey, Jr., Barna Brigham, Constant Ruggles, Henry Kingman, Oliver Smith, Jr., Ezra Brown, John Rankin, Jr., Cyrus Kingman, John Parmenter, David Abercrombie, Horace Gray, John Jones, A. C. Kieth, John F. Dyer, C. D. Eaton, Minor Gold, and perhaps others have served the town in the capacity of Justice of Peace. Probably Henry Kingman was as notable as any. He came to Pelham from Bridgewater early in this present century, being the first of that name in the town. For many years he was appealed to for professional services. Many important cases were brought before him for trial as his docket or record book gives abundant evidence. Civil and criminal cases were numerous seventy-five years ago. Squire Kingman was a fine penman, and his services were sought for in drawing up transfers of property, such as deeds and mortgages, etc., and also in the settlement of estates. J. W. Keith, Mrs. J. W. Keith and Silas S. Shores are the Justices now under commission in the town.

Physicians.

Dr. Robert Cutler, the son of Rev. Robert Cutler of Greenwich, was born at Epping, N. H. He began the study of medicine at Hardwick ; began practice in Pelham in 1770; married Widow Esther Guernsey of Northampton, and daughter of Elisha Pomroy, Dec. 22, 1773. He was a physician at Pelham until 1787, when he removed to Amherst. Dr. Cutler was a prominent man in town affairs and served on the school committee. He was not in sympathy with the insurgent element led by Capt. Daniel Shays in 1786-'87 and vigorously opposed the plans of the rebel leader. The Shays men were determined that he should fall into line with them and appointed a night on which he was notified they should call upon him and insist on his accompanying them to Springfield in the capacity of surgeon. The doctor was not at home when they called. Being disappointed in not finding him they demanded food of Mrs. Cutler and she set before them what food there was in the house. When the food was eaten they demanded cider and liquor. Mrs. Cutler placed herself in front of the door leading to the cellar, and declared that all cider or liquor obtained would be secured by passing over her dead body. The rebels made some threats, broke some dishes but went their way without tasting the Doctor's cider.

Dr. Nehemiah Hinds was a man of affairs as well as a physician and his name appears very often in town and church records from 1780 to 1825.

Dr. Isaac Powers was in town early in this century.

Dr. Henry Williams name is found in connection with his services attending the poor of the town.

Dr. Abiah Southworth was another prominent man as well as physician from 1785 to 1828.

Dr. Olney Potter lived at the west end of the town on the farm now owned by George P. Shaw.

Dr. Albigence King was practicing in town as early as 1817, perhaps earlier; he also served the town as school committee.

Dr. Daniel Thompson was a native of Pelham and was a practicing physician for twelve years before removing to Northampton. He served as school committee.

Dr. Nathaniel Ingraham was a physician in 1839.

Dr. Israel H. Taylor was also a native of the town and was a successful physician in his native town before removing to Amherst.

Dr. Adam C. Craig was in town a few years. .

Dr. Code was in town for a short time.

Dr. Rhodes was connected with the Orient house for several seasons, as was Dr. Beers.

Dr. Herman Heed was the proprietor of the Orient Springs House when it was destroyed by fire in 1881. Since his removal from town there has been no resident physician in Pelham.

BLACKSMITHS.

Robert Peibols one of the leading men in the purchase of the tract of land and starting the settlement, was the first blacksmith. Where his shop was located is not known, but the ring of Peibols' anvil was the first heard in the settlement.

Doubtless other blacksmiths came when Peibols laid down his hammer for the last time, but no record tells who they were during the latter part of the eighteenth century. Early in the Nineteenth, Thomas Harlow worked as a blacksmith at the west end of the town near the Methodist church.

Jonathan Pratt had his forge in the Valley, and David Hannum had a blacksmith shop on the county road at the west end of the town.

Abijah Bruce was a blacksmith in the Hollow for many years and lived on the place now occupied by John Vanstone. His shop was on the opposite side of the highway.

Nathaniel Dodge was a farmer and blacksmith on the main road from the center of the town to Packardville and was succeeded by his son, Ellison Dodge.

Samuel W. Russell and his brother John S. Russell worked at blacksmithing at that part of the town called Packardville.

In more recent years Ansel Hill was the village blacksmith, a short distance west of the center of the town.

At present Justin W. Canterbury works at the business towards the south part of the town, and Charles A. Holcomb towards the south part, but nearer the center than Canterbury.

Population of Pelham and Amherst Compared.

YEARS.	PELHAM.	AMHERST.	YEARS.	PELHAM.	AMHERST
1765	371	1045	1855	789	
1776	729		1860	748	3206
1790	1040		1865	737	
1800	1144	1352	1870	673	
1810	1185		1875	633	
1820	1278	1917	1880	614	4298
1830	904		1885	549	
1840	956	2550	1890	486	
1850	983		1895	486	4785

RELIGIOUS SOCIETIES.

The First Presbyterian Church History gathered from the town and parish records, the old church records having been lost or destroyed.

THE PRESBYTERIAN CHURCH.

As all records of the organization of the Scotch Presbyterian church at Pelham are lost or not accessible it is impossible even to fix upon the exact date of its organization. It is well known that the settlers of the town begun to build the meeting house in 1739 and that the first service was held long before it was finished.

Services were continued from that time until the Rev. Robert Abercrombie began to preach to the people of the town in 1742, who these "supplyers" were we find no record. Mr. Abercrombie was settled in 1744 and was the pastor for twelve years,—including the two years that he preached before his ordination. After his dismissal by the Presbytery there was no settled pastor for nine years, or until the settlement of Rev. Richard Crouch Graham in 1763. It was during this long interval that the town was without a settled orthodox minister, that the town was prosecuted or indicted by the grand jury of Hampshire county and ordered to appear in court to answer for the neglect; the record in detail being given elsewhere. During the years from 1754 to 1763 it is probable there was preaching most of the time, sometimes by preachers sent by the Presbytery and sometimes by the action of the people of the town in sending a man as a committee or agent to secure a minister for the town. In 1755, the year after Mr. Abercrombie was dismissed, there were three ministers that received pay for services supplying the pulpit. Rev. Mr. Dickinson was allowed £2—12s, Rev. Mr. Mc-Clintock, £4—8s, and Rev. Mr. John Houston £5—8s.

How many others supplied the pulpit that year is not known, but as £45 was voted for the support of the Gospel that year the services of Messrs. Dickinson, McClintock and Houston could not have covered the entire year. About £40 was allowed for the support of the Gospel each year following 1755 up to the settlement of Mr. Graham but who the ministers were that preached for these Presbyterians all these years is not clear from the town records.

In October, 1760 John Crawford was chosen to go to New Jersey to " Gett a Minister to supply the Pulpit," and on another occasion a man was sent to Pennsylvania on the same errand. The long horseback journeys involved in seeking a minister is evidence that no pains or expense were spared in searching for pulpit supply by the people of Pelham at that time.

At a meeting Jan. 24, 1763, it was "voted that Richard Crouch Graham is to be their Gospel Minister," and £60 a year fixed as the salary of Mr. Graham. He was ordained and began his labors as pastor and a new house was built for him. The only means of information as to the location of the house is the following vote concerning the location of a road: " That there is a two Rode Road established from ye two Rode Road south of Mr. Grahams New House by s^d house to the County Road. Consented to by R Crouch Graham March 4, 1765."

Notwithstanding the protest of twenty-one men against the action of the majority in voting to settle Mr. Graham, (three of them being men who protested against the settlement of Mr. Abercrombie) he seems to have been successful in his work for the seven years he was spared to labor with them. Mr. Graham died on the 25th of February, 1771 in the 32d year of his age, and the town was again left without a settled pastor.

In October, 1772, the Rev. Andrew Bay was invited to settle as pastor, and £80 granted as a settlement; but Mr. Bay was not settled, and the church was without a settled pastor until 1775 when Rev. Nathaniel Merrill was installed, a call having been extended to him Nov. 23, 1774. At a meeting August 28, 1775, it was "Voted there is preperation to be made for the installment of Rev. Mr. Merrill, and that said preperation be for Ministers & other Gentlemen of Liberal Education." Thomas Cochran, Robert Hamilton and James Halbert were chosen committee to make the necessary arrangements for the entertainment of the dignitaries invited to take part in the installation.

From what part of the country Mr. Merrill came from is not indicated, but Jonathan Gray was allowed " £1, 14s expense Money for Bringing up Mr Merrill and family." £70 was voted as settlement and £80 yearly salary; and £60 was added to his salary in 1778.

This income was probably necessary owing to the depreciated currency. Further increase of his salary was found desirable, and in 1779 £420 was added to Mr. Merrill's salary, but this vote was recalled subsequently, as was the increase of £60 previously voted and the pastor was left with the original salary, and its value in currency much depreciated.

Mr. Merrill made a strong appeal to the people of the town after the above reconsideration and the result of his appeal caused the people to do justice to their pastor; and at a meeting Dec. 10, 1779 the £420 was again voted and the vote stood firm. Mr. Merrill's plain statement of facts concerning himself was what the town meeting of Dec. 10, 1779 was called to consider. It was placed before the town in the form of a warrant for their consideration and is found on page 138.

March 23, 1780 it was. "Voted that there is £2000 added to the Rev Mr Merrills £500 for the Present year,"—amounting to £2500 in depreciated continental currency.

On the 18th of May, 1781 there was a town meeting at which the town " Voted Twenty three Hundred and twelve pound ten shillings, old Continental Money to be assessed to Enable the Treasurer to settle with Rev. Mr. Merrill."

July 30, 1781. Article in warrant for town meeting:

"To see if the town will reconsider a vote passed in April last to raise £2312 –10s continental money to redeem a note given to Mr. Merrill by the Treasurer."

There is no record of action on this article; but the vote to raise £30 in hard money for the supply of the pulpit at this meeting indicates that Rev. Mr. Merrill had been dismissed, although no record of dismissal appears upon the records,—the dismissal of ministers being by action of the Presbytery or Council.

The Presbyterian church and town was without a pastor again for quite a number of years and dependent upon the "Supplyer." It was during this long period in which there was no settled pastor that the church and town had the experience with the unregenerate impostor, Stephen Burroughs, in 1784, and the year and more of turmoil and excitement of the Shays Rebellion in 1786-87. The second parish had been organized and consequently the first parish was obliged to do the same and the business of securing supplyers devolved upon the parish instead of the town from 1786 to 1822.

First Parish Records, 1786 to 1822.

The call for the first meeting of the first parish was issued by Ebenezer Mattoon, Jr., of Amherst, Justice of the Peace, and was directed to John Rinkin, Dec. 25, 1786. The parish was organized Jan. 4, 1787 with the following officers: Ebenezer Gray, moderator: Andrew Abercrombie, parish clerk; Lieut. Joseph Packard, Hugh Johnston, Capt. John Thompson, parish committee; John Harkness, Joseph Hamilton, Lieut. Nathaniel Sampson, assessors; John Peebles, parish treasurer.

Sept. 18, 1787, " Voted to authorize Collector to take produce for parish Rates at following prices :

"Voted that the collector shall take flaxseed at 4^s pr Bushel—Wheat at 4^s–6^d pr bushel—Rye at 3^s pr bushel, Indian corn at 2^s-4^d pr bushel,—oats at 1^s-4^d per bushel,—Peas at 4^s per bushel,—Butter at 7^d pr pound. Voted that the above said stipulated articles shall be transported by each individual that has rates to Pay to the Parish treasurer, that each carry his produce to the Collector, and the latter not obliged to take flaxseed after Sept. next."

A committee was given full power to settle with the second parish concerning pews in dispute by allowing the owners one-third of the first cost if good security is given for the pews. "Voted that committee allow half way between one half and one third of the first cost of pews in the first parish meeting house."

Meeting, Oct. 5, 1787 "Voted that Pews lately purchased of the second parish shall be disposed of by seating them to those that have no Pews and pay the highest taxes, shall have their choice of Pews by paying the sum which was offered for them when they were formerly seated."

Oct. 15, " Voted that there be made one tear of pews on the side Gallery and that they be offered to the highest in valuation that has no pews—so in the same proportion till the whole is compounded."

Meeting, Feb. 7, 1791.

" Chose Lt John Rinken, Lt Nath^{ll} Sampson, Mr Hugh Johnson, Mr Jonathan Leach, Lt Benoni Shurtlieff a committee to fix on a sum or sums for the Settlement and Sallery of Mr Jabez Pond Fisher.

Voted to give Mr. Fisher £145 Settlement, ½ of it in one year from the time of Settlement and the other ½ in two years from said time. Voted to give Mr. Fisher £65 a year for two years then add £2–10^s

yearly till it amounts to £80." But Jabez Pond Fisher was not settled in Pelham.

Mr. Merrill was dismissed in 1780 and until August 27, 1793 they were without a settled pastor. Patrick Peebles and Robert McCulloch had gone to bring Rev. William Oliver's family (probably from Londonderry, N. H.) to Pelham, Mr. Oliver having accepted their call. At this distance from the period of which we are writing it is impossible to state what obstacles may have been in the way of having settled ministers instead of supplyers, but the fault must have rested largely with the people themselves. Just how many ministers they had called to settle cannot be determined accurately but it was a fact that in the early part of 1791 they had given calls to Rev. Jabez Pond Fisher and Rev. Solomon Spalding, but for some reason that does not appear upon the record the call was not accepted in either case. Mr. Freeman and a Mr. Stone and probably others had preached as supplyers.

Mr. Oliver accepted their call in 1792, but one condition of his acceptance was, the paying one-half of the £160 settlement within two months after his ordination and the other half within one year, instead of one year to pay the first half, and two years to pay the second, as first voted. Possibly the knowledge had become general that the people of Pelham did not have the united and harmonious relations with their ministers to be desired, or if such relations existed at the settlement of a minister they did not continue long, and under the circumstances it would be a good move to have a good part of the settlement paid early. The ordination had taken place and there was now a settled minister in the first church and parish as we learn by the record of the meeting, Oct. 28, 1793.

Meeting, June 10, 1794.

" Article 3 To see if it is the minds of the Parish to Direct the Parish Committee to proceed in Colouring the backside of the Meetinghouse according to a former vote of the Parish.

Article 4 To see if it is the minds of the Parish to Grant Dr Southworth and others the Privilege of Putting in a window for the use of the Pulpit in the first Parish Meetinghouse."

On article 3, it was " Voted to Direct the Parish Committee to postpone Cullering the backside of the Meetinghouse for the Present." No action on the proposition of Dr. Southworth to place a window in the meeting house to allow the light to shine into the pulpit.

The assessors were directed "to asses the salery of Rev. Mr. Oliver and the remainder part of his Settlement as soon as May be." This indicates that his settlement was not paid according to the vote when he was settled.

Meeting, May 14, 1799.

"Voted to seat the singers in the gallerys. Voted to give the Singers all the front seats and all seats in the East gallery, and one half of the seats in the West gallery."

Both Parishes had begun to realize that it was not easy to run two parishes in the town, and in a call for a meeting of the first parish, May 29, 1805, appears this article:

" To see if it is the Minds of the Parish to Chose a committee to consult with the Committee from the East Parish on the Expediency of the Parishes Joining in the Support of the Gospel and Pass any vote on the subject that shall be thought Necessary on the Subject."

Acting on the above article it was " Voted to chose a Committee of five—Lt Rinken, Dea Gray, Landlord Hach, Major Conkey and Esquire Abercrombie—said Committee to treat with the Second Parish on the Expediency of the Parishes Joining in the Support of the Gospel."

The labors of Rev. Andrew Oliver had ended in the first parish, for, at a meeting Oct. 7, 1805, the warrant calls for action on the following business:

" To see what sum the Parish will Grant for the yearly support of the Rev[d] Mr. Brainard in Case he takes the Pastoral Charge of this Church and Congregation and Pass any vote the Parish shall think Necessary on the Subject."

Actions on above article :—" Voted to raise the Rev Mr. Elijah Brainard $350 for his yearly support so long as he Performs the Ministerial Duties in this Church and Congregation.

Choose Dea. Ebenezer Gray, Dea. Nathaniel Sampson and Mr. John Rinken Committee to Make arrangements for the Installation of Rev. Mr. Elijah Brainard."

March 23, 1806 " Voted to Choose two men to go to Randolph to Sarch out Mr. Brainard's Carictor :—Said men is Dea. Thompson and Dea. Gray."

Unquestionably the Committee went to Randolph to "Search the Character" of Mr. Brainard as at a Meeting in May following, Dea. Gray was allowed $15.29 for a journey to Randolph and Dea. Thompson $17.00 for a journey to Randolph:—the latter was also allowed $4 for the use of a horse on the same journey and Dea. Gray was allowed $5 for his time.

The murmurings of the anti-Brainard party seemed to come up continually as shown by an article in the warrant for a Parish Meeting, November 25,1806, based on a petition sent in by anti-Brainard men. What they petitioned for is herewith set forth:—

" To see if the Parish will Remit the Parish taxes of all those who do not attend the Administration of the Rev. Elijah Brainard nor wish to support him as their Minister."

"Voted not to Remit taxes of those who do not attend the Administration of the Rev. Mr. Brainard."

Meeting May 3, 1809. The commendable freedom from trouble in the church and parish for two years past could not be continued, and the old opposition to Rev. Mr. Brainard crops out again, as per warrant:—

" Article 2. To see if the parish will Choose a Committee to converse with Mr. Brainard at this session and state to him the situation of supporting him as their Minister and Make and Receive propositions for his removal from the Charge of this Church and Congregation, and make report of it at s^d Meeting and poll all votes relative to the above subject."

Action on above article. " Voted to choose a committee to treat with Mr. Brainard Respecting taking a Dismission,—James Abercrombie, Wm. Dunlap, Lt. Taylor, Lt. Rankin and Samuel Clark, committee."

A special Meeting of the Parish was called Oct. 17, 1811, with an article in the warrant, of which the following is a true copy.

"Article 2. To see if the inhabitants of the first Parish of Pelham will vote to Dismiss the Rev. Elijah Brainard from his Pastoral care and Charge of this Church and Congregation of said Parish."

Action on warrant:—" Doct. Abiah Southworth chosen Moderator:—Voted to Dismiss Rev. Mr. Brainard in a legal Mode.

Voted to choose a agent to Attend Presbytery Respecting the Dismission of Mr. Brainard, said Agent is James Abercrombie.

Voted to send Ensign John Rinken to Presbytery with Mr. Brainard."

The Presbytery made the Pelham people two propositions for them to select from in dismissing Mr. Brainard, and at a Meeting, Nov. 18, 1811, they "Voted to Except the first proposal of the Presbytery, that is, to pay Mr. Elijah Brainard $160 according to the Proposal of the Presbytery.

Voted to raise $160 to meet the above vote."

The dismissal of Mr. Brainard was accomplished at last after a rather stormy pastorate of about five years. He was settled by installation near the last of the year 1805 or early in 1806. Early in the spring following the mutterings of dissatisfaction began and a committee of two Deacons were sent to Randolph "To Sarch out Mr. Brainard's Carictor," and from that time on there was a Brainard and an Anti-Brainard party until he was dismissed.

It is probable that Mr. Brainard still remained a resident of the town after his dismissal from the pastorate, as in a copy of the tax bills of the first parish for the year 1813 the name of Elijah Brainard appears as a tax payer.

In 1812 Andrew Hyde, David Harkness, George Macomber, Isaac Otis, Jun., John Harkness, Jr. and David Hannum petitioned the General Court to be set off to Amherst for parochial purposes, and an order of notice was served on the parish by Ebenezer Mattoon sheriff. The parish voted promptly not to set off the petitioners and choose a committee to oppose the petition in the General Court.— They were not set off.

Meeting, Dec. 4, 1812.

Warrant, Article 2. "To see if the Parish will Chose a Committee to Converse with the Committee of the Second Parish of Pelham respecting forming a union of the two Parishes so far as relates to Ministerial affairs."

Committee's Report.

"To the Inhabitants of the first Parish in Pelham, in this Meeting, Assembled. Gentlemen:—We your Committee appointed to Consult with a Committee from the Second Parish of Pelham, have meet According to Appointment and have agreed to propose to the several Parishes as follows: (Viz.) That the first Parish should raise one hundred Dollars and the Second Parish one Hundred Dollars and that the aforesaid sums be laid out for the support of a publick teacher of religion and Morality, the publick meetings to be held three fifths of the time in the first Parish Meeting house and two fifths in the Second. The time proposed for said Agreement to Commence is the first of April next.

Ebenezer Gray, John Rankin, James Abercrombie, Committee. Pelham, Dec. 31, 1812."

Committees of both parishes agreed upon a basis of union in Dec. 1812 to take effect April, 1813, but no union was effected.

As there was no settled pastor now the sum of $200 was thought sufficient for the support of the Gospel for the year 1814.

Meeting, Jan. 2, 1815. "Voted to give Rev. Winthrop Bailey a call for Settlement.—Voted to give him $400 per year providing he will settle with us as long as he remains our Minister."

March 24, 1817. About this time there began to be some dissatisfaction with the Old Meeting house. Some seemed to be in favor of general repairs on the old building and others were anxious for a new one. This difference of opinion was the cause of disagreement and contention. The parish would vote to build a new house, and order plans:—then reconsider, and vote to repair the old one by subscription. Adjournment would be carried at this stage of the proceedings and on assembling a vote to build a new Meeting house would be carried. This change of sentiment and reconsideration of votes continued through many meetings for a year or more and then settled down to making an agreement with the proprietors of the old Meeting house, July 4, 1818, as follows: "Voted to give and relinquish to the proprietors of the pews in the Meeting house the pew ground and seats in the front of the body pews on the lower floor in lieu of the $200 voted on the 27th of May last to assist said proprietors in repairing the Meeting house."

April 10, 1820. It is possible that the vote of the previous year to allow Doct. Abiah Southworth $5 for sweeping the Meeting house, "Extra and Common," had caused a belief that the Doctor was getting too much of the parish money into his hands, and the care of the Meeting house was struck off to the lowest bidder. Eliot Gray got the plum for $2.17 for the ensuing year. The meeting was adjourned several times and the last to July 4th.

A large measure of harmony and contentment seemed to prevail under the ministration of the Rev. Winthrop Bailey and the people were not called together in parish meeting during the time from July 4, 1820, to April 3, 1821—which was a long time for them. Rev. Mr. Bailey was a man greatly respected by the people of Pelham and had much more pleasant relations with them than some of the pastors that preceded him. He was on the school committee for several years, and was chosen as delegate from the town to the

Constitutional Convention held at Boston on the 3d of Nov. 1820, for the revision of the Constitution. He owned a farm in the town and probably devoted a portion of his time to tilling it. Mr. Bailey was dismissed in September 1825 and was the last Presbyterian pastor settled in Pelham. Some years elapsed before another pastor was called and during this interval there was a change to Congregationalism. Mr. Bailey moved to Deerfield in 1825,—taught in the Deerfield Academy: and preached at the Unitarian Church at Greenfield, now known as All Souls Church, from 1825 to 1830. Descendants of Mr. Bailey lived in Pelham for many years and there are some in Northampton at the present time.

Taxing the property of the whole town for the support of the minister began to be a source of irritation, and considerable opposition arose, not only in Pelham but all over the state from those of different religious sects that had began to appear in the towns. In Pelham when the Scotch Presbyterians were in the ascendency, the few Quakers, Baptists, Universalists and Unitarians that had come in objected to having their property taxed to support the Presbyterian Church. The feeling became so strong in the state that in 1833 the Eleventh Amendment to the Constitution was adopted which put an end to the taxation of any mans property for the support of the Gospel without the consent of the owner, and the result of this change tended to lessen the amount raised for the support of the Presbyterian Church and to cause a neglect of the ordinances of the gospel on the part of some of the people of Pelham.

In the foregoing records of the first parish the frequent applications for abatement of a parish tax because parties taxed claimed to belong to the Baptist persuasion, or of some other belief than the "standing order" or that they were Quakers, gave the Scotch Presbyterians not a little vexation, and it will be remembered that they required those who desired to be relieved from taxation for the support of the Gospel, to prove they were of another faith before the tax was levied upon them. While no such documentary proofs appear on the parish record book they are found on the town records, copies of a few follow:

"Belchertown, July 14 day A. D. 1806.

This may Serve to Sertify the Town of Pelham the first Parish in Particular that Mr. Oliver Smith of Pelham is Member of the Baptist Society in Belchertown and Pays towards the support of the Gospel thair.

JEREMIAH HASKEL, Teacher."

"We certify that Lewis Draper, William Gaskin, Levi Newell, Solomon Braley, Collins Braley, Jesse Allen, Esick Baker, Joseph Howard, Silas Bayington, Laben Alby, Ezra Brown, Jesse F. Peck, Isaac Otis Jun., Oliver Curtice, Nathan Jilson, Sen., Reuben Waiscoat, John Taylor, Aaron Dwelley attend the Baptist Meeting in Shutesbury and when held elsewhere, and pay to us the Baptist order in Shutesbury there fore, these are to Desire that they may be Exempted from Taxes as the Law Directs."
JOSEPH SMALAGE, LISCOMB BRIGHAM, LUTHER SPEAR, Committee.
Shutesbury, Nov. 11th, 1811."

"We certify that Joseph Whipple of Pelham Belongs to the Religious Society in the town of Dana, Called Universalists.
Dated this first Day of April 1812.
STEPHEN JOHNSTON, AARON JOHNSON, Committee."

Pelham, Third Mo. the 28th, 1820.
"We the Subscribers, Overseers of the Meeting or Society of Friends Called Quakers in the Town of Pelham in the County of Hampshire do hereby certify that Samuel Willard Usually attends with us in our Stated Meetings for Worship.
ASAHEL ALDRICH, CLERK."

FROM THE RECORDS OF THE SECOND PRESBYTERIAN CHURCH AND PARISH OF PELHAM, FROM 1786 TO 1822.

After a long contest on the part of the people living East of the West Branch of Swift River they succeeded in securing the passage of an act of incorporation through the legislature for a Second parish, to include all that part of Pelham East of the River, and also included some people living in New Salem.

The act passed both houses of the General Court and was signed by Gov. James Bowdoin, Jan. 28, 1786.

The first parish meeting was held Aug. 24, 1786.—Moderator, Dr. N. Hinds; Clerk, Lamond Gray; Treasurer, James C. McMillin; Parish Committee, Dr. N. Hinds, Alexander Berry, John Linsey; Assessors, Wm. Conkey, Jun., Lt. John Hamilton, William Berry; Collector, Eliot Gray; Daniel Grey, Surety for the Collector.

With the above officers chosen the Second Parish of Pelham was organized.

£10 was voted for the support of the Gospel and £10 for defraying parish expenses for the year, ending in April, 1787, when a new set of officers was chosen and £10 voted for the support of the Gospel.

In March, 1788, It was "Voted to send a man to inform Mr. Chatman that we are making preparations to give him a Call.

Voted Daniel Gray should be s⁴ Messenger.

Voted to appoint a Minister to hold a day of fasting to Moderate the Call for the settlement of Mr. Chatman.

Voted that the Rev. Moses Baldwin should be s⁴ Minister.

Voted to give Mr. Chatman a call.

Voted six shillings per week in summer and seven shillings in winter for boarding the Minister."

April 14, 1788. "Voted to give Mr. Chatman £150 Settlement and from £50 to £70 Sallary—Payable thus,—£50 yearly for three years—then £55 the fourth year and advancing £5 a year until £70 and that be his sallery as long as he remains the Minister of s⁴ Parish."

Dec. 9, 1788. " Voted that the Committee of said Parish should proceed in building the Meeting house as fast as they Conveniently Can.

There is no record of the settlement of Mr. Chatman over the Second church, Oct. 25, 1790.

" Voted to invite Mr. Jabiz Pond Fisher to settle with us in the Ministry.—Then Voted him settlement and sallery just as was voted to Mr. Chatman—with the addition of twenty cords of wood annually."

No record of the settlement of Jabiz Pond Fisher.

April 12, 1793. Voted to send for Mr. Fish to supply the pulpit four Sabbaths."

Dec. 20, 1793. " Voted to give the Rev. Matthias Cazier a call to settle in the Ministery in this 2⁴ Parish of Pelham. Voted to give the Rev. Matthias Cazier £100 Settlement and £65 and 20 cords of wood to be his yearly sallery."

Mr. Cazier was settled over the church and parish. The new Meeting house was still unfinished and there was not entire harmony and satisfaction with Mr. Cazier, as the very grave remonstrance presented against the action of the council indicates.

Action of the remonstrants to calling Mr. Cazier, from the church records.

" To the Rev⁴ Eccleseastical Council Convened at Pelham Second Parish for the purpose of introducing Mr. Matthias Cazier into the work of the Gospel Ministery over the church and people in this place.

Gentlemen :—We the subscribers belonging to said parish view with great concern the measures taken by this people for the settlement of a Gospel Ministry among us as now proposed ; we as individuals remonstrate against the proceedings of both Church and Parish and seriously request of the Venerable Council that they will not be active in supporting the gentleman proposed to the work of the Ministry over us contrary to our inclination and remonstrance.

Our reasons against such measures are the following, Viz;

1. That we are total strangers to the gentlemen's character and know not whether it is religious or moral.

2. The church and parish we consider to have been hasty and premature in their invitation of him to a settlement before the people would have convenient opportunity to cultivate such an acquaintance with him as to form a satisfactory opinion respecting him.

3. We are by no means agreed with Mr. Matthias Cazier in religious sentiment so far as we have been able to learn them from his public preaching the few Sabbaths he has been with us, and desire to have no such public teacher placed over us the tendency of whose instructions we concieve to be subversive of all morality.

4. The conduct of Mr. Matthias Cazier on all matters relative to his settlement among us has been so opinionative and dictatorial as to give us grounds to apprehend that he is not possessed of that spiritual prudence which is requisite in a gospel minister, and of a Soverign disposition to Lord it over God's heritage.

The above, Gentlemen, is sufficient to convey our sentiments respecting Mr. Matthias Cazier: we earnestly desire to have a gospel minister settled among us whose religious sentiments are similar to our own: and will cheer fully unite with this parish in the choice and settlement of such a gentlemen when Providence shall open a door for it.

But permit us to assure your venerable council that if this man is settled amongst us we will take the earliest opportunity to petition the general assembly of this Commonwealth that agreeably to the Constitution of this state we may severally be annexed to those towns upon the religious institutions of which we can conscientiously and profitably attend.

We are with greatest respect, Gentlemen, your friends and servants.

WILLIAM CONKEY, ALEXANDER CONKEY, WM. COWAN, THOMAS CONKEY, JOSEPH AIKEN, DANIEL GRAY, JOEL CONKEY, SAMUEL SLOAN. Pelham, March 23^d, 1794.

A true copy of the original. Attest
REUBEN MOSS, Scribe."

Rev. Reuben Moss was the pastor of the church in Ware and was doubtless present as pastor of his church at the council convened for the ordination of Rev. Mr. Cazier, and as scribe, made the copy of the remonstrance.

May 9, 1794. "Voted to take away the south poarch from the Meeting house and finish the place where it stands. Voted to make an alteration on the north side pews in the Meeting house to have an Elder seat. Voted to have a hunge cannapy."

March 30, 1795. "Voted to remit Capt. Daniel Shays rates for the settlement of Mr. Cazier."

March 28, 1796. "Voted to call a council to decide the difficulties between the parish and Mr. Cazier, also voted for the parish to chuse a committee to request Mr. Cazier to join with the church in calling a Mutual Council to try the charges that have been brought against Mr. Cazier."

That the matters which were troubling the good people of the second parish at this time may be better understood we copy from the church records the charges of Dr. Hinds against Rev. Matthias Cazier over his own signature.

"To the Church of Christ in Pelham, East Parish :—

The subscriber as Plaintiff exhibits the following complaints as matter of grievance against the Moral Character of the Reverend Matthias Cazier.

He considers the following articles as what may be confirmed by legal evidence and as contrary to the laws of God,—what he would wish to submit to the judgement and decision of the Church.

The articles of aggrievance are as follows, Viz:

1. A disregard to the truth, repeatedly, first in declaring previous to his installation that he would give up his settlement whenever he should be dissmissed from Pelham, if the Council judged he was in the blame, and at another time denying that he ever made such a promise.

Secondly.—his reporting that he had sent a letter to Mrs. Cazier that he should set out from Pelham to Castleton on the 12th day of May, and then saying that if he did not set out on the 5th of May in the same year, he should dissappoint Mrs. Cazier and fail of being at the sd Castleton at the time he had sent to her in the above sd letter.

Thirdly.—In representing and declaring that his great opposer Reuben Marston of Castleton had manifested that he had wronged him, and made retraction for it which is not a truth.

Fourthly.—In falling from a bargain he made with me to procure him lumber for his house.

Fifthly.—In declaring that he believed only a less part of Creation would be saved, and afterwards denying that he ever said a less part would be saved but the greater part.

Sixthly.—Profaneness. In saying that he would not pray for the Reverend Mr. Williams of Leveritt because he was in error; but if he did he must pray as the other man did.—O Lord! Damn such damnable doctrines.

Neh'h Hinds."

Meeting, April 6, 1797. Chose parish officers etc. "Voted to have a dog whipper—choose John Gray Dog Whipper by giving four mills.

Voted to invite a number of Ministers to consult and advise the parish under their present difficulties.—Voted to invite the Rev. Joseph Blodgett of Greenwich, the Rev. Andrew Oliver of Pelham, the Rev. David Parsons of Amherst and the Rev. Thomas Holt of Hardwick for s^d Advisers."

Thomas Gray, Robert Crossett and Dr. Hinds was chosen a committee to present the case to the four ministers and they heard the case of the parish on the last Wednesday in April 1797 at the house of Dr. Hinds. May 3, '97 the parish voted to ask the church to call a mutual council before which the difficulties might be brought for final decision, and a committee was chosen to lay the case before the council, and also instructed to provide for the entertainment of the of the council which was to convene at the house of Dr. Hinds, and which they desired to have convene before the first of July.

The church made answer to the request for a mutual council by letter to the committee of the parish, a copy of which follows.

The reply of the Church to the demand of the Parish for a council to examine into the charges against Rev. Matthias Cazier by Dr. Nehemiah Hinds.

"Pelham, May 5, 1797.
To the Church of Christ in the 2^d Parish in Pelham:
To Doctor Nehemiah Hinds, Mr. William Berry and Mr. William McMillen, a committee chosen by the 2^d Parish of Pelham who applied to us by their letter dated May 3^d, 1797, to call an Ecclesiastical Council for the purpose of examining into certain difficulties which the said Parish may have with their Pastor:—
Gentlemen.—This church beg leave to inform you that they feel in duty bound in chusing and calling an Ecclesiastical Council, to abide by the principles upon which Mr. Cazier was settled in this place.—We also inform you that we are willing to join with the Rev. Matthias Cazier in chusing a Mutual Council, one half to be chosen by this church and the other half of the Council to be chosen by Mr. Cazier,—for the purpose of looking into our Difficulties and bringing them to a final issue.
Whenever the Parish, individuals of the Parish, or an individual, will bring in a written complaint to the Church against our pastor, signed by those who will engage to support it,—and give the names of two or more witnesses for the support of each charge in the complaint, and that the Parish shall vote Money for the support of said Council when convened,—then the Church will proceed to the choice of a council, and send letters Missive to Churches which may be called to by their pastor and delegates to the house of Doctor Nehemiah Hinds,—at a time which shall be appointed by the Church when they shall send letters for a council.
Wishing that our present conduct may be influential to our mutual good.
We remain yours affectionately,
By order of the Church,
MATTHIAS CAZIER, Moderator,
JAMES MCMILLEN, Clerk of the Church.
A true copy from the original,
JAMES C. MCMILLEN, Clerk of the Church."

The letter of the church concerning the mutual council was not satisfactory to the parish and a vote was passed not to accept it. It was also " Voted that all that are willing to enjoy Mr. Cazier as their minister may have that privelige and all that are not go where they please."

At a Meeting of the Parish May 9, 1797 John Maklam was chosen to present the answer of the church to Rev. David Parsons of Amherst for his consideration and for him to pass judgment upon the same. Rev. Joseph Blodgett of Greenwich was also invited to review the answer of the church to the parish.

Whatever the advice of the two eminent ministers may have been is not stated, but the parish " Voted May 11th to accept the answer or terms of the Church, except the word *engage*, and the granting of money."

Letters Missive were sent out and the Council was called on the 14th of June, 1797, at the house of Dr. Hinds to consider his charges. No record of the action of the Council is found, but at a parish Meeting held July 3, 1797 it was "Voted that the result of Council should be read.—Also voted to accept the result of the Council."

Meeting Feb. 21, 1798.

" Dr. Hinds moderator. —Motioned and seconded that all those that are not for Mr. Cazier as their Minister under present existing circumstances to move to the west end of the Meeting house and also twenty-nine moved to the west end of the Meeting house, which was the whole of the voters present."

This would indicate that the council of June 14, 1797 did not reconcile the people to Mr. Cazier. There was a council called on March 14, 1798 which voted to dismiss Mr Cazier, after hearing the facts. Rev. David Parsons of Amherst was moderator and Rev. Thomas Holt scribe. The council in their report reviewed the troubles of parish and pastor at length, and the vote for dismission was unanimous, after giving good advice to the church, pastor and parish.

However injudicious and imprudent Mr. Cazier may have been as pastor of the second church in Pelham he was evidently a man of much ability, a fine penman, and wrote in a pointed yet respectful manner in his address to the church which follows :

"Pelham, April 25, 1796.
An address to the Church of Christ in the 2ᵈ Parish in Pelham.

DEARLY BELOVED BRETHREN :—As I consider the sole right of impeaching my character is invested in you,—I shall always view your conduct as justifiable, in making use of all the light which can come to you by any means, in order to see whether my character deserves impeachment.—I also consider that you are under an obligation by your own articles, as well as by the general laws of Christ,—to attend to creditable reports existing against the character of any of your members.—I would beg leave also to observe that all reports have some degree of credit until experience shall determine you to conclude that any person, who makes a report, has done that, which in your view ought to destroy the credit of his reports.—Under a sense of your duty to be a city set upon a hill—I would observe,—that whereas I have heard a report—that Mr. David Wait has intimated in a Parish Meeting that he has a difficulty with me. Therefore I would request that you would take such a method as your wisdom shall direct to search into the nature of his difficulty and the evidence which Mr. Wait has to convince you that he has a just foundation for the difficulty. I would also observe that it would discover partiality in you in favor of me to presume that Mr. Wait would give the most distant hint in a publick manner,—that he was burdened with me, without being always ready to give you sufficient evidence, that his burden is justly founded.

Therefore proper respect to Mr. Wait requires you to make enquiry into his difficulty and the evidence which he may give to convince you that he ought to have the difficulty.

I am Dear Brethren Yours
in the fellowship of the Gospel,
MATTHIAS CAZIER."

MEETING APRIL 17, 1798.

The church and parish being destitute of a settled pastor, Daniel Gray, Wm. McMillen, Wm. Berry, Robert Crossett and James Linsey was chosen a committee to supply the pulpit and another long term without a settled pastor began. "April 13, 1801 it was voted that the sexton shall be the lowest bidder, and was struck off to Jonathan Millen for $1.23. He is to repair the windows by putting into them nine squares of glass, and sweep the Meeting house once if no preaching and four times if preaching. Chose Doc't Hinds and Capt. Millen Dog Whippers. Voted to have a candidate to preach in this parish. Voted the place for the candidate should be the Lowest bidder and was struck off to Jonathan Millen for 8s—3d per week for Boarding him and keeping his horse." In 1802 a committee was chosen to converse with Mr. Tobey on terms of settlement but there is no record of Mr. Tobey being settled. Mr. Sebastian C. Cabbot was engaged to preach three months, in October, 1806, and he continued to preach for sometime; $150 was voted for his support in December of that year, " on condition that Mr. Sebastian Cabbot shall have the privilege to be Dismist in one year after giving notice to the parish that he was dissatisfied by lodging his reasons in the Clerk's office ; and whenever a Majority of the Inhabitants shall vote against him as minister by a Dissatisfaction of his Moral Carricter he shall be Dismist in one year after being notified of such Vote." The time was afterwards changed to six months.

March 27, 1807. "Voted that the Ecclesiastical Council now convened shall go on and settle Mr Sebastian C. Cabbot to the work of the Gospel Ministry, etc." At the same meeting the parish voted " Fifthly for the parish to act and pass all such votes as shall be thought necessary to keep peice and harmony with themselves and the world of Mankind."

August 21, 1809. " Voted to Join with the Church to agree with Mr. Sabastian Cabbot to call a mutual council for his dismission." Mr. Cabbot was dismissed but probably not until February, 1810. No record of the work of the council is found on the parish records.

The people were without a pastor again and dependent upon committees to supply the pulpit.

The records speak of negotiations with the West Parish for the mutual support of the Gospel as early as 1816, and these negotiations were continued from time to time by both parishes but there is no record found of their joining in the good work up to the time Prescott was set off as a town in 1822.

The name of Rev. Mr. Marcy appears in a way to indicate that he preached for the Second Parish in 1816.

Rev. Mr. Cazier was settled early in 1794 and dismissed March 14, 1798, after a pastorate of four years. Rev. Mr. Cabbot was settled in 1807 and the pastoral relation was ended in 1809, so that for only about six years did the people of the second parish have a settled ministry from 1786 to 1822, a period of 36 years. Besides the two ministers that were settled we find personal mention of only a few ministers of the many that must have preached there during the period named. Rev. Mr. Chatman, Rev. Jabiz Pond Fisher, Rev. Mr. Fish, Rev. Mr. Marcy, Rev. Mr. Tobey, and Rev. Mr. Moss are all the records make mention of as supplyers of the pulpit. when there was no settled minister. A Congregational church was organized in Prescott in place of the Presbyterian church in 1823.

CONFESSION OF FAITH AND ENGAGEMENTS OF THE EAST CHURCH IN PELHAM.

"Whereas in divine Providence we are formed into a Society by ourselves, we, to promote the worship of God, the interest of the Redeemer, and our Mutual Edification thereto under Christ as our Head in one church by the Name of the East Church in Pelham. In testimony of our Union, Faith and Fellowship, we adopt the following Confession of Faith and Engagements.

1. We believe the Scriptures of the Old and New Testaments to be the Word of God and the only rule of Faith and Manners.

2. We own and believe the Doctrines contained in the Westminister Confession of Faith approved by the Church of Scotland, to be founded upon the Word of God, and we acknowledge the same as the Confession of our faith, and we will firmly and constantly adhere thereto, assert, maintain, and defend the same to the utmost of our Power and Ability.

3. We are persuaded that the Presbyterian Government and Discipline of the Church of Christ as have been practiced in the Church of Scotland, are founded upon the Word of God, and agreeable thereto, and we promise to submit to the Said Government and Discipline, and to concur with the same and endeavor to maintain, to support and defend the said Presbyterian Government and Discipline as far as our position and Circumstances will admit thereof.

4. We promise and engage to do our endeavor to maintain the Peace and Unity of the Church, the Worship of God, the honor of Christ and the interest of his Kingdom according to our respective, Places and Relations.

5. We promise and engage as fellows citizens with the Saints, and of the Household of God, Constantly and perseveringly to walk together in all the ordinances of Christ's house and in all the Precepts of his holy religion, to pray for one another, and to watch over one another, not for our halting, but for our mutual good unto the edification of the Body of which we are joint members.

MOSES GRAY,	AARON GRAY,	DANIEL GRAY,
JAMES C. MCMILLEN	JOHN LINSEY,	PATRICK MCMILLEN,
JOHN HAMILTON,	JOHN MCMILLEN,	ALEXANDER BERRY,
	WILLIAM BERRY,	THOMAS MCMILLEN."

The Persons belonging to the Church in the Second Parish when it was incorporated we learn from a paper bearing the names in the Volume of Ancient Church records, and which is carefully copied.

"A List of the Members both male and female of the Church of Christ in the Second Parish in Pelham,—you are to observe the Men's Names are taken down and their wives Names in one line.

The Names of Men whose wives have joined the church and they have not are set against their wives Names.

Mens Names		
Deacon Patrick McMillen,	Mary McMillen,	
Deacon Daniel Gray,	Mary Gray,	
Aaron Gray,	Ruth Gray—Isabel Gray,	
Moses Gray,		
Alexander Berry,	Martha Berry,	
James C. McMillen,	Sarah McMillen,	
William Berry,	Naomi Berry,	
John McMillen,	Mary McMillen,	
	W^d Rebacah Maklem,	
	Eunice Sloan,	Samuel Sloan,
	Abigail Shays,	Capt. Daniel Shays,
Isaac Baker,	Rebeccah Baker,	
	W^d Mary Linsey,	
	W^d Anne Linsey	
Jeremiah Gray		
James Linsey	Mary Ann Linsey,	
	Alice Willson,	William Willson,
	Sarah Crosett,	Archibald Crosett,
William Linsey,	Susannah Linsey,	
Joel Gray,	Martha Gray,	
Isreal Crosett,	Martha Crosett,	
	Lyda Gray,	Thomas Gray,
	Jean McMillen,	Wm. McMillen."

During the pastorate of Rev. Matthias Cazier, Capt. Joel Gray was in command of one of the Militia companies, and William Linsey a member of the Company and also a member of the Second Church became intoxicated on training day,—was sorry for it, and made a confession which we copy. It is undoubtedly the composition of Mr. Cazier and in his handwriting, and probably expressed the erring one's sense of sin and need of forgiveness much better than he could have done it himself.

"Pelham, Oct. 15, 1797.

To the Church of Christ of the Second Parish of Pelham, under the care of Rev^{1d} Matthias Cazier,—from William Linsey a member of said Church:

BELOVED BRETHREN:—As on last Monday, at the Meeting of Capt. Joel Gray^s Company, I was overtaken with the drinking of more Spirituous liquor than my nature could bare, and thus by my conduct I have given an occasion to my fellow men to speak reproachfully of the Christian Cause of which I am an unworthy professor. Therefore I think it my duty to acknowledge my offence in a public manner. Therefore I now confess with shame and sorrow that I am guilty of the sin of intoxication,—and I pray God against whom I have sinned that he would, for the sake of the Lord Jesus Christ, pardon my great offense, and preserve me for the future from this and all other kinds of sins. I ask also the forgiveness of all whom I have offended by my sin.—

I desire brethren, that you would accept of this my confession, and that you would pray for me, that God would, in mercy, overrule my past sins to his own glory, the good of his cause, the good of this church and the good of him who now confesses his sin.—That it would please God, by his grace to preserve from falling again into sin.—I remain, Dear brethren, your unworthy brother, but sincere in the faith and fellowship of the Gospel.

WM. LINSEY."

This confession was read in public and accepted by the Church, October 15, 1797.

Jeremiah Gray became prejudiced against Rev. Mr. Cazier, took action against him, and absented himself from the sacrament of the Lord's Supper. He acknowledged his error sorrowfully. The confession of his error and sin is in the handwriting of Mr. Cazier and Mr. Gray affixed his signature to the document.

" Pelham, May 20th, 1797.

To the Church of Christ of the Second Parish of Pelham under the pastoral care of Revd Matthias Cazier from Jeremiah Gray a member of said Church.

BELOVED BRETHREN —As my voluntarily absenting myself from the communion with the church, the last time the Sacrament of the Lord's supper was administered in this place, is well known both to the church and congregation.—I feel myself in duty bound to make Christian satisfaction for my great offense against God.

Therefore I am willing to acknowledge before the church and congregation,—That I am guilty of breaking covenant with the Church of Christ in this place.—I also acknowledge with shame and sorrow for my sin, that I have indulged an unreasonable prejudice against our Pastor, and wickedly made his sin my excuse for committing the sin of breaking covenant with you.

I pray the Lord to forgive my sins through the blood of that glorious Redeemer, Jesus Christ, whose cause I feel I have wounded.—I desire forgiveness of you the Church of Christ in this place, to whom I have given a just occasion of being offended.—I desire forgiveness of our Revd Pastor, and I desire forgiveness of all whom I have offended by my sins,—I desire brethren, that you will receive me as a returning prodigal, into your Christian embrace, and that you would pray for me, that God would in mercy, overule my past sins to his own glory, the good of his cause, the good of this church, and the good of him who now confesses his sins.

That it would please God by his grace to preserve me from falling again into sin.—I remain Dear brethren your unworthy brother, but sincere in the faith and fellowship of the Gospel.

JEREMIAH GRAY."

RECORDS OF CHURCH AT PELHAM CENTER FROM 1822 TO 1897.
CALVINISTIC CHURCH ORGANIZED IN 1822.

From recently discovered records of the church at Pelham Center during the pastorate of Rev. Winthrop Bailey.

RECORD OF CHURCH MEETING APRIL 4, 1822.

At a meeting of the church, notified and held for the purpose the following measure was unanimously adopted.

"As the members of this church entertain different views of some doctrines which all regard as important; and as some of the Members are desirous on this account of constituting a church by themselves, that they may enjoy christian ordinances in a way consistent with their own views of truth and Duty: therefore Voted that with feelings of Friendship and Goodwill towards each other, and without aspersing or implying any censure on either part, we do now separate into two distinct and independent churches: the one to be known as the Congregational church and the other as the Calvinistic Church in Pelham, and we request so to be regarded by our sister churches; and also the Table furniture shall be held in common and be equally for the use of both.

Attest, WINTHROP BAILEY, Moderator.

A true copy of Church Records, Attest, W. BAILEY.
Pelham, April 11, 1822."

"At a meeting of certain members of the church not adhering to the change of sentiment taken place in the Rev. Winthrop Bailey" action was begun.

Letters Missive were sent out by John Rankin Jr. and William Oliver to Rev'd Messers Crosby of Enfield, Perkins of Amherst and Woodbridge of Hadley to "meet and take into view our situation, and if they think proper, to organize us into a church by the name of the Calvinstic Church in Pelham."

These letters were sent out May 21, 1822.

On the 28th of the same month the three ministers met at the house of John Rankin Jr. A statement of facts was made by the "Independent Brethren" to the above named elders, and upon the statements made to the elders, they judged it expedient to advise that a church to be known as the Calvinistic church of Pelham be organized. At 4 o'clock of the same day they proceeded to the old meeting house and organized the church agreeable to the vote. Rev. Joshua Crosby was Moderator and Rev. Nathan Perkins Scribe.

PELHAM CENTER FROM THE SOUTH.

DAISIES AMONG THE GRAVES.—OLD BURYING GROUND.

Articles of Faith and a form of Covenant were drawn up and adopted.

ORGANIZED MEMBERS OF THE CALVINISTIC CHURCH OF PELHAM.

Ebenezer Gray,
William Oliver,
John Rankin,
James Rankin,
Ezra Lee,
John Gray,
John Millen,
John Rankin Jr.,
Oliver Hamilton,
Samuel Ingalls,
John Dunlap,
Levi Crafford,

Agnes Gray,
Anne Rankin,
Betsey Gray,
Hannah Millen,
Mary Lee,
Diana Ingalls,
Mary Cook,
Mary Dunlap,

Polly Rankin,
Patty Crafford.

The following persons were admitted after the church was organized as per dates :

June 30, 1822. Sarah Gray, Cynthia Rankin, Anna Hamilton, Betsey Hamilton.
May 18, 1823. Silas Rankin, Sally Rankin, Susanna Cowan, Margerett Thompson.
Jan. 1, 1823. Clarissa Boyden.
Nov. 6, 1825. Thankful Turner.
July 6, 1825. John Gray 2^d, William Oliver.
Oct. 28, 1827. Sylvia Hamilton, Hannah Conkey.

With the above records of admissions the history of the Calvinistic church as organized in 1822 ends.

It seems the Rev. Winthrop Bailey was charged with a "change of sentiment," by those that organized the "Calvinistic Church," which probably means that Mr. Bailey had become a Congregationalist, or more liberal in his views than was pleasing to those who took the name of Calvinists. Who preached for the Calvinistic church does not appear from the record, but it is certain that Mr. Bailey was not dismissed until 1825 and must have preached to all that were left after the organization of the Calvinistic church.

During the period from 1827 to 1837 there was a great decline in religious observances; there seems to have been no stated preaching in the old meeting house by any church organization. It was during this period that the Methodists under the preaching of Rev. John Stoddard gained a standing in the town by holding services in the old meeting house in 1831 and later.

Possibly Rev. Luther Smith and Rev. L. A. Spofford may have preached sometime previous to 1837 but no records are found.

The state of affairs, as pretaining to religious organization and observance is stated in a record of Oct. 26, 1837.

"The original Congregational and Calvinistic churches in this Place having been disbanded for years, and the regular ordinances of the Gospel not enjoyed."—

Rev. William Tyler, a relative of Prof. W. S. Tyler of Amherst, and settled at South Hadley, became interested in Pelham and was instrumental in organizing the church and society.

An ecclesiastical council was called at the house of Nathaniel Pratt at Pelham on the 25th of October, 1837 in response to letters missive from John Gray, Henry Walker, Jonathan Turner and others. Churches in Amherst, Belchertown, Prescott, and Enfield were represented by pastor and delegate. The council deemed it advisable to organize a church and the name adopted was the Evangelical Congregational church of Pelham.

Articles of faith and covenant were adopted. The following person subscribed thereto and were duly organized into a distinct church:

John Gray,	Sarah Thompson,	Clarissa Boyden,
Jonathan Turner,	Livia Gold,	Charlotte Eaton,
Betsey Gray,	Nancy Packard,	Hannah Conkey,
Eliza Turner,	Mary Dunlap,	Francis Eaton,
Sally Kingman,	Mary Walker,	Lydia Wood,
Anne M. Kingman,	Betsey Smith,	Mary Conkey,
Mary Hayden.		

After the council had organized the church,—there being no settled pastor it was proposed that a standing moderator be chosen, and Rev. Nathan Perkins of Amherst Second church was chosen, and John Gray was also chosen to act when Mr. Perkins could not be present. Rev. L. A. Spofford was acting pastor for a year or more after the organization of the church and Daniel Packard was clerk and treasurer in 1838. It was in connection with this renewed interest in religious matters at Pelham the Rev. Frederick Janes was settled. How long he preached is not known. Then the movement was made for a new church building and the work was begun in 1839, Rev. Nathan Perkins laying the corner stone. The first child baptized in the new church was Frances Atessa Eaton. From the records of the Hampshire East Association it appears that Rev. A. C. Page of Pelham was a member of that body in 1842, but there is no record of his installation at Pelham, yet it is highly probable that Mr. Page was installed in 1842 or 1843, and continued in charge of the church until 1850, perhaps longer. In 1851 a new confession of faith and covenant was adopted. Rev. Samuel Wolcott was moderator at the meeting.

In 1855 Rev. Zenas Bliss was acting pastor. Rev. Mr. Witherell was preacher at one time, also Rev. Mr. Howard.

The above is nearly all there is of record concerning the church at Pelham center for some years. There was another period during which there was little religious zeal, and the organization of the church was again broken up. Not until after 1860 was much interest manifested in church and parish matters.

July 1, 1861, Rev. W. H. Dowden came to Pelham and began his labors as acting pastor of the church.

In March, 1862, James M. Cowan, a native of the town, then in business at the hollow, and on the board of selectmen, interested himself in the reorganization of the society. A petition, addressed to Judge Ithamar Conkey of Amherst, was drawn up and signed by the following persons, asking for a warrant under which to hold a meeting for organization :

James M. Cowan,	Lemuel R. Chapin,	Gilbert G. Hunt,
Russell Hildreth,	Wm. B. Downing,	Joseph R. Hunt,
W. H. Dowden,	Albert A. Grout,	Charles H. Taylor,
Nathan Canterberry,	Moses L. Ward,	Frederick Dane,
E. S. Richardson,	Milo W. Field,	John Dane,
John B. Davis,	Horace Stacy,	Lyman Jenks.

April 8th, 1862, the organization was effected with the following officers: Clerk, M. W. Field ; Treasurer, W. B. Downing ; Executive Committee, J. M. Cowan, M. L. Ward, L. R. Chapin, E. S. Richardson ; Collector, W. B. Downing.

April 15th, it was voted to engage Rev. W. H. Dowden to supply the pulpit for the year ending April 1, 1863.

In September 1862, a move was made to secure a bell for the church. The bell was purchased and presented to the society " for its use so long as the society sustains evangelical preaching in the meeting house, but should the society fail to do this for the term of two years, the bell may be disposed of as the donors may direct."

Names of doners :

Ladies' Sewing Circle, $25.00,
E. S. Richardson, $26.79,

James M. Cowan, $15.00,
Luther Chapin, $5.00,
Samuel Williston, $15.00,
J. P. Williston, $25.00,
J. H. Gamble, $10.00,
Wells & E. Southworth, $20.00,
L. M. Hills & Son, $10.00,
Wm. B. Downing, $5.00.

The bell which Lord Pelham is said to have donated to the town in response to the honor paid him in giving the town his name never was received, but the new steel bell from the above named donors still hangs in the church belfry, and its clear tones can be heard across the great hollow, on Prescott Hill, and when the wind is favorable it can be heard at the western border of the town.

Rev. W. H. Dowden was very successful in his work at Pelham, from the first, and a goodly number were received into the church by letter, and May 6, 1862, sixteen persons were received on profession of faith ; these additions were the result of religious interest the previous winter.

Nov. 5, 1863, Rev. W. H. Dowden was ordained and installed over the church, Rev. Dr. Eddy of Northampton preaching the sermon. First church at Northampton, Amherst Second and College church, Prescott, Belchertown, New Salem, Enfield and Greenwich churches being represented.

August 6, 1864, Rev. Mr. Dowden received and accepted a call to the Congregational church at Carlyle, Mass. Was dismissed from the church at Pelham and began his labors at Carlyle, Sept. 1, 1864.

From 1864 to 1871 there was no settled minister. On the 21st of March, 1865, instructions were given to employ Rev. R. D. Miller for a year, and for two years after Mr. Millers' service, Rev. Matthew Kingman supplied the pulpit. Rev. William K. Vaille was settled over the Union Church at Packardville on the 28th of June 1871 and an arrangement was entered into by the churches whereby Mr. Vaille was to preach Sunday mornings at Packardville and in the afternoon at Pelham center. Mr. Vaille preached to both churches until 1887 when he resigned, but the arrangement has been continued until now under various acting pastors, being for the most part students from Amherst College. Their names will be found in the notice of the Union Church at Packardville.

QUAKERS OR FRIENDS.

Pelham was settled by Presbyterians of the straightest sect, and the Church they established was the only Church organization in town until the second parish was incorporated in 1786 and the " East Church in Pelham " was organized, and this church also was pledged to " maintain, support and defend Presbyterian government and discipline "

A few Baptists had moved into town as well as a few Universalists and Unitarians,—just enough to complain about being taxed for the support of the Gospel as preached by the Presbyterians, and not enough to support a church organization of either creed. Eseck Cook, a Quaker, came to Pelham from Cumberland R. I. in 1806, and he was instrumental in gathering together a small society of his faith and erecting a plain one storied building at the westerly part of the town for use as a house of worship, and it was always known as the " Quaker Meeting House." The building stood upon the edge of a somewhat level tract of land bordering upon the " highway leading from Amherst to Boston. " as expressed in the deeds of the property, and was purchased of Samuel Arnold and deeded by him and Rhoda his wife " to William Bassett of Richmond, Cheshire County, N. H. Alice Turner and Benjamin Dexter of Orange in the County of Hampshire, Massachusetts, for, and in behalf of the Monthly Meetings of the People called Quakers, Known by the name of the Richmond Monthly Meeting." There was about four acres of land sold to the Quakers March 12, 1808. On this lot the plain Meeting House was erected, and there the Quakers worshipped in their quiet way for many years, until there were but few left, and the society was broken up. The " Monthly Meeting " continued to hold the property until "fourth month, fourth day, eighteen hundred and fifty five " when it was sold to Ziba Cook for $86.50 by the Uxbridge Monthly Meeting. Edward Earle of Worcester, Clerk, acting as agent. The four acres of land had one small plot in which the Quakers buried their dead, and the deed to Ziba Cook contains the following reservation.

" Reserving for ever a right of passage way in and over said land to the graveyard belonging to the said society situated in the rear of said lot of land, which graveyard is to be retained for the use of said society, and is not intended to be conveyed by this instrument. "

The Quaker Meeting house, brown with age and the absence of paint stood on the brow of the hill long years after services were entirely suspended, as through patiently waiting for the plainly dressed demure worshippers to return but they never came. The property was sold as already described and the Old Meeting house was turned to use as a barn, and is still standing.

Baptists at Packardville.

In 1831 a petition signed by a number of persons in the north part of Belchertown, the south part of Pelham and the north-west part of Enfield was addressed to the First Baptist church of Belchertown asking permission to organize a district society of the Baptist denomination at Packardville, the distance from Packardville and vicinity being too great for the people to go to the first church at Belchertown.

The request of the petitioners was granted and a society organized, and a meeting house was built at Packardville not long after. The society was quite prosperous for perhaps thirty years under the charge of the following pastors: Rev. Messrs. Bigelow, Burt, Vaughn, Smalledge, Snell and Emerson Hill, and then there was a decline in the work and services by the Baptists were almost if not entirely suspended for some years, or until there was a movement to organize a society that should include those of every evangelic faith who might be living in the neighborhood from which the Baptists had come, which was started in 1868.

The Methodists.

In the early part of the year 1831 Rev. Isaac Stoddard, a member of the New England Conference was invited to Pelham to preach, and he came. Other Methodist preachers had occasionally preached in town before Mr. Stoddard came but had not succeeded in making much impression in favor of Methodism. Mr. Stoddard was well received, as at that time there was no stated preaching in the old Meeting House of the Presbyterians except now and then by a few Unitarians, and Mr. Stoddard held meetings there. As a result of his visit to Pelham the New England Conference saw fit to appoint Mr. Stoddard to the town for the year 1831 and he was reappointed for the year 1832. During the first year of Mr. Stoddard's ministry in Pelham there was a notable revival and as a result Methodism secured

UNION CHURCH, PACKARDVILLE.

METHODIST CHURCH, WEST PELHAM.

a permanent hold upon the people of the town, and the members of the society numbered about one hundred and twenty-five at the close of Mr. Stoddard's labors.

Rev. John Case was the successor of Mr. Stoddard in this field of labor and was with the new society one year, and in 1834 Rev. Erastus Otis and Rev. William Gordon was appointed to take charge of the work. Pelham and Greenwich being connected by the conference. In 1835 Rev. O. Robbins were appointed to take charge of the Pelham church which continued to increase and extend its usefulness, but in the second year of Mr. Robbins pastorate and for several years following there was a visible decline in the prosperity of the society, owing to prominent members leaving town for more enterprising places of business.

Up to 1836 the Methodists had occupied the Old Meeting House, —built by the original settlers of the town soon after purchasing the tract of land in 1738-9. It was in 1836 that the first movement was made towards erecting a church for themselves, but it was not successful, and they continued to occupy the old meeting house.

In 1837 Rev. James O. Dean was appointed to labor with this people. He was continued in the work for two years. Mr. Dean was an earnest worker and gave his best efforts to build up the church. He reported 77 person's names on society or class papers when he commenced his labors and that fourteen or fifteen persons joined the society during the two years of his labors, yet the net gain was small on account of deaths and removals from town.

Rev. Mr. Dean was a much beloved pastor of the Methodist church of Pelham and was greatly respected by the people of the town generally. The earnestness and zeal of Mr. Dean, and the work he accomplished for the society over which he had been appointed as pastor for two years led to the expression of an earnest desire for a reappointment and the conference returned him to the Pelham field in 1843 and 1844. It was while giving his best service to the Methodist society that he was stricken with lung fever and died. He died on the 10th of October 1844, and was buried in the Valley Cemetery. Perhaps no pastor of the Methodist church was more sincerely mourned, or was held in more grateful remembrance than Mr. Dean.

The effort to build a meeting house once abandoned or postponed was renewed in 1838 and during the following years the project was pushed as fast as the limited means of the society would permit.

Augustus Webster donated a site on which to build and through the efforts of Rev. Mr. Dean the building of the meeting house was hastened. The work was accomplished and the church was dedicated in the autumn of 1840. Deeds of the pew holders were subscribed by Thomas Buffum, Zadock Presho and Pliny Hannum, being a committee of proprietors, and the church property has never been under control of the conference.

The society did not secure a parsonage until 1857 when the original parsonage was deeded to the following trustees: Rufus Grout, David Newell, Lemuel C. Wedge, Horace Gray, Zadock Presho, Ansel A. Rankin and John Sisson, and as stated in the document, "for the benefit of such men as shall be employed by the Methodist Episcopal Church to preach in the west part of Pelham." The original house was used by the various Ministers sent by the conference until Aug. 11, 1875 when the building was sold and a new one erected on the old location.

In 1865 during the pastorate of Rev. John Cadwell the church was repaired, a pulpit after the more modern style built, and the vestry finished in the basement, with adjoining kitchen, added later. In 1891 while Rev. J. O. Dodge was pastor a new barn and sheds were added at the parsonage. In 1866 during the pastorate of Rev. O. W. Adams 70 persons united with the church, and in 1868 36 members took letters to the newly organized Methodist church at Amherst, and to other churches.

The Ministers who have followed Rev. James O. Dean's pastorate in 1837 are as follows: Rev. Joseph W. Lewis for the year 1839; Rev. John Cadwell 1840; Rev. William P. White 1841 and '42; Rev. James O. Dean 1843 and '44; Rev. Winsor Ward 1845 and '46; Rev. Increase B. Bigelow 1847 and '48; Rev. William Bardwell 1849; Rev. Judah Crosby 1850 and '51. Rev. R. W. Wright 1852 and '53; Rev. Franklin Fisk 1854; Rev. John Jones 1855 to '57; Rev. John W. Lee in 1858 and '59; Rev. J. L. Esty and Lorenzo Bosworth 1860; Rev. L. A. Bardwell 1861; Rev. Gilbert R. Bent 1862; Rev. John H. Gaylord 1863; Rev. John Cadwell 1864 and '65; Rev. O. W. Adams 1866 and '67; Rev. John Noon 1868 and '69; Rev. George Hewes 1870; Rev. N. H. Martin 1871 and '72; Rev. W. H. Adams 1873; Rev. Nathan A. Soule 1874; Rev. Jonathan Neal 1875 and '76 ; Rev. George E. Chapman 1877 and '78 ; Rev. John Noon 1879 and '80; Rev. Joseph Wood 1881 and '82 ; Rev. Lorenzo White 1883 ; Rev. E. P. Herrick 1884; Rev. Henry A. Jones 1885 and '86; Rev. F. S. Miller 1887 ; Rev. W. H. Dockham 1888 ; Rev. E. H. Turnecliff 1889 ; Rev. W. P. Blackmer 1890.

Mr. Blackmer did not accept the appointment and the society was supplied by students from Wilbraham part of the year and Rev. Isaac Yerkes came during the latter part of the year.

Rev. J. O. Dodge 1891 ; Rev. George Hudson 1892 and '93 ; Rev. Sherman Meracle 1894; Rev. Eaton B. Marshall 1895, '96, '97 ;

During the first pastorate of Rev. John Cadwell in 1840 the Meeting house was finished and dedicated; and the year was also notable as the year the camp-meeting of the Springfield District Conference was held in Pelham. The ground selected was perhaps a half mile from the new meeting house ; a grove on lands of Savannah Arnold and not far from Mr. Arnold's residence. There were great crowds in attendance during the whole week, and as none could come by railroad there were many horses to be cared for. Long processions of teams loaded with visitors came daily from Amherst and other towns. There were no hotels nearer than Amherst and no cottages on the camp grounds in those days, so that all visitors who spent the night slept in the tents, which were ranged in a circle around the grounds; the preachers stand being on the western edge of the circle, and within the circle of tents the seats for the audience were placed ; advantage being taken of the general slope of the camp ground to the west to give all a chance to see the preachers on the stand and to hear them more readily by having the preachers placed at the lowest point in the circle.

Union Society at Packardville.

The following are the names of those who signed the call for the organization of the Union Congregational Society Dec. 4, 1868.

Albert Firman,	Asahel B. Shaw,	Horton B. Ward,
Oren Sykes,	David Randall,	George W. Knight,
Philander S. Knight,	Ansel C. Shaw,	A. A. Howard,
Lorenzo W. Miller,	George S. Calkins,	Ziza A. Hanks.

The meeting was held Jan. 4, 1869.

First Officers of the Union Society.

Albert Firman, Clerk; Ansel Shaw, Treasurer; Lorenzo W. Miller, Auditor; Prudential Committee, Albert Firman, Ziza A. Hanks, Philander S. Knight.

"Voted that the prudential committee be empowered to appoint three disinterested persons to appraise the pews in the Meeting house and sign vouchers in behalf of the society for complying with the conditions required in asking aid from Congregational Union, and to make such repairs in and about the Meeting house as are judged necessary."

The Society having completed its organization, found in 1869 that the old meeting house that had been in use by the Baptist society, which preceded them, was in a somewhat dilapidated condition and must be repaired or a new one built in its place. It was while repairs were in progress on the old Baptist meeting house that it caught fire and was burned.

At a meeting March 26, 1869 a committee was chosen to estimate the cost of a suitable house of worship after having inspected churches and houses of worship in other places. Lorenzo W. Miller, Aretas J. Cadwell and Albert Firman were the committee, and after due consideration reported that a building 36 x 45 feet would be large enough for the needs of the society and the committee were instructed to go forward and erect such a house as they thought for the best good of the people. The present church was built at a cost of about $6,500 and was first occupied in 1870 for the funeral of David Randall.

The society were without a settled pastor for several years, after the organization, the pulpit being supplied mostly by Professors of Amherst College or students from that institution.

April 29, 1871 the society voted to join with the church in calling Rev. Wm. K. Vaille of Shutesbury to settle over the church and society, and it was further voted to pledge Mr. Vaille $450 as an annual salary—this sum to include the aid promised by the Mass. Home Missionary Society, which was $300 annually.

Letters missive were sent to the following churches; First, Second, College, North, and South Congregational churches of Amherst, Congregational churches in Enfield, Belchertown, Granby, Greenwich, Pelham, Prescott, Shutesbury, Sunderland and South Hadley, and the Methodist Episcopal church at West Pelham.

The council deciding it desirable to install the Rev. Mr. Vaille, the exercises were held June 28, 1871, Prof. W. S. Tyler preaching the sermon. Rev. J. L. Jenkins being Moderator of the council and Rev. Payson W. Lyman Scribe. There was a debt upon the society for the church building and the churches represented by the council voted to assume it if the church at the center of the town would accept Mr. Vaille as their pastor also, he holding services Sunday morning at Packardville and at the center in the afternoon. The church at the center finally accepted the proposition and Rev. Mr. Vaille continued to be pastor of the Union Society, preaching in the two churches until 1887 when he resigned his charge but continued to reside on his farm in the south part of the town until his death in 1889. His death being caused by fatal burns received in trying to save his property when his house burned in May of that year.

Since the resignation of Mr. Vaille the society has had no settled pastor, the pulpit having been supplied almost entirely by students from Amherst College, and among them who have officiated acceptably to the present time are Erving Burnap, Amherst College, class of '88, one year; E. N. Billings, class of '92, one year; Andrew H. Mulnix, class of '91, one year; J. A. Goodrich, class of '93, one year; Alfred Lockwood, class of '96, two years; J. Elmer Russell, class of '96, one year; L. B. Chase, class of '97.

REV. ROBERT ABERCROMBIE

AND THE CHURCH AT PELHAM.

The settlement of Rev. Robert Abercrombie as the first minister of Pelham in 1744 has already been given from the records of the town; also some of the troubles and disagreements between pastor and people, beginning soon after his settlement and continuing for a good portion of the ten years of his pastorate, as we are led to believe, from the far from full and clear information obtainable from the town records.

That pastor and people, or a portion of the people of his charge were not in accord, is quite evident, but a careful reading of all the data on the town record books referring to the differences, fail to give us a clear and distinct idea of what it was all about.

That the people were not prompt in the payment of the meagre salary is made plain by the records, but anyone after learning all that the records afford upon the failure of the people to pay Mr. Abercrombie's salary when due, will be forced to the conclusion that there were other causes of disagreement and contention of which the records do not give intelligent information, only hints of what may have been.

The protest signed by a goodly number of the leading men among the proprietors or settlers, and probably members of the church, against the action which others, and probably the majority of the voters had taken, in extending a call to Mr. Abercrombie to settle in 1743, led to the formal or informal postponement of the business of settling the first minister for about a year. This gives reason for the belief that there was an anti-Abercrombie party before his settlement, but the basis of their objection and protest is not made plain. The protest was much feebler in 1744 than the year previous but it is possible that while those who protested over their names in 1743 were many of them holding the same opinions and beliefs as to the expediency of settling Mr. Abercrombie;—they had cooled down perhaps, but had not changed their minds materially on the question of settlement.

On the other hand we must believe that Mr. Abercrombie had a strong following of the church members and voters with him, who were equally persistent in pushing forward the important business of settling a pastor, and were for settling Mr. Abercrombie.

While we do not understand the reason or reasons why a portion of the voters of the town were opposed to settling Mr. Abercrombie, or on what grounds the majority urged and demanded that he should be settled ; it is quite easy to learn from these unfortunate conditions that the town and church was divided from the beginning, and consequently in a state of mind not conducive to harmony and mutual helpfulness so desirable in any community between pastor and people, and especially unfortunate in this newly settled colony where prosperity and happiness depended upon unity of action in all matters pretaining to church and town.

The people composing these two factions, who disagreed about settling the first minister, were much alike in the possession of strong wills, each party doubtless believed that it was working for the best interests of the little settlement, and at the same time may have been at a loss to understand how the opposite faction could take the stand they did.

Each individual Scotchman in the opposing factions had all the characteristic persistence of purpose common to that nationality, and consequently not much inclined to make concessions for the sake of harmony and unity ; and might have been much more inclined to argue with strength and vehemence in sustaining his own individual position, and that of the faction to which he was joined.

Rev. Robert Abercrombie, from all that can be learned of him, was a man in whom the Scotch characteristics of resolute persistence and determination were very marked. He was a descendent in an unbroken line of Abercrombies dating back to the twelfth century in Fifeshire, Scotland ;—was educated at the Edinburg university, where he had the reputation of being a profound scholar, familiar with Latin, Greek, Hebrew and Syriac ; and brought testimonials from the Presbytery of Edinburg and Kirkaleby, also recommendations from distinguished Scotch divines. A man of sound sense and ability, well equipped for his chosen profession ; a strict disciplinarian, and possessed of a resolute purpose to demand rigid adherence to the doctrines and requirements of the Presbyterian church of Scotland. After landing at Boston in the autumn of 1740, as a licensed preacher, he preached among Presbyterians at Boston, Worcester and other places, going about on horseback and in this work became acquainted with Scotch-Irish Presbyterians who went from Worcester to Pelham, before they had become fully established in their new settlement.

The foregoing outline of the differences and disagreements between Mr. Abercrombie and the people of Pelham, and a proper consideration of the tenacious and unyielding character of pastor and people when they honestly believed themselves in the right, should help to a better and more charitable understanding of the facts as they appear on the records, as we review and study them more carefully.

It was on May 11, 1742, that the people of Pelham "Voted to intercede with Mr. Robert Abercrombie to be our Supplayer as far as he can for this summer."

In 1743, May 26, Ephriam Cowan, Samuel Gray and Robert Piebles were chosen a committee "to invite three neighboring ordained ministers to keep a day of fasting and prayer with us and to consult with the same whome we shall call to be our minister." Although the time for holding this day of fasting and prayer was postponed from time to time, they being directed first " to desire the Ministers to attend on the last Thursday in June ;" and at a meeting June 21 the committee was directed to "call it when they can have it with the best convenecy." We will assume that it was held though the date does not appear. Subsequent to this day of fasting and prayer a formal call was extended to Mr. Abercrombie to become their minister, but the date thereof does not seem to have been entered on the book. The next thing that attracts attention on the records is the protest already referred to. There are twenty-two names signed to the document, but as the name of James Gilmore appears twice there were only twenty-one protesting voters,—though it was possible one of the Gilmores was James, Jun., as there was such a man.

The Protest.

"Pelham, August 31, 1743.

We ye Subscribers Being Freeholders & Inhabitants of said town Do protest against ye Proceedings of Part of ye inhabitants of ye s^d town in their calling of ye Rev. Robert Abercrombie to be their minister in s^d town.
Test ye Subscribers,
James Gilmore, William Fergerson,

Samuel Fergerson, Adam Petterson, John Gilmore, Thomas Dick, James Thornton, James McCulloch, Alexander McCulloch, Hugh Gray, Robert King, William Thornton, John Stairling, James Gilmore, Robert Fergerson, John Fergerson, Robert McCulloch, James Fergerson, James Dunlap, Thomas Petterson, George Petterson, John Dick."

No reasons were given for this protest,—and it is impossible to determine by the document itself whether they disliked the idea of settling Mr. Abercrombie, or whether they were opposed to settling any minister at that time; but the effect of the protest was the same as a formal order to halt, and all further action was abandoned until the next spring.

A glance at the names appended to the protest shows conclusively that there was earnest opposition to the action of the town. Among the names are such prominent men as James Thornton, one of the two men who led off in purchasing the tract and organizing the settlement. John Fergerson, at whose house the first meeting of the proprietors in Pelham was held; Thomas Dick and his brother John Dick were the men who built the meeting house, and both were important personages in the history of the settlement. Later on John Dick was town clerk thirty-five years in succession; and there must have been others among the protesting faction whose influence in church and town affairs was an important factor. Taking the protest with names appended as a whole, it was of sufficient importance to cause delay and hesitation on the part of those most zealous for settling Mr. Abercrombie as pastor of the church at Pelham.

The Ministers' Letter of Endorsement.

" Whereas we ye Subscribers have had some considerable acquaintance with Rev. Mr. Abercrombie, Preacher of y^c Gospel, and what we know of his qualification by Information and personal acquaintance, we advise ye people of God in Pelham to Invite ye s^d Mr. Robert Abercrombie to settle in ye Work of ye Ministrie among them as their Pastor—as Witness our hands this 30th of August 1743.

JONATHAN EDWARDS, DAVID WHITE, DAVID MCGREGORIE, DAVID PARSONS, JUN."

The above recommendation by the ministers which is dated, Aug. 30th, the day before the call was probably extended,—tends to sustain the belief that the formal call was made Aug. 31, and that the protest followed quickly, and was given the same date.

WARRANT FOR TOWN MEETING, MARCH 5, 1743-4.

The first article in the warrant for the town meeting, March 5, 1743-4 was:

"To see if the town will order their vote of August ye 31 1743 concerning Mr. Robert Abercrombie's Call to Stand thus there being read in the meeting a Call from ye Inhabitants of Pelham unto Mr. Robert Abercrombie to be Minister in Said Place."

The record of action on the above article is as follows:—"Ye meeting did Unanimously concur therewith and Voted upon his being Approved, Accepting of Said Call and Settling With them he shall be Minister in said Town."

(The date of the meeting. March 5, 1743-4 is really March 5,1744, because of the practice of beginning the business of the new year March 25 rather than on January first. All dates up to March 25 were given as belonging to the year that ended with the previous December.)

Article 2. "To see if they will appoint a Committee to represent their Call unto & acquaint said Mr. Robert Abercrombie with their proposals and Receive His Answer."

Article 3. "To act upon Every Perticular that may be found Necesery in Consequence of His Answer to Compleat his settlement.

Pelham, March ye 5th 1843-4.

ROBERT PEIBOLS, ALEXANDER CONKEY, JOHN ALEXANDER, JOHN GRAY Selectmen of Pelham."

John Stinson was chosen moderator. "It is Voted & Concorded with according as it is Mentioned in the Warrant.

Voted that Alexander Conkey, Ephriam Cowan, Matthew Gray & Robert Peibols be a Committe to Present a Call to Mr. Robert Abercrombie & Receive His answer & also this Meeting is adjourned for one Houre & a half to ye Meeting House to Receive ye Report of s^d Committee.

Then Meet and also voted y^t ye Proposals of Mr. Robert Abercrombie is Concord With By a Great Majority,—and also Voted that there be a Committee chosen to Complete ye Work from time to time from this time to ordination.—Said Committee is George Cowan, John Stinson & Robert Peibols,—this meeting is adjourned to ye first tusday of April Nixt at ten of ye Clock in ye forenoon at ye Meeting House of said Pelham.

JOHN STINSON, Moderator."

"March ye 5th 1743-4.
These May Certifie y^t James Thornton his entered His Protest against ye above Meeting."

Of the twenty-two men who the year previous recorded a formidable protest against the action of "Part of ye inhabitants of the town," only James Thornton comes to the front in opposition to similar action at this time.

Rev. Robert Abercrombie's Acceptance of the Call.

"Pelham March ye 5th 1744.

Messers:—You may Signifie to your Constituents y^t Having Considered ye Call from ye Congregation Concured in by them togither With the Circumstances of ye place I am at last Willing to Submit myself to be tried as to my fitness for such a Charge & Being found Qualified shall Consent to be Ordained & Indever in ye Strength of Divine Grace to Exercise ye Ministerial office among them as God shall enable me Provided y^t in Place of what Proposals they have made for my Incouragement & Support they secure to me ye land sett apart for ye first Settled Minister of this town wth a yearly Sallery of 50 pounds Lawful Money to be paid at ye present value of ye Bills of New tenor in case they should Depreciate upon ye Expiration of eight years if God pleases to continue us so long togither Consider of their ability & my Needsesity Reqnire anything to be added thereto and act as they find cause or if they can propose anything Better for us both I should willingly Consent.

I am &c.
R. Abercrombie."

The Ordination of the First Minister.

The ordination of Robert Abercrombie took place on the 30th of August, 1744 and was a notable occasion for the newly incorporated town.

"At a meeting adjourned from ye first Tuesday of July to the 30th day of July 1744 Then Meet on said Day and was nominated Mr. Jonathan Edwards, Mr. John Moorehead, Mr. David McGregorie, Mr. David Parsons, Mr. David White, Mr. Billings, Mr. John Graham to be invited to our Ordination ye time agreed upon is ye 30th Day of August Nixt."

Warrant for Town Meeting, August 28, 1744.

"at 2 of ye Clock in ye afternoon then and there to hear What their Committee appointed to see Mr. Abercrombie's Settlement Finished may have to Say before them & Act upon Whatsoever Particulars may be found Necery to Compleat ye same & Make Everything Relative thereto Effectual and firm. Hereof fail Not & Make return of your Doings Sometime before said Meeting to one of us Subscribers as Witness our Hands & Seal this 9th Day of August 1744 and in y° 18th year of His Majesties Reights.

MATTHEW GRAY, EPHRIAM COWAN, GEORGE & JOHN STINSON."

There is no record of action under the above warrant.

The Ordaining Council was composed of the following ministers and laymen : Rev. Jonathan Edwards, of Northampton ; Rev. John Moorhead, of Boston ; Rev. David McGregorie, of Londonderry, N. H.; Rev. David Parsons, Jun., of Amherst ; David White, Mr. Billings and John Graham. No residence of the last named members of council is given, but they probably did not live far from Pelham.

Rev. Jonathan Edwards preached the sermon on this important occasion, and the great business of settling the first minister was accomplished.

Homelot No. 1 was turned over to Mr. Abercrombie, together with the second and third divisions of land that went with lot No. 1.

On Lot No. 1, on the north side of the middle range road, the ministers' house was erected, and it was there that Mr. Abercrombie lived during his ten years pastorate, and there is no record to show that he did not continue to reside there until his death March 7, 1786.

In a warrant for a town meeting to be held on the 15th of April, 1746, appears the following article :—

"6ly to See What Method y° town will take in Paying y° Rev. Mr. Robert Abercrombie his Sallery this Present year."

Recorded action on this article follow : " Voted that y° Rev. Mr. Robert Abercrombie be paid this Present year's Sallery by Pole & Improvement."

There is nothing upon the records to indicate that there was any trouble between pastor and people for the first two years of Mr. Abercrombie's pastorate but the following copy of an order of the Court of Sessions shows that trouble had begun and the Court was appealed to by the pastor to settle some difficulty between them or compel payment of overdue salary. Just what the trouble was the brief court order does not inform us.

" Robert Abercrombie of Pelham, Clerk, Complaint against the Town of Pelham, for &c.--Ordered that the Selectmen of s^d Town be notified to appear at the next Court and make answer thereto to which for further consideration thereof is referred.
Northampton, May 19, 1746, Court of Sessions."

The following document copied the exact size of the original was addressed to the selectmen by the town treasurer, Jan. 13, 1746-7.

"To The Select men of Pelham"

Pelham Jan the 13th 1746/7
Gentmen pleas to Insert in
your warrent as an artecale
to see whether I shall pay
the Revd mr Crombe Last years
salery without a Discharge
for the forman year seeing it is
payed for he Refases to giue it
to see if the Town is willin
to giue him ten or twelue pounds
for the fall of money which
he Demands of me therinfor
I Desier that you would do me
Justes to take the Blame off
me Jams Conkey Jr Tresarer.

The Warrant of March 11 for a town meeting, March 19, 1746-7 contained the following articles:—

"2^ly To see if ye town Will Impower the Committee that was chosen at ye Feb^r Meeting Meet ye 9th of Said Month 1746-7—and Impower them With all Necery Power to Wite to Imploy a Councler & a Retorney if in Case the Rev. Mr. Ebercrombie Suess ye town—

3ˡʸ to See if yᵉ town Will Except of the report that the Committee his to Lay Before yᵉ town Concerning the Pepers that William Gray Hath and to see what ye town Will Do Concerning Said Peper—

8ˡʸ To see what the town Will Do with yᵉ Money that Lays in the treasurer's Hands for Mr. Ebercrombie Hath Refused to take itt."

Recorded action of the town under the warrant for meeting, March 19, 1746-7 :

" Voted that ye Committee that was chosen att ye Febʳ Meeting ye Ninth One Thousand Seven Hundred & Fourty Six-Seven is Impowered to Imploy a Councler & Retorney if in Case yᵉ Rev. Mr. Ebercrombie Sue the Town.

Voted that yᵉ Old Committee that was chosen to Look over yᵉ Pepers is Impowered to go and Receive yᵉ said Pepers and Deliver them to ye Present Clerk.

18ˡʸ Voted that James Conkey, treasurer, is to keep ye Money that is in his Hands till yᵉ first of May unless yᵉ Rev. Mr. Ebercrombie Demand it from yᵉ aforesaid treasurer."

Immediately following the record of action at the meeting, March 19, 1746-7 there is a protest, and an agreement spread upon the records which are copied in full.

The Protest.

"We ye Subscribers Enter our Protest against ye Proceedings of Chusing a Committee to go to Law with ye Rev. Mr. Ebercrombie Relating to his Sallery as Witness our Hands this 19ᵗʰ Day of March 1747.

William Gray, Thomas Hamilton, John Stinson, John Savige, Matthew Gray, Thomas Lowden, John Gray, Robert Pebles, Thomas Cochran, John Hunter, Patrick Pebels, James Johnson."

Rev. Mr. Aberbrombie's Agreement.

" That for five years from my Settlement be payed fifty pounds in Bills of the New Tenor as ye same is Collicted that upon no part of it being Kept back Longer than demanded and the last of it Payed Yearly I promise to aCept of it as My Sallery for these years and discharge aCordingly. Pelham August 1ˢᵗ 1747.

R. Abercrombie."

Meeting, February 17, 1748-9.

Two articles in the warrant :—

" First to see if yᵉ town Will Chuse a Committee To Send to yᵉ Rev. Mr. Ebercrombie to See What Vote yᵉ town Hath voted against Mr. Ebercrombie that is Contrary to ye Law.

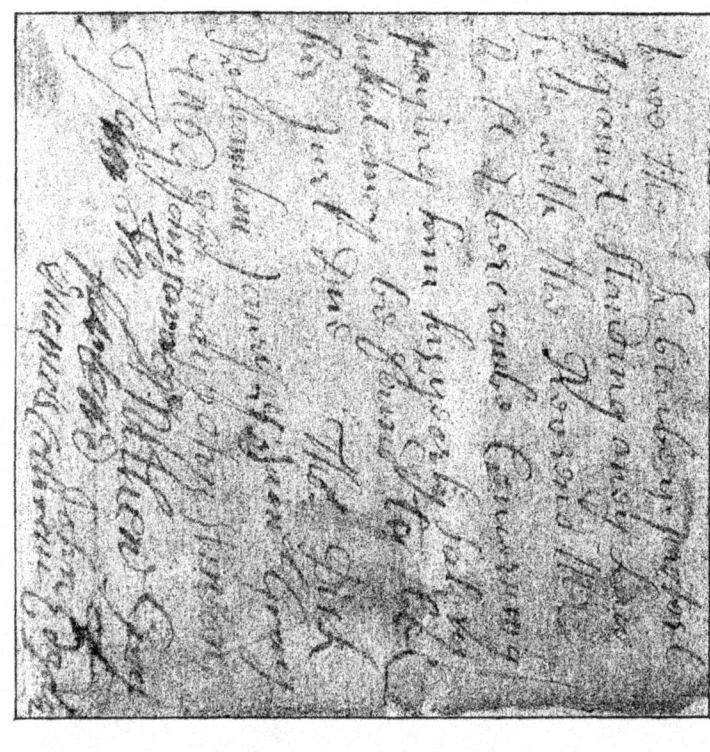

FACSIMILE OF PROTEST, PAGE 302.

GRAVE OF ADAM JOHNSON.

2ly to see What the Town Will be willing to add to ye Rev. Mr. Robert Ebercrombies Sallery for this Present year."

"Voted that there be Nothing acted on y^e first article of ye Warrant.

Voted that there be one Hundred Pound aCording to ye old tenor added to ye Rev. Mr. Ebercrombies Sallery for this Present year.

WILLIAM GRAY ye 2^d Moderator."

MEETING, APRIL 4, 1749.

In the warrant for the meeting there were articles concerning the town debt and credit,—about the roads,—the schools.—and about building a bridge on the West Branch of Swift River and then,—

" 5^{ly} to See if ye town Will Consider those votes that Injours Mr. Ebercrombie in his Character as he says—

6^{ly} to see if ye town Will Reconsider ye votes that is Contrary to ye town agreement With Mr. Ebercrombie as He says—

7^{ly} to See if ye town Will Chuse a Man or Men to Represent ye town at ye Presbytrie if ye town and Mr. Ebercrombie Don't agree."

"Voted there be nothing acted on ye fifth and sixth articles of ye Warrant.

Voted that Robert Maklem is to Represent the the town at the Presbytrie—

GEORGE COWAN, Moderator."

"We ye Subscribers Enter our Protest against ye vote of Not acting upon those votes Mentioned that is Grivioroos to Mr. Ebercrombie :—

William Gray, Patrick Pebels, John Gray, John Edeger, Matthew Gray, John Stinson, Thos Hamilton, Thomas Cochran, John Hamilton, James Taylor, John Lucore, Thomas Lowden."

The 5th and 6th articles which were not acted upon and thereby caused the above protest, were called up again in another warrant for a meeting Sept. 9, 1752 and the injurious votes were recalled.

It is evident that the Presbytery had taken a hand in the trouble between Mr. Abercrombie and the people and were expected to make charges against the town at a session soon to be held at Pelham. In view of serious charges that might be made a town meeting was called on the 31st of May, 1749, to deliberate, and take such action as might be thought proper. There was but one article in the warrant.

MEETING, MAY 31, 1749.

Warrant.—"To see if the town Will think it Proper to Chuse a Man or Men to answer the Presbytrie in behalf of the town.

Voted that John Savige, Ephriam Cowan, Thomas Dick, James McConel, Robert Maklem, John Clark & John Johnson be a committee for to answer at ye Presbytrie in Behalf of said town.

THOMAS DICK, Moderator."

WARRANT FOR MEETING, APRIL 30, 1751.

In the warrant for a town meeting on the above date this article is found :

6^{ly} to see if the town Will be Willing to send a man to the Presbytrie with a pition to Have them Meet here in Respect to our Deficualty Espacly Baptism to Chirdling."

Infant Baptisim was a subject over which there was radical disagreement between pastor and people and the article in the warrant indicates that the question of submitting the matter to the Presbytery had been considered and the town was called upon to decide whether they would send a man to ask the Presbytery to hold a session with them in regard to the existing troubles and especially the important question of Infant Baptism. What action was taken by the town when assembled cannot be learned from the record as no mention of action on the 6th article appears.

MEETING, JANUARY 8, 1750-51.

The warrant for this meeting contained five articles or "particulars" as follows :—

" First to see if town Will Continue Mr. Ebercrombie's Sallery as it Was last year.

2^{ly} to see if ye town Will Chuse a Committee to Prosecute John Stinson at ye Law for afals Record that he Give to ye Clerk.—Att ye request of ye Rev^d Mr. Robert Ebercrombie ye following articles is Inserted.

3^{ly} to see if ye town will Confirm and fulfill their agreement With Mr. Ebercrombie.

4^{ly} to see if ye town will Confirm Mr. Ebercrombie's Proposals upon which he Settled with them, or oppose Him in ye Law Provided he apply to ye Civil Authority to Settle this matter and fix his Sallery.

5^{ly} to see if ye town will chuse a Committee to Withstand Mr. Ebercrombie in ye Law Provided he apply to the same."

Action of the meeting on the above warrant follows : " Att a Meeting of ye freeholders & other Inhabitants of ye town of Pelham Legally Assembled on tuesday, the Eighth Day of January, 1750-51.

Then Meet on Said Day and then was chosen Thomas Dick, Moderator.

First voted to Confirm & fulfill their agreement with Mr. Ebercrombie aCording to His Proposals upon which he Settled With them.

2^{ly} Voted that Mr. Ebercrombie's Sallery be Continued as it Was last year.

3^{ly} past Negitivly that there be no Committee Chosen to Prosecute John Stinson at ye Law."

"We ye Subscribers Enter our Protest against ye Vote of Mr. Ebercrombie's Proposals Being Confirmed & fulfilled.

James Conkey, Ephriam Cowan, George Cowan, John Blair, John Clark, James McConel, David Thomas, Alexander Turner, James McColloch, Robert Loutheridge, William Gray ye 3^d, John Johnson, James Johnson, James Gilmore, Jun."

The town record contains no account of the council or Presbytery that suspended or dismissed Mr. Abercrombie, but certain records indicate that the pastoral relation had been severed and that the Presbytery had appointed certain preachers who were to act as supplies for the church at Pelham, and in this connection we copy the warrant for a town meeting, Nov. 29, 1754 and the action of the voters on the several articles.

Warrant for Meeting, Nov. 29, 1754.

"2^{ly} To see if the town Will allowe the Selectmen to keep the Meetinghouse for ye Supplies ordered by the Presbytrie or Chuse others in there Room.

3^{ly} To see Who ye town will order to Entertain the Ministers that is ordered to supply untill ye Nixt Presbytrie."

"2^{ly} Voted that the Selectmen Keep the Meeting house for the Supplies that the Presbytrie ordered.

3^{ly} Voted that the Selectmen Provide for the Entertainment of the Ministers that is ordered By the Presbytrie to supply.

WILLIAM CROSETT, Moderator."

"We ye Subscribers Inhabitons of Pelham Protest Against the Second and third Vots Past in atown Meeting in Said Pelham ye twenty Ninth of Novb^r one thousand Seven Hundred & fifty-four.

Thomas Dick, John Hamilton, William Petteson, Thomas McMullen, John Stinson, James Sloan, James Taylor, Joseph Rinken, Thomas Cochran."

Judging from the nature of the "Second and Third" votes passed at the meeting of Nov. 29, which is the basis of the protest, we come to the conclusion that the men who signed the document were feeling very unpleasantly over the suspension of Rev. Mr. Abercrombie by the Presbytery and were not in a state of mind to accept of the ministers the Presbytery in their good judgment had selected to supply the Pelham pulpit. They probably cast their votes against allowing the meeting house to be opened for these ministers to preach in, and also against providing for their entertainment.

To aid in a better understanding of the articles in the foregoing warrant and the action thereon by the town, it can be said that the Rev. Mr. Abercrombie had been charged by the Presbytery with having acted contrary to Presbyterian principle and rules governing the church and Mr. Abercrombie had been suspended from the exercise of the duties of his pastorate, while under this order of suspension. At the same meeting of the Presbytery "Supplies for the Pelham pulpit were appointed," and an order was directed to the selectmen to shut the doors of the meeting house against Mr. Abercrombie, and only allow preaching by those the Presbytery should send.

The Selectmen recognizing the Presbytery as authority shut the doors of the meeting house against Mr. Abercrombie as directed. Then came the warrant for the town meeting, Nov. 29, 1754, and the action of the town was as above recorded.

The first "Supply" or minister that came was Rev. Mr. McDowel and the reception he met with we quote from Mr. Abercrombie's account of it. "Mr. McDowel called at my house; He introduced himself with large Protestations of his aversion to come; He asked if I would willingly resign the pulpit to him? I absolutely refused: and told him I should look upon it as an unwarrantable *Intrusion* if he took it. I invited him to lodge at my house, which he refused.— He went off and immediately concluded with the Selectmen not to take the meeting house upon the Sabbath but upon the Monday; which he accordingly did: The Selectmen keeping the doors shut until he came: and they, with one or two of the elders hurrying him into the pulpit,—while the Selectmen forcibly kept me from entering the same: where in a most *precipitant* manner he began his service." Rev. Mr. Burns was the next supply, he was followed by Rev. Mr. McClintock. The troubles which led to the suspension of Mr. Abercrombie will be gone into more fully later on, but it may be well to say now that it was as early as 1753 that the controversy with the Presbytery began and after he had expressed a desire to be dismissed from the pastorate at Pelham, and the Presbytery had declined to comply with his request.

MEETING, JAN. 14, 1756.

The warrant for this meeting had but two articles or "Particulars."

" First To see if the town Will Chuse a Committee to Defend the Complant That Mr. Abercrombie His Laid In Against the town for His Sallery.

2^{ly} to See What Method the town Will take to Get the Minits of the Presbytrie that Will be Needed.

Acting on the first article the town "Voted that there be a Committee Chosen in Behalf of the town to Attend the Court at Northampton. Said Committee is John Savige & Allexander Turner.

2^{ly} Voted that John Blair is to Get the Minits of the Presbytrie.

3^{ly} Voted that William Gray is to assist the Present Clerk to Put the Minits on the town Book that William Gray Minited.

WILLIAM GRAY, Moderator.

From the court records at Northampton:

"Robert Abercrombie Complaint against the town of Pelham in ye County of Hampshire for not paying him his salary as per Complaint on file. The parties appeared and ye Courts having considered the Complaints and ye parties pleas. It's considered that ye Complaints be dismissed and ye said Town Recover against y^c said Abercrombie 12—3 lawful money allowed them for Costs.

Court set the second Tuesday of February 1756."

Rev. Mr. Abercrombie, having lost one suit against the town in February, 1756 for overdue salary very soon brought another, and in March of the same year Alexander Turner was chosen to answer the complaint in behalf of the town. The case dragged along year after year and Turner and others, including John Savige, were chosen to represent the town until it finally came to trial at Northampton in 1759, and the court records that follow are interesting:

"ROBERT ABERCROMBIE VS. THE TOWN OF PELHAM.

Robert Abercrombie of Pelham in the County of Hampshire, Clerk Plaintiff or the Inhabitants of the town of Pelham in said County Defendants in a Plea of Trespass on the Case wherein said Abercrombie demands against the said Inhabitants of Said Town the sum of One Hundred & Seventy seven Pounds Sixteen shillings lawful Money being ye arreas of the salery due him from s^d town as their Minister &c as is at large set forth in the writ on file.—The Parties in this Case appear Viz: the said Robert personally and the said Town by Alexander Turner their Agent and attorney, and enter into a Rule of Court to refer this Case and also to submit all Contracts Actions disputes controversies and Demands respecting any per-

sonal Matters now subsisting between them. The Plaintiff chose Oliver Partridge of Hatfield Esq. The Defendants chose Thomas———— of Deerfield Esq, and the Court appointed Timothy Woodbridge Esq of Stockbridge who are to hear the Parties, consider the Case and all personal matters submitted to them, and make report to the next Court whose Determination or any two of them is to be final, and the Action is Continued in the Meantime.
February 13, 1759."

"1759 ABERCROMBIE VS. THE INHABITANTS OF PELHAM.

Robert Abercrombie of Pelham in the County of Hampshire Clerk Pltf or The Inhabitants of the Town of Pelham aforesaid Defendants in a Plea of Trespass on the Case for that the Inhabitants of said Pelham having invited and Called the Plaintiff to be their Settled and ordained Minister he on the 5th of March 1743 at Pelham afore said by his Answer in Writing to the said Inhabitants qualified by Law to vote in the choice of a Minister these legally met in Town Meeting accepted their Invitation & Call aforesaid and the said Inhabitants of said Pelham promised and obligated themselves and successors Inhabitants of said Pelham that in Case he the said Abercrombie would settle and be ordained their Minister to pay him the annual salery of fifty Pounds to be fixed at the then Value of Bills of the New Tenor in Case of Depreciation for every year after his settling so long as he should continue their Minister and further comply with and perform all the other Terms and Conditions by him required in his Answer aforesaid and that in pursuance of the Call & Choice made of him said Robert by and with the advice of three Neighboring Ministers he on the 29th day of August 1744 at Said Pelham was duly ordained Minister and Pastor of the same Town & the Church to be gathered therein, and that he is and then was a person qualified as the Law requires for the Ministerial office and has ever since continued their settled Minister and Pastor and during the whole time performed and discharged the proper functions of his office and Trust aforesaid and on the 9th of September last four of said annual Sums or yearly Salery at the rate aforesaid for years then Compleat being of the value of Forty four Pounds nine shillings lawful money for each year became due and arrear being in the Whole one hundred & Seventy seven Pounds Sixteen shillings, yet the Defendants tho often requested have not paid the same nor any part thereof but neglect and refuse to pay it to the Damage of the Plaintiff two hundred Pounds all which is more largely set forth in the Plaintiffs writ on File. This Case was originally commenced at the Inferior Court of Common Pleas held at Northampton on the 2d Tuesday of February last when and where the Parties entered into a rule of Court to refer to the Case with all Contracts Actions Disputes Controversaies and Demands respecting any personal Matters subsisting between them as per Records of sd Court appears. And now the Referees to whom the Case &c was referred Report that they met at Pelham where the Pltfs & ye Dfts by their Agent were present who agreed to refer to their Consideration the Matters Contained in the Writ only and that after a full hearing of the Parties thereon they adjudge and determine that the said Robert shall recover of the said Inhabitants of said Pelham thirty Pounds, one shilling and Eight Pence & Cost of Court together with the Cost of this Reference and the Cost of the Referees.

It is therefore Considered by the Court that the Pltf shall recover against the Defts the sum of thirty Pounds one shilling and Eight pence lawful Money Damages and Cost of Court with the Cost of the Referees as per Bill allowed at Nine Pounds Eleven Shillings and Eight Pence. Execution issued 6 July 1759."

The receipts or discharges which Mr. Abercrombie gave when money was paid him on his salary has his peculiar autograph and hand writing. Space is allowed for one of them.

Now that the long drawn out lawsuit against the town which Mr. Abercrombie had been pushing since his dismission had been settled it would seem but a natural result of such long continued litigation that the people of the town would feel incensed, and perhaps a revengeful spirit developed which would seek an opportunity to get even with their former pastor should a favorable opportunity present itself. But the people did not seem to be affected that way, or to lose respect for him in the least, so far as we may judge by recorded action. An opportunity to display revengeful feeling toward Mr. Abercrombie, if any such feeling existed, came very soon.

In the warrant for a town meeting Oct. 2d. 1760, was the following article.

" To see if the town Will agree to Petition the General Court to Have all the unImproven Land taxed for two years at one penny per acer to finish the Meetinghouse and Charges arising on the town except what Land Mr. Abercrombie owns."

Recorded action upon the above article :

"Voted that they Prefer a Petition to the General Court to Have all the unImproven Land taxed for two year at one Penny pr acer Except what Land Mr. Abercrombie owns.

THOMAS DICK, Moderator."

At this distance we cannot understand why Mr. Abercrombie should be exempt from taxation on such lands as he owned that it was proposed to tax, and can conceive of no reason for making an exception in his favor unless it was because of the great esteem in which he was held by the people of the town, who, remembering his services as their minister for ten years were still desirous of showing their great regard for him when a fitting opportunity presented itself. Whether the recorded vote was unanimous does not appear, but there is no recorded protest against the action taken, and yet the people were not halting or backward in recording a protest against anything that it was possible to protest against. They seemed at times to be watching for an opportunity to record a protest.

In a warrant for a town meeting Dec. 2, 1763, article 4 reads as follows:

"Fourthly To see if the town will agree to free Mr. Abercrombie's Party from paying their respective Proportion of Mr. Graham's Settlement & yearly Sallery and Consent that they and all such as Joyn with them in this requist may be allowed to Pay there several Proportions of Yearly Sallery to Mr. Abercrombie."

On this article the recorded action was,—"Voted that there is nothing acted on the Fourth article of this warrant."

This action of the town was the cause of the Abercrombie party taking their case to the General Court, and the town was obliged to take notice of a citation which had been served upon the town of the petition which had been filed at Boston, giving the town opportunity to oppose its being granted.

The persistence of Mr. Abercrombie's friends in clinging to him is shown by their action in petitioning the General Court, and by an article in a warrant for town meeting, Jan. 16, 1764, ten years after he had been dismissed and denied the right or privilege of preaching at Pelham.

"Article 8. Whereas there has been a petition lodged in the General Court of this Province by a Number of Petitioners Belonging to this town to Wite :—

Some adherents to Mr. Abercrombie and others to the Intent that they may be freed from Paying any Settlement or Sallery to Mr. Graham.

That the town chuse a Man or Men to represent their case and make answer to the General Court in their Nixt Sessions, to said Petition according to the Citation we have Received from said Court."

Hugh Johnston, Isaac Gray, George Cowan, John Savige and William Crosett were chosen a committee to answer the said petition. The General Court could not grant such an unreasonable request and they failed in their purpose to pay their assessments for the support of the Gospel to Mr. Abercrombie rather than to Mr. Graham.

After Mr. Abercrombie's dismissal from the church at Pelham there is little of record on the town books to show that he took a very active part in town affairs or that he preached any more to his former people. He lived on his farm in a quiet manner, preaching occasionally in other towns, there is a record of his preaching on one occasion at Amherst, and he probably preached in other places near by and may have supplied more distant churches.

AT A TOWN MEETING, JUNE 21, 1774,

The following vote was passed: "Voted that the Rev. Mr. Abercrombie is cleared from all his Rats that is already assessed on him, —also voted that Mr. Abercrombie is cleared from Paying any Rats for the future.   THOMAS COCHRAN, Moderator."

The above vote covers all the record of action at the meeting, and exhibits the kindly and generous feeling of the town toward their former pastor.

AT A TOWN MEETING, APRIL 16, 1779,

"Rev. Robert Abercrombie was chosen a committee to meet other committees at Northampton at a County Convention to Consider the question of a Constitution for the state." And at a meeting, March 23, 1780 it was "Voted that Mr. Abercrombie is allowed nine pounds for time and expenses for going to Northampton in behalf of the town."

This is believed to be the first and only occasion that Mr. Abercrombie was called to serve the people of Pelham in any Public capacity after being released from his pastorate.

At a meeting of the town Jan. 9, 1782, near the close of the Revolutionary war and eight years after the action of the town in June, 1774 clearing Mr. Abercrombie from taxes already assessed, and also relieving him from paying any in future, there was an article in the warrant to see if the town would reconsider the vote of June 21, 1774 and it was voted to reconsider it. Whatever the reasons were that led the people to exempt Mr. Abercrombie from taxation during all the years of the war we may not be able to determine, but it indicates that the people over whom he had been settled thirty years before the vote of June 21, 1774 was passed, and who had been dismissed twenty years when the exemption was extended, still retained so kindly an interest in his welfare as to be willing to exempt him from taxation when all the people had been so sorely pressed to meet the expenses of the struggle for liberty.

After Mr. Abercrombie retired from active labor in the ministry he seems to have spent his life in tilling his lands and in the care of his family of eight sons and three daughters.

REV. ROBERT ABERCROMBIE AND THE PRESBYTERY.

In the year 1755, in letters to a friend, Rev. Robert Abercrombie gave an account of the proceedings of the Presbytery against him. In the same letters he criticizes their action and questions their authority to act as they did in the premises. The action of the Presbytery caused Mr. Abercrombie's suspension from the exercise of his functions as a minister, and later his dismission from the pastorate at Pelham.

Mr. Abercrombie claimed that the first springs of differences between him and the Presbytery arose from the fact that he could not comply with all the measures of the Presbytery;—that he could not in faithfulness to his own convictions do so, and consequently desired the Presbytery to dismiss him from the pastorate of the church in Pelham on the 15th of June, 1748, but his request was declined at that time and his differences with the Presbytery increased.

We gather from the printed letters to a friend, that certain members of the church at Pelham were not such as should be admitted to the sealing ordinances of the church, as in the judgment of Mr. Abercrombie, it would be contrary to scripture and to Presbyterian principles. There seems to have been an inclination on the part of some to be more liberal in belief than a strict disciplinarian could allow, and until such members had purged themselves from such sins Mr. Abercrombie felt it his duty to withhold the ordinance of baptism from the children of such members. With this condition of affairs and while his application for dismissal was pending, the " Presbytery proceeded to ordain Rev. Mr. Moorehead. Either now or on his return from Colrain to use the assistance of the Session of Pelham (in case Mr. Abercrombie declines it) in inquiring into the Christian conversation of those in Pelham who have children to baptize ; and to baptize them whom he finds upon enquiring to have the Right to that privilige."

Mr. Abercrombie having been suspended from his duties this action on the part of the Presbytery and of Mr. Moorhead in allowing the children of unfit parents to have the benefit of the ordinance of baptism, and without giving him (Mr. Abercrombie) sufficient time

Pelham March 24th 1748

Accounted with James Conky Treasurer for my Sallery for the Year from Aprile the 30th 1748 was and received fifty Pounds in Bills of the new Tenor which I accept of as my Sallery for said Year and fully Discharge him and the Town from all further Demands of the Same

Ro: Abercrombie

FACSIMILE OF A RECEIPT GIVEN BY REV. ROBERT ABERCROMBIE.

for consideration before Mr. Moorhead acted in the matter, was displeasing to Mr. Abercrombie and he gave in a paper to the Presbytery in which he made a representation or criticism of the conduct of that body. The document is long and able. The Presbytery met at Palmer, Mass., Nov. 14, 1753, and the document was received by that body there. The opening paragraph was as follows:

"That whereas, next to the purity of Doctrine, which belongs to the Principles, a Dicipline agreeable to the word of God, which may regulate the Practice of the Members, is necessary to the Well-being of every Christian Society; the first of these the Presbytery seem to have taken some care of, by requiring every Probationer, under their care, to subscribe to the Westminster Confession of Faith and Catechisms: But I apprehend, we are still defective in the *last*: and therefore I would now represent some things to the Presbytery concerning our past Conduct and what I apprehend to be our present Duty."

The representation embraced four points or heads, and under the first head he claimed that the Presbytery should bring all under such regulations that discipline might be exercised upon offenders, and such kept back from sealing ordinances until proper satisfaction be given, and ordinances only administered to such as are found worthy. Mr. Abercrombie claimed that the admission of unfit persons to sealing ordinances had, he feared, already been productive of many scandals and offences; and had "given to just ground of complaint, to those who complain of our being too inclinable to favour a lax admission to sealing ordinances etc."

Under the second head he argued that it was necessary for the Presbytery to reconsider their sentence in the affair of P—— and again take it into consideration; in other words, to review their findings in the case, at the same time declaring that the sentence (of suspension) did not stand upon sufficient grounds.

Part third of the paper is an argument for reconsideration of their determination in the affairs of Pelham, on the ground that the Presbytery "had no right at that time to meddle in the affair of baptizing the children of that congregation.—No reference was made to them, —no complaint entered, and no time nor indeed opportunity was given to answer upon that head." Mr. Abercrombie also claimed that his being excluded from the deliberations of the Presbytery was what they had no right to do. "That they had no right to appoint one to moderate in the session, and baptize the children in case he declined; and that their conduct in that point was both irregular and without precedent." Again we quote:

"What ignorant, what profane, what scandalous people will pay the least regard to their own Ministers, who know their conduct and would bring them to censure, when they can find those who will readily administer ordinances to them upon easier terms?"

Further: "It is well known to any who are in the least acquainted with the Presbyterian Constitution that where the Case of a Minister is to be tried, there are at least to be *three Ministers* present: Whereas, in the present case there were only *two*."

In the fourth and last division of the paper, Mr. Abercrombie calls attention to the rules and principles of the Reformed Church of Scotland in relation to procedure: "which declare that the Constitutions, so far as agreeable to the Word of God, is the rule of proceedure in our judicatories."

He then calls attention to the danger to the church that might be expected from the endless disputes and protestations, "to the dishonor of religion, and hurt, if not the utter ruin, of this society at the last," and closes with the following appeal:

"I hope therefore, the Reverend Presbytery will take these things into serious Consideration, and do what may be for the Glory of God and the edification of those under our care. Which is the earnest desire of your Brother in the Work of the Gospel. R. ABERCROMBIE.
Palmer, Nov. 14, 1753."

At the next meeting of the Presbytery the "Representation" submitted by Mr. Abercrombie was considered and the following minute concerning it recorded.

"The Presbytery finding among their papers a long Representation put in by the Rev. Mr. Abercrombie at their last session and left by the said Session to the Consideration of this, in which are several things which at present appear Matters of high Charge Against the Presbytery. Voted unanimously, that as the author of said paper is absent, in order that no advantage may be taken of his Absense, the Consideration of said paper shall be left till next session, when the Author is expected to be present, and to make good those things that are Matters of Charge, either against the Presbytery, or any particular Member of it; and he is seasonably to be served with a copy of this Minute. SAMUEL MCCLINTOCK, Scribe.
A true copy attest."

The position taken by the Presbytery that the "Representation" brought serious charges against the Presbytery and that the author must appear before that body and make good what they construed as grave charges against the body itself or individuals composing it, and that he was called upon to appear and be tried before them,—*they*, whom he was charged with making accusations against, to be judges, —was in Mr. Abercrombie's opinion, contrary to the principles of the Presbyterian body and in disregard of the rules governing the Presbytery. In other words if the Presbytery was the party accused it was contrary to all precedent that the accused should hear the case and render decision.

The first session after the "Representation" was received, was held at Boston, Mr. Abercrombie not being able to attend. The session following was at Newberry. At this session Mr. Abercrombie was appointed to preach Mr. Boyd's ordination sermon at Greenwich but before the time, received a message from Rev. Mr. Moorhead forbidding him to do so.

At the next session, as Mr. Abercrombie claims, the Presbytery made repeated requests to have him withdraw the offensive " Representation." These requests were declined, and being called upon to support the "Representation," he respectfully declined to do so, because he was not to be heard as a representer, but as an accuser, and the accused were to be his judges.

Mr. Abercrombie then submitted a proposition to refer the case to the General Assembly of the church of Scotland, or to a number of Congregational ministers to be mutually chosen. These propositions were declined by the Presbytery.

At this session Mr. McGregorie read a long paper covering the whole case exhaustively,—declaring that the papers of Mr. Abercrombie contained

" * * diverse insinuations and reflections, also sundry more direct assertions against this judicatory, and declined their authority. * * * Upon the whole the Presbytery judge that the said Mr. Abercrombie is guilty of insinuating things against the Presbytery false and groundless, and that he ought to be solemnly admonished and rebuked for his sin against God and the church, and exhorted to walk with more circumspection in future.

That if he submits to said rebuke, he will be esteemed in his former standing, with this Judicatory ; but if not he is *suspended* from the exercise of his Ministerial office four weeks from this time.

Mr. Abercrombie being called upon and refusing to submit to the rebuke the Moderator in the Name of the Presbytery proceeded to suspend him from the exercise of the Ministerial office, according to the foregoing vote.

From the Minutes of the Session at Newbury August 20th 1754.

Per SAMUEL McCLINTOCK, Scribe."

A few days later a man was sent to the Pelham people, and read to them the minutes of the Presbytery, and by an order from that body "discharged all from hearing Mr. Abercrombie."

The suspension for four weeks was on August 20, 1754, and Mr. Abercrombie was continued under suspension until the meeting of the Presbytery in Pelham on April 15, 1755. At the session of the Presbytery in Pelham April 15, 1755 Mr. Abercrombie submitted another document, addressed as follows:

"Unto the Gentlemen calling themselves the Presbytery to meet at Pelham April the 15th 1755."

In this paper as in the first he plead with them to receive the discipline of the Church of Scotland in her purest times, and to practice in such a manner that immoral and illiterate persons may not be admitted into the sacred office of the ministry, and those unworthy among the people may be kept back from sealing ordinances. He declined to accept them as worthy to decide in his case because to quote his words: "by your former conduct you have unqualified yourselves to sit in judgement upon any case wherein I am concerned. * * and I absolutely refuse to submit to your judgement."

The closing paragraph of the paper follows:

"I appeal from you as Judges, unto the first free and impartial Synod Assembly or Council, to whom I may in Providence have access to apply, and who will redress those injuries you have done me. And finally, if the all wise Jehovah, in his adorable Providence see meet so to dispose of matters that such Synod, Assembly or Council cannot be obtained in Time, I appeal from your unrighteous Judgment, unto the Righteous Judge of all the Earth, to whom I desire to commit my cause, before whose awful bar you and I must ere long appear to answer for our conduct, stand an impartial trial, and receive the final sentence, from which there is no appeal. Even so, Come Lord Jesus.   Amen.   R. ABERCROMBIE.
Pelham, April 15, 1755.

At this meeting of the Presbytery the people of Pelham submitted a paper to that body desiring light upon the matter of suspension of their pastor and expressing doubt as to the legality of the proceedings, and setting forth at length their reason for so believing, and closing with a desire that the Presbytery give answer in writing. The answer of the Moderator was that they had joined with a man the Presbytery had laid under suspension, and that going to hear him was against the wishes of the Presbytery, consequently the Presbytery had no more to do with them.

At a meeting or session of the Presbytery at Boston, May 14, 1755, they reported that they had proven many of the charges against Mr. Abercrombie, although he was absent and declared :

* * " that his usefulness at Pelham was at an end. Therefore the Presbytery by their vote dissolve the particular relation between said Mr. Robert Abercrombie and the Church and Congregation at Pelham :—and they do hereby in the name of the Lord Jesus Christ, the great head of the Church, and by virtue of the authority committed by him to them, actually disolve the relation of Pastor and people : between the said Mr. Robert Abercrombie and the Chnrch and Congregation of Pelham ; prohibite and discharge him to exercise the office of the holy ministry or any part thereof in said Pelham, under the pain of the highest censure of the church : and furder; seeing Mr. Robert Abercrombie has rejected all proposals, made to him ; by the Presbytery for an accomodation, and refuses to retract from or make satisfaction for the false and injurious things insinuated : we do in the same name suspend the said Mr. Abercrombie from the Exercise of the Ministry and every part of it until the next session of the Presbytery, or such time as he shall be orderly restored therefrom : under the pain of Deposition.

J. MOORHEAD, Mod'r.

Signed per order SAMUEL MCCLINTOCK, Clerk.

Boston, May 14^{rh} 1755."

In criticism of the decision of the Presbytery at its session at Pelham on the 15th of April 1755, Mr. Abercrombie remarks to his friend :

" I am threatened with the highest Censure of the Church, if I exercise any part of the Ministry in Pelham. I should be glad to know, whence it comes to be thought so highly censurable and criminal for me to exercise my Ministry in Pelham, more than in any other place. But not having the papers, upon which, it may be supposed, this sentence is founded, I cannot give you that light concerning it, which I would desire. I shall only say this Method, that the Presbytery have taken to condemn a man, without letting him or the world know for what, I look upon as mean unreasonable and injurious. While a man is thereby deprived of an opportunity to clear up the truth, to vindicate himself, the world are left in the dark, yea, are necessarily left to think it must be some *gross* immorality, some *heinous crime* for which he is so severely treated, and has such awful threatenings denounced against him.

When the case was examined at Pelham none but Messers Moorhead, McGregorie, McDowel and Burns with their Elders were present.—It is customary to change the Elders every meeting : and at this, Mr. McDowel and Elder were absent. Messrs Parsons and Boyd, with their Elders, now present, had *never* heard the case *examined*; nor those Elders who were not at Pelham. Mr. Moorhead was continued Moderator. So that of *ten* members who were to judge, *seven* had not heard the case examined. In

short, if *they* gave any *judgment* it must not be thought to result from their own knowledge, upon having heard the case and enquired into the affair; but grounded upon the testimony of Messrs Moorhead, McGregorie and and Burns, and if so, I can't see why these *three* could not have done the business *alone*; unless the others wanted to give their followers an *example* of practicing upon the principles of implicit faith, and convince them that they required of other men no more than they themselves were willing to do. 'Tis plain there was not a majority of the Presbytery to act upon the affair. And so according to Presbyterian Principles, their sentence is of no force and claims no regard. R. ABERCROMBIE.
Pelham, May 30, 1755."

It has been claimed that certain members of the church and society at Pelham appeared before the Presbytery and preferred complaints against their pastor. This was doubtless true, as there were people in Pelham who protested against the action of the town in calling Mr. Abercrombie at first, and may have carried their opposition along until another good opportunity came to express it publicly. In more recent times it is seldom that there cannot be found a small minority in any church or parish that do not like the settled minister whoever he may be. If one minister is dismissed and another settled, the same chronic grumblers and fault-finders begin their opposition to the new minister where they left off with the old. Notwithstanding the fact of personal opposition to Mr. Abercrombie in Pelham, there is also indisputable evidence that he had a strong following among them through his entire ministry, and during his life until his death.

Whatever the cause or causes of the trouble between the Rev. Mr. Abercrombie and the Presbytery, or upon whom rests the blame for trouble between the pastor and the people of Pelham it was most unfortunate for pastor and for people,—unfortunate for all concerned. The absence of united and harmonious feeling and action between pastor and people worked for harm continually, and could only result in preventing the new settlement from becoming as strong and flourishing as it would have been, had all of the disturbing disagreements been absent. The people of Pelham should have been more largely benefitted by the labors of such an highly educated, talented man as Mr. Abercrombie, and would have profited thereby to a much greater degree had they been united in supporting him by prompt payment of salary, and in giving him a more united moral support. Strict disciplinarian as was the pastor, it is possible he was not as lenient as some more liberal members of his church thought he should be, and too much inclined to exact entire and unquestioned compliance with the Westminster Confession of Faith. He was a man of strong mind and will, and his convictions of duty would not allow him to preach smooth things, or allow any falling away from the strict letter of church discipline without reproof. His people were also Scotch and it is quite possible were firmly convinced that the pastor was too exacting and strict in church discipline, and disinclined to bow humbly under correction. Mr. Abercrombie was unfortunate in having a strong element of opposition to contend with from his first connection with the people of Pelham as shown by the strong protest against his settlement. There was also a strong Abercrombie element or party that clung to him for years after his connection with the church was severed by the Presbytery.

Stephen Burroughs, The Supplyer.

From 1739 to 1784, or for forty-five years the people of the town had enjoyed the services of a settled minister only about twenty-four years. From 1744 to 1754, during the pastorate of Rev. Robert Abercrombie, from 1764 to 1771 under Rev. Richard Crouch Graham, from 1774 to 1781 under Rev. Nathaniel Merrill. During all the years not covered by the pastorates of these three eminent ministers the town had received the Gospel from supplyers; sometimes through the aid and recommendation of the Presbytery, at other times by their own exertions in securing a preacher. The cause of this state of things, judging from what the records contain of the troubles and trials of the people lay largely with the people themselves. They were all sturdy and zealous in their belief, conscientious and scrupulous in the matter of discipline,—consequently each man considered his individual ideas and opinions those that should be adopted. The result was a division of opinion and no spirit of concession for sake of harmony and unity.

Mr. Abercrombie continued to live in the town after his dismission, and the strong minority of followers and adherents which his presence in the town kept together and active in their allegience to him, could not fail to have a discordant effect, and had a tendency to prevent unanimity and harmony in the matter of calling a new minister, as well as tending to keep up and encourage dissentions. We would not wish the reader to think that we have any desire to charge Mr. Abercrombie with having a hand in preventing harmonious action and unity among the people, but we do say that his presence in the town, and the loyalty of his friends, must have been harmful rather than beneficial, and we can but feel that to this fact among others, the trouble in settling and retaining men in the pastoral relation was due.

That ministers without settlements were not very numerous is attested by the records showing where men were paid for journeying to "the Jersey College and to Pennsylvania after a minister," and there is a possibility that the good deacons of Pelham became a little careless in demanding the fullest and undoubted endorsement before accepting the services of a supplyer.

However this may have been it is certain that a Godless adventurer at last obtained entrance to the pulpit and was accepted as supplyer for a limited period.

The reader should bear in mind that at this time nearly all travel over the country was on horseback or on foot, and that the means of communication by mail were at long intervals and uncertain, It was not as easy to learn the antecedants of men as now. There was no quick communication by railroad, telegraph or telephone,—no daily mail,—no detective agencies through which the records of suspicious persons could be looked up. The ministerial office was above suspicion. A ministerial imposter and deceiver was unheard of, and yet the continual demand for supplyers was the means of these good people having experience with a first-class specimen of the genus so much more common now than then. The reader should be charitable in his consideration of the experience of these people at Pelham, having in mind their environment, and compare it with that of other towns and communities which have had experience with the hypocritical religious cheat, and ministerial wolves in sheep's clothing, and who have been deceived and cheated by such graceless imposters, while every modern facility for enquiry and investigation was at hand.

STEPHEN BURROUGHS: ALIAS REV. MR. DAVIS.

On a Tuesday afternoon in April or May 1784, a bright active young man nineteen years of age, rode up the steep hillside highway to Pelham, West Hill. He sought Dea. Ebenezer Gray and presented a letter of recommendation written by Rev. Mr. Baldwin, then minister at Palmer, which introduced the young man as Rev. Mr. Davis, and as one well equipped to discharge the duties of supplyer for the pulpit of the church at Pelham, at that time without a settled minister, Rev. Mr. Merrill having been dismissed. Dea. Gray read the letter of Rev. Mr. Baldwin and having great confidence in the latter as a man of piety and good judgment, he consulted with other prominent members of the church to whom Mr. Baldwin's letter was submitted. The result of the careful consideration of the letter and its recommendation, including the fact that the young man had preached acceptably to the good people of Ludlow the previous Sunday, was, that they engaged the applicant as supplyer for four weeks at five dollars per Sunday beside board and horsekeeping.

The young man's garb at the time was anything but ministerial, or that would be considered so at the present day. He wore a light gray coat with silver-plated buttons, green vest and red velvet knee breeches, and seems to have entered upon his duties as supplyer without any objection being made to his unministerial robes. Possibly they might have supposed that he had more fitting raiment for the pulpit within his capacious saddle-bags. Whatever he may have had in the way of clothing within the saddle-bags, he did have ten old sermons written by his father which he had purloined on leaving home. These sermons were his only reliance for success in his new field of labor in addition to his abundant assurance, fearlessness and cheek, with which he was well equipped.

STEPHEN BURROUGHS.

There seems to have been satisfaction with the preaching of the new supplyer during the four weeks of his engagement, as a new contract was then made with him to supply the pulpit for four months longer.

It was not long after he entered upon the performance of the duties of his second engagement before some of the watchful ones began to have certain vague suspicions that the new supplyer was not all that he claimed to be, and might be more and worse than he claimed;—the people became suspicious, consequently watchful, and alert.

Deaths occurred among these hardy people occasionally and there was at least one death during the ministrations of this bright but wicked pretender, and the supplyer officiated at the funeral. Sermons were required often at funerals among these people at that time, and it is said that this funeral being at a private house the supplyer did not have a position where he could easily read his sermon and at the same time be sure that none present could get a glimpse of it. Some one present looked over his shoulder and saw that the manuscript did not have the fresh, crisp appearance that should mark the newly written sermon; on the contrary it was yellow and dingy with age, and this fact being noised about roused a suspicion that the supplyer was preaching old sermons, and not of his own composition.

The suspicion based upon what was seen at the funeral was spread from man to man until the whole town was discussing the situation. Doubtless this topic was the main one for days, until the ability of the new supplyer to write a sermon, or to preach without obtaining one already written became seriously questioned. This was a very important matter for the Scotch Presbyterians, and a plan was laid to test the young supplyer's ability to preach without a written sermon of his own or another's composition, and the plan was carried out. The following Sunday, a short time before the supplyer entered the church, he received a call from the leading members and was requested to preach from the words found in the first clause of the fifth verse of the ninth chapter of Joshua,—which reads as follows: " And old shoes and clouted upon their feet".

The supplyer without any show of surprise or appearance of being disconcerted, walked up the winding stairs to the high pulpit and opened the services preliminary to the sermon, and having only the intervening time to think out a sermon based upon such a strange and barren passage of scripture as the one thrust upon him.

He seems to have been equal to the situation however, and with a coolness and deliberation worthy of a more honest man and a less solemn occasion, he proceeded to preach a sermon that commanded the attention of the audience, and at the same time convinced his critics of his ability to preach an old sermon or a new one, if written, —more than that,—it satisfied them of his ability to preach without any sermon at all, though they might not have accepted with becoming grace the personal application of the subject with which he scored them at the close. His exordium consisted of a short narrative of the Gibeonites, and a history of their duplicity in general and toward the Jews especially. The subject was divided into three heads :

First—The place of shoes.
Second—The significance of old shoes.
Third—Of clouted shoes.

Under the first head he discussed the nature and use of shoes,—calling attention to the fact that man is but a sojourner in the world for a season; all traveling to another and better state of existence where all would arrive at last. He dwelt upon the necessity of being prepared for the journey, of being well and fittingly shod to render the journey easy; that the truly good man was careful to have his feet shod with the preparation of the Gospel of peace. He called upon them to remember that there was no such thing as remaining inactive during this earthly probation, all are moving rapidly forward to their final end ; and the way is not smooth,—it is filled with stones as well as briars and thorns, and unless well shod, we are wounded at every step. Mankind has learned that the way is rough and thorny and seeks such covering for the feet as they imagine will be a sure protection.

Secondly, of old shoes ;—he informed his hearers they represented those who had been hewing for themselves broken cisterns that could hold no water. Generation after generation follow each other on the same road,—they follow in the footsteps of those that have gone before them, and their feet are shod with the same old shoes.

The old shoes also represent old sins. The spirit of jealousy and discord, of suspicion and lack of confidence among men is but a display of old sins,—of old shoes that are as old as any worn. Jealousy is an old sin, and of this old sin Solomon said "Jealousy is more cruel than the grave." It causes men to hate each other,—it breaks up and destroys churches and all organizations wherever it is allowed to enter. Woe be to those who cherish and nourish the seeds of jealousy.

Thirdly, of clouted shoes.—Those who wear old shoes, who become suspicious and jealous of their fellowmen know very well how hateful and odious they become to all who are subjected to their wicked practices. Ministers and people, husbands and wives, parents and children fall a sacrifice to this unseemly jealousy. Such people know this is all wrong, know that it is sinful and are ashamed, and they have recourse to patching and clouting; they cover themselves with false pretenses to hide their deserved shame and disgrace.

Jealousy is a most debasing sin, and the least excusable of all. My hearers, he said, you know that when this sin has taken possession of your souls all comforts and joys flee away, and this first born son of hell triumphed in your bosoms. O jealousy, that green-eyed monster that makes the meat it feeds on.

The conclusion of the sermon from this strange text was a stinging application of the subject which must have made the suspicious Scotchmen writhe under the lash laid upon them by this nineteen years old stripling, from the high pulpit of the old meeting house.

"My Hearers, where shall I apply this doctrine? Is it calculated for a people only at some great distance? Can we not bring it home, even to our own doors? Search and see. Try yourselves by the sanctuary and if there your garments are not washed in innocence, you will find 'Mene, Mene, tekel upharsin' written on your walls. Will you suffer this hateful monster to rage among you? Will you wear these old filthy clouted shoes any longer? Will you not rather be shod with the preparation of the Gospel of peace?"

The people who had selected the text for the "Supplyer" under the suspicion that he had been preaching sermons written by others because he was unable to write them himself were abundantly satisfied that it was not necessary for him to write sermons in order to preach, and they were comparatively quiet for awhile. The supplyer had preached the four Sundays that Dea. Ebenezer Gray with the advice of other prominent members of the church had hired him for and had begun on his second engagement of sixteen Sundays at five dollars per Sunday besides board and horsekeeping. He had secured for himself more fitting clothing, and had purchased a new horse, saddle and bridle; had disposed of the horse and outfit that he first came to town with and he seemed to be going along swimmingly. But there was trouble in store for this wicked pretender that all of his smartness failed to avoid. No one of his acquaintances knew where young Burroughs was or what he was doing save Joseph Huntingdon, a young man whom he had known at Dartmouth college. Burroughs kept up a correspondence with Huntingdon and the latter proposed to visit Pelham on his way from College to his home in Coventry, Conn., sometime in September, 1784.

Joseph Huntingdon came to Pelham and remained several days

and during his stay on several occasions addressed the pretender Davis, by his true name Burroughs. This was noticed by those that heard it and it excited suspicion that Davis was not his real name. Huntingdon, concluded his visit, and set out on a Monday morning for Coventy, Conn., on horseback. Burroughs accompanied him, and when the two young fellows were riding past the house of Rev. Mr. Forward, the pastor of the church at Belchertown, the latter came forth and desired them to call, saying that Rev. Mr. Chapin from Windsor was within and he wished Davis or Burroughs to make his acquaintance.

Burroughs knew Chapin already and declined, stating that he was in haste to move on with his friend Huntingdon, but while making excuses, Rev. Mr. Chapin came forth from Mr. Forward's house and addressed the supplyer as Burroughs. It was in vain that he tried to convince Chapin that his name was Davis. Chapin was not deceived by talk of that sort and persisted that he knew the man before him and that his name was not Davis but Burroughs. Burroughs and Huntingdon then rode on towards Palmer, the former leaving Mr. Forward and Mr. Chapin with not a little assumed indignation at being addressed as Burroughs instead of Davis.

Burroughs and Huntingdon parted some distance below Belchertown. Huntingdon to pursue his journey to Coventry, Conn., and Burroughs turned back towards Pelham, by the same road that led past Mr. Forward's house; and after passing the house he heard some one shouting from the parsonage to him calling Mr. Davis, and also Mr. Burroughs, but he turned not back. Continuing along the hilly road toward Pelham, the supplyer had time to reflect upon the effect which the unpleasant interview with Mr. Chapin and Mr. Forward would have upon the people of his charge at Pelham when they came to know all about it as it was plain they would, the next day at farthest, when his true name and character would be laid bare to the people of Pelham, already suspicious, and who lacked but the information that Mr. Chapin could give them to cause the indignation of the people to burst forth and fall upon him in full measure. He had preached fifteen of the sixteen Sundays of his second engagement, and to meet the cost of new and fitting ministerial robes and his new horse, saddle and bridle had drawn all the salary that would be due after another Sunday's labors should be given, and as any further engagement was now impossible, he hastily decided upon leaving the town without the formality of bidding the people farewell. Arriving at his boarding place at Pelham that evening he put his horse in the usual place at the barn and went to bed as usual. When the family were all asleep he gathered his personal effects together, passed quietly from the house, took his horse from the stable, mounted and rode to the house of a trusted friend whom he calls Lysander. Who this man was or in what part of the town he lived is not known, probably in the easterly part. To Lysander he told the incidents of the day and what would befall him on the morrow if he fell into the clutches of those before whom he had been parading as a minister. Lysander secreted the guilty pretender in his house and hid the horse in his barn, and then they waited to see what a day would bring forth.

When the landlord of Davis, the supplyer, rose on that bright September morning in 1784 and learned that his guest of the summer had departed in the night, leaving not a trace, he was greatly astonished and excited. He informed the neighbors and the news spread like wildfire. A man came from Belchertown and gave information showing that the supplyer who said his name was Davis was a fraud and impostor, which added fuel to the flames of indignation that had begun to blaze. The whole town was in uproar. They mounted their horses and rode in all directions seeking for information that would lead to the discovery of Davis. Just what they proposed to do if they could find him cannot be clearly understood now but it is enough to know that those good people had been outraged, scandalized, by this unsanctified pretender who had been occupying the sacred desk of their meeting house, and they were all intent upon discovering the way he had gone and his whereabouts if possible.

During all that day of exciting thought and action among the people Burroughs was in the house of his friend, Lysander, and a witness of the hurrying to and fro of the angry people to whom he had been preaching for five months.

About 12 o'clock at night, after the people had quieted down, Burroughs mounted his horse and took leave of his friend Lysander and family and rode out into the darkness, going eastward towards Greenwich. He could, and doubtless did have a review of the past five months of his life in Pelham, now so suddenly terminated as he rode out of the town alone in the darkness of night. About one o'clock Burroughs overtook a man in the town of Greenwich named

Powers whom he had known before coming to Pelham. He accused Powers with having been searching for himself with the Pelham people, which Powers at first denied but later confessed that it was true. Burroughs explained the situation to Powers and endeavored to have the latter promise not to divulge his whereabouts. Powers hesitated and then Burroughs frightened him into taking a solemn oath that he would not, and they rode along together until Powers reached his house and Burroughs kept on, having decided to ride to Rutland, and reached there about eight o'clock in the morning.

As soon as Burroughs had parted with Powers the latter forgot his oath and turned back to Pelham, giving the alarm and rousing the people into the greatest excitement again on learning the direction Burroughs had taken.

A goodly number saddled their horses and pushed on after the fleeing imposter. Burroughs was in the store of a friend named Frink when he heard the tramping of horses hoofs. Looking out the window near which he was standing he recognized a crowd of Pelham people rushing into town on horseback, and he very well knew the errand that brought them there. His first thought was to elude them by flight; he made a rush for the rear door of his friend's store or shop, when near the door he met a Mr. Conkey, one of the angry Pelham men, who tried to lay hold of him. Burroughs struck Conkey across the arm with a stick with such force as to break his arm. Rushing past Conkey, now disabled, he ran around the end of the shop or store and turning the corner he met two of the Pelham deacons; turning again to avoid them, all of the angry Pelham people gave chase, shouting " Stop him! Stop him!" as they chased Burroughs down the hill. The fact of being pursued by the people he had been preaching to for the past five months, the shouting, and not very complimentary language of his pursuers angered their late Supplyer and he halted, picked up a stone and faced them, declaring that he would kill the first man who came near him. At this defiant attitude, the pursuers all halted in astonishment except Dr. Hinds, a prominent man of Pelham, who coming within reach of Burroughs, received a blow on the head which felled him to the ground. Burroughs seeing a crowd of Rutland people coming to see what it was all about, moved forward towards a small barn, his late people following at a respectful distance. Entering the barn, he climbed to the top of the haymow, taking a scythe snath along for defense. Rutland people came into the barn with the angry men from Pelham, and the former wanted to know what the disagreement was based upon.

Deacon McMullen of Pelham then explained that the man on the haymow was an imposter who had come to Pelham, calling his name Davis while it was Burroughs and had grossly deceived them by claiming to be a preacher, and preached to them all summer, and they had paid him for one Sunday that he had not preached.

The last statement seemed to strike the Rutland people as wrong, but as the Sunday had not yet come on which he had been engaged to preach, it constituted a mitigating circumstance.

Deacon McMullen then charged that Burroughs had nearly killed Dr. Hinds and Mr. Conkey and ought to be arrested and punished,. he also spoke of the intimidation and threatening of Powers at Greenwich the previous night.

There was a wordy discussion between the pursuers of Burroughs from Pelham and the Rutland people who had followed into the barn where Burroughs had taken refuge. Dea. McMullen and the party with him insisted that the law should take hold of Burroughs, and the Rutland people were not sure that he had done any great wrong by preaching under an assumed name if his preaching was good ; neither did they think that collecting money in advance for a Sunday's preaching, that he had not given them, was any very grave offense. Finally the Rutlanders proposed, that as Burroughs had collected five dollars of the Pelham people beyond what he had given an equivalent for, the whole business should be settled up by an adjournment to Wood's tavern where Burroughs was to expend the five dollars at the bar for the benefit of all those who were thirsty, whether native Rutlanders or people from Pelham. This proposition was finally adopted. Burroughs descended from the hay loft, where he had climbed for safety, and the party went to the tavern where Burroughs called for drinks for all hands, and an era of good feeling and satisfaction was rapidly setting in when Dr. Hinds, who had been knocked down for venturing to near while Burroughs was retreating to the barn, put in an appearance and began to foam with rage at the turn things had taken. Dr. Hinds was a prominent man in Pelham, was the heaviest tax payer as well as a noted physician at home,—and smarting under the pain of the blow from the stone in the hands of Burroughs was in no mood to condone the grave offences of an imposter, such as he had ridden from Pelham to Rutland to overhaul. There was a consultation between the leading Pelham men to decide upon what their action should be, and it is said they decided to take Burroughs back to Pelham. The result of the consultation and the decision to force their late supplyer to go back to Pelham was made known to Burroughs in some way, probably by the Rutlanders, and having decided objections to returning to Pelham as a prisoner, he decided on a plan to escape. Being in a room on the second story of the tavern, Burroughs locked himself in. The Pelham men went to the room to take the fugitive supplyer, finding the door locked, an axe was sent for. Burroughs jumped out of a window to the slooping roof of a shed and from that to the ground, landing close by where the men were looking for an axe to break down the door of the room. Burroughs then ran and obtained a good lead before the fleetest of the irate Pelham men knew that their hoped for prisoner had escaped. Burroughs eluded them. Being unable to find their man, they gave up the idea of taking him back with them and returned to the tavern, mounted their horses and set out for Pelham, filled with vexation and anger over the failure of their expedition to secure and punish the wicked supplyer.

Burroughs returned to Frink's store after Dea. McMullen and party had departed, spent the night in Rutland and the next morning started towards Providence, enquiring as he travelled, for a place to preach. On the way to Providence he learned that the people at Attleboro were without a preacher and desirous of obtaining one.

Arriving in Attleboro he offered his services to the proper persons and was engaged for a short season. Burroughs ministered to the people of Attleboro for four Sundays only, refusing to remain longer, because he had engaged to preach at Danbury, Conn., and desired to visit his friend Huntingdon at Coventry in the same state.

While it is not our purpose to go fully into the life of Stephen Burroughs there is one episode which should be given in connection with what has gone before. Burroughs was intimate with the man Lysander, a citizen of Pelham and with whom he was a guest for twenty-four hours after he disappeared from his boarding place as already stated. Who this Lysander was or what his family name was cannot be determined with certainty, but it was through Lysander that Burroughs became interested in a process of transmuting copper into silver which Lysander informed him was known to one

Phillips, who was working with the noted Glazier Wheeler, a counterfeit money-maker at New Salem. This secret Phillips had agreed to communicate to Lysander. Burroughs was greatly interested in the story, and Lysander wished to have his friend share in the wealth which he (Lysander) believed was to come from transmuting copper into silver, and personally had the greatest confidence in the practicability of the business, but his wife was not hopeful, on the contrary was doubtful. In order to make sure that there was no deception practiced by Phillips it was arranged that Burroughs should accompany Lysander to New Salem and together witness the process and note results. The visit was made in the night because it was thought it might cause unpleasant suspicions should it become known that they had been seen in the vicinity of Glazier Wheeler's place in the daytime, especially for one supplying the pulpit of the Presbyterian church at Pelham.

They arrived at New Salem at ten o'clock at night, and informed Phillips of the purpose of their visit. Phillips kindly consented to gratify his visitors with practical evidence of his power to transmute ordinary copper to the best of silver.

Phillips weighed out half an ounce of copper and put it into a crucible,—put the curcible into the fire; after a short time had elapsed Phillips put something wrapped in a paper into the hot crucible containing the copper.

The contents of the crucible then began to foam and boil, continuing in that state for ten minutes when it settled down into a clear fluid which was poured off and cooled. It was good silver and weighed half an ounce. It withstood nitric acid and other well-known tests, so that there was no doubt as to the quality of the product turned from the crucible. The only unsatisfactory thing with Burroughs was the nature of the so-called powder in the paper which Phillips had thrown into the crucible at a certain stage of the process. Phillips contended that it absorbed the verdigris of the copper leaving the remainder pure silver.

Burroughs desired to see some of the powder, and after satisfying himself that it was really a powder as claimed, he then wished Phillips to perform the experiment again and put the powder in open, without the covering of paper. Phillips said it was not quite as good a plan to do that way, but consented to gratify his visitors' curiosity. The experiment was then repeated in all respects the same as before, except that the transmuter, Phillips, laid a large flat piece of coal over the mouth of the crucible after putting in the copper. The result was the same;—half an ounce of pure silver was poured from the crucible as before.

Burroughs then desired Phillips to furnish him with materials and allow him to proceed, with the details of the experiment and the handling of the crucible, while Phillips should remain at a distance from the fire. Phillips assented to this proposition. Burroughs weighed out the copper, put it in the crucible and at the proper time put in the powder and when the contents were foaming Phillips, standing at a distance from the forge, cried out to Burroughs to stir the contents of the crucible. The only thing at hand with which the crucible's contents could be stirred was an iron rod about the size of the old-fashioned nail rod, such as blacksmiths of those days hammered out their own nails for horse and cattle shoes. Burroughs seized the rod and stirred the contents of the crucible, although he did not remember that Phillips stirred the crucible when attending it himself. On pouring out the contents of the crucible they weighed up a half ounce of pure silver as on the two previous occasions.

Burroughs begged for still further indulgence in the investigation and this time he stipulated that Phillips should not be even a spectator; that he should leave the room and remain out while Burroughs and his friend Lysander selected the materials for the crucible and manipulated it in the fire; to this Phillips gave assent. The two weighed out the half ounce of copper, placed it in the crucible, and when it was fully melted added the mysterious powder and stirred the contents with a short piece of walking stick, the nail rod not lying handy at the time. In stirring the contents of the crucible, about four inches of the stick was burned away, but as the stick of itself was worthless no thought was given to it at the time. After pouring out the contents of the personally managed crucible and giving it time to cool, a half ounce of pure silver was weighed up as in each of the former tests.

Satisfaction could not be more complete, and late that night Burroughs and his friend Lysander returned to Pelham filled with visions of fabulous wealth which was within easy reach, and they began perfecting plans to get this wealth in hand.

After two years in Dartmouth college, which he was forced to leave before the completion of the course, by fault of his own rather than

that of others; he left his father's house at Hanover, N. H. and went
to Newburyport and shipped on a packet having letters of marque
for Nantes, France, shipping in the capacity of physician for the
ship. On the passage out the packet halted at Sable Island, a lonely
uninhabited island on which there was only a hut for the protection
of such as might be shipwrecked on the surrounding reefs, and some
wild hogs that might be used as food by such unfortunates, if by any
possibility they could be killed.

The proposition which Burroughs and his friend Lysander considered was to charter a vessel, load her with copper, coal and provisions, besides the necessary outfit for transmuting copper into
silver and then take up their residence on Sable Island so that they
might pursue the wealth getting business without interruption, expecting, doubtless to bring back a ship load of silver instead of copper.

The consideration of this money making scheme was an all-absorbing one with Burroughs and Lysander, when the sudden exposure of
Burroughs came by the visit of his friend Huntingdon, and the unfortunate collision with Mr. Chapin and Mr. Forward at Belchertown,
made it imperative for Burroughs to leave Pelham. This broke off the
consideration of their plans for a time, but Burroughs who had become
an ardent believer in free silver, was desirous of completing the plans
already begun, and after visiting his friend Huntingdon at Coventry,
several weeks subsequent to his escape from the clutches of the
enraged Pelham people at Rutland, he determined to return to Pelham to renew the consideration of the plans so suddenly broken off.
He made the journey to Massachusetts and to Pelham, arriving at
the house of his friend Lysander at one o'clock in the night.

He was received with hearty expressions of satisfaction by Lysander and his family, and Burroughs was as effusive in his greetings as
they. There was a mutual recapitulation of the exciting occurrences
connected with his departure from Pelham and the scenes at Rutland
of which Lysander had of course received exparte statements from his
neighbors who were witnesses of the doings at Rutland. They
laughed over the ludicrous antics of the leading citizens when they
learned that Mr. Davis, the supplyer had disappeared, and over the
anathemas and execrations that his pursuers heaped upon the Rutlanders for not joining heartily with them in securing the imposter
and bringing him to punishment.

After all the incidents and happenings of the chase after Burroughs had been rehearsed and nothing of information concerning the great business of securing wealth by changing copper to silver had been volunteered by Lysander, Burroughs ventured to ask how he was progressing in the business, and with much show of distress and disappointment was informed by Lysander that the scheme for getting rich was exploded. "Burroughs, we have all been deceived by Phillips, that king of villians," said Lysander, and then he went on to explain how the deception was practised and made so plain as to fully convince them of its being a real transmutation of copper to silver.

When the half ounce of copper was placed in the crucible at the first test, Phillips put in a half ounce of silver wrapped in the paper with the powder which consumed the copper and left the silver. The second test was made to appear real by resorting to the following manipulations which neither Burroughs nor Lysander detected at the time.

As Burroughs desired to see the powder the silver could not be enclosed in the paper containing it, so Phillips unobserved laid the silver on the forge and covered it with a flat piece of charcoal broad enough to cover the top of the crucible, and with the tongs raised the silver with the charcoal and laid the coal across the crucible, the silver falling from the under side of the charcoal into the crucible when the tongs were removed. The third test was the one which Burroughs managed with Phillips standing at a distance from the forge and was directed to stir the contents of the crucible, which he did with a horse nail rod that lay handy on the forge. On the end of this rod the silver was fixed and blackened to look exactly like the iron rod itself,—when used to stir the contents of the crucible the silver melted off.

The last test was performed by Burroughs and Lysander alone, they weighed out the copper, put in the mysterious powder at the right time and stirred the mass in the crucible with a short piece of walking sticking,—the only thing in reach at the time,—no thought being given to the disappearance of the iron rod which had been laid aside unnoticed and the innocent piece of walking stick left within easy reach to be sought to stir the contents of the crucible at the right stage of the operation. The handy portion of walking stick was burned off for about five inches at the end and there was hidden the necessary half ounce of silver to complete the test and show up when cool as pure silver.

This statement of fact by Lysander caused a collapse in the hopes of great wealth which had filled the mind of Burroughs and had caused him to journey from Coventry to Pelham, when he was aware that neither Dr. Hinds nor Dea. McMullen cared to see him except to put him under arrest as the worst imposter they had ever known. Burroughs had lost in his expectations but his pocket had not suffered from the skillful manipulations of the one-armed bunco man, Phillips at New Salem, but Lysander and others had been fleeced in the sum of $2000, for Lysander was not the only one that Phillips was letting into the secret for a money consideration. It cost Lysander $100 in money and a fine horse to learn that he had been duped. Phillips, having secured all that he thought it possible with safety to seek, disappeared and left his dupes in the lurch, including Glazier Wheeler, to whom he had promised half the swag he should collect from those anxious to learn the business of transmutation of metals.

According to the statement of Burroughs, Lysander then decided to try to better his financial condition by securing a quantity of Glazier Wheeler's counterfeit silver dollars, which the latter turned out at the rate of three spurious for one standard dollar, and in the face of the pleadings of his wife and the arguments of Burroughs against it signified his intention to put them in circulation. He proposed to go to Springfield after certain drugs which Wheeler was in need of to fill an order he had placed in Wheeler's hands for more spurious money, and to take some of the bad money along to make the purchases. Arguments and pleadings were in vain, and because of his high regard for Lysander and his family Burroughs offered to take twenty counterfeit dollars and ride to Springfield to purchase the drugs which Lysander said must be obtained and for which he had determined to go in person.

Burroughs arrived in Springfield at 11 A. M. called at the drug store, ordered the drugs, and turned over some of the twenty bogus dollars in payment, and was arrested in a printing office opposite the drug store a few minutes later.

Burroughs was thrown into jail to await trial, and it was while in prison that he decided upon the course which he would pursue at the trial. Instead of implicating Lysander in the business of passing bad money he concluded to keep his mouth closed and take the punishment dealt out by the courts because of the great suffering the implication of his friend Lysander would cause his innocent wife and family. Burroughs was convicted and sentenced to three years imprisonment in Northampton jail.

Stephen Burroughs was the only son of Rev. Eden Burroughs of Hanover, N. H. He had spent one year in preparation for Dartmouth college, was in that institution two years; went on a voyage to Nantes, France, as ship physician at seventeen; taught school at Haverhill and Oxford, N. H., after his return from France; was obliged to leave home on account of being concerned in the robbery of a bee-house near Hanover, and for his attentions to a married woman at Oxford. When nineteen years old he follows the Connecticut river valley to Massachusetts; preaches his first sermon at Ludlow, and rides up the long Pelham slopes and bargains with good Deacon Ebenezer Gray to preach for four Sundays at five dollars a Sunday including board and horse keeping. Having followed the career of this talented young imposter so far as it has connection with the people of Pelham, as preacher or as passer of counterfeit money, we now take leave of him, with a good start in a career which became notorious, and whose operations covered a goodly portion of New England. The main facts of this Burroughs episode are condensed from the "Life of Burroughs," written by himself and published by M. N. Spear of Amherst.

The Hay Mow Sermon.

The famous Hay Mow Sermon of Stephen Burroughs has been a subject of great interest for more than a century. It has been asserted many times that it was preached from the hay mow in Rutland by Burroughs, to the people of Pelham who had pursued him from the tavern, and when hard pressed he had entered a barn and mounted the hay mow for safety. From the hay mow as a pulpit Burroughs doubtless made some pointed remarks in response to the incriminating charges that came up to him from the mixed audience on the barn floor of pursuing Pelham men, and the curious Rutlanders who were interested to see the outcome of the strange spectacle of a foot race between the staid churchmen from Pelham and their late "Supplyer," who had proven to be a wolf in sheep's clothing. But it is quite evident that the episode at the Rutland barn was only used to furnish on attractive name for a document issued several years later in pamphlet form, and probably never preached at all.

The opening paragraphs refer to the several ministers that had been settled in Pelham before Burroughs was engaged as " Supplyer " viz.: Rev. Robert Abercrombie, Rev. Richard Crouch Graham and Rev. Mr. Merrill. Rutland is mentioned truthfully as a land of hills and valleys—and the collision between Burroughs and Dr. Hinds, in which the latter received a blow on the head from a stone in the hands of the former is a matter of history.

Then the trouble between the Lincolnites and the Pelhamites is taken up. This refers of course to the Shays rebellion of 1786-7: proving conclusively that the Hay Mow Sermon was not preached extempore from the Rutland hay mow, but written after the rebellion had been crushed out, or not until three or four years after Burroughs climbed the hay mow. This feat having been accomplished in the autumn of 1784 after " supplying the vacant pulpit at Pelham for perhaps twenty Sundays and skipping the town with one Sunday more paid for than he had preached.

That part of the so-called sermon which touches upon St. Patrick and the race question was one upon which the people were very sensitive, as Burroughs well knew, and the charge that they could not pronounce the word faith, at all,—the nearest approach being the shorter and more quickly spoken word " fath " accompanied by the distinctive Irish brogue tended to make the Scotch people very angry, for they much disliked the title of Scotch-Irish often applied to them, and coming from Burroughs, the irreligious and wicked youth who had by sanctimonious pretentions been able to deceive them and gain admission to the pulpit for several months, made it all the more unbearable.

The above comments and explanations will help to a better understanding of the circumstances under which the much too highly extolled sermon was evolved from the brain of the notorious Burroughs, and will take away much of the sprightly novelty and spice commonly supposed to be found in the extempore effort of Burroughs from the Rutland hay mow.

The Sermon.

" In those days the Pelhamites being gathered together, from the East and from the West, from the North and from the South : Stephen the Burrowite being the Prophet of Pelham, ascended the *hay mow*, and lifted up his voice, saying, "hear ye the voice of the Lord which crieth against the Pelhamites,—for the anger of the Lord speaketh with furious indignation against you for the follies which you committed against the Lord and against his annointed. For verily, saith the Lord, I have given you my prophets, rising up early, and sending them: But the first* you soon rejected:—The second† on account of your cruelty, I took to myself:—The third‡ you drove away with great wrath, and pursued with great rage, malignity, and uproar.— "Then," said the Lord "I will give them a Minister like unto themselves, full of all deceit, hypocricy, and duplicity. But whom, among all the sons of men shall I send? Then came there forth a *lying Spirit*, and stood before the Lord, saying "I will go forth, and be a spirit in the mouth of Stephen the Burrowite." And the Lord said "go." Then rose up Stephen the Burrowite, of the tribe of the Puritans, and family of Ishmael, and went forth to Pelham, sorely oppressing the *Pelhamites*, taking from them ten shekels of silver, a mighty fine horse, and changes of raiment, and ran off to Rutland.

Then the *Pelhamites* were moved with rage, like the moving of the trees of the forest by a mighty tempest, and gathered themselves together, and pursued their Prophet down to Rutland.

And now, I your prophet and minister, being ascended on the *hay mow*, declare unto you, that I see an angel flying through heaven, crying "Wo! Wo! Wo! to the *Pelhamites*. The first wo is past, but behold two other woes shall come, which will sweep you away with a mighty besom of destruction."

Then arose up Nehemiah the son of Nehemiah, Daniel the son of John, and John the son of John, who was a trader in potash and were about to lay violent hands on the Prophet.

Then the Prophet lift up his rod, which he held in his hand, and smote John§, the trader in potash across the right arm, and broke it asunder, but the rod breaking and falling out of his hand, he caught up a great mill stone, and cast it on the head of Nehemiah‖ and sunk him to the ground.

This Rutland being a land of hills and valleys, where groweth the sycamore tree, the fir tree, and the shittim wood, by the wayside, as thou goest unto Dan, which in the Hebrew is called Abandone, but in Syriac Worcester; it being the place of a Skull: And not that Dan which is called by Tom Paine and Philistines Laith. The Prophet travelling through this land by the way of Ur of the Chaldeans, sought him five smooth stones out of the brook, and put them into his wallet; lest, haply, Syhon King of Hespbon, and Ogg King of Bashan, should come out against him. But it went out all round about the land of Edom saying, "The Burrowite is not, but is fled and gone over the brook *Cedron*."

Therefore they blew a trumpet, saying, "Every man to his tent O *Pelhamite!*" So they all went up from following after the Prophet; but when

---
*Mr. Abercrombie.   †Mr. Graham.   ‡Mr. Merrill.   §Konkey.   ‖Dr. Hinds.

they came to the pass of *Jourdan* behold a strong army had taken possession of the ford of the river! at which the *Pelhamites* were sore dismayed, and sought by guile to deceive the army of the *Lincolnites*; therefore, they say unto the *Lincolnites*. "We be strangers from a far country, with old shoes, and clouted on our feet." Then said the *Lincolnites* unto the men of *Pelham*, "Say Faith!" Then the *Pelhamites* said "fath," for they could not say *faith*. Then the *Lincolnites* knew them to be *Pelhamites* and fell upon them and slew them so that not one was left to lean against the wall.

When it was told in *Pelham*, saying, "Our old men are slain, and our young ones are carried away into captivity, and our holy places are polluted with the abomination which maketh desolate, there was great lamentation, weeping and wailing; every family mourned apart and their wives apart—and their mourning was like the mourning of *Hadradimmon* in the valley of Megidon;" and they said "alas! for the glory is departed from *Pelham*; the second wo which the Prophet foretold is surely come to us; and when the third wo shall come who shall be able to stand.—The beauty of *Pelham* is slain upon the high places! is slain! is slain upon East Hill. The Grays, the McMullens, the Hindses and the Konkeys are fallen upon the dark mountains of the *shadow of death*! Tell it not in *Greenwich*, publish it not in *Leverett*, lest the daughters of the uncircumcised rejoice; alas, for our wives and our little ones! So the hearts of the *Pelhamites* were troubled, and they drew around the alter of St. Patrick, and bowed down before the alter saying, "O great Spirit! how have we offended that thou hast left us to be destroyed by our enemies! Shall we go up again to fight against the *Lincolnites*, and shall we prosper?" But they received no answer, by Urim nor Thummim, by voices nor dreams; and the *Pelhamites* were greatly dismayed. Then said Ahab, the *Tishbite*, "Hear O *Pelhamites*! There liveth in the wilderness of Sin, as thou goest unto the land of *Shinar*, a cunning woman, whose name is Goody McFall, who has a familliar, and dwelleth alone, even with her cat. To this woman let the fathers and leaders of the tribe of *Pelham* repair and peradventure she may tell us what we ought to do."

Then the chief men of *Pelham*, captains of tens, captains of twelves and captains of twenties, arose up and disguised themselves in the habits of honest men, and went forth to Goody McFall, saying, "Bring us up a Spirit,"—and she said "Whom shall I bring up?" And they say unto her "Bring up Father Abercrombie." Then Goody McFall laid hold of her instrument of Enchantment and stamped on the ground, and then cried out, alas! for you have deceived me, for you are *Pelhamites* and not honest men. And they said unto her "fear not." Then the ground was troubled and began to move—and they said unto her, "Whom sawest thou?" And she said "Abercrombie." Then came there forth old Father Abercrombie; and with a countenance which made the Pelhamites quake with fear, said, "Why hast thou troubled me, even in my grave?" Then answered the *Pelhamites*, and said, "Because we are sore troubled.—We have fallen by the hands of the *Lincolnites*, and when we enquired at the altar of our great Prophet, we were not answered by Urim nor Thummim, by voices nor dreams." Then said Abercrombie,—"You shall go out to-morrow against the *Lincolnites*, and shall fall by their hands, and be utterly destroyed,— your wives and little ones shall be led away into captivity, for your measure of iniquity is full." Then the men of *Pelham* fell all along on the ground, and their hearts sunk within them.—Then fear and sore dismay spread through all the town of *Pelham*, and the *Pelhamites* fled into the wilderness, and hid themselves in caves and holes of the earth.

And lo! it was told in the army of the *Lincolnites*, saying,—The *Pelhamites* have fled!" Then arose up the *Lincolnites* and pursued after the men of *Pelham*, sorely discomfiting them, and led many away captive to the city of Dan. Then Benjamin the *Lincolnite* blew a trumpet, and all the men left pursuing after the *Pelhamites*.

And the *Pelhamites* who were carried away captive to the city of *Dan*, besought Jammy the Bostonian, saying, "We be evil men, dealing in lies and wickedness; we have sought to destroy the goodness of the land! we digged a pit and fell therein; we have trusted to St. Patrick to deliver us, but he has utterly forsaken us;—therefore O Jammy, in thy wrath remember mercy; and we will leave assembling ourselves together to talk politics, and follow our occupation of raising potatoes."—Then Jammy the Bostonian had compassion on the *Pelhamites*.

They then sung the following hymn, after which, the Prophet passed out of their hands and fled from their sight.

THE HYMN.

Says Irish Teague I do not know,
 From whence came our Nation;
"I to St. Patrick's shrine will go,
 And there get information.
Great genius of our Nation, tell
 By whom we are befriended,
For the Irish are so much like hell,
 I fear they from thence descended.
At which the grumbling spirit spoke,
 Poor Teague, I will befriend thee;
Since now my aid you do invoke,
 My help I'll freely lend thee.
Once on the coast of Gadareen,
 As flocks and herds were feeding,
A great herd of two hundred swine,
 Which shepherds these were leading.
Were by a Legion then possessed—
 * * of minds were bent on slaughter."

Any further reprint of the hymn is impossible as the ancient copy is so worn and torn that the above is all there is left.

VIEW IN WEST PELHAM, NEAR THE FISHING ROD FACTORY.

Pelham in the Wars.

French War.—Revolutionary War.—War of 1812.—Mexican War. —The Great Rebellion.

FRENCH AND INDIAN WARS.

Information concerning the part Pelham men had in the French and Indian wars is not easily obtainable. The ancient muster rolls had headings printed in a business like manner, giving a heading for all information for the identification of every soldier, term of service, miles marched, amount of pay, etc., and yet the one heading, "Town From," that would locate each man definitely is left blank on most of the rolls. These rolls are pasted into large blank volumes, ten or more in number, and not yet fully indexed, so that one must examine each roll for the names of men that have a familiar sound or that was a common family name in the town one is specially interested in. If one finds a muster roll of Hampshire county men it is scrutinized closely for names of men from the town whose soldier record is being looked up. Absolute accuracy is hardly attainable under the circumstances.

The first man whose name appears as serving in the French and Indian wars is given on the authority of the town records, as follows: At a meeting, March 19, 1746-7, "Voted that James Fergerson is freed from Paying Rats ye 1746 for his being in ye War." At the same meeting it was "voted that Isaac Hunter and John Starling is freed from Paying Rats last year and this year." Robert Fergerson was also "freed from paying Rats last year and this year." The record does not state that the last three men were freed from paying taxes in consideration of their being in the war, but it may not be unfair to assume that the four men were in his Majesty's service fighting the French and Indians.

A muster roll of Capt. Isaac Wyman's company in 1755, has the name of John Gray as in service of that company,—no town being given but it is a Pelham name and it is assumed that he was probably from that town.

On the 15th of Sept. 1755, the regiment of militia under Col.

Abraham Williams was mustered and thirty-nine men enlisted therefrom by order of Lieut.-Gov. Phipps and among these names was that of Benoni Shirtlieff, afterwards innkeeper, constable, and a man of position in Pelham.

When such an order was sent out to the commander of any regiment the quota was filled by enlistment from the enrolled men in the regiment, or if men enough did not volunteer, men were " impressed " to make up the quota.

A demand was made upon the regiment of Lt.-Col. Thomas Williams, May 4, 1756, and not enough enlisting, Matthew Gray was impressed, and the squad was mustered in at Hatfield. Matthew Gray was a Pelham man.

Levi Gray's name appears in the list of men from Col. Joseph Dwight's regiment who enlisted for service at Crown Point, May 4, 1756. Levi Gray lived on the farm known as the Eseck Cook farm.

John Dunlap was in Capt. Samuel Moody's company, Sept. 10, 1755, and Robert Dunlap in the company of Capt. David Dunning.

Robert Gilmore enlisted for service at Crown Point, Oct. 7, 1755, and William Oliver enlisted from Col. Jacob Wendall's regiment for service at the same place, Oct. 2, 1755, as did William Patterson. It is not absolutely certain that the last two names were of Pelham men but there were men of these names in the town and in the absence of statement on the rolls as to the towns the men came from it is quite possible they were from Pelham.

Joshua Conkey and James Turner were doubtless soldiers in the French and Indian wars sometime previous to 1761, and it is believed that during their service they traversed some part of Washington county, New York, and it is supposed that the land in that section pleased them and caused the men to go out there in the spring of 1761 and secure a tract of land on the flats where the village of Salem, N. Y., now stands.

" A Muster Roll of the Company under Command of Capt Robert Lotheridge in the Regiment of which Isreal Billings is Colonel, which marched by the Captain Generals orders for the relief of the Garrison and Troops at Fort William Henry at the time it was invested in the year 1757 in which is given the names of men, their Quality, the number of miles Marched, the whole term of service in Days, the number of Horses, the amount of each mans wages, and the number of meals that were eat upon the credit of the Province, annexed to the names of those who eat them."

Names.	Quality.	No. of Horses.	Wages.	Meals to be Deducted.
Robert Lotheridge,	Capt.	Horse	£3—12—-4	—
John Johnson,	Lieut.	Horse	2—14—-5	—
William Crosett,	Ensign	Horse	2—-3—-8	1
James Conkey,	Cler.	—	2—00—-7	1
Andrew Maklem,	Serg't	—	2—00—-7	1
Hugh Johnson,	do	—	2—-1—-3	1
Isaac Gray,	do	—	2—00—-7	1
John Hamilton,	Corp'l	—	2—00—-7	—
Oliver Selfridge,	do	—	1—19—-5	1
William Selfridge,	Cert.	—	1—19—-5	—
Patrick McMallan,	—	—	1—18—-2	1
George Patterson,	—	Horse	1—18—10	1
James Hood,	—	Horse	1—18—10	—
Isaac Hunter,	—	—	1—18—-2	—
Robert McCulloch,	—	—	1—18—-2	—
John Peebels,	—	Horse	1—18—10	—
Robert Hamilton, Jun.,	—	—	1—18—-2	—
Hugh Moors,	—	—	1—18—-2	1
Robert Peebels, Jun.,	—	Horse	1—18—10	—
Archibald Crosett,	—	—	1—18—-2	1
Jonathan Gray,	—	—	1—18—-2	1
Robert Maklam,	—	—	1—18—-2	1
James Hamilton,	—	Horse	1—18—10	1
James Turner,	—	—	1—18—-2	1
Thomas Cochran,	—	Horse	1—18—10	1
James Cowan,	—	—	1—18—-2	—
Arthur Crozier,	—	—	1—18—-2	1
Thomas Johnson,	—	Horse	1—18—10	1
John Lynsey,	—	—	1—18—-2	1
John Crozier, Jun.,	—	—	1—18—-2	1
Wm. Gilmore,	—	—	1—18—-2	—
James Harkness,	—	Horse	1—18—10	1
James Hamilton,	—	—	1—18—-2	1
Daniel Gray,	—	Horse	1—18—10	1
Alexander Conkey, Jun.,	—	—	1—18—-2	—
John Thompson,	—	—	1—18—-2	1
Samuel Stinson,	—	—	1—18—-2	—
James Thompson,	—	Horse	1—18—10	1
John McCartney,	—	—	1—18—-2	1
James Halbert,	—	—	1—18—-2	—
James Barry,	—	Horse	1—18—10	1
John Blaire,	—	—	1—18—-2	—
John Gray, Jun.,	—	—	1—18—-2	1
John McNiell,	—	Horse	1—18—10	1
Wm. Gray, Jun.,	—	—	1—18—-2	1
William ———	—	—	1—18—-2	1

Number of miles, 200. Time of service in days, 14⅓.

About one quarter of the paper on which the above muster roll was written, is missing, so that as many as sixty officers and men from Pelham marched to the relief of Fort William Henry in 1757, though but 46 are now on the muster roll.

A billetting roll of Capt. Salah Barnard's company in Colonel William Williams' regiment has the names of the following men; year not given:

David Johnson,	Isaac Davis,
Robert King,	Robert Gilmore,
James Peebles,	Eliot Gray,
James Powers,	Adam Gray,
Isaac Stevenson,	John Peeble,
Seth Rowland,	Robert Peeble,
David Gowden,	Isaac White.
Robert Cochran,	

These men enlisted May 2, served 33 days, and each received £1—2s.

"A Return of Men in Col Isreal Williams Regiment to be put under the immediate command of Jeffry Amherst for the invasion of Canada in 1759," has the names of the following Pelham men. Their ages are given, and each man furnished his own gun and enlisted April 2:

David Cowden	35	Arthur Crozier		19
Robert Hamilton	28	John Edgar Jun		20
John Crozier Sen	59	John McCartney		40
William Gray	18	John Halbert		18
James Hamilton	18	James Halbert		24
Isaac Hunter	19			

Arthur Crozier, son of John Crozier. James Hamilton son of John Hamilton.

A return of men enlisted for His Majesty's service in the reduction of Canada in 1760. Enlisted April 10: mustered April 12.

William Gray	19	Adam Clark Gray		17
Arthur Crozier	19	James Sloan		18

In the pay-roll of Capt. Thomas Cowdine's company for service from April, 1761 to December following there is just one Pelham name: Robert Clarke, Serg't.

The following signed document indicates that John Stinson, Stenson or Stevenson, the first town treasurer and father-in-law of Rev. Robert Abercrombie saw service in the army:

"(Vol. 96, page 98, Archives.) NORTHAMPTON, MAY 3, 1758.

To Col. Ruggles: Please pay unto Capt Daniel Robinson our respective Billetting,—we being soldiers in his Company and you will oblige subscribers. JOHN STINSON."

A muster roll of Capt. Samuel Robinson's company dated April 4, has the name of John Stevenson, Rutland, son of John Stevenson, age 18. John Stevenson appears on a list of men in South Regiment, Capt. Mirah's company, Col. John Worthington's regiment.

(Page 346, Vol. 96, Archives.) "Billetting roll. List of men under Capt. Samuel Robinson, Col. Timothy Ruggles' regiment: John Stevenson, £12—5s."

John Savage, a noted citizen of Pelham from 1747 or earlier until about the year 1766, "Was appointed a captain of a company of volunteers in 1758 and served under Gen. Bradstreet in his expedition against Fort Frontenac and under Gen. Abercrombie in the assault of Fort Ticonderoga."—(From Salem Book, 1896.)

THE REVOLUTIONARY WAR.

The temper of the men of Pelham concerning the oppressive acts of Great Britain in the year just previous to the opening of the Revolutionary war is shown in many places on the town records, and all of these items of record show that all were intensely patriotic and outspoken concerning the oppression of the Mother Country and ready for any demands that might be made upon them by the Continental Congress. There is no hint upon the records of any tories or tory sentiment among the people of the town.

The following iron clad oath, though without date, was evidently drawn up and subscribed to by the five men whose names appear, just before the war broke out. Just why these five and no more should sign the document is without explanation, so the paper is made part of the history of Pelham in the Revolutionary war without attempting to explain more than is done by the iron clad oath itself.

"I—A—B Truly and Sincerly acknowledge profess certify and declare that the Commonwealth of Massachusetts is and of Right ought to be a free Soverign and Independant state and I do Swear that I will Bear true faith and allegeance to the said Commonwealth—And that I will defend the same against Traitorous Conspiricies and all hostile attempts whatsoever and that I do Renounce and objure all allegiance subjection and obedience to the King Queen or government of Great Brittain (as the case may be) and every other foreign Power whatsover, and that no foreign Prince Person Prelate State or Potentate hath or ought to have any Jurisdiction Superiority Preeminence authority Dispensing or other Powers in any Matter Civil Ecclesiastical or Spiritual within this Commonwealth except the authority which is or may be rested by their Constituents in Congress of the United States and I do further testify and declare that no man or body of men hath or can have any right to absolve or discharge me from the Obligations of this oath Declaration or Affirmation,—and that I do make this acknowl-

edgement, Profession, testimony, Declaration, Denial, renunciation and obligation heartily and truly according to the common meaning and acceptation of the foregoing words without equivocation mental evasion or secret reservation whatsoever.   So help me God.   JOHN RANKIN,
JOHN HASKINS,
ANDREW ABERCROMBIE,
ALEXANDER BERRY,
NATH'L SAMPSON."

The town responded promptly to the call for men in the spring of 1775 and Captain David Cowden with a company composed of Pelham men was dispatched to the seat of war near Boston. The date of service of these men began April 19, 1775.

To better present this service of the Pelham men the old muster rolls have been copied and will be reproduced so far as may be thought advisable, or as fully as can be in type.

Capt. Cowden's company was connected with Col. Benjamin Ruggles Woodbridge's regiment, and the date of the service is the earliest found. Some of the muster rolls have no date and it is impossible to fix the year of service of some of the men for that reason.

A minute roll of the company under the command of Capt. David Cowden in Col. Benj'm Ruggles Woodbridge's regiment:

Pelham Men's Names.	Rank.	Time of Service. Weeks. Days.		Whole Amount Paid.			
				£	s	d	Far.
David Cowden,	Capt.	1	4	2	6	4	3
James Taylor,	Ensign	2	3	2	16	10	
Ebenezer Gray,	Sargent	1	4		18	10	1
Thomas Johnson,	Corporal	1	4		17	3	1
Timothy Rice,	Private	2	3	1	18	7	2
James Barns,	"	2	3		15	8	2
John Alexander,	"	1	4	"	"	"	
Isaac Bennett,	"	"	"	"	"	"	
Wm. Fergerson,	"	"	"	"	"	"	
James Harkness,	"	"	"	"	"	"	
John Hood,	"	"	"	"	"	"	
William Hunter,	"	"	"	"	"	"	
James Hill,	"	"	"	"	"	"	
John Killogg,	"	"	"	"	"	"	
John McKee,	"	"	"	"	"	"	
James Patterson,	"	"	"	"	"	"	
Joseph Ranken,	"	"	"	"	"	"	
Samuel Rush,	"	"	"	"	"	"	
Robert Salfrage,	"	"	"	"	"	"	
John White,				Total, 23	7	11	1

Time of service from April 19, 1775.

A muster roll of the company under command of Capt. David Cowden in Col. Benj. Ruggles Woodbridge's regiment to the first of August, 1775, has the following additional names of Pelham men :

James McCulloch,
William Hays,
Joshua Conkey, drummer,
Silas Conkey, fifer,
Ethanon Cowing,
John Cowden,
James Fergerson,
David Gilmore,
William Gray,
William Haskins,
John Hamilton,
Daniel Hathaway,
John Kelley,
John McCartney,
John White, Jun.

These were from enlistments in May and July mostly, most of the men having served more than three months.

A return of Capt. Cowden's company was made Sept. 28, 1775 from a point near Prospect Hill, shows all the above names save those of James McCulloch, David Gilmore, John Hamilton, Joshua Conkey and Silas Conkey, but with the addition of Adam Patterson and David Green. The absence of Joshua and Silas Conkey, drummer and fifer, respectively, may be because of their transfer to some other company or regiment as musicians.

Robert Salfrage or Selfridge, enlisted at the Lexington alarm as it is probable all of Capt. Cowden's original company did. He was a son of Edward Selfridge who died in Pelham in 1761, and Robert, a minor son, was placed under the guardianship of John Dick until he became of age. His service under his first enlistment was for eleven days. An order for Bounty Coat was dated at Prospect Hill, now Somerville, Nov. 13, 1775 and made payable to Capt. Cowden. He enlisted for another term of service Aug. 17, 1777 and is reported as discharged Aug. 20 of that year. He marched on alarm at Bennington. Sept. 23, 1777, he enlisted in Capt. John Thompson's company, Col. Porter's regiment, and was discharged Oct. 17, after a service of one month and a day. He marched on alarm to reinforce the Northern army under Gen. Gates.

Robert Selfridge was the only man of the name that served in the Revolutionary war from Massachusetts. The surname is spelled Selfridge, Selfridg, Selfrage, Sulfrage, Salfrage, Salfridg. Sometime after the close of the war he removed to Argyle, Washington county, New York.

A muster roll of the company under Capt. Isaac Gray in Col. Jonathan Brewer's regiment to Aug. 1, 1775.

Isaac Gray, captain,
John McLem, serg't,
Thomas McMullen, serg't,
Alexander Conkey, corp.,
Wm. Crossett, corp.,
James Abercrombie, private,
David Abercrombie, private,
James Barnes, private,
James Baker, private,
Alexander Conkey, private,

John Donoley, private,
Robert Gray, private,
Andrew McGray, private,
John Thurston, private,
Zebulon Richmond, private,
Bartlett Robinson, private,
Thomas Thompson, private,
Elijah Wilson, private,
Amos Whitney, private,
Jacob Conkey, private.

These men enlisted May 1, term of service three months and eight days, miles travelled 80, pay 6s—8d at one penny per mile.

In a muster roll of the Eighth regiment of the Continental Army at Dorchester commanded by John Fellows, the name of Timothy Rice of Pelham appears and the only one from that town on the roll, and the record shows that Rice went to Quebec with the Company to which he belonged; no date is given.

In a roll of Captain Coburn's company of Colonel Bridge's regiment dated Sept. 26, 1775, appears the name of Gardner Gould of Pelham.

William Haskins of Pelham was serving in Capt. Ezra Badlam's company of Colonel Gridley's regiment Oct. 8, 1775.

At a town meeting in Pelham Dec. 31, 1776, Abizer Edson and Andrew Abercrombie were chosen assessors, "In room of John Hamilton and James Caldwell McMullen Gone to the War." Hamilton's name appears on the muster rolls but that of James Caldwell McMullen does not though he probably was in the service.

A return of Capt. William Todd's company in Col. Crafts regiment of Artillery in Boston, Nov. 30, 1776, shows that David Sloan was in service in that company and drew pay for 83 miles' travel to his home in Pelham.

An abstract of the Travel of Company commanded by Cap't. Reuben Dickinson of Amherst—Col. Woodbridge's regiment, to Ticonderoga and from thence home.

One penny per mile per day, one day for 20 miles—in year 1776.

Daniel Shays, serg't.
Alexander McCulloch, serg't,
David Cowden, lieutenant,
Silas Conkey, fifer,
John Crafford, private,
Thomas Hamilton, private,
Thomas Montgomery, private,
George Elliot, private,
John Cochran, private,
Wm. Haskins, private,
Wm. Blare, private,
John Donnelly, private.

John Robinson, private,
John Crossett, private,
James Baker, private,
Wm. Gillmore, private,
Jacob Conkey, private,
David Abercrombie, private,
Thomas Johnston, private,
John Kelley, private,
Dinnis Charlton, private,
James McCotton, private,
James Abercrombie,

Number of miles, 307, 1 penny per mile, £1—5s—7d, 1 day for 20 miles, £2—6s—0d—1far, average per man, £1—5s—7d, average amount for the whole, per man, £2—6s—0d—1far.

Very little can be learned of the militia companies of Pelham previous to the Revolution or later, as no records have been found up to this writing to give light upon the make up of militia companies. A document dated South Hadley, March 16, 1776, and containing a record of election of officers for militia companies as the law directs, in the towns of South Hadley, Granby, Greenwich and Pelham the following officers were elected for the Pelham company: John Thompson, captain; James Halbert, 1st lieut.; John Hamilton, 2d lieut.

Muster Roll of Cap't. Oliver Lyman's company, in Col. Dike's regiment, 3 months to March, 1777, had two Pelham men on it.

William Berry, Corp'l,
James Harkness.

No. miles, 90, 1 penny per mile, 7s—6d, wages travelling home at 28 miles per day, 7s—1d, whole amount, 14s—7d, time in service, 7 days.

Company marched to East Hoosick on the alarm of August 17th. Cap't Oliver Lyman made oath to the above before Jabez Fisher, Justice Peace.

"AMHERST, MAY 15, 1778.

A return of men procured by Capt. Eli Parker to serve in the Continental Army.

Nehemiah Dunbar Pelham, enlisted or hired for the town of Amherst served under Capt. Maxwell—Col. Bangliss,—time of engament 8 months, time ends Decem 1778.
Enlisted for state of Massachusetts Bay."

List of men mustered in the Continental Army for nine months services from the County of Hampshire in the State of Massachusetts.

Pelham Men.	Age.	Height.	Color of Hair.	Regiment.	Company.
Hugh Johnson,	50	5 ft. 9 in.	Brown	Col. Porter's	Capt. Thomson's.
James Hill,	49	5 ft. 9 in.	"	"	"
James Cammel,	33	5 ft. 8 in.	"	"	"
John Cowden,	35	5 ft. 10 in.	Dark	"	"
Amos Gray,	16	5 ft. 6 in.	Brown	"	"

"South Hadley, June 17, 1778.

MR. JOHNSON.—SIR: You are Hereby directed to march the men committed to your care the directest Road & with convenient dispatch to Fishkill and deliver them together and not suffer them to do any damage to any of the Inhabitants of Towns through which they may March, and they are hereby directed to obey your orders on their March.

NOAH GOODMAN, Superintendant for the County of Hampshire.

12 Men in Squad: Leverett 2, So. Hadley 1, Granby 1, Hatfield 1, Chesterfield 1, Northampton 1, Pelham 5—12."

In a list of men raised in the several Counties in the state of Massachusetts Bay for the purpose of completing the fifteen battalions of Continental troops to be raised in the state for the period of Nine Months from the time of their arrival, agreeable to the resolve of April 6, 1778, the name of James Camble of Pelham is enrolled. It may be intended for Campbell.

The return of militia of Hampshire County who were drafted to march to Horse Neck under the command of Col. Sam'l How, that did not join the regiment, has the name of of Wm. McMullen of Pelham. He was in Cap't Thompson's company.

There were enlistments of men for short terms of service, three, six and perhaps eight months, and the dates are sometime omitted; among them we find a list of Pelham men—the date is indistinct and the record torn,—we copy all that it was possible to make out and the list follows:

	Age.	Stature.	Complexion.
Isaac Bennett,	21	5 ft.—11 in.	Ruddy
Charles Handy,	21	6 ft.—	Dark
James Baker,	33	5 ft.—9 in.	Ruddy
Samuel Abercrombie,	18	5 ft.—9 in.	"
John Hamilton,	18	5 ft.—9 in.	Dark
Andrew McGray,	21	5 ft.—10 in.	Ruddy

In 1779, the following Pelham men were in Col. Moseley's regiment and Capt. Fowler's company serving on the Tours quota:

William McMullen,
David McMullen,
Joel Winship,
Peter King,

Joseph Gray,
Alexander McCulloch,
John Dart.

In the list of men received for nine months' service from Noah Goodman, Esq., superintendent for Hampshire county June 9, 1779, are the names of Pelham men as follows:

	Age.		Age.
Daniel Ranham, black,	19	Nehemiah Dunbar, brown,	17
Reuben Hollan, brown,	19	Nathan Richards, brown,	17
Josiah Dunbar, light,	18		

Col. Porter's regiment; Captain Thompson's company.

Descriptive list of men engaged to reinforce the Continental Army for eight months agreeable to the resolve passed June 9, 1779.

From Pelham.	Age.	Size.	Col. Porter's Regiment.	Capt. Thompson's Company.
Wm. McMullen,	26	6 ft.—	"	"
David McMullen,	17	6 ft.—	"	"
Joel Winship,	21	5 ft.—6 in.	"	"
Peter King,	22	5 ft.—7 in.	"	"
Joseph Gray,	17	5 ft.—6 in.	"	"
Alexander McCulloch.	16	5 ft.—2 in.	"	"
John Pratt,	16	5 ft.—4 in.	"	"

All dark complexion.

Additional men mustered by Col. Elisha Porter, Aug. 10, 1780, and furnished by the town of Pelham's selectmen July 30.

Names.	Age.	Statue.	Complexion.
Samuel Thatcher,	63	5 ft.—6 in.	Dark
John Coffin,	58	5 ft.—6 in.	"
James Conkey,	57	5 ft.—6 in.	"
James Hill,	44	5 ft—10 in.	"
Lamnen Gray,	27	5 ft.—10 in.	"

In the company of Captain Dwight of Belchertown were the following Pelham men by record made June 22, 1780.

Names.	Age.	Size.	Complexion.
Wm. McFall.	67	5 ft.—7 in.	Dark
Christopher Stevenson,	28	5 ft.—11 in.	"
Benjamin Edson,	21	5 ft.—11 in.	Light
James Cowan,	19	5 ft.—11 in.	"
Eziah Baker,	16	4 ft.—10 in.	"
Howard Alden,	19	5 ft.—4 in.	"
Micah Pratt.	22	5 ft.—10 in.	"
John Stevens,	16	5 ft.—	"
Jonathan Ingraham,	21	5 ft.—6 in.	"

The eleventh division of six months men marched from Springfield under or with Ensign Bancroft, July 11, 1780, and George Hacket of Pelham was on the rolls, probably as a private.

The 29th division of six months men marched from Springfield July 26, 1780, and Joel Winship of Pelham, 21 years old and of ruddy complexion marched with them.

In the 41st division of six months' men who marched from Springfield Oct. 26, 1780 under Lieut. Cary was Peter King of Pelham,—light complexion, 5 ft. 10 in. in height.

The 39th division of six months' men marched from Springfield under Ensign Simonds Sept. 7, 1780. In it was William Baldwin of Pelham, described as of dark complexion, 5 ft. 8 in. high and 30 years old.

John Harkness of Pelham, 20 years old, 5 ft. 11 in. high and dark complexion, marched from Springfield with the 40th division of six months' men October 1780.

According to a Resolve of the General Court, Oct. 5, 1781, empowering the selectmen to make out pay rolls for the six months from the year 1780, the following roll was submitted:

> John Hamilton marched to camp June 25; discharged Dec. 25.
> Steven Perin, marched to camp Aug. 7; discharged Feb. 7.
> Peter King, marched to camp Aug. 2; discharged Feb. 2.
> Charles Kundy, marched to camp, June 31; discharged Dec. 31.
> John Hacket, marched to camp June 6; discharged Dec. 6.
> Abner Smith, marched to camp July 30; discharged Jan. 30.
> Seth Wood, marched to camp July 10; discharged Jan. 10.
> George Hacket, marched to camp July 10; discharged Jan. 10.
> John Harkness, marched to camp Sept. 20; discharged Dec. 15.
> James Baker, marched to camp June 25; discharged Dec. 25.
> Isaac Bennett, marched to camp June 25; discharged Dec. 25.
> Andrew McGray, marched to camp June 9; discharged Dec. 9.
> Samuel Abercrombie, marched to camp July 9; discharged Dec. 9.
> Amos Bran, marched to camp June 25; discharged Dec. 25.
> Joel Winship, supposed to be deserted.

Whole time of service, 6 months, 8 days; number of miles from home, 160; total amount of wages, £12—10s—8d.

The original sworn to before William Conkey, town clerk.

From record of town meeting at Pelham, March 1783: " Voted to Amos Bran thirty pounds for his serving the town as a soldier in the war for three years or during the war.—Abram Livermore, In behalf of the Selectmen."

Pay-roll for the wages and traveling allowance of Capt. Oliver Coney's company, Colonel Sears' regiment of levies raised for the Continental service for three months. Captain Coney was from Ware. Men from Pelham:

Joshua Conkey,
Ezekiel Conkey,
Daniel Sampson,
Edward Brown,

Samuel Crossett,
Cato Dansett,
John McKlurn.

These men enlisted Aug. 12, 1781 and were discharged Nov. 15. Pay, £6—3s—4d.

A return of men belonging to the town of Pelham in the Continental Army for three years or during the war, January 1781.

Robert Conkey, enlisted Jan. 30., 1777; enlisted by Lieut. Taylor in 2d Mass. regiment, Capt. Drew's company.
George Eliot, enlisted Mar. 15, 1780; enlisted by Lieut. Taylor in 2d Mass. regiment, Capt. Alden's company.
Nehemiah Dunbar, enlisted Mar. 15, 1780; enlisted by Lieut. Taylor in 2d Mass. regiment, Capt. Alden's company.
Nathaniel Richmond, enlisted Dec. '79; enlisted by Capt. Howard in 2d Mass. regiment Capt. Alden's company.
Amos Bryant, enlisted Jan. 13, '81; enlisted by Col. Greaton in 3d Mass. regiment, Capt. Alden's company.
Wm. Haskins, enlisted Nov. 12, '79; enlisted by Lt.-Col. Newhall in 5th Mass. regiment, Capt. Trotter's company.
John Pratt, enlisted Nov. 23, '79; enlisted by Calvin Sawyer in 5th Mass. regiment, Capt. Trotter's company.
Dan'l McDaniel enlisted May '79; enlisted by Lt. Lunt in 7th Mass. regiment, Capt. Trotter's company.

A list bearing date 1781 has the following names of Pelham men:

Bartlett Robinson, time of engagement Mar. 27, age 28, complexion dark, stature 6 ft. 3in., occupation farmer.
Abijah Bruce, time of engagement Mar. 27, age 45, complexion dark, stature 5 ft. 7 in., occupation farmer.
Joseph Ganson, time of engagement April 11, age 20, complexion light, stature, 5 ft. 10 in., occupation farmer.
Joseph Lamb, time of engagement April 6, age 18, complexion light, stature 5 ft. 5 in., occupation farmer.
Isaac Bennett, time of engagement April 20, age 22, complexion light, stature 5 ft. 10 in., occupation farmer.
James Hill, time of engagement May 15, age 48, complexion light, stature 5 ft. 11 in., occupation farmer.
Wm. Cando, time of engagement April 27, age 27, complexion black, stature 5 ft. 5 in., occupation farmer.
James Baker, time of engagement May 15, age 24, complexion light, stature 5 ft. 4 in., occupation farmer.
John Atkinson, time of engagement May 14, age 46, complexion light, stature 5 ft., occupation farmer.
Ebenezer Searls, time of engagement April 10, age 32, complexion light stature 6 ft. 2 in., occupation doctor.

These men enlisted for three years.

"PELHAM, APRIL 5, 1781.

This may certify that the subscribers have Inlisted to serve Three years in the Continental Service for the town of Pelham & also we have Rec'd

Ninety Pounds in hard money as a hire for s^d service—We say received by us,

JAMES BAKER, ABIJAH BRUCE, JOSEPH LAMB, JOSEPH GANSON, ISAAC BENNETT."

James Baker was discharged by Gen. Washington, June 9, 1783, Baker having procured a man to serve in his place.

"In obedience to the General Court Act of Dec 1780 we have raised & marched the quota of men sent for according to the Schedule in s^d order and these are the names of the men raised as folows with the sum annexed to each mans name Given to him as Hier or Bounty in Hard Money.

Abijah Bruce £90, James Baker £90, Joseph Ganson £90, Isaac Bennett £90, David Cowden £98—8s, Bartlett Robinson £90, 'Ebeneser Sarls £80. Whole amount £686—8s—0.

This is to certify that the Selectmen appeared before me and gave oath to this return. EBENEZER GRAY, Town Clerk.
Pelham, Jan. 12, 1781."

"PELHAM, APRIL 18, 1781.

Then Received of the class of Mr. Benjamin Edsons the sum of £78—8s for serving in the Continental Service for three years for said class.

I say Received by me, DAVID COWDEN.

Receipts from Bartlett Robinson and Ebeneser Sarls for the money are on file."

Return of men enlisted or Drafted into the Continental Army from the Fourth battalion of militia in the county of Hampshire from Pelham.

Isaac Bennett, enlisted in Capt. Shay's company, Col. Putnam's battalion.
Bartlett Robinson, enlisted in Capt. Shay's company, Col. Putnam's battalion.
James McDaniel, enlisted in Capt. Shay's company, Col. Putnam's battalion.
Jacob Turrell, enlisted in Capt. Shay's company, Col. Putnam's battalion.
James Baker, enlisted in Capt. Shay's company, Col. Putnam's battalion.
Job Ransom, enlisted in Capt. Maxwell's company, Col. Bayley's battalion.
Robert Conkey, enlisted in Capt. Maxwell's company, Col. Bayley's battalion.
Cato—Negro, enlisted in Capt. Maxwell's company, Col. Bayley's battalion.
Daniel McDaniel, enlisted Capt. Day's company, Col. Alden's battalion.
James Conkey, enlisted in Capt. Millington's company, Col. Wigglesworth's battalion.
Joseph Rankin, enlisted in Capt. Maxwell's company, Col. Bayley's battalion.
Patrick McMullen, enlisted in Capt. Maxwell's company, Col. Bayley's battalion.
William Conkey, enlisted in Capt. Maxwell's company, Col. Bayley's battalion.
John McRankin, enlisted in Capt. Maxwell's company, Col. Bayley's battalion.
John Prebble, enlisted in Capt. Maxwell's company, Col. Bayley's battalion.

No date to the above return. Moses Ransom was also in the service, but perhaps not in this battalion. These men enlisted from Capt. Thomas' company.

In a list of men without officers names, or date, but including men from Western Mass. the following list of men from Pelham are given :

Isaac Bennett,	Joel Winship,
Charles Handy,	John Hacket,
James Baker,	Amos Brand,
Samuel Abercrombie,	William Baldwin,
John Hamilton,	John Harkness,
Andrew McGray,	Seth Ward.

The Surname, Abercrombie, is spelled variously on the old muster rolls, viz.: Abercrombie, Abercromney, Abecrombey, Abercumby, Abercrombee, Abercromby, Abicrombey, Abercrumbe, Abercrome, Crombe, Ebercrombie. The common pronunciation in Pelham 60 years ago was the same as though the name was spelled Crummy, the first two syllables (Aber) were dropped entirely except when written.

A muster roll to draw billiting money for a company of militia under the command of Capt. Elijah Dwight of Belchertown, which included the following Pelham men,—no date.

John Thompson, lieutenant,	Abraham Livermore,
Asa McConkey, drummer,	Mathew Clark,
Daniel Gray,	John Pebles,
James Crossett,	Adam Clark,
Eliot Gray,	Isaac Craford.

Elijah Dwight, captain. These men were paid 14s each for 168 miles travel at one penny per mile.

Capt. Joshua Parker's company, Col. Nathaniel Ward's regiment. At service in Rhode Island. No date :

James Harkness, corporal,	Peter King, private,
Thomas Harlow, private,	John Harkness, private.

Nathaniel Gray, father of "Cooper" John Gray, and grandfather of Horace Gray of Northampton and of Nathaniel Gray of San Francisco, deceased, is said to have died in the service at 32 but in what company or regiment is not known.

PELHAM MEN IN THE WAR OF 1812.

The records of the service in the war of 1812 to 1815 are not easily accessible. On enquiring at the State House one is referred to Washington, D. C., and no satisfying results are obtained as a reward for diligent and painstaking effort at the capital.

Not very many Pelham men were called out for service in the war of 1812, and those who were called out did not see much active service. The few that were called marched from Pelham to Cambridge where they were in camp or quartered for some time. The writer used to listen to the tales some of those men told of their experience during the time they were serving their country while in camp at Cambridge and they were not tales of suffering and fatigue from long marches and other hard service, but rather of jolly times in camp while awaiting marching orders which never came. All returned home in a few weeks or months at most as there was no further need of men in active service.

One or two of these stories may not be out of place here. Leonard Ballou, one of the Pelham militia that was called out by the war of 1812, marched to Cambridge with others and was probably no worse than others in raiding the country along the line of march for supplies. Toward morning of one night of the march to Cambridge the crowing of a cock in a large apple tree near a farm house attracted the attention of some of the young men and a plan formed to get the rooster. It was pretty dark and not easy to see just where in the tree the bird was. Two cider barrels that were found under the tree were used by placing one on the top of the other, and Ballou was lifted to the top of the two barrels standing on end and he quietly waited for the rooster to crow again so that he might locate him. After awaiting in silence for some time the rooster started to crow again as in duty bound to usher in daylight in the east. The bird was within reach and Ballou seized him by the neck cutting off the clarion notes with a strangled sound caused by the grip, about its neck, of Ballou's right hand. In the effort made in seizing the rooster, the cider barrels canted sideways and Ballou and the barrels came to the ground, but he held fast to the rooster.

Uncle Eseck Cook, the Quaker, was a non-combatant in principle, but he took pity on young Ballou in being suddenly ordered to march to Cambridge, and loaned his long gray overcoat to him. Ballou accepted the offer of the coat and wore it when the weather demanded it and sometimes when it did not. The coat came down nearly to his ankles and was ample in size and Ballou found it very convenient and useful to hide an occasional fish from a peddlar's wagon that came to camp, when opportunity offered by the peddlar's attention being drawn aside. The folds of the long coat hid many things dur-

ing the stay at Cambridge and was returned to Uncle Eseck when
the Pelham contingent arrived home, and young Ballou thanked him
for the loan, at the same time telling how handy he found it to secrete
things-the soldiers needed.   Uncle Eseck was thunder-struck, but his
only remark was : " I think it would have been better if thee had not
had the coat."

The following list of Pelham men is all we have been able to
obtain of those who were called out at that time.   There may have
been more but the inability to reach the muster rolls makes it useless
to claim a full and complete list.   The names and rank were as
follows :

Capt. John Taylor, and privates
John T. Conkey,
Grove W. Hannum,
Luther Lincoln,
James Smith,
Amasa Jillson,

Leonard Ballou.
Sidney Hannum,
Henry Hannum,
Luther Thompson,
Joseph Barrows.

Capt. John Taylor was in command on the march from Pelham to
Boston.

The Mexican War.

The Mexican war was not a long one and very few men from
Massachusetts were called out for service then, and so far as can be
learned no Pelham man saw service in Mexico.

Record of Pelham Soldiers in the Rebellion.

The record of the town in its contribution of men and means for
the suppression of the great rebellion of 1861 to 1865 is an honorable one.   The population of the town in 1860 was 748 and the valuation $162,635.   The number of men between the ages of 18 and
45 on the rolls for military duty in 1861 was only 100.   Seventy-
five men were contributed to the great work of saving the country
from destruction by those who had risen up in arms against it, and
most of them by voluntary enlistment, or five more than the town
was called upon to send.

In common with many other towns in the state it was found
impossible to fill by enlistment the quotas of men called for by the
state authorities with as much celerity as the need of men demanded,
and there was a draft from the enrolled militia in 1863 of 20 men, a
list of them being given in full.   Of this number seven passed exami-

nation and were accepted. Two of the seven went to the front and the other five paid $300 commutation money and remained at home. In 1864 the draft was resorted to again, when ten of the enrolled men were drawn; five were declared fit for military duty and each paid $300 commutation money, and the other five were exempted, or failed to appear for reasons unknown or not fully shown by the town record.

The enlistments and service of Pelham men in the war of the rebellion are given in the order of enlistment as gathered from the rebellion record kept by the town and from regimental histories, the Adjutant General's report, and other reliable sources.

The first enlistment from the town was that of Joseph Freeland Bartlett, born in Ware, July 25, 1843. He enlisted in the 10th Massachusetts regiment June 21, 1861, and served with that regiment three years, when, having re-enlisted, he was transferred to the 37th Massachusetts regiment. and in June, 1865, was transferred to the 20th regiment, from which he was discharged July 28, 1865, having served continuously at the front during the entire war, with the exception of three months when he was in the hospital with wounds. He was promoted 2d lieutenant, 37th Massachusetts regiment, May 24, 1865; 1st lieutenant, 20th Massachusetts regiment, June 1, 1865. He participated in 33 of the great battles of the war. including all the battles around Richmond in 1862, Antietam, Fredericksburg, Chancellorsville, Gettysburg, Wilderness, Sheridan's battles in the Shenandoah valley, Petersburg, Sailor creek, and Appomattox at the surrender of Lee. He was also with the 6th army corps in. North Carolina when Johnson surrendered to Sherman. He was slightly wounded in the battle of Fair Oaks and severely at battle of the Wilderness.

Manley Jillson, 45, born in Pelham, enlisted as a private June 21, 1861, mustered into 10th Mass. regiment, Company C, for three years June 21, 1861; discharged for disability Nov. 29, 1862.

Henry E. Wheeler, 26, born in Pelham, enlisted as a private Sept. 21, 1861, mustered into the 27th Mass. regiment Sept. 30, 1861 for three years, Company G; discharged July 29, 1862.

Solomon Rhoads, 18, born in Pelham, enlisted September 1861 as a private, was mustered into the 27th Mass. regiment, Sept. 20, 1861 for three years, Company I; discharged Dec. 24, 1863 to re-enlist; mustered in the second time Dec. 24, 1863, discharged June 26, 1865, at expiration of service.

George A. Griffin, 20, born in Pelham, enlisted Sept. 29, 1861, mustered into 27th Mass. regiment, Company G, Sept. 29, 1861 for three years; term of service expired Sept. 27, 1864.

Charles Griffin, 35, born in Pelham, enlisted Sept. 30, 1861, mustered into 27th Mass. regiment, Company C, for three years; discharged Sept. 4, 1862. Enlisted again July 11, 1864 in the Third Heavy Artillery. Received $175 bounty from the town, discharged July 27, 1864, at Gallops Island on surgeon's certificate of disability.

Otis B. Griffin, 23, born in Pelham, enlisted Oct. 11, 1861, was mustered into 27th Mass. regiment, Company G, for three years, Oct. 11, 1861; discharged Aug. 29, 1862.

Erastus S. Southwick, 40, born in Pelham, enlisted Oct. 8, 1861, mustered into 27th Mass. regiment Oct. 15, 1861, Company G, for three years; discharged July 29, 1862.

Stephen Rhoads, 28, born in Pelham, enlisted Oct. 21, 1861, mustered into 31st Mass. regiment, Company C, for three years, Oct. 21, 1861; discharged on surgeon's certificate of disability at New Orleans, April 18, 1864. No bounty.

Francis A. Blodgett, 22, was mustered into the 31st Mass. regiment, Company C, Nov. 20, 1861; he was discharged that he might re-enlist Feb. 14, 1864. He was a sergeant, discharged Sept. 9, 1865 at expiration of service. Bounty $423.33. Record says New Salem was place of residence.

Charles R. Cleveland, 41, born in Pelham, enlisted Oct. 21, 1861, mustered into 31st Mass. regiment, Company F, for three years, Oct. 21, 1861; transferred to Veterans' Relief Corps April 20, 1864.

William S. Pratt, 43, enlisted from Pelham in 31st Mass. regiment, Company C, or was credited to the town, was mustered in Oct. 21, 1861; deserted Dec. 7, 1861. No bounty.

Sanford M. Lovett, 55, born in Cumberland, R. I., enlisted Nov. 1, 1861, mustered into 31st Mass. regiment, Company F, for three years as a private Nov. 1, 1861; discharged Nov. 18, 1862 for disability. The Adjutant Generals' report says he was 44 when he enlisted, but 55 is believed to be his right age at that time.

Harrison L. Horr, 19, born in Pelham, enlisted Nov. 4, 1861, mustered into 31st Mass. regiment, Company F, as a private, for three years, Nov. 4, 1861; discharged Dec. 20, 1864, at New Orleans, his term of service having expired. He held the rank of sergeant.

Charles H. Horr, 26, born in Pelham, enlisted Nov. 22, 1861, mustered into the 31st Mass. regiment, Company F, as a private for three years, died at New Orleans Dec. 7, 1864 from wounds received in the service. He was first sergeant of his company. The town record says that Horr enlisted Nov. 22, 1861, and the Adjutant Generals' report states that he was mustered in Oct. 22.

John Shaw, 40, born in Granby, enlisted Aug. 9, 1862, as a private in 27th Mass. regiment, was not sent to the front; discharged in a few days. Received $100 bounty from town, lived in town until his death.

Otis B. Hill, born in ———, enlisted Aug. 9, 1862 as a private in the 27th Mass. regiment, was not sent to the front; discharged in a few days. Received $100 bounty from the town.

Patrick Bailey, born in Ballybane, County of Cork, Ireland, enlisted Aug. 9, 1862, as a private for three years, mustered into the 27th Mass. regiment Dec. 21, 1863; discharged June 15, 1865, by order War department. Received $100 bounty from the town.

Henry Barrows, 22, born in Pelham, enlisted for three years, Aug. 9, 1862, as a private in the 27th Mass. regiment, did not go to the front; discharged Aug. 29, 1862. Received $100 bounty from the town.

Otis Kimball, 21, born in ———, enlisted as a private Aug. 9, 1862, for three years, mustered into the 27th Mass. regiment, Company H, Aug. 26, 1862; discharged July 2, 1863, for disability. Received $100 bounty from the town.

Franklin Bramble, 35, born in ——— enlisted Aug. 9, 1862, for three years as a private, mustered into the 27th Mass, regiment, Company K, Aug. 29, 1862; discharged to re-enlist Jan. 1, 1864, mustered second time Jan. 2, 1864; term expired June 26, 1865. Received $100 bounty from the town.

John F. Nichols, 22, born in ——— enlisted as a private for three years, Aug. 8, 1862, mustered into the 27th Mass. regiment, Company D, Aug. 11, 1862; discharged Dec. 31, 1863, at Norfolk, Va. Re-enlisted, discharged Dec. 31, 1863, at Annapolis Md. June 15, 1865; was in Libby prison 18 days. Received $100 bounty from the town.

Joseph D. Whitney, 25, born in East Boylston, enlisted as a private, for three years, Aug. 25, 1862, mustered into the 27th Mass. regiment Company I, Aug. 25, 1862; discharged June 23, 1863, at

New Berne, N. C. for physical disability. Received $100 bounty from the town.

Joseph E. Boynton, 18, born in Pelham, enlisted as a private, for three years, Aug. 25, 1862, mustered in Aug, 25, 1862, died at Baltimore, Md. Dec. 4, 1864. Received $100 bounty from the town.

Frederick Dane, 24, born in Pelham, enlisted for three years as a private, unassigned, mustered in Aug. 25, 1862, and was discharged Sept. 10, 1862, at Camp Day for disability. Received $100 from the town.

Stillman Abercrombie, 32, born in Pelham, enlisted as a musician Aug 27, 1862, for nine months in Company G, 52d Mass. regiment, mustered in Oct. 11, 1862, regiment started for Louisiana in November 1862, returned to Massachusetts Aug. 3, 1863; discharged Aug. 14, 1863. Received $100 bounty from the town.

Joseph D. Allen, 18, born in Pelham, enlisted as a private, Sept. 1, 1862, for nine months, was mustered into the 52d Mass. regiment, Company G, Oct. 11, 1862, left Massachusetts for Louisiana Nov. 20, 1862, regiment returned to the state Aug. 3, 1863; discharged Aug. 14, 1863. Received $100 bounty from the town.

Dexter R. Barnes, 19, born in Pelham, enlisted as a private Aug. 27, 1862, for nine months service, was mustered into the 52d regiment, Company G, Oct. 11, 1862, the regiment marched for Louisiana, Nov. 20, 1862, did not return until Aug. 3, 1863; discharged Aug. 14, 1863. Received $100 bounty from the town.

William P. Montgomery, 30, born in Enfield, enlisted Aug. 22, 1862, as a private for nine months, was mustered into the 52d Mass. regiment, Company G, Oct. 11, 1862, regiment marched for Louisiana Nov. 20, 1862, returned Aug. 3, 1863; discharged Aug. 14, 1864. Received a bounty of $100 from the town. Re-enlisted Sept. 3, 1864, in the First regiment Heavy Artillery, mustered in Sept. 3, 1864, mustered out June 4, 1865, at expiration of service. Received $450 bounty.

Charles H. Sanger, 18, born in Pelham, enlisted as a private for nine months, mustered into the 52d Mass. regiment, Company G, Aug. 11, 1862, marched south with the regiment Nov. 20, 1863, returned Aug. 3, 1862; mustered out Aug. 16, 1863. Received $100 bounty from the town.

Amos D. Leonard, 28, born in Minerva, N. Y., enlisted as a private for nine months, Sept. 3, 1862, mustered into the 52d Mass. regiment, Company G, Oct. 11, 1862, went with the regiment to Louisiana, Nov. 20, 1862, returned Aug. 14, 1863; mustered out Aug. 14, 1863. Received $100 bounty from the town. His last known residence was in Minnesota.

Daniel Cook, 32, born in Pelham, enlisted as a private for nine months, Aug. 27, 1862, mustered into the 52d Mass. regiment, Company G, Oct. 11, 1862, was made corporal, went south with the regiment, Nov. 20, 1862 returned Aug. 3, 1863; mustered out Aug. 14, 1863. Received $100 bounty from the town.

Edmund S. Ellsbree, 19, born in Pelham, enlisted Sept. 1, 1862, as a private for nine months, mustered into the 52d Mass. regiment, Company G, Oct. 11, 1862, sailed for Louisiana, Nov. 20, 1862, returned Aug. 3, 1863 ; mustered out Aug. 20, 1863. Received $100 bounty from the town.

Amaziah Robinson, 38, born in Jamaica, Vt., enlisted as a private for nine months Aug. 24, 1862, mustered into the 52d Mass. regiment, Company G, Oct. 11, 1862, went with the regiment to Louisiana, returned Aug. 3, 1863 ; mustered out Aug. 11, 1863. Received $100 bounty from the town. Has resided in Pelham since the war.

Nelson Witt, 29, born in North Dana, enlisted as a private for nine months, Aug. 30, 1862, mustered into the 52d Mass. regiment, Company G, Oct. 11, 1862, went with the regiment to Louisiana, Nov. 20, 1862, was wounded at Irish Bend, lived to come back Aug. 3, 1863. Died at Belchertown. Received $100 bounty from the town.

Thomas Linds, 40, born at —— enlisted June 2, 1863, for three years, mustered into the Second Heavy Artillery, Company A, July 28, 1863 ; discharged Sept 3, 1865, at expiration of service.

James D. Mower, 20, born at Brattleboro Vt. was drafted in 1863, Examined and excepted, mustered into the 22d Mass. regiment, July, 20, 1863, Company I, transferred to 32d Mass. regiment, Oct. 6, 1864, Company M ; company was mustered out when Mower was at home on a furlough in the spring of 1865.

Joel Cutting, 31, born at East Boylston, drafted in 1863, examined and accepted, mustered into the 32nd Mass. regiment, Company B, Sept. 14, 1863 ; mustered out June 1, 1865, by order of War department.

John O. Rhoads, 22, born in Pelham, enlisted as a private Dec. 1, 1863, for three years, in First Regiment Heavy Artillery, Company I, mustered in Dec. 1, 1863, discharged Aug. 5 1865.

George A. Gardner, 24, born in —— enlisted Dec. 1, 1863, for three years as a private, mustered into the 4th Mass. cavalry, Jan, 27, 1864, Company E; mustered out Nov. 14, 1865, at expiration of service. Bounty $325.

George W. Allen, 44, born in —— enlisted Dec. 7, 1863 as a private for three years, mustered into the 1st Mass. Heavy Artillery, Company I, Dec. 7, 1863. Died of wounds Oct. 29, 1864 at Petersburg, Va.

Truman Squares, 18, born in Shutesbury, enlisted Dec. 21, 1863, as a private for three years, in 57th Mass. Infantry, Company B, mustered in Jan. 24, 1864. Killed at Spottsylvania, May 7, 1864. Bounty $325.

Thomas Fergerson, 32, born in —— enlisted as a private for three years, Dec. 26, 1863, mustered into the 4th Mass. Cavalry regiment, Company E, Jan. 27, 1864; mustered out Nov. 14, 1865 at expiration of service. Bounty $325.

Garrett O'Neal, 22, born in Northampton, enlisted for three years as a private, Dec. 28, 1863, mustered into the 27th Mass. regiment, Company G.

Philander Pike, 38, born in Petersham, enlisted as a private for three years, mustered into the 27th Mass. regiment, Company I, Jan. 5, 1864; discharged Dec. 7, 1864. Bounty $325.

Simeon Gilbert, 42, born in —— enlisted for three years as a private, mustered into the 2d Mass. Heavy Artillery, Company G, Dec. 7, 1863. Died July 29, 1864, at Andersonville, Ga. Bounty, $325.

William O. Kimball, 23, born in Amherst, enlisted in 1st Mass. regiment Heavy Artillery for three years, July 11, 1864, mustered into Company I, July 11, 1864. Discharged April 2, 1865. Bounty $325.

Charles A. Abbott, 18, born in Wilbraham, enlisted in 1st regiment Heavy Artillery, Company C, mustered in Aug. 1, 1864; discharged Aug. 16, 1865, at expiration of service, in Company M. Bounty $325.

George E. Witherell, 22, born in —— enlisted in 1st regiment Heavy Artillery, Company I, mustered in Sept. 3, 1864; discharged June 4, 1865 at expiration of service. Bounty $181.32.

Henry Wood, 31, born in —— enlisted in 1st regiment Heavy Artillery, Company H; discharged March 13, 1864, to re-enlist, mustered in March 14, 1864; discharged April 1, 1865 for disability. Bounty $421.99.

Madison L. Fales, 18, born in Pelham, enlisted for three years in Company C, 1st regiment Heavy Artillery, mustered in Sept. 7, 1864. Died March 31, 1865. Bounty $234.

Norman S. Fales, 19, born in Pelham, enlisted in First regiment Heavy Artillery, Company C, for three years, mustered in Sept. 7 1864, died Dec. 18, 1864, in the 2d Corps hospital. Bounty $181.

Frederick Grover, 18, born in —— enlisted in First regiment Heavy Artillery, Company C, for three years, mustered in Sept. 7, 1864; discharged June 4, 1865, at expiration of service. $125 town bounty.

Dennis V. Champlin, 23, born in Amherst, enlisted for three years in the 54th Mass. regiment, transferred to the 55th regiment, Company B, mustered in Dec. 28, 1864; discharged Aug. 26, 1865, at expiration of service.

Joseph R. Hunt, 23, musician, mustered into 46th regiment, Company H, October, 1862; discharged for disability, Jan. 14, 1863.

Levi G. Osborn, 38, mustered into 52d Mass. regiment Oct. 11, 1862; discharged Aug. 14, 1863.

William B. Fales, 30, born in Pelham, mustered into 52d Mass. regiment, Aug. 27, 1862; was in the battles of Oak Ridge, Irish Bend and the siege of Port Hudson; discharged Aug. 14, 1863.

Lauriston Barnes, enlisted as a private Aug. 29, 1862, mustered into the 52d regiment, Company G, Oct. 11, 1862; discharged Aug. 14, 1863.

Murray B. Lovett, 22, born in Pelham, mustered into 10th regiment, Company K, June 21, 1861; died June 4, 1862, at Fair Oaks, Virginia.

William Jones, 19, mustered into the 1st Infantry, March 8, 1865. Bounty $325.

The number credited to the town by the re-enlistments of Joseph F. Bartlett, John T. Nichols, Wm. P. Montgomery, Franklin Bramble, Francis A. Blodgett, Solomon Rhoads, Charles Griffin and Henry Wood carries the number up to 69. After the draft in June, 1864 there were five or six enlistments made in Boston, near the close of the war, of men who probably did not go to the front and whose names are not known, making 75 men that the town should have credit for, or five men above all calls made upon the town.

FALLS ON PERGY BROOK.

AMHERST AS SEEN FROM PELHAM BEFORE 1850.

The men were distributed among various military organizations. Mass. 27th regiment, 16; 52d regiment, 13; 1st Heavy Artillery 10; 31st regiment, 7; 10th regiment, 3; 2d Heavy Artillery, 3; 3d Heavy Artillery, 2; 4th Calvary, 2; 37th regiment, 1; 20th regiment, 1; 46th regiment, 1; 55th regiment, 1; 57th regiment, 1; besides those who were unassigned. We are indebted to Rev. John Jones, who was chairman of the recruiting committee during the war, for valuable aid in perfecting the roll of Pelham men who served in the army; many of whom he enlisted and took to the recruiting officers, and personally attended to the collection of bounty money for them.

The Shays Rebellion of 1786-87.

The rebellion against the government of the state of Massachusetts in 1786-87, whose acknowledged leader was Capt. Daniel Shays, a citizen of Pelham, makes it necessary to give a more extended notice of this insurgent outbreak than would be necessary in writing the local history of almost any other town in the state, as it was here the leading spirit, that gave the rebellion its name resided as a respected citizen, who was honored by election to positions of trust and responsibility. It was at the old Conkey tavern in the "Hollow" that he met the dissatisfied turbulent spirits who were weighed down with debts and numerous other real or imagined grievances, and discussed the situation before the wide open fire places of the hostelry, and when protracted argument and excitement caused thirst, they quenched it by sampling the well assorted liquors which Landlord Conkey was noted for keeping in his cellar.

Shays doubtless enjoyed the good cheer as well as any who gathered there with him to talk over their mutual troubles; he joined with them in charging the State with oppression; was as ready as they to declare for the removal of the General Court from the City of Boston;—to shout down with the lawyers; to demand the abolition of the courts; to cry for a revision of the constitution and to clamor for paper money and other things which they may have honestly believed were necessary for the relief of the people. And as the excitement increased and the mutterings of the people turned to open threats of opposition by force of arms, the experience of Capt. Shays as a soldier became of value in organizing and drilling the men in the manual of arms.

It must be conceded that the people were in much distress from the pressure of hard times and honestly believed they were oppressed with grievances unbearable; but it is by no means certain that they had any intention at the beginning of the agitation to take up arms against the state. They must have believed it perfectly proper to gather in conventions for consultation, for the nineteenth article of the Constitution of Massachusetts declares : " The people have a right, in an orderly and peaceable manner, to assemble to consult for the common good ; give instructions to their representatives, and to request of the legislative body, by way of addresses, petitions or remonstrances, redress for the wrongs done them, and the grievances they suffer ; " Certainly the earlier conventions were not to be considered disorderly, but seem to have been conducted " in an orderly and peaceable manner ". These conventions for the consideration of " grievances " began to be held in Western Massachusetts as early as 1781 or before the close of the war of the Revolution, but these gatherings did not attract much attention until the summer of 1786. This course would seem to have been a proper one for the people to bring the attention of the General Court to whatever real grievances the people were suffering under. Doubtless these conventions became less peaceable and orderly as the unrest and discontent increased under the leadership of rash and unscrupulous men who joined the movement, until the people found themselves with arms in their hands in rebellion against the constituted government of the state.

One of the most important conventions held, as the people believed under a constitutional right, for the redress of grievances, was held at Hatfield August 22, 1786. Fifty towns of Hampshire county were represented and the convention was continued for three days, Caleb Keith and Mathew Clark being delegates from Pelham.

They first " Voted, that this Meeting is Constitutional. " The further action of the convention is given with list of grievances.

" The Convention from a thorough conviction of great uneasiness, subsisting among the people of this county and Commonwealth, then went into an inquiry for the cause ; and upon mature consideration, deliberation and debate, were of the opinion that many grievances and unnecessary burdens now lying upon the people, are the sources of that discontent so evidently discoverable throughout this Commonwealth. Among which the following articles were voted as such :

" 1st. The existence of the Senate.

2nd. The present mode of representation.

3rd. The officers of Government not being annually dependant on the representatives of the people, in General Court assembled, for their saleries.

4th. All the Civil Officers of Government, not being annually elected by the people in General Court assembled.

5th. The existence of the Court of Common Pleas, and General Sessions of the Peace.

6th. The Fee Table as it now stands.

7th. The present mode of Appropriating the import and excise.

8th. The unreasonable grants made to some of the officers of the Government.

9th. The Supplementary Aid.

10th. The present mode of paying government securities.

11th. The present mode adopted for the payment and speedy collection of the last state tax.

12th. The present mode of taxation as it operates unequally between the polls and estates and between landed and mercantile interests.

13th. The present method of the practice of attorneys at law.

14th. The want of a sufficient medium of trade to remedy the mischiefs arising from the scarcity of Money.

15th. The General Court sitting in the town of Boston.

16th. The present embarassments on the press.

17th. The neglect of the settlements of important Matters depending between the Commonwealth and Congress, relating to Monies and Averages.

18th. Voted, This convention recomends to the several towns in this County, that they instruct their Representatives, to use their influence in the next General Court, to have emitted a bank of paper Money, subject to a depreciation : making it a tender in all payments, equal to silver and gold to be issued in order to call in the Commonwealth secureties.

19th. Voted, That Whereas several of the above articles of greivances, arise from defects in the constitution, therefore a revision of the same ought to take place.

20th. Voted, that it be recommended by this convention to the several towns in this county that they petition the Governor to call the General Court immediately together in order that the other grievances complained of may by the legislature be redressed.

21st. Voted, That this convention recommend it to the inhabitants of this country, that they abstain from all Mobs and unlawful assemblies, until a constitutional method of redress can be obtained.

22nd. Voted, That Mr. Caleb West be desired to transmit a copy of the proceedings of this convention to the Convention of the County of Worcester.

23rd. Voted, That the Chairman of this Convention be desired to transmit a copy of the proceeding of this Convention to the County of Berkshire.

24th. Voted, That the Chairman of this convention be directed to notify a County Convention upon any motion made to him for that purpose if he judge the reasons offered be sufficient, giving such notice, together with the reasons thereof in the public papers of this county.

25th. Voted, that a copy of the proceedings of this convention be sent to the press in Springfield for publication."

Daniel Gray of Pelham was chairman of a committee chosen to issue an address to the people for their better understanding of the causes or reasons for their being under arms; they discharged the obligation laid upon them with zeal and earnestness, and though mistaken as to the means chosen to correct the evils complained of, we believe there was a large measure of honesty in the mass of the insurgent forces under arms, and that Daniel Gray believed he was serving in a righteous cause.

"An address to the people of the several Towns in the County of Hampshire, now at arms. Gentlemen We have thought proper to inform you of some of the principel causes of the late risings of the people, Also of their present movements Viz:

1st. The present expensive mode of collecting debts, which, by reason of the great scarcity of cash, will of necessity fill our goals with unhappy debtors, and thereby a reputable body of people rendered incapable of being serviceable either to themselves or to the community.

2d. The Monies raised by imports and excise being appropriated to discharge the interest of the government securities, and not the foreign debt, when these securities are not subject to taxation.

3d. A suspension of the writ of Habeas Corpus by which those persons who have stepped forth to assert and maintain the rights of the people, are liable to be taken and conveyed even to the most distant part of the Commonwealth, and thereby subjected to an unjust punishment.

4th. The unlimited power granted to justices of the Peace and Sheriffs and Constables, by the Riot Act, indemnifying them to the prosecution thereof; when perhaps, wholly actuated from a principle of revenge, hatred and envy.

Furthermore,—Be assured, that this body, now at arms, dispise the idea of being instigated by British Emessaries, which is so strenuously propagated by the enemies of our liberties: And also wish the most proper and speedy measures may be taken, to discharge both our foreign and domestic debt. Per Order, DANIEL GRAY,
Chairman of Committee for the above purpose.

Thomas Grover of Worcester, an insurgent leader took upon himself the liberty to fulminate his individual ideas of some of the grievances the people were suffering under in the *Hampshire Herald*;

"To the Printer of the *Hampshire Herald*: Sir. It has somehow or other fallen to my lot to be employed in a more conspicuous manner than some of my fellow citizens in stepping forth in defence of the rights and privileges of the people, more especially of the County of Hampshire.

Therefore, upon the desire of the people now at arms, I take this method to publish to the world of mankind in general, particularly the people of this Commonwealth, some of the principal grievances we complain of and of which we are now seeking redress, and mean to contend for, until a redress can be obtained, which we hope, will soon take place; and if so, our brethren in this Commonwealth, that do not see with us yet, shall find we shall be as peaceable as they be.

In the first place, I must refer you to a draft of Grievances drawn up by a committee of the people, now at arms under the signature of Daniel Gray, Chairman, which is heartily approved of; some others also are here added, viz.:

1st. The General Court, for certain obvious reasons, must be removed out of the town of Boston.

2d. A revision of the Constitution is absolutely necessary.

3d. All kinds of government securities now on interest, that have been bought of the original owners for two shillings, three shillings, four shilling, and the highest for six shillings and eight pence on the pound, and have received more interest than the principal cost the speculator who purchased them,—that if justice was done, we verily believe, nay positively know, it would save the Commonwealth thousands of pounds.

4th. Let the lands belonging to this Commonwealth, at the eastward, be sold at the best advantage, to pay the remainder of our domestic debt.

5th. Let the monies arising from impost and excise be appropriated to discharge the foreign debt.

6th. Let that act, passed by the General Court last June by a small majority of only seven, called the Supplementary Aid, for twenty-five years to come, be repealed.

7th. The total abolition of the Inferior Court of Common Pleas and General Sessions of the Peace.

8th. Deputy Sheriffs totally set aside, as a useless set of officers in the Community; and Constables who are really necessary, be empowered to do the duty, by which means a large swarm of lawyers will be banished from their wonted haunts, who have been more damage to the people at large, especially to the common farmers, than the savage beasts of prey.

To this I boldly sign my proper name, as a hearty well wisher to the real rights of the people.   THOMAS GROVER.
Worcester, Dec. 7, 1786."

Possibly Grover issued his manifesto from Worcester, but at other times his name appears as Capt. Thomas Grover of Montague.

The causes which led to the prevailing discontent, the calling of conventions, and the formulation of a long list of grievances and the resort to arms, may need further explanation for the better understanding of the disturbed condition of the people 112 years ago, by those who may read this portion of the history of Pelham.

CAUSES OR REASONS WHICH LED TO REBELLION.

The War of the Revolution had been ended but a few years. It had been an expensive war. The state debt was £1,300,000 besides £250,000 due to officers and soldiers. The state's portion of the

Federal debt was £1,500,000. Every town was more or less embarrassed by advances of money which they had made to equip the frequent requisitions of men, called for by the state, and for supplies to support the army, which had been done upon their own particular credit.

This burden of debt was enormous as compared with that before the war,—when it was less than £100,000.

Tax payers now will appreciate the burdens laid upon the people at that time, when they know that the third part of all sums raised by taxation was laid upon the rateable polls alone, and the rateable polls little exceeded 90,000 in the state.

The people had secured freedom from Great Brittain, but were under grievous embarrassments which pressed upon them sorely. For eight or nine years they had been fighting for liberty and now they felt as though they were fighting for life,—for mere existence as it were. Upon the right management of the public debt depended the tranquility and happiness of the people.

They were strongly prejudiced against raising money by duties of impost and excise, for paying running expenses of government, or for paying public debts. It was considered anti-republican by the leading men of that day. The paper currency was depreciating day by day and it seemed an impossibility to save the public credit, upon which the happiness of the people depended.

The opposition of the people to paying interest is another thing which astonishes us in these times when interest paying by states, counties, towns and individuals is so common. They said it was "*a cankerworm that consumed their substance without lessening their burdens.*" We should have said, fund the debt and pay interest annually and the principal by installments. But the installment plan had not been invented at that time. They wanted to pay the debt at once, but could not.

Another cranky notion was this: That trade,—commerce,—the importation of goods, led to luxury and vice. The commercial men said all trouble came from the regulations under which commerce had to be carried on. To destroy commerce would not lessen the evils complained of; and finally the opposition to impost and excise duties began to give way. The export trade was almost destroyed, and if goods were imported they must be paid for in specie,—which tended to drain the country of ready money.

The private, or individual indebtedness was large ; those who had been fighting for liberty came home and found indebtedness they had left, unpaid, and more modern debts had been added to the old. Paper money was of little value, and specie was not easily obtained, while creditors were pressing for payment. The Tender Act of July 3, 1782, provided that private debts might be paid in neat cattle and certain other personal property at an appraisement by men under oath. The law did not satisfy debtors or creditors. It had the effect to suspend lawsuits in some cases, but also served as the signal for hostilities between creditors and debtors and really because of this law debtors thought their creditors were under their control.

The pressure of creditors had made the people irritable and turbulent, and the burdensome taxes made the load heavier still; and there was clamor for another issue of paper money for relief, but it was not issued.

The lawyers brought suit in the courts for creditors and attached personal property if it could be found. If a debtor had a stock of cattle the sheriff seized them and drove them off the farm. The debtor could not offer a receiptor for the cattle, as now, until trial. The effect of such action being to absolutely block the work of the farm, and there is little wonder that the farmers became sullen and angry and cast about for successful opposition to such practices. That they were in dead earnest to get rid of lawyers is shown by the foregoing draft of grievances by Thomas Grover of Worcester, which doubtless expressed the prevailing sentiment of the people toward lawyers.

There was great increase of these suits for debt, pushed by lawyers, urged on by creditor clients anxious to realize on accounts long overdue. This persistence on the part of lawyers caused the impecunious debtors to hate lawyers without stint. Inflamatory newspaper articles against lawyers increased this hatred. The leading insurgents insisted that " this class of professional men ought to be abolished." They instructed the representatives elected to the General Court in 1786 " to annihilate lawyers " but they failed to accomplish it. Perhaps it would have been better for the country if they had. They practically excluded lawyers from the General Court for the session of 1786, and convinced the House that their distresses were greatly increased by the exhorbitant fees exacted by lawyers and attorneys, and passed a bill through the House fixing the fees for attorneys and providing for their taking an oath previous to pleading, in every cause, that they would not receive more than the lawful fees, but it failed to pass the Senate.

The lawyers being odious to the people the next step was a logical one;—the lawyers were intimately connected with the courts of justice, and the courts somewhat under their control, so the extension of this hatred of lawyers so as to include the courts was a natural one, so the clamor for the abolishment of courts became loud, and the purpose to stop the courts by force of arms was soon formed, and carried out in many instances.

On the last Tuesday in August 1786, only a few days after the Hatfield convention where they urged the people to abstain from all mobs and unlawful assemblies, 1500 men under arms assembled in Northampton, took possession of the court house and effectually prevented the sitting of the court. The next week the court was prevented from holding session in the court house at Worcester but held court in a private house. The foregoing brief explanation of the reasons or causes which led the people to resort to arms for the relief they sought is perhaps sufficient, though it may not be satisfactory to those who may read it.

Enlistment and Organization of the Insurgents.

The massing of armed men for raids upon the courts in the shire towns of the counties in the state required organization and some sort of method for securing and enlisting men. A meeting for the consideration of this important business was held, and a committee of seventeen insurgents was appointed to raise and organize a large force of men in Hampshire county; among the members of this committee were Capt. Shays of Pelham and Capt. Billings of Amherst. The form of enlistment used in recruiting these forces was as follows:

"We do Each one of us acknowledge our Selves to be Inlisted into a Company Commanded by Capt. —— & Lieut. Bullard & in Colo Hazeltons Regiment of Regulators in Order for the Suppressing of tyrannical government in the Massachusetts State, And we do Ingage to obey Such orders as we shal Reseeve from time to—to time from our Superior officers, and to faithfully Serve for the term of three months from the Date in Witness hereof we have hereunto Set our names—the Conditions of Will Be for a Sarg^t Sixty Shillings Pr Month Cop^l Fifty Shillings a Month Privet Forty Shillings a Month and if git the Day their will be a Consedrable Bounty Ither Forty or Sixty Pounds."

The enrollment of men went on under the direction of the above committee among the restless and turbulent element until a large number of the able bodied men in many of the towns were drawn in, and were in arms against state authority under local leaders; constituting a formidable insurgent body who were determined to prevent the sitting of the courts, in the belief that if they could stop the sessions of the courts they would stop the entry and trial of suits for debt by impatient creditors who employed the lawyers.

The insurgents took possession of court houses in Middlesex county and at Worcester, also at Great Barrington in Berkshire. They also determined to prevent the sitting of the court at Springfield on the 27th of Sept. 1786. Six hundred of the state militia under Gen. Shepard were ordered to take possession of the court house which they did. Capt. Daniel Shays with more than 600 insurgents appeared on the scene and sent a request to the judge that none of the late rioters who were under arrest should be indicted. The court did little business, and after three days' session adjourned, after resolving that it was not expedient to proceed to Berkshire for a session of the court in October following.

In October, Capt. Shays marched his men through the streets of Springfield in the face of Gen. Shepard's men, by permission of the General; it is said the one condition of the permission was, that the insurgents behave well; which it is said they did. There was a gathering of insurgents at Great Barrington the same month because they feared that an attempt would be made to hold court, but there was no attempt to hold a session.

The legislature which was called together on the 27th of Sept. 1786 had passed some stringent measures which caused Capt. Shays to issue the following order:

"PELHAM, OCT. 13, 1786.

GENTLEMEN:—By information from the General Court they are determined to call all those who appeared to stop the court to condign punishment. Therefore I request you to assemble your men together to see that they are well armed and equipped with sixty rounds each man, and be ready to turn out at a Minute's warning: likewise be properly organized with officers. DANIEL SHAYS."

The General Court adjourned on the 18th day of November, 1786 after suspending the Habeas Corpus act and passing other acts that it was hoped would pacify the excited people of the state. At that time it was estimated that one-third of the entire population was in sympathy with, or in active action against the constituted authorities, and in some sections of the state the proportion of insurgents was larger. On the 23d of November there was a convention of insurgents at Worcester after the courts had been unable to enter the court house on the 21st, and obliged to hold court in a tavern.

Governor Bowdoin then began to take active measures for the suppression of this uprising. The militia in Middlesex was called out and four regiments in Essex. The insurgent leaders having rejected offers of pardon, warrants were issued for the arrest of the leaders, and Parker, Page, and Job Shattuck, leaders in the eastern part of the state, were arrested in Groton.

Shays with the largest part of the insurgents left Worcester after stopping the courts on the 21st and marched to Rutland where he remained until Dec. 3d when he returned to Worcester, but marched back to Rutland again on the 9th of the same month where he remained for some time, some of his men freezing to death on the march. There was a great scarcity of provisions, and 'tis said that Shays made known his willingness to leave the people to themselves and accept of pardon if the Government would offer it.

WARRANTS FOR THE ARREST OF REBEL LEADERS.

On the 10th of January, 1787, Gov. Bowdoin issued Warrants to the sheriff of Hampshire county for the arrest of

Capt. Asa Fisk of South Brimfield.
Alpheus Colton of Longmeadow.
Luke Day of West Springfield.
Capt. Gad Sacket of Westfield.
Capt. Aaron Jewett of Chesterfield.
Capt. John Brown of Whately.
Samuel Morse of Worthington.
Capt. Daniel Shays of Pelham.

Joseph Hinds of Greenwich.
Capt. Joel Billings of Amherst.
Obed Foot of Greenfield.
Capt. Abel Dinsmore of Conway.
Capt. Mathew Clark of Colrain.
Samuel Hill of Charlemont.
Capt. Thomas Grover of Montague.
John Powers of Shutesbury.

These men were the leaders of the insurgents in Western Mass. of whom the governor wrote the sheriff as follows: " That the enlargement of the above named persons is dangerous to the Commonwealth, its peace and safety." Sheriff Elisha Porter reported to the governor:—" Day, Colton, Clark and Brown, jailed,—the others not found."

Gov. Bowdoin found that calling out a few men here and there was having no good effect in quelling these rebellious citizens and by the advice of the Council 4400 men were called out, 700 of them from Suffolk, 500 from Essex, 800 from Middlesex, 1200 from

Hampshire and 1200 from Worcester counties, with two companies of artillery, detached from Suffolk and two from Middlesex. The troops from Suffolk, Essex and Middlesex were ordered to gather near Boston on the 19th of January, 1787. Those from Hampshire county at Springfield on the 18th. Troops from Worcester to join those of the eastern counties at Worcester. All were raised for thirty days' service, unless sooner discharged. Major-Gen. Benjamin Lincoln was placed in command.

The state treasury was so low at that time that there was not money enough to place the troops in the field and private citizens furnished the money to do it. Gov. Bowdoin issued his orders to Gen. Lincoln to take command and protect the courts, to apprehend all hostile persons, etc.,—and closed with this paragraph:

"On these attempts to restore system and order I wish the smiles of heaven, and that you may have an agreeable command, the most perfect success, and a speedy and safe return; I am with much esteem, sir, your most obedient servant, JAMES BOWDOIN.
HON. MAJOR GEN. LINCOLN."

THE REBELS MARCH TOWARD SPRINGFIELD.

Capt. Shays and his insurgent forces had withdrawn from Worcester toward the western part of the state. Gen. Lincoln arrived at Worcester on the 22d of January. The court was to sit on the 23d, and it did without any trouble. Gen. Lincoln and his army prevented any outbreak.

Gen. Shepard was in command of 1100 men from Hampshire county guarding the arsenal and stores at Springfield and the insurgents under Capt. Shays and others were concentrating there for an attack. Luke Day had 400 men at West Springfield. Shays with 1100 men was on the Boston road while Eli Parsons was at Springfield, North Parish (Chicopee) with 400 more. Most of these men were old Continental soldiers.

Shays informed Day that he proposed to attack the post at Springfield on the 25th, which was the next day. Day replied that he could not assist on the 25th, but would be ready on the 26th, but his letter was intercepted by Gen. Shepard. Shays thinking it was all right marched his forces from Wilbraham to the attack. Day in the meantime had sent a preëmptory demand to Gen. Shepard that the troops under his command be surrendered to him, but it did not terrify the General as Day perhaps hoped it might.

Gen. Lincoln was two days' march from Springfield, but hurrying forward through the deep snow. With more insurgent troops near him than he had militia, Gen. Shepard discovered Capt. Shays and his forces approaching from the Boston road about 4 P. M. on the afternoon of the 25th of January, moving toward the arsenal which he had been ordered to defend. The General sent an aid accompanied by two citizens to Shays, several times, to ask what the latter's intentions were and to warn him of danger. Shays was informed that the militia was posted there by order of the Governor, and of Congress and if he should advance further the militia would certainly fire upon his men. Shays declared that he would have possession of the barracks, "Barracks I will have and stores," and marched to within 250 yards, when Gen. Shepard ordered his men to fire the cannon; but the first two shots were fired over the heads of Shays and his men, who continued to march upon the arsenal. The third shot was aimed at the center of the advancing column and fired with deadly effect.

There was a cry of "murder," and old soldiers though they were, the whole body of men were thrown into confusion. Shays tried to rally his men but could not, and his whole force was soon in full retreat in the direction of Ludlow, leaving three dead and one wounded upon the field. Shays joined forces with Eli Parsons at Chicopee on the next day but the arrival of Gen. Lincoln on the 27th prevented another attack by the Shays men.

Gen. Lincoln had four regiments, three companies of artillery, and one company of horse or cavalry as they would be called now. At 3-30 the same day, Gen. Lincoln crossed the Connecticut river on the ice after Day and his men, but they fled in confusion and spent the night on the march to Northampton. On the 28th, Gen. Lincoln began the march after Shays who had retreated through South Hadley towards Amherst. The pursuit of Shays and his followers began at 2 o'clock in the morning of the 28th, and Gen. Lincoln pushed along as fast as the drifted snow would permit. Capt. Shays had a pretty good lead and kept out of the way of his pursuers, arriving in Amherst quite a little in advance of Gen. Lincoln, but knowing he was not far behind, pushed on toward Pelham.

A short time after the Shays men had gone from Amherst, ten sleigh loads of provisions from Berkshire came to East Amherst and stopped to feed their horses at the tavern kept by Oliver Clapp.

Landlord Clapp knew that Gen. Lincoln was in pursuit of Shays and his men and that the men were about famished. He told the men in charge of the provisions not to think of stopping to feed the horses, but to push on towards Pelham before they were gobbled up by Lincoln. The teams hurried on after Shays and the famished men got the provisions which they would have failed to receive, had not Landlord Clapp, who was a personal friend of Shays, hurried up the teams. Gen. Lincoln and his army arrived in Amherst and on being informed of the passing of Shays and his men towards Pelham, decided not to pursue them further that day.

The people who were in the farm houses along the road from Amherst to Pelham, West Hill, consisting mostly of women and children, saw a very strange and unusual sight as they looked out to the west along the deeply drifted snow-covered highway on the afternoon of the 28th of January, 1787. Straggling along the untrod road, they saw 1100 armed men, foot-sore and weary, toiling slowly along up the hills after their long march from Springfield. No such sight had they ever seen before, and never since that day has so large a body of armed men been seen in the town.

Captain Shays they knew, and their husbands and sons and brothers also, but the men from Middlesex, Worcester and Berkshire counties they did not know. The travel-worn army of rebels was halted on the common in front of the old meeting house. A portion of the men camped as comfortably as it was possible with the great lack of tents or camp equipage, and the other half, with the rebel captain moved on through the snow of that old fashioned winter down the slope to the "Hollow" where the old Conkey tavern was located, and then up to the summit of Pelham, East Hill, where they camped, Capt. Shays making himself comfortable at the old tavern he knew so well. That 1100 men could be maintained in any sort of comfort on these bleak hills in the dead of winter would seem almost impossible to anyone who will visit them any year in January; but they were quartered on these hills from Jan. 28 to Feb. 3 and none were frozen so far is known. Doubtless the ten sleigh loads of provisions, which Landlord Clapp hurried along after Capt. Shays' rebel army, helped to make their stay in Pelham more agreeable than it otherwise would have been.

General Lincoln made an examination of the houses at Amherst and discovered that they contained mostly women and children, most of the men being with the insurgents under Shays. He also learned about the ten sleigh loads of provisions which had gone forward. He then forbade the remaining inhabitants from furnishing any supplies to the insurgents; and pushed on to Hadley where he might find cover for his weary troops.

As we have already said the Shays men were quartered in some sort of comfort on these two hills in Pellham and Capt. Shays was at his old headquarters at Landlord Conkey's tavern in the great hollow between the east and west hills. Gen. Lincoln was at Hadley ten to twelve miles west of Pelham, with his forces and from his headquarters sent the following letter to Captain Shays on the 30th of January, 1787.

"Whether you are convinced or not of your error in flying to arms, I am fully pursuaded that before this hour, you must have the fullest conviction upon your mind that you are not able to execute your original purposes.

Your resources are few, your force is inconsiderable, and hourly decreasing from the disaffection of your men; you are in a post where you have neither cover nor supplies, and in a situation in which you can neither give aid to your friends nor discomfort to the supporters of good order and government. Under these circumstances you cannot hesitate a moment to disband your deluded followers. If you should not, I must approach, and apprehend the most influential characters among you.

Should you attempt to fire upon the troops of the government, the consequences must be fatal to many of your men, the least guilty. To prevent bloodshed, you will communicate to your privates, that if they will instantly lay down their arms, surrender themselves to government, and take and subscribe the oath of allegiance to this Commonwealth, they shall be recommended for mercy. If you should either withhold this information from them, or suffer your people to fire upon our approach, you must be answerable for all the ills which may exist in consequence thereof."

To this letter General Lincoln received the following reply:

"PELHAM, JANUARY 30TH, 1787.

TO GENERAL LINCOLN, COMMANDING THE GOVERNMENT TROOPS AT HADLEY, *Sir.*—The people assembled in arms from the counties of Middlesex, Worcester, Hampshire and Berkshire, taking into serious consideration the purport of the flag just received, return for answer, that however unjustifiable the measures may be which the people have adopted, in having recourse to arms, various circumstances have induced them thereto.

We are sensible of the embarrassments the people are under; but that virtue which truly characterizes the citizens of a republican government, hath hitherto marked our paths with a degree of innocence; and we wish and trust it will still be the case. At the same time, the people are willing to lay down their arms, on the condition of a general pardon, and return to their respective homes, as they are unwilling to stain the land, which we in the late war purchased at so dear a rate, with the blood of our brethren and neighbors.

Therefore, we pray that hostilities may cease, on your part, until our united prayers may be presented to the General Court, and we receive an answer, as a person is gone for that purpose. If this request may be compiled with, government shall meet with no interruption from the people; but let each army occupy the post where they now are.

DANIEL SHAYS, Captain."

On the following day three of the insurgents from the camp at Pelham appeared at General Lincoln's headquarters at Hadley with the following communination :

THE HONORABLE GENERAL LINCOLN, *Sir.*—As the officers of the people now convened in defence of their rights and privileges, have sent a petition to the General Court, for the sole purpose of accommodating our present unhappy affairs, we justly expect that hostilities may cease on both sides, until we have a return from our legislature. Your Honour will therefore be pleased to give us an answer.

Per order of the committee for recconcilliation,

FRANCIS STONE, Chairman,
DANIEL SHAYS, Captain,
ADAM WHEELER.

Pelham, January 31, 1787."

General Lincoln sent answer to the foregoing letter as follows:

" HADLEY, JANUARY 31, 1787.

GENTLEMEN.—Your request is totally inadmissible, as no powers are delegated to me which would justify a delay of my operations. Hostilities I have not commenced. I have again to warn the people in arms against the government, immediately to disband, as they would avoid the ill consequences which may ensue, should they be inattentive to this caution.

B. LINCOLN.

TO FRANCIS STONE, DANIEL SHAYS, ADAM WHEELER."

It was while this correspondence was going on that the time for the assembling of the General Court arrived according to adjournment, but owing to the unsettled state of the people the legislators did not arrive at Boston in sufficient numbers until the 3d of February. On the 4th a declaration of rebellion was passed by the Senate and concurred in by the House. When General Shepard and General Lincoln dispersed the rebels at Springfield the latter discharged 2000 militia becausped he believed they would not be wanted, but when Captain Shays posted his men at Pelham, the rebellion began to assume more importance, and Governor Bowdoin issued orders for 2600 of the militia in the middle counties to take the field.

The petition, which Shays and his associates of the committee of reconcilliation referred to as having been sent to the General Court, reached Boston and was duly presented to the honorable body. It was in language as follows:

"PETITION OF THE OFFICERS OF THE COUNTIES OF WORCESTER, HAMPSHIRE, MIDDLESEX AND BERKSHIRE NOW AT ARMS.

Humbly Sheweth:—That your petitioners being sensible that we have been in error, in having recourse to arms, and not seeking redress in a Constitutional way; we therefore heartily pray your honours, to overlook our failing, in respect to our rising in Arms, as your honors must be sensible we had great cause of uneasiness, as will appear by your redressing many grievances, the last session; yet we declare, that it is our hearts desire, that good government may be kept in a constitutional way; and as it appears to us, that the time is near approaching, when much human blood will be spilt, unless a recconcilliation can immediately take place, which scene strikes us with horror, let the foundation cause be what it may.

We therefore solemnly promise, that we will lay down our arms, and repair to our respective homes, in a peaceable and quiet manner; and so remain, provided your honours will grant to your petitioners, and all those our brethren who have recouse to arms, or otherwise aided or assisted our cause, a general pardon for their past offences. All of which we humbly submit to the wisdom, candour and benevolence of your honours, as we in duty bound shall ever pray. FRANCIS STONE,

Chairman of the Committee for the above Counties.
Read and accepted by the Officers. Pelham, January 30, 1787."

The General Court took the petition in hand and at once "Voted that the said paper cannot be sustained," and gave seven distinct reasons for their action, a few of them we copy. "First, because those concerned therein openly avow themselves in arms, and in a state of hostility against the government, and for this reason alone, the said paper would be unsustainable, even if the tenor of the application had discovered a spirit suitable to the object of it. Fourthly, The said applicants appear to view themselves on equal, if not better standing than the legislature, by proposing 'a reconcilliation.' Fifthly, They appear to threaten the authority and Government of the Commonwealth, with great effusion of blood, unless this 'reconcilliation can immediately take place.'"

In a letter written by General Lincoln to Governor Bowdoin dated at Hadley, Feb. 1, 1787, he says:

"I have just been honored with the receipt of your Excellency's favor of the 25 ult. * * * I wait with a degree of impatience for such weather as will permit my reconnoitering Shays' post, which as I have advised you before is a very strong one. Every exertion will be made to bring this matter to a happy close. B. LINCOLN."

It is probably true that there was a reconnoisance of Capt. Shays' position by order of Gen. Lincoln and it doubtless caused the rebel leader to set his forces in motion towards Petersham.

The terse answer of General Lincoln Jan. 31, 1787, did not satisfy the committee of insurgents of which Capt. Shays was one, and a private conference was sought by one of the leading rebels to further consider the subject of promise of pardon. It was granted and the conference was held at Hadley, Feb. 3, 1787, the day the General Court assembled. While the conference was in session Capt. Shays, who seems to have forgotten the petition that had been sent to the legislature, concluded not to wait for the result of the conference, at Hadley, but while it was going on the wily Captain started his men on the march across the hills and through the valleys towards Petersham.

Dr. Nehemiah Hinds kept a tavern at that time on Pelham East Hill, where a part of Capt. Shays' men were gathered while in Pelham. It stood on the site of the present Congregational parsonage in Prescott, and Landlord Hinds had for a sign the painting of a horse held by a groom. The board on which this sign was painted was hung on a post or pole set in a solid rock in front of the tavern. The tavern and the sign are gone but the rock with the hole six inches in diameter and about two feet deep remains. The rains in summer keep the hole filled with water and the children of all generations from 1787 to this day have made mud pies on that rock.

It was by this rock with the tavern sign above it that Capt. Shays is said to have treated his men, (probably the officers of his insurgent force) as they were leaving the town by the snowy highway, continuing their flight from the larger and stronger body of State Militia under General Lincoln encamped at Hadley, that Capt. Shays knew would continue the pursuit just as soon as General Lincoln became aware that the private conference was sought only for the purpose of gaining time, and the General should learn of his leaving Pelham.

This march of the rebels to Petersham was the last move in any considerable numbers of the insurgent forces. There was trouble from small bodies of rebels afterwards for some time in various parts of the state, but it is not thought best to follow up this sort of guerrilla war that was kept up for several months.

The march of General Lincoln's army from Hadley to Petersham, as given in Minot's History of the insurrection:

"Information that Shays had put his forces in motion and left Pelham was carried to Gen. Lincoln at Hadley at noon of the same day (Feb. 3, 1787) but it was first thought that he had only marched the men on the West Hill to join those on the East Hill of Pelham.

Gen. Lincoln issued orders to his army to be ready to march at a moments notice and to have three days provisions ready. At 6 o'clock that day news came that Shays had really left his position at Pelham and gone eastward. In two hours from the time or at eight o'clock in that winter night Lincoln and his army were on the march after the rebels. Through Amherst, Shutesbury and New Salem they marched as fast as the deep snows would permit, hour after hour without any unusual incident of note save the bitter cold. At two o'clock in morning they were in New Salem. By this time a violent snow storm had begun, accompanied by a fierce north wind, which sharpened the cold to an extreme degree. The route lay across high lands, and the falling snow filled the road. The soldiers were exposed to the full effect of these circumstances, and the country being thinly settled did not afford a covering for them within the distance of eight miles. Being thus deprived of shelter by want of buildings, and of refreshment by the intenseness of the cold, which prevented their taking any in the road, their only safety lay in closely pursuing a march, which was to terminate at the quarters of the enemy. They therefore advanced the whole distance of thirty miles subject to all these inclemencies without halting for any length of time. Their front reached Petersham by nine o'clock in the morning, (Feb. 4) their rear being five miles distant."

Shays and his men had been comfortably housed during the cold and storm, while Lincoln and his army were greatly worn by the fatigue of the march and suffering from the intense cold. It would seem that Shays had the advantage, but he did not seem to know it, or Gen. Lincoln didn't give him an opportunity to use it, for the latter advanced into the town with some artillery in front. Shays was taken by surprise,—he had not the least suspicion that any danger of attack was possible; and in his fear the only thought seemed to be his own personal safety, and he and his men immediately evacuated the houses where they had been quartered and thronging into a back road, fled towards Athol, without scarcely stopping to fire a gun. Many of the privates retired to their own homes,—others including officers fled to Vermont, New Hampshire and New York.

After the breaking up the main body of the rebels under Capt. Shays at Petersham, Gen. Lincoln marched his forces back to the Western part of the state to look after and disperse other small bands that still kept up a noisy but not a very dangerous campaign.

As some may ask whether any of these rebels were ever punished, it may be best to say right here that the state government had no desire to execute the extreme penalties of the law against these rebels, but they wished to show that it was dangerous business to rebel. A commission was appointed consisting of Gen. B. Lincoln, Hon. Samuel Phillips and Hon. Samuel Allen Otis for granting indemnity to some persons concerned in rebellion, and 790 persons came under its benefits, of whom 12 were convicted of treason in the western part of the state and sentenced to death. Seven or eight of these were extended a free pardon by the governor on the 30th of April, 1787, and a reprieve granted to the others on the 21st of June following, but the sheriff of Hampshire Co., was directed not to open his orders until the criminals had arrived at the gallows and all arrangements for the execution attended to. Among these was one man from Pelham and his name was Henry McCulloch.

A member of the House of Representatives was arrested by a state warrant for sedition and sentenced to sit upon the gallows for a time, to pay a fine of £50 and give bonds to keep the peace for five years and the sentence was executed.

Those who had been guilty of favoring the rebellion were excluded from the jury box for three years. Unless they could get a vote of the town to restore them. In some towns there were hardly men enough in town not tinctured with rebellious sentiments for town officers, and all town officers were required to take and subscribe to the oath of allegiance for some years.

Shays and Parsons and others of the leaders sued for pardon in February 1788 and it was granted to Shays in the following June.

Although Capt. Daniel Shays was the acknowledged leader of the insurrection, and the disturbance received its name as the Shays rebellion from the fact of his leadership, he escaped the notoriety of being sentenced to death for his crime against the state, and the honor or disgrace fell upon Henry McCulloch, being the only man from Pelham who had the death penalty passed upon him.

Henry McCulloch was a farmer and his farm was the whole or a part of home lot 48 originally drawn by John Stinson on the middle range road about a mile west of the Old Meeting House and now occupied by Mr. C. P. Hanson a soldier of the Civil War. The site of the residence of McCulloch is back from the highway and northeast of the farm house of Mr. Hanson. Some stones of the foundation remain and the well with its moss covered stones and abundance of pure water can be seen by the visitor interested in tracing such lines of history.

Henry McCulloch of Pelham, Jason Parmenter of Bernardston, David Luddington of Southampton, James White of Colraine and Alpheus Colton of Longmeadow, were tried in April 1787 and found guilty. McCulloch was sentenced to death by hanging on the gallows for participating in the insurrection, the date was fixed and he was confined in jail at Northampton awaiting the fatal day.

Petitions numerously signed for a reprieve were forwarded to Gov. Bowdoin and the following order for delay in the execution of the sentence was forwarded to High Sheriff Porter.

" BOSTON, MAY 17, 1787.
ELISHA PORTER, ESQ., Sheriff of the County of Hampshire.

Warrant deferring the execution of Henry McCulloch and Jason Parmenter. We therefore by and with the advice of the Council do hereby direct you to suspend and delay the sentence aforesaid until Thursday the twenty-first day of June next, and hereby require you then, between the hours of 12 and three o'clock in the daytime to execute the said sentence of death in execution against them and cause them to be hanged up by the neck until they be dead as directed in the warrant. JAMES BOWDOIN."

After the reprieve petitions for his pardon and release were circulated. There was a petition from Hatfield signed by 73 people of that town : one from Hadley having 44 names : one from Colraine and from other towns. Pelham people were greatly interested for the release and pardon of McCulloch and the following petition with appended list of names shows that almost all of the male inhabitants must have signed it.

" PETITION TO HIS EXCELLENCY, JAMES BOWDOIN, ESQ.

Govenor of the Commonwealth of Massachusetts and the Honorable Council. The Subscribers, Petitioners, Inhabitants of the town of Pelham, in the County of Hampshire, in behalf of Henry McCulloch of said Pelham, now a prisoner within the goal in Northampton under a sentence of death for treason against the Government most humbly shews :—That, very deeply affected with the unhappy condition of the said Henry McCulloch and anxiously desirious to do everything within their power and to use every proper and regular method in order to avert if possible his impending Fate, they have presumed to approach your Excellency & Honors with their most Honorable petition in favour of the said Henry begging the clemency and mercy of the government to spare his forefited Life and Pardon his offences for which he is sentenced to die.—They beg Leave to assure your Excellency and Honors that although he stands convicted of so high and aggravated an offence, yet he is by no means in other respects of an abandoned Character but has been in the vicinity where he dwells considered as benevolent and useful citizen, and that it is the opinion of your Petitioners that in case his Life might be saved he would be induced from his past errors, misfortunes and Dangers to yield due submission to the Laws of the Government and make all possible atonement for Past Offenses, by future obedience;—your Petitioners further beg leave to suggest to your Merciful and compassionate consideration the distresses of an aged and impotent Parent, and all the tender agencies of surrounding Neighbors and Friends, and likewise to spare your Excellencie's and Honor's in case the said unhappy Prisoner would receive a pardon it would be considered by your Humble Petitioners and by the Inhabitance of their town in general, as such an act of clemency as would lay them under the most particular obligations to use their utmost influence in future in order to promote and secure a due submission to Government and obedience to the Laws : your Petitioners therefore Most Humbly Pray that the said Prisoners life may be spared, and he may receive a full pardon for his offences, and as in duty bound shall ever pray, May 1787.

Ebenezer Liscom,
Hugh Johnson,
John Crawford,
John Bruce,
Ephriam Church,
Adam Clark,
Orles Keith,
Wm Johnston
Joseph Packard,
Joseph Thompson,
James McMilleon,
Jonathan Gray,
Mathew Brown,
Barnabas Blackmer,
John McCulloch,
James Taylor,
Jonathan Hood,
David Conkey,
Levi Packard,
Robert Houston,
James Thompson,
Elihu Billings,
Thomas Dick,
Eliakim Barlow,
Joseph Tinkham.
M Clark,
James King,

(Blotted) Peebles,
John Hood,
John Harkness 2d,
Ebenezer Gray,
Adam Johnson,
William Dunlap,
Reuben Lothridge,
Robert Crossett,
Starling King,
Wm Wells,
Nathn'l Sampson,
Thomas McMillan,
James McMillan,
James Thomson,
John Rinken,
Jacob Gray,
Andrew Conkey,
——— Thompson,
James Abercrombie,
Isaac Conkey,
Jonathan Leach,
Stephen Fish,
Daniel Tyler,
Jonathan Engram,
Alase Crosther,
Hugh Holland,
Ezekiel Baker,

John Peebles,
John Hamilton,
Samuel Hyde,
Thomas Harlow,
Ezekiel Conkey,
David Houston,
Alexander Conkey,
Alexander Conkey, Jr.
John Coal,
Levi Arms,
Isaac Barlow,
Joel Crawford,
John Thompson,
Mathew Gray,
Isaac Abercrombie,
Robert McCulloch,
Wm Baldwin,
Robert Abercrombie,
Peter King,
Joseph Rinken,
Mathew Rinken,
Isaac Dodge,
Gideon Hacket,
George Hacket,
Ichabod Hayward,
John Abbott,
Andrew Abercrombie,
Thomas Montgomery,
Samuel Holley,
Samuel Stevenson,
John Johnson,
Stephen Andrews.
James Cowden,
Uriah Southworth,
Abner Amsdill,
Robert Sekell,
Elisha Conkey,
James Latham,
William Choate, Jr.
James Cowan, Jr,
James Cowan,
Joseph Hamilton,
George Eliot,
Jeremiah McMillan,
James Kim,
Wm Hays,
Savanna Hays,
David Harkness,
John Harkness.
Timothy Engram,
James Hyde,
Timothy Clapp,
Nathan Perkins,
Thomas Fuller,
Clement Marshal,
Daniel Harkness,
John Barber,
James Rinken,
Jonathan Snow,
Alexander Torrence,
Ebenezer Sarls,
Samuel Rhods,
Thomas Conkey,
Robert Maklam,
Wm Conkey, Jr.
Robert Young Peebles,
Ebenezer Wood,
James Hunter,
Isaac Baker,
Lewis Baker,
Elam Brown,
Wm Ashley,
David Sloan,
Samuel Fenton,
Aaron Gray,
Mathew Gray, Jr.
Eliot Gray,
Barber Gray,
Patrick Gray,
Joel Gray,
Thomas Gray,
Jeremiah Gray,
James Conkey,
James Baker,
James Conkey, Jr.
Patrick McMillan,
Jonathan McMillan."

The above petition was forwarded to Gov Bowdoin, at Boston.

Gen. Ebenezer Mattoon, who it is said counted McCulloch among his personal friends, wrote to Lieut. Gov. Thomas Cushing in which he said.

" I am fearful McCulloch will suffer for want of proper knowledge of his character. He is rash and bad in many of his expressions, exceedingly so, yet when he is out of bad company and himself, I declare I know not of a person of more honesty and fidelity, nor a person more generous according to his ability ; *surely less guilty* than either of the four who are pardoned. I am certain of it, from my own knowledge.—He is forward: had a good horse and was frequently called upon by Shays, Gray and other leaders in Pelham.——He frequently told me he wished he were out of it, but he could not live in Pelham unless he joined them. Have been acquainted with him a number of years and knew him in private life. I should have been happy while at Springfield with the Government troops, and Shays in Amherst, If I had known that my family were protected by McCulloch.

I have suffered much in person and property by these people,—I have been obliged to move my family to a Neighboring town for Shelter.—Notwithstanding all this I must beg for McCulloch. I cannot express my feelings on this subject, but am sure McCulloch is not the person to make an example of. EBENEZER MATTOON, JUN.
TO MAJOR THOMAS CUSHING, Boston.
Northampton, May 8, 1787."

The earnestness and feeling displayed in the above letter shows that Gen. Mattoon had more than an ordinary interest in McCulloch and a story that has come down from the time of the insurrection touching Gen. Mattoon's relations with McCulloch may explain to some extent this peculiar interest.

McCulloch and Mattoon were said to have been associated together in years previous to the Shays rebellion when they were young men and they made a compact or agreement each with the other that in after life should one become well to do and the other be poor and in need, he should have the privilege of making his wants known and receive needed assistance. Later in life McCulloch was in rather straightened circumstances, and it is said, used to come to Gen. Mattoon's home at Amherst and say to the General, "Dost thou remember the compact?" and in response McCulloch's bags were at once filled with grain from the General's well filled granary, which the former would take home to his family in Pelham.

As Henry McCulloch and Jason Parmenter were associated together in the warrant for execution and in the reprieve it may not be out of place to state that active measures were taken by Parmenter's friends for his pardon.

A petition for the reprieve of Jason Parmenter was sent to the Govenor dated at Sudbury, May, 11, 1787, signed by,

RUTH PARMENTER, (mother.)

Brothers of Jason
{ MICAH PARMENTER,
DELIVERANCE PARMENTER,
ISRAEL PARMENTER,
SILAS PARMENTER.

There was also a petition sent to the governor by the condemned Jason and signed by himself alone, in which he pled earnestly for pardon. The result of the various petitions and letters poured in upon Govenor Bowdoin seemed to have the desired effect and not only reprieve for a few weeks but a "full, free and ample pardon" was granted. Whether there was any real purpose to hang these men, on the part of the state authorities may be questioned, but the men under sentence of death were led to believe that the state would punish rebels by death.

Governor Bowdoin went out of office before the final decision was made concerning the cases of the two condemned rebels and they were pardoned by Governor John Hancock. The document which relieved the men from their fears and set them at liberty read substantially as follows, only the important and effective portions being copied.

"We therefore by and with the advice and consent of the Council of our Special grace do hereby remit to the said Henry McCulloch and Jason Parmenter a full free and ample pardon of all the Pains and Penalties they were liable to suffer and undergo by Vertue of the Sentences and Judgements aforesaid and of which the Sheriff of our said County of Hampshire is in an especial manner to take notice.   JOHN HANCOCK, Governor.
Boston, Sept. 12, 1787."

While the friends of Henry McCulloch were doing their best to get him pardoned and set at liberty during the spring and summer of 1787, the rank and file of the Pelham people who had been engaged in rebellion against the state government had taken the oath of allegiance and had been at work on their farms as law abiding citizens.

From the rolls among the records at the State House the following list of men from Pelham, who had been in rebellion, has been copied in full. Some delivered up guns they had used against the state ; some did not, while others offered such excuses as they had for their conduct.

"Pelham men who took oath of allegiance April 16, 1787, because they had been engaged in the insurrection.

Thomas Johnson,
George Eliot,
John Harkness 2ᵈ,
Daniel Harkness Jun,
David Hays,
James Baker Feb. 27, 1787,
Stephen Andrews,

Joseph ✛ Rinken, (his mark)
John Hamilton, Jun.,
James Cowan, Jun.,
James Johnston,
Joel Crawford.
Moors Johnston,

Stephen Pettingall	Jacob Edson, gun,
Abner Amsdill,	John Bruce, Gun,
Samuel Rhods, gun,	Eleakim Barton,
George Hacket, gun,	Isaac Abercrombie,
Uriah Southworth, gun,	Abiah Southworth.
Joseph Tinkham, gun,	Justus Cowan,
William Cowan,	Jonathan Baker,
John Cowan,	Eliot Gray,
Lewis Ames, gun,	Jonathan Snow,
John Cole, gun,	Joel Rinken.

Thirty persons on the right hand of this column (meaning the first thirty names) Personally appeared and took and subscribed the oath of allegiance to the Commonwealth on the 16 day of April 1787.

Coram (before me.)   E. MATTOON, JUN., Justice Peace."

"Hugh Johnston subscribed March 14, 1787 Excepting the words 'Ecclesiastical or Spiritual.

March 16 Ebenezer Gray carried no arms he said.

March 19 Simeon Smith delivered his Gun.

March 20 Medad Moody 'lent a gun unwillingly.'

March 21 Joshua Whitney aided only by leading home his brothers horse.

Feb 6 Elias Smith, Samuel Smith Received their arms at Amherst.

Henry Lee Never bore Arms.

March 23, 1787, Ezekiel Conkey,	David Conkey,
James Abercrombie,	James McMillan,
David Pratt,	Robert Crosett,
Samuel Robins,	Jeremiah McMillan,
Eliott Gray 2ᵈ,	Wm. McMillan,
Thomas Clelland,	Jonathan McMillan.
Joseph Johnston,	Wm. Johnston,
Ezekiel Conkey,	Elisha Gray,
Thomas Thompson,	Joseph Waiscoat,
Ezekiel Baker,	Thomas Conkey,
John Thompson Jun.,	John Hunter.
Andrew Hyde,	

Before ISAAC POWERS, Justice Peace."

"Sept. 10, 1787, Lieut. Timothy Packard of Pelham took oath before me E. Mattoon, Jun."

"HAMPSHIRE SS FEB. 1, 1787.

Then John Hood, Adam Johnson, Jonathan Engram, Samuel Engram of Pelham informally appeared before me and took and subcribed to the oath of Allegiance.   Before me ABNER MORGAN.

ELISHA BALDWIN,
SAMUEL WRIGHT."

Lieut. Timothy Packard was one of the last to take the oath, while Hood, Johnson and the two Ingrams were the earliest; the date on which they subscribed to the oath of allegiance was one of the four days that Capt. Shays and his men were quartered at Pelham after his repulse at Springfield and before he marched to Petersham. Baldwin and Wright were Pelham men and doubtless subscribed to the oath but the record was not filled out.

HOME OF CAPTAIN SHAYS.

THE ABIAL ROBINSON FARM HOUSE.

Captain Daniel Shays.

Daniel Shays is said to have been born in Hopkinton, Mass. in 1747. His parents being poor, and his early education neglected. It is also said that he removed from Hopkinton to Great Barrington before the Revolutionary war. How long before the war his removal occurred we have no record, neither is there any means of determining when he came to Pelham. But he was there when the Lexington alarm was sent out and joined a company of minute men under Capt. Reuben Dickinson of Amhetst. This Company served eleven days. Shays was an ensign in this company. Capt. Dickinson organized another company May 1, 1775, which served three months and eight days and Daniel Shays was sergeant in this company. He was promoted for bravery at the battle of Bunker Hill. Shays was in Capt. Reuben Dickinson company of Col. Ruggles Woodbridge's Regiment on the expedition to Ticonderoga in 1776; was appointed lieutenant in Col. Varnum's regiment in 1776 and detached on recruiting service; enlisted a company which he took to West Point, whose engagement to serve was conditioned upon his being appointed captain. He was not appointed captain and the men were apportioned to different corps. Shays was at the surrender of Burgoyne and at the storming of Stony Point. In 1779 he received a captain's commission and was with Col. Putnam's regiment at Newark, N. J., in 1780, when he resigned and left the service.

Capt. Shays probably returned to Pelham soon after resigning his position in the army. Landlord Conkey was a friend of the Captain and there had been business transactions of some sort between them as shown by the following receipt:

"Sudbury February 11 1779
Received of William Conkey, Jun, the som four hundred dollars. I say Re'cd by me.   ABIGAIL SHAYS."

Abigail Shays was the Captain's wife, and the dating of the paper at Sudbury may indicate her place of abode while her husband was in the army.

On the 9th of March 1781, Capt. Shays was chosen a member of Committee of Safety at Pelham; was chosen again in 1782 on the same committee, and the committee were directed to attend the County Convention. He was also chosen one of the town Warden for several years, and held that office the year the insurrection broke out. He was sent as a delegate to several of the conventions for the consideration of grievances which began to burden the people before the war closed. It was while he was a member of the Committee of Safety that he filed the following petition or bill for services at conventions:

"Pelham March 18 1782
This is to see if the town will allow me 1£—17s—8d for tending the Convention held at Hatfield and Hadley nine days and seven nights.
DANIEL SHAYS."

March 26, 1783, Capt. Shays was allowed 12s for attending a County Convention. The last office to which he was chosen in Pelham was as delegate to attend a convention at Hadley in October, 1786—but he was excused and another man chosen in his place.

The farm on which Capt. Shays lived is on the Prescott side of the West Branch of Swift river; for the last hundred years known as the "Johnson place." The farm house now on the place is not the one occupied by the rebel captain, but is only a little removed from the site of the one that preceded it. The farm lays along the middle range road and the Old Conkey Tavern was half a mile or so farther down the road in the Hollow. Capt. Shays was no stranger at Landlord Conkey's tavern, nor at the hostelry of Dr. Nehemiah Hinds on the East Hill, living as he did between the two.

The open fire-place in the bar room of Landlord Conkey's tavern was a pleasant place during the long winter evenings, when the hard times began to be felt by the debt burdened farmers, after the war was ended. What more fitting place to talk over their troubles than beside the great open fire place with its blazing logs, and the well filled decanters on the shelves of the bar in the corner behind. Here Capt. Shays met the people who came to consult him in regard to their grievances. Here the first mutterings of opposition in this vicinity were heard, and later developed into defiance of the state government, and armed resistance to the Courts and laws. In the open space in front of the tavern Capt. Shays drilled the men in the use of arms, and as the insurrection assumed greater proportions he was called to other parts of the state to organize the excited people.

Capt. Shays was doubtless poor in a financial sense, and possibly cramped and hampered by debts he was unabled to pay, as many of

FACSIMILE OF CAPTAIN SHAYS' HANDWRITING.

his neighbors were; and felt as keenly as they the distress caused by the lack of money and the other grievances complained of by the people. Whether he had large indebtedness is not known, but a note still in existance is evidence that he was unable to settle small indebtedness with cash.

Capt. Shays' Note.

"For Value re'cd I promise to pay to William Conkey or Order the sum of Eighteen shillings six pence, to be paid by the first of January next with interest for the same, as witness my hand. Daniel Shays.
Pelham Sept 1, 1786."

The above note was overdue when he led his deluded followers from Springfield back to Pelham on the 28th of January, 1787, and was never paid, Milo Abbott of Prescott holds the note. The small sum represented by the note may have been a loan from his friend Conkey, to whom Shays had extended aid and comfort in previous years as shown by the following letter, which is of interest, being a copy of an autograph letter of the Captain while stationed at Putnams' Heights. The letter is also of use in forming an intelligent idea of the character and capacity of the insurgent leader; who, though not well educated, had some military experience,—was popular and companionable among the people, and had some capacity for organizing and directing the movements of the excited insurgents, but it seems fair and reasonable to admit that he was not so able a leader as might have been chosen from the large number of insurgents in the state.

"Putnams Heighth" June 25th 1778.
Mr. Conkey, Sir: After my kind Requist to you I wish to inform that I am well & in good health, hoping that these will find you & your family as well as these leave me. I have wrote to you once before but hearing you have not Rec'd my Letter from me & understand that you have been Drafted with these last men I write to you now for you to inform the selectmen of the town by showing thim this Letter that you have hired Jacob Toorell for to do eighteen months service for you on consideration of your paying him ten pounds for that space of time which I saw you pay him the money.

Thinking that these few lines will be sufficient for to clear you for the present time I thought I would embrace this opportunity to write to you for your Security. Having nothing Remarkable for news & hoping these will find you and yours well I must Conclude.
Your Friend and Servant, Daniel Shays.
To Mr. William Conkey, Tavern Keeper in Pelham."

Capt. Daniel Shays defended his action in the rebellion in an interview with Gen. Rufus Putnam, the revolutionary soldier, seventeen days before the attack upon the Springfield Armory. General Putnam reported the interview to Governor Bowdoin:

"RUTLAND, JANUARY 8, 1787.

SIR:—As I was coming through Pelham the other day I met Mr. Shays in the road alone, where we had a conversation, some of which was of a very particular kind. I shall state the whole, by way of dialog, as far as I can recollect; but in order to understand the meaning of some parts of it, it is necessary you should know that the week before they stopped Worcester court the last time, I spent many hours with Shays and his officers, endeavoring to dissuade them from their measures, and persuade them to return to their allegiance.

Mr. Shays—Do you know if the petition drawn up at Worcester has been sent to the governor or not?

Putnam—I am surprised to hear you inquire that of me; you certainly ought to know whether you have sent it, or not—however, since you ask the question I tell you I have been credibly informed that so late as last Friday it had not been presented.

Shays—They promised to send it immediately, and it was very wrong they did not; but I don't know that it will alter the case, for I don't suppose the governor and council will take any notice of it.

Putnam—You have no reason to expect they will grant the prayer of it.

Shays—Why not?

Putnam—Because many things asked for it is out of their power to grant; and besides that since you and your party have once spurned at offered mercy, it is absurd to expect that another general pardon should be ever granted.

Shays—No! Then we must fight it out.

Putnam—That as you please, but it's impossible you should succeed, and the event will be that you must either run your country or hang, unless you are fortunate enough to bleed.

Shays—By God I'll never run my country.

Putnam—Why not? It's more honorable than to fight in a bad cause, and be the means of involving your country in a civil war; and that is a bad cause; you have always owned to me; that is, you owned to me at Holden, the week before you stopped Worcester court, that it was wrong in the people ever to take up arms as they had.

Shays—So I did, and so I say now, and I told you then and tell you now, that the sole motive with me in taking the command at Springfield, was to prevent the shedding of blood, which would absolutely have been the case, if I had not; and I am so far from considering it as a crime, that I look upon it that the government are indebted to me for what I did there.

Putnam—If that was the case, how came you to pursue the matter? Why did you not stop there?

Shays—I did not pursue the matter; it was noised about that the warrants were out after me, and I was determined not to be taken.

Putnam—This won't do. How came you to write letters to several towns in the county of Hampshire, to choose officers and furnish themselves with arms and 60 rounds of ammunition?

Shays—I never did; it was a cursed falsehood.

Putnam—Somebody did in your name, which it can never be presumed was done without your approbation.

Shays—I never had any hand in the matter; it was done by a Committee, and Doctor Hunt and somebody else, who I don't know, put my name to the copy and sent it to the Governor and Court.

Putnam—But why did you not take the benefit of the act of indemnity, as soon as it passed? But instead of that, you ordered the whole posse collected and marched as far as Shrewsbury, in order to go and stop the Court at Cambridge.

Shays—I never ordered a man to march to Shrewsbury, nor anywhere else, except when I lay at Rutland. I wrote to a few towns in the counties of Worcester and Hampshire. You are deceived; I never had half so much to do with the matter as you think for, and the people did not know of the act of indemnity before they collected.

Putnam—If they did not you did, for you told me at Holden that you knew everything that passed at Court; and that when you talked with Gen. Ward at Shrewsbury you was able to correct him in several things which he advanced.

Shays—I could tell you—but—

Putnam—I don't wish to know any of your secrets. But why did you not go home with the Hampshire people from Holden, as you told me in the evening you would the next morning?

Shays—I can tell you, it would not have done. I have talked with Maj. Goodman. I told him what you said, and he gave it as his opinion the act would not have taken us in.

Putnam—Suppose that to be the case, yet the General Court might have extended it to you; the chance in your favor was much greater before than after you had stopped Worcester Court. Why did you not petition, before you added that crime to the score?

Shays—It would have been better; but I cannot see why stopping that Court is such a crime that if I might have been pardoned before, I should be exempted now.

Putnam—When offered mercy has been once refused, and the crime repeated, Government never can with any kind of honor and safety to the community pass it over without hanging somebody; and as you are at the head of the insurgents, and the person who directs all their movements, I cannot see you have any chance to escape.

Shays—I at their head! I am not.

Putnam—It is said you are first in command, and it is supposed they have appointed you their General.

Shays—I never had any appointment but that at Springfield, nor did I ever take command of any men but those of the county of Hampshire; no General Putnam, you are deceived, I never had half so much to do with the matter as you think for, nor did I order any men to march, except when at Rutland, as I told you before.

Putnam—Did you not muster the party to go to Springfield the other day?

Shays—No, nor had I any hand in the matter, except that I rode down in a sleigh.

Putnam—But I saw your name to the request presented to the justices—that you won't deny?

Shays—I know it was there, and Grover put it there without my knowledge; I wan't got into Springfield when it was done,—the matter was all over before I got there and I had no hand in it.

Putnam—But is it a truth that you did not order the men to march to Springfield the other day?

Shays—Yes—I was sent to and refused, and told them I would have nothing to do in the matter.

Putnam—But why?

Shays—I told them it was inconsistent after what we had agreed to petition, as we did at Worcester, and promised to remain quiet and not to meddle with the courts any more, till we knew whether we could get a pardon or not.

Putnam—Have you not ordered the men to march to Worcester the 23d of this month?

Shays—No. I was sent to from Worcester county to come down with the Hampshire men; but I told them I would not go myself nor order any men to march.

Putnam—Who has done it? Hampshire men are certainly ordered to march.

Shays—Upon my refusing to act they have chose a committee, who have ordered the men to march.

Putnam—But how do you get along with these people, having been with them so long; how is it possible they will let you stay behind?

Shays—Well enough. I tell them that I never will have anything more to do with stopping Courts, or anything else, but to defend myself, till I know whether a pardon can be obtained or not.

Putnam—And what if you can not get a pardon?

Shays—Why, then I will collect all the force I can and fight it out; and, I swear, so would you or anybody else, rather than be hanged.

Putnam—I will ask you one question more, you may answer it or not, as you please—it is this—Had you an opportunity, would you accept of a pardon, and leave these people to themselves?

Shays—Yes—in a moment.

Putnam—Then I advise you to set off this night to Boston, and throw yourself upon the mercy and under the protection of Government.

Shays—No, that is too great a risk, unless I was first assured of a pardon.

Putnam—There is no risk in the matter, you never heard of a man who voluntarily did this, whose submission was not accepted; and if your submission is refused, I will venture to be hanged in your room.

Shays—In the first place, I don't want you hanged, and in the next place, they would not accept of you.

The only observation I shall make is, that I fully believe he may be brought off, and no doubt he is able to inform Government more of the bottom of this plot than they know at present.

I have the honor to be Sir your Ex'y's most obed't and humble servant,

RUFUS PUTNAM.

GOV. BOWDOIN.

Capt. Shays retreated in much haste from Petersham as far as Winchester, N. H., after he was surprised February 4, 1787, by Gen. Lincoln's remarkable march through the snowstorm, and three days later he had nearly 300 men with him. These dispersed gradually, and Shays probably went through Vermont into New York state, as many of his followers did.

On the 9th of February 1787, Gov. Bowdoin issued a proclamation ordering the arrest of Daniel Shays of Pelham, Luke Day of West Springfield, Adam Wheeler of Hubbardston, and Eli Parsons of Adams; designating them as "Principals and abetters," and a reward was offered for their apprehension. The reward was renewed by the state authorities in the hope that Capt. Shays might be delivered up by officers in whatever state he might be, but he escaped arrest and trial for more than a year and then Shays proffered a petition for pardon in February 1788, couched in the most humble terms. The legislature then in session failed to agree upon granting pardon to Shays, but a full pardon was granted in the summer of 1788. After he was pardoned he is said to have returned to Pelham, but there is no known record of his living in Pelham after the collapse of the rebellion. Nor is there any reliable evidence that he returned to his native state as a place of residence, though he may have done so. There is general agreement that he did not prosper in business whereever he was located. After living in several different places in New York state he drifted to Sparta, Livingston county, where he lived in extreme poverty. He died in 1825, when he was 78 years old. His grave is said to be marked by a flat stone in the beautiful cemetery of Conesus near Scottsburg. Something like ten or twelve years ago there was a movement to set up a large boulder inscribed with his name to mark the grave of Capt. Shays; but it may not have been accomplished. Letters of enquiry sent to the local authorities at

Sparta concerning the rebel captain, his death and place of burial, were not answered, and the generally conceded statements given above must be accepted as the most authentic obtainable.

After the rebellion was quelled the movement itself and Capt. Shays in particular was the target for ridicule of all sorts. The would-be poets of the time exercised their talents upon him and various effusions of poetical doggerell have come down to the present time. " The Confession of Capt. Shays " follows; also a more extended version which was sung by the choir of the Olivet church, Springfield, at the celebration of the one hundredth anniversary of the attempt of Shays upon the arsenal in January, 1887:

UP THE EAST HILL, (PRESCOTT).

THE CONFESSION OF CAPT. SHAYS.

In former days my name was Shays,
   In Pelham I did dwell, sir;
But now I'm forced to leave that place,
   Because I did rebel, sir.

But in this State I lived till late:
   By Satan's foul invention;
In Pluto's cause against the laws
   I raised an insurrection.

In hell 'twas planned by obscure hand
  All laws should fail before me,
Though in disgrace the populace
  Like Persia did adore me.

On mountain's steed we did proceed,
  Our federal stores to plunder;
But there we met with a back set
  From Shepard's warlike thunder.

They killed four; they wounded more;
  The rest they run like witches;
Roswell Merrick lost his drum,
  And Curtis split his breeches.

Which proved too hard for my front guard,
  For they still growing stronger,
I'm resolved to go to the shades below
  And stay on earth no longer.

When I arrived at the water side,
  Where Charon kept the ferry,
I called for quick passage o'er,
  For I dare no longer tarry.

Then Damon came to Charon's boat,
  And straightly gave him orders
To bring no more such rebels o'er,
  If they had no further orders.

For I have orders sent to me
  That's very strict indeed, sir,
To bring no more such rebels o'er,
  For they're of Charon's breed, sir.

Then Damon ordered Shays away
  To gather up his daises;
And the service done by him is
  They gave him many praises.

SHAYS'S REBELLION.

My name was Shays; in former days,
  In Pelham I did dwell, sir;
But now I'm forced to leave that place,
  Because I did rebel, sir.

Within the state I lived, of late,
  By Satan's foul invention,
In Pluto's cause, against their laws
  I raised an insurrection.

'Twas planned below, by that arch foe,
  All laws should fall before me;
Though in disgrace, the populace
  Did Persian-like adore me.

On mounted steed I did proceed
  The federal stores to plunder;
But there I met with a bold salute
  From Shepard's war-like thunder.

He kindly sent his aid-de-camp
  To warn me of my treason;
But when I did his favors scorn,
  He sent his weighty reason,

Which proved too hard for my front guard,
  And they still growing stronger,
I planned to go to world below
  And live on earth no longer.

And when I reached the river Styx,
  Where Charon kept the ferry,
I called for speedy passage o'er
  And dared no longer tarry.

But Charon's boat was freighted with
  Four ghosts from Springfield plain, sir;
He bade me tarry on the wharf
  Till the boat returned again, sir.

But while I tarried on the wharf,
  My heart kept constant drumming,
And conscious guilt made me believe
  'Twas Lincoln's army coming.

Then Charon hoists his sable sails,
  The lazy gales seemed ling'ring;
I leaped into the sulph'rous stream,
  To cross the flood by swimming.

Then Demon came to Charon's boat
  And strictly gave him orders
To take no more such rebels o'er,
  Till he enlarged his borders.

" For I have orders sent to me
  That's very strict indeed, sir,
To bring no more such rebels o'er,
  They're such a cursed breed, sir."

"Go tell that rebel to return,
  And he shall be well-guarded,
And for the service done for me
  I'll see him well rewarded."

Then Charon ordered Shays right back
  To gather up his daisies,
And for the service done for him
  He gave him many praises.

Then Shays was wroth, and soon replied,
  " O ! Charon, thou art cruel !"
And challenged him to come on shore
  And fight with him a duel.

Then Charon straightway ordered Shays
  To leave the river's bank, sir;
For he would never fight a man
  So much below his rank, sir.

Then Shays returned to Vermont state
  Chagrined and much ashamed, sir;
And soon the mighty, rebel host
  Unto our laws were tamed, sir.

Oh, then our honored fathers sat
  With a bold resolution,
And framed a plan and sent to us
  Of noble constitution.

America, let us rejoice
  In our new constitution.
And never more pretend to think
  Of another revolution.

Settlement of Salem, N. Y.

BY PELHAM PEOPLE IN 1764.

Less than twenty years after the incorporation of the town of Pelham the restless unsatisfied spirit developed itself as it always does among the true pioneers who push out to the edge of civilization and beyond to establish new settlements, and in the spring of 1761 James Turner and Joshua Conkey, Pelham men but not among those who drew home lots in the first division of land in 1739, started out to begin another settlement in the forests of New York state in the neighborhood of Crown Point where it is probable both men had seen service, in the French and Indian war which resulted in the conquest of Canada in 1760.

These men may have discovered that the lands in that section were not so rough and stony as the tract of land on which they had settled in Hampshire county and made up their minds to improve their condition. At any rate they set out from Pelham in the spring of the year 1761 and made the journey through the wilderness, to Charlotte county, New York, since changed to Washington county, and selected lands on the flats where the village of Salem is now situated. Turner and Conkey spent the summer there and returned to Pelham to spend the following winter. In the spring of 1762 they set forth again on horseback for White Creek, as the new settlement was called by these settlers from New England, while other settlers in that neighborhood, Scotch Presbyterians from Ballibay, Ireland in 1765, insisted upon calling the settlement New Perth, from Perth, Scotland. On this journey they were accompanied by Hamilton McCollister another Pelham man, and these three were the original settlers of the town now known as Salem, and the spot where their cabin was built is now occupied by the On-da-wa House. Each man selected a tract of land for himself. Turner taking the land west of the cabin, and McCollister went up the creek a little for his selection, while Conkey went up the creek for a mile or so and located. The summer was spent upon the lands they had selected and when winter came they returned to Pelham. The summer of 1763 was spent in making improvements on their lands and the journey back to Pelham was made late in the autumn for the winter sojourn.

In the spring of 1764 the three men, two with families, set out from Pelham to make the journey to White Creek on horseback, with all their household effects also strapped upon the backs of horses. In this way they journeyed through the forests, and forded the many streams along the route.

These people were the first actual settlers in Washington County. Other families from Pelham, Colraine, Sturbridge and perhaps other Massachusetts towns joined them in years following and the settlement was quite properly known as the "New England Colony." They were the founders of the Salem Church known as "The first Incorporated Presbyterian Congregation in Salem, County of Washington, and State of New York."

The following tribute of respect, and estimate of the character of the settlers from Pelham and other Massachusetts towns, we copy from an Historical Sketch of the Presbyterian Church of Salem by Rev. Edward P. Sprague pastor, 1876.

"The settlers from Massachusetts were persons of a character to place the very highest estimate upon all religious privileges, and whose first care after providing houses for their families would certainly be to secure for them the sacred influences of the church and the preached Gospel.

Whatever they might feel compelled to forego on occount of their location and circumstances, they would never consent to neglect the establishment and maintainance of the ordinances of religion. We find therefore as we might expect, that previous to their leaving New England they took measures for securing to themselves a distinct church organization. And this design they never abandoned, even after the settlement of Dr. Clark's Colony (from Ballibay, Ireland) furnished them with the opportunity of attending Christian worship.

They might have joined themselves with the church thus transplanted hither from Ireland, and the two colonies thus have been merged in one ecclesiastically, as well as socially, but the points of difference between themselves and the Scotch seem in the main to have presented almost insurmountable obstacles. There were at intervals certain more favorable seasons when such a union was contemplated, and even appeared ready for consumation, but it was never actually accomplished, and the New England people remained, what they had been from the first, a distinct religious congregation."

The desire and purpose of those who had journeyed from Pelham for the early establishment of Gospel privileges in the new settlement seems to have been the same as was manifested by the settlers of Pelham, and the first sermon ever preached in White Creek or Salem was delivered in the cabin of James Turner by Rev. Dr. Clark a Scotchman from Ballibay. Three years after the settlement of Conkey, Turner and McCollister with their families, or in the year 1767, and soon after there had been further accessions of Massachusetts people, they felt that they must secure a preacher of the Gospel to settle among them, and a letter was written to Rev. David McGregorie of Londonderry, N. H. a member of the Presbytery which was organized or constituted in 1745 by Rev. John Moorehead of Boston, Rev. David McGregorie of Londonderry, N. H., Rev. Robert Abercrombie of Pelham with Messrs Alexander Conkey of Pelham and James McKeon and James Hughes, at a meeting in Londonderry on the 16th of April of that year, and called the Boston Presbytery.

The reason for writing to Rev. Mr. McGregorie was unquestionably the fact that many of the Pelham men who had settled at White Creek were acquainted with Mr. McGregorie, having met him at Pelham before moving to the state of New York. The letter follows.

To the Reverend Mr. DAVID McGREGORIE

Reverend and Dearly Beloved — Grace and Peace be Multiplied, &c.

This Comes to you by the hand of Dea. McMullen A Gentleman Chosen and Appointed by us for the purpose viz.—Once more to Implore your presence and assistance, in our Destitute Circumstances in order to open a way for the resettlement of the Gospel among us — The reason which induce us to send for yourself Rather than for any other of our Fathers in the presbytery are our Sensibility of your more peculiar acquaintance with our People, Backed by their unanimous Voice for you in particular,—We hope that the knowledge you have of our State, the Love and Regard we trust you bear for us, together with the prospect you herein have of the promotion of the Interests of our Common Lord, will by no means fail to preponderate in our Favor—and that our Sister Church will sympathise with us so far as cheerfully to part with you till you can come over to our Macedonia once more to help us, since we hope that God is in his tender providence putting an end to our Difficulties in some good measure and that this is one of the Last times we shall be necessitated to entreat your presence in an affair of like Nature. For further particulars Please enquire of Deacon McMullen. And now that God may incline your heart to assist us, Bring you safe on your Journey and make your Coming and our concerns to terminate Ultimately in his own Glory is the prayer of Reverend Sir

Your servants in Christ,

JOHN GRAY, JOHN SAVAGE, ALEXANDER TURNER, JAMES BERRY, Elders.

These names signed to the above letter are all of them men who had only recently come from Pelham and joined the pioneers, also from Pelham, who first took up lands at White Creek in 1761. John Savage, married Eleanor Hamilton of Rutland Jan. 16, 1733.

The name of John Savage appears on the records of Pelham as early as 1747 when he was chosen to represent the town at the Presbytery.

He was on a committee to provide school masters April 30, 1751, was moderator of a town meeting in 1752, was on a committee to see about legalizing certain town meeting actions, 1753, was on committee to represent the town at the Superior Court at Springfield, in 1757, was on a committee whose duty it was to make answer to a petition that had been sent to the General Court in Jan. 1764.

John Savage was allowed 12 shillings for pasturing horses at the ordination of Rev. Richard Crouch Graham in 1764, John Savage and James Harkness were alloted pew No. 10 in the Old Meeting House at Pelham March 28, 1766.

From this last date the name of John Savage does not again appear on the records of the town, nor is there mention of his leaving the state of Massachusetts, but there can be no doubt of his removal from Pelham in 1766. Pelham lost an able and valuable citizen and the settlement of White Creek gained one.

John Gray, another of those whose names are subscribed to the letter to Mr. McGregorie, married Martha Savage, April 17, 1755. His connection with the Savage family is reason sufficient for his being at White Creek at about the same date as John Savage.

Alexander Turner was one of the original settlers of Pelham and drew home lot No. 46, and built a sawmill.

The surname Berry was not among the original settlers of Pelham but there must have been men of that name in town not long after the first settlers took up the tract, and there never has been a time since until now when there were not families of that name in the town or its immediate vicinity.

James Turner of Pelham was married to Susannah Thomas of Worcester, April 1, 1760. Joshua Conkey and Dinah Dick, both of Pelham, were married April 13, 1762. These last are the two young men who spent the summer of 1761 on lands they had secured at White Creek, only one of them married at the time.

Joseph McCracken, of Worcester, was married to Sarah Turner, of Pelham, Feb. 12, 1760. Miss Turner was doubtless the sister of James Turner. McCracken was a prominent man at White Creek and a captain in the Revolutionary war.

Thomas Morrison, of Londonderry, N. H., was married to Martha Clark, of Pelham, Feb. 11, 1762. He was an early settler at White Creek.

Hamilton McCollister, the companion of Conkey and Turner on their return to White Creek from Pelham in the spring of 1762 and who was with them in 1764 when they made the new settlement their permanent abiding place, came back to Pelham three years later, and was married to Sarah Dick, Oct. 15, 1767.

The royal grant of the land on which the New England colony settled was given August 17, 1764; it consisted of 25,000 acres, and was granted in response to a petition presented by Alexander and James Turner, and twenty-five others in January 1763. The terms were an annual quit-rent of two shillings for each hundred acres, with all the mines, and all pine trees above a certain size, reserved to the crown. One-half of this tract they conveyed by deed to Oliver DeLancey and Peter Dubois of New York. Following the plan they knew was adopted at Pelham twenty-five years previous, the tract of land was divided into 304 lots, each half a mile long and containing 88 acres. Three lots drawn by DeLancey and Dubois and three belonging to "the proprietors" were reserved for the support of the minister and a schoolmaster.

The colony from Ballibay, Ireland, that came in 1765, purchased DeLancey's and Dubois's land under Dr. Clark the leader of the colony. The two colonies, viz. the Scotch colony from Ballibay and the New England colony lived near by each other under the most friendly relations socially, but a certain society rivalry sprang up between them and prevented them from joining harmoniously in one church organization under Rev. Dr. Clark as their minister. The New England colony charged the people of the Scotch colony with a desire to secede from them. A document drawn up by Joshua Conkey, one of the three first settlers from Pelham, explaining the purposes of the New England colony, bearing as an endorsement "The petition presented to Dr. Clark and his Elders," dated Sept. 16, 1771, exhibits to some extent the disturbed feeling existing between the two Presbyterian bodies.

"Whereas we for sometime have had it in our hearts to Build a house of Publick Worship for God & for fear of further Disputes & Contention we think proper to enter into agreement in writing as we have hade some Evidence of late of a separation by those who take to themselves the name of seceders by there staying from publick Worship when a member of the Philadelphia Signod priched in this place who was Regerly sent forth to prich and administer ordinances wherever he might be cold in this vacant part of Gods vinyard—therefore We the subscribers do unanomesly agree to joyn in building a house for the Worship of God with those who subscribe the foloing articles, viz.

1. that we the Subscribers do bind our selvs we shall have and give free liberty to ordain or install a minister of the philadelphia Signod or one in connection with them in said house or at least to joyn in the ordination or Instalment of any one that shall be coled by the Majority of the Inhabitance of this place that subscrice to this.

2. that we shall not be consigned to that set of people Coled soceders. White Creek, 16 Jept. 1771.

Joshua Conkey,	James Moor,	Alexander Turner,
Edward Savage,	Hugh Moor,	John Gray,
Frances Lammon,	John Nevens,	Samuel Hyndmand,
Hamilton McCollister,	John Savage,	Edward Long,
Timothy Titus,	James Turner,	James Savage,
Ebenezer Russell,	Joseph McCracken,	Reuben Turner,
Daniel McCollister,	Moses Martin,	Launard + Webb. (his mark)

The foregoing document with the signatures was not received with satisfaction by Dr. Clark and his people, and at a session of that society it was taken up and considered carefully and replied to.

There was quite a little spicy correspondence between the two societies resulting from the document written by Joshua Conkey and the result was, to make a union of the two societies impossible, and the New England colony proceeded to carry out their purpose to continue as an independent organization and to build a meeting house for their own use. Their first meeting-house was sometime building and perhaps not used much previous to 1774, and was never finished.

They began to worship in it when there was only a roof to protect them from the weather, and before the sides were boarded or a floor laid. After the Revolutionary war broke out the uncompleted meeting house was used first as a barrack by the patriot forces and then strengthened and made to serve as a fort. Logs set close together in the ground made a stockade about sixty feet from the building and extending around it, and was finished July 26, 1777. The meeting house having been changed into a fort it was first called the

Salem fort, the name was afterwards changed to Fort Williams, in honor of Gen. John Williams.

In the autumn following the erection of the stockade all the people, save perhaps a few tories, were obliged to leave the place, leaving their homes and property because of the advance of Gen. Burgoyne and his forces upon the town. The meeting house fort was burned to the ground during the last days of August or early September.

Col. Joseph McCracken, was at one time in command of the patriot forces that occupied the meeting house fort,—and the same man already referred to as the husband of Sarah Turner of Pelham. He was a brave soldier and later lost an arm at the battle of Monmouth.

At the close of the Revolutionary war the people of the New England colony were very poor, having lost heavily by reason of Burgoyne's army invading the town, and no attempt was made to erect a meeting house in place of the one burned for about ten years, and in the mean time they worshiped with the people of the other presbyterian church or had a minister occasionally to preach to their own people.

A new meeting house was erected on the same lot on which the first one stood, and a part of Hamilton McCollister's original tract, which is held in trust by the society for use as a church and for no other use. In 1788, Nov. 14, Savage and Conkey attorneys for the propritors executed a deed which conveyed to the trustees of the New England congregation the three lots, numbered 91, 188, and 192 " for the sole use of supporting a regular gospel minister of the presbyterian persuasion belonging to the Synod of New York and Philadelphia, in and over said congregation in Salem." The second meeting house was seventy-five feet long and sixty feet wide with the pulpit and sounding board on one side of the audience room, and the pews were the usual square high box-like enclosures of the olden time.

The first pastor settled over this church was the Rev. John Warford of Amwell N. J. who commenced his labors in 1788, laboring with great success until his death in 1802.

The original membership of the first incorporated presbyterian congregation in Salem, the one founded by New England people, quite a number of whom were from Pelham, Mass., consisted of fifty-two persons. For fifty years following the membership is said not to have exceeded one hundred. In 1828 there was a membership of two hundred and eighty. In 1832 the number had increased to four hundred and twenty-six. This was the highest number ever reached, and from that time the decrease in membership began. In 1842 there was only three hundred and five members, in 1876 the number was one hundred and seventy-three, and a little over two hundred in 1896.

The little settlement begun by James Turner and Joshua Conkey in 1761 makes a much better showing to-day than the old town of Pelham from which they sallied forth, and plunged into the wilderness to reach and establish their new home.

The village of Salem contains about twelve hundred inhabitants and in the whole town there was about four thousand, while Pelham has only four hundred and eighty-six. The main facts of the above sketch of the settlement of Salem were gathered from The Salem Book printed in 1896, and other historical pamphlets relating to the town of Salem, N. Y.

The people who went out from Pelham through the forests to begin a new settlement at White Creek were quite peaceable men and women who respected the rights of others and at the same time resented any and all invasions of their own rights and privileges, and would not hesitate to oppose any one whom they believed was endeavoring in any way to prevent the full enjoyment of their liberties. They made no exceptions when the King's officers came among them armed with authority from the King's representatives, if they knew the charges had no basis of fact to rest upon; any officer who came among them under such circumstances was liable to meet with a hot reception. This estimate of the temper of Scotch farmers of that time is borne out by the reception extended to Sheriff Solomon Boltwood of Amherst who made an official visit to Pelham on the twelfth of February 1762. Just what his official business may have been does not appear, but the manner in which he was received makes it quite clear that the official errand was considered an affront which justified resistance by every means at hand, the men and the women taking part in resisting him, the weapons selected being those that were most handy when the determination to resist seized them.

The resistance to the sheriff evidently occured on the twelfth of February 1762, but the record of the trial and acquittal is dated a year later and is copied from the court records at Northampton.

"NORTHAMPTON FEB. 18, 1763.

DE REX VS SAVAGE &c.

John Worthington Esq. Attorney to our Soverign Lord the King in this behalf here instantly complains and give this court to understand and be informed that John Savage of Pelham in the County of Hampshire Gent.

Alexander Turner Yeoman, Alexander Turner Jun. Yeoman, James Turner, Yeoman, Robert Gilmore, Yeoman, Hamilton McCollister, Yeoman, Jane Savage, Spinster, wife of John Savage Jun., Elisibeth Savage, Spinster, Eleanor McCollister, Spinster, and Sarah Drane, Spinster, all of Pelham aforesaid, did at said Pelham on the 12th day of February last past, with force and arms, that is to say, with Axes, Clubs, sticks, hot water and hot soap in a riotous and tumultinous manner and riotously and unlawfully meet and assemble themselves together to disturb the peace of the said Lord the King, and the said John Savage, Alexander Turner, Alexander Turner Jun., James Turner, Robert Gilmore, Hamilton McCollister, Jane Savage, Eleanor Mc-Collister, Elisibeth Savage, and Sarah Drane, being so met and assembled together did then and there with force and arms made an assault on one Solomon Boltwood of Amherst, then, and ever since being a Deputy Sheriff under Oliver Partridge Esq. Sheriff of said County, he being then in due execution of his said office and in the peace of God and of the said Lord the King, and then and there uttered menace and threatenings of bodily hurt and death against said Solomon, and then and there, with force and arms, obstructed, opposed, hindered and wholly prevented said Solomon from the due execution of his said office contrary to law, and against the peace of the said Lord the King, his crown and dignity, and now comes before ye court the said John Savage, Gent., and Alexander first above named, the said Jane, Elisibeth, and Sarah being held by Recognisance for this purpose, the said James, Robert and ye other Alexander not being present, and being set to the bar and severally put to plead and answer to the premise, they the said def'ts severally plead that they were in nothing guilty of the same and thereof put themselves on ye County.

A Jury being sworn according to law to try the issue between our said Lord the King, and the said Def'ts after a full hearing return their verdict therein, that is, the jury on their oath say the said Def'ts are not guilty. It is thereupon ordered that the Def'ts be dismissed and ye go without day."

The result of the trial being a verdict of not guilty for the heinous offence charged was so complete a vindication of those whose names appear in the indictment that we are forced to the conclusion that "axes, clubs, sticks, hot water, and hot soap" were fit weapons for resistance to injustice of some sort at the hands of the sheriff of said Lord the King.

We cannot but admire the grit and vim displayed by these men and women in resistance to what this King's officer was commissioned to preform if they knew there was no valid reason for his presence among them. It seems to have been a case of justifiable self defence, and the jury by their verdict were evidently unanimous in that view of the case. A year later and some of these men and women started out on horseback on the long journey through the forest to begin the settlement at White Creek now Salem, Washington county N. Y. If there could have been any question of their qualifications for pioneering and taking care of themselves in a new settlement the above episode from the court records would be amply sufficient to dispel all doubts on that score. Not all of the self-reliant and plucky men and women went out from Pelham to White Creek, there were others of the same self-reliant positive sort left in the old town.

Professional and Business Men,

NATIVES OF PELHAM.

The Southworths. — The Southworth family, a branch of which settled in Pelham during the latter part of the last century and probably after the Revolutionary war, is traced in an unbroken line from Sir Gilbert Southworth of Southworth Hall, Lancaster, England, in the fourteenth century through ten generations in that country. The following is the line: Sir Gilbert, Sir John, Sir Thomas, Richard Southworth of Salisbury, Sir Christopher, Sir John, Sir Thomas of Warrington, Richard of London, Sir Thomas, recorder of wills, Somersetsthire, to Edward who in 1598 married Alice Carpenter, daughter of Alexander Carpenter.

Mr. Edward Southworth with his two sons Thomas and Constant, fled to Holland with the Pilgrim Fathers who left England on account of the persecution of Dissenters by the Church of England. After a few years residence in the city of Leyden Mr. Southworth died. Alice Southworth the widow of Edward came over to this country in 1623 and married Governor William Bradford second Governor of the colony at Plymouth. Her sons Thomas and Constant followed their mother to America in 1628. Constant was born in 1614. In 1639 he married Elizabeth Coltier of Duxbury, and three sons were born to them Edward, Nathaniel and William.

Edward, son of Nathaniel, had four sons, Constant, Edward, Samuel and Benjamin.

Edward married Lydia Packard, Dec. 16, 1750, to them were born Uriah, Perez, Desire, Edward, Abiah, Bridget, Lydia and Fear. All of these children of Edward and Lydia, except Perez, removed from Bridgewater to Pelham.

Abiah Southworth married Kesiah Boltwood of Amherst in 1794.

Wells Southworth. — Was the son of Dr. Abiah Southworth and Kesiah Boltwood Southworth, and was born in Pelham August 17, 1799. He first engaged in business at Pelham in 1823

WELLS SOUTHWORTH.

as a merchant, continuing the business at the center of the town until 1828 when he disposed of his store and the family homestead without consulting his father, so it is said. Dr. Southworth was somewhat disturbed at first, but having such great confidence in his son's good judgement and business foresight that he acquisced in the business change thereby necessitated, and the family removed to South Hadley Falls, where Wells opened as a merchant.

Wells Southworth removed to Chicopee Falls and continued in the mercantile line until 1839 when he removed to Mittineague, West Springfield, where he built a mill for manufacturing fine writing papers, now owned by the Southworth Paper Co. and for many years was the president of the corporation.

In 1854 Mr. Southworth removed from West Springfield to New Haven, Conn. In the spring of the following year he organized the City of New Haven Fire Insurance Company and was president of the company for ten years. He was a stockholder and director in the Tradesman's Bank of New Haven for many years from its organization. Mr. Southworth was also a large stockholder in the New York, New Haven and Hartford railroad, and engaged in other business enterprises. In early life he was a Whig in politics and later a republican was elected a member of the Massachusetts legislature for two years from Springfield, and one year represented West Springfield in the House. Mr. Southworth was living in Pelham when Amherst College was established at Amherst and was greatly interested as a young man in the enterprise, and did what he could to aid in building south college, the first building erected. He drove a yoke of cattle from Pelham with the first load of stone delivered on College hill for the foundation of south dormitory, and they to-day are doing their part in supporting the walls of that well known and most ancient building on the college grounds.

Mr. Southworth was married three times. His first wife was Miss Rebecca C. Woodburn of Salem, Mass., she died in 1839. For his second wife he married Mrs. Frances R. Lyon, daughter of Mrs. E. T. Smith of South Hadley. In 1845 he married Miss Harriet M. Jillet of Rome, N. Y.

The other members of Dr. Southworth's family were as follows: Rufus, Mary, Edward and Martha.

Rufus was born in 1796 and died at Charleston S. C. in 1828.

Edward, born in 1804 and died in 1869. Mary, born Nov. 6, 1797, died in Pelham, 1872. Martha, born May 10, 1807, married Robert Curtis of Bridgewater.

Dr. Abiah Southworth died at South Hadley Falls, Dec. 27, 1835. His wife, Kesiah Boltwood, died in April of the same year.

Edward Southworth, son of Dr. Abiah Southworth, and brother of Wells and Rufus was born in Pelham July, 3, 1804. Attended the public schools of the town until he was sixteen, was then sent to Amherst academy where he prepared for college. He entered Harvard College in 1822 and was graduated in 1826 in a class which numbered many eminent men among its members. After graduation he went to Charleston S. C. as instructor in ancient languages, in an academy which his brother Rufus had established, and was the principal. Rufus died in 1828 at 32, and Edward succeeded him as principal of the school, but was obliged to return to the north in 1833 on account of ill health. On his return from Charleston he was engaged in business at South Hadley Falls for several years, then removed to West Springfield and with his brother Wells established The Southworth Manufacturing Company, for making fine writing papers; was postmaster several years at West Springfield, and in 1853 was elected as representative to the Legislature and served two years. He was elected state senator in 1854 but would not take his seat which had been contested by another candidate, although the seat was accorded to him and against his opponent by vote of that honorable body.

With his cousin John H. Southworth of Springfield and his brother Wells he organized the Hampshire Paper Company of South Hadley Falls, and The Hampden Paint and Chemical Company of Springfield Mass; was treasurer of the Southworth Manufacturing Company; director of the Fire and Marine Insurance Company of Springfield, and of the Agawam bank of the same city, and of the Massasoit paper company of Holyoke, and a trustee of the Hampden Savings Bank of Springfield.

He was a trustee of Mount Holyoke Seminary from its opening until his death in 1869 at West Springfield. Mr. Southworth was for many years a member of the First Congregational Church at West Springfield and for thirty years one of its deacons.

He was married three times and six children survived him.

EDWARD SOUTHWORTH.

Daniel Thompson, M. D., son of James and Matilda Thompson, was born in Pelham, Jan. 14, 1800, where his father and grandfather had passed most of their lives as farmers. The maiden name of his paternal grandmother was Mary Cowan, a surname that appears among the first settlers of the town, and Mary Cowan was of Scotch descent. His mother was Matilda Pierce of Middleboro, Mass. He was educated by attendance at the public schools of his native town, and at Amherst Academy. His medical education was obtained at Northampton, supplemented by the full course of lectures at the Berkshire Medical Institution at Pittsfield during the years from 1823 to 1825.

He began the practice of his profession at Pelham in 1825 and remained there twelve years. In 1827 he married Caroline A. Hunt, daughter of Dr. David Hunt of Northampton, and in 1837 Dr. Thompson removed to Northampton. In 1839 he entered into copartnership with Dr. Benjamin Barrett, with whom he had studied, and they were associated together for seven years when Dr. Barrett retired from active practise, and from the firm.

His next partner in business was his brother Dr. James Thompson also a native of Pelham, and the brothers were associated in business until the death of Dr. James, Aug. 6, 1859. Dr. James Thompson was a skillful physician and had an extensive practice in Northampton and vicinity. After the death of Dr. James, Dr. Daniel naturally turned to his nephew Dr. A. W. Thompson who was then admitted to partnership for a few years, and then it was dissolved, and from that time until his death May 25, 1883, he pursued his chosen profession alone.

Dr. Daniel Thompson was a skillful and successful physician who secured a competance by his profession, and was noted for generosity and liberality in the use of the means he had gathered during his long professional career.

Austin W. Thompson, A. M., M. D., was born in Pelham, May 22, 1834.

His father, Peleg P. Thompson, died when his son Austin was but four years old and the boy was received into the family of Dr. Daniel Thompson then living at Pelham, and a few years later went with the Doctor's family to Northampton.

He laid the foundation of his education by attending the public schools and later was a student in the Northampton Collegiate Institute. After finishing his course at the Institute he decided upon a thorough college course and was fitted for college by Rev. Rufus Ellis.

He graduated at Harvard College in 1854, having the "salutatory" oration. After graduation he read law a few months with Judge Huntington. Tiring of the study of law he decided to turn his attention to medicine and began his studies with his uncle Dr. Daniel Thompson, and on completing them began practise, making a specialty of mental diseases, and was appointed assistant superintendent at the Northampton Lunatic Hospital, which he held for two years.

Resigning his position on account of failing health he resumed general practice, and later established the institution known as Shady Lawn, a medical home for invalids.

He was president of the Hampshire County Medical Society in 1856 and 1857, and was a member of the Massachusetts Medical Society.

Ira P. Rankin was born in Pelham, Jan. 10, 1817, in that part of the town known as "The Valley." He was a son of Zebina Rankin. Zebina Rankin's ancestors were from the north of Ireland, where many of the people of Scotland had lived previous to their coming to Massachusetts and to Pelham. The surname first appears upon the records written Rinkin, then Rinken, and later Rankin.

Zebina Rankin removed from Pelham to Ohio when Ira P. was about fourteen years of age. The son plead with his father to be allowed to remain in Massachusetts and his request was finally acceded too. After the removal of his father and the rest of the family to Ohio, Ira went to Enfield and entered the store of Oliver Bryant, where he was employed for several years.

Mr. Rankin was married to Miss Caroline Bryant, a cousin of William Cullen Bryant at Northampton, in 1841. Mrs. Rankin died in 1881, leaving no children. From Enfield he went to Boston.

After residing in Boston for nearly twenty years he removed to San Francisco. This was about the year 1852, soon after the diccovery of gold and the rush for that state was on.

He engaged in business there, was successful, became a member of The Chamber of Commerce and continued a member for twenty-seven years; was a prominent church man and a liberal giver of his wealth to benevolent purposes originating with the churches and otherwise.

IRA P. RANKIN.

Mr. Rankin received the appointment as collector of the port of San Francisco from President Abraham Lincoln, and performed the duties of that responsible position with ability, and great credit to himself and to the satisfaction of the merchants of San Francisco as well as to the government at Washington.

Mr. Rankin's first business venture in San Francisco was in a general commission firm on Front street, under the name of Rankin & Co. This was so successful that after a few years he was enabled to sell out at a profit and became a partner in the Pacific Iron Works. The firm name, Goddard & Co., was changed to Rankin & Brayton after his entrance. This firm was one of the largest of its kind on the coast. It dealt in mining machinery, marine and milling goods. After many years Mr. Rankin absorbed all the interests of the firm, and at his retirement, when the Pacific Iron Works became absorbed in the Union Works he was sole owner.

The political interests of Mr. Rankin were always on the side of the Republican party. He took an active part in the formation of the party in the state. Before that he took an active interest in the People's party. He was a most pronounced Whig. In 1856 and again in 1875 he was the Republican candidate for Congress, and was defeated each time.

The positions of public trust that Mr. Rankin has filled in San Francisco are numerous. He was one of the original Trustees of the College of California, and did active work for the bill incorporating it as a University. During the iron moulders' strike Mr. Rankin was placed at the head of the Manufacturers' Association, organized against them. For twenty-seven years he was a member of the Chamber of Commerce, and in 1889 was its President. He was a Trustee of the Lick Trust, and President and life member of the Mercantile Library.

Mr. Rankin was actively interested in philanthropic matters, and for that reason was many years a Trustee in the Society for the Prevention of Cruelty to Children, the Society for the Prevention of Cruelty to Animals, and the Society for the Suppression of Vice. He was Chairman of the State Board of Commissioners for selecting a site for the Deaf and Dumb Asylum, and also Chairman of the Building Committee of the same institution. He was President of the Engineers' and Foundrymen's Association, of San Francisco, and interested in all matters pertaining to the iron business.

Mr. Rankin died October 1, 1895, highly esteemed as a business man and christian. His funeral was attended by many of the first citizens and business men of the city of San Francisco. After the close of the exercises a stranger stepped forward and announced himself as Edward Rankin, a brother of the deceased.

None present had ever seen the man nor had anyone ever heard of Ira P. having a brother or even relatives of any degree nearer than cousins. The stranger backed his claims by offering to bring forward proofs of his kinship, which he did to the satisfaction of all. Edward Rankin proved by indisputable facts and records that he was a son of Zebina Rankin, born in Ohio, and that he came to California about three years after Ira came from Boston, and he had resided within fifty miles of San Francisco during all the years,

DR. JAMES DUNLAP.

since 1854. He had known of his brother by hearing of his prominence as a business man and public officer, but had not taken pains to claim blood relationship until he learned of the death of his distinguished brother.

Edward Rankin is a carpenter by trade. An industrious, honest man.

James Dunlap, M. D., was the son of John and Mary Dunlap, born in Pelham, February 13, 1819.

The name Dunlap appears on the records of the town as early as 1743, but no one of the name was among those who drew home lots after the first survey in 1739.

The family is of Scotch descent and the Dunlap farms were located about a mile southwest of the center of the town. There appear upon the records the names of Andrew, James, and William Dunlap, besides John already alluded to. William was familiarly known as Uncle Billy, and was noted for his broad Scotch accent in conversation. Dr. Dunlap attended the district schools of his native town and became a teacher, or schoolmaster, in Pelham, and possibly in other nearby towns. He was a student at Williston Seminary, in the first class at the opening of the institution, and fitted for admission to Amherst College and entered that institution in 1843, where he remained until 1845. Five years later he graduated at the College of Physicians and Surgeons in New York City, and at once entered upon the practice of his profession at Northampton, where he continued actively engaged for forty-five years or more, or until his death, August 3, 1896.

At the time of his death Dr. Dunlap was the oldest practising physician in the city. He was devoted to his profession and never refused to answer a call for his services, whether it came from the rich or the poor. His office was always open for consultation to those who needed his services, and during the latter part of his life answered calls to visit the sick that much younger men in the profession had declined because of the distance, the cold or storm. He never took a vacation from his business, and was never married. He was quiet and retiring in his tastes, was rarely seen in social assemblies, and seldom took an active part in any movement of public interest, he seemed to detest anything like personal publicity and never sought to gain a reputation for himself by the common methods employed by many good men. Dr. Dunlap never sought offices of trust and responsibility, yet he was called to serve as a director in the Hampshire County National Bank at the time of its incorporation, and held the position until he resigned, in 1880. He was also one of the Trustees of the Hampshire Savings Bank for many years, and at the time of his death was senior Vice-president of the institution. He served as President of the Hampshire County Medical Society for several years and was much interested in everything pertaining to the welfare of the organization. He gave much time and attention to forwarding the establishment of the Dickinson Hospital, was on the staff of hospital physicians and was cared for at the hospital during the last weeks of his life. Owing to his frugal mode of life and constant attention to his profession he succeeded in accumulating a handsome property variously estimated at from $30,000 to $50,000 and even higher. No portion of his property was donated to the city or to public institutions but was distributed by will to relatives.

Dr. Dunlap was taken ill about the first of July, and believing that the pure air on the hill-tops of his native town would restore him to health and strength again, he took rooms at Hotel Pelham, and remained about a week, but as there was no improvement, he was taken back to Northampton, and was cared for at the Dickinson Hospital until his death.

In all of his long professional life at Northampton he was trusted and respected by a wide circle of families who had need of his professional services, and outside the city, in the surrounding towns, his services were also in demand; and in some families he had been called to attend the sick for nearly half a century. During his long life his influence was given in favor of those measures that were for the best interests of the people among whom he dwelt.

The Harkness Family was one of note, and of much influence in the affairs of the town, as well as in the social relations of the section in which they lived. They were earnest, active, industrious people, thoroughly honest and capable, and of Scotch descent. They occupied large farms in the western part of the town and their lands extended to the dividing line between Amherst and Pelham.

William Harkness, the first of the name in this vicinity, was the son of William and came from Scotland to Massachusetts in 1710,

DR. HARVEY WILLSON HARKNESS,

when but seven years old. He married Ann Gray, July 28, 1748, a daughter of one of the Grays who settled in Pelham, and possibly this was the reason of his being drawn to Pelham after the settlement of the town.

The children of William Harkness were John, William, David, James, Daniel, Jonathan and Nancy. The children of these six sons and one daughter numbered fifty, forty-four of them bearing the surname Harkness. Nancy Harkness married Dea. Nathaniel Sampson who lived on the farm occupied for many years by Rev. John Jones in the west part of the town. Of the fifty children of the six sons and one daughter of William Harkness, twenty-six were daughters, and twenty-four were sons. John Harkness had eight children ; William, seven ; David, three ; James, nine ; Daniel, nine ; Jonathan, eight ; and Nancy, six. The descendants had nearly all removed from Pelham before 1850.

The descendants of these Pelham-born people are scattered in almost every state in the Union. Huron county, Ohio, Fulton and Peoria counties, Illinois, hold many of he descendants of James Harkness. Descendants of John are more widely scattered : some in California, some in Utah, others in Covington, Tioga county, Pa., still others in Elmira, N. Y. Of the descendants of Nancy, some went to Vermont, others are scattered in various parts of the country. Descendants of Daniel are in Peoria county, Illinois, and in Ohio. Descendants of William are found in Huron county, Ohio, and in Auburn, N. Y. Daniel's descendants are in Peoria county, Illinois. While those of David and Jonathan are not as definitely located. The following sketches of members of the Harkness family are of the descendants of John, and sons of John jr., born in Pelham.

A son of William[4] is living in Biloxi, La. and has a large family. His name is John Harkness and he removed to the South before the war of the Rebellion. There are a few of the name in Amherst, also descendants of William, but there is not one of the name in the town whence they sprang, in short—

"They are scattered far and wide, o'er Mount and Stream and Sea."

Harvey Willson Harkness, M. D., was born May 25, 1821, in the farm house still standing on the south side of the county road, a little west of the site of the Orient House—the farm at that time and for some years previous, being a part of a large tract of land owned by the Harknesses. He attended the public schools of the town during the years usually devoted to getting a common school education in the country towns at that time, supplementing it by several terms at Williston Seminary. He then entered upon the study of medicine in the office of Drs. Barrett and Thompson, at Northampton.

Leaving Northampton he went to the Berkshire Medical College, at Pittsfield, where he graduated in 1847. Dr. Harkness then went west and located in St. Joseph, Missouri.

When the news of the discovery of gold in California caused the breaking out of the gold fever and the consequent exodus for the newly discovered gold fields, in 1849, Dr. Harkness with others set out across the untravelled plains west of the Missouri with ox-teams and after a long weary journey, the party arrived in California in September of that year.

He located at Sacramento and commenced the practice of his profession among those of the eagar gold-diggers who fell sick. The town increased in population very fast, owing to the influx of eastern men in search of gold, and soon the need of schools forced the people to organize them and Dr. Harkness became a leader in the movement which resulted in establishing a permanent system of schools in the City of Sacramento, and he was elected the first school superintendent.

The citizens of Sacramento appreciated his services in organizing and superintendance at the time, and a few years since, after erecting a fine school building, named it the Harkness School in recognition of his services for the schools in the early days, and that the memory of his services might be kept fresh for years to come.

Dr. Harkness was present by invitation at the formal opening of the Pacific railroad, May 10, 1869, when the lines were connected that made passage across the continemt by rail possible, and in behalf of the State of California, presented the golden spike used on that occasion in making the final connection of the rails of the two roads—one having been built from California east, and the other over the mountains and across the plains toward the west.

Retiring from active practice of his profession in June, 1869, he visited Europe and the East, and was present as an invited guest at the opening of the Suez Canal, on the 17th of November of the same year.

Having retired from the practice of medicine Dr. Harkness devoted his time and attention to scientific investigation and removed to San Francisco. Since his removal to San Francisco he has been an active member of the California Academy of Sciences for the past fifteen years, having served eight years as its President.

In 1886, and while Dr. Harkness was President of the Academy of Sciences, the society erected a magnificent building for the better accommodation of its scientific departments, library and museum, at an expense of $450,000.

Dr. Harkness has spent much time in foreign travel for pleasure and scientific investigation, visiting Europe on four different occasions, and spending two winters in Northern Africa.

He was elected a life member of the British Association in 1877, and is honorary member of several European scientific societies.

At present, though 76 years of age, the Doctor is serving as one of the Regents of the Stanford University, and is actively engaged in microscopical research in various lines, giving special attention to the Mypogaci of the Pacific coast.

In 1895 Dr. Harkness declined further service as President of the Academy of Sciences and was succeeded by Prof. David Starr Jordan.

Martin Kingman Harkness, a brother of Dr. H. W. Harkness, was born in Pelham, in 1831, at the farmhouse on the highway leading from the county road at West Pelham to Belchertown, known for many years as the Sylvester Jewett place, and at present occupied by Charles P. Jewett.

Mr. Harkness attended the public schools of the town and at 17 years of age accompanied his brother on the ox-team journey across the plains to California in 1849. He has been engaged in mining most of the time somewhere in the mining regions of the Pacific slope, and for the past twenty years has been a resident of Salt Lake City, engaged as superintendent for a Pittsburg mining company.

Henry Harkness, youngest brother of Dr. H. W. Harkness, was born at the Sylvester Jewett farm, near the western line of Pelham, in 1833. He spent his boyhood on the home farm until the death of his oldest brother Sumner, and in 1852 set out for California by way of the Isthmus of Panama to join his brothers already there. He engaged in mining most of the time until his death at Auburn, Cal. in March, 1895.

Sumner J. Harkness, son of Sumner Harkness and a nephew of Dr. H. W. Harkness, was born at the Jewett farm in Pelham, and joined his uncles on the western shore of the continent about the year 1873. He is a resident of Scofield, Utah. Has served as Judge of Probate and is engaged in mining and stock raising.

William Pomeroy Daniels was born in Pelham, May 11, 1815. His parents, Joseph and Lucy Daniels, moved to Pelham from Worcester, Mass., where they lived on a farm located at the site of the present Union station. Their Pelham residence was in a little house near the Orient house on the south side of the road leading to the Methodist church. The subject of our sketch had almost no school privileges, a few terms at the district school being the limit of his opportunity. Before he was fifteen years of age he was " put out to work." A boy of that age to-day would count it a hardship to be obliged to start for his work by four o'clock in the morning, with lunch and dinner in his hand to be eaten frozen, with snow deep and no companion to share the hours and then to chop wood in the wilderness until dark. Such was the experience of this boy. He often told of it in later days but with no consciousness of hardship beyond the loneliness of the work. He served an apprenticeship as carpenter and for a considerable time was connected with the factories of Barre, Mass., as carpenter and repairer. It was the custom in those days for the native born girls to be factory help and the best girls left farm and country villages for this purpose. Here in Barre he became acquainted with Miss H. Ann Stark of Hanover, N. H., who became his wife June 4, 1837. They began their home life on a farm in Lyme, N. H., where they resided, Mr. Daniels dividing his time between the farm and his trade as carpenter, until 1853, when the family consisting of four sons and one daughter, removed to Worcester, Mass. Here he became a builder and contractor, and later a lumber merchant owning one of the prosperous lumber yards of the growing city. He never sought or held public office, but was known as an honorable business man, interested in the welfare of the city. Of a puritan type of thought, he loved his Bible, the Lord's Day and his Church. During the later years of his life he was a large and constant contributor to Christian institutions. His mind early turned with abhorance to the iniquities of slavery and he was an abolitionist long before the war appeared as arbiter of righteousness. He

JUDGE ITHAMAR CONKEY.

BIRTHPLACE OF JUDGE ITHAMAR CONKEY.

gave to his country in the war of the Rebellion the costly offering of two sons, both victims of the battle field. Then he gave to the freedmen of the south his hearty sympathy in their efforts for Christian education. He was a Republican in politics in those days when great moral questions were maintained by its platform. Many far away schools, churches and christian workers shared his unostentatious charities. He delighted to give loving helpful sympathy to those whom the less thoughtful might overlook. Of a quiet, undemonstrative temperament, of Quaker origin, his life was one of deeds more than words. In the summer of 1873 during a season of ill health he felt a great desire to spend a little time with his cousin Thomas Buffum of Pelham. Here within one mile of his birthplace, which he had left more than forty years before as a lad, he died on the nineteenth of September, 1873, aged fifty-eight years and five months. His daughter became the wife of Hon. Frank T. Blackmer, a prominent lawyer in Worcester. One of his sons holds an influential position in the same city as the general superintendent of the Washburn, Moen Manufacturing Company. The other son is an alumnus of Amherst college and a well known minister of the Congregational denomination, having been recently elected to the responsible position of corresponding secretary of the American Board of Commissioners for Foreign Missions, with residence in Boston.

Ithamar Conkey was the seventh son of John Conkey and Margaret Abercrombie, and was born May 7, 1788, there were besides, three daughters. His father was a leading man in the town, and his mother was a daughter of Rev. Robert Abercrombie, the first settled minister at Pelham. He studied law with Noah Dickinson Mattoon at Amherst and opened a law office in his native town in 1814. He was elected town clerk of Pelham in 1816 and for the two following years. In 1818, N. D. Mattoon having removed to the west, Mr. Conkey succeeded to the business of the office at Amherst and removed to Amherst; was chosen special commissioner for Hampshire county in 1828, and was elected county commissioner in 1830; was appointed Judge of Probate for the county by Lieut. Governor Armstrong, acting as Governor, in 1834 and held the office continually until 1858; was a member of the Constitutional convention for the revision of the Constitution in 1853. Judge Conkey married Elizabeth Clapp Kellogg, daughter of Deacon John Kellogg of North

Amherst, Jan. 26, 1820. Miss Kellogg lived in the family of Gen. Ebenezer Mattoon from the age of seven until marriage, her mother, Roxana Mattoon, was a sister of the General. Judge Conkey had four children, but all died when quite young except Ithamar F. Conkey, who studied law and became the leading lawyer of Amherst until his death Aug. 8, 1875, aged 52. Judge Conkey was a leading member of the Second Congregational church and his residence and law office were in that part of the town known as East Amherst. He delivered the address at the Centennial celebration of the incorporation of the town of Pelham, Jan. 16, 1843. After his services for twenty-eight years as Judge of Probate, he retired form active interest in legal business and directed the work upon his farm until his death, October 30, 1862. He was the last of the family of seven sons and three daughters, children of John and Margaret Conkey of Pelham, whose names follow :

Israel	born April, 1774—	died May,	1814.
Daniel	" Sept., 1775—	" July,	1855.
Joshua	" Feb., 1777—	" April,	1790.
John	" Dec., 1778—	" May,	1853.
Isaac	" Dec., 1780—	" ——	1822.
Sarah	" May, 1782—	" June,	1855.
Eleazer	" Feb., 1784—	" Feb.,	1808.
Anna	" April, 1786—	" Sept.,	1835.
Ithamar	" May, 1788—	" Oct.,	1862.
Mehitable	" Feb., 1791—	" ——	——.

Adam Johnson was a son of Adam Johnson, one of the original settlers of the town who drew home lots Nos. 34 and 52, and built his house on No. 34, which is the farm now occupied by S. F. Arnold Esq., whose house can be seen upon the Pelham slope, looking straight east from Amherst college. It was on this farm that Adam Johnson the subject of this sketch was born about 1753, and he continued to live on the home lot, No. 34, until 1800, when he disposed of his farm to Samuel Arnold for $3000. He was somewhat incapacitated for the heavy farm work by lameness, which was probably the cause of his retiring from the labors of the farm. Mr. Johnson removed to the Valley and afterwards lived on the John Gray farm, now occupied by Levi Moulton. It is believed that he had other money or property than that received for his farm, and having no family and but few near relatives, save perhaps a sister and one brother ; when more than 70 years old and in declining health the matter of the disposition of his property became a question for consideration. Amherst College had but recently been incorporated and had erected but one building, (South College) and was in sore need of a chapel. The era of rich men and liberal donors to the struggling college had not arrived, and some of the trustees and friends of the college presented the great need of a chapel to Mr. Johnson for his consideration; and either at first, or later, the proposition to have the proposed new chapel known as "Johnson Chapel," in case he should decide to bequeath his property to the trustees for use in erecting the much needed building, was added, as an inducement or appeal which they hoped would be effectual in influencing Mr. Johnson to make his will as they desired to have him. The trustees were successful. Samuel F. Dickinson, Esq., of Amherst, who had made frequent calls upon Mr. Johnson to present the needs of the college, was called upon to write the will which bequeathed the accumulations of a lifetime to the trustees of Amherst College. There was but a few thousand dollars but it was probably the largest bequest the college had received up to that time.

The total inventory under the will was $6,559.12. Of this sum $4,000 was donated for the use of "The Collegiate Charity Institution in Amherst." The will was executed on the 6th of February, 1823, but the final decision that the will should stand was not made by the court until 1826, owing to the strong and persistent attempt to have the will set aside, which was made by Thomas Johnson, the testator's brother, on the ground that undue influence had been brought to bear upon the testator, who, as Thomas claimed, was in a weakened and unfit condition of mind to dispose of his property. In 1827, Thomas Johnson, who was a poor man living in Greenfield, having been cut off by his brother Adam with a paltry legacy of $12, issued a pamphlet of twenty-four pages, entitled "The Last Will and Testament of Thomas Johnson of Greenfield, County of Franklin, in favour of the Trustees of Amherst College."

In this last will Thomas bequeathed the trustees a good generous piece of his mind concerning the covetous tactics he believed had been employed in getting possession of his brother Adam's property. The pamphlet abounds in Scripture quotations which he believed applicable to the Amherst trustees, a few paragraphs of which may be interesting here.

"And although imperfection cannot keep the law perfectly, yet if we are volunteers in coveting and taking our neighbors' property, contrary to the law of God, then the transgressor must be condemned by the law: which brings me to consider what was the cause of dispute between the heirs of Adam Johnson, late of Pelham, deceased, and the trustees of Amherst College; to which I answer, the dispute was because Amherst trustees were making merchandise of the poor, the widow and the fatherless, all of which is in direct opposition to God's law, which brings down the judgements of God in this world, and eternal damnation, which the word of God makes manifest, as you may see. 2 Peter ii-3: And through covetousness shall they with feigned words make merchandise of you, whose judgment now of a long time lingereth not, and their damnation slumbereth not. Secondly, Luke 20, 47: Which devour widows houses, and for a show make long prayers; the same shall receive greater damnation. Yea Mathew and Mark give the same account respecting damnation to hypocrites and devourers of widows houses. See Matt. xxiii, 14; Mark xii, 40. With respect to covetousness, inspiration saith:—There is a generation whose teeth are as swords, and their jaw teeth as knives, to devour the poor from off the earth and the needy from among men."

The closing paragraph follows:

"Nevertheless, as Amherst trustees never rested until they got the principal part of my brothers property into their possession; and as I am an old man, and therefore must be near the close of life, and my earthly property all consumed, yet would attempt to *will and bequeath*, as a memorandum this composition of Scripture truth, for the benefit of Amherst TRUSTEES, with all interested in the college, with which I close this essay, in the words of the Apostle Paul, namely, Am I therefore become your enemy, because I tell you the *Truth?*—THOMAS JOHNSON."

In the West burying ground, at the head of Mr. Johnson's grave, is a plain white marble slab with the following inscription : "Adam Johnson, Esq. Died August, 1823, aged 70 years. Erected by the trustees of Amherst College in testimony of their gratitude for the Johnson Chapel."

James N. Smith only son of James Smith and Betsey Otis Smith was born in Pelham, March 25, 1826. He came of Revolutionary stock and was a lineal descendant in the maternal line of James Otis, well known as one of the most powerful and persistent opponents of the acts of the British Parliament for taxing the American colonies.

The early life of young Smith was spent at Pelham where he laid the foundation of his education in the public schools of the town. Later he attended the celebrated Leicester Academy at Leicester, Mass., from which he was graduated and while quite a young man

COL. JAMES N. SMITH.

went West. Before going west he engaged in railroad building by contract and it was while engaged in building a railroad at Lock Haven, Pa. that he was first married, but his first experience in railroad building was in superintending railroad work at Willimantic, Conn. He was engaged in railroad building at Oskalousa, Ia. when the war of the Rebellion broke out. He joined the 7th Iowa regiment as a line officer and hurried to the front, and subsequently commanded a cavalry regiment. After the war Colonel Smith became actively engaged in railroad building again in New York, Pennsylvania, the New England and Western states, under the firm name of Smith & Ripley. When Commodore Vanderbilt and the men associated with him determined upon the gigantic scheme for sinking the tracks of the New York Central and Hudson River railroad from the Grand Central station toward Harlem the contract was awarded to Dillon, Clyde & Co., Mr. Clyde being the active manager of the work, but when work was only about half done Mr. Clyde died and Colonel Smith assumed full management of the great and difficult contract which he completed. Other large contracts on which Colonel Smith was engaged were: The extension of the Delaware, Lackawanna & Western road, a large section of the Northern Pacific railway, the Enterprise, Atlantic Coast & Indian River railroad in Florida, besides many branch lines in various parts of the country. Colonel Smith assisted in the formation of the Brooklyn, Flatbush & Coney Island railroad company and built the road as sole contractor, and served for sometime as President of the company. Among his business associates were many of the leading capitalists of the time in New York, including Hon. William H. Barnum, chairman of the Democratic National committee and Sidney Dillon, President of the Union Pacific railway, who was his brother-in-law. Colonel Smith contracted for the double tracking of the Morris & Essex railroad from Madison to Morristown, and from Dover, N. J. to Easton, Pa. He was senior partner of the firm that built the Weekawken tunnel for the West Shore road.

Few men were more conspicuous or instrumental in developing the railway system of the country, and none more conscientious or efficient in the execution of the great contracts committed to him. He was a man of prodigious energy and of great executive ability, and noted for his uncompromising fidelity to his professional obligations.

Politically, Colonel Smith was a stalwart republican. As a warm friend and admirer of General Grant and Roscoe Conkling, he always clung to that wing of the party. He contributed liberally always for the legitimate campaign needs of the party, and took an active part in the leadership among republicans of the twentieth ward and frequently represented the party at local and state conventions. He was a candidate for the republican congressional nomination in the third New York district in 1884, and again in 1886, being defeated the first time by Darwin R. James, and later by S. V. White, but he did not allow defeat to cool the ardor of his party faith and interest. During the pastorate of Rev. H. W. Beecher at Plymouth church, Colonel Smith was a prominent member of the church and a warm friend of the people.

His city residence was 265 Clinton Avenue, Brooklyn. His summer home was a fine farm well stocked with the best Holstein and Alderney cattle, a few miles out of Litchfield Conn., and it was to his farm that he retired when his health failed him and he had failed to receive permanent benefit from a visit to Europe and treatment at Carlsbad.

Colonel Smith died at Litchfield July 31, 1888. He was married three times.

Nathaniel Gray was the son of John Gray and Betsey Rankin Gray, and was born at Pelham July 20, 1808. He attended the public schools of the town and learned the trade of stone cutter as did many other young men of the town, and worked at it for some years before his marriage. He was married at Brattleboro Vt., Dec. 29, 1832, to Miss Emeline A. Hubbard, daughter of Giles Hubbard of Sunderland. In 1833 Mr. Gray and wife removed to the city of New York, where he continued working at his trade for six years, and then became a local missionary in the employ of the City Tract Society at a salary of $700 a year. He was a member of the West Presbyterian church of that city and was elected ruling elder in 1840. He was engaged in the missionary work for twelve years, and in 1850 removed to San Francisco, via the Isthmus of Panama, the journey taking the time from February 12 until June 12 on account of delays and sickness.

In 1852 Mr. Gray was elected coroner for the county of San Francisco, and in 1863 was elected a member of the California legislature on the independent republican ticket.

NATHANIEL GRAY.

Much of his time was devoted to the interest of various charitable institutions of the city and state and he served in them as follows; president of Old Peoples Home, president of San Francisco Benevolent Society, trustee of California Bible Society, director of San Francisco Theological Seminary, director of California Prison Commission, and trustee of the Young Men's Christian Association. Mr. Gray was successful in business and built a fine residence at 758 Tenth Street, Oakland, where the golden wedding of Mr. and Mrs. Gray was celebrated on Dec. 29, 1882, in the presence two hundred invited guests, among them was his brother William D. Gray and wife, and Mrs. Harriett Steuben. The latter was a witness of the marriage at Brattleboro fifty years before, and Mr. W. D. Gray was a witness of the marriage of William W. Oliver and Miss Lorania Gray, the later was a sister of Nathaniel and William, at Pelham, Oct. 4, 1826, Mr. and Mrs. Oliver also being present and celebrated the fifty-six anniversary of their marriage.

The children of John Gray, father of Nathaniel and Lorania included also the following; Mary Gray, Ira Gray, Sarah H. Gray, (afterwards Sarah H. Thompson,) William D. Gray, Hinckley R. Gray, and Horace Gray. All of these left Pelham early in life except Horace and Mrs. Sarah H. Thompson, and the descendants of those who went out from their native town are scattered in the states of New York, Pennsylvania, Ohio, Indiana, Illinois, Kansas, Nevada, and California.

The children of Nathaniel Gray are as follows; Giles H. Gray, a prominent lawyer of San Francisco, Henry M. Gray, Edwin P. Gray, George D. Gray and Emma A. Gray, now Mrs. Cyrus S. Wright of Oakland. The birth place of Nathaniel Gray was the farm in that part of the town known as "The Valley" on which is situated the quarry from which so many building stones are quarried, and known for the last twenty years or more as the Joseph G. Ward place. John Gray the father of Nathaniel lived there and was known as "Cooper" John Gray to distinguish him from another John Gray, son of Dea. Ebenezer Gray, who lived on the farm near by now owned by Levi Moulton, who was known as "Tanner" John Gray. "Cooper" John was a farmer and made good barrels, "Tanner" John was a practical tanner and worked at the business in connection with the work of the farm. Both were useful men in the community, "Cooper" John Gray and "Tanner" John Gray were from different races of Grays and were not related to each other by blood.

Nathaniel Gray's business in San Francisco was that of undertaker; beginning July 1, 1850, and continuing until his death April 24, 1889, and during that time he attended to thirty thousand five hundred and forty-nine burials. He was liberal in his gifts to educational and other benevolent institutions. He gave $5000 to the San Francisco Theological Seminary towards the endowment of a professorship, and other property now valued at $30,000; and to educate the young women of the state he gave Mills Seminary, in Alameda county, $10,000, and also a sum sufficient to establish a scholarship so that at least one young woman could obtain free tuition; he also gave a site for the hospital for children and training school for nurses, but the many smaller gifts would aggregate a much larger sum. He was always laboring for the relief of the needy and the distressed. The board of trustees of the Old Peoples Home of San Francisco, of which Mr. Gray was president, in the resolutions at the time of his death, gave expressions to the following: "An able factor in every Charitable cause in which he took part. He possessed a robust constitution, and the mind of a pioneer of the city of his residence, he possessed business qualifications which made him the peer of the business men of his day, both in worldly accomplishments and success. At the same time he posesssed a religious fervor, an eminently pious character, and a most benevolent and charitable disposition to the poor, the aged, the sick, and the oppressed, which commanded from him respect alike in business circles and is Christian brotherhood." There were Grays among the original settlers of Pelham, and there have been families of that name in town until recent years, but at present not a person of that name resides in town. In 1799 there were fourteen voters bearing that surname, as follows: Jacob Gray, Mathew Gray, Ebenezer Gray, John Gray, Jonathan Gray, Elliot Gray, Adam C. Gray, Justin Gray, Daniel Gray, John Gray, Thomas Gray, Patrick Gray, Moses Gray 2d, and Joel Gray.

Israel H. Taylor. M. D., was born in Pelham 1811. He was a son of John Taylor and Martha Thompson Taylor. The family consisting of five sons and two daughters, besides the subject of this sketch there were Alfred, John, Stewart and James. The daughters were Lucy, afterwards Mrs. Lucy Houston, and Martha, afterwards Mrs. Colton of Springfield.

REV. ALDIN GROUT.

BUFFUM BROOK.

Israel laid the foundation of his education in the common schools of the town ; began the study of medicine with Dr. Daniel Thompson of Northampton, who was at that time associated with Dr. Barrett. He supplemented his study with Drs. Thompson and Barrett by attendance at the Pittsfield Medical School, and later by attendance upon medical lectures in New York city. He commenced the practice of medicine in Pelham in 1833.

In 1842 he married Miss Lavinia C. Crossett of Prescott, and brought his wife to Pelham. Dr. Taylor continued in the practice of his profession in Pelham until 1848, when he removed to Amherst and soon increased his business very much, at the same time continued to answer calls from the many friends he had left in his native town. He continued in active service for forty years after his removal to Amherst, making a total of fifty-five years of active service as a physician. He was for several years the leading physician in the town, and very highly respected among a large number of the citizens of the town in whose families he had ministered in the many years of his residence among them. His kindly cheerful manner, while making professional calls, endeared him to many families who looked upon him as a kind friend as well as family physician. For two years or more before his death he did little in the line of his profession, and he died Oct. 15, 1890.

Rev. Aldin Grout was a son of Joel and Aseneth Grout ; he was born at Pelham, Mass., Sept. 2, 1803 ; graduated at Amherst College 1831, and Andover Seminary, 1834 ; married Miss Hannah Davis, Nov. 17, 1834 (who died in 1836); ordained at Holden, Mass., 1834. He sailed from Boston Dec. 3, 1834, on the bark Burlington with five other missionaries and their wives, sent out by the American Board to establish a mission in South Africa, or rather two missions, but both among the Zulus. One was to be in the interior, and the other on the coast, to be called the Maritime Mission. Rev. David Lindley, Rev. H. I. Venable, and Dr. Alexander E. Wilson, with their wives, were to form the interior mission, while Rev. Aldin Grout, Rev. George Champion, and Dr. Newton Adams, with their wives, were designated to Natal, for the Maritime Mission. Landing together at Cape Town, Feb. 5, 1835, the first company went to the country of Umzilikaze (Moselekatse) who was the father of Lobengula, the Matabele king. But this mission secured no foothold among the Matabele. The other party, consisting of Messrs. Grout, Champion, and Adams, reached Port Natal (Durban) Dec. 20, 1835, and after visiting the Zulu chief Dingaan received permission to remain as missionaries among his people. Two years later the mission was broken up and Messrs. Grout and Champion came to the United States in 1838. But with undaunted courage Mr. Grout returned to Natal in 1840, remaining for thirty years in the Zulu Mission, till, in 1870, at the age of sixty-seven, he retired from the work. Of the twelve persons who thus commenced work among the Zulus only one is now living, Mrs. Venable, residing in Kansas, at the age of eighty-one. Of the men, the last to be called from earth was Rev. Aldin Grout, who died at Springfield, Mass., Feb. 12, 1894 having resided there since he returned to the United States in 1870.

In the beautiful cemetery at Springfield, Mass., there may now be seen a plain marble shaft, with an appropriate inscription, over the grave of Rev. Aldin Grout. A most interesting fact connected with this monument is that it was erected by the gifts of Zulus in South Africa with whom Mr. Grout lived and labored for thirty-six years. It is a custom among the Zulus, when a friend leaves them not to return, to present him with what is called "grave money," to be used in procuring a suitable burial. When Mr. and Mrs. Grout returned from Natal in 1870 such a gift was made him by the Zulus of Umvoti. This sum was sufficient to meet the funeral expenses of Mr. Grout and also to erect this comely monument at Springfield.

The family of Joel and Aseneth Grout consisted of nine children :

Martin born May 30, 1792 ; settled at Grout's Corner, now Millers Falls.
Rufus born March 13, 1794 ; married Clarissa Hall.
Aseneth born —— ——; married Whipple Cook.
Orpha born —— ——; married Mr. Moon of Westfield.
Orra born Oct. 17, 1800 ; married Malinda Randall.
Aldin born Sept. 2, 1803 ; married 1st, Miss Hannah Davis; 2d, Miss Charlotte Bailey.
Austin born Nov. 26, 1805 ; married Susan Hall.
Josiah W. born July 24, 1809 ; married Harriett Peck.
Annis born March 4, 1813 ; married Samuel Robbins.

Albert Brown Robinson, M. D., is the son of Abial Robinson and Mary Ann Packard Robinson and was born in Pelham, Mass., April 12, 1835. At the age of twelve years his parents moved to Ware and he entered the high school there, but pursued his academic studies at Monson, Mass., and was graduated at the University of Buffalo, N. Y., medical department, in the year 1857. He practiced in Amherst, Mass., a few months and then settled in Holden, Mass., where he married in 1859 the daughter of the late Cyrus Chenery of New York. Her great-grandfather was Dr. Isaac Chenery, who was a surgeon in the Revolutionary war, and whose great-grandfather was Major Logan of revolutionary fame. In August, 1862, he was commissioned assistant surgeon of the 10th Regiment Mass. Volunteers (Col. Briggs) and in May following he was commissioned full surgeon of the same regiment. After the expiration of the three years' term of the regiment's enlistment, June 1864, he, with the regiment, was mustered out of the United States service after being in every battle of the army of the Potomac, from Gen. McClellan on the Peninsula to Gen. Grant at Petersburg, Va. The next month he was commissioned surgeon of the 42nd Regiment to serve 100 days at the defences of Washington, D. C., and was mustered out the following November. In April 1865 he settled in Boston where he has been in the active practice of his profession since. In the autumn of 1865 he was appointed professor of surgery in the New England Female Medical College of Boston. In 1858 he was an admitted member of the Mass. Medical society and in 1865 a member of the Norfolk District Medical society. In 1866 a comrade and surgeon of Post 26, Grand Army of the Republic. In 1867, was made a mason of Washington Lodge F. & A. M. During his residence in Boston he has been medical examiner for various insurance companies and beneficiary associations, and is at present a member of many literary and secret societies.

William Smith Otis, the inventor of the steam shovel, or the American steam excavator (as styled in the patent), was the son of Isaac Otis and Tryphina Smith Otis, and was born in Pelham Mass., September 20, 1813. He came of good old Revolutionary stock; both of his grandfathers having been soldiers in our Revolutionary army; his maternal grandfather having resided and died in Pelham.

At the time of his invention he was residing in Philadelphia, Pa., engaged in railroad construction, and he patented it about 1836. The first machines were built by Eastwick & Harrison (the firm that under the style of Harrison, Wynans & Eastwick, went to Russia, where they constructed all of the locomotives and rolling stock for the St. Petersburg & Moscow R. R., a road over four hundred miles long, and where they accumulated large fortunes). The Russian government bought two of the excavators (built by E. & H. in Philadelphia), which were used in the construction of this road.

OTIS PATENT STEAM EXCAVATOR.

The first steam excavator was used by Mr. Otis on a contract on the B. & O. R. R. somewhere in Maryland, and the second near Springfield, Mass., on the Boston & Albany R. R. in 1837,–'38,–'39. A machine was sent with an agent to England about this time, but the English contractors refused to use it, though since the expiration of the patent they have constructed and used large numbers, about twenty having been employed on the excavations of the Liverpool & Manchester canal. One was sold to the Peruvian government, which they used on one of their Guano islands, in excavating and loading into cars the fertilizer deposited by the birds. The French and Germans have also built and used many of them, in fact, they are used the world over where ever any heavy excavations are to be made.

Mr. Otis was the first person to hang a shovel on a revolving crane, and was the progenitor of a large class of dredges used in excavating hard material.

At the time of his invention, engines and boilers were large and clumsy, entirely unsuited for the excavator, and Mr. Otis designed an engine and boiler of the style in use at this day; the only improvement made since his death in steam excavators has been in enlarging and strengthening them. The most of our prominent railroads own one or more of them, using them in their gravel pits, and they are employed on some of the Lake Superior iron mines in digging the ore.

William S. Otis, while engaged in constructing a portion of the Boston & Providence R. R. near Canton, Mass., married on June 23, 1835, Miss Elizabeth Everett, daughter of Leonard Everett, a merchant of that place. They had two daughters and one son, the latter died in infancy, and one of the daughters at an early age; the oldest, Helen E., married John D. Dunbar, of Canton, Mass., April 4, 1855. They are both deceased, leaving several sons, one of whom is an employee of the Pennsylvania R. R. at Altoona, Pa., and the others are doing well. Mr. Otis died in Westfield, Mass, November 13, 1839, aged 26 years, one month, and 23 days.

Isaac Otis was the fourth of that name, and the seventh generation in descent from the first settler who came from England in 1635.

William Smith Otis was the oldest of eleven children. His mother being the daughter of Capt. Oliver Smith of Pelham, but she was born in Walpole.

John Otis, the first of that name in this country, settled near Otis Hill in Hingham Mass., and was the son of Richard Otis of County Somerset, England. John Otis, first, had a son John second, who had four sons, viz: John, Stephen, Joseph, and Job. From John many noted men have descended, among them James Otis the "patriot of the Revolution," and Harrison Gray Otis, first Mayor of Boston, and a United States Senator.

Capt. Isaac Abercrombie, youngest son of Rev. Robert Abercrombie, was born in Pelham, Mass., Sept. 30, 1759. When a lad he went to Brookline and lived with Mr. William Hyslop, a wealthy Englishman and friend of Rev. Robert. In his early manhood he returned to Pelham. He married Martha McCulloch, daughter of Robert and Sarah (Cowan) McCulloch, June 26, 1790. They lived in the old parsonage for many years, and at the parsonage their nine children were born. He was a man of fine presence, erect and stately in figure. He filled many offices of honor and trust in the town and county before his removal from town. He represented the town in the General Court in 1799, 1800, 1801, 1802, 1804, 1806, 1809 and 1819; was on the board of selectmen often and was commissioned a Justice of the Peace for Hampshire and Hampden counties, and a captain in the militia. He removed from his native town to New Salem first, and then to Greenfield and Deerfield where he died Dec. 4, 1847.

Isaac Abercrombie was a much respected and influential citizen, and noted for his strength of mind. His service in the Revolution was while living at Brookline, consequently his name does not appear among the list from Pelham. David, Samuel, John and James, sons of Rev. Robert, also served in the Revolutionary war. David, the eldest son, was in the battles of Bunker Hill, Stillwater, Saratoga and Ticonderoga ; was taken prisoner by the British, sent to England and never returned. It is claimed that few, if any, able-bodied men remained in Pelham during the war—the old men, and the women doing what work was done on the farms.

Otis Abercrombie, M. D., son of Capt. Isaac Abercrombie, was born in Pelham, June 25, 1802. He married Dorothy Lovina, daughter of Major Daniel and Mary (Sawyer) Putnam of Lunenburg, Mass., June 16, 1835. He was graduated at Williams College in 1823 and began the study of medicine at the Medical School in Richmond, Va., and finished his studies at New Haven, Conn., receiving his degree in 1827. Later in that year he was licensed to practice medicine by the Mass. Medical Society and located in Ashburnham, Mass. He removed to Fitchburg in 1829 and was associated with Dr. Jonas A. Marshall. After nine years of successful practice in Fitchburg, failing health obliged him to retire from active practice and he removed to Lunenburg. At the last named town he was postmaster for several years, served on the board of selectmen and took active interest in public affairs. Dr. Abercrombie died at Lunenburg, Jan. 24, 1851.

Ira Abercrombie, son of Isaac, was born in Pelham, Jan. 28, 1805. He was educated in the schools of the town and at New Salem Academy; taught school when a young man; went to Houlton, Me., as a clerk in a store; returned to Massachusetts and engaged in trade at Deerfield (Cheapside) with his brother Isaac. They were also engaged in boating on the Connecticut river. Mr. Abercrombie became prominent in town, served as selectman in Deerfield for six years and often moderator of the town meetings; represented the town in the General Court in 1850 and 1861; served as trustee of the Smith Charities; was state director of the Troy & Boston R. R.; was one of the incorporators of the Franklin County bank, then a director. In 1863, was chosen president, a position which he held until his death July 14, 1870. He was also trustee of the Greenfield Savings bank. Ira and Isaac were never married, a sister being their housekeeper for many years.

Asiel Abercrombie, son of Isaac, was born in Pelham, Oct. 21, 1807. He was educated in the schools of the town and at New Salem Academy; worked on the farm in Pelham; removed to New Salem where he was a merchant; moved to Deerfield (Cheapside) where he was engaged in the hotel business until the railroads were opened. He then turned his attention to farming. Mr. Abercrombie was not in public office very much. He was a director in the Franklin County National bank at Greenfield, also a trustee of the Greenfield Savings bank, and a trustee of the Deerfield Academy until his death, March 10, 1874. He married Miss Elizabeth B. Fuller of Deerfield.

Isaac Abercrombie, son of Isaac, was born in Pelham, July 20, 1793. His education was obtained at the common schools, and at New Salem Academy. He taught school in the neighboring towns in winter. For one term in Ludlow his pay was a " Straight rifle " which he treasured all his life, and bequeathed it to a nephew by will. His father was interested in a tract of land conveyed by Robert Brooks, governor of Virginia, in Lewis and Randolph counties, by patent dated Richmond, Nov 7, 1796.

The grantees met at South Hadley, June 3, 1810, and " drew by lot " their several portions. Isaac was sent to Virginia in 1814, with others, to locate the shares of land. The trip was made on horseback, he having been furnished with a certificate of good moral character by Daniel Stebbins, Notary Public, of Northampton. Two trips to Virginia were made on business connected with these lands.

Mr. Abercrombie was a deputy sheriff in Hampshire county for several years before removing to Greenfield, Mass., where he held the position of deputy sheriff and jailer under Epaphras Hoyt, Sheriff in 1828. He was also interested, with others, in running a line of mail stages between Boston, Troy and Albany. Selling out his interest in the stage route he engaged in trade with his brother Ira, at Deerfield, (Cheapside.) The firm did an extensive wholesale and retail business, extending over a large portion of the county and into Vermont. They ran a line of boats on the Connecticut river, between Cheapside and Hartford, loading with country produce on the down trip, and general merchandise on the return. The opening of the Connecticut River R. R. in 1846 destroyed their trade and boating business. He then turned his attention to the care of his property and to farming. He held offices in the town of Deerfield; was director in the Greenfield bank, and trustee of the Smith Charities. In business circles he was known as a man of strict integrity. He died at Deerfield, Sept. 10, 1872.

Thomas Buffum was born in Pelham in August, 1846, the son of Thomas Buffum. He spent his boyhood there and obtained a common school education. When he was eighteen years old he went to

THOMAS BUFFUM.

Easthampton and began work under Edmund H. Sawyer in the Nashawannuck mills. He began at the bottom and worked up, learning the entire business. In a few years he was placed in charge of the finishing department and this position he held for 26 years.

He possessed a large amount of executive ability, and he was a man who was not satisfied with allowing things to drift, but rather took delight in driving things. He was one of that class of men who achieve results when they set out on a given line. Mr. Buffum was of jovial nature, and loved congenial companionship and sociability. He went about much, and was known in every town up and down the valley. He was a shrewd business man, and was always a steady worker. He was generous and kind-hearted, and the people who worked under him in Easthampton were his friends. This was shown by the presents that were given him and the kind words that were spoken by the employes at the time he severed his connection with the company. He possessed a power for observation, and with his travels accumulated a vast amount of knowledge, especially of men and human nature. His hobby was a good driving horse, and "Handsome Tom," as he was familiarly known about the county, was never known to drive a slow horse. He resigned his position at the Nashawannuck mills in 1895, and since then he had been connected with Dibble & Warner in the same business. He was with this firm at the time he was taken with his last sickness. He was twice married. His first wife was Miss Mary E., daughter of Martin Graves of Northampton. They were married in 1870. His second wife was Miss Sarah Chase of Easthampton. Mr. Buffum removed to Northampton in the autumn of 1896 where he died on the 18th of February, 1897.

James M. Cowan, born in Pelham, August 5, 1827, was the son of John Cowan and Susan Hildreth. He attended the public schools in Pelham, and afterward learned the machinist's trade. He went to Chicopee Falls in 1852, where he ran a grist mill for two years. He returned to Pelham at the end of that time and began the manufacture of bobbins and spools for cotton and woolen factories. The firm name was James M. Cowan & Co., his partner being L. M. Hills of Amherst, at that time the president of the First National bank in that town. The business was a profitable one, especially during the war, and the firm built up a large business. He sold his interest in the mill in 1867 to his partner and removed to Springfield, where he entered the employ of the Boston & Albany railroad as foreman of the car shops. He gave up this position and went in business for himself about 1875, being engaged in the retail meat and coal trade.

He afterward gave up the meat business and had been engaged in handling coal until the time of his illness. His yards are along the Boston & Albany railroad tracks. He formerly occupied the entire ground on Lyman street where the station now stands. He had a branch yard on the New England road opened in 1893, where he received his Lehigh coal. Mr. Cowan was successful in business, confining his energies to the one line. It was while living in his native town that the war of the Rebellion broke out, and as a member of the board of selectmen, he was able to render the town valuable service in filling the quota of men called for from time to time during the war. He also rendered much assistance in support of the Congregational church at the center of the town, and it was largely through the efforts of Mr. Cowan that the bell, now hanging in the steeple of the church, was secured and placed in position.

Mr. Cowan was a member of the North church, Springfield but sometimes attended the Park church, near his home. He was much interested in church and missionary enterprises and until recent years had been an active worker in the railroad Young Men's Christian Association. His first wife was Miss Almariah Bartlett of Enfield, Mass., and he was married to her in May, 1851; she died Aug. 5, 1862. His second wife, who was Miss Ellen Mitchell of Palmer, survives him with two children, Miss Mary E. Cowan, and J. Edward Cowan, who was associated in business with his father. Mr. Cowan died Feb. 14, 1897.

The Cowan family was a well known and much respected one in the town from its first settlement. George and Ephraim Cowan were among those who drew Home lots in 1739. George drew lot 21 and Ephraim lot 42, the latter being about a mile east of the Methodist church. The name of Cowan appears on the town records for many years, and probably until Mr. James M. Cowan removed from town in 1867. George Cowan the first settler was from Concord, in the county of Middlesex, while Ephraim was from Worcester where most of the settlers of the town came from. Whether these two men were brothers cannot be determined by the records, but they may have been. In 1757 there was a Samuel Cowan, also a James Cowan; they were both married that year. Sept. 8, 1781, James Cowan was married to Mary Dunbar of Winchendon. On a list of voters for the year 1799 the names of James and George Cowan appear.

Dr. Morton Monroe Eaton was the son of Monroe Eaton and Clarissa Boyden, and was born in Pelham, April 21, 1839. He attended the schools of the town, supplemented by several terms in the schools of Amherst and removed to Illinois in 1855 being at that time sixteen years old. In Chicago he studied medicine with Prof. Daniel Brainard, formerly president of the Rush Medical College. Dr. Eaton graduated from this college in 1861. He was then resident physician of the city hospital for two years. He then removed to Peoria where he was made surgeon of that post in the war of the Rebellion. During the Rebellion he made five trips through the South for the Sanitary Commission, under the direction of Gov. Yates of Illinois, distributing sanitary stores and assisting the wounded and needy to get home or to suitable hospitals.

Dr. Eaton was a prolific writer for medical journals, and also wrote and published books. His most noted book was a volume of over 800 pages, profusely illustrated, and had, and is still having an extensive sale. Dr. Eaton was president of the City Homeopathic Medical Society of Cincinnati. He was vice-president of the State Society of Illinois; also a member of the American Institute of Homeopathy, and an honorary member of several other state and other societies, including the International Congress of Paris, France. In 1881 he attended the World's Homeopathic convention in London.

Dr. Eaton removed to Cincinnati in 1877 and to Walnut Hills in May, 1886. He practiced medicine as partner with Prof. S. R. Beckwith. He was a hard student and was successful both as practitioner and as a business man, saving a pretty large fortune. Dr. Eaton was twice married. His first wife was Miss Eliza J. Payne of Galesburg, Ill., with whom he lived seventeen years. His second wife was Miss Sutherland of Peoria, Ill. Dr. Eaton died Oct. 21, 1889, leaving besides his wife, two daughters and a son, who is also a physician, his mother and a step brother, Shelby M. Cullom, who was at one time governor of Illinois. In religion Dr. Eaton was a Congregationalist and attended the Walnut Hills Congregational church. He was also a member of the N. C. Harmony lodge of Masons.

Dr. Francis Lapier Eaton was the son of Monroe Eaton and Clarissa Boyden, and was born in Pelham, March 5, 1843. He attended the schools of his native town in boyhood until his parents moved to the West, where his education was completed and he selected medicine as a profession. After completing his course of study he began practice at St. Louis, Mo., but later Dr. Eaton settled in Cincinnati, Ohio, and for twenty years or more was a most zealous and active worker in the interests of his chosen profession, having been corresponding secretary for some years of the Cincinnati College of Pharmacy, then trustee, and later president of the college. He served with honor during the war of the Rebellion and was an honored member of the Geo. H. Thomas Post G. A. R. of that city. He died in Cincinnati, Jan. 24, 1887, when but 44 years of age.

Lebbeus Gaskell, Esq., was the son of William Gaskell and Phebe Cook, and was born in Pelham in 1809. He attended the schools of the town until he left home to learn the wagon-makers' trade at Woonsocket, R. I. After becoming master of the practical part of the business, young Gaskell decided to go into the business for himself and having saved $300 used it as capital, it being all that he had. His venture proved a success after a while and the money made, was saved and as his savings increased he loaned money to the manufacturers about Woonsocket at good rates of interest. He also engaged in the real estate business and was successful in that also. He became director in one of the banks at Woonsocket and later was chosen president of the institution and served in that capacity for several years. Mr. Gaskell died at Woonsocket, R. I., in 1875. He was twice married, and had two daughters, one of them inheriting nearly all of the large fortune her father accumulated, and married Dr. Bailey, a noted fancy farmer and lecturer upon agricultural topics.

The Gaskell family came to Pelham from Cumberland, R. I. Other members of William Gaskell's family were: Orinda, Silas, Lyman, James M., Lucy D., Joanna, Chester, and Philena, ten in all. Chester and Philena, the only living members of this large family, now reside in Amherst.

Dr. E. Ward Cooke, was born in Pelham on the 18th day of May 1851. He was the sixth son of Nathaniel and Bethiah Ward Cooke and grandson of Eseck Cooke, the Quaker farmer of early times. He received his early education in the old Valley district school, and later became a pupil of Minor Gold, a noted teacher of Pelham. Being naturally ingenious and possessed of mechanical ideas, he

DR. E. WARD COOKE,

UNCLE ESECK COOK'S FARM HOUSE.

early acquired a knowledge of the joiner's trade, at which he worked in this and adjoining towns and later in Providence, R. I. Afterwards, he went to South Carolina where he was engaged in the Sea Island cotton trade. It was while there he met and formed the acquaintance and friendship of an eminent physician and surgeon and through his influence, he determined upon a professional career, whereupon he took up a course of reading and study and after two years, returned to his native state and entered the office of Dr. Horace C. Smith of Athol, Mass., as a dental student. Subsequently he matriculated at the Philadelphia Dental College in Philadelphia, Pa., and completing his course of study there, he returned to Athol, where he began the practice of dentistry on his own account. On June 16, 1875, he was married to Miss Etta I. Lewis, daughter of Enoch T. Lewis, an old and prominent resident of the town. In 1882, he removed to Cambridge, Mass., where there were broader fields in which to labor, and where he has achieved most marvelous success, having contributed much toward the advancement and progress of the dental profession. Dr. Cooke is a prominent man in the dental profession in the city of Cambridge.

Johnson J. Thompson, son of Asa and Ruth Thompson, was born in Pelham, Oct. 14, 1832. He attended the public schools of the town, studied medicine with Drs. Smith and Taylor of Amherst for several years; attended medical lectures in Albany and Brooklyn, N. Y.; located at Davenport, Iowa. He married a niece of Judge Conkling of Brooklyn, N. Y., and a cousin of Hon. Roscoe Conkling. He practiced medicine with much success for thirty years or more, and died at Davenport, March 24, 1894. His wife dying the same night, within less than an hour of his death. He was a contributor to leading medical journals, and was honored by election to offices of trust and responsibility in the city of Davenport, and was largely instrumental in founding an orphan asylum in the city. Four children, two sons and two daughters, survive.

There are other successful business men who were natives of Pelham besides those given more extended notice. Among these are: Edwin and Oliver Bryant; L. V. B. Cook of West Springfield; Lucius W. Cook, Williamsport, Pa.; Marcus D. Cook, Denver, Colo.; Dwight M. Cook, Chicopee Falls, sons of Olney Cook; W. H. H.

Ward, Amherst ; Henry C. Hamilton, Springfield ; Augustine H. Rankin, Blackstone; M. F. Robinson and L. F. Jenks, Springfield; Charles P. Aldrich, Greenfield ; R. J. D. Westcott, Ware, for many years cashier of First National bank, Amherst; Wm. S. Westcott, merchant, Amherst ; William A. Bailey, contractor, Northampton ; Zimri Thurber, shoe manufacturer, Brockton ; Seth B. Hall, capitalist, Lowell; Charles O. and Lemuel W. Hall, Lowell, sons of John B. Hall; Warren C. Wedge, Chicopee ; Marcus C. Grout, Providence, R. I.; John T. Fales, Newport, R. I.; Leander L. Bartlett, Montague City; Eugene P. Bartlett, Pelham ; Sanford M. Robinson, Pittsburg, Pa.; Oliver C. Smith, Rock Springs, Wy.; Homer Eaton, Northampton ; Frank Kingman, Enfield ; Osmyn Houston, Springfield ; S. W. Rankin, Springfield ; G. P. Smith, Jersey Shore, Pa.; Alfred Taylor, Kansas City, Mo.; Otis S. Lyman, Lagrange, Ill.; George and Albert Davis, clothing dealers, Prescott, Ont.; Edwin Chapman, contractor, Needham ; Levi D. Hall, Lowell.

John Savage was one of the most remarkable men among the settlers of Pelham. He was not one of the original settler of the town but came to Pelham with his wife in 1745 or 1747 and was one of the towns' ablest and most trusted citizens for about twenty years, serving the town in almost every position of trust and responsibility while he dwelt within its borders. He was chosen to represent the town before the presbytery in 1747 ; committee to provide schoolmasters in 1781 ; moderator at town meetings, and selectman in 1752 ; on committee to legalize acts of town meetings before the General Court, and also one of the selectmen in 1753 ; on committee to represent the town at the superior court in Springfield in 1757 ; chosen agent to represent the town before the court of General Sessions in 1762 ; was on a committee to represent the town and make answer to a petition that had been presented to the General Court in 1764. The above are a few of the important positions of service to which he was called as shown by the record. Hardly a year but John Savage was in active service in some capacity from the time when his name first appears until he removed from the town in 1767 to Salem, Washington county, N. Y.

A lineal descendant has kindly furnished the following interesting **sketch** of the life of John Savage. "The ancestors of Captain John **Savage** were French, being Huguenots they were driven from France by the revocation of the edict of Nantes in 1685. They settled in or near Londonderry in the north of Ireland. The father of John Savage married a Scotch lady, Miss Eleanor Hamilton; he died leaving three sons, who came to America with their mother and stepfather in 1717, and settled at Rutland, Mass. John Savage was ten years old at that time and followed the seas as a sailor during the early part of his life. He gradually accumulated property and became sole owner of the vessel which he commanded. In a storm the vessel was wrecked off Cape Breton, his men and cargo being all lost, and he barely escaped with his life. After this experience he abandoned the sea, and in 1733 married a daughter of his stepfather also a Miss Hamilton, and settled upon a farm in Pelham, Mass.

In 1758 he was selected as captain of one of the Massachusetts companies in the old French War, and served under General Bradstreet in his expedition against Fort Frontenac, and under General Abercrombie in his disastrous assault upon Fort Ticonderoga. Captain Savage was lame at the time of the latter engagement, but notwithstanding this he placed himself at the head of his men and led them into the fight.

After residing twenty-two years in Pelham, Captain Savage moved to Salem, Washington county, N. Y., in 1767, where he died Jan. 27, 1792, aged eighty-five years, and now rests in Evergreen Cemetery, at Salem.

The following is the quaint and curious inscription upon his tombstone.

"Near this stone are deposited the remains of Captain John Savage, whose useful life (which Heaven protected to an unusual length) was distinguished by the dangerous hardships and deliverences he experienced in a long series of adventures both by land and sea.

In recounting these to his latest moments, he gratefully acknowledged the wisdom, goodness, and power of Divine Providence ; that he was attentive to the duties of religion; that he undauntedly advocated the faith which he firmly believed; that amidst the temptations peculiarly incident to the stations of a seaman and soldier, he preserved an unsullied and exemplary character, diligently discharging the several duties of life was his distinction.

Mr. Savage was born in the Kingdom of Ireland about the year 1707, in his youth he emigrated to America and settled in the Province of Massachusetts. In the year 1767, he, with his family removed from Pelham to this town, (Salem) then an uncultivated wilderness.

January 27, 1792, aged eighty-five year; his pilgrimage being ended in the certain hope of a blessed immortality. He rested in Jesus."

The descendants of John Savage have been distinguished for ability and learning. Edward Savage, son of John, was born in Rutland, Mass., and removed to Salem, N. Y., with his father when the latter left Pelham in 1767, being then 21 years of age. He married Mary McNaughton and was the first sheriff of Washington County, N. Y., after the Revolutionary war; he was also surrogate; and a member of the state legislature for twenty-one years, and was three times elected a member of the council of appointment. He was in the battle of Plattsburg in 1814, and died in 1833, aged 87. His son John Savage was born in Salem in 1779, educated at Salem Academy and Union College; studied law and opened a law office in Salem in 1803; served two terms in Congress in 1814 and 1816; in the latter year he married Ruth Wheeler of Lanesboro, Mass.; resided in Albany from 1821 to 1837, when he removed to Utica. He was chief justice of the Supreme Court of the state of New York from 1822 to 1836. He died at Utica, October 19, 1863, aged 84.

The opinions of Judge Savage on legal questions while chief justice are quoted in law reports of the various states, and are cited in the current volumes, having stood the test of nearly a century.

John Stinson and descendants. John Stinson or Stevenson was one of the original settlers of the town of Pelham and drew Home Lot No. 48, situated on the middle range road nearly a mile west of the center of the town, and is the farm now owned by C. H. Hanson. His father's name was John who came to this country with other Scotch-Irish immigrants in 1718, and died at Rutland in 1743, leaving a will of which John Savage was sole executor.

John Stinson, the subject of this sketch, was known as a man of responsibility upon whom the early settlers could rely, and consequently he was chosen treasurer of the town at the first town meeting after the act of incorporation on the 19th of April, 1743. He was moderator of the town meeting held in June of the same years and filled many other responsible offices in the town during the year until 1774. He, with his son Isaac Stevenson, were soldiers in the colonial wars, and John went with the New England expedition to Lake George in 1758.

Isaac Stevenson married Thankful Savage, daughter of Capt. John Savage of Rutland, Oct. 23, 1764. Capt. Savage was afterwards a prominent citizen of Pelham until 1767. Isaac removed to Enfield about the year 1789 and a bought a pew in the church there when first built, paying £8 therefor.

Margarett Stevenson, daughter of John, became the wife of Rev. Robert Abercrombie, the first settled minister of Pelham, Jan. 7, 1743 and was the mother of eleven children, eight sons and three daughters.

Samuel, son of John Stinson or Stevenson, married Martha Sloan of Pelham and was a voter in Pelham in 1799.

Mary Stevenson, daughter of Isaac and Thankful, married Alden Lathrop, first town treasurer of Enfield, Mass., and a descendant of John and Priscilla Alden. Their son Sylvanus Lathrop, was born in Enfield and was a noted builder in early life, having erected the steeple of the church at Enfield before he was twenty-one years of age, and became a noted civil engineer and contractor. His first extensive contract was on the Erie canal, and later executed a contract on a canal at Akron, Ohio. He built the third rolling mill at Pittsburg, Pa., and engaged in the iron business. The first acqueduct over the Allegheny river at Pittsburg was built by Sylvanus Lathrop in 1829, and he was the first to plan a bridge over the Mississippi river at St. Louis.

Concerning the Women of Pelham.

The names of very few women appear upon the town records from 1738 to 1825 inclusive. They did not vote even in church affairs. They did not teach school, and were hardly allowed to attend school in the early years. They were taught to sew, to spin, to knit and to weave; these plain useful accomplishments were thought to comprise all that it was necessary for women to possess. That the wives of the Scotchmen of Pelham exerted great influence, as they always do, is unquestionably true: but they made their influence tell at home rather than as directors of the sewing society, as managers of the woman's board of missions, or as members of women's clubs.

We know that they must have taken a lively interest in all that pertained to the well being of the town and the church, and must have taken sides in the troubles which existed for much of the time during the pastorate of the first minister, but they are not on record. They had borne their share of the burdens of the war for liberty and saw their husbands and sons march away to fight against King George, and were pinched and oppressed by the heavy taxes imposed to carry on the war. While their husbands were away with the army, they were left at home on the farms with the old men and boys, doing the best they could to keep their children fed and clothed. Yet not a written word of their struggles and their self-denying actions is left on record for our perusal now, when we would be pleased to learn about it.

That the women of Pelham held radical opinions concerning that clerical impostor and rogue, Stephen Burroughs, does not admit of a doubt, and that they used their tongues in denouncing the wily youth quite as freely and effectively as did their husbands, sons and brothers cannot be questioned for a moment; but no criticism of their's has come down to us. They felt the pressure of debts and sympathized with their husbands when the burdens pressed heavily and creditors seemed intent upon evicting them from their homes almost in their determination to force payment of claims; they criticized the laws and lawyers, and inveighed against the courts as volubly as their husbands during the stirring times of the Shays rebellion; but we can only guess the strong expressions they used, for the records are a blank on the subject. Probably the first name of a woman on the records of the town is that of Eloner Gray in 1760. It appears in the record of a town meeting, Nov. 14, 1760,—"first voted that there is Six Pound thirteen Shilling & four pence allowed for the Support of Eloner Gray for the Present year."

Eloner Gray was poor, possibly a widow and alone in the world. Her's is the first name of a woman assisted by the town. Later, came others whose names appear regularly for years, or until death relieved them of their poverty and distress. At a meeting Jan. 20, 1764, "It was Likewise Voted that Elizabeth Clark is allowed four Shilling for Tendance at Ordination time." The services of Elizabeth Clark that brought her four shillings reward by vote of the town, was at the ordination of Rev. Richard Crouch Graham. She was probably one of those helpful women that know just what needs to be done on all occasions, whether it be a wedding, a funeral or an ordination, and it was well that the town appreciated her services, and still better to show their appreciation by an appropriation of money from the town treasury as partial payment—it could not have been but partial payment, for services rendered by such a woman as we conceive Elizabeth Clark to have been was worth much more than four shillings for "tendance" at such an interesting occasion as an ordination. In the warrant of another town meeting is the following:—

"To see what Method the town will take to help Rebeckah Selfradge for Maintaining and taking care of her Mother Elisibeth Selfradge."

This name is more frequently written Selfridge, and there were several men of that name who held responsible positions as officers of the town; so that both Rebeckah and her mother were unquestionably worthy people, and it is fair to infer from the language of the town warrant, that Rebeckah had striven heroically to take good care of her mother and maintain her without calling upon the town, and that her efforts had been noticed by some people, who had, without any suggestion from the Selfridges, taken this method of calling the attention of the people of the town to the unselfish and plucky struggle of Rebeckah. Edward Selfridge died in 1761 and his widow Elizabeth lived until 1799 or 1800 when she died aged 95 years,

Rebeckah caring for her all of the nearly forty years of her widow hood.

At a town meeting, April 1, 1793, the town "Voted Rebeckah Conkey £1—10s for Boarding and Nursing Lydia Miller and child eighteen days." There is no explanation of the circumstances under which Rebeckah Conkey rendered the service for which the town voted the above sum from the town treasury, but it being an unusual form for service rendered the town poor, we assume that it was a special case of suffering, and there was need of special service, which Rebeckah Conkey rendered.

From these few isolated cases in which the names of the women of Pelham appear on the public records of a century or more ago, we are bound to assume that in the limited sphere to which the habits and customs of the times in which they lived restricted them, and under which they lived and moved and had their being, they exercised all the womanly qualities as opportunity offered, and were not troubled very much by reason of being kept in the background. They cared for the sick; they helped the unfortunate; they sympathized with the distressed. No young woman's marriage outfit was complete without the little linen wheel. The whir and hum of these little linen wheels in their humble homes was as melodious and more harmonious than the sounds that come from many a modern home piano under the merciless thrumming of the girls of to-day, who are no more successful in producing harmonious sounds than they would be in trying to spin flax on the little wheel.

Then came a time when the little wheel for spinning flax was laid aside because the cultivation of flax was suspended. And as factory made goods came into use, the larger and more noisy wheel for spinning wool, that had been carded into rolls either by hand or at the carding machine, was stored in the attic and was at rest. Early in this century the braiding or plaiting of split straw braid was taken up by the women. About the middle of June a rye field was selected where the growth was thick and vigorous, which was usually on new land from which the wood had been cut the year previous, and the green rank growth of rye was cut and tied in small bundles. These bundles were placed in hot water for a short time and then spread upon the ground, and in a few days was bleached nearly white. This straw was cut into length at the joints, submitted to the fumes of burning brimstone and the white supple straw was split in narrow splints and the women plaited them into braids of various kinds which was gathered by dealers and sold for making ladies bonnets, it being paid for by the yard. Many women occupied the spare time from domestic duties in plaiting this domestic braid. About the year 1827 the palm-leaf hat business was started. Palm-leaf cut from the trees in Cuba was imported, bleached and split by men, and distributed among the women of Pelham and other towns to be braided into hats. The women and girls and boys of the town were employed for many years at this work, and many thousands of hats were turned out yearly. Then came the weaving of palm-leaf into webs for making Shaker Hoods. This weaving by the women was commenced first about 1840, and was continued at intervals until after the War of the Rebellion when it was suspended, because women and girls preferred hats to the close unwieldly Shaker Hood, and it went out of use because fashion decreed it. Very few women braid palm-leaf hats at present, as the rebellion in Cuba prevents the importation of palm-leaf.

The women of Pelham, wives and daughters of the first settlers, were none of them brought up in the lap of luxury; there were none of the farmer settlers who were rich, or able to live without work, consequently all worked,—both men and women, and the latter have been noted for their industrious habits during all the years since the town was settled.

There are a few pages of the record books on which the names of women are found but they are not the pages on which the records of the many annual and special business town meetings are spread, but it is on the few pages, where the publication of marriage intentions— marriages and the deaths are found. Omitting the record of deaths, the record of publications and marriages furnish almost the only source from which the names of women who lived in town can be obtained. No attempt will be made to give the marriages from the settlement of the town down to the present time, but from the earliest records,—the marriages from 1746 to 1822 are given so far as they are obtainable from the early record books, and the "publications" from 1769 to 1815, or such of them as do not show a record of marriage of the parties whose marriage intentions appears. Publication was good evidence that marriage should and did follow; breach of promise of marriage was not common 125 years ago.

MARRIAGES.

Aug. 25, 1746, Robert McKee and Mary Gray, both of Pelham.
Sept. 25, 1746, John Dick and Jean McCulloch, Pelham.
Nov. 10, 1746, Ephraim Whiler and Hannah Marks, of Quabin, so-called.
Jan. 23, 1747, Jacob Ramsdell and Hannah Owens, of Quabin, so-called.
April 2, 1747, James Hood and Easter Gray, Pelham.
April 16, 1747, James Conkey and Isabel Maklem, Pelham.
Jan. 7, 1748, Alexander Conkey and Sarah Maklem, Pelham.
April 25, 1748, Joseph Rinken and Elisebeth Gray, Pelham.
May 18, 1748, Andrew Smith, Holden, and Jean Clark, Pelham.
Nov. 13, 1746, Robert McCulloch, Pelham, and Margarett Smith, Kingstown.
Dec. 4, 1746, James Fergerson and Ester Thornton, Pelham.
July 28, 1748, William Harkness and Ann Gray, Pelham.
Oct. 27, 1748, James Smith, Kingstown, and Margarett McCulloch, Pelham.
April 14, 1749, Alex'd^r McNutt and Elisebeth Maklem, Pelham.
May 18, 1749, William Petteson and Margarett King, Pelham.
Feb. 8, 1750, Robert McCulloch and Sarah Cowan, Pelham.
April 24, 1750, David Thomas and Elisebeth Cowan, Pelham.
May 16, 1751, Robert Barber and Sarah McFarland, Pelham.
Jan. 16, 1753, Nathaniel Tagert, Blandford, and Janet Hamilton, Pelham.
Feb. 8, 1753, John Crawford and Susanna Kelso, Pelham.
Sept. 10, 1754, Isaac Gray and Mary Maklem, Pelham.
Feb. 20, 1755, Alexander McCulloch and Sarah Peebels, Pelham.
April 17, 1755, John Gray, Jun., and Martha Savige, Pelham.
Nov. 17, 1755, William Conkey aud Rebeckah Hamilton, Pelham.
Nov. 18, 1755, David Thomas, Pelham, and Elisebeth Harper, Lancaster.
Dec. 11, 1755, Samuel Cowden, Worcester, and Margarett Gilmore, Pelham.
April 8, 1756, Sam'l Wallas, Rutland, and Mary McClelland, Pelham.
Dec. 28, 1756, Oliver Selfridge and Ester Smith, Pelham.
Jan. 4, 1757, Sam'l Cowan and Margarett Hunter, Pelham.
Mar. 8, 1757, Patrick Pebbles and Margarett Taylor, Pelham.
Mar. 17, 1757, Willm Selfridge, Pelham, and Catrin McMaster, Palmer.
April 7, 1757, James Harkness and Nancy Gray, Pelham.
April 19, 1757, Robert Hamilton and Elisebeth Kid, Pelham.
April 26, 1757, David Stoughton, Londonderry, and Mary Pebels, Pelham.
Oct. 27, 1757, Henry Strongman, Greenfield, and Jennet Alexander, Pelham.
Nov. 17, 1757, Rev. John Houston, Bedford, and Mrs. Ann Peebles, Pelham.
Dec. 8, 1757, William Brown, Blandford, and Agness King, Pelham.
Dec. 13, 1757, John Thompson and Prudence Clark, Pelham.
Dec. 22, 1757, James Cowan Jun. and Elisebeth Hunter, Pelham.
Jan. 19, 1759, James Hamilton and Sarah Lucore, Pelham.
Feb. 22, 1759, John Young and Margerett Conkey, Pelham.
Aug. 17, 1759, John Pebels, Pelham, and Mary Cunningham, Brookfield.
Sept. 13, 1759, Abraham Nut, Pequige, and Sarah Gray, Pelham.
Sept. 13, 1759, Robert Oliver, Pequige, and Lydia Gray, Pelham.

CONCERNING THE WOMEN OF PELHAM. 455

Dec. 27, 1759, John Hamilton and Agness Sloan, Pelham.
Jan. 15, 1760, William Henry, Coldrain, and Isabel Gilmore, Pelham.
Feb. 12, 1760, Joseph McCraken, Worcester, and Sarah Turner, Pelham.
April 1, 1760, James Turner, Pelham, and Susanna Thomas, Worcester.
Oct. 21, 1760, John McCreelless, Coldrain, and Hannah Conkey, Pelham.
Oct. 23, 1760, Daniel Gray and Mary Dick, Pelham.
Feb. 26, 1761, James Tafts, Worcester, and Martha Gray, Pelham.
Nov. 23, 1760, James Halburt and Janet Hunter, Pelham.
Oct. 13, 1761, John Walless, Coldrain, and Agness Linsey, Pelham.
Nov. 24, 1761, Samuel Wilson, Coldrain, and Sarah Cowan, Pelham.
Dec. 3, 1761, John Sloan, Salem, and Mary Butler, Pelham.
Dec. 17, 1761, John Lindsey and Mary Thompson, Pelham.
Feb. 2, 1762, John Clark, Blandford, and Ann Maklem, Pelham,
Feb. 11, 1762, Thomas Morrison, Londonderry, and Martha Clark, Pelham.
Mar. 2, 1762, Robert Clark, Pelham, and Mary Patrick, Rutland.
April 13, 1762, Joshua Conky and Dinah Dick, Pelham.
Dec. 9, 1762, Thomas Hamilton, Jun., and Jennet McCulloch, Pelham.
June 2, 1763, Robert Gilmore and Jean Gray, Pelham.
Oct. 27, 1763, Isaac Hunter and Ketrin Dick, Pelham.
Feb. 14, 1764, James Hamilton, Coldrain, and Phebe Henderson, Pelham.
Nov. 15, 1754, Isaac Stevenson, Pelham, and Thankful Savage, Rutland.
Nov. 22, 1764, William Clark, Coldrain, and Mary Petteson, Pelham.
Dec. 20, 1764, Robert Young, Athull, and Elisebeth Gray, Pelham.
Dec. 27, 1764, John Halbert, Chesterfield, and Elenor Colester, Pelham.
Jan. 10, 1765, John Sloan and Ann Fergerson, Pelham.
Feb. 19, 1765, James Clark, Coldrain, and Mary Clark, Pelham.
Oct. 17, 1765, George Gilmore, New Cambridge, and Elisebeth Blair, Pelham.
Dec. 5, 1765, George Thompson and Mary Crosett, Pelham.
Dec. 19, 1765, Samuel Hyde and Hannah Meklem, Pelham.
June 17, 1766, Jonathan Sprague, Ashfield, and Elesebeth Clark, Pelham.
July 24, 1766, James Thompson and Mary Cowan, Pelham.
Oct. 9, 1766, Thomas Torrance, Braintree, and Agness Cochran, Pelham.
Oct. 30, 1766, Mathew Gray and Sarah Barber, Pelham.
Nov. 18, 1766, William Campbell, Murryfield, and Mary Young, Pelham.
Dec. 11, 1766, James Hunter and Susanna Fergerson, Pelham.
Dec. 25, 1766, John Black, Murrayfield, and Jennet Blair, Pelham.
Feb. 12, 1767, Ebenezer Gray and Sarah Johnston, Pelham.
June 18, 1767, Robert Cochran, Bennington, and Mary Gilmore, Pelham.
July 11, 1767, John Anderson, Deerfield, and Jenny McCraken, Pelham.
Oct. 1, 1767, Robert Hamilton, Rutland Dist., and Margaret Conkey, Pelham.
Oct. 21, 1767, James Gilmore and Margerett Berry, Pelham.
Oct. 15, 1767, Hamilton McCollester, White Creek, and Sarah Dick, Pelham.
Dec. 9, 1767, Samuel Wilson, Coldrain, and Agness Dunlap, Pelham.
May 5, 1768, James Pebels and Rachel Young, Pelham.
May 6, 1768, Robert Hamilton and Isabel Conkey, Pelham.
July 7, 1768, Ephraim Hamilton, Blandford, and Margaret Hamilton, Pelham.

Oct. 27, 1768, John Hinncks, Shelborn, and Margarett Gray, Pelham.
Nov. 8, 1768, John McCulloch, New Cambridge, and Isabel Blair, Pelham.
July 25, 1769, Timothy Rice, Chesterfield, and Mary Halbert, Pelham.
Mar. 15, 1770, Seth Morton, Hatfield, and Mary Sloan, Pelham.
June 7, 1770, James Campbell and Mary Ann Dick, Pelham.
June 14, 1770, John Blair, Murrayfield, and Elisebeth Halbert, Pelham.
Aug. 2, 1770, William Johnston and Margerett Meklem, Pelham.
Nov. 8, 1770, Reuben Lothridge and Margery Nolten, Pelham.
Dec. 20, 1770, William Fergerson and Jennet Hood, Pelham.
Dec. 27, 1770, Nathaniel Gray and Sarah Blair, Pelham.
Feb. 7, 1771, Benjamin Kid, Chesterfield, and Agness Johnston, Pelham.
June 20, 1771, James Dunlap and Margarett Dick, Pelham.
Oct. 10, 1771, Alex. McCulloch, New Cambridge, and Jennet Cowden, Pel'm.
Jan. 9, 1772, John Maklem and Martha Thomas, Pelham.
June 4, 1772, John Conkey, Jun., and Margarett Abercrombie, Pelham.
Dec. 3, 1772, Jacob Croset, Pelham, and Eloner English, Greenwich.
Dec. 3, 1772, Abizer Edson and Rhoda Peterson, Pelham.
Feb. 4, 1773, John Buck, Worthington, and Elisebeth Selfridge, Pelham.
April 29, 1773, David Conkey and Sarah Hunter, Pelham.
Nov. 11, 1773, Joseph Hamilton and Ann Oliver, Pelham.
Nov. 22, 1773, Andrew Abercrombie and Mary Conkey, Pelham.
Dec. 23, 1773, Robert Cutler, Pelham, and Mrs. Esther Garnsey, Amherst.
Nov. 25, 1773, Jonathan Cluff, Belchertown, and Elisebeth Croset, Pelham.
Nov. 30, 1773, Charles Kid, Chesterfield, and Frank Hamilton, Pelham.
Dec. 7, 1773, Samuel Finton, Greenwich, and Martha Croset, Pelham.
Mar. 8, 1774, Jonathan Gray, Pelham, and Elisebeth Willey, Worcester.
May 19, 1774, William Ree, Greenwich, and Mary Croset, Pelham.
June 2, 1774, David Sloan, Pelham, and Elisebeth Scot, Leicester.
June 16, 1774, Moses Cooley, Petersham, and Sarah Sloan, Pelham.
June 30, 1774, Joseph Thompson and Margaret Croset, Pelham.
July 29, 1774, Samuel Rush and Elisebeth Cowden, Pelham.
Oct. 3, 1774, Jonathan Hood and Sarah Holland, Pelham.
Oct. 6, 1774, John Rinken, Pelham, and Mary Torrance, Belchertown.
Nov. 29, 1774, James Caldwell McMullen and Sarah McCulloch, Pelham.
Nov. 29, 1774, Joseph Henry, Coldrain, and Margerett McCulloch, Pelham.
Dec. 1, 1774, Nehemiah Hinds, Greenwich, and Anne Pebels, Pelham.
Feb. 2, 1775, Asa Conkey and Margaret Hamilton, Pelham.
June 1, 1775, Oliver Holland and Martha Rinken, Pelham.
March 6, 1776, John Lawson, Shelburn, and Margeret Barber, Pelham.
June 11, 1776, Alexander Conkey, Jun., and Mary Pebels, Pelham.
July 4, 1776, James White and Mary Cowden, Pelham.
Sept. 6, 1776, Philip Freker, Hardwick, and Elisebeth Ransom, Pelham.
Sept. 6, 1776, Timothy Ingram and Persela Richmore, Pelham.
Sept. 19, 1776, Mathew Brown, Murrayfield, and Elisebeth Dick, Pelham.
Oct. 17, 1776, Simeon Peck, Amherst, and Frances Zuillo, Pelham.
Oct. 24, 1776, Moses Ransom and Jennet Fergerson, Pelham.

Dec. 18, 1776, James Gilmore, Conway, and Jean McCulloch, Pelham.
May 13, 1777, David Heirs, Coldrain, and Jean Dick, Pelham.
May 15, 1777, John Johnston and Jean Johnston, Pelham.
June 26, 1777, Mathew Rinken and Martha Torrance, Pelham.
Sept. 11, 1777, Thomas Thompson and Jean Maklem, Pelham.
Sept. 25, 1777, Mathew Gray and Catrin Dick, Pelham.
Nov. 18, 1777, Moses Fulton, Colrain, and Lydia Clark, Pelham.
Dec. 11, 1777, James Petteson and Mary Green, Pelham.
Dec. 18, 1777, John Brooks, Hadley, and Margaret Clark, Pelham.
Jan. 9, 1778, James Cowdin, Pelham, and Rebeckah Hamilton, Shutesbury.
Jan. 29, 1778, Thomas McMullen and Martha Cowdin, Pelham.
May 26, 1778, Jonas Conkey, Pelham, and Ruth Bridge, Shutesbury.
May 26, 1778, Lamond Gray and Isabel Hamilton, Pelham.
June 11, 1778, William Harkness, Jun., and Isabel Gray, Pelham.
July 7, 1778, Adam Petteson, Shutesbury, and Jennet Rinken, Pelham.
Aug. 21, 1778, James Rinkin and Sarah Hunter, Pelham.
Dec. 3, 1778, William Cowdin and Sarah Crawford, Pelham.
Dec. 10, 1778, William Croset, Pelham, and Jenny Thomas, Worcester.
Sept. 9, 1779, James King and Elisebeth McCulloch, Pelham.
Nov. 30, 1779, Samuel Sloan and Eunice Dick, Pelham.
Jan. 27, 1780, William Berry and Naomi Petteson, Pelham.
Feb. 29, 1780, John Alexander, Bennington, and Elisebeth Berry, Pelham.
Mar. 6, 1780, William Mills and Jean McConel, Pelham.
April 27, 1780, Thomas Dick and Mary McMullen, Pelham.
Aug. 21, 1780, George Elot and Eloner Bears, Pelham.
Aug. 24, 1780, Samuel Hathey, Middleberry, and Sarah Stevens, Pelham.
Aug. 31, 1780, Thomas Thompson and Mary Smith, Pelham.
Sept. 21, 1780, Nathaniel Sampson and Nancy Harkness, Pelham.
Sept. 21, 1780, John Berry, New Salem, and Mary Haskell, Pelham.
Sept. 26, 1780, James Blair, Belchertown, and Mary Dick, Pelham.
Sept. 26, 1780, Jacob Gray, Pelham, and Jean Smith, Holden.
Nov. 15, 1780, James Abercrombie and Margery Conkey, Pelham.
Dec. 5, 1780, Isaac Conkey and Rebekah Maklem, Pelham.
Feb. 13, 1781, John Gittee, Black Creek, and Sarah Gray, Pelham.
Mar. 24, 1781, Alexander Torrance and Precila Heket, Pelham.
May 29, 1781, Aaron Gould and Lydia Gray, Pelham.
Dec. 8, 1782, David Harkness and Sarah Gray, Pelham.
Dec. 8, 1782, Robert Croset and Nancy Hood, Pelham.
Mar. 22, 1784, Robert Huston and Katherin Taylor, Pelham.
May 26, 1784, Jonathan Leach, Pelham, and Annie Williams, Shutesbury.
Mar. 30, 1786, William Conkey and Mary Maklam, Pelham.
Nov. 15, 1793, William Hunt, Shutesbury, and Polly Crosher, Pelham.
Dec. 2 1793, Joseph Hinds, German Flats, and Jennet Crosett, Pelham.
Dec. 5, 1793, William Lawson, Greenfield, and Polly Montgomery, Pelham.
April 3, 1794, David Haskell, and Polly Gray, Pelham.
June 25, 1794, John Baker, Pelham, and Hannah Smith, Hardwick.

July 11, 1794, Jonathan Field, Amherst, and Elisebeth Johnson, Pelham.
July 18, 1794, Froa Shirtleiff, and Anne Taylor, Pelham.
Dec. 4, 1794, Ameriah Belew, and Anne Lotherige, Pelham,
Dec. 30, 1794, Robert King, and Sarah Conkey, Pelham.
Jan. 15, 1795, Archibald Fergerson, Hadley, and Polly Latham, Pelham.
May 14, 1795, Frank Peebles, and Polly Billings, Amherst.
Feb. 19, 1795, Daniel Car Gray, and Susannah Crawford, Pelham.
Mar. 2, 1795, Bildad Searl, Southampton, and Phebe Gray, Pelham.
Mar. 12, 1795, Isaac Cowan Hunter, Greenwich, and Alice Wilson, Pelham.
Aug. 27, 1795, Patrick Gray, Pelham, and Lois Hunter, Greenwich.
Oct. 13, 1795, Bezebel Whitney, aud Lucy Shays, Pelham.
Oct. 22, 1792, Jacob Shaw, Shutesbury, and Isabel Gray, Pelham.
Mar. 2, 1796, Joel Conkey, and Molly Thompson, Pelham.
June 2, 1796, Gideon Ingraham, Amherst, and Mary King, Pelham.
June 10, 1796, Gideon Hackett, and Lydia Peeso, Pelham.
Nov. 10, 1796, Aaron Gray, Pelham, and Ruth Powers, Shutesbury.
Nov. 20, 1796, Squire Abbott, and Martha Thompson, Pelham.
Nov. 27, 1796, Seth Sudden, Hadley, and Sally Latham, Pelham.
Dec. 17, 1796, Levi Crawford, and Martha Gray, Pelham.
Jan. 7, 1797, Robert Gitte. Hebran, New York, and Martha Conkey, Pelham.
Jan. 20, 1797, David Conkey and Eunice Thompson, Pelham.
Mar. 2, 1797, Salvenus Wood, and Polly Gray, Pelham.
July —, 1797, Stewart James Park, and Nancy Gray, Pelham.
Aug. 24, 1797, William Berry, New Salem, and Sally Ray, Pelham.
Sep. 7, 1797, David Winter, and Patty Newcomb, Pelham.
Nov. 20, 1797, Samuel Hyde, and Margerett Dickinson, Pelham.
Nov. 29, 1797, Ephriam Weler, Shutesbury, and Rebecca Crosett, Pelham.
Dec. 28, 1797, Titus Randel, Greenwich, and Patty Davidson, Pelham.
Dec. 28, 1797, Ebenezer Gates, and Sally Washburn, Pelham.
April 3, 1798, William Berry, and Nancy McMillen, Pelham.
Jan. 10, 1799, James Harkness, Salem, N. Y., and Polly Rhodes, Pelham.
May 2, 1799, Isreal Conkey and Hannah Conkey, Pelham.
May 29, 1799, Collister Gray and Phebe Tolynan, Pelham.
June 20, 1799, John Taylor and Martha Thompson, Pelham.
Sept. 27, 1799, Joseph Peck, Amherst, and Isabel Hyde, Pelham.
Aug. 7, 1800, Stephen Graves, Deerfield, and Lucy Clark, Pelham.
Nov. 3, 1800, William Oliver and Polly Macomber, Pelham.
Nov. 20, 1800, Samuel Allen Jun and Betsey Davison, Pelham.
Nov. 27, 1800, Robert Lotheridge and Mary King, Pelham,
Dec. 23, 1800, Seth Dunbar, Causenovia, N. Y., and Anne Collah, Pelham.
Dec. 25, 1800, Ebenezar Gray Jr. and Anne Peebles, Pelham.
Dec. 25, 1800, Samuel Peeso and Polly Davinson, Pelham.
Feb. 6, 1801, Robinson Shepard, Hamilton, N. Y., and Nabby Leech, Pelham.
Feb. 13, 1801, John Clark, Buckland, and Susannah Clark, Pelham.
July 2, 1801, David Conkey and Patty Washburn, Pelham.
Aug. 6, 1801, Patrick Peebles and Jenny Gray, Pelham.

Sept. 16, 1801, Daniel Harkness and Betsy Hollan, Pelham.
Sept. 18, 1801, George Macomber and Anne Harkness, Pelham.
—— ——, Daniel Thompson and Sarah Conkey, Pelham.
Jan. 7, 1802, John Stevenson, Greenwich, and Elizabeth Maklam, Pelham.
Feb. 2, 1802, Patterick Peebles and Anne Hamilton, Pelham.
Nov. —, 1802, Asahel Phelps, Northampton, and Annie Hamilton, Pelham.
Dec. 7, 1802, John Rinken Jr. and Anne Hunter, Pelham.
Dec. 7, 1802, William Bosworth and Lucy Thorp, Pelham.
Dec. —, 1802, Samuel Abercrombie and Lucinda Castle, Pelham.
Dec. 30, 1802, Uziel Taylor, South Hadley, and Polly Clark. Pelham.
Dec. 30, 1802, Timothy Leach and Hannah Cutter, Pelham.
Mar. 1, 1803, James Conkey and Batty Cowan, Pelham.
May 20, 1803, Caleb Tilson, Greenwich, and Elizabeth Thirsten, Pelham.
Oct. 27, 1803, William Wilson and Margerett Abercrombie, Pelham.
—— ——, James Peebles, Hamilton, N. Y., and Polly Millen, Pelham.
Nov. 17, 1803, David Peebles, Hamilton, N. Y., and Elisebeth Hamilton, Pelham.
Dec. 20, 1803, William Smith and Rebecca Abercrombie, Pelham.
Jan. 7, 1804, William Lewis, Northfield, and Sally Sears, Pelham.
Mar. 7, 1804, Patrick Phillips, Boston, and Mary Gaven Oliver, Pelham.
—— 1804, John Lotherige and Nancy King, Pelham.
Oct. 4, 1804, Laben Bates, Bellingham, and Chloe Sampson, Pelham.
Nov. 26, 1804, Job Smith and Mahetable Abercrombie, Pelham,
Nov. 29, 1804, William Hunter Conkey, and Olive Bryant, Pelham.
Nov. 27, 1804, William Pratt and Betsey Hathaway, Pelham.
Dec. —, 1804, Elisha Baker and Esther Cutler Lathem, Pelham.
Dec. 15, 1804, Andrew Johnson and Juda Chace. Pelham.
Jan. 19, 1805, Nathan Thayer, Boston, and Phebe Clough, Pelham.
Mar. 26, 1805, Barna Brigham and Anna Hinds, Pelham.
July 1, 1805, Job Packard and Patty Clark, Pelham.
Nov. 28, 1805, Joseph Rinken and Polly Harkness, Pelham.
Dec. 27, 1805, Andrew Gray and Sally Harkness, Pelham.
Mar. 13, 1806, Abraham Follet, Cumberland, R. I., and Roxilana Mitchel, Pelham.
Nov. 26, 1806, Levi Cook and Anna Hardin, Pelham.
Mar. 10, 1806, Joseph Whipple and Dolly Cahoon. Pelham.
—— —, 1807, Warren Conkey and Mary Conkey, Pelham.
Feb. 24, 1807, David Griffin and Betty Cleveland, Pelham.
Feb. 24, 1807, Samuel Caruth Jr. and Susannah Thompson, Pelham.
Mar. 16, 1807, John Dunlap and Mary Oliver, Pelham.
Mar. 16, 1807, Samuel M. Pond Esq., Norton, and Marguerett Danforth, Norton.
July 14, 1807, Smith Arnold, Cumberland, R. I., and Susannah Hall, Pelham.
July 14, 1807, Gardner Sloan and Sally Berry, Pelham.
May 16, 1807, Aaron Clough and Mary Andrews, Hadley.
May 16, 1807, James Stevenson, Greenwich, and Anne Conkey, Pelham.

April 26, 1807, John Thayer, Belchertown, and Polly Hayward, Pelham.
Aug. 10, 1807, John Wheeler, Greenwich, and Sally Vaughn,, Pelham.
Mar. 2, 1808, Eli Haskell, Belchertown, and Betty Fowler, Pelham.
April 26, 1808, Isaac Lazell, Wardsborough, and Lucy Wilson, Pelham.
June 23, 1808, James Hunter, Ware, and Polly Edson, Pelham.
July 6, 1808, Pliny Hannum, Belchertown, and Polly Arnold, Pelham.
Oct. 30, 1808, Pliny Wilson, Belchertown, and Hannah Thompson, Pelham.
Sept. 21, 1808, Samuel Orcut, Wendall, and Mary Wood, Pelham.
Oct. 13, 1808, Ephraim Arnold, Belchertown, aud Mary Crozier, Pelham.
Jan. 26, 1809, William McFall and Judith Parkins, Pelham.
May 25, 1809, Daniel Chapman, Belchertown, and Nancy Smith, Pelham.
Mar. 10, 1810, John Torrance, Belchertown, and Chloe Bartlett, Pelham.
Feb. 1, 1810, Ezra Brown and Polly Lincoln, Pelham.
Aug. 22, 1810, Ansel Shaw and Lidia Vaughn, New Salem.
Jan. 2, 1810, Daniel Willson, Belchertown, and Vesta Harkness, Pelham.
Feb. 19, 1811, Isaac Hamilton and Rachel Hoar, Pelham.
Mar. 12, 1811, Joel Hamilton and Abigail Hoar, Pelham.
Nov. 19, 1811, James Rankin and Margerett Pratt, Pelham.
May 30, 1811, Luke Willington, Starling, and Eliza Bennett, Pelham.
Mar. 24, 1812, Henry Kingman and Sally Robinson, Pelham.
April 30, 1812, Gardner Sloan and Roxana Gray, Pelham.
May 7, 1812, John M. Thompson and Hannah Millen, Pelham.
Dec. 19, 1812, James Crosett and Polly Conkey, Pelham.
April 5, 1813, Dea. Joseph Hamilton and Mrs. Eunice Cowan, Pelham.
May 18, 1813, John Conkey 2^d and Sila Cowan, Pelham.
June 24, 1813, Thomas Vaughn Jun., Pelham, and Louisa Shaw, Greenwich.
Sept. 27, 1813, Patrick Peebles, Madison, and Rebeckah Conkey, Pelham.
Nov. 10, 1813, Thomas Fisher, Pelham, and Abigail Dickinson, Shutesbury.
Dec. 2, 1814, Mr. Josiah Learned and Miss Lucia Childs, Ware.
CONSTANT RUGGLES, Justice of Peace.

"PELHAM, April 29, 1815.
The following persons have been married by me since March last:
April 19, 1815, Giles Rider, Belchertown, and Mary Brown, Pelham.
April 20, 1815, Zebina Rankin and Nancy Packard, Pelham.
WINTHROP BAILEY, Minister of Pelham."

"A list of persons joined in marriage by me the year past:
Mr. Alexander Bartlett, Greenwich, and Miss Lucy Jones, Pelham.
Mr. James Lewis and Miss Rachel Abercrombie, Pelham.
Mr. Benjamin Newell and Charlotte Newell, Pelham.
Mr. Chester Chapin, Heath, and Miss Pamelia Gray, Pelham.
Mr. Wm. Millen and Miss Hannah Thompson, Pelham.
ISAAC ABERCROMBIE, Justic of Peace.
Pelham, March 6, 1815."

Nov. 27, 1815, Samuel Clark, Jr., and Susan Gray, Pelham.
Jan. 18, 1816, David Abercrombie and Mary Eaton, Pelham.
July 28, 1816, Perez Brown, Belchertown, and Polly Andrews, Pelham.

BETSEY OTIS SMITH, WIFE OF JAMES SMITH, AT 80.
Mother of Col. James N. Smith and Mrs. Sidney Dillon.

Dec. 31, 1814, William Millen Sr., and Widow Hannah Thompson, Pelham.
Mar. 5, 1815, James Lewis and Rachel Abercrombie, Pelham.
July 1, 1815, Benjamin Newell and Charlotte Newell, Pelham.
Oct. 1, 1815, Chester Chapin, Heath, and Pamela Gray, Pelham.
Nov. 27, 1815, Samuel Clark Jr. and Susanna Gray, Pelham
Jan. 18, 1816, David Abercrombie and Mary Eaton, Pelham.
Jan. 28, 1816, Periss Brown, Belchertown, and Polly Andrews, Pelham.
Feb. 15, 1816, John Hunt, Belchertown, and Esther Hooker, Pelham.
Mar. 23, 1816, James Smith and Betsey Otis, Pelham.
Feb. 15, 1816, John Hunt, Belchertown, and Esther Hooker, Pelham.
April 24, 1816, Absalom Lord, Athol, and Clarissa Hodgkins, Pelham.
April 25, 1816, Adin Ruggles and Cyntha Snow, Pelham.
June 20, 1816, Henry Richardson and Saloma Snow, Pelham.
July 4, 1816, James Shaw, Granby, and Eunice Fales, Pelham.
July 4, 1816, John Lindsey Millen and Polly Hyde, Pelham.
Dec. 12, 1816, William Harkness and Abigail Turner, Pelham.
Feb. 5, 1817, Charles Billings, Cazenovia, and Sarah Hayden, Pelham.
Mar. 27, 1817, Cyrus Kingman and Phebe Hayden, Pelham.
April 2, 1817, Whipple Cook and Aseneth Grout, Pelham.
May 8, 1817, Chester Gray, Pelham, and Lydia Shaw, New Salem.
May 15, 1817, David Millen and Laura Wetherby, Pelham.
May 27, 1817, Charles Staples and Susanna Mellen, Pelham.
June 10, 1817, Francis Adams, New Braintree, and Naomi Gray, Pelham.
Sept. 23, 1817, Ira Millen, Temple, N. H., and Patty Jones, Pelham.
Oct. 28, 1817, Reuben Newell and Serena Packard, Pelham.
Dec. 24, 1817, Arba Albee and Sally Lewis, Pelham.
Dec. 25, 1817, Robert Barton, Enfield, and Elinor Conkey, Pelham.
Jan. 15, 1818, Zebina Cook and Mary Gray, Pelham.
Jan. 20, 1818, Andrew Sloan, Waterford, N. Y., and Mehetable Conkey, Pelham.
April 12, 1818, Samuel Currier, Belchertown, and Malinda Danforth, Pelham.
May 3, 1818, Joseph Hamilton and Sylvia Cowan, Pelham.
May 21, 1818, Barnabas Sears, Jr., and Polly Gray, Pelham.
May 21. 1818, Daniel Robins Boston and Harriett Willson, Pelham.
Oct. 10, 1819, Cullen Warner, New Marlboro, and Lucy Cooley, Pelham.
Nov. 10, 1819, John Rider, Pelham, and Rebeckah Woods, Enfield.
Nov. 28, 1819, Patrick Millen and Judiath Chadwick, Pelham.
May 23, 1819, Moses Davis, Milford, and Sally Boynton, Pelham.
June 8, 1819, Lyman Draper and Sally Newell, Pelham.
June 17, 1819, John O. Houston and Lucy Taylor, Pelham.
Sept. 30, 1819, David Packard, Enfield, and Azubah Whipple, Pelham.
Nov. 11, 1819, Alanson Chapin and Almira Harrington, Pelham.
Jan. 29, 1820, Lucius Millen, Marcellus, N. Y., and Abigail Mills, Pelham.
April 4, 1820, Grove W. Hannum and Amelia Brown Newell, Pelham.
Mar. 1, 1821, Lewis Cook and Nancy Fales, Pelham.
Mar. 22, 1821, Silas Ballou, Cumberland, R. I., and Sally Harlow, Pelham.

April 19, 1821, Arba Randall, Belchertown, and Esther Smith, Pelham.
May 27, 1821, Jason Carpenter, Hardwick, and Sarah Gray, Pelham.
Oct. 8, 1821, Moses Crosier, Pelham, and Lucinda Danforth, Belchertown.
Nov. 11, 1821, Lemuel C. Wedge and Cyntha Westcott, Pelham.
Nov. 21, 1821, Earl Johnston and Nancy Oliver, Amherst.
Dec. 6, 1821, Learned O. Draper and Anna Comstock, Pelham.
Dec. 6, 1821, Chester Hyde, Bethlehem, N. Y., and Katherine Packard, Pelham.
Dec. 25, 1821, Jonas Bridge, New Salem, and Nancy Ayres, Pelham.
Dec. 26, 1822, Abial Rankin and Mary A. Bryant, Pelham.

Nearly all the marriages from Nov. 27, 1815, to December 1821 were solemnized by Rev. Winthrop Bailey.

"THEN ENTERED IN PUBLICATION"

The usual form of entry of marriage intentions was as in the following record of actual cases.

"March Y^e 21st, 1772, Then Entered in Publication John Conkey Juner & Margarett Abercrombie Both of Pelham."

"July Y^e 3^d 1773 Then Entered in Publication Andrew Abercrombie & Mary Conkey Both of Pelham."

The time elapsing between publication and marriage varied from a few weeks preceding marriage to several months, as in the two cases above cited, of these the marriage records follow.

"June 4th 1772 Then was John Conkey Jun. & Margerett Abercrombie, Both of Pelham Joyned in Marriage."

"Nov. 22^d 1773 Then was Joyned in Marriage Andrew Abercrombie, & Mary Conkey, Both of Pelham."

Cases of publication and a failure of consummation by marriage were substantially unknown; and the publications of marriage intentions are given as the next best thing in the absence of a record of many marriages, which were probably not solemnized in Pelham, or not found on the records.

Sept. 3, 1769, Starling King, Chesterfield, and Mary Henderson, Pelham.
Mar. 17, 1770, John Peebles, Pelham, and Anne Shaw, South Brimfield.
Sept. 9, 1770, Elijah McFarland, Pelham, and Elisebeth Heas, Belshiretown.
Sept. 14, 1771, Mathew Clark, Pelham, and Hannah Stevens, Salisbury.
Sept. 3, 1773, Adam Clark, Pelham and Jean Stewart, Braintree.
Nov. 29, 1773, Frederick Denio, Greenfield, and Lucy Wood, Pelham.
April 2, 1774, William Cowden and Jean Maklem, Pelham.

April 22, 1775, John McKee, Pelham, and Lucy Ramsdell, Greenwich.
Mar. 9, 1776, William Blair and Silence Leach, Pelham.
April 27, 1776, Joseph Hulet, Belshiretown, and Jean Johnston, Pelham.
May 4, 1776, Ebenezer Gray and Agness Berry, Pelham.
Sept. 1, 1781, John Harkness and Keziah Edson, Pelham.
Oct. 28, 1781, John Harkness 2^d, Pelham, and Rachel McNall, Union.
Sept. 8, 1781, James Cowan, Pelham, and Mary Dunbar, Winchendon.
Nov. 3, 1781, William McMillen, Pelham, and Hannah Smith, Holden.
Nov. 20, 1781, Benjimen Hanks, Belchertown, and Anne Edson, Pelham.
Dec. 29, 1781, James Dunlap and Nane Selfridge, Pelham.
Mar. 14, 1782, Joshua Conkey, Pelham, and Millicent Briggs, Shutesbury.
Mar. 29, 1782, John Boltwood, Amherst, and Harmony Briggs, Pelham.
June 2, 1782, Samuel Boyc, Blandford, and Ann Dick, Pelham.
June 27, 1782, Patrick Gray, Pelham, and Abigail Sloan, New Salem.
Sept. 6, 1782, Levy Dickinson, Amherst, and Margarett Peebles, Pelham.
Oct. 28, 1782, Elisha Conkey and Susannah Thompson, Pelham.
Nov. 15, 1782, Reuben Holland and Sarah Conkey, Pelham.
Dec. 9, 1782, Barnabas Faye, Belshiertown and Chloe Packard, Pelham.
Jan. 18, 1783, William Baldwin and Sarah Dunlap, Pelham.
Feb. 17, 1783, Samuel Wilhay, Worcester, and Eanor Conkey, Pelham.
Mar. 22, 1783, Jonathan Killogg, Amherst, and Mary Holland, Pelham.
April 1, 1783, Jos Hunter, Pelham, and Sarah Nilson, Goshen.
April 17, 1783, John White, Belchiertown, and Elisebeth Sloan, Pelham.
April 25, 1783, Peter King and Abigal Ingram, Pelham.
Aug. 25, 1783, Richard Haden and Ellis Hyde, Pelham.
Aug. 31, 1783, William Harkness, Pelham, and Easter Bridge, Shutesbury.
Oct. 24, 1783, Abner Ramsdale and Susannah Scheil, Pelham.
Dec. 3, 1783, Stephen Anderson, Ware, and Bridget Southworth, Pelham.
Dec. 6, 1783, Silvanus Pratt and Lydiah Southworth, Pelham.
Dec. 17, 1783, Hugh Smith and Jennet McFall, Pelham.
Mar. 7, 1784, Robert Johnston and Katherine Taylor, Pelham.
May 21, 1784, Thomas Conkey, Pelham, and Elisebeth Duluphe, Conway.
July 24, 1784, Joseph Latham and Eunice Dunbar, Pelham.
Sept. 15, 1784, James Harkness and Betsey Edson, Pelham.
Sept. 25, 1784, Doct James Wood, Springfield, and Ana Holland, Pelham.
Oct. 6, 1784, Isaac Dodge, Chalton, and Nancy Mcdonnal, Pelham.
Oct. 21, 1784, John Boltwood, Amherst, and Sarah Hayze, Pelham.
Dec. 24, 1784, Ezekiel Conkey and Elizebeth Thompson, Pelham.
Jan. 26, 1785, David Houston and Sarah Pebbles, Pelham.
Mar. 8, 1785, Jonathan McMillen, Dedham, and Sally Freeman, Greenwich.
May 8, 1785, John Maclam, Blandford, and Unice Croset, Pelham.
May 8, 1785, Benjimin Bartlet and Rebeckah Hill, Pelham.
July 17, 1785, John Barber and Zubee Warran, Pelham.
Oct. 6, 1785, George Nukop and Mary Fuller, Pelham.
Oct. 6, 1785, Thomas Gray and Lidia Crbset, Pelham.
Oct. 6, 1785, Daniel Harkness and Lidia Hacket, Pelham.

Feb. 12, 1786, Obed Hunt, Shutesbury, and Dolly Barber, Pelham.
Mar. 5, 1786, Cato Dunsett, Stamford, and Zube Pratt, Pelham.
April 2, 1786, William Ashley and Nancy Pumroy, Pelham.
May 11, 1786, Josiah McKee and Deborah Barloe, Pelham.
May 11, 1786, Luice Baker, Dedham, and Loise Walker, Hardwick.
May 21, 1786, John Hamilton, Jun., and Mary Thomas, Pelham.
July 16, 1786, Mathew Gray ye third and Sarah Croset, Pelham.
Sept. 16, 1786, Samuel Keruth, Barry, and Martha Thompson, Pelham.
Oct. 15, 1786, Joel Gray, Pelham, and Martha Linsey, New Salem.
Oct. 19, 1786, Levi Wood and Bethanie Fuller, Pelham.
Oct. 25, 1786, William Chote Jun., and Mary Conkey, Pelham.
Jan. 1, 1787, Oliver Herroen, Cambridge, and Molly McCulloch, Pelham.
Jan. 6, 1787, Henry McCulloch and Martha Hamilton, Pelham.
Feb. 11, 1787, James Hyde and Martha Thompson, Pelham.
Feb. 11, 1787, Eliot Gray 2^d and Hannah Crawford, Pelham.
Mar. 13, 1787, William Cowan and Eunice Dunbar, Pelham.
Mar. 31, 1787, Samuel Stevenson and Martha Sloan, Pelham.
April 28, 1787, Obed Hunt, Shutesbury, and Lucy Whitney, Pelham.
May 17, 1787, Then personally appeared Mary Barloe of Pelham and made Solloam oath that Obed Hunt of Shutesbury solloamly promised to join with her in marriage previous to her (Lucy Whitney) entering on Publication with him.
Oct. 21, 1787, Eli Hamilton, Greenfield, and Avis Southard, Pelham.
Nov. 24, 1787, Andrew Conkey, Shutesbury, and Martha Marsh, Pelham.
Feb. 2, 1788, Dea. Mathew Gray, Pelham, and Jemina McCorceles, Colrain.
Mar. 4, 1788, James Thompson 2^d and Hannah Gray, Pelham.
Mar. 11, 1788, William Dunlap and Jennett Conkey, Pelham.
Mar. 31, 1788, John McCulloch and Molly Thompson, Pelham.
May 12, 1788, Nehemiah Dunbar, Pelham, and Mary Hunter of Greenwich.
June 10, 1788, Levi Tinkham and Polly Barloe, Pelham.
June 10, 1788, Joseph Renkin, Pelham, and Jemina Keet, Leverick.
June 28, 1788, David Billings, Amherst, and Hannah Hyde, Pelham.
July 11, 1788, Jonathan Ingraham and Mary Haward, Pelham.
Aug. 21, 1788, John Thompson, Jun., and Katuron Clark, Pelham.
Aug. 21, 1778, Jedediah Jewett, Killinglee, Ct., and Mary Atkinson, Pelham.
Oct. 30, 1788, Isreal Crosett, Pelham, and Martha Hamilton, Shutesbury.
Dec. 15, 1788, John Hench and Parses Blair, Pelham.
Jan. 3, 1789, James Lindsey and Margeret Gray, Pelham, second Parish.
Feb. 13, 1789, Winchester Peck, Amherst, and Lydia Pirkens, Pelham.
Mar. 14, 1789, Elihu Hollan, Pelham, and Elisebeth Bradshaw, Amherst.
April 12, 1789, Edward Foster, Jun., and Vise Shurtlieff, Pelham.
April 19, 1789, Elihu Haward and Tryol Hayward, Milford.
July 31, 1789, Jonathan Harkness and Elisebeth Thompson, Pelham.
Aug. 23, 1789, William Lindsey and Susannah McMillen, Pelham, 2^d Parish.
Sept. 6, 1789, Anthony Cutler and Jemima Conkey, Pelham.
Dee. 5, 1789, Esqr Isaac Abercrombie and Martha McCulloch, Pelham.

Jan. 8, 1790, Paul Thurston, Pelham, and Mary Rodgers, Ware.
April 15, 1790, Ichabod Hayward and Ruth Hacket, Pelham.
May 21, 1790, John Atkinson, Pelham, and Mary Woods, Shutesbury.
Aug. 22, 1790, Jeremiah Gray and Margeret Gray, Pelham.
Feb. 14, 1791, Thomas Johnston, Pelham, and Sarah Bell, Newport, R. I.
Mar. 7, 1791, James Forbs, Shoreham, Vt., and Sarah Conkey, Pelham.
April 10, 1791, William Forbush Peebles, Salem, N. Y., and Elisebeth Religh, Pelham.
April 10, 1791, James Bell, Salem, N. Y., and Isabel Harkness, Pelham.
June 10, 1791, Jeremiah Hase and Levince White, Pelham.
June 18, 1791, Alexander Conkey and Elenor McConel, Pelham.
Aug. 20, 1791, Joseph Shaw, Canterbury, Conn., and Prudence Robertson, Pelham.
Aug. 2, 1791, Elihu Gray, Pelham, and Martha Wilson, Oakham.
Sept. 5, 1791, Thomas Brooks and Martha Knapp, Pelham.
Sept. 5, 1791, Ebijah Edson and Sally Atkinson, Pelham.
Oct. 3, 1791, Jeremiah McMillen and Nancy Lindsey, Pelham.
Nov. 17, 1791, George Lindsay and Anne McMillen, Pelham, 2^d Parish.
Jan. 10, 1792, David Huston and Martha Pratt, Pelham.
Jan. 20, 1792, David Clarey, Leverett, and Rhoda Hayward, Pelham.
Feb. 12, 1792, Justus Gray, Pelham, and Lucy Tekiel, Deerfield.
Mar. 11, 1792, Thomas Harlow, Pelham, and Sally King, New Salem.
Mar. 25, 1792, John Gray and Susannah Hunter, Pelham.
June 30, 1792, Isaac Barlow and Hannah Hacket, Pelham.
July 30, 1792, Thomas Johnston, Pelham, and Lucy Ashley, Adams.
Sept. 17, 1792, William Crosett, Hebron, N. Y., and Margeret Gray, Pelham.
Sept. 30, 1792, William McMillen, Pelham, and Jean Linsey, New Salem.
Nov. 10, 1792, Samuel Hyde and Rachel Peebles, Pelham.
Jan. 5, 1793, James Joans, Shutesbury, and Sarah Leach, Pelham.
Jan. 18, 1793, Andrew Hyde, Pelham, and Mary Morton, Amherst.
Feb. 5, 1793, Hugh Moore Johnston, Pelham, and Levina Powers, Shutesbury
Feb. 5, 1793, Seth Foster and Hannah Shays, Pelham.
July 8, 1793, Moses Gray, Pelham, and Marcy Whiteham, New Salem.
Sept. 22, 1793, Joseph Robeson, Greenwich, and Sarah Wilson, Pelham.
June 23, 1794, John Eaton, Jun., Pelham, and Sally Cudworth, Barkley.
June 23, 1794, Jonathan Field, Amherst, and Elisebeth Johnston, Pelham.
Sept. 7, 1794, Abisha Sampson, Pelham, and Damaries King, Taunton.
Oct. 20, 1794, Abiah Southworth, Pelham, and Keziah Boltwood, Amherst.
Jan. 19, 1795, John Cole, New Salem, and Sarah Thompson, Pelham.
Feb. 19, 1795, Robert Stutson, Greenwich, and Isa Crosett, Pelham.
Jan. 10, 1796, Berthiah Holcomb Granger, Hadley, and Sarah Peeso, Pelham.
Mar. 6, 1796, James Thompson, Pelham, and Mitilda Parce, Shutesbury.
April 3, 1796, Jonathan Leach, Pelham, and Lydia Amerson Pettengall, Belchertown.
Oct. 25, 1796, Aaron Gray, Pelham, and Ruth Powers, Shutesbury.
July 2, 1797, Eliphaz Eaton, Pelham, and Polly Barns, Greenwich.

Sept. 24, 1797, John Gray 3ᵈ, and Batsey Rinken, Pelham.
Oct. 14, 1797, Calvin Ashley and Matilda Mun, Pelham.
July 22, 1798, David Winter and Polly Newton, Pelham.
July 22, 1798, William Barry 2ᵈ, New Salem, and Sally Ray, Pelham.
Sept. 13, 1798, Levi Gray, Pelham, and Abigail Robbins, Belchertown.
Oct. 14, 1798, Seth Bryant and Nabby Baker, Pelham.
Oct. 14, 1798, Morrel Leach and Rebekah Howard, Pelham.
Mar. 24, 1799, Elias Shaw, Belchertown, and Mary Thurston, Pelham.
Aug. 11, 1799, Patrick Gray, Pelham, and Battsey Moor, Chester.
Oct. 5, 1799, Henry Strobridge, Northfield, and Anne Montgomery, Pelham.
Oct. 7, 1799, Robert Abercrombie and Mary Thurston, Pelham.
Oct. 10, 1799, Gaius Right, Pelham, and Lucy Sheldon, Ludlow.
Nov. 17, 1799, Samuel Briten, Pelham, and Bashaba Haskins, New Salem.
May 11, 1800, Seth Draper, Belchertown, and Polly Haden, Pelham.
May 25, 1800, Ebenezer Lyskem, Pelham, and Hannah Lach, New Salem.
June 22, 1800, Stephen Graves, Deerfield, and Lucy Clark, Pelham.
July 19, 1800, James Bruce, Greenwich, and Sally Wright, Pelham.
Sept. 7, 1800, Nathan Falten and Mary Hinds, Pelham.
Sept. 29, 1800, Lockwood Barry and Polly Childs, Pelham.
Dec. 18, 1800, Samuel Miller and Jinney Sloan, Pelham.
Sept. 28, 1801, William Hunter, Pelham, and Abigail Andros, Belchertown.
Nov. 15, 1801, Oliver Hamilton and Battsey Gray, Pelham.
Mar. 7, 1802, Amos Blackamore, Greenwich, and Margeret Gray, Pelham.
June 27, 1802, Calister Gray, Pelham, and Hannah Cahoon, Greenwich.
Oct. 24, 1802, Agnostius Chase, Pelham, and Mary Arnold, Belchertown.
May 2, 1803, George Smith and Battsey Cleveland, Pelham.
Oct. 15, 1803, Eliab Packard, Pelham, and Lyda Forde, Abingdon.
Nov. 26, 1803, William Shaw, Belchertown, and Eunice Baker, Pelham.
April 9, 1804, James Sloan and Hannah Leach, Pelham.
Aug. 14, Obed Dickinson, Pelham, and Experience Smith, Whately.
Nov. 11, 1804, Andrew Johnston and Judah Chase, Pelham.
Dec. 25, 1804, William Paul, Greenwich, and Catrin Rice, Pelham.
Mar. 3, 1805, Nathan Peso, Pelham, and Lucretia Dorety, Hardwick.
May 20, 1805, Joseph Howard, Pelham, and Olive Lanord, New Salem.
Sept. 30, 1805, Major John Conkey, Pelham, and Polly Dolan, New Salem.
Oct. 21, 1805, John Falton, Pelham, and Mary Cahoon, New Salem.
Oct. 27, 1805, Thomas Fisher, Pelham, and Venis Simons, Shutesbury.
Oct. 27, 1805, Thomas Sampson, Pelham, and Bettsey Darling, Amherst.
Nov. 25, 1805, David Gray, Pelham, and Ester Clough, Belchertown.
Dec. 1, 1805, Nathanial Gray, Pelham, and Philena Macomber, Shutesbury.
Dec. 1, 1805, Andrew Gray and Sally Harkness, Pelham.
Dec. 15, 1805, Seth Field, Leverett, and Margery Lotherige, Pelham.
Aug. 31, 1806, Paul Thurston, Pelham, and Mary Moody, Amherst.
Nov. 23, 1806, Levi Cook and Anne Montgomery, Pelham.
Jan. 11, 1807, John Ward Jr., Belchertown, and Polly Davison, Pelham.
Feb. 4, 1807, Theverick Weeks, Petersham, and Lydia Borden, Pelham.

CONCERNING THE WOMEN OF PELHAM. 467

June 6, 1807, Rufus Mellin and Eunice Hyde, Pelham.
June 19, 1807, Isaac Powers, Madison, N. Y., and Anne Mellin, Pelham.
Aug. 13, 1807, Isaac A. Conkey and Vesta Hinds, Pelham.
Oct. 10, 1807, Jasper Stearns, Pelham, and Patty Wyman, Winchendon.
Oct. 27, 1807, Eli Gray and Elizabeth Conkey, Pelham.
Nov. 14. 1807, Barzillia Packard, Belchertown, and Olive Rider, Pelham.
Dec. 5, 1807, Amos Tylor, Hinsdale, and Widow Phinneus Larrabee, Pelham.
Jan. 2, 1808, Alexander Conkey Jr., Pelham, and Lucy McColough, Colrain.
Jan. 23, 1808, Joel Johnson, Pelham, and Alenda Fails, Holden.
June 25, 1808, Nathaniel Wheeler, Shutesbury, and Faithful Herrington, Pelham.
July 9, 1808, Elisha Graves, Leverett, and Sarah Hinds, Pelham.
Aug. 27, 1808, Samuel Orcutt, Wendal, and Widow Mary Wood, Pelham.
Sep. 16, 1808, David Mellin, Pelham, and Hannah Patch, Stowe.
Oct. 1, 1808, David Ide, Amherst, and Lucy Draper, Pelham.
Oct. 8, 1808, Pliny Wilson, Belchertown, and Hannah Thompson, Pelham.
Nov. 8, 1808, Oliver Smith, Pelham, and Sarah Gay, Walpole.
Nov. 25, 1808, Nathan Pettengall, Belchertown, and Lavinia Tower, Pelham.
Feb. 17, 1809, Isaac Tower Jr., Pelham, and Polly Haskell, Belchertown.
Mar. 1, 1809, Noble Keep, Jeffrey, N. H., and Anna Johnson, Pelham.
May 6, 1809, Haffield Gould, Pelham, and Betsey Phelps, Holden.
May 6, 1809, John Berry and Betty Millen, Pelham.
July 27, 1809, Levi Millen and Patty Sears, Pelham.
Aug. 12, 1809, Rozel Knowlton, Belchertown, and Prudence Conkey, Pelham.
Sept. 9, 1809, Rev. Sebastian Collumbus Cabott, Pelham, and Electa Osburne, Belchertown.
Sept. 12, 1809, William Millen, Jr., Pelham, and Sally Snow, Greenwich.
Nov. 4, 1809, Pattrick Millen, Pelham. and Livena Sadler, Ashfield.
Mar. 1, 1810, James Cook, Pelham, and Martha Moody, Amherst.
Mar. 15, 1810, Andrew Thompson and Almedia Keep, Pelham.
Mar. 24, 1810, Patrick Gray Jr., Pelham, and Sally Pierce, New Salem.
Dec. 8, 1810, John Harkness Jr., Pelham, and Esther Willson, Belchertown.
Jan. 11, 1811, Samuel Kimball, Shutesbury, and Polly Cook, Pelham.
April 8, 1811, Josiah Pierce Jr., Pelham, and Ruth Ayers, Greenwich.
June 1, 1811, Thomas Packard, Pelham, and Estha Powers, Greenwich.
July 6, 1811, Rufus Nowley and Olive Prat, Pelham.
Aug. 3, 1811, Benony Streter, Cumberland, R. I., and Sally Allen, Pelham.
Jan. 4, 1812, Luther Pomroy, Amherst, and Elizabeth Tower, Pelham.
Mar. 10, 1812, Nahum Wedge, Pelham, and Rhoda Chapin, Heath.
Mar. 27, 1812, Daniel Dodge, Pelham, and Esther Brown, Belchertown.
April 15, 1812, John Berry and Dorcas Thompson, Pelham.
April 18, 1812, Benjamin Bard, Belchertown, and Lucy Davison, Pelham.
Sept. 26, 1812, William Abercrombie and Abigail Bell, Pelham.
Dec. 9, 1813, Silas Rankin, Pelham, and Sally Robbins, Belchertown.
Mar. 20, 1813, David Millen and Patty Rankin, Pelham.
Aug. 16, 1813, Jonathan F. Sears, Pelham, and Polly Town, Greenwich.

Aug. 21, 1813, James Hood and Nancy Harkness, Pelham.
Sept. 27, 1813, Collins Braly and Lurana Jilson, Pelham.
Jan. 29, 1814, Josiah Smith, Boston, and Chloe Harkness, Pelham.
Jan. 29, 1814, Oliver Smith, Boston, and Lovicey Harkness, Pelham.
Jan. 29, 1814, Samuel J. Lincoln, Pelham, and Diana Brown, Belchertown.
June 24, 1814, Alvan Hill, Shutesbury, and Polly Cleavlin, Pelham.
Aug. 29, 1814, Lieut. John Gray, Pelham, and Patty Smith, Rutland.
Sept. 3, 1814, James Cowan and Lovina Miller, Pelham.
Oct. 3, 1814, Daniel Reeniff, Pelham, and Rhoda Comins, Shutesbury.
Oct. 7, 1814, Moses Williams, Amherst, and Teurah Bartlett, Pelham.
Mar. 17, 1815, Daniel Woods, New Braintree, and Widow Nabby Joslin, Pelham.
Sept. 2, 1815, Benjamin Wheeler, New Malborough, and Anna Dunn, Pelham.

NOTE.—The names of those married or published, are printed as written upon the records.

BIRTHS.

It is not our purpose to undertake publishing a list of births for any long period after the settlement of the town, but some of the earlier births may have interest. The earliest birth record was a paper covered blank book, and the earliest entries have become so worn and torn that not all of the entries can be made out clearly, though as originally written they were very plain and distinct, though somewhat too closely written. One of the earliest, if not the first birth record was that of a daughter to Thomas Dick and Margarett Dick, but that portion of the leaf on which the names of children were written has been lost. We give the full list of Thomas and Margerett's children:

Dau. born Dec. ye 18, 1738.
Dau. born Jan. ye 4th, 1740.
Dau. born Aug. ye 29th, 1742.
Son born Oct. ye 7th, 1743.
Dau. born May ye 4th, 1744.
Dau. born Sept. ye 31st, 1746.
Dau. born Sept. ye 17th, 1748.
Son born May ye 12th, 1750.
Dau. born June ye 15th, 1752.
Dau. born June ye 14, 1754.

The family of the first settled minister, Rev. Robert Abercrombie and Margarett Stevenson Abercrombie :

David, said to have been taken prisoner at Bunker Hill.
Andrew, married Mary Conkey, Nov. 22, 1773.
James, married Margery Conkey, Dec. 5, 1780.
Margerett, married John Conkey, Jr., 1772.
Samuel, married Lucinda Castle, Dec. 1802.
John, died at Fort Edward.
William, married 1st Jemima Darling; 2d, Mrs. Nabby Pease.
Sarah, born Oct. 11, 1756, never married, died Dec. 8, 1854.
Robert, married Mary Thurston.
Isaac, born Sept. 30, 1759, married Martha McCulloch, Jan. 6, 1790.
Mehetable, born July 4, 1767, married William Akers.

The family of Rev. Richard Crouch Graham, the second settled pastor, and Molly Graham :

William Lee, born Mar. 7, 1762.
Becca, born Feb. 7, 1764.
Nabby Peggy, born June 23, 1766.
David, born Aug. 8, 1769.

"Rev. Richard Crouch Graham, Husband to Madam Molly Graham Departed this life Feb. ye 26, 1761."

The family of Rev. Andrew Oliver, the fourth settled pastor, and Battsey Oliver :

Mary Given, born July 11, 1786.
Jenny Fulirton, born June 16, 1788.
Wm. Morrison born in Londonderry, Oct. 15, 1791.
Battsey Ormston, born in Londonderry, Feb. 22, 1793.
Nancy, born Nov. 4, 1796.
Margarett, born Nov. 4, 1798.
Robert Ormston, born May 2, 1802.

Probably the first four in the list were all born in Londonderry, N. H., and the last three in Pelham. The size of the families in the earlier years of the town is indicated by transcripts from the birth records of a few families copied from the much worn pamphlet used from the first settlement of the town; it also gives evidence of the numbers who bore the surname of Thompson. Children of John and Prudence Thompson :

Mary, born July 5, 1758.
Thomas, born April 20, 1760.
Susanna, born Mar. 19, 1762.
Elesebeth, born April 10, 1764.
John, born Aug. 6, 1766.
Martha, born Aug. 13, 1768.
Molly, born Oct. 6, 1770.
Sarah, born Jan. 5, 1773.
George, born July 15, 1775.
Daniel, born May 4, 1777.
Eunice, born Oct. 1, 1780.

Children of Joseph and Margarett Thompson :

Jacob, born Nov. 7, 1774.
Jane, born Nov. 17, 1775.
Mirriam, born April 27, 1777.
William, born Sept. 29, 1778.
Joseph, born Mar. 13, 1780.
James, born Sept. 9, 1781.
Elesebeth, born June 5, 1783.
Molly, born Mar. 16, 1785.
Martha, born Sept. 11, 1787.
Achsah, born May 23, 1789.
Joel, born April 23, 1791.
Sarah, born May 11, 1793.

The usual form of death record was as follows :

"James Peebles departed this life March 6th 1784—Husband to Rachel Peebles."

"Levi Thompson Departed this life Nov. 19, 1791—Son to Thomas and Jean Thompson."

"Rebeckah Selfridge Departed this life January 3^d 1815, daughter to Edward and Elisebeth Selfridge."

"Margeret Cowan departed this life June 22nd 1808—wife to James Cowan."

No ages were ever given upon the record book, of those whose deaths were recorded.

Mount Lincoln.

Mount Lincoln is about a mile and a half from the old meeting house, or town hall, in a southwesterly direction. When covered with forest it was known as Pine Hill. The height is given by the state survey as 1220 feet above tide water. It is not remarkably high when compared with Greylock, the highest point in the state, which is 3500 feet above the sea, or with Wachusett which lifts its head 2500 feet above tide. But the wide extent of the view from Mt. Lincoln is quite remarkable. The route to the mountain from Amherst is by the old county highway, and from the west line of Pelham a part of the way it is the same as the sixth chartered turnpike built in Massachusetts, which began at the east line of Amherst and extended to Worcester, the company being chartered June 22, 1799. The ascent really begins as soon as the limits of Pelham are reached, and one on a trip to the mountain must be content to take time and drive slowly. When the summit is reached one finds himself in position to sweep the entire circle of the horizon with unobstructed vision as there is no higher land near by to prevent.

To the west and seemingly close at hand Amherst, with its colleges, its straw factories, its churches, residences and farm houses, is in full view; Hadley's two spires, Hatfield with one, Northampton, Easthampton, Westhampton, Williamsburg, Worthington and other hill towns of Western Hampshire beyond the Connecticut river valley and the farther away hills of eastern Berkshire can be seen. At the left Mount Holyoke and Tom crowned with mountain houses, and south of them the towns of Granby and South Hadley and the cities of Holyoke and Springfield; while still farther south, across the state of Connecticut, we believe East and West Rock may be seen under best conditions of atmosphere.

Toward the northwest Whately, Conway, Sunderland, South Deerfield, and farther on the wild country of Franklin county; while the mass of blue far beyond is the rounded top of Greylock, and the Green mountain range of southern Vermont. Sugar Loaf, with its red sandstone cliff seems but a hillock, and farther to the right are

TOWER ON MOUNT LINCOLN.

BOILING CIDER.

MOUNT LINCOLN.

VIEW FROM THE ENFIELD ROAD TO THE HIGHWAY LEADING TO PELHAM CENTRE.

the rounded masses of Mt. Toby, while beyond them are distant mountains in Southern Vermont.

To the north the steeples of the two churches at Shutesbury are seen above the high land in the north part of Pelham, and beyond the church at Pelham center, New Salem is in full view. In the same direction Mount Monadnock in New Hampshire looms up, and farther to the east, Wachusett in this state is visible. Portions of Enfield, Prescott, Hardwick and New Braintree appear more directly east, while far away Rutland and other western Worcester towns can be located when the afternoon sun shines clearly upon them. To the south portions of Belchertown and Granby are not far away, but owing to the height of "Great hill" in the northern part of the former town the center of the town cannot be seen; the ranges of hills and mountains beyond are located in eastern Hampden or farther away. Close at hand the eye rests upon forest or young growth of trees with now and then a farm-house; probably more of the tract now known as Pelham and purchased of John Stoddard of Northampton can be seen here than from any other point.

It was from Mt. Lincoln that beacon fires flashed forth during the Revolutionary war when it was necessary to give alarm to the sturdy yeoman in this section of the state; and during the geodetic survey of the state the surveyors established a station from which triangulations could be made with other stations of similar character miles away.

Looking toward the west from the summit of Mt. Lincoln the nearest farm buildings are those of Uncle Reuben Allen and Charlotte Johnson Allen, his wife. Here, far up the slope of the mountain, and perhaps three-fourths of a mile from the nearest neighbor, Mr. Allen cultivates the acres of his farms, raises potatoes and corn, gathers hay enough to keep his horse and two cows, and every Saturday in sunshine or storm drives down from his high perch to Amherst with butter and eggs to his customers, and carries back groceries and other necessaries for the coming week in his home and on the farm. Sunday he rests, and on Monday resumes his labors again on the farm; the days go by one by one until another Saturday comes and the customary trip to market is undertaken in the same thrifty business-like way as the previous week. The weeks of summer pass with a repetition of the simple round of duty and labor little varied from week to week, and when the winter comes and the chilling winds pile the snow into drifts, the days are passed in hauling wood from the nearby forest, cutting it for the fires, the care of his horse, his cows, and his hens, until the market day comes with its imperative duty.

EAST SCHOOL HOUSE.

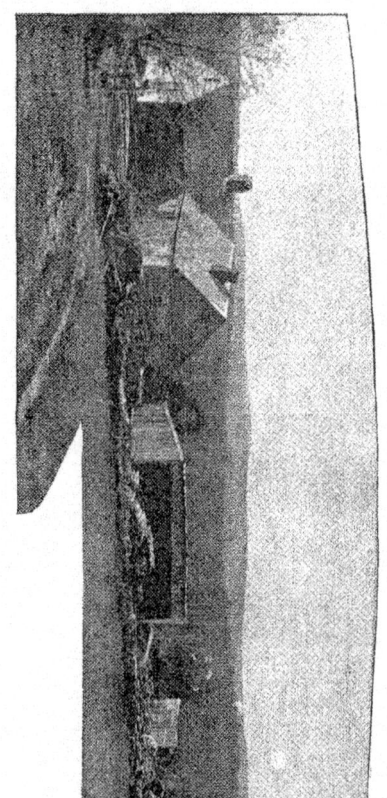

THE REUBEN ALLEN FARM BUILDINGS.

SAMUEL DAVIS'S RESIDENCE.

Old Burial Places.

A SKETCH OF EACH OF THE ELEVEN BURIAL PLACES OF PELHAM.

THE OLD BURIAL GROUND AT THE CENTER.

When the sturdy Scotch Presbyterian settlers took possession of the tract of land now known as Pelham in 1739, it was surveyed and plotted by William Young, surveyor, and ten acres was set apart on the West Hill for use as "common, training field and burial ground." The old burial ground in the rear of the ancient town hall, which the settlers began to build for use as a church almost as soon as they settled, was the first established burial place in the town and is within the ten acres set apart as stated above.

Perhaps an acre and a half of ground is included by the heavy stone fence. Here the early settlers were laid to rest when they died, and the ancient moss-covered stones, stand as sentinels above them. Enough of the inscriptions can be read to show that Scotch names predominated where none are heard now. Such names as McMillan, Patterson, Peebles, Gilmore, Thurston, Dunlap, Houston, Cowan and Johnston are frequently found on these rough stones.

The first settled minister, Rev. Robert Abercrombie, was buried here though no stone marks his grave; and 'tis said that the old church now used as a town hall was moved back into the burial ground, covering some of the graves, and that of the first minister among the rest. Recently, however, this has been disproved and the location of Mr. Abercrombie's grave has been established, it is thought, and a large boulder with a suitable inscription is to be placed at the head of his grave, behind the town hall and near the west wall of the enclosure. Not all accept this as the true location, however.

Rev. Richard Crouch Graham, second pastor of the Pelham Presbyterian church, died at the age of 32, and a large stone marks his grave showing that he died in 1771. One of the oldest fairly legible inscription is on a stone above the grave of Margaret Hood who died in 1758.

Perhaps the oldest record of burial by an inscribed stone is that of " Margerett, Wife of Alexander Conkey, who died Nov. 13, 1756 in ye 75th year of her age." There are many graves which show only as low mounds with no stones at the head or foot, and others with only rough stones without inscriptions and sunk to a level with the mounds they were intended to mark. Of the inscribed stones very few are of marble, but black slate slabs are common. A coarse dark grey stone was much used and was probably quarried, split out and inscribed by the people here. These gray stones are covered with moss and the inscriptions are so much obliterated as to make it almost impossible to decide whose remains lie beneath them. The storms of a century and a half have beat upon them, the frosts of winter have heaved them, some lean one way, others the opposite way, few stand erect, and some have fallen and cover the mounds; others are broken and stand against the wall of the enclosure where some kindly hand has placed them.

No burials have been made in this ancient burial ground for many years ; and of many lying here it can be said none bearing their names are now living in town. The grass that grows among the grave-stones is mowed every summer and carried away, so that the chance visitor can walk among the graves of the first settlers and recall their sturdy virtues, but not much money is expended to beautify and adorn the place. In the early summer the white daisy blooms in profusion among the time worn slabs and upon the graves.

THE WEST BURYING GROUND.

A mile or so west by the main or middle range road is another ancient burial place. It was laid out as early as 1760, and is located upon a hillock which commands a magnificent view down the valley westward, with Amherst, the Holyoke range and the Connecticut river valley in the distance. As it is reached by an untravelled by-way leading off from the main road, no one passing through the town on a carriage drive ever passes this old burial place. It is somewhat larger in area than the one just described at the center of the town and is used occasionally for burials now.

Here we find many well remembered names of families that were large and prosperous during the first half of this century. Descendants of Rev. Robert Abercrombie, are buried here. William and Isaac Abercrombie with their families are here, the former buried

THE OLD GRAVE YARD AT THE CENTER.

J. W. KEITH'S RESIDENCE.

in 1811 and the latter in 1837. Descendants of another family of original settlers are found here, the Grays. John Gray, ruling elder, died in 1782, aged 82, his wife in 1799 at 92. Nathaniel Gray, in 1777 at 32, Dea. Ebenezer Gray, probably the good deacon to whom Stephen Burroughs offered his services as "Supplyer," and showed his letter of recommendation from the Palmer pastor in 1784, was laid to rest in 1834 when 90 years old; James Gray died in 1802, Amos Gray in 1823 and another John Gray in 1852. Stone posts with connecting chains enclose the graves of the Grays.

The Rankins were once numerous in town, there are none now. John Rankin was buried in 1786, John Rankin, Esq., in 1829, Lieut. Rankin in 1830, another John Rankin in 1860. Another common name was Harkness, but it is heard no more in town save as the lettered stones speak. Lieut. Harkness was buried in 1779, aged 57. David Harkness died Mar. 19, 1816, when 59 years of age. Capt. Thomas Dick, one of the original settlers and an officer in the army or militia, was buried here in 1774, aged 70. Robert McCulloch's head-stone tells of his death in 1800 at 80.

Four solid stone posts and an iron fence rusty with age enclosing a lot just large enough for one grave, also encloses a stone which informs the visitors that Nancy Park, 26, wife of Stuart Park, with infant child, were buried in the same grave in 1803. There are graves of Macombers, Westcotts, Robinsons, Eatons, Kingmans and other well known names. Adam Johnson, a liberal doner to Amherst College was buried here in 1823, and a white marble slab bears the following inscription: "Erected by the trustees of Amherst College in testimony of their gratitude for the Johnson Chapel." Not a very generous or adequate testimonial of gratitude on the part of the trustees for benefits received, nor what was promised to Johnson, if current history of the matter is true.

THE QUAKER BURYING GROUND.

At one time during the early part of this century there was a small body of Quakers or Friends in town, led by Uncle Eseck Cook, whose kindly *thee* and *thou* the writer remembers, and their "meeting house" was about half a mile east of the West Pelham Methodist church. Here the little band used to gather on Sunday and await in silence for the spirit to move. Out on the plain west of the meeting house, which is now used as a barn, the "Friends" were buried as one after another they finished their earthly course. The space set apart was not large nor was it ever enclosed by fence or wall. Thirty or forty perhaps were buried here but no marble headstones inform the visitor who they were or when they shuffled the mortal coil. Some of the graves show like low swelling mounds of grassy turf with ordinary stones gathered from the field at the head and feet. Many tenants have occupied the small farm but the plow has never invaded the little burial place upon the plain. No name-inscribed stones are seen, no dates, nothing to indicate who the dead are who lie here, and possibly no person living can identify a single grave or tell whose remains lie beneath one of the slightly raised mounds covered with green sward of June. Once 'tis said an inscribed stone was set up on this spot to mark the grave of Dr. Gulley Potter, a young medical student, who was a son of Dr. Olney Potter, whose parents were Quakers. This act of sacrilege was not looked upon with favor by the Quaker brethren and it is said the stone was twice removed after being erected, as a gentle hint that it was not wanted. As the stone was contributed by fellow students at the medical school, and Dr. Olney Potter wished to have it stand above his son's grave, he was obliged to disinter the remains and bury them elsewhere.

THE ARNOLD BURYING GROUND.

Thirty or forty rods north of the little Quaker burial place, on a sandy hill slope is the burial place opened by the father of S. F. Arnold. The pines are thick on the north and west sides, and a wall of stone incloses the whole. Here rests the families of Arnolds, Stephen and Leonard Ballou, Pliny Hannum, the Cundals, Lovetts, Braileys, Croziers, Jillsons, etc. Here we find the grave of Dr. Gulley Potter, referred to above, and find that he died June 20, 1821, aged 26. Beneath the inscription is the following terse declaration of fact, "Life, how short, Eternity, how long!" The most costly stone here is that erected in memory of Col. Chas. C. C. Mower, who died of cholera in New York in 1849.

THE JOHNSON FAMILY BURIAL PLACE.

High up on the west slope of Mt. Lincoln and within half a mile of the summit George Johnson, a protestant Irishman from Dundalk, Ireland, settled in the year 1837. Here he lived and brought up his family of girls. One married John Gardner and a child by this mar-

TOMB IN THE SMITH PRIVATE CEMETERY.

THE ARBA RANDALL FARM HOUSE.

riage sickened and died of what was thought to be small-pox. Consequently burial was refused in the public burial places and Mr. Johnson buried his grandchild upon a plot of land near his home. A few square rods of land is walled in and fifteen or twenty burials of his family and relatives have been made within the little enclosure. George Johnson the ancestor of the family was buried in 1853 and among the graves are those of two soldier sons-in-law, Lieut. George Johnson of the 25th Mass. and Patrick Bailey of the 27th Mass. and each Memorial Day flags are planted above them which float in the wind until worn out by the blasts that career about Mt. Lincoln.

THE SMITH PRIVATE BURIAL GROUND.

In 1843 or thereabouts James Smith, Daniel Holbrook and Arba Randall set apart a small tract of land upon the farm of the last named and it has been used since for the burial of the members of these families and their friends and neighbors until there are quite a cluster of graves. The yard is pleasantly situated a little to the right of the county road leading to Enfield and a mile and a half from the Methodist church. More has been expended here in beautifying the spot and in erecting costly monuments than in any private burial place in town. A heavy bank wall surmounted by an iron rail surrounds the grounds and a weeping willow waves near the tomb at the northeast corner. James Smith and his wife, Betsey Otis Smith, together with their daughters and daughter's husbands or some of them are buried here. There are Randalls and Browns and Chapmans and Lymans and Smiths, all more or less related to the original founders of the grounds. Robert Brown a soldier of the Revolutionary war is buried here; he died in 1849 at the age of 84, and his son, Martin V. B. Brown, who recently died in Hadley, was the youngest son of a revolutionary soldier in this state if not in the whole country, he being but 55 years of age. James Smith and Betsey Otis Smith his wife, the father and mother of Sidney Dillon's wife, the great railroad builder and millionaire, president of the Union Pacific railroad, recently deceased at New York, are resting here near their old home farm on the hilltop beyond.

BURIAL GROUND NEAR GEORGE KNIGHT'S.

A mile or more along the same county road towards Packardville is another burial ground close by the roadside and not far from the reservoir at the head of Springfield's water supply. It is well cared for except now and then a plot that shows the lack of loving friends. Three tall spruce trees stand near together within the enclosure, otherwise there are few trees or other attractive features. Here we find the names of Browns, Wards, Pratts and Westons and in the southeast corner of the grounds we found the grave of Rev. William K. Vaille, for some years pastor of the Union church at Packardville and the Congregational church at Pelham center. The most unique inscription of all is found upon a white marble slab not far from the road side fence, which reads as follows :

>Warren Gibbs,
>Died by arsenic poison
>March 23, 1860 Aged 36 years
>5 months and 23 days.
>Think my friends when this you see
>How my wife hath dealt by me
>She in some oysters did prepare
>Some poison for my lot and share
>Then of the same I did partake
>And nature yielded to its fate
>Before she my wife became
>Mary Felton was her name.
>Erected by his brother
>Wm Gibbs.

No punctuation marks seem to have been used in the above charge of crime where it was possible to get along without, and the marble worker doubtless followed copy.

PACKARDVILLE BURYING GROUND.

Close by the Union church, where the ground begins to slope to the north is a small number of graves, ten or a dozen in all : quite a number of the stones bearing the name of Hanks, and there is a monument to the memory of the wife of Levi W. Gold. That so few are buried here, is accounted for by the fact that a larger and older burial ground is not far away just over the town line in Enfield which has been used, and is still by both towns.

THE VALLEY CEMETERY

is very pleasantly located in what is known as the Valley district of West Pelham, it is on a sandy hillock above the highway and is one of the later and better cared for of all the burial places visited. It was opened for burials in 1848 and the first person buried here was a Mrs. Wylie, a sister of Asahel Gates, whose farm is not far away. Among the well cared for lots are those of John B. Ward, a citizen of Amherst, Joseph G. Ward, Asahel Gates, Levi B. Hall, and Rufus

Grout. Thomas Buffum and many of his family are lying here. Horace Gray, a former resident of the town, now of Northampton, and a descendant of the Grays that lie in the West burying ground, above described, has a fine monument erected here. Here we read the names and ages of three wives of a well known man now living, who died at 20, 22 and 26 years of age. A monument bears the date of birth and death of four wives of a man now living happily with his fifth wife: the dates of their deaths are as follows, 1855, 1871, 1882 and 1889. The space set apart is nearly all plotted and the lots taken, but more equally high and dry land surrounds it, and is available when needed.

THE WEST PELHAM BURYING GROUND

is located on the county road not far from the Orient grounds, so called, and was laid out about the year 1830, William Harkness being the first person interred in it. Here lie ten or twelve of the same name, once so common. The father, mother, brothers and sisters of Dr. H. W. Harkness of San Francisco are among them. There are other well known names of men prominent in town affairs fifty years ago, among the fifty to seventy-five persons who are buried in this quiet resting place.

In these burial places of the town there are resting many more people than are living in the town now, and many more than were ever living in it at any period since the town was settled. Other causes besides death have been instrumental in removing people from the old town until by the last census there are but 486 inhabitants, where more than double that number dwelt in more prosperous days. The young and active have been going out from the old farm houses where they were born to seek success in the far away cities or at business centers not so remote, until the abandoned farms and the cellars of deserted homes are quite common. Of the living who went forth to battle with the world for success, there is a noteworthy record. Of those who lived here until their life work was finished and whose remains were deposited in one or another of these hillside burial places we may truthfully say:

> " In these villages on the hill,
> Never is sound of smithy or mill :
> The houses are thatched with grass and flowers
> Never a clock to toll the hours ;
> The marble doors are always shut,
> You cannot enter hall or hut ;

> All the villagers lie asleep:
> Never again to sow or reap;
> Never in dreams to moan or sigh,
> But silent and idle and cold they lie."

THE CEMETERY ON THE PRESCOTT SIDE OF EAST HOLLOW.

Having described ten separate burial places in the present town of Pelham it is necessary to include at least one that was in Pelham before Prescott was set off as a town and where many of the people whose names appear quite often among the active men of the town on the records of town and church, are now resting after life's fitful fever. This cemetery was probably opened as a burial place sometime previous to 1780 and is situated on a sandy bluff perhaps 150 feet above and overlooking the west branch of Swift river, whose waters are spread over the low ground by the dam near the bridge until it has the appearance of a small lake or inland pond, making a pretty view looking westward from the northwestern portion of the enclosure. To the east, the great ridge on which Prescott center is located, looms up, seemingly covered by a thick forest growth. Toward the northeast and less than half a mile away is the site of the old Conkey tavern. Near the northwestern corner of the cemetery, William Conkey, the first landlord of the tavern lies at rest. He died Nov. 5, 1788, aged 70, and his wife, Rebeckah Hamilton, is not far away; she died in 1811, aged 84. William Conkey, the second landlord of the tavern, died Jan. 8, 1841, in his 90th year. The moral lesson engraved upon his stone is as follows:

> " 'Tis but a few whose days amount
> To three score years and ten;
> And all beyond that short account,
> Is sorrow toil and pain."

The second William was known to everybody during life as "Uncle Billy." Mrs. Mary Maklem Conkey, wife of the second William, died Sept. 13, 1819, in her 66th year. Mr. John Conkey died in 1784 at 76. John Conkey, Esq., died April 15, 1824, aged 77. His wife, Margaret Abercrombie, died Feb. 1, 1800, aged 53. David Conkey died in 1828, aged 80, and his wife, Patty, in 1840, aged 74. Another David Conkey died in 1861, aged 85. The wife of the latter died in 1819, aged 73. There are many other Conkeys, both old and young, resting here, and among them Ansel and Robert, sons of Uncle Billy.

James Peebles finished his work Mar. 6, 1787 at 48. Another stone informs us by its sculptured story that " Mrs. Rachel Hyde successively the wife of James Peebles and Dea. Samuel Hyde died June 25, 1795." Capt. Isaac Gray, the revolutionary soldier, died in September, 1786, in his 57th year. Dea. Daniel Gray, a leading agitator during the Shays' rebellion, died in December, 1803, at 77. James Abercrombie died in 1836 at 82 years of age. Margery, his wife, died in 1832, aged 75. James Abercrombie, Jr., died in 1859, aged 69. David Abercrombie died in 1851, aged 55. The McMullens—Millens—Mellens, are here; twenty or more graves with this well known surname, but spelled in different ways according to usage at the time they lived. Dr. Nehemiah Hinds, the active physician and man of affairs, lies here; he died July 11, 1825, aged 79. On the stone at the head of his grave is the following inscription:

> "This friend lamented is not dead,
> But gone the path we all must tread:
> He, only to that distant shore
> Where all must go, has gone before,"

Anna, relict of Dr. Hinds, died in 1835, aged 81. Nehemiah Hinds, Jr., Lazetta, a daughter, and John Hinds, the latter dying at 47 in 1826, are also lying here. Barna Brigham, Esq., son-in-law of Dr. Hinds, is also near by. He died in 1834, aged 49 years.

The plot containing the remains of the Chapins is surrounded by an iron fence of elaborate pattern. Within this enclosure lie the descendants of Luthur Chapin, a prominent citizen in his time. His son Alanson had several wives and on the stone marking the grave of Almira Harrington, first wife of Alanson, is the following inscription:

> Died Jan. 16, 1824, aged 24 years.
> "Affliction sore long time I bore,
> Physicians were in vain;
> Till God was pleased to give me ease,
> And free me from my pain."

There are also Cowans, and Smiths and Berrys beside other well known families, who lived and labored actively in the years that are gone, for the best interests of the church and the town, who having finished their labors have been brought here for their long rest. This cemetery is in use now by people in Pelham as well as Prescott. It has been well cared for generally and has an iron fence along the roadside front. The oldest stones are moss grown and worn by storms, and the finger of time has nearly obliterated many names and dates.

Taverns and Landlords.

THE TAVERN OF THOMAS DICK.

Thomas Dick was the first taverner and landlord, and he opened by license in 1749. He continued in the business until 1770 or thereabouts. Further notice of Landlord Dick and his tavern will be found on page 249.

THE OLD CONKEY TAVERN.

No man driving along the dusty highway leading past the site of the old Conkey tavern in the lonely valley of the west branch of Swift river, would ever suspect that in the old tavern, sitting beside the wide open fire-places, the hardy yeomanry of this section gathered to mutter of grievances, and later to sally forth in armed rebellion against the constituted authorities, and government of Massachusetts. But so it was.

It was the ideal spot to gather together the discontented and debt burdened country people from far and near, to rehearse their grievances with each other, and to devise ways and means for relief. There were no telegraph lines, no telephones; no reporters lurking about to hear what was said, and learn of their plans, for there were no morning papers that could be reached in which to publish exciting accounts of rebellious gatherings in the old Conkey tavern, and probably no mail that came oftener than once a fortnight. However loudly they threatened there was no danger of their doings being spread before the public the next morning. They were as safe and secure from interruption as it was possible to be anywhere within the state. The East hill was high and steep, and across the west branch of Swift river rose the companion ridge known as Pelham West hill. Look in whatever direction one chooses as he stands on the site of this old tavern to-day, not a building or habitation can be seen, and so it must have been in 1786-7 when these excited and determined men plotted rebellion, and from the old tavern sallied forth under arms to encounter disaster and defeat.

The tavern was built by William Conkey in 1758. The upright part was two stories in height but low studded and contained but two rooms on the ground floor, and the same number above on

OLD CONKEY TAVERN SIGN, (Front and Back.)

THE OLD CONKEY TAVERN.

the second story. The rooms were all roughly sheathed, no plastering anywhere. The tavern faced the south and the east room was the dining room and the west room was the all important bar-room ; between the two rose the great stone chimney, ten feet or more square at the base. There were large open fire-places in the dining and bar rooms. Across the north side of the upright part a leanto was built for the long ample kitchen with a pantry at each end. In the middle of the south side of the kitchen was the great fire-place where the long back log was rolled to its position to receive the assaults of blazing brands thrust underneath, and piled upon the forestick and backlog. At the right of the great fire-place was a door that led from the kitchen to the bar-room, where the bar with its array of bottles and decanters was set up across the southwest corner. On the left of the great kitchen fire-place was the door leading to the dining room. On the wide stone lintel over the great fire-place in the kitchen was this inscription " William Conkey, June ye 21 A. D. 1776." Another stone lintel inscribed " WilliamConkey," but having no date, was over the fire-place in the bar-room.

The date was cut in the stone to mark the year that changes and improvements were made at the tavern. Silas S. Shores of Pelham has these lintels in use as thresholds in the basement of his house. The front door opened into a narrow hall from which a narrow stairway wound up to the two chambers already mentioned ; turning to the left on entering the front door led to the bar-room, and a turn to the right into the dining-room.

On the southeast corner of the main building swung the tavern sign, consisting of a board perhaps two feet in length by one and one-half feet in width ; on one side was painted a mounted horseman and on the reverse side was a horse held by a groom. This sign is in possession of Milo Abbott of Prescott, who also has the old clock that ticked off the time at the tavern. The furniture of the tavern was of the plainest kind, made for use rather than for show.

In the open space in front of the tavern Captain Shays drilled the man, who gathered at the headquarters, in the manual of arms. The wide casing on the big beam in the ceiling of the bar-room showed many a circular indentation answering in form to the muzzles of the muskets which the thirsty insurgents carried, and which they thrust against the smooth board overhead while impatiently waiting for their turn in front of the bar.

The cellar of the tavern was important because it was there that Landlord Conkey stored his large stock of liquors, as well as a good supply of cider. It was of good depth and the walls instead of being built perpendicular, inclined outward from the bottom. It was in this cool receptacle that the barrels of West India rum and casks of wine and brandy, orange and clove, were stored, and drawn from to replenish the bar. The cellar also furnished storage for a goodly supply of salt pork and beef as well as an ample supply of potatoes and garden vegetables. East of the house was the well with the long well-sweep from which was hung the pole and bucket for drawing the cool water. West of the house were located the barns and other out buildings usually needed upon a farm, and further west towards the West Branch were the acres of mowing and cultivated land belonging to Landlord Conkey's farm from which he filled his barns.

Landlord Conkey kept a good supply of assorted liquors in his cellar sufficient to drown the griefs of discouraged farmers and no doubt the men organizing the rebellion improved the opportunity when argument and discussion became dull and unsatisfying. We offer a copy of one bill of liquors that Landlord Conkey put in his cellar as early as 1772 to show his liberality in providing for the thirst of his patrons:

BOSTON, OCT. 31, 1772.
MR. WILLIAM CONKEY bought of JOHANNET & SEAVER.

```
2 Bbls rum 63 gallons at 12 shillings                      £37—16—0
32 Galls West India Rum at 22 shillings 6d                  36—00—0
4   "   Brandy 30 shillings,—Keg 13 shillings 6             10—13—6
4   "   Annas seed 17   "        "  13     "   6            4— 3—6
6   "   Clove—at 17—6—Keg 15            "                   6— 0—0
3 3-4 " Orange 17—6          "   13 6                       3—19—2
1       Wine 30—                                            1—10
                                                           _____
                                                           £100— 2—2
```

BOSTON, OCT. 31, 1772.
£6—0—0   Received of Wm Conkey six pounds in lawful money on account.   JOHANNET & SEAVER.

BOSTON, FEB. 11, 1773.
Received the within to balance in full.   JOHANNET & SEAVER.

Another bill of liquors that went into the cellar of the old tavern two years later is added proof of Landlord Conkey's liberality in providing for the comfort of his guests many years before men gathered at his hostelry to plot armed opposition to the state government, and before the Revolutionary war began.

ZIBA COOK'S TAVERN.

WATERFALL ON THE DUNLAP BROOK.

BOSTON, 11 FEB'Y, 1774.
MR. WILLIAM CONKEY AND SON WILLIAM bot of JOHANNET & SEAVER.

4 Bb'ls Rum	32		
	32		
	21½		
	29½	125 Galls a 13s	81— 5— 0—
1 Bb'l West India		30½ " a 22—6	34— 6— 3—
15½ Galls Brandy		a 3—6	29— 1— 3—
13¾ Galls Molasses		a 2—6	8— 5— 5—
8⅞ Galls Wine		a 30	13— 6— 3—
8 Galls Orange ⎱ 18⅛ Galls			
10½ Galls Clove ⎰		a 15	13—11—10—
1 Bb'l 27—6 ½ Bbl 22—6			2—10—
1 Bb'l Sugar		2—3—8	
		19	
		——— a £15	39—15— 7—
		£2—2—17	
			£222— 1—7—

William Conkey, the original builder and landlord of the tavern was succeeded by his son William, who continued business at the old stand after his father died. Both father and son were prominent in town affairs for many years. The latter was known to everybody during the latter part of his life as "Uncle Billy" Conkey, and he lived until 1841, and died in his 90th year. East and West Hills remain substantially as they were in 1786-87 and the great hollow lies between. The snow covers all in winter as it did at the time of the insurrection, though not as deeply as then, but is white and cold just the same. The men, armed and excited, who were marching over the hills and through the Hollow and gathered at the old tavern,—have all gone; all marched over into the silences eternal. The old tavern has disappeared, but we can, in a measure, bring back to mind the exciting scenes enacted within and about the old hostelry long years ago. The people who now live upon these two hills and in the great Hollow are at peace; and if not rich, are not so burdened and distressed by debt as those who gathered about the old tavern more than a century ago.

DR. HINDS' TAVERN.

Dr. Nehemiah Hinds was a noted landlord as well as physician and business man. His tavern was on the East hill and was first licensed in 1783. He continued as taverner until 1802.

Landlords Benoni Shurtlieff, Christopher Patten, John Bruce, Harris Hatch, and John Cole appear quite often on the town records, as town meetings were adjourned to the tavern of these landlords, and about in the order named. It should not be understood that these taverns were all in existence at the same time, but it may have been the same tavern stand with successive landlords. The tavern must have been near the old meeting house in order that an adjournment of fifteen minutes to the tavern could be made and business resumed in so short a time, and the tavern must have been on the West Hill.

KINGMAN'S TAVERN.

Martin Kingman was in the field as a popular landlord on the West Hill as early as 1820. The location of his tavern was on the site of the residence of Town Clerk J. W. Keith, perhaps the same building. Kingman was in the business until 1838 almost continuously. Calvin D. Eaton was the next landlord of this hostelry beginning in 1842, and the last license as innkeeper issued to him was for the year 1848. Mr. Eaton was a popular landlord and the tavern was a noted place for gatherings of young people who danced the time away until the small hours to the music of "Old" Fenton's fiddle.

COOK'S TAVERN.

Ziba Cook's tavern was about half a mile south of the Methodist church on the road to Enfield. It was opened as a tavern in 1829, and the last license was issued in 1835. It was a popular resort during the few years it was open to the public. At that time the large carriage factory of Knowles & Thayer at East Amherst was in full blast, employing perhaps 125 young men, and delegations of these workmen were often guests at Cook's tavern until late at night, and went home towards daybreak in a jolly mood which attested the good cheer dispensed at the tavern on the hillside.

RANDALL'S TAVERN.

In 1837 another tavern was opened on the county road beyond Cook's tavern on the way to Enfield, and on the highest point of land before descending towards Enfield. Benjamin Randall was landlord and the daily line of stages from Northampton to Worcester or West Brookfield halted there morning and evening. The old tavern remains much the same as it appeared 50 years ago when the county road was used for passenger travel and for mails.

THE ORIENT HOUSE.

William Newell, shoemaker, a native of the town, who had become quite a mineralogist by making it a study in odd hours when business was dull, and who owned the tract afterwards known as the Orient Springs property, thought he detected mineral qualities in the water of springs that gushed forth in a ravine near Amethyst brook, and

THE ORIENT HOUSE.

HOTEL PELHAM.

analysis showed the presence of iron, sulphur and other mineral substances in solution. This was in 1853 and the water became quite celebrated locally, and many visitors came to drink the water, and some invalids came and boarded in the neighborhood to avail themselves of the benefit of continued use of the waters of the springs. The increasing popularity of the waters led Mr. Newell to build a small house in the ravine on the north side of the brook for the better accommodation of transient visitors. A bowling alley and other attractions were added and in 1858 two brothers named Ballou from Rhode Island, purchased an interest and erected a three story building, using the smaller building already spoken of for an ell or wing to the larger structure. This was in 1858, but before the building was furnished it was destroyed by incendiary fire. The popularity of the waters continuing to increase, notwithstanding the misfortune attending the efforts to accommodate people who wished better accommodations, and in the spring of 1861, Dr. Sornborger of Northampton purchased twenty-five acres or more of land and commenced the erection of a summer hotel, 100 feet long and three stories high. The breaking out of the Rebellion that spring had a depressing effect upon such new undertakings, but it was rushed to completion and opened for business that season.

This building did not occupy the site of those burned, but was on an elevated plateau near the county highway, having a magnificent outlook toward the west and southwest, the foundation of the building being higher than the tower on Johnson Hall, one of the more prominent of the Amherst College buildings at Amherst. Dr. Sornborger was not successful as a manager of the property and it passed into other hands. One proprietor succeeded another with varying success, but with no satisfactory financial results. The last proprietor was Dr. Herman Heed, a well educated physician, and pleasant gentleman who was in possession when the building accidentally took fire and was burned to the ground Feb. 23, 1881.

HOTEL PELHAM.

In 1889 Theodore F. Cook began to remodel and enlarge the Lyman Jenks' house at Pelham center to fit it for a hotel, and in 1890, having completed the improvements, the house was opened to the public under the above name. The house is roomy and well kept and every season there are some who come up to the ancient hilltop to enjoy the pure air and sunshine, and to rest from the cares of business, as guests at Landlord Cook's Hotel Pelham.

Old Advertisments, Etc.

STRAY CATTLE, ETC.

Early after the incorporation of the town the custom of recording the description of stray animals that had been "taken in damage" and otherwise began, and we find in the back part of the first book of records a long list of descriptions of stray animals from which some interesting selections are herewith submitted. The earliest entry is as follows:

"Oct ye 16 1747 Entered by Abraham Gibs of Quabin—A yearling Hefer white With Black Legs a black head & Neck—& a yearling Hefer Colord black with brown Ears & a Brown List on ye Back & some White on ye Belley—& a yearling Hefer Colored Ride With a Short tail with some White under her Belley.

March ye 7, 1748 Entered by Rob't King of Pelham—a black stear coming in two, with apice Cutt of ye Near Ear, letter W ye top of ye Near Horn.

Oct ye 19, 1748 Entered by John Hunter of Pelham two Hefers Coming in three and a steer coming in three one of y^e is Colored ride & ye other two hefers is Ride with white Belley & Some White on ye tail ye steer is Colored Black with white spots these hefers his a Swallow tail Cutt of ye Right Ear.

Nov ye 5 1757 Entered by David Cowden of Pelham a steer a yearling Past Colored aPeal Ride Cropt in ye Near Ear & a Slit in ye off Ear with White on His Belly and White on His Rump & white on his tale.

June 12, 1758 Entered by Robert Hamilton of Pelham—a Darkish Bay Meere Supposed to be Eight past With S pon ye Near hind thigh Both Hind feet white & a long Scrach of white Down Hir forehead a Neatrel troter. Also entered by Said Hamilton a Horse Colt Collerid a Dark Brown supposed to be three past Branded With HD on His off shoulder With some White Hears on ye Middle of His forehead Neatral troter. Also Enterd by Said Hamilton a Yearling horse colt Collored abayesh Sorrel with a larg Bleas in ye forehead Neatrel paser.

Taken up by me the subscriber one yoak of oxen supposed to be four years old Last Spring one of them is a dark Brown with a white Spot on his left thigh as big as half a dollar. Sum Little whight under his Belly the other a Brite Rid with sum little white under his Belly the owner may have them again by applying to me the Subscriber and proving property and paying Charges.   NAHUM WEDGE.
Pelham, July 10 1799."

"ADVERTIZEMENT"

Broke into the inclosure of the Subscriber one two year old Stear about the twenty third of June last having no Artificial mark. Dark brown line Back with White and some other spots of white about his face and legs the owner is Desired to prove property Pay Charges and take him away.
    DAVID HARKNESS.
Pelham July 25 1798."

"Oct ye 19 1764 Taken up In Damige Present by Isaac Gray of Pelham a Black Roand Meer Colt Supposed to be three years old with White on Hir Hind feet & Some White on Hir forehead & a small Bell Hung with a Small Strap.—Paser.

May the 15, 1771 Taken up in Damige present by John Clark of Pelham a Brown & White Cow Supposed to be about Six years old with a white face & a White Strike along Hir Back with a Pice Cut off Hir off Ear Gives No Milk.

August the 19 1771 Taken in Damige Present by John McHertney of Pelham Two White Meers one Supposed to be about ten years old, the other about nine; one a little gray a Bout the head. One Branded on the Near Buttock with the figer of Eight—they both trote & Pace—one of Said Meers his abel on.

Taken up by the subscriber on the sixth instant light Dun Bull Abought Nine Months old the owner is desired to prove property pay charges and take him away. JOHN HARKNESS.
Pelham, Nov. 8, 1789."

" Broke into the inclosure of me the Subscriber one year old heffer on the 16th day of July 1805 a pale Rid with no Artificial Marks on hir the owner is Desired to prove property Pay Charges and take hir away.
JOHN FELTON.
Pelham July 21st 1805."

"MARKS FOR CREATURS."

" Mr Seth Edsons Mark is a Swallow Tail Cut off the Near Ear and a slit in the off Ear."

" May 9, 1794 Mr. Jonathon Grays Mark for Sheep is a crop off the Near Ear."

" May 9 1794 Mr Eliot Grays Mark for Sheep is a swallow Tail out of Both Ears."

" Dec 29, 1796 The Reverand Mathias Cazier puts on his hogs and Sheep a hole in each ear and a half penny cut out the lower side of the ear."

" June 31 1802 Mr. Levi Crawfords mark for sheep is a crop off the Near Ear."

" June 3 1802 Thomas Conkeys mark for sheep is a crop off the off ear and a slit in the Near Ear."

" Aug 9, 1809 Nathan Jilsons Mark for Sheep is half Penny on the upper side of the Left Ear and a half penny on the Wright Ear the under side."

" May 31 1813 Riley Jilsons Mark for Sheep is a slit in the right ear."

" Nathan Jilson Juns Mark for Sheep is a half penny on the upper side of the right Ear."

Of course there were others.

POSTING OF WARRANTS FOR TOWN MEETINGS AND MANNER OF MAKING RETURN ON WARRANTS.

Sometimes the warrants were given to two constables and they notified the voters personally. Then the returns were made by each officer separately, one constable endorsing upon the warrant as follows:

" By varture of the within warrant I have warned ye Inhabitons of Pelham from the Cross Road East, Qualified to vote in town affairs to Assemble & meet at time & place within mentioned."

The other officer would make the same return except that he would affirm that he had warned the " Inhabitons " west of the cross road; which was the road running north and south and crossing the Middle

Range road at the center of the town. Later the two constables would affirm that they had together warned the inhabitants east and west of the cross road. In 1770, meetings were called by notifications posted up by a constable, (place of posting not stated). In 1771 James Hunter, constable, made return that he had notified the qualified voters to meet at time and place " By posting up a Notification on the tree at the Meeting House." Nathaniel Gray, constable in 1772 made a return stating that he had " Posted up a copy of said warrant on the tree Some Rods Southwest from the Meeting house." Another constable posted a copy of his warrant upon "The Chestnut tree near the Meeting house." In 1782 Constables Andrew Abercrombie and Abraham Livermore made the following return : " The Directions of the within Warrant heath been Duly observed to the Within Described Persons Residing East & West of the Cross Road." John Conkey, constable, notified and warned the freeholders and others in 1785 by " setting up an Advertisement on the Meeting House east of the South door." The same constable made the return on another warrant the same year in these words, " By vartue of the within warrant I have observed the Directions of the Same." Andrew Abercrombie made return of his official act in posting a warrant for a meeting, Nov. 26, 1787 as follows :

" By Vartue of the within Warrant I have Set up Advertizments on the old and New Meeting houses (refering to the West and East parish meeting houses) Mentioning the Within articles and Giving Notice Said time and place."

The same constable made this return on warrant for meeting Feb. 15, 1788 :

" By Vartue of the Within Warrant I have Warned Some and Endeavoured that the Rest should have Notice."

Benoni Shurtlieff made a concise return while he was in office, of which the following is a specimen :

"Hampshire ss. by this warrant I have Endeavoured to warn the West parish as the Law Directs."

His brother officer's style was equally direct and pointed :

" Hampshire ss. by Vartue of the within warrant I have Warned Second Parish as the Law Directs.   WILLIAM JOHNSTON, Constable. Pelham June 4 1790."

James Thompson was a popular constable and spread upon the back of the warrants a handsomely turned notice of his official action. A specimen of his style follows :

" By vartue of a Warrant committed to me from the selectmen of Pelham I have Warned and given Notice to the freeholders and other Inhabitance of s^d Town by satting up a Notification on Each Parish Meeting House to meet at time and place within Mentioned. May 4th 1789.
JAMES THOMPSON, Constable.

Stories—Pleasant, and Otherwise.

DE REX VS. HYDE.

Not long after the settlement of Pelham a very worthy family bearing the surname Hyde settled in the Hollow. Among the children was one named Samuel. He was probably full of fun and up to all sorts of mischief as a boy and young man, playing his tricks without thought of the consequences, and was shrewd enough to escape detection for the most part, but there came a time when he was so unfortunate as to get caught. John Worthington, Esq., attorney for ye Lord ye King, was appealed to and Samuel was brought up with a round turn, placed under arrest and brought into court at Northampton to answer for his misconduct. The charges against him are explained by the court records which follows:

"De Rex vs. Hyde 1765. John Worthington Esq attorney for ye Lord ye King in this behalf comes here and gives this Court to understand and be informed that Samuel Hyde of Pelham in ye County of Hampshire yeoman in the night next following the third Day of May Instant did with force and arms privately and secretely and in the night time set up and erect a large Log against one of ye Doors of ye Dwelling house of William Fergerson of said Pelham yeoman and did also set up and erect as aforesaid a large Hoggs Trough against another of ye Doors of said House all with intent to obstruct and hinder ye passage through ye Doors aforesaid and also that s^d Hyde on ye same Night did with force and arms and Secretly as aforesaid take six shirts ye Goods and chattels of ye Said William Conkey from a fence near his house aforesaid where they were then hanging and ye same shirts ye said Hyde did then and there in ye Manner aforesaid throw on ye Ground or rowl in the Dirt so that said Shirts were thereby much Damnified. Also that said Hyde did then and there in like manner break and destroy fourteen Goose Eggs the proper goods and chattels of said William then being in said William's barn and also then and there with like force and Secrecy throw down twenty rods of fence partly surrounding one Close of William Conkey of said Pelham yeoman, and did then and there take off from ye hinges with force and arms and secretly as aforesaid one barn door from ye barn of William Conkey of said Pelham yeoman, and ye same Door put under water in a pond there and heaped stones on ye same to keep it Sunken and Secreted under ye water, all which is against Law and Contrary to ye peace of ye said Lord ye King his Crown and dignity. The said attorney of ye Lord ye King appears and ye said Samuel being held comes here and being set to ye Bar and put to plead says he will not Contend with ye King. It is therefore considered by the Court now here that ye said Samuel for his said offence shall pay a fine of two shillings to ye King &c and Costs of prosecution taxed at two Pounds five Shillings and four pence two farthings.—Standing Committed &c"

There is no evidence that Samuel Hyde was ever complained of afterwards for any such malicious mischief, and there is evidence that he became a much respected citizen and deacon of the Scotch Presbyterian church; was often chosen moderator of town meetings, and was an able town officer. He lived, during the latter part of his life, in the southwest corner of the town of Pelham on the farm now occupied by Hiram Ballou. The highway leading from his house north to the Harkness or Jewett farm was laid out Sept. 13, 1792 and "was built by the town for the accommodation and at the request of Dea. Samuel Hyde;" which gives evidence of the influence he had in town affairs, being sufficient to cause the selectmen to lay out a highway in place of a cart path, for the good deacon's use.

Dea. Samuel Hyde has been lying at rest for more than eighty-eight years, and the inscription on the stone that marks his grave in the West Burying Ground informs the visitor that he departed this life in the year 1810 at the age of 67. The Hyde family has no representatives in Pelham at present, but there are descendants of Samuel Hyde in Amherst who retain all the good qualities of their ancestry.

REV. ROBERT ABERCROMBIE AND THE CHURCH COMMITTEE.

Among the stories that have come down from the time of the pastorate of Mr. Abercrombie over the Scotch Presbyterian church at Pelham, is one which could hardly happen now at the close of the Nineteenth Century, but something might have happened away back in the middle of the Eighteenth century that has been used as a frame work which in the years since has been padded up until it is an enjoyable story that in substantially its present form has been repeated for many years. The Scotch people of Pelham were not total abstainers from spirituous liquors;—total abstinence was unknown;—there were no societies or individuals advocating total abstinence or even the temperate use of intoxicants. While these men were not restrained by temperance reformers they did not often indulge to excess; they were men of strong wills, and their religious faith and training acted as an additional restraint in the social use of strong drink so prevalent among all classes at that time. If the pastor called upon members of his church it was considered of the utmost importance to set before him something to drink, and as good as the house afforded; and when a member of the church or parish called on the minister he did not fail in the social requirements of the time, and flip or toddy was set before his callers promptly, and both partook of the steaming drinks without thought of wrong doing or of the possibility of harm coming to themselves, or of a bad example being set for others. Weddings without wine or other enjoyable social beverage were the exception. The raising of a bridge over the West Branch, of a house, or the frame of a barn without flip or toddy was thought impossible. The first meeting house was raised, but not without a cost of "£11—05s—00 paid to John Crawford for Rum to the Meeting house raising."

While the social events of the times required the presentation of liquors, and all men drank more or less, excessive drinking was not common and the men who became habitual drunkards were but a small percentage of the whole. It was under such circumstances and conditions of the social life of the town and country that the occurrence we are to relate took place and we wish them kept in mind while reading the oft repeated story of Rev. Robert Abercrombie and the church committee. Mr. Abercrombie had many warm friends among the people of his church and parish as well as some not so friendly, and it is fair to presume that some of his church, not any more friendly than they ought to be, started the charge that the pastor was indulging in strong drink much more than the social customs of the times required or allowed; and the charge became so oft repeated that the church as a body was obliged to notice it in justice to themselves, and a church meeting was duly called to consider the grave charge that was in circulation against the pastor. After due deliberation and discussion it was deemed best to choose a committee of three members of the church to wait upon the pastor and in a Christian spirit and temper advise him of the grave charge that had been brought to the attention of the church and in the same kindly spirit to remonstate with him upon the gravity of the charge, and if by any possibility there had been any basis for the alleged over indulgence they were instructed to point out the necessity for the exercise of becoming restraint upon himself in future, so that no repetition of the alleged offence might occur. After having attended to the duty to which they were chosen they were to report at the next regular church meeting. Mr. Abercrombie, though not present at the meeting at which the committee were chosen, was advised of the action taken, and was also advised of the evening on which the committee proposed to discharge the duty laid upon them by calling upon the pastor in their official capacity.

Pastor Abercrombie went home and told his wife he was expecting visitors on such a night, and on their arrival he directed her to follow the usual practice on such occasions, i. e. to mix the flip or toddy, which his visitors would expect to have served; the first time with a small quantity of spirit and a goodly quantity of water. After a reasonable time she was to mix another round of flip, with less water and more spirit than was used the first time, and if the visit was extended considerably a third round of flip was to be prepared using little if any water, but composed almost entirely of rum.

The committee arrived on their mission as Pastor Abercrombie had been informed, and as the custom of the time demanded, the flip was brought in and the committee did not feel it wrong to accept the proffered beverage. The committee and the pastor passed the time in pleasant conversation for sometime,—the committee not finding it quite so easy a matter to broach the business which they had been entrusted with as they expected; but finally mustered up courage to make known their business after the second round of flip, with more rum and less water than the first, had loosened their tongues.

Pastor Abercrombie much to their surprise did not take offence, but on the contrary expressed sorrow that he should have given cause for such action by the church;—if there had been real cause for the charge he expressed himself as thankful for the kindly and Christian spirit manifested by the committee in the discharge of the duty laid upon them, and hoped that the report of the committee to the church would be made in the same spirit of Christian charity and kindliness.

The committee having discharged their whole official duty laid aside their dignity and reserve as well as all thought of having come with a serious charge against their pastor, and proceeded to enjoy the occasion as an exceedingly pleasant social call.

It was quite late in the evening when the last round of flip, composed wholly of rum, and a generous quantity of it, was brought in, and the committee drank freely thereof.

It was not long before the enjoyment of the occasion had so completely overcome the committee that they were unable to go to their homes, and were lying prone upon the floor.

Daylight was showing beyond the line of Pelham East hill when two of them began pulling themselves together to make a start for home, and the drenched nature of the third member of the committee "lay in swinish sleep" until the next forenoon, and some affirm until the afternoon of the day following their official call upon the Parson, before he had sufficient command of himself to set out for his home.

Unlike many other committees who make up reports to lay before the body that gave authority to investigate and report at some future occasion, this committee did not allow the public to learn of what happened at the Parson's on that eventful night, nor what their report was to be at the next regular meeting of the church. For obvious reasons the committee maintained a most determined silence while they awaited the arrival of the time for the stated church meeting.

The days went by one by one until the much dreaded occasion came at which the report of their official visit must be made. The day for the meeting came at last. After some informal matters of business had been disposed of, the committee who were chosen to wait upon Pastor Abercrombie to remonstrate with him for over indulgence on social occasions were called upon for a report.

The spokesman arose to discharge a very unpleasant duty, not so much on account of Pastor Abercrombie as on that of the committee. The report was very brief, and expressed in language which did not lead to discussion or inquiry, as follows:

" The committee chosen at the last church meeting to call upon our pastor, have attended to their duty and desire to report,—*That he gave us Christian satisfaction.*"

REV. DR. PARSONS OF AMHERST, AND THE PEOPLE OF PELHAM.

The Pelham people were much interested in establishing a college at Amherst, and considerable building material was contributed for the first college building by Pelham people, and Adam Johnson left $4,000 to erect Johnson Hall.

After the college was once established there was for many years a systematic and persistant recourse to begging for the institution. Ministers journeyed from church to church to present the needs of Amherst college. A collection followed such sermons in all cases, and much money was obtained in that way. Not only did these solicitors go out to some distance, but they did not forget to present the needs of Amherst college to the churches of near by towns. Pelham did not escape from these importunate calls for funds from regular authorized collectors, nor was all the funds raised by regular solicitors. It was considered a proper thing for any minister to ask for a collection for Amherst college wherever he might be called upon to preach.

One Sunday Rev. Dr. Parsons preached at Pelham, and at the close of his sermon asked for a collection for Amherst college. The boxes were duly passed around the old meeting house, but came back as empty as they started on the tour of the pews.

The Doctor returned to Amherst and on Monday called upon Aunt Rene Cowles, one of his friends, and during his call told Aunt Rene of his experience at Pelham the day previous. "Just think of it" said he, "I went to Pelham to preach yesterday, and at the close of the afternoon sermon I asked for a collection for Amherst college, and if you can believe it not one cent did the collectors get." "Is it possible?" exclaimed Aunt Rene. "Yes," said the Doctor, "didn't get a cent, but you can't guess what hymn I gave out to be sung after I learned that not a cent had been contributed." "Of course not" said Aunt Rene, "but what was it." "Well" said the Doctor, "I gave out the one of Doctor Watts', beginning : ' Oh ! what a wretched land is this, that gives us no supplies.'" "Did they sing it?" inquired Aunt Rene. "Yes they did, and with a will" replied Dr. Parsons.

Doubtless the people of Pelham, with other towns, had been called upon for contributions for the college until it had become monotonous, and withheld money for that reason, and it would not be supprising if they caught on to the grim humor of Parson Parsons in the selection of the closing hymn and sang with a will in appreciation of the Doctor's dry thrust at them for not contributing money for Amherst college at his suggestion.

FARMER HARKNESS AND THE TRAVELLER.

John and William Harkness, brothers, were owners of large farms situated along the county road leading from Amherst through Pelham. Their lands extended from the west line of Pelham three-quarters of a mile or more east and a part of the way on both sides of the highway, and included the lands on the north side of the road where the Orient House stood. The houses they lived in are still standing. John lived in the house now occupied by Joseph R. Powell, and William in the house owned by Mrs. Annette Morgan. They were successful farmers and their pastures extended to the west line of the town, and the stone bridge on the town way south of J. R. Anderson's was built for a cattle pass through which and under the highway their cattle might reach the pastures further west. East of the house John lived in and on the same side of the way are gravelly knolls that were often plowed and sowed to winter rye in the fall for harvesting next season.

Once when John Harkness was plowing these knolls and had halted his cattle to rest near the highway, a gentleman driving a fine pair of horses attached to a nice carriage, containing himself and family was slowly climbing the hills towards Pelham center, and seeing the farmer resting his team of cattle near by, stopped his fine turnout and bidding the farmer good morning, received the usual salutation in return. "I wish to ask you one question," said the gentleman. "What is it?" returned the plowman. "What will such land as you are plowing bear, is what I desire to know." Just then the farmer gave the word for the cattle to go forward and as he resumed the plow handles replied, "It will bear manure, sir."

Quite satisfied of the truthfulness of the farmer's answer the gentleman resumed his journey up the hills towards Pelham.

CRIMES.

Not many crimes of a serious nature have been committed in Pelham since its incorporation. In 1859 Prince Dwelly lost his life at the hands of some drunken companions at the house of Seth Davis on the Second Range Road. Charles Wiley, of Amherst, a companion of Davis at the time, was arrested plead guilty to manslaughter and was given eighteen months in the House of Correction at Northampton. Davis was arrested for assault upon Dwelly, plead guilty and was given five months in the House of Correction, after testifying for the state against Wiley.

On the 11th of April 1881, a dance was held at a building near the center of the town, sometimes used as a cider mill. At this dance Charles A. Briggs, 21, and Charles Stetson, 23, were present. There had been trouble between the two before this meeting, caused by jealousy, and the two had unpleasant words relating to their differences and both went outside the building. Stetson, being near the edge of the highway, when after a few words Briggs drew a revolver and fired three shots at Stetson which struck him in the head, killing him almost instantly. Briggs was arrested and tried for the crime and sentenced to state prison for life, but was pardoned after about ten years. Stetson and Briggs were not natives of Pelham but were living in or near the town temporarily.

On the 26th of December, 1882, there was a great crime committed at the house of Horatio Marsh in the south part of the town on the farm known as the Ellison Dodge place, by Marion Montgomery, who shot his four years old son in the forehead killing him instantly; the shot was in response to the child's request,—" Kiss me papa." The boy was standing on a hand-sled in the kitchen, one that his father had brought as a Christmas present. After killing the boy, Montgomery stepped into the sitting-room and pointed his pistol at the head of his daughter six or seven years of age, but it missed fire and the child ran. Firing again Montgomery shot the girl in the cheek, the ball passing out on the side of the neck without making a serious wound. Montgomery's wife was the daughter of Mr. Marsh and was not living with her husband. He had come to spend Christmas, and the day of the murder, when about to leave asked his wife if she would live with him again; to this she replied in the negative. He then asked if he could have the children, and received the same answer. Then the killing occurred. Mr. Marsh heard the firing and rushing into the house grappled with the murderer, threw him on the floor, face downward, and held him until cords were brought with which Montgomery was bound and taken to the jail at Northampton. He was tried and sent to state prison for life, but received a pardon after a few years. Montgomery was not a resident of Pelham, and his family had resided in town but a short time.

VIEW OF PRESCOTT FROM THE NORTH.

VIEW FROM WEST BURYING GROUND.
Mt. Orient in Pelham on the right, Mt. Holyoke on the left, distant mountains in Western Hampshire.

Sketch of Henry Pelham.
(1696—1754.)

FROM MEMOIRS OF HENRY PELHAM, BY WILLIAM COXE, VOL. II, 301—304.

"Towards him, even political rivalry seems scarcely to have engendered either prejudice or animosity; and, in the estimate of the principles, by which he was guided, the ends which he pursued, and the means which he employed, both his opponents and friends, with little exception, cordially agree.

His knowledge was rather useful than extensive; his understanding more solid than brilliant. His abilities did not burst forth with that splendor which has distinguished the opening career of many statesmen, but were gradually developed by experience and practice, and seemed to grow equal to the occasions, by which they were called into action. He was slow and cautious in deciding, yet firm and persevering, when his resolution was once formed; though he knew the proper time and occasion, to bend to popular prejudice, or public opinion. Instead of declining under the weight of years, his energies continued to increase; and, at no period did he better assume the spirit and authority of a great minister, than in that which immediately preceded his dissolution.

His temper was naturally equable and conciliatory; and his disposition candid and unassuming. He was cautious in raising expectations, but faithful in the performance of his promises. These qualities, instead of being deteriorated by the exercise of power, distinguished to the latest period, the minister as well as the man; and to them he owed more friends, and a stronger attachment, than the most profound and refined art could have acquired. Even his opponents felt the value of such merits; and, however disposed to question the propriety of his measures, they seldom failed to render justice to his sincerity, disinterestedness, and integrity. Indeed, a better proof cannot be given, of the suavity of his manners, and the impression produced by his manliness and candor, than the treatment he expe-

rienced in his intercourse with the sovereign. Notwithstanding the
irritability of temper, and the pertinacity of opinion, which marked
the character of George II., his Majesty invariably behaved towards
Mr. Pelham with kindness and attention; always listened to his
advice with complacency; and, in numerous cases, yielded to his
representations, though frequently opposed to his favorite plans of
continental policy. When he was informed of his death, he testified
his regret by the exclamation, ' Now I shall have no more peace!'

In manner, Mr. Pelham united dignity and ease. Though naturally grave, yet no one was more free from affected reserve or repulsive austerity; and, in his, social hours, no one could more gracefully unbend, and mingle in the playfulness of conversation.

In his public character, he was uniformly moderate and disinterested; and, it is mentioned to his honor, by almost the only author who has treated him with obloquy, that he lived without abusing his power, and died poor. In a word, Mr. Pelham may be ranked among the few ministers who enjoyed at once the esteem of the sovereign, the confidence of the parliament, the respect of opposition, and the love of the people.

Without the natural gifts of a great orator, he always spoke with good sense and effect; and his speeches, though rarely marked with bursts of eloquence, or decorated with rhetorical graces, were remarkable for judgment and perspicuity. Though occasionally too colloquial and redundant, they were delivered with such·candor and simplicity, as to convince his hearers that they directly conveyed the real sentiments of his heart; and were rendered still more effective, by the general conviction which prevailed of his honesty, economy, and patriotism.

By his well known attachment to true liberty, and the respect he ever preserved for the principles of the constitution, he dispelled all suspicions of the slightest intention to extend the royal prerogative beyond its due bounds, or in the least degree to incroach upon the rights of the people. He may indeed be classed among those sound patriots, whom Mr. Burke distinguishes by the name of the Old Whigs, who were equally free from faction on the one hand, and servility on the other.

In the development of his financial arrangements, he is said to have proved himself a worthy pupil of Sir Robert Walpole; and, in many instances, is admitted to have been scarcely inferior to his able master. As a minister, however, he was certainly deficient in a knowledge of the general system of European policy. Indeed, he seems to have limited his cares and ambition to his own peculiar province, the finances and domestic economy of the country; and when he did venture to interfere with the management of foreign affairs, it was rather from necessity than inclination. From this principle, he felt all the sensibility of a financier, with regard to the state of public credit; and gave cause for the complaints of his colleagues, that he sometimes manifested too much despondency and alarm in the House of Commons. Sometimes, also, like Sir Robert Walpole, he was carried by his love of peace to too great an extent of concession. As the head of the financial department, he was a frugal steward of the public money; and, having experienced the difficulties and embarassments attending protracted and unsuccessful hostilities, he was led to consider even a doubtful peace as preferable to the most successful war; and to think no sacrifice too great for the preservation of national tranquility.

To the agriculture, manufactures, and commerce, of the country, he was vigilantly attentive; and not only rose superior to the narrow principles of preceding times, but suggested or promoted a greater number of useful and practical regulations, than any other individual, in a similar period of time, since the Revolution.

The great feature of his administration, is the reduction of the interest on the national debt, and the consolidation of the public funds. This important operation was not only accomplished with peculiar prudence, but with equal justice towards the public and the fundholder; and no better proof can be adduced of its merits and effects, than the ready acquiescence with which it was attended, and the general satisfaction since expressed in its favor.

In his private life, Mr. Pelham was equally moral and regular. He had, as Lord Chesterfield observes, many domestic virtues, and no vices. He was a tender husband, an indulgent father, and a kind master; and though peculiarly liberal in his religious opinions, he was a zealous member of the Church of England."

Representatives to the General Court.

There was no representative from Pelham in the Colonial legislature. Not until after the adoption of the Constitution in 1780 did the town take upon itself the responsibility of electing a man to represent it in the General Court, and assume the burden of paying the man chosen. The amount of money received by members was small, but was paid by the town in the form of a tax. This fact is sufficient to account for the record, "Voted not to send," found quite often on the record books. Pelham did not feel like sending a man every year. In 1857 the district system was adopted, and the smaller towns were thereby substantially shut out from selecting candidates for the General Court, consequently Pelham has not been allowed to select the representative since 1880, and has been represented by one of its own citizens but sixty-one years since 1780. From 1780 to 1782, there was no election, but in the spring of 1783, it was decided to have the town represented. The following is believed to be a complete list of men who have represented the town in the General Court, and the years they served:

Thomas Johnson—1783, 1784.
Lieut. Joseph Packard—1787. Mr. Packard was also chosen to represent
 the town at the Convention for framing the Constitution, 1779-80.
Adam Clark—1788, 1789, 1790, 1792, 1793, 1795, 1796, 1797. He was also a
 member of the Convention of 1788.
Captain Isaac Abercrombie—1799, 1800, 1801, 1802, 1804, 1806, 1809, 1819.
Nathaniel Sampson—1805.
John Conkey—1808.
James Abercrombie—1810, 1811.
Moses Gray—1813.
Henry Kingman—1816, 1820.
Rev. Winthrop Bailey—Member Constitutional Convention of 1820.
Oliver Smith—1824.
Ezra Brown—1827.
Cyrus Kingman—1828. Also member of the Senate, 1849, 1850.
Ziba Cook—1829, 1830, 1831, 1832.
Lewis Draper—1833, 1834.
Whipple Cook—1835.
Luther Chapin—1836.
Rev. Luther Pierce—1837.
Joseph Barrows—1839.
David Abercrombie—1840, 1852.
John Parmenter—1841.
George B. Pitman—1842.
James Thurston—1843.

Calvin D. Eaton—1844, 1848. Also member of the Constitutional Convention of 1853.
Nehemiah W. Aldrich—1851.
Thomas Buffum—1854.
Rufus Grout—1855.
Marcus C. Grout—1861.
Rev. John Jones—1866.
Sylvester Jewett—1870.
Asahel Gates—1874.
Charles O. Parmenter—1880.

In 1890, James R. Anderson of Pelham, received the nomination in the Fifth Hampshire district, but failed of an election because of political combinations, and not because of any lack of ability or fitness for the position.

Town Officers.

Town officers elected at the annual meetings from 1743 to 1762, inclusive, will be found in full on pages from 77 to 112. Moderators, Town Clerks, Treasurers and Selectmen, are given from 1763 to 1898, inclusive. EXPLANATION :— Following the year, the first name is that of Moderator ; second, Town Clerk ; third, Town Treasurer. The three or five names following these are the Board of Selectmen for that year.

1763. *Moderator*, William Croset; *Town Clerk*, John Dick; *Treasurer*, Thomas Dick ; *Selectmen*, Robert Meklem, Hugh Johnston, George Petteson, Isaac Gray, James Cowan.

1764. William Croset; John Dick; Hugh Johnston; Isaac Gray, William Croset, Alexander Conkey, Thomas Johnson, John Crawford.

1765. Thomas Dick; John Dick; Hugh Johnston; William Croset, Daniel Gray, Patrick McMullan, Thomas Cochran, James Halbert.

1766. Thomas Dick; John Dick; Hugh Johnston; John Crawford, Thos. Johnston, George Petteson, Thomas Dick, James Cowan.

1767. William Croset; John Dick; Hugh Johnston; James Halbert, Archibald Croset, Robert Maklem, William Conkey, James Harkness.

1768. William Croset; John Dick; Hugh Johnston; William Conkey, Robert Hamilton, Archibald Croset, John Dick, David Cowden.

1769. William Croset; John Dick; Alexander McColloch; James Halbert, David Cowden, John Crawford, Robert Hamilton, George Petteson.

1770. William Croset; John Dick; Alexander McColloch; Robert Hamilton, David Cowden, George Petteson, James Berry, Archibald Croset.

1771. William Croset; John Dick; Alexander McColloch; James Berry, Robert Hamilton, George Petteson, John Dick, James Halbert.

1772. William Croset; John Dick; Alexander McColloch; John Hamilton, John Dick, Hugh Holland, Robert Hamilton, William Croset.
1773. John Crawford; John Dick; Alexander McColloch; William Harkness, Daniel Gray, John Crawford, John Thompson, Robert Hamilton.
1774. William Croset; John Dick; Alexander McColloch; Thomas Cochran, David Cowden, Daniel Gray, Hugh Johnston, John Crawford.
1775. John Crawford; John Dick; Alexander McColloch; Daniel Gray, Hugh Johnston, Robert Hamilton, George Petteson, John Crawford.
1776. William Croset; John Dick; Ebenezer Gray; William Harkness, James Dunlap, Jonathan Gray, Hugh Johnston, John Thompson.
1777. Daniel Gray; John Dick; Ebenezer Gray; Isaac Gray, George Petteson, James Cowan, Mathew Clark, Ebenezer Gray.
1778. John Crawford; John Dick; Ebenezer Gray; Joseph Packard, Daniel Gray, James Taylor, Jonathan Hood, Abraham Livermore.
1779. Hugh Johnston; John Dick; Ebenezer Gray; Hugh Johnston, Geo. Petteson, William Dunlap, Jonathan Hood, Daniel Packard.
1780. Hugh Johnston; John Dick; Ebenezer Gray; Hugh Johnston, Jacob Edson, John Rankin, Samuel Hyde, Thomas Johnson.
1781. Daniel Gray; John Dick; Ebenezer Gray; Joseph Packard, Daniel Gray, Nehemiah Hinds, David Cowden, Caleb Kith.
1782. Samuel Hyde; William Conkey, Jr.; Ebenezer Gray; Aaron Gray, Joseph Hamilton, Jonathan Hood, William Dunlap, Thomas McMullen.
1783. Samuel Hyde; William Conkey, Jr.; Ebenezer Gray; Aaron Gray, Jonathan Hood, William Dunlap, Joseph Hamilton, Thomas McMullen.
1784. Samuel Hyde; John Rinken; Ebenezer Gray; Joseph Hamilton, Nathaniel Sampson, Timothy Packard, John Pebbles, James King.
1785. Joseph Packard; John Rinken; Ebenezer Gray; Timothy Packard, John Conkey, Mathew Clark, John Bruce, James Taylor.
1786. Nehemiah Hynds; John Rinken; Ebenezer Gray; Mathew Clark, John Rinken, Joseph Hamilton.
1787. Alexander Berry; John Rinken; Ebenezer Gray; Nathaniel Sampson, John Bruce, Alexander Berry.
1788. Capt. John Conkey; Joseph Hamilton; Ebenezer Gray; Jonathan Hood, Capt. John Conkey, John McMullen, Adam Clark, William Choat.
1789. John Rinken; Joseph Hamilton; Ebenezer Gray; Jonathan Hood, James C. McMillen, Mathew Clark, David Conkey, Lieut. John Rinken.
1790. Capt. John Conkey; Joseph Hamilton; Dea. Ebenezer Gray; Mathew Clark, James Dunlap, David Conkey, Lt. John Rinken, Robert Mcklam.
1791. Samuel Hyde; Joseph Hamilton; Dea. Ebenezer Gray; Lieut. John Rinken, Alexander Berry, Lieut. Nathaniel Sampson, David Conkey, Robert McKliem.
1792. Dr. N. Hinds; Jos. Hamilton; Dea. Eb. Gray; Capt. John Conkey, Lieut. John Rinken, Lieut. Mathew Gray, Wm. Conkey, Rob't Croset.
1793. Capt. John Conkey; Jos. Hamilton; Dea. Eb. Gray; Dr. N. Hinds, David Conkey, N. Sampson, James C. McMillen, Capt. John Conkey.
1794. Dr. N. Hinds; Joseph Hamilton; Dea. Eb. Gray; David Conkey, Jonathan Hood, Lieut. I. Abercrombie, Alexander Berry, Capt. Joel Gray.
1795. Alexander Berry; Joseph Hamilton; Dea. Eb. Gray; Lieut. John Rinken, David Conkey, Lieut. Isaac Abercrombie.
1796. Maj. John Conkey; Joseph Hamilton; Ebenezer Gray; Mathew Clark, James C. McMillen, Patrick Pebbles, Robert Croset, John Barber

TOWN OFFICERS.

1797. Dr. N. Hinds; Joseph Hamilton; Dea. Eb. Gray; John Barber, John Pebbles, Adam Clark, Esq., Alexander Conkey, Dr. N. Hinds.

1798. Dr. N. Hinds; Joseph Hamilton; Dea. Eb. Gray; David Conkey, Dr. N. Hinds, Lieut. John Rankin, Alexander Berry, John Peebles.

1799. Dr. N. Hinds; Joseph Hamilton; Dea. Eb. Gray; David Conkey, Lieut. John Rinken, John Hood, Dr. N. Hinds, Robert Croset.

1800. Lieut. John Rinken; Joseph Hamilton; David Conkey; Robert Croset, J. McKliem, Dea. N. Sampson, Dan'l Harkness, Rob't Huston.

1801. Dr. N. Hinds; Joseph Hamilton; David Conkey; John Maklam, Robert Croset, Jonathan Hood, Joel Grout, Lieut. John Rinken.

1802. N. Hinds; Jos. Hamilton; D. Conkey; Maj. John Conkey, Ensign David Wright, Lieut. Samuel Joslin, John Maklaim, Robert McCollah.

1803. Dr. N. Hinds; Joseph Hamilton; David Conkey; Maj. John Conkey, Lieut. Sam'l Joslin, Lieut. John Rinken, John Miller, Ensign David Wait.

1804. Dr. N. Hinds; Joseph Hamilton; David Conkey; Maj. John Conkey, Lieut. J. Rinken, Lieut. Sam'l Joslin, Lieut. J. Miller, Lieut. Moses Gray.

1805. Maj. John Conkey; Joseph Hamilton; David Conkey; Lieut. John Rinken, Jonathan Packard, Joel Grout, Jos. Akins, Jos. Hamilton, Esq.

1806. Joseph Aikin; Joseph Hamilton; David Conkey; Maj. Conkey, Wing Kelley, James Abercrombie, Joseph Aikins, Joseph W. Hamilton.

1807. Maj. John Conkey; Isreal Conkey; David Conkey; Capt. Samuel Joslin, Lt. J. Rankin, I. Abercrombie, Esq., J. W. Hamilton, Capt. M. Gray.

1808. Maj. John Conkey; Isreal Conkey; David Conkey; Maj. J. Conkey, Wing Kelley, Seth Edson, Nathan Felton, Joseph W. Hamilton.

1809. Maj. John Conkey; Isreal Conkey; David Conkey; Maj. John Conkey, Oliver Smith, Lewis Draper, Nathan Felton, Jon't'n. Richardson.

1810. Isaac Abercrombie; Isreal Conkey; David Conkey; Maj. John Conkey, Isaac Abercrombie, Andrew Hyde, Roland Sears, J. Richardson.

1811. Isaac Abercrombie; John Rankin, Jr., David Conkey; Isaac Abercrombie, Andrew Hyde, John Rankin, William Miller, Moses Gray 2d.

1812. Nehemiah Hinds; Isreal Conkey; David Conkey; John Conkey, Esq., Oliver Smith, Jesse F. Peck, Jonathan Richardson, Dea. R. Sears.

1813. Isaac Abercrombie; John Rankin, Jr.; Samuel Clark; Isaac Abercrombie, Henry Kingman, Daniel Harkness, Moses Gray, William Miller.

1814. Isaac Abercrombie; John Rankin, Jr.; Samuel Clark; Henry Kingman, Jonathan Packard, Lemuel Hall, Capt. M. Gray, Barna Brigham.

1815. Isaac Abercrombie, Esq.; John Rankin, Jr.; Samuel Clark; John Rankin, Jr., Luther Chapin, Jesse F. Peck, Moses Gray 2d, B. Brigham.

1816. Isaac Abercrombie; Ithamar Conkey; Samuel Clark; John Rankin, Jr., Henry Kingman; John Taylor, David Miller, James Crosett.

1817. Isaac Abercrombie, Esq.; Ithamar Conkey; Samuel Clark; John Rankin, Jr., J. F. Peck, Lt. L. Chapin, C'pt. M. Gray 2d, Constant Ruggles.

1818. Jesse F. Peck; Ithamar Conkey; Samuel Clark; John Rankin, Jr., Lieut. Luther Chapin, Jesse F. Peck, M. Gray 2d, Barna Brigham.

1819. Jesse F. Peck; Abia Southworth; Samuel Clark; Henry Kingman, Dr. Abiah Southworth, John Gray, David Miller, Joseph Pierce.

1820. Jesse F. Peck; David Abercrombie; Abia Southworth; Samuel Clark, Capt. Oliver Smith, David Conkey, Jr., Moses Gray, B. Brigham.

1821. Jesse F. Peck; David Abercrombie; Dr. Abia Southworth; Oliver Smith, Jr., David Conkey, Jr., Daniel Fales, Barna Brigham, Josiah Pierce.

1822. Luther Chapin; David Abercrombie; Samuel Clark, Jr.; Capt. Oliver Smith, David Conkey, Jr., Daniel Fales.

1823. Luther Chapin; David Abercrombie; Samuel Clark, Jr.; Henry Kingman, Lemuel Hall, Luther Chapin.

1824. Lieut. Luther Chapin: David Abercrombie; Samuel Clark, Jr.; Capt. Oliver Smith, Ezra Brown, Reuben Westcott.

1825. Isaac Abercrombie; David Abercrombie; Reuben Westcott; Oliver Smith, Jr., Ezra Brown, Reuben Westcott.

1826. Isaac Abercrombie; David Abercrombie; Martin Kingman; Oliver Smith, Jr., Ezra Brown, Reuben Westcott.

1827. Isaac Abercrombie; Samuel Clark, Jr.; Martin Kingman; Oliver Smith, Esq., Ezra Brown, Reuben Westcott.

1828. Isaac Abercrombie; Samuel Clark, Jr.; Samuel Clark, Jr.; Ezra Brown, Cyrus Kingman, Pliny Hannum.

1829. David Abercrombie; Samuel Clark, Jr.; Samuel Clark, Jr.; Cyrus Kingman, Ziba Cook, Rufus Grout.

1830. Luther Chapin; Martin Kingman; Samuel Clark, Jr.; Rufus Grout, Samuel Clark, Jr., Benjamin Randall.

1831. Cyrus Kingman: Dr. Daniel Thompson; Dr. Daniel Thompson; Oliver Smith, Jr., Reuben Westcott, David Conkey.

1832. Cyrus Kingman; Daniel Thompson; Daniel Thompson; Reuben Westcott, Martin Kingman, Ezra Brown.

1833. Cyrus Kingman; Cyrus Kingman; Cyrus Kingman; Oliver Smith, Jr., Martin Kingman, Ezra Brown.

1834. Dr. Daniel Thompson; Cyrus Kingman; Cyrus Kingman; Ezra Brown, Asahel Aldrich, Whipple Cook.

1835. Cyrus Kingman; Cyrus Kingman; Cyrus Kingman; Ezra Brown, Rufus Grout, Luther Chapin.

1836. Cyrus Kingman; Lemuel C. Wedge; Lemuel C. Wedge; Luther Chapin, John Harkness, James Thurston.

1837. Cyrus Kingman; Rufus Grout; Rufus Grout; Luther Chapin, Cyrus Kingman, Joseph Barrows.

1838. Col. Cyrus Kingman; Rufus Grout; Rufus Grout; Luther Chapin, Levi B. Hall, Jared T. Westcott.

1839. Luther Chapin; Asa Thompson; Asa Thompson; Jared T. Westcott, Levi Gates, Cheney Abbott.

1840. Martin Kingman; Calvin D. Eaton; Calvin D. Eaton; George B. Pitman, Nathaniel Aldrich, James Thurston.

1841. David Abercrombie; Calvin D. Eaton; Calvin D. Eaton; George B. Pitman, N. W. Aldrich, James Thurston.

1842. David Abercrombie; Calvin D. Eaton; Calvin D. Eaton; Cyrus Kingman, Asahel Aldrich, James Thurston.

1843. David Abercrombie; Calvin D. Eaton; Calvin D. Eaton; Cyrus Kingman, Asahel Aldrich, Benjamin Randall.

1844. Cyrus Kingman; Calvin D. Eaton; Calvin D. Eaton; Cyrus Kingman, Asahel Aldrich, Wyatt Richardson.

1845. Cyrus Kingman; Lyman Jenks; Lyman Jenks; Cyrus Kingman, Ziba Cook, John T. Thurston.

1846. Cyrus Kingman; Calvin D. Eaton; Calvin D. Eaton; Cyrus Kingman, Levi B. Hall, Joel Packard.

1847. Thomas Buffum; Calvin D. Eaton; Calvin D. Eaton; Levi B. Hall, Cheney Abbott, George B. Pitman.

1848. David Abercrombie; Calvin D. Eaton; Calvin D. Eaton; C. D. Eaton, Thomas Thurston, Austin W. Conkey.

STONE BRIDGE OVER THE DUNLAP BROOK.

HIGH WATER IN THE WEST BRANCH, 1897, VANSTONE'S MILL AND THE BRIDGE.

TOWN OFFICERS. 507

1849. Francis Kingman; Francis Kingman; Francis Kingman; Austin W. Conkey, Thomas Thurston, N. W. Aldrich.
1850. Cyrus Kingman; Lyman Jenks, Lyman Jenks; Austin W. Conkey, Ansel A. Rankin, Philander Bartlett.
1851. Monroe Eaton; Lyman Jenks; Lyman Jenks; C. D. Eaton, N. W. Aldrich, David Abercrombie.
1852. Monroe Eaton; William Conkey; William Conkey; N. W. Aldrich, Monroe Eaton, Lemuel H. Newell.
1853. Monroe Eaton; Erastus P. Boyden; Erastus P. Boyden; A. A. Rankin, Moses L. Ward, Philo D. Winter.
1854. D. Abercrombie; E. P. Boyden; E. P. Boyden; A. A. Rankin, P. D. Winter, Emery Ballou.
1855. Alfred Taylor; Lyman Jenks; Lyman Jenks; Thomas Thurston, N. W. Aldrich, Philander Bartlett.
1856. Alfred Taylor; Lyman Jenks; Lyman Jenks; Thomas Thurston, P. D. Winter, D. Abercrombie.
1857. Philander Bartlett; Lyman Jenks; Lyman Jenks; T. Thurston, I. B. Barrows, D. Abercrombie.
1858. P. Bartlett; D. Abercrombie; D. Abercrombie; C. D. Eaton, M. C. Grout, Horace Gray.
1859. P. Bartlett; David Abercrombie; David Abercrombie; Calvin D. Eaton, James M. Cowan, Lemuel H. Newell.
1860. P. Bartlett; D. Abercrombie; D. Abercrombie; Lemuel H. Newell, James M. Cowan, John Jones.
1861. P. Bartlett; C. D. Eaton; C. D. Eaton; James M. Cowan, Warren Randall, Asahel Gates.
1862. P. Bartlett; C. D. Eaton; C. D. Eaton; James M. Cowan, L. H. Newell, P. Bartlett.
1863. Alfred Taylor; C. D. Eaton; C. D. Eaton; John Jones, Dexter Thompson, Alfred Taylor.
1864. S. Jewett; C. D. Eaton; C. D. Eaton; John Jones, A. Taylor, D, Thompson.
1865. S. Jewett; C. D. Eaton; C. D. Eaton; John Jones, Alfred Taylor, A. J. Cadwell.
1866. S. Jewett; C. D. Eaton; C. D. Eaton; John Jones, A. Taylor, P. Bartlett.
1867. Freeman C. Carver; C. D. Eaton; C. D. Eaton; Marcus C. Grout, A. Firman, A. A. Rankin.
1868. F. C. Carver; C. D. Eaton; C. D. Eaton; Marcus C. Grout, Albert Firman, A. A. Rankin.
1869. S. Jewett; C. D. Eaton; C. D. Eaton; M. C. Grout, Sanford Boyden, A. A. Rankin.
1870. F. C. Carver; C. D. Eaton; C. D. Eaton; Moses L. Ward, Lewis Dodge, Samuel B. Davis.
1871. F. C. Carver; George W. Shepherd; George W. Shepherd; Moses L. Ward, T. W. Stratton, S. B. Davis.
1872. F. C. Carver; A. C. Keith; A. C. Keith; S. Jewett, T. W. Stratton, A. C. Randall.
1873. P. Bartlett; A. C. Keith; A. C. Keith; S. Jewett, T. W. Stratton, A. C. Randall.
1874. P. Bartlett; A. C. Keith; A. C. Keith; S. Jewett, T. W. Stratton, A. C. Randall.

1875. John Jones; A. C. Keith; A. C. Keith; S. Jewett, James Hanks, Israel Taylor.
1876. John Jones; A. C. Keith; A. C. Keith; S. Jewett, James Hanks, T. W. Stratton.
1877. John Jones; A. C. Keith; A. C. Keith; S. Jewett, T. W. Stratton, A. C. Randall.
1878. P. Bartlett; A. C. Keith; A. C. Keith; S. Jewett, T. W. Stratton, John Jones.
1879. P. Bartlett; A. C. Keith; A. C. Keith; S. Jewett, M. E. Boynton, D. Shores.
1880. S. Jewett; Adam Cole; Adam Cole; S. Jewett, Myrett E. Boynton, David Shores.
1881. S. Jewett; Adam Cole, Adam Cole; S. Jewett, M. E. Boynton, Asahel Gates.
1882. S. Jewett; John L. Brainard; John L. Brainard; S. Jewett, M. E. Boynton, A. Gates.
1883. John F. Dyer; Justin W. Keith; Justin W. Keith; S. Jewett, M. E. Boynton, A. Gates.
1884. George D. Jones; J. W. Keith; J. W. Keith; S. Jewett, M. E. Boynton, A. Gates.
1885. G. D. Jones; J. W. Keith; J. W. Keith; S. Jewett, M. E. Boynton, C. B. Shores.
1886. G. D. Jones; J. W. Keith; J. W. Keith; S. Jewett, M. E. Boynton, Israel Taylor.
1887. G. D. Jones; J. W. Keith; J. W. Keith; S. Jewett, M. E. Boynton, Dwight Presho.
1888. G. D. Jones; J. W. Keith; J. W. Keith; S. Jewett, M. E. Boynton. Eugene P. Bartlett.
1889. Charles B. Shores; J. W. Keith; J. W. Keith; S. Jewett, M. E. Boynton, H. R. Davidson.
1890. Charles B. Shores; J. W. Keith; J. W. Keith; S. Jewett, M. E. Boynton, H. R. Davidson.
1891. John A. Page; J. W. Keith; J. W. Keith; S. Jewett, M. E. Boynton, H. R. Davidson.
1892. John D. Ward; J. W. Keith; J. W. Keith; M. E. Boynton, E. P. Bartlett, C. E. Humphrey.
1893. John D. Ward; J. W. Keith; J. W. Keith; M. E. Boynton, C. E. Humphrey, John L. Brewer.
1894. John D. Ward; J. W. Keith; J. W. Keith; M. E. Boynton, C. E. Humphrey, J. L. Brewer.
1895. John D. Ward; J. W. Keith; J. W. Keith; M. E. Boynton, C. E. Humphrey, Henry S. Allen.
1896. John D. Ward; J. W. Keith; J. W. Keith; C. E. Humphrey, H. S. Allen, J. L. Brewer.
1897. John D. Ward; J. W. Keith; J. W. Keith; C. E. Humphrey, Lysander H. Ward, John A. Page.
1898. John D. Ward; J. W. Keith; J. W. Keith; C. E. Humphrey, John L. Brewer, C. P. Hanson.

INDEX TO MEN.

Abbott, Charles A 363
Abbott, Cheney 231, 232, 239, 506
Abbott, John 387
Abbott Milo 237, 394, 483
Abbott, Squire 167, 458
Abby, Sabin 177
Abercrombie, Abercromney, Abicromby, Abercrome, Ebercrombie, Crombe, etc.
Abercrombie, A n d r e w 122, 131, 136, 140, 141, 144, 145, 149, 152, 160, 161, 164, 169, 237, 250, 264, 346, 348, 387, 456, 462, 490
Abercrombie, Asiel 439
Abercrombie, David 192, 200, 231, 258, 348, 438, 461, 502, 505, 506, 507
Abercrombie, General 345
Abercrombie, G e o r g e 206
Abercrombie, Ira 192, 438, 439
Abercrombie, Isaac 171, 174, 175, 177, 180, 181, 182, 183, 185, 187, 190, 191, 228, 229, 230, 231, 237, 251, 252, 258, 266, 387, 390, 437, 438, 439, 460, 464, 474, 502, 504, 505, 506
Abercrombie, J a m e s 149, 177, 180, 181, 258, 267, 268, 348, 386, 390, 438, 457, 481, 502, 505
Abercrombie, James, Jr. 481
Abercrombie, John 434
Abercrombie, Otis 438
Abercrombie, R o b e r t, 35, 45, 46, 47, 49, 62, 72, 73, 78, 81, 112, 117, 180, 261, 294, 295, 296, 297, 298, 299, 300, 301, 302, 303, 304, 305, 306, 307,
308, 309, 310, 311, 312, 313, 314, 315, 316, 317, 318, 319, 320, 337, 339, 344, 405, 425, 437, 449, 468, 473, 474, 492, 493, 494, 495
Abercrombie, Robert 2d 387, 466
Abercrombie, S a m u e l 350, 352, 355, 438, 459
Abercrombie, Stillman 207, 361
Abercrombie, William 177, 467, 474
Adams, Francis 461
Adams, Newton 433
Adams, O W 290
Adams, Samuel 143
Adams, W H 290
Airs, Beunos 177, 230
Akers, Joseph 174, 175, 237
Akers, William 468
Albee, Arba 461
Alby, Laben 271
Alden, Colonel 354
Alden, Howard 351
Alden, John 449
Aldrich, Asahel 271, 506
Aldrich, Charles P 232, 446
Aldrich, Martin 204
Aldrich Nathaniel 506
Aldrich, Olney 204
Aldrich, Tyler D 204
Aldrich, Nehemiah W 199, 503, 506, 507
Alexander, James 17, 22, 24, 26, 31, 33, 40, 46, 52, 53, 79, 81, 84
Alexander, John Jr 96
Alexander, John 17, 24, 31, 39, 46, 47, 49, 77, 79, 117, 124, 128, 298, 346, 457
Allen, David H 204
Allen, George W 363
Allen, Henry S 233, 508
Allen, Jesse 271
Allen, Joseph D. 361

Allen, Lewis W 241, 242
Allen, Matthew 13, 17
Allen, Reuben 472
Allen, Samuel Jr 458
Ames, Lewis 390
Amherst, Jeffry 344
Amsdill, Abner 387, 390
Anderson, James R 233, 497, 503
Anderson, John 104, 226, 455
Anderson, Stephen 463
Andrews, Stephen 387, 389
Andross, Stephen 177
Anthony, Mr 242
Arms, Levi 387
Arnold, Ephraim 1 7 7, 460
Arnold, Samuel 176, 177, 179, 180, 287, 291, 426
Arnold, Savannah 243
Arnold, Samuel F. 204, 206, 426, 476
Arnold, Smith 459
Ashley, Calvin 466
Ashley, William 251, 387, 464
Atkins, Joseph 177, 273, 505
Atkinson, John 353, 465
Avery, William 204
Ayers, William Jedediah 157
Baker, Elisha 459
Baker, Eseck 271
Baker, Ezekiel 169, 386, 390
Baker, Eziar 351
Baker, Isaac 149, 280, 387
Baker, James 348, 350, 352, 353, 354, 355, 387, 389
Baker, John 177, 230, 239, 457
Baker, Jonathan 390
Baker, Lewis 387, 464
Badlam, Ezra 348

34

Bailey, Patrick 360, 477
Bailey, William A 446
Bailey, Winthrop 186,
 188, 190, 191, 231, 269,
 270, 282, 283, 460, 462,
 502
Balden, William 149, 166
Baldwin, Elisha 390
Baldwin, Rev 321
Baldwin, Moses 272
Baldwin, William 177,
 352, 355, 387
Ballard, Jeremiah 122
Ballard, Joshua 177
Ballou, Emery 507
Ballou, Hiram 176, 199,
 213, 492
Ballou, Leonard 356, 357,
 476
Ballou, Silas 461
Ballou, Stephen 178, 476
Bancroft, Ensign 351
Bangliss, Colonel 349
Bannister, Andrew 229
Barber, John 155, 227,
 229, 230, 387, 463, 504,
 505
Barber, Robert 19, 24, 27,
 31, 454
Bard, Benjamin 467
Bardwell, L A 290
Bardwell, William 290
Barlow, Eliakim 386
Barlow, Isaac 387, 465
Barnard, Salah 344
Barnes, Ansel 206
Barnes, Dexter R 361
Barnes, Estus 204, 206
Barnes, James 346, 348
Barnes, Lauriston 364
Barnum, William H 429
Barrett, Benjamin 415,
 422, 433
Barrows, Henry 204, 206,
 360
Barrows, Isaac B 200,
 507
Barrows, Joseph 357, 502,
 506
Barrows, William 231,
 232, 256
Barrus, John, 157
Barry, Lockwood 466
Barry, William 2d 466
Bartlett, Alexander 460
Bartlett, Benjamin 463
Bartlett, Eugene P 242,
 248, 446, 508

Bartlett, Emerson 204
Bartlett, Joseph F 358,
 364
Bartlett, Leander L 242,
 446
Bartlett, Philander 203,
 206, 212, 507, 508
Barton, A S 204
Barton, Eliakim 390
Barton, Robert 461
Bassett, William 287
Bates, Laben 459
Bay, Andrew 124, 262
Bayley, Colonel 354
Bayington, Asa 178
Bayington, Ebenezer
 178
Bayington, Silas 178, 206,
 230, 264
Beckwith, S R 443
Beecher, H W 430
Beers, Dr 259
Belcher, Jonathan 10
Belew, Ameriah 458
Bell, James 465
Bent, G R 206, 290
Bennett, Isaac 346, 350,
 351, 353, 354, 355
Bennett, Peter 129, 137
Berry, Barry
Berry, Alexander 146,
 160, 161, 169, 177, 180,
 227, 228, 229, 250, 251,
 271, 279, 280, 343, 346,
 504, 505
Berry, James 98, 100, 120,
 225, 405, 503
Berry, John 457, 467
Berry, William 271, 275,
 277, 279, 280, 349, 457,
 458
Bigelow, I B 232, 290
Bigelow Rev 288
Billings, David 464
Billings, Charles 461
Billings, Elihu 251, 386
Billings, E N 293
Billings, Isreal 342
Billings, Joel 373, 375
Billings, Mr 299, 300
Black, John 455
Blackmar, W P 291
Blackmer, Barnabas 386
Blackmer, Frank T 424
Blackamore, Amos 466
Blair, James 457
Blair, John 81. 85, 88, 89,
 90, 91, 92, 93, 94, 96, 97,

 100, 101, 120, 225, 305,
 307, 343, 456
Blair, Robert, 88, 90, 91,
 92, 97, 117
Blair, William 144, 348,
 463
Bliss, Colonel 143
Bliss, Zenas 285
Blodgett, Francis A 359,
 364
Blodgett, Joseph, 275,
 276
Boltwood, John 463
Boltwood, Solomon 46,
 47, 410, 411
Boltwood, William 115
Boyden, Erastus P 507
Boyden, Sanford 204,
 206, 507
Bosworth, Lorenzo 290
Bosworth, William 459
Bowdoin, James 375, 376,
 380, 381, 385, 387, 389,
 398
Boyc, Samuel 463
Boyd. Rev 315
Boyd, William 8
Boynton, Joseph E 361
Boynton, Myrett E 204,
 233, 255, 508
Bradford, William 412
Bradstreet, General 345
 447
Brailey, Collins 81, 82,
 223, 243, 271, 468
Brailey. John 243
Brailey, Solomon 177, 270
Brainard, Elijah 266, 267,
 268
Brainard, Daniel 443
Brainard, John L 232,
 233, 508
Bramble, Franklin 204,
 360, 364
Brand, Amos 352, 355
Breakenridge, James 24,
 31, 33
Brewer, John L 233, 247
Brewer, Jonathan 347
Bridge, Colonel 348
Bridge, Jonas 462
Briggs, Charles A 498
Briggs, Isaac 231
Briggs, Mr 239
Briten, Samuel 466
Brigham, Barnabas 177,
 230, 250, 258, 459, 481,
 505

INDEX TO MEN.

Brigham, Liscomb 177, 230, 252, 271
Brooks, John 457
Brooks, Thomas 465
Brown, Edward 352
Brown, Elam 387
Brown, Ezra 178, 191,244, 58, 271, 460, 502, 506
Brown, Isaac L 231
Brown, John 375
Brown, M V B 477
Brown, Matthew 18, 49, 386, 456
Brown, Osborn 123
Brown, Perez 461
Brown, R 184
Brown, Robert 477
Brown, Waltham 129
Brown, William 178, 454
Bruce, Abijah 260, 353, 354
Bruce, James 466
Bruce, John 143, 148, 151, 152, 155, 159, 250, 251, 386, 485, 504
Bryant, Amos 353
Bryant, Edwin 445
Bryant, Ichabod 177
Bryant & Kingman 253
Bryant, Oliver 231, 253, 416, 445
Bryant, Seth 466
Bryant, William Cullen 416
Buck, John 456
Buffum, George 244
Buffum, Myron 204
Buffum, Thomas 198, 200, 203, 206, 245, 246, 290, 440, 441, 479, 503, 506
Buffum & Ward 242
Bullard, Lieutenant 373
Burgoyne, General 409
Burnap, Erving 293
Burns, Rev 306, 317
Burroughs, Eden 336
Burroughs, Stephen 70, 71, 156, 263, 321, 326, 327, 328, 329, 330, 331, 332, 333, 334, 335, 336, 337, 450, 475
Burt, Rev 288
Butler, Daniel 177
Butler, Moses 164
Butterworth, John 178

Cabbot, Sebastian C 278, 467
Cadwell, Artus J 204, 292
Cadwell, A J 507
Cadwell, John 290, 291
Caldwell, Mr 46
Calkins, George S 291
Cambel, Mr 117
Campbell, James 349,350, 456
Campbell, William 455
Cando, William 353
Canterbury, Justin W 260
Canterbury, Nathan 285
Canterbury, Nathan C 204
Capron, Otis 178
Carpenter, Daniel 178
Carpenter, Jason 462
Caruth, Samuel Jr 459
Carter, John 231
Carver, Freeman C 211, 507
Cary, Lieutenant 351
Cazier, Matthias 272,273, 274, 275, 276, 277, 278, 280, 281, 489
Chamberlain, Freedom 173
Chamberlain, John 121
Champion, George 433, 434
Champlin, Dennis V 364
Chandler, Cornal 46
Chandler, John 17, 18, 34, 35, 36, 37
Chandler, John Jr 13, 16, 17, 19, 20, 21, 22, 23, 24, 27, 28, 33, 47
Chapin, Alanson 191,199, 231, 461, 481
Chapin, Calvin 239
Chapin, Chester 461
Chapin, Lemuel R 204, 206, 286
Chapin, Luther 206, 231, 252, 286, 481, 502, 505, 506
Chapin, Rev 326, 333
Chapman Edwin 446
Chapman, Daniel 460
Chapman, G E 291
Charlton, Dinnis 348
Chase, Agnostius 466
Chase, Judah 466
Chase, L B 293

Chatman, Rev 271, 272, 278
Cheever, Samuel 228
Chesterfield, Lord 501
Chenery, Cyrus 435
Chenery, Isaac 435
Child, John 121
Choate, William Jr 387, 464, 504
Church, Ephraim 386
Clapp, Oliver 377, 378
Clapp, Timothy 387
Clark, Adam 17, 24, 31, 162, 355, 386, 462, 502, 504, 505
Clark, Chauncy 194
Clark, James 455
Clark, John 32, 52, 58, 59, 78, 81, 83, 85, 87, 88, 96, 100, 104, 120, 225, 304, 305, 455, 458, 489
Clark, John Jr 251
Clark, Matthew 137, 144, 151, 152, 153, 155, 158, 159, 164, 168, 237, 355, 367, 375, 386, 462, 504,
Clark, Robert 344, 345
Clark, Samuel 178, 267, 505
Clark, Samuel Jr 192, 461 505, 506
Clark, Thomas 404, 405, 407, 480
Clark, William 100, 117, 455
Clary, David 465
Clelland, Thomas 390
Clemens, Curtis 117
Cleveland, Charles R 204, 359
Clifford, Daniel P 177
Clough, Aaron 459
Clough, Orcutt W 247
Clough, Warren 206
Cluff, Jonathan 456
Coburn, Captain 348
Cochran, John 348
Cochran, Robert 344, 455
Cochran, Thomas 86, 87, 90, 98, 100, 103, 112, 117 120, 124, 127, 128, 129, 262, 302, 305, 311, 343, 503, 504
Code, Doctor 259
Cole, Adam 214, 508
Cole, John 250, 251, 254, 387, 390, 465, 485

512   HISTORY OF PELHAM, MASS.

Coffin, John 351
Coles, Ensign John 168
Colton, Alpheus 375, 385
Comstock, William 204
Coney, Oliver 352
Conkey, Alexander 73, 77, 79, 81, 83, 92, 99, 100, 111, 120, 121, 132, 151, 178, 224, 226, 230, 273, 298, 348, 387, 405, 454, 465, 503, 505
Conkey, Alexander Jr 83, 84, 177, 230, 231, 343, 348, 387, 456, 467, 502
Conkey, Andrew 386, 464
Conkey, Ansel 238
Conkey, Asa 250, 456
Conkey, Austin W 239, 507
Conkey, David 167, 169, 170, 171, 172, 174, 178, 194, 227, 228, 229, 237, 386, 390, 456, 458, 480, 504, 505, 506
Conkey, David 2d 178
Conkey, David Jr 121, 177, 178, 230, 505
Conkey, Elisha 178, 230, 387, 463
Conkey, Ezkiel 352, 387, 390, 463
Conkey, Isaac 149, 178, 252, 386, 457
Conkey, Isaac A 468
Conkey, Isreal 173, 178, 230, 458, 505
Conkey, Ithamar 11, 12, 231, 285, 425, 426, 505
Conkey, Jacob 348
Conkey, James, 79, 81, 83, 85, 86, 87, 88, 89, 90, 93, 106, 110, 177, 301, 302, 305, 343, 351, 354, 387, 454, 459
Conkey, James Jr 387
Conkey, Joel 169, 273, 458
Conkey, John 58, 59, 77, 79, 83, 84, 86, 87, 88, 89, 90, 92, 93, 96, 97, 99, 102, 110, 120, 145, 155, 162, 163, 176, 178, 180, 181, 224, 251, 252, 266, 480, 490, 504, 505
Conkey, John Jr 122, 149, 178, 230, 250, 251, 258, 426, 456, 462, 468, 480

Conkey, John 2d 460
Conkey, Major John 466
Conkey, John T 357
Conkey, Jonas 457
Conkey, Joshua 342, 347, 352, 403, 405, 406, 407, 408, 410, 455, 463
Conkey, Reuben 178
Conkey, Robert 154, 238, 353, 354
Conkey, Silas 347, 348
Conkey, Thomas 177, 229, 230, 239, 273, 387, 390, 463, 489
Conkey, W 507
Conkey, Warren 178, 255, 459
Conkey, William 77, 79, 83, 84, 87, 88, 90, 92, 93, 95, 96, 97, 98, 99, 100, 101, 105, 111, 112, 117, 122, 130, 169, 177, 226, 227, 228, 229, 236, 237, 238, 239, 249, 250, 251, 255, 273, 352, 454, 480, 482, 483, 484, 485, 491, 503
Conkey, William Hunter 459
Conkey William Jr 162, 163, 176, 178, 180, 181, 224, 271, 354, 364, 387, 391, 394, 457, 480, 504
Conklin, Henry 204
Conkling, Judge 445
Conkling, Roscoe 430, 445
Cook, Aaron 204
Cook, Adams 178
Cook, Ammon 231
Cook, Daniel 362
Cook, Dwight M 445
Cook, Eseck 178, 179, 180, 224, 287, 342, 356, 357, 444, 475
Cook, Henry 204
Cook, James 178, 232, 467
Cook, Levi 459, 466
Cook, Lewis 461
Cook, Lucian W 445
Cook, L V B 445
Cook, Marcus D 445
Cook, Nathaniel 444
Cook, Nathaniel H 208
Cook, Olney 198, 206, 445
Cook, Silas 178

Cook, Simon 231
Cook, James M 242
Cook, Theodore F 204, 208, 238, 254, 487
Cook, Whipple 434, 461, 502, 506
Cook, Zebina 461
Cook, Ziba 197, 206, 253, 256, 287, 486, 502, 506
Cooke, E Ward 444, 445
Cooley, Moses 456
Cooley, Obadiah 177, 230, 231, 247, 248
Cowan, Ephraim 17, 24, 26, 31, 32, 42, 46, 47, 49, 77, 79, 81, 82, 85, 87, 88, 89, 117, 120, 223, 224, 296, 298, 300, 304, 305, 442
Cowan, George 17, 24, 31, 33, 40, 45, 46, 47, 48, 53, 59, 77, 78, 83, 85, 87, 88, 89, 90, 91, 93, 97, 98, 112, 229, 298, 303, 305, 310, 442
Cowan, George Heirs 178
Cowan J Edward 442
Cowan, James 93, 98, 99, 112, 115, 120, 178, 229, 343, 351, 387, 442, 463, 468, 469, 503, 504
Cowan, James Jr 387, 389, 454
Cowan, James M 203, 204, 206, 238, 285, 286, 441, 442, 507
Cowan, John 390
Cowan, Josiah 178
Cowan, Justus 390
Cowan, Samuel 442, 454
Cowan, Willard 178
Cowan, Wm 273, 390, 464
Cowden, David 88, 89, 93, 97, 100, 101, 108, 111, 112, 117, 119, 120, 121, 122, 127, 129, 137, 144, 145, 150, 225, 344, 346, 347, 348, 354, 488, 503, 504
Cowden, Jas 121, 387, 457
Cowden, John 347, 349
Cowden, Samuel 454
Cowden, William 121, 457, 462
Cowdine, Thomas 344
Cowing, Ethanon 347
Cowles, Edwin 238
Cowles, Mala 238

INDEX TO MEN. 513

Crafts, Colonel 348
Craig, A G 232, 259
Crawford, Isaac 355
Crawford, Joel 386, 389
Crawford, John 46, 47, 56, 81, 98, 99, 100, 101, 111, 127, 129, 133, 141, 146, 226, 227, 235, 262, 348, 386, 454, 493, 503, 504
Crawford, John Jr 88
Crawford, John and Levi 178
Crawford, Levi 184, 229, 230, 283, 458, 489
Crosby Joshua 282
Crosby, Judah 290
Crosier, Moses 462
Crozier, Arthur 343, 344
Crozier, John 106, 111
Crozier, John Jr 343
Crossett, Archibald 92, 93, 97, 98, 109, 120, 121, 280, 343, 503
Crossett, Ichabod 120
Crossett, Isreal 280, 464
Crosett, Jacob 456
Crossett, James 177, 355, 460, 505
Crossett, John 348
Crossett, Robert, 177, 228, 229, 247, 275, 277, 386, 390, 457, 504, 505,
Crossett, Samuel 352
Crossett, William 32, 42, 46, 47, 56, 77, 81, 83, 84, 85, 87, 88, 89, 90, 91, 92, 93, 95, 97, 98, 99, 100, 101, 120, 124, 128, 132, 133, 141, 149, 150, 305, 310, 343, 348, 457, 465, 503, 504
Cullom, Shelby M 443
Currier, Samuel 461
Curtis, Oliver 178, 230, 271
Curtis, Robert 414
Cushing, J 75, 76
Cushing, Thomas 387, 388
Cutler, Anthony 464
Cutler, Robert 242
Cutler, Dr Robert 141, 226, 243, 258, 456
Cutting, Joel 208, 362

Dane, Frederick R 204, 208, 285, 361

Dane, John 285
Danforth, Elijah 178
Daniels, Joseph 424
Daniels, William P 424
Dansett, Cato 352, 354, 464
Dart, John 350
Davenport, Eisha 122
Davis, Albert 446
Davis, George B 204, 208, 446
Davis, Isaac 344
Davis, John B 285
Davis, Moses 461
"Davis, Rev Mr" 321, 333
Davis, Samuel B 206, 507
Davis, Seth 204, 497, 498
Davidson, John 117
Davidson, Herbert R 216, 233, 508
Davidson, Phinneas 178
Day, Captain 354
Day, Luke 385, 376, 398
Dayton, James 47
Dean, James O 289, 290
DeLancey, Oliver 407
Denio, Frederick 462
Dexter, Benjamin 287
Dick, John 17, 19, 24, 27, 28, 31, 40, 46, 47, 50, 51, 59, 63, 83, 85, 86, 87, 88, 89, 90, 92, 93, 96, 97, 98, 100, 101, 111, 117, 119, 120, 121, 122, 123, 124, 127, 128, 146, 216, 219, 224, 297, 347, 454, 503, 504
Dick, Thomas 17, 24, 31, 48, 50, 51, 52, 53, 54, 55, 56, 57, 58, 59, 60, 61, 62, 63, 64, 65, 66, 81, 83, 84, 85, 86, 87, 88, 89, 90, 92, 93, 94, 96, 98, 99, 101, 112, 119, 120, 123, 124, 219, 224, 227, 249, 251, 254, 297, 304, 305, 309, 386, 457, 468, 475, 482, 503
Dickinson, Edward 201
Dickinson, Levi 463
Dickinson, Lieut 138
Dickinson, Mr 96
Dickinson, Rev 261
Dickinson, Obed 466
Dickinson, Obadiah 137, 139

Dickinson, Reuben 348, 391
Dillon, Clyde & Co 429, 477
Dillon, Sidney 429, 475
Dinsmore, Abel 375
Dix, Benjamin 247
Dockham, W H 291
Dodge, Daniel 178, 467
Dodge, Ellison 260, 498
Dodge, Hollis 204, 206, 208
Dodge, Isaac 164, 387, 463
Dodge, J O 290, 291
Dodge, Lewis 204, 206, 507
Dodge, Nathaniel 178, 204, 250, 260
Dodge, Samuel B 204
Donoley, John 348
Dowden, William H 206, 232, 285, 286
Downing, E 238
Downing, William B 204, 206, 212, 285, 286
Draper, Learned O 195, 462
Draper, Lewis 178, 194, 231, 271, 502, 505
Draper. Lewis L 253, 255, 256
Draper, Lyman 461
Draper, Seth 466
Dubois, Peter 407
Dunbar, John D 437
Dunbar, Josiah 136, 178, 350
Dunbar, Nehemiah 349, 350, 353, 464
Dunbar, Seth 458
Dunlap, Alexander 8
Dunlap, Andrew 8, 419
Dunlap, James 8, 86, 98, 120, 129, 130, 150, 166, 178, 419, 456, 463, 504
Dunlap, Dr James 419, 420
Dunlap, John 178, 283, 342, 419, 459
Dunlap, Robert 342
Dunlap, Thomas 8
Dunlap. William 136, 140, 150, 151, 178, 228, 267, 386, 419, 464, 504
Dunning, David 342
Dwelly, Aaron 178, 271
Dwelly, Prince 497

Dwight, Elijah 351, 355
Dwight, Joseph 342
Dwight, Timothy 46, 47, 50, 56, 79, 80, 96, 166
Dyer, John F 232, 233, 258, 508

Earle, Edward 287
Eaton, Calvin D 117, 202, 203, 205, 206, 209, 213, 231, 232, 253, 254, 258, 486, 503, 506, 507
Eaton, Darias 242
Eaton, Eliphaz 465
Eaton, Francis 284
Eaton, Francis L 443, 444
Eaton, Heman D 204, 208
Eaton, Homer 446
Eaton, John Jr 465
Eaton, M M 443
Eaton, Marston 176, 178, 230, 252, 254
Eaton, Monroe 198, 231, 232, 443, 507
Eaton, Walter 178, 252
Eastwick & Harrison 435
Edgar, John 87, 94, 106, 303
Edgar, John Jr 344
Edgar, William 112
Eddy, Rev 286
Edson, Abizer 131, 348, 456
Edson, Benjamin 351, 354
Edson, Ebijah 465
Edson, Jacob 141, 157, 390, 504
Edson, Seth 178, 227, 230, 489, 505
Edwards, Jonathan 10, 75, 297, 299, 300
Eggleston, Major 167
Eliot, George 164, 348, 353, 387, 389
Ellis, Rufus 416
Elot, George 457
Ellsbree, Edmund S 362
Engram, Jonathan 386, 390
Engram, Samuel 390
Engram, Timothy 387
Esty, J L 290
Everett, Leonard 437

Fairbanks, Stephen 239, 240
Fales, Abijah 206, 246
Fales, Daniel 505
Fales, James 204
Fales, John T 208, 446
Fales, Sewal 178
Fales, Madison L 364
Fales, Norman S 364
Fales, William B 364
Fay, Mr 203
Faye, Barnabas 463
Fellows, John 348
Felton, John 466, 488
Felton & Conkey, 177, 180, 238
Felton, Nathan 177, 230, 238, 250, 251, 252, 254, 466, 505
Fergerson, Archibald 458
Fergerson, James 93, 94, 97, 99, 100, 104, 117, 225, 297, 341, 347, 454
Fergerson, John 17, 24, 31, 37, 39, 46, 47, 87, 91, 92, 93, 95, 97, 98, 99, 100, 218, 249, 297, 491
Fergerson, Robert 100, 297
Fergerson, Samuel 51, 100, 297
Fergerson, Thomas 363
Fergerson, William 87, 92, 97, 98, 100, 101, 111, 117, 119, 120, 128, 296, 346, 456
Fenton, Samuel 387
Field, Jonathan 458, 465
Field, Milo W 204, 206, 232, 285
Field, Seth 466
Fields, Esquire 171
Finton, Samuel 456
Firman, Albert 206, 291, 292, 507
Firman, Erlon G 204
Firman, Gilbert H 204, 208
Fish, Cummings 231
Fish, Lewis B 232
Fish, Rev 272, 278
Fish, Stephen 386
Fish, Jabez 349
Fisher, Jabez Pond 264, 265, 272, 278
Fisher, Thomas 360, 466
Fisk, Asa 375
Fisk, Franklin 290

Fletcher, Abel 232
Fletcher, Solomon 247
Follett, Abraham 459
Foot, Obed 375
Forbs, James 465
Forward, Rev 326, 333
Foster, Edward, Jr 464
Foster, Lieut 122
Foster, Seth 465
Fowler, Captain 350
Freeman, Mr 265
Freker, Philip 456
Fuller, Thomas 387
Fulton, Moses 457

Gamble, J H 286
Ganson, Joseph 353, 354
Gardner, George A 208, 363
Gardner, John 475
Gaskill, Chester 198, 199, 231, 232, 256, 271
Gaskell, Lebbeus 444
Gaskell, William 178, 444
Gates, Asahel 204, 206, 232, 233, 503, 507, 508
Gates, Ebenezer 458
Gates, General 347
Gates, Levi 506
Gaylord, Flavel 247
Gaylord, J H 290
Gibbs, Abraham 488
Gibbs, Warren 478
Gibbs, William 478
Gilbert, Simeon 363
Gillespie, George 71
Gilmore, David 347
Gilmore, George 454
Gilmore, James 8, 17, 24, 31, 32, 33, 47, 50, 81, 83, 84, 86, 87, 88, 121, 127, 226, 296, 455, 457
Gilmore, James Jr 38, 46, 47, 83, 297, 305, 348
Gilmore, John 297
Gilmore, Robert 342, 344, 411, 455
Gilmore, William 86, 88, 104, 110, 120, 221, 343
Gitte, Robert 458
Gittee, John 457
Goddard, David Jr 193
Gold, Levi W 204, 206, 208, 478
Gold, Martin D 256
Gold, Minor 200, 202, 206, 231, 232, 239, 258, 444
Gold, Theodore 204

INDEX TO MEN. 515

Goodell, Abner 192
Goodman, Major 396
Goodman, Noah 143, 350
Goodrich, J A 293
Gordon, William 289
Gould, Aaron 457
Gould, Gardner 348
Gould, Haffield 178, 230, 467
Gould, Jared 257
Gray, Aaron 111, 117, 145, 150, 152, 279, 280, 387, 458, 465, 504
Gray, Adam 344
Gray, Adam Clark 137, 138, 139, 344, 432
Gray, Amos 349, 475
Gray, Andrew 459, 466
Gray, Barber 387
Gray, Calvin D 204, 206, 208, 241, 242
Gray, Chester 231, 461
Gray, Collester 458, 466
Gray, David, 466
Gray, Daniel 59, 88, 89, 90, 91, 92, 93, 95, 96, 97, 99, 112, 118, 120, 128, 129, 131, 134, 135, 136, 144, 145, 148, 150, 151, 271, 272, 273, 277, 279, 280, 343, 355, 368, 369, 388, 432, 455, 481, 503, 504
Gray, Daniel Car 458
Gray, Ebenezer 63, 122, 128, 129, 145, 151, 155, 159, 161, 162, 166, 170, 179, 229, 238, 251, 258, 264, 266, 268, 283, 321, 325, 336, 346, 354, 386, 390, 431, 432, 455, 463, 475, 504, 505
Gray, Ebenezer Jr 458
Gray, Ebenezer and John 178
Gray, Edwin P 431
Gray, Eli 468
Gray, Elihu 465
Gray, Elliot 130, 131, 179, 228, 230, 269, 271, 344, 355, 387, 390, 432, 489
Gray, Eliot 2d 390, 464
Gray, Elisha 390
Gray, George D 431
Gray, Giles H 431
Gray, Henry M 431
Gray, Hinckley R 431

Gray, Horace 206, 232, 241, 247, 258, 290, 355, 431, 479. 507
Gray, Hugh 29, 32, 77, 79 297
Gray, Ira 431
Gray, Isaac 99, 101, 107, 111, 112, 120, 131, 140, 141, 142, 151, 310, 343, 347, 348, 454, 481, 488, 503, 504
Gray, Jacob 386, 432, 457
Gray, James 475
Gray, Jeremiah 177, 280, 281, 387, 465
Gray, John 8, 24, 31, 33, 34, 37, 39, 42, 43, 44, 45, 46, 47, 48, 51, 62, 63, 77, 79, 81, 84, 85, 89, 94, 95, 97, 98, 99, 101, 106, 110, 117, 118, 120, 178, 179, 230, 231, 246, 298, 302, 303, 341, 405, 406, 408, 465, 475
Gray, John Jr 17, 99, 112, 120, 274, 283, 343, 454, 505
Gray, John 3d 466
Gray, Lieut John 468
Gray, "Cooper" John 284, 355, 431
Gray, "Tanner" John 247, 283, 426, 431, 432
Gray, Joel 280, 387, 432, 464, 504
Gray, Jonathan 90, 97, 98, 103, 120, 130, 262, 343, 386, 432, 456, 489, 504
Gray, Joseph 350, 351
Gray, Joshua 117
Gray, Justin 432
Gray, Justus 465
Gray, Lamond 160, 271, 351, 457
Gray, Levi 169, 342, 466
Gray, Matthew 31, 32, 34, 37, 38, 39, 40, 51, 46, 47, 55, 77, 78, 81, 83, 85, 94, 98, 102, 112, 117, 120, 137, 138, 139, 226, 235, 298, 300, 302, 303, 342, 387, 432, 455, 457, 464, 504
Gray, Matthew Jr 16, 24, 387
Gray, Matthew 3d 464

Gray, Moses 59, 117, 229, 230, 279, 280, 280, 465, 502, 505
Gray, Moses 2d 177, 231, 432, 505
Gray, Nathaniel 81, 355, 430, 431, 432, 456, 466, 475, 490
Gray, Patrick 177, 387, 432, 458, 463, 466
Gray, Patrick Jr 177, 467
Gray, Robert 348
Gray, Samuel 17, 19, 21, 24, 26, 36, 38, 40, 41, 45, 46, 47, 48, 49, 52, 53, 77, 79, 81, 82, 83, 84, 209, 223, 296
Gray, Thomas 273, 275, 381, 432, 463
Gray & Son 242
Gray, William 34, 38, 39, 40, 41, 42, 43, 44, 45, 46, 47, 48, 49, 50, 52, 53, 77, 79, 81, 82, 84, 87, 110, 111, 117, 120, 121, 122, 218, 223, 303, 307, 344, 347
Gray, William Jr 17, 24, 31, 32, 86
Gray, William 1st 87, 302
Gray, William 3d 83, 85, 86, 303, 305
Gray, William D 431
Graham, John 299, 300
Graham, Richard Crouch 62, 116, 117, 118, 123, 124, 128, 131, 261, 262, 310, 320, 337, 406, 451, 469, 473
Granger, Berthiah H 465
Grant, U S 430, 435
Graves, Elisha 468
Graves, Martin 441
Graves, Stephen 458, 466
Green, David 347
Green, John 177
Greenwood, Daniel 178
Gridley, Colonel 348
Griffin, Charles 359, 364
Griffin, David 178, 459
Griffin, George A 359
Griffin, Jonathan 178
Griffin, Otis 204
Griffin, Otis B 359
Grout, Albert A 204, 285
Grout, Aldin 433, 434
Grout, Austin 434

Grout, Joel 178, 229, 230, 433, 434, 505
Grout, Josiah 434
Grout, Marcus C 204, 206, 238, 446, 503, 507
Grout, Martin 434
Grout, Orra 434
Grout, Rufus 196, 199, 200 231, 232, 290, 434, 479, 503, 506
Grover, Frederick 364
Grover, Thomas 370, 372
Grover, Thomas 373

Hacket, George 351, 352, 387, 390
Hacket, Gideon 387, 458
Hacket, John 352, 355
Halbert, James 107, 110, 115, 118, 128, 129, 262, 343, 344, 349, 455, 503,
Halbert, John 344, 455
Hall Charles O 446
Hall, John B 231, 446
Hall, Lemuel 179, 230, 505, 506
Hall, Lemuel W 446
Hall, Levi 245, 246
Hall, Levi B 478, 506
Hall, Levi D 446
Hall, Seth B 446
Hamilton, Andrew 120
Hamilton, Eli 464
Hamilton, Ephraim 455
Hamilton, Frank 456
Hamilton, Henry C 446
Hamilton, James 88, 94, 343, 344, 454, 455
Hamilton, Isaac 177, 460
Hamilton, Joel 460
Hamilton, John 42, 49, 77, 79, 81, 85, 86, 87, 89, 99, 117, 127, 129, 131, 141, 151, 160, 161, 303, 305, 343, 344, 347, 348, 349, 350, 352, 355, 387, 455, 504
Hamilton, John Jr 112, 271, 279, 389, 464
Hamilton, Joseph 150, 158, 159, 177, 206, 228, 264, 387, 456, 460, 461, 504, 505
Hamilton, Joseph W 175 252, 505
Hamilton, Oliver 177, 231 283, 466

Hamilton, Robert 94, 96, 119, 121, 124, 127, 128, 262, 344, 454, 455, 488, 503, 504
Hamilton, Robert Jr 343
Hamilton, Thomas 77, 79, 83, 86, 89, 92, 93, 98, 99, 107, 111, 120, 125, 302, 303, 348
Hamilton, Thomas Jr 105, 455
Hancock, John 143, 389
Handy, Charles 350, 355
Hanks, Benjamin 463
Hanks, James 232, 233, 257, 508
Hanks, Warner 204, 257
Hanks, Ziza 204, 291, 292
Hannum, David 179, 230, 251, 260, 268
Hannum, Grove W 200, 231, 357, 461
Hannum, Henry 357
Hannum, Pliny 179, 230, 290, 460, 476, 506
Hannum, Sidney 357
Hannum, William 204
Hanson, C P 385, 448, 508
Harkness, Daniel 179, 228, 387, 421, 459, 463, 505
Harkness, Daniel Jr 389
Harkness, David 179 227, 268, 387, 421, 457, 475, 488
Harkness, H W 421, 422, 423, 479
Harkness, Henry 423
Harkness. James 94, 97, 98, 99, 100, 101, 107, 113, 117, 120, 124, 128, 343, 346, 349, 355, 406, 421, 454, 458, 463, 503
Harkness, Joel 177
Harkness, John 121, 150, 154, 161, 167, 179, 187, 229, 246, 247, 264, 352, 355, 387, 421, 463, 489, 497
Harkness, John Jr 268, 467
Harkness, John 2d 386, 389, 463, 506
Harkness, Jonathan 421, 464
Harkness, Martin K 423
Harkness, Sumner J 424

Harkness, William 56, 93, 97, 99, 101, 111, 112, 117, 120, 128, 130, 228, 231, 246, 420, 421, 454, 463, 497, 504
Harkness, William Jr 457, 461, 479
Harkness, Lt William 475
Harlow, Thomas 177, 259, 387, 355, 465
Harris, W J 244, 256
Haward, Elihu 464
Hase, Jeremiah 464
Haskell, David 457
Haskell, Eli 460
Haskell, Jeremiah 270
Haskins, James 243
Haskins, John 346
Haskins, William 347, 348, 353
Hatch, Hach
Hatch, Harris 172, 173, 174, 230, 251, 252, 256, 485
Hathaway, Jonathan 177
Hathaway, Samuel 347
Hathey, Samuel 457
Hawley, Joseph 55, 59, 61, 62
Hayes, Haze, Hase, Hays
Hays, David 389
Hays, Savanna 387
Hays, William 347, 387
Hayden, Haden
Hayden, Richard 463
Hayden, Thomas 177, 230
Hayden, Thomas Jr 231
Hayward, Heywood, Haward
Hayward, Ichabod 387, 465
Heywood, Daniel 19, 20, 23, 26, 28, 34. 218
Hazelton, Colonel 373
Heed, Herman 232, 259, 487
Heirs, David 457
Hemmenway, Hardin, 255
Hench, John 464
Henry, Joseph 456
Henry, William 455
Herrick, E P 291
Herroen, Oliver 464
Hewes, George 290

INDEX TO MEN. 517

Hildreth, Russell 204, 206, 285
Hill, Alvan 468
Hill, Ansel 260
Hill, Emerson 288
Hill, James 346, 349, 351, 353
Hill, Lucian 204, 206
Hill, Otis B 360
Hill, Samuel 375
Hills, Elijah 255
Hills, H F 238
Hills, L M 238, 255, 286, 441
Hincks, Huncks
Hinncks, John 456
Hincks, Thomas 249
Hinds, Hynds
Hinds, John 481
Hinds, Joseph 375, 457
Hinds, Nehemiah 148, 150, 151, 152, 159, 162, 166, 169, 171, 172, 173, 174, 177, 180, 237, 250, 251, 252, 259, 271, 274. 275, 276, 277, 328, 329, 335, 337, 382, 392, 456, 481, 485, 504, 505
Hinds, Nehemiah Jr 481
Hoar, Horr
Hoar, Calvin 177
Hoar, John 177, 238, 239
Horr, Charles H 360
Horr, Elbridge F 204
Horr, Harrison L 204, 359
Hobby, C H 232
Holbrook, Daniel 477
Holcomb, Charles A 260
Holland, Hollan
Holland, Elihu 464
Holland, Hugh 112, 386, 504
Holland, Oliver 456
Holland, Reuben 350, 463
Holly, Samuel 387
Holt, Thomas 275, 276
Holt, William 238
Hood, James 17. 24, 31, 33, 46, 77, 83, 106, 110, 120, 343, 468
Hood, John 346, 385, 390, 454, 505
Hood, Jonathan 121, 135, 145, 150, 170, 179, 180, 226, 227, 386, 456, 504, 505

Hooker, Benjamin 171
Hopkins, Mr 46, 47
Houston, Huston, Husten
Houston, David 56, 60, 62, 111, 120, 166, 177, 225, 387, 463, 465
Houston, John 96, 261, 454
Houston, John O 461
Houston, Osmyn 446
Houston, Robert, 177, 227, 228, 386, 457, 505
How, Samuel 350
Howard, A A 291
Howard, Joseph 179, 271, 466
Howard, Labbeus 251
Howard, Rev 285
Hoyt, Epaphras 439
Hubbard, F 92
Hubbard, Giles 430
Hudson, George 291
Hughes, James 73, 232, 405
Hulet, Joseph 463
Humphrey, Charles E 233, 508
Hunt, Alden 177
Hunt, David 415
Hunt, Gilbert G 204, 285
Hunt, John 461
Hunt. Joseph R 204, 206, 285, 364
Hunt, Obed 464
Hunt, William 457
Hunter, Isaac 341, 343, 344. 455
Hunter, Isaac Cowan 458
Hunter, James 387, 455, 460, 490
Hunter, John 87, 89, 99, 100, 119, 120, 224, 226, 302, 390, 488
Hunter, Joseph 463
Hunter, Wilkins 177, 180
Hunter, William 226, 346, 466
Huntington, Joseph 325, 326, 333
Huntington, Judge 416
Hyde, Andrew 168, 175, 176, 179, 181, 182, 243, 390, 465, 505
Hyde, Chester 462
Hyde, James 177, 268, 387, 464

Hyde, Samuel 121, 136, 141, 145, 150, 151, 152, 153, 154, 155, 160, 168, 176, 179, 199, 455, 458, 465, 481, 491, 492, 504
Hyndmand, Samuel 408
Hyslop, William 437

Ide, David 467
Ingram, Engram, Ingraham
Ingram, Timothy 128, 456
Ingraham, Gideon 458
Ingraham, Jonathan 351, 464
Ingraham, Nathaniel 231, 259
Jackson, Jeremiah 128
James, Darwin R 430
James, Frederick 284
Janes, Stephen 177
Jenison, William 18, 21, 27
Jenks, Charles H 208
Jenks, L F 446
Jenks, Lyman 199, 206, 255, 285, 506, 507
Jenkins, J L 293
Jennings, Roswell 177, 230
Jewett, Ansel 217
Jewett, Aaron 375
Jewett, Benjamen 229
Jewett, Jedediah 464
Jewett, Sylvester 202, 204, 206, 209, 213, 214, 216, 217, 232, 233, 503, 507, 508
Jillson, Gillson, Jilson
Jillson, Amasa 241, 357
Jillson, Manley 358
Jillson, Nathan 178, 180, 240, 271, 489
Jillson, Nathan Jr 178, 489
Jillson, Riley 241, 242, 247, 489
Johannet & Seaver 484, 485
Johnson, Jonson
Johnson. Aaron 271
Johnson, Adam 17, 24, 31, 88, 177, 191, 386, 390, 426, 427, 428, 475, 495
Johnson, Andrew 459
Johnson, David 344

518   HISTORY OF PELHAM, MASS.

Johnson, Earl 462
Johnson, George 476, 477
Johnson, Lt George 477
Johnson, Hugh 60, 90, 94, 99, 100, 104, 112, 117, 120, 121, 122, 128, 130, 132, 135, 136, 137, 140, 141, 144, 149, 150, 151, 310, 343, 349, 386
Johnson, James 96, 98, 302, 305
Johnson, Joel 467
Johnson, John 17, 24, 31, 33, 47, 48, 53, 77, 79, 86, 87, 88, 89, 93, 96, 304, 305, 343, 386
Johnson, Rev 40, 78
Johnson, Silas 230
Johnson, Thomas 59, 85, 89, 90, 91, 92, 94, 97, 101, 104, 120, 122, 124, 137, 141, 150, 151, 225, 343, 346, 389, 427, 428, 502, 503, 504
Johnson, William 8, 19, 24, 28, 31, 240, 242, 386
Johnston, Jonston, Jonson
Johnston, Andrew 466
Johnston, Hugh 61, 62, 63, 64, 65, 155, 158, 159, 236, 237, 264, 390, 503, 504
Johnston, Hugh Moor 465
Johnston, James 46, 389
Johnston, John 45, 46, 48, 53, 457
Johnston, Joseph 390
Johnston, Moors 389
Johnston, Robert 463
Johnston, Silas 178
Johnston, Stephen 271
Johnston, Thomas 55, 58, 59, 152, 155, 156, 159, 348, 465
Johnston, William 390, 490
Jones, Joans
Joans, James 465
Jones, George D 508
Jones, H A 291
Jones, John 207, 208, 209, 212, 232, 233, 258, 290, 421, 503, 507, 508
Jones, William 364
Joslin, Josline, Joslyn
Joslin, Joseph 177

Joslin, Samuel 505
Josline, Samuel 173
Judd, Sylvester 248

Keep, Chelles 252
Keep, Noble 467
Keith, Keath, Kith
Keith, Ariel C 213, 258, 507, 508
Keith, Caleb 144, 145, 146, 147, 148, 149, 150, 151, 159, 160, 162, 226, 227, 367, 504
Keith, Justin W 215, 216, 258, 486, 508
Keith, Orles 386
Kelley, John 347, 348
Kelley, Wing 178, 230, 505
Kellogg, Killogg, Kelog
Kellogg, Giles C 194
Kellogg, Horace 201
Kelog, Jels Creach 128
Kellogg, John 346
Kellogg, Dea John 425
Killogg, Jonathan 169, 463
Kellogg, Ralph 253
Keruth, Samuel 464
Kid, Benjamin 456
Kid, Charles 456
Kim, James 387
Kimball, Charles 204
Kimball, Mr 246
Kimball, Otis 360
Kimball, Samuel 206, 467
Kimball, William O 249, 363
King, Albigence 231, 259
King, James 229, 386, 457, 504
King, Peter 178, 350, 351, 352, 355, 387, 463
King, Robert 86, 297, 344, 458, 488
King, Rufus P 204
King, Starling 386, 462
Kingman, Cyrus 191, 192, 193, 194, 231, 255, 258, 461, 502, 507
Kingman, Francis 446, 507
Kingman, Henry 178, 179, 181, 183, 184, 187, 189, 190, 192, 230, 231,

258, 460, 486, 502, 505, 506
Kingman, Martin 189, 190, 191, 192, 194, 196, 231, 251, 253, 254, 255, 506
Kingman, Matthew 286
Kingman & Packard 254
Knight, George W 204, 291, 477
Knight, John W 233
Knight, Philander S 206, 291, 292
Knight, William 177
Knowlton, Rozel 467
Knowles & Thayer 486
Conkey, McConkey, Conky, McKonkey, Konky
Konkey, Alexander 45, 46, 47
Konkey, Alexander Jr 46
Konkey, James 48, 51, 52
Konky, John 45, 46, 47, 50
Konky, William 46, 47
Kundy, Charles 352
Lamb, Joseph 353, 354
Lammon, Francis 408
Latham, Francis 204, 206
Latham, James 168, 387
Latham, Joseph 463
Latham, O S 204, 206
Lathrop, Alden 449
Lathrop, Sylvanus 449
Lawson, John 456
Lawson, William 457
Lazell, Isaac 460
Leach, Jonathan 178, 264, 386, 457, 465
Leach, Marvelous 178
Leach, Morrell 466
Leach, Timothy 459
Learned, Josiah 460
Lee, Ezra 283
Lee, Henry 390
Lee, John W 290
Leland, Gillett and Gilbert 238
Leonard, Amos D 361
Lesure, Jesse 206
Lewis, Enoch T 445
Lewis, James 461
Lewis, Joseph W 290
Lewis, William 459
Lincoln, Benjamin 376, 377, 378, 379, 380, 381, 382, 383, 384, 398

INDEX TO MEN.

Lincoln, Abraham 417
Lincoln, Isaac 178
Lincoln, Luther 357
Lincoln, Samuel J 468
Linds, Thomas 362
Lindsey, Linsey, Linsley
Lindley, David 433
Lindsey, George 465
Lindsey, James 250, 251, 277, 280, 464
Lindsey, John 109, 110, 120, 271, 279, 343, 455
Lindsey, Stacy 231, 252
Lindsey, William 86, 98, 280, 281, 464
Little, Joseph 229
Lyskam, Liscome, Liskam
Liscom, Ebenezer 386
Liskam, Ebenezer 226
Lyskem, Ebenezer 466
Livermore, A b r a h a m 132, 152, 352, 355, 490, 504
Lockwood, Alfred 293
Logan, Major 435
Long, Edward 408
Loomis, Curtis 250
Lord, Absalom 461
Lotheridge, Lotheredge, Lotridge, Latridge
Lotheredge, John 459
Lotheridge, Reuben 135, 140, 142, 151, 173, 386, 456
Lotheridge, Robert 17, 19, 21, 24, 26, 31, 36, 38, 42, 46, 52, 53, 54, 55, 56, 58, 77, 79, 81, 83, 90, 99, 101, 168, 173, 225. 305, 342, 343, 458
Lovett, Murray B 364
Lovett, Sanford M 204, 359
Lowden, Thomas 17, 24, 31, 90, 99, 102, 110, 118, 302, 303
Lucore, John 77, 87, 90, 120, 235, 303
Luddington, David
Lumbard, Abial 230
Lyman, John 245
Lyman, Oliver 349
Lyman, Otis S 446
Lyman, Payson W 293
Lyon, Asaph 251
Lysander 330, 331, 332, 333, 334, 335, 336

Macomber, George 178, 268, 459
Maklem, Meklam, McClaim, McLam, McLem, Macllom
Maklam, John 121, 142, 144, 145, 149, 151, 177, 180, 276, 348, 456, 463, 505
Meklam, Andrew 32, 40, 47, 77, 81, 83, 90, 120, 122, 225, 343
Meklam, Robert 32, 47, 59, 77, 79, 81, 83, 85, 88, 97, 103, 110, 111, 112, 117, 120, 121, 166, 304, 343, 387, 503, 504
Marcy, Rev 278
Marsh, Elisha 18
Marsh, Horatio 498
Marshall, Clement 387
Marshall, E B 291
Marshall, Jonas A 438
Marston, Reuben 274
Martin, Moses 408
Martin, N H 290
Mathers, Doctor 143
Metoon, Captain 148
Mattoon, Ebenezer Jr 264, 388, 390, 425
Mattoon, Ebenezer 243, 387
Mattoon, Noah D 425
Maxwell, Captain 349, 354
May, Isaac 178
McCartney, John 120, 226, 343, 344, 347
McClallan, Colonel 153
McClellan, General 435
McCollister, Daniel 408
McCollister, Hamilton 403, 405, 407, 408, 409, 411, 455
McConel, James 77, 85, 87, 98, 99, 117, 120, 304, 305
McCotton, James 348
McClintock, Samuel 96, 261, 306, 314, 315, 317
Conkey, McConkey, Conky, McKonkey, Konkey, Konky
McConkey, Alexander 17, 24, 31
McConkey, Asa 355
McConkey, James 24, 31, 33

McConkey, John 17, 24, 31
McConkey, William 33
McCraken, John 226
McCraken, Joseph 407, 408, 409, 455
McCrelless, John 455
McCulloch, McAllah, McAllach, M c C o l- lough, M c C u l l o g h, McCollah
McCulloch, Alexander 33, 57, 59, 60. 62, 63, 81, 90, 100, 111, 120, 128, 297, 348, 350, 351, 454, 456, 503, 504
McCulloch, Henry 151, 152, 161, 178, 227, 229, 250, 384, 385, 387, 388, 389, 464
McCulloch, James 34, 37, 38, 39, 40, 46, 47, 81, 83, 84, 85, 87, 88, 89, 218, 297, 305, 347
McAllach or McCulloch, John 17, 24, 31, 386, 456, 464
McCulloch, Robert 151, 152, 161, 178, 227, 229, 250, 265. 343, 387, 437, 454, 475, 505
McDaniel, Daniel 353, 354
McDaniel, James 354
McDowell, Rev 112, 306, 317
McFall, William 165, 166, 168, 169, 351, 460
McFarland, Andrew 21, 24, 26, 31, 34, 36, 46, 52, 235
McFarland, Elijah 462
McFarland, John 94, 106, 235
McGray, Andrew 348, 350, 352, 355
McGregorie, David 73, 297, 299, 300, 315, 317, 405, 406
McHertney, John 489
McKee, John 346. 463
McKee, Josiah 464
McKee, Robert 33, 85, 105, 454
McKeon, James 73, 405
McKlurn, John 352
McLachay, Samuel 49
McLeane, John 146

McMillin, Millin, Mullen, Mellen
McMillen, Archibald 228
McMillen, James 386, 390
McMillen, James C 271, 275, 279, 280, 504
McMillen, Jeremiah 166, 387, 390, 465
McMillen, John 279, 280, 283
McMillan, Jonathan 387, 390, 463
McMillan, Patrick 387
McMillan, Thomas 386
McMillen, William 277, 280, 390, 463, 465
McMullin, Mullin, Mellin
McMullin, David 350, 351
McMullen, Deacon 329, 330, 335, 405
McMullen, James Caldwell 131, 247, 348, 456
McMullen, John 504
McMullen, Patrick 57, 59, 60, 90, 92, 94, 98, 114, 120, 225, 279, 280, 343, 354, 386, 503
McMullen, Thomas 89, 119, 150, 279, 305, 348, 457, 504
McMullen, William 350, 351
McNaughton, 448
McNiell, John 343
McNitt, Alexander 108
McNutt, Alexander 92, 100, 112, 454
McRankin, John 354
Meracle, Sherman 291
Merrick, Roswell 400
Merrill, Calvin 243
Merrill, Nathaniel 116, 128, 130, 133, 134, 135, 138, 139, 140, 145, 147, 262, 263, 320, 321, 337
Mellen, Mellin, Millan
Millen, Captain 277
Millen, David 461, 467
Millen, Ira 461
Millen, John Lindsey 461
Millen, Jonathan 177, 180, 277
Millen, Levi 177, 467
Millen, Lucius 461
Millen, Patrick 461, 467

Millen, Rufus 467
Millen, William 177, 230, 275
Millen, William Sr 461
Millen, William Jr 467
Miller, David 505
Miller, David and William 177
Miller, F S 291
Miller, Job S 248, 255
Miller, John 229, 230, 505
Miller, John and Rufus 177
Miller, Jonathan 230
Miller, Lorenzo W 291, 292
Miller, Moses 178
Miller, Robert 232
Miller, R D 286
Miller, Samuel 178, 466
Miller, William 177, 180, 183, 229, 230, 505
Millington, Captain 354
Mills, Brigham 177
Mills, James 177
Mills, William 457
Mirah, Captain 345
Mitchel, Andrew 242
Montague, Luke 251
Montgomery, Marion 498
Montgomery, Thomas 149, 155, 228, 233, 348, 387
Montgomery, William P 361, 364
Moody, Medad 390
Moody, Samuel 342
Moor, Mr 434
Moor, James 408
Moorhead, John 9, 73, 299, 300, 312, 313, 315, 317, 405
Moors, Hugh 343, 408
Morgan, Abner 390
Morse, Samuel 375
Morrison, Thomas 407, 455
Morton, Seth 456
Moseley, Colonel 350
Moss, Reuben 273, 278
Moulton, John F 204
Moulton, Levi 426, 431
Moulton, Levi H 204, 247
Mower, C C C 476
Mower, James D 208, 362

Mulnix, Andrew H 293
Murray, Colonel 151
Murray, James A 256
Murray, John F 256
Myrick, Edmund 241
Myrick, William L 204, 206

Nash, Samuel 172
Neal, Jonathan 291
Nevens, John 408
Newell, Benjamin 461
Newell, David 290
Newell, David Jr 178
Newell, Lemuel H 206, 507
Newell, Levi 178, 271
Newell, Reuben 461
Newell, William 200, 254, 486, 487
Nickerson, Joshua 204
Nichols, John F 204, 206, 360, 364
Noon, John 290
Nowley, Rufus 467
Nukop, George 463
Nut, Abraham 454

Ober. Asa 244
Oliver, Andrew 265, 266, 275, 469
Oliver, Robert 454
Oliver, William 178, 230, 282, 283, 342, 458
Oliver, William W 431
O'Neal, Garrett 363
Orcutt, Samuel 460, 467
Ormston, Robert 174, 250, 251, 252, 254
Osborn, Levi G 364
Otis, Erastus 289
Otis, Harrison Gray 437
Otis, Isaac 435
Otis, Isaac Jr 178, 241, 271
Otis, James 428
Otis, John 437
Otis, Samuel Allen 384
Otis, William Smith 435, 436, 437
Packard, Abram 184
Packard, Barzillia 467
Packard, D F 204, 206, 208
Packard, Daniel 178, 230, 284, 504
Packard, David 461

INDEX TO MEN.

Packard, Eliab 178, 228, 229, 466
Packard, Elijah 178
Packard, Eliphaz 252
Packard, J Monroe 257
Packard, Jacob Jun 178, 230, 251
Packard, Job 178, 459
Packard, Joel 253, 257, 506
Packard, Jonathan 178, 229, 230, 231, 505
Packard, Joseph 133,135, 136, 142, 143, 144, 145, 147, 148, 150, 151, 159, 160, 162, 264, 386, 502, 504
Packard & Kingman 252
Packard, Levi 386
Packard, Thomas 178, 468
Packard, Timothy 137, 142, 155, 160, 226, 390, 504
Page, A C 232, 284
Page, John A 245, 508
Parker, Eli 250
Park, Joseph 204
Parker, Joshua 355
Park, Stewart James 229, 251, 458, 475
Parmenter, Charles O 204, 503
Parmenter, Deliverance 388
Parmenter, Israel 388
Parmenter, Jason 385, 388, 389
Parmenter, John 197,231, 242, 247, 258, 502
Parmenter, Micah 388
Parmenter, Silas 388
Parsons, David 243, 275, 276, 297, 299, 300, 495, 496
Parsons, David 495, 496
Parsons, Eli 376, 377, 398
Partridge, Oliver 308, 411
Patton, Christopher 169, 259, 251, 485
Patterson, Petterson, Peterson, Peteson, etc
Patterson, Adam 17, 24, 31, 46, 47, 83, 86, 89, 297, 347, 457
Patterson, George 59, 61, 63, 64, 88, 97, 98, 101, 111, 120, 122, 127, 128, 129, 136, 225, 297, 343, 503, 504
Patterson, James 346, 457
Patterson, Thomas 297
Patterson, William 305, 454
Paul, William 466
Peables, Peibols, Peabels, Pebils, Pebles, Peebles, etc
Peebles, David 459
Peables, Patrick 17, 19, 20, 24, 26, 31, 47, 48, 56, 57, 58, 59, 62, 63, 79, 85, 86, 89, 90, 91, 94, 95, 102, 110, 117, 120, 122, 224, 265, 302, 303, 454, 458, 459, 460, 504
Peebles, Frank 458
Peables, James 117, 134, 142, 226, 344, 455, 459, 469, 480, 481
Peables, Robert 10, 13, 14, 15, 16, 17, 19, 21, 23, 24, 26, 29, 31, 32, 33, 34, 37, 39, 41, 45, 46, 47, 48, 49, 50, 75, 76, 77, 79, 81, 82, 84, 86, 89, 94, 95, 96, 97, 98, 222, 259, 296, 298, 302, 344
Peables, Robert Jr 343
Peables, Robert Young 387
Peebles, William Forbush 465
Peables, John 32, 85, 86, 88, 90, 95, 98, 103, 111, 120, 148, 150, 159, 169, 227, 228, 264, 343, 344, 355, 387, 454, 462, 504, 505
Peables, John Jr 120
Peck, Jesse F 178, 183, 184, 230, 231, 271, 505
Peck, Joseph 458
Peck, Simeon 456
Peck, Winchester 464
Pelham, Henry 74, 196, 286, 499, 500, 501
Perin, Steven 352
Perkins, Nathan 282,284, 387
Peso, Nathan 466
Peso, Samuel 178, 229, 230, 458
Pettengall, Mr 184
Pettengall, Nathan 467
Pettengall, Stephen 227, 390
Phelps, Asahel 459
Phelps, C 54, 60
Phipps, Lieutenant-Governor 342
Phillips, Mr 331, 332, 333
Phillips, Patrick 459
Phillips, Samuel 384
Pierce, Joseph 505
Pierce, Joseph Jr 231
Pierce, Josiah 231, 505
Pierce, Josiah Jr 467
Pierce, Luther 231, 502
Pike, Philander 363
Pitman, George B 197, 231, 232, 506
Pitman, Fred 241
Pitman, John N 204, 206, 208
Pond, Samuel M 459
Pomroy, David 243
Pomroy, Ebenezer 13, 17
Pomroy, Elisha 258
Pomroy, Luther 467
Porter, Ebenezer 61
Porter, Eleazer 44. 92
Porter, Elisha Sheriff, 375, 385
Porter, Elisha 347, 351
Potter, Gulley 476
Potter, Olney 178, 230, 231, 259, 476
Powell, Edwin J 256
Powell, Joseph R 497
Powers, Isaac 468
Powers, Capt Isaac 148, 153, 390
Powers, Doct Isaac 177, 230, 259
Powers, James 344
Powers, John 153, 375
Pratt, Albert 208
Pratt, David 390
Pratt, John 351, 353
Pratt, Jonathan 260
Pratt, Micah 351
Pratt, Nathaniel 284
Pratt, Sylvanus, 463
Pratt, William 459
Pratt, William S 359
Prebble, John 354
Presho, Dwight 233, 508
Presho, Zadock 206, 290
Proute, Jacob 149
Purington, Daniel 199, 247

Putnam, Colonel 354, 391
Putnam, Daniel 438
Putnam, Rufus 395, 396, 397, 398
Pynchon, William 18

Ramsdale, Abner 463
Ramsdell, Anson 257
Ramsdell, Jacob 454
Randell, Alonzo C 204, 206, 507, 508
Randell, Arba 206, 245, 462, 477
Randall, Benjamin 253, 486, 506
Randall, David 291, 292
Randall, Elijah 184, 231
Randall, Ephriam 178, 230
Randall, Gideon 178
Randall, Titus 458
Randall, Warren 204, 206, 507
Ranham, Daniel 350
Rankin, Rinkin, Renken
Rankin, Abial 462
Rankin, Ansel A 206, 212, 213, 231, 232, 290, 507
Rankin, Augustin H 446
Rankin, Austin 232
Rankin, Edward 418, 419
Rankin, Ira P 416, 417, 418
Rankin, James 178, 229, 282, 387, 457, 460
Rankin, John 130, 131, 136, 137, 141, 145, 148, 150, 151, 153, 155, 158, 159, 160, 171, 174, 175, 178, 182, 194, 227, 228, 236, 264, 266, 268, 282, 283, 346, 386, 456, 475, 504, 505
Rankin, John Jr 177, 178, 184, 230, 231, 258, 282, 283, 459, 505
Rankin, Ensign John 267
Rankin, John Esq 475
Rankin, Joseph 87, 89, 92, 112, 117, 122, 305, 346, 354, 387, 389, 454, 459, 464
Rankin, Lieutenant 267, 475
Rankin, Nathan 250

Rankin, S W 446
Rankin, Silas 283, 467
Rankin, William C 231
Rankin, Zebina 416, 460
Rinkin, Joel 390
Rinken, Mathew 387, 457
Ransom, Job 354
Ransom, Moses 355, 456
Redding, Moses 208, 209
Reeniff, Daniel 468
Reniff, Abisha 178, 230
Reniff, Morey 178
Ree, William 456
Reed, William F 204
Reid, John 72
Rhodes, Rhoads, Rodes, etc
Rhodes, Doctor 259
Rhodes, John O 362
Rhodes, Samuel 164, 387, 390
Rhodes, Solomon 358, 364
Rhodes, Stephen 82, 204, 223, 359
Rice, Timothy 346, 348, 456
Richards, Nathan 350
Richardson, Cyrenas T 204
Richardson, Enos S 255, 285
Richardson, Henry 461
Richardson, Isreal 122
Richardson, John 252
Richardson, Jonathan 177, 181, 505
Richardson, Marcenus B 204, 206
Richardson, Wyatt 506
Richmond, Nathaniel 353
Richmond, Zebulon 348
Rider, Giles 460
Rider, Isaac 178
Right, Gaius 466
Robins, Daniel 461
Robins, Samuel 390, 434
Robbins, Amariah 252
Robbins, O 289
Robeson, Joseph 465
Robinson, Abial 434
Robinson, Albert B 434
Robinson, Amaziah 362
Robinson, Bartlett 348, 353, 354
Robinson, Daniel 344

Robinson, John 348
Robinson, M F 446
Robinson, Samuel 344, 345
Robinson, Sanford M 446
Root, John 204
Rowland, Seth 344
Ruggles, Adin 461
Ruggles, Constant 230, 258, 460, 505
Ruggles, Timothy 344
Rush, Samuel 346
Rush, Samuel 456
Russell, Ebenezer 408
Russell, J Elmer 293
Russell, John 199, 202
Russell, John S 260
Russell, Samuel W 260
Rust, Mr 56

Sabin, Timothy 233
Sampson, Samson
Sampson, Abisha 465
Sampson, Daniel 352
Sampson, Lieutenant 153, 155
Sampson, Nathaniel 144, 145, 147, 148, 152, 158, 160, 161, 162, 171, 228, 229, 230, 236, 250, 251, 264, 266, 346, 386, 457, 502, 504, 505
Sampson, Samuel 150, 250
Sampson, Thomas 466
Sanger, Charles H 361
Sarls, Ebenezer 387, 353, 354
Sackett, Gad 375
Savage, Savige
Savage & Conkey 409
Savage, Edward 408, 448
Savage, James 408
Savage, John 85, 88, 89, 90, 91, 92, 93, 98, 112, 113, 114, 118, 120, 224, 235, 302, 304, 307, 310, 345, 405, 406, 408, 410, 446, 447, 448
Savage, John Jr 411
Savage, Judge John 448
Sawyer, Edmund H 440
Searl, Bildad 458
Sears, Barnabas Jr 461
Sears, Colonel 352
Sears, Ebenezer 353, 354
Sears, Jonathan F 467

Sears, Roland 177, 181, 505
Sekell, Robert, 387
Selfridge, Edward 83, 85, 87, 88, 89, 97, 109, 347, 451, 469
Selfridge, Oliver 98, 109, 117, 343, 454
Selfridge, Robert 346, 347
Selfridge, William · 98, 100, 117, 343, 454
Shattuck, Job 375
Shaw, Andrew 119
Shaw, Ansel 460
Shaw, Ansel C 291, 292
Shaw, Asa 230
Shaw, Asahel B 291
Shaw, Daniel 148, 153
Shaw, Edwin 241
Shaw, Elias 466
Shaw, Ezra
Shaw, George 204, 206
Shaw, George L 256
Shaw, George P 246
Shaw, Jacob 458
Shaw, James 461
Shaw, John 204. 360
Shaw, Joseph 465
Shaw, William 466
Shepard, General 374, 376, 380, 401
Shepard, George W 507
Shepard, Robinson 458
Shiells, Robert 71
Shirley, William 75, 76, 91, 92
Shores, David, 232, 239, 245, 246, 508
Shores, Charles B 233, 508
Shores, Silas S 257, 258, 483
Shurtlieff, Benoni 164, 165, 166, 249, 251, 264, 342, 485, 490
Shurtlieff, Froa 458
Shurtlieff, Landlord 162, 164
Shute, Governor 8
Sloan, Andrew 177, 461
Sloan, David 154, 250, 348, 387, 456
Sloan, David and Gardner 177
Sloan, Gardner, 459, 460
Sloan, James 108, 120, 305, 344, 466

Sloan, John 455
Sloan, Samuel 177, 273, 280, 457
Sloan, Samuel Jr 177
Smallage, Joseph 271
Smalledge, Rev 288
Smith, Abial B 253
Smith, Abner 352
Smith, Andrew 454
Smith, Elias 390
Smith, G P 446
Smith, George 466
Smith, Horace C 445
Smith, Hugh 463
Smith, Job 459
Smith, James 357, 454, 461, 477
Smith, James N 428, 429, 430
Smith, John 172
Smith, Josiah 468
Smith, Luther 284
Smith, Oliver 178, 231, 245, 270, 467, 468, 502, 505, 506
Smith. Oliver Jr 191, 258, 505, 506
Smith, Oliver 437, 506
Smith, Oliver C 446
Smith, Samuel 390
Smith, Simeon 390
Smith, William 178, 179, 230, 252, 459
Snell, Rev 288
Snow, Jonathan 387, 390
Shays, Shess, S h a s s, Sheas
Shays, Daniel 145, 148, 150, 151, 152, 156, 160, 162, 258, 274, 280, 348, 354, 366, 373, 374, 375, 376, 377, 378, 379, 380, 381, 382, 383, 384, 388, 390, 391, 392, 394, 395, 396, 397, 398, 399, 400, 402, 483
Shay, John 204
Sikes, Oren 291
Simonds, Ensign 352
Sisson, John 290
Slater, Solomon 208
Sornborger, Doctor 487
Soule, Nathan A 290
Southwick, E S 204
Southwick, Erastus B 359
Southworth, Southard

Southworth, Abiah 149, 162, 164, 185, 189, 230, 231, 259, 265, 267, 269, 390, 412, 413, 414, 465, 505
Southworth, Christopher 412
Southworth, Constant 412
Southworth, Edward 286, 412, 414
Southworth, Gilbert 412
Southworth, John 412
Southworth, John H 414
Southworth, Richard 412
Southworth, Rufus 253, 255, 413
Southworth, Thomas 412
Southworth, Uriah 387, 390
Southworth, Wells 253, 255, 286, 412, 413
Spaulding, Solomon 265
Spear, Luther 271
Spear, M N 336
Spofford, L A 284
Sprague, Edward P 404
Sprague, Jonathan 455
Squares, D N 204
Squares, Truman 363
Squares, William 208
Stacy, Horace 285
Staples, Charles 461
Staples, Elias 177
Starling, Luke Wellington 460
Starling, John 90, 297, 341
Sterns, Jasper 178
Stearns, Jasper 467
Stebbins, Daniel 439
Stetson, Charles 498
Stevens, Abraham 257
Stevens, John 351
Stevenson, Stinson, Stenson, Stevison
Stevenson, Christopher 351
Stevenson, Isaac 344, 448, 455
Stevenson, James 459
Stevenson, John 120, 344, 345, 459
Stevenson, John 59
Stevenson, Samuel 387, 464

Stickney, John 251
Stinson, John 17, 19, 24, 26, 31, 32, 45, 46, 47, 48, 50, 53, 77, 78, 79, 80, 81, 83, 84, 85, 86, 87, 90, 117, 225, 298, 300, 302, 303, 305, 344, 448
Stinson, Samuel 343, 449
Stockwell, Peter 177, 230
Stoddard, Isaac 231, 288, 289
Stoddard, John 9, 10, 13, 14, 16, 17, 18, 20, 21, 46, 77, 78, 471
Stoddard, Roswell 14
Stone, Eliab 206
Stone, Francis 380, 381
Stone, James 105
Stoddard, John 283
Stone, Mr 265
Stoughton, David 454
Stratton, Francis 157, 170
Stratton, John 227
Stratton, Thomas W 507, 508
Streter, Benony 467
Strong, Caleb 143
Strongman, Henry 454
Strowbridge, Henry 466
Stutson, Robert 465
Sudden. Seth 458
Swan, Duty and Robert 178
Swan, William

Tagart, Nathaniel 454
Taft, James 59, 117, 455
Taft, Jared 178
Taft, Levi 230
Tally, James 164
Taylor, Alfred 231, 432, 446, 507
Taylor, C H 204, 285
Taylor, Israel 204, 508
Taylor, Israel H 199, 200, 232, 255, 259, 432, 433, 445
Taylor, James 17, 24, 31, 40, 46, 47, 49, 77, 81, 85, 86, 88, 89, 120, 148, 150, 151, 155, 159, 224, 226, 234, 236, 237, 303, 305, 346, 386, 432, 504
Taylor, John 178, 229, 230, 271, 357, 432, 458, 505
Taylor, Lieutenant 267

Taylor, Lyman 177
Taylor, Samuel 224
Taylor, Stewart 432
Taylor, Thomas Thompson 164
Taylor, Uzzial 459
Thayer, John 184, 460
Thayer, Jonathan 227
Thayer, Nathan 459
Thatcher, Samuel 350
Thomas, Captain 355
Thomas, David 83, 88, 89, 91, 92, 93, 94, 95, 96, 97, 98, 99, 305, 454
Thomas, Samuel 17, 24, 31
Thompson, Thomson, Tomson, Tompson
Thomson, Alexander 49
Thomson, James Jr 178, 230, 386
Thompson, A W 415
Thompson, Andrew 467
Thompson, Asa 198, 255, 445
Thompson, Daniel 178, 193, 231, 259, 415, 416, 422, 433, 459, 506
Thompson, David 194
Thompson, Deacon 266, 267
Thompson, Edmund 206
Thompson, George 121, 206, 455
Thompson, Capt George 138, 140, 141, 142, 145, 146, 148, 152, 159
Thompson, John 454, 469
Thompson, John Jr 355, 390, 464
Thompson, John M 460
Thompson, John 264, 343, 347, 349, 350, 351, 504
Thompson, James 99, 100, 105, 112, 120, 149, 178, 343, 386, 455, 465, 490
Thompson, James Jr 178, 230, 386
Thompson, James 2d 464
Thompson, Dr James 415
Thompson, Johnson J 445

Thompson, Joseph 227, 386, 456, 469
Thompson, Levi 469
Thompson, Luther 357
Thompson, Peleg P 415
Thompson, Philo 204, 208
Thompson, Thomas 149, 178, 348, 390, 457, 469
Thornton, Elisha 204
Thornton, James 10, 13, 14, 15, 16, 17, 19, 21, 23, 24, 29, 31, 37, 38, 39, 40, 41, 42, 45, 46, 47, 48, 49, 53, 85, 86, 219, 297, 299
Thornton, Matthew 24, 31
Thornton, Samuel 84
Thornton, William 24, 27, 28, 31, 32, 33, 297
Thurber, William 206
Thurber, Zimri 446
Thurston, Thusten, Thirsten
Thurston, James 502, 506
Thurston, John 257, 348
Thurston, John T 506
Thurston, Paul 178, 231, 465, 466
Thurston, Thomas 157, 227, 506, 507
Tilson, Caleb 459
Tinkham, Joseph 386, 390
Tinkham, Levi 464
Titus, Nathan 252
Titus, Sylvester 177, 230
Titus. Timothy 408
Tobey, Mr 277, 278
Todd, William 348
Torrance, Alexander 387, 457
Torrance, John 460
Torrance, Thomas 455
Tower, Isaac Jr 178, 230, 467
Tufts, George 204, 206
Turnecliff, E H 291
Turner, Torner
Turner, Alexander 17, 24, 31, 46, 47, 55, 56, 59, 77, 79, 86, 87, 92, 93, 95, 99, 100, 105, 110, 111, 120, 225, 305, 307, 405, 406, 407, 408, 411
Turner, Alexander Jr 411

INDEX TO MEN.

Turner, James 111, 112, 118, 343, 403, 405, 406, 407, 408, 410, 411, 455
Turner, Jonathan 284
Turner, Reuben 408
Turrell, Terel
Turrell, Jacob 354
Terel, Noah 178
Tuttle, Alfred 233, 256
Tuttle, Hiram 204, 206
Twohig, Richard 204
Twohig, Timothy 204
Tyler, Tylor
Tylor, Amos 467
Tyler, Daniel 386
Tyler, W S 284, 293
Tyler, William 284

Vaille, William K 213, 232, 286, 292, 293, 478
Vanstone, John 238, 239, 260
Vaughn, Rev 288
Vaughn, Thomas 177, 230
Vaughn, Thomas Jr 460
Varnum, Colonel 391
Venable, H I 433, 434

Wade, Cyrus A 208
Wait, David 228, 277, 505
Waldo, Cor-nel 18
Walker, Henry 284
Wallas, Samuel 454
Walless, John 455
Walpole, Robert 500, 501
Ward, Charles L 233, 285
Ward, John 179, 206
Ward, John Jr 466
Ward, John D 508
Ward, John B 204, 206, 478
Ward, Joseph G 95, 204, 206, 242, 246, 431, 478
Ward, Hosea 206
Ward, Horton B 291
Ward, Lysander H 508
Ward, Moses L 204, 206, 233, 507
Ward, Nathaniel 355
Ward, Seth 355
Warren, T 131
Ward, W H H 446
Ward, Winsor 29
Ward & Latham 242
Warford, John 409
Warner, Cullen 461

Washburn, James 230
Washburn, Jason 232
Washington, George 354
Wason, John 83
Watkins, James 164
Webb, Lannard 408
Webster, Augustus 290
Wedge, Wage
Wedge, Lemuel C 191, 255, 290, 462, 506
Wedge, Nahum 170, 172, 179, 230, 467, 488
Wedge, Warren C 232, 256, 446
Weeks, Nathan 253
Weeks, Theverick 466
Wells, Augustin 179
Wells, William 386
Wendell, Jacob 342
West, Caleb 368
Westcott, Waistcoat
Westcott, Jared T 194, 255, 506
Waistcoat, Joseph 390
Westcott, Reuben 179, 191, 194, 230, 231, 271, 506
Westcott, Reuben J D 446
Westcott,, William S 238, 446
Wetherell, Barney 200, 248
Wheeler, Weler
Wheeler, Adam 380, 398
Wheeler, Benjamin 468
Wheeler, Chancellor 255
Wheeler, Glazier 331
Weler, Ephriam 454, 458
Wheeler, John 460
Wheeler Joseph 178
Wheeler, Henry 204
Wheeler, Henry E 358
Wheeler, Nathaniel 193, 468
Whipple, Joseph 271, 459
Whipple, Russell Jr 206
Whipple, Russell W 204
White, David 297, 299, 300
White, Isaac 344
White, James 385, 456
White, John 129, 157, 227, 346, 463
White, John Jr 347
White, Lorenzo 291
White, Samuel 228
White, William P 290

Whitney, Amos 348
Whitney, Benjamin 118
Whitney, Bezebel 458
Whitney, Elmer 257
Whitney, Joseph D 360
Whitney, Joshua 390
Whitting, Amos 127
Wild, Silas 121
Wiley, Charles 497, 498
Wilhay, Samuel 463
Willard, Samuel 271
Willard, J 75, 76
Williams, Abraham 342
Williams, Elisha 17, 42, 43, 46, 47
Williams, Henry 179
Williams, Dr Henry 259
Williams, John 409
Williams, Israel 42, 43, 47
Williams, Col Israel 344
Williams, Major 83
Williams, Moses 468
Williams, Silas 230
Williams, Thomas 342
Williams, William 344
Willis, John 204, 208
Williston, J P 286
Williston, Samuel 286
Willson, Daniel 460
Willson, Samuel 455
Willson, William 179, 280, 459
Willson, William Jr 179
Wilson, Alexander E 433
Wilson, Elijah 348
Wilson, George H 204, 206, 208
Wilson, Pliny 460, 468
Winship, Joel 350, 351, 352, 355
Winslow, Lucian 204
Winter, Philo D 232, 507
Winter, David 458, 466
Witherell, George E 363
Witherell, Rev 285
Witt, Nelson 204, 206, 362
Wolcott, Roger 13, 17
Wolcott, Samuel 285
Wood, Ebenezer 387
Wood, Henry 363, 364
Wood, James 463
Wood, Jonathan 176, 179
Wood, Joseph 291
Wood, Levi 464
Wood, Seth 352

Wood, Sylvanus 458
Woodbridge, Benjamin Ruggles, 346, 347, 348, 391
Worthington, John 345
Woodbridge, Rev 282
Woodbridge, Timothy 308, 345
Woods, Daniel 468
Woods, John 157

Worthington, John 115, 410, 491
Wright, Ebenezer 170, 179
Wright, Gad 177
Wright, Gaius 177
Wright, John 227
Wright, R W 290
Wright, Samuel 214, 390
Wyman, Isaac 341

Yates, Governor 443
Yerkes, Isaac 291
Young, John 108, 454
Young, Robert 455
Young, William 22, 23, 26, 27, 28, 32, 36, 37, 48, 49, 56, 66, 84, 473

INDEX TO WOMEN.

Abercrombie, Margaret 456, 459, 462
Abercrombie, Mehetable 459
Abercrombie, Rachel 461
Abercrombie, Rebecca 459
Allen, Sally 467
Alexander, Esther 108
Alexander, Jennett 454
Andrews, Mary 459
Andrews, Polly 461
Andros, Abigail 466
Arnold, Mary 466
Arnold, Polly 460
Ashley, Lucy 465
Atkinson, Mary 464
Atkinson, Sally 465
Ayers, Nancy 462
Ayers, Ruth 467

Baker, Eunice 466
Baker, Nabby 466
Baker, Mrs Rebeccah 280
Bailey, Charlotte 434
Barber, Dolly 464
Barber, Margarett 456
Barber, Sarah 455
Barloe, Deborah 464
Barloe, Mary 464
Barloe, Polly 464
Barns, Polly 465
Bartlett, Almariah 442
Bartlett, Chloe 460
Bartlett, Teurah 468
Bears, Eloner 457
Bell, Abigail 467.
Bell, Sarah 465
Bennett, Eliza 460
Berry, Agness 463
Berry, Elisebeth 457
Berry, Margerett 455
Berry, Mrs Martha 280
Berry, Mrs Naomi 280
Berry, Sally 459
Billings. Polly 458
Blair, Elisebeth 455
Blair, Isabel 456

Blair, Jennet 455
Blair, Parses 464
Blair, Sarah 456
Boltwood, Keziah 465
Borden, Mrs Lydia 466
Boyden, Clarissa 283, 284, 443
Boynton, Sally 461
Bradshaw, Elisebeth 464
Brewer, H B 232
Brewer, Louise M 233
Bridge, Easter 463
Bridge, Ruth 457
Briggs, Harmony 463
Briggs, Millicent 463
Brown, Diana 468
Brown, Esther 467
Brown, Mary 460
Bryant, Caroline 416
Bryant, Mary A 462
Bryant, Olive 459
Butler, Mary 455

Cahoon, Dolly 459
Cahoon, Hannah 466
Cahoon, Mary 466
Canada Girls 193
Castle, Lucinda 459, 468
Cazier, Matthias Mrs 274
Chace, Juda 459
Chadwick, Judith 461
Chapin, Almira Harrington 481
Chapin, Rhoda 467
Chase, Sarah 441
Childs, Lucia 460
Childs, Polly 466
Clark, Elisabeth 118, 451, 455
Clark, Jean 354
Clark, Katuron 464
Clark, Lucy 458, 466
Clark, Lydia 457
Clark, Margerett 457
Clark, Martha 407, 455
Clark, Mary 455
Clark, Patty 459
Clark, Polly 459
Clark, Prudence 454
Clark, Susannah 458

Cleavlin, Polly 468
Cleveland, Betty 459
Cleveland, Battsey 466
Clough, Phebe 459
Clough, Ester 466
Cochran, Agness 455
Collester, Elonor 455
Coltier, Elisebeth 412
Colton, Mrs 432
Comstock, Anna 462
Comins, Rhoda 468
Conkey, Anne 459
Conkey, Eanor 463
Conkey, Elinor 461
Conkey, Elizebeth 467
Conkey, Hannah 283, 284, 455, 458
Conkey, Isabel 455
Conkey, Jennett 464
Conkey, Jemima 464
Conkey, Mahetable 461
Conkey, Mary Maklem 480
Conkey, Mary 284, 455, 456, 459, 462, 462, 464, 468
Conkey, Martha 458
Conkey, Margery 457, 468
Conkey, Margarett A 480
Conkey, Mrs Margarett 474
Conkey, Margarett 454, 455
Conkey, Prudence 467
Conkey, Polly 460
Conkey, Sarah 458, 459, 463, 465
Conkey, Rebeckah Hamilton 480
Conkey, Rebeckah 452, 460
Cook, Bethiah Ward 444
Cook, Mary 283
Cook, Phebe 444
Cook, Polly 467
Cooley, Lucy 461

Cowan, Batty 459
Cowan, Elisebe,h 454
Cowan, Mrs Eunice 460
Cowan, Mary E 442
Cowan, Mary 455
Cowan, Mrs Margaret 469
Cowan, Sarah 120, 454, 455
Cowan, Sila 460
Cowan, Susuanna 283
Cowan, Sylvia 461
Cowden, Elisebeth 456
Cowden, Jennet 456
Cowden, Martha 457
Cowden, Mary 456
Cowles, Aunt Rene 496
Crawford, Hannah 464
Crawford, Patty 283
Crawford, Sarah 457
Crawford, Susannah 458
Crosett, Elisebeth 456
Crosett, Isa 465
Crosett, Margerett 456
Crosett, Martha 456
Crosett, Sarah 464
Crosett, Mrs Sarah 280
Crossett, Eunice 463
Crossett, Jennet 457
Crossett, Lavinia C 433
Crossett, Lydia 463
Crossett, Mrs Martha 280
Crossett, Mary 455, 456
Crossett, Rebecca 458
Crosher, Polly 457
Crosther, Alase 386
Crozier, Mary 460
Cudworth, Sally 465
Cunningham, Mary 454
Cutler, Mrs Dr 258
Cutter, Hannah 459

Danforth, Lucinda 462
Danforth, Malinda 461
Danforth, Margerett 459
Darling, Bettsey 466
Darling, Jemima 468
Davenport, Eliza
Davis, Hannah 433, 434
Davison, Betsey 458
Davison, Lucy 467
Davison, Polly 466
Davidson, Patty 458
Davinson, Polly 458
Dick, Ann 463
Dick, Catrin 457
Dick, Dinah 406, 455

Dick, Elisebeth 456
Dick, Eunice 457
Dick, Jean 457
Dick, Ketrin 455
Dick, Margarett 249,456, 468
Dick, Mary 455, 457
Dick, Mary Ann 456
Dick, Sarah 407, 455
Dickinson, Abigail 460
Dickinson, Margarett 458
Dolan, Polly 466
Dorety, Lucretia 466
Dulphe, Elisebeth 463
Dunbar, Eunice 463, 464
Dunbar, Mary 442, 463
Dunlap, Agness 455
Dunlap, Mary 283, 284
Dunlap, Sarah 463
Dunn, Anna 468
Drane, Sarah 411
Draper, Lucy 467

Eaton, Charlotte 284
Eaton, Frances Atessa 284
Eaton, Mary 461
Edson, Annie 463
Edson, Betsey 463
Edson, Keziah 463
Edson, Polly 460
English, Eloner 456
Everett, Elisebeth 437

Fails, Alenda 467
Fales, Eunice 461
Fales, Nancy 455
Fergerson, Ann 455
Fergerson, Jennet 456
Fergerson, Susanna 455
Ford, Lyda 466
Fowler, Betty 460
Freeman, Sally 463
Fuller, Bethanie 464
Fuller, Mary 463

Gay, Sarah 467
Gilmore, Isabel 455
Gilmore, Margerett 454
Gilmore, Martha 249
Gilmore, Mary 455
Gold, Livia 284
Graham, Mrs Molly 123, 124, 469
Graves, Mary E 441
Gray, Agnes 283
Gray, Ann 421, 454

Gray, Battsey 466
Gray, Bettsey 283, 284
Gray, Easter 454
Gray, Elinor 118, 451
Gray, Elisebeth 454, 455
Gray, Emma A 431
Gray, Hannah 464
Gray, Isabel 457, 458
Gray, Mrs Isabel 280
Gray, Jean 455
Gray, Jenny 458
Gray, Lorania 431
Gray, Lydia 454, 457
Gray, Mrs Lydia 280
Gray, Margerett 456, 464, 465, 466
Gray, Martha 455, 458
Gray, Mrs Martha 280
Gray, Mary 431, 461
Gray, Mrs Mary 280
Gray, Nancy 454, 458
Gray. Naomi 461
Gray, Pamelia 461
Gray, Phebe 458
Gray, Polly 457, 458, 461
Gray, Roxana 460
Gray, Mrs Ruth 280
Gray, Sarah 283, 454, 457, 462
Gray, Sarah H 431
Gray, Susan 460
Green, Mary 457
Grout, Annis 434
Grout, Aseneth 433, 434, 461
Grout, Orpha 434
Guernsey, Esther (widow) 258, 456

Hacket, Heket
Hacket, Hannah 465
Hacket, Lydia 463
Hacket, Ruth 465
Heket, Precila 457
Halbert, Elisebeth 456
Halbert, Mary 456
Hall, Clarissa 434
Hall, Susan 434
Hall, Susannah 459
Hamilton, Anna 283
Hamilton, Annie 459
Hamilton, Betsey 283
Hamilton, Eleanor 406, 446
Hamilton, Elisebeth 459
Hamilton, Isabel 457
Hamilton, Janet 454

INDEX TO WOMEN.

Hamilton, Margerett 455, 456
Hamilton, Martha 464
Hamilton, Rebeckah 454, 457
Hamilton, Sylvia 283
Hamilton, Widow 130
Hardin, Anna 459
Harkness, Anne 459
Harkness, Chloe 468
Harkness, Lovecey 468
Harkness, Isabel 465
Harkness, Nancy 421, 457, 468
Harkness, Polly 459
Harkness, Sally 459, 466
Harkness, Vesta 460
Harlow, Sally 461
Harper, Elisebeth 454
Harrington, Almira 461
Hathaway, Betsey 459
Haskell, Mary 457
Haskell, Polly 467
Haskins, Bashaba 466
Hawley, Rebecca 75
Hayden, Haden
Haden, Polly 466
Hayden, Mary 284
Hayden, Phebe 461
Hayden, Sarah 461
Haward, Mary 464
Hayward, Polly 460
Hayward, Rhoda 465
Hayward, Tryol 464
Hayze, Sarah 463
Heas, Elisebeth 462
Henderson, Mary 462
Henderson, Phebe 455
Herrington, Faithful 467
Hill, Rebeckah 463
Hinds, Hynds
Hinds, Anna 459
Hinds, Mary 466
Hinds, Sarah 467
Hinds, Vesta 467
Hoar, Horr
Hoar, Abigail 460
Hoar, Rachel 460
Hodgkins, Clarissa 461
Holland, Hollan
Holland, Ana 463
Hollan, Betsey 459
Holland, Mary 463
Holland, Sarah 456
Hood, Jennet 456
Hood, Margerett 473
Hood, Nancy 457
Hooker, Esther 461

Houston, Mrs Lucy 432
Howard, Mary 464
Howard, Rebekah 466
Hubbard, Emeline A 430
Hunter, Anne 459
Hunter, Elisebeth 454
Hunter, Janet 455
Hunter, Lois 458
Hunter, Margerett 454
Hunter, Mary 464
Hunter, Sarah 456,.457
Hunter, Susannah 465
Hyde, Hannah 464
Hyde, Isabel 458
Hyde, Ellis 463
Hyde, Eunice 467
Hyde, Polly 461
Hyde, Mrs Rachel 480

Ingram, Abigal 463
Ingalls, Diana 283

Jillit, Harriet M 413
Jilson, Lurana 468
Johnson, Anna 467
Johnson, Elisebeth 458, 465
Johnson, Mary 192
Johnson, Rachel 192
Johnston, Agness 456
Johnston, Jean 457, 463
Johnston, Sarah 455
Jones, Lucy 460
Jones, Patty 461
Joslin, Nabby(widow)468

Keep, Almedia 467
Keet, Jemima 464
Keith, Mrs J W 258
Kellogg, Elisebeth C 425
Kelso, Susanna 454
Kidd, Kid
Kid, Elisebeth 454
Kidd, Margerett 109
King, Agness 454
King, Damaries 465
King, Margerett 454
King, Mary 458
King, Nancy 459
King, Sally 465
Kingman, Annie M 284
Kingman, Sally 284
Knapp, Martha 465

Lanord, Olive 466

Larrabee, Phinneus (widow) 467
Latham, Esther Cutler 459
Latham, Polly 458
Latham, Sally 458
Leach, Hannah 466
Leach, Nabby 458
Leach, Sarah 465
Leach, Silence 463
Lee, Mary 283
Lewis, Etta I 445
Lewis, Sally 461
Lincoln, Polly 460
Lindsey, Linsley, Linsey
Lindsey, Anne (widow) 280
Linsey, Agness 455
Lindsey, Jean 465
Lindsey, Martha 464
Lindsey, Mary (widow) 280
Lindsey, Mrs Mary Ann 280
Lindsey, Nancy 465
Lindsey, Mrs Susanah 280
Lotheridge, Anne 458
Lotheridge, Hannah 120
Lotherige, Margery 466
Lotheridge, Mary 173
Lucore, Sarah 454
Lyon, Frances R 413

Macomber, Philena 466
Macomber, Polly 458
McClelland, Mary 454
McCollister, Eleanor 411
McConel, Elenor 465
McConel, Jean 457
McCorceles, Jemima 464
McCraken, Jenny 455
McCulloch, McAllah, McAllach, McCollough, McCullagh, McCollah
McCallough, Lucy 467
McCulloch, Anne 458
McCulloch, Elisebeth 457
McCulloch, Jean 454, 456
McCulloch, Jennett 455
McCulloch, Margerett 454, 456
McCulloch, Martha 437, 464, 468
McCulloch, Molly 464
McCulloch, Sarar 456

McCulloch, Sarah Cowan 437
McDonnal, Nancy 463
McFall, Goody 339
McFall, Jennet 463
McFarland, Sarah 454
McMaster, Catrin 454
McNall, Rachel 463
Maklem, Meklam, McClaim, McLam, McLem, Macilom
Maklem, Ann 455
Maklem, Elisebeth 454, 459
Maklem, Hannah 455
Maklem, Isabel 454
Maklem, Jean 457, 462
Maklem, Margaret 456
Maklem, Mary 454, 457
Maklem, Rebeckah 457
Maklem, Rebeccah (widow) 280
Maklem, Sarah 454
Marks, Hannah 454
Marsh, Martha 464
Mattoon, Roxana 426
Mellin. McMullin, McMellin, Mullen, Millan
McMillen, Anne 465
McMillen, Mrs Jean 280
McMullen, Mary 457
McMillen, Mrs Mary 280
McMillen, Nancy 458
McMillen, Mrs Sarah 280
McMillen, Susannah 464
Mellin, Anne 467
Mellen, Susanna 461
Millen, Betty 467
Millen, Hannah 283, 460
Millen, Polly 459
Mills, Abigail 461
Miller, Lovina 468
Miller, Lydia 452
Mitchel Ellen 442
Mitchel Roxilana 459
Moody, Martha 467
Moody, Mary 466
Moor, Bettsey 466
Montgomery, Polly 457
Montgomery, Anne 466
Morgan, Mrs Annette 497
Morton, Mary 465
Mun, Matilda 466

Newcomb, Patty 458

Newell, Amelia Brown 461
Newell, Charlotte 461
Newell, Sally 461
Newton, Polly 466
Nilson, Sarah 463
Nolton, Margery 456

Oliver, Ann 456
Oliver, Battsey 469
Oliver, Mary 459
Oliver, Nancy 462
Oliver, Mary Gaven 459
Osburne, Electa 467
Otis, Betsey 461
Otis, Tryphena Smith 435
Owen, Hannah 454

Packard, Chloe 463
Packard, Katherine 462
Packard, Lydia 412
Packard, Nancy 284, 460
Packard, Serena 461
Paice, Matilda 465
Park, Mrs Nancy 475
Parkins, Judith 460
Parmenter, Ruth 388
Patch, Hannah 467
Patrick, Mary 455
Patterson, Naomi 457
Patterson, Roxana 106
Payne, Eliza J 443
Pease, Mrs Nabby 468
Peck, Harriett 434
Peebles, Mrs Ann 454
Pebels, Anne 456
Peebles, Anne 458
Peebles, Margarett 463
Pebels, Mary 456
Peebels, Mary 454
Peebles, Rachel 465
Peables, Mrs Rachel 469
Peebles, Sarah 454, 463
Peeso, Lydia 458
Peeso, Sarah 465
Peterson, Rhoda 456
Pettengall, Lydia Amerson 465
Petteson, Mary 455
Phelps, Betsey 467
Pierce, Matilda 415
Pierce, Sally 467
Pirkins, Lydia 464
Powers, Estha 467
Powers, Levina 465
Powers, Ruth 458, 465
Pratt, Margarett, 460

Pratt, Martha 465
Pratt, Olive 467
Pratt, Zube 464
Pumroy, Nancy 464
Putnam, Dorothy L 438
Putnam, Mary S 438

Queen, Elisebeth (widow) 117

Ramsdell, Lucy 463
Randall, Malinda 434
Rankin, Anne 283
Rankin, Cynthia 283
Rankin, Jennet 457
Rankin, Martha 456
Rankin, Patty 467
Rankin, Polly 283
Rankin, Sally 283
Ransom, Elisebeth 456
Ray, Sally 458, 466
Religh, Elisebeth 465
Rice, Catrin 466
Richmore, Persela 456
Rider, Olive 467
Rinken, Batsey 466
Rhodes, Polly 458
Robeson, Widow 165
Robertson, Prudence 465
Robbins, Abigail 466
Robbins, Sally 467
Robinson, Mary A P 434
Robinson. Sally 460
Rodgers, Mary 465

Sadler, Livena 467
Saltonstall, Mary 13, 14
Sampson, Samson
Sampson. Chloe 459
Savage, Elisebeth 411
Savage, Jane 411
Savage, Martha 406, 454
Savage, Thankful 455
Schiel, Susannah 463
Scot, Elisebeth 456
Sears, Patty 467
Sears, Sally 459
Selfridge, Mrs Elisebeth 120, 451, 456
Selfridge, Nane 463
Selfridge, Rebeckah 469
Shaw, Anne 462
Shaw, Louisa 460
Shaw, Lydia 461
Shays, Mrs Abigail 280, 391

INDEX TO WOMEN.   531

Shays, Hannah 465
Shaye, Lucy 458
Sheldon, Lucy 466
Shurtlieff, Vise 464
Simons, Venis 466
Sloan, Abigail 463
Sloan, Agness 455
Sloan, Elisebeth 463
Sloan, Mrs Eunice 280
Sloan, Jinney 466
Sloan, Martha 449, 464
Sloan, Mary 456
Sloan, Sarah 456
Smith, Betsey 284
Smith, Mrs Betsey Otis 477
Smith, Mrs E T 413
Smith, Ester 454
Smith, Esther 462
Smith, Experience 466
Smith, Hannah 457, 463
Smith, Jean 457
Smith, Margarett 454
Smith, Mary 457
Smith, Nancy 460
Smith, Patty 468
Smith, Rebecca 252
Smith, Sally 192
Snow, Cynthia 461
Snow, Sally 467
Snow, Saloma 461
Southworth, Southard
Southworth, Alice 412
Southworth, Avis 464
Southworth, Bridget 463
Southworth, Kesiah Boltwood 412
Southworth, Lydiah 463
Stark, H Ann 424
Steuben, Mrs Harriett 431
Stevens, Hannah 462
Stevens, Sarah 457
Stevenson, Margarett 449
Stevenson, Mary 449
Stewart, Jean 462
Sutherland, Miss 443

Taylor, Anne 458
Taylor, Katherin 457, 463

Taylor, Lucy 461
Taylor, Margarett 454
Tekiel, Lucy 465
Thomas, Jenny 457
Thomas, Martha 456
Thomas, Mary 464
Thomas, Susanna 455
Thomas, Susannah 406
Thompson, Thomson, Tomson
Thompson, Dorcas 467
Thompson, Elisebeth 463, 464
Thompson, Eunice 458
Thompson, Hannah 460, 467
Thompson, Wid Hannah 461
Thompson, Mrs Jean 469
Thompson, Margaret 283
Thompson, Mrs Margaret 469
Thompson, Martha 458, 464
Thompson, Matilda 415
Thompson, Mary 455
Thompson, Molly 458, 464
Thompson, Mrs Prudence 469
Thompson, Ruth 445
Thompson, Sarah 284, 465
Thompson, Sarah H 431
Thompson, Susannah 459, 463
Thornton, Ester 454
Thorp, Lucy 459
Thurston, Elisebeth 178, 459
Thurston, Margerett 108
Thurston, Mary 466, 468
Tolyman, Phebe 458
Torrance, Martha 457
Torrance, Mary 456
Tower, Elisebeth 467
Tower, Lavinia 467
Town, Polly 467
Turner, Torner
Turner, Abigail 461

Turner, Alice 287
Turner, Eliza 284
Turner, Sarah 407, 409, 455
Turner, Thankful 283

Vaughn, Lydia 460
Vaughn, Sally 460

Walker, Loise 464
Walker, Mary 284
Ward, Mrs M L 232
Warren, Zubee 463
Washburn, Patty 458
Washburn, Sally 458
Wetherby, Laura 461
Westcott, Cynthia 462
Wheeler, Ruth 448
Whipple, Azubah 461
White, Lovince 465
White, S V 430
Whiteham, Marcy 465
Whitney, Lucy 464
Willey, Elisebeth 456
Williams, Annie 467
Willson, Wilson
Willson, Mrs Alice 280
Willson, Esther 467
Willson, Harriett 461
Wilson, Alice 458
Wilson, Lucy 460
Wilson, Martha 465
Wilson, Sarah 465
Wood, Mary 460
Wood, Lucy 462
Wood, Lydia 284
Wood, Mary (widow) 467
Woodburn, Rebecca C 413
Woods, Rebeckah 461
Woods, Mary 465
Wright, Sally 466
Wylie, Mrs 478
Wyman, Patty 467

Young, Mary 455
Young, Rachel 454

Zuillo, Frances 456

www.ingramcontent.com/pod-product-compliance
Lightning Source LLC
Chambersburg PA
CBHW071132300426
44113CB00009B/946